THIRD EDITION

# Windows PowerShell Cookbook

D1258365

*Lee Holmes*

O'REILLY®

Beijing · Cambridge · Farnham · Köln · Sebastopol · Tokyo

**Windows PowerShell Cookbook, Third Edition**

by Lee Holmes

Published by O'Reilly Media, Inc., 1005 Gravenstein Highway North, Sebastopol, CA 95472.

O'Reilly books may be purchased for educational, business, or sales promotional use. Online editions are also available for most titles (*http://my.safaribooksonline.com*). For more information, contact our corporate/institutional sales department: 800-998-9938 or *corporate@oreilly.com*.

| | |
|---|---|
| **Editor:** Rachel Roumeliotis | **Proofreader:** Rachel Monaghan |
| **Production Editor:** Kara Ebrahim | **Indexer:** Angela Howard |
| | **Cover Designer:** Randy Comer |
| | **Interior Designer:** David Futato |
| | **Illustrator:** Rebecca Demarest |

| | |
|---|---|
| October 2007: | First Edition |
| August 2010: | Second Edition |
| January 2013: | Third Edition |

**Revision History for the First Edition:**

2012-12-21    First release

See *http://oreilly.com/catalog/errata.csp?isbn=9781449320683* for release details.

ISBN: 978-1-449-32068-3

[LSI]

# Table of Contents

Foreword................................................................... xvii

Preface..................................................................... xix

## Part I. Tour
A Guided Tour of Windows PowerShell........................................... iii

## Part II. Fundamentals

**1. The Windows PowerShell Interactive Shell...................................... 19**

1.1. Run Programs, Scripts, and Existing Tools                          19
1.2. Run a PowerShell Command                                           23
1.3. Resolve Errors Calling Native Executables                         24
1.4. Supply Default Values for Parameters                              26
1.5. Invoke a Long-Running or Background Command                       28
1.6. Program: Monitor a Command for Changes                            32
1.7. Notify Yourself of Job Completion                                 35
1.8. Customize Your Shell, Profile, and Prompt                         36
1.9. Customize PowerShell's User Input Behavior                        39
1.10. Customize PowerShell's Command Resolution Behavior               40
1.11. Find a Command to Accomplish a Task                              43
1.12. Get Help on a Command                                            45
1.13. Update System Help Content                                       47
1.14. Program: Search Help for Text                                    49
1.15. Launch PowerShell at a Specific Location                         50
1.16. Invoke a PowerShell Command or Script from Outside PowerShell    52
1.17. Understand and Customize PowerShell's Tab Completion             55
1.18. Program: Learn Aliases for Common Commands                       59
1.19. Program: Learn Aliases for Common Parameters                     61

1.20. Access and Manage Your Console History   64
1.21. Program: Create Scripts from Your Session History   66
1.22. Invoke a Command from Your Session History   68
1.23. Program: Search Formatted Output for a Pattern   69
1.24. Interactively View and Process Command Output   70
1.25. Program: Interactively View and Explore Objects   72
1.26. Store the Output of a Command into a File   79
1.27. Add Information to the End of a File   80
1.28. Record a Transcript of Your Shell Session   81
1.29. Extend Your Shell with Additional Commands   82
1.30. Use Commands from Customized Shells   84
1.31. Save State Between Sessions   85

**2. Pipelines.** . . . . . . . . . . . . . . . . . . . . . . . . . . . . . . . . . . . . . . . . . . . . . . . . . . . . **89**
2.1. Filter Items in a List or Command Output   90
2.2. Group and Pivot Data by Name   91
2.3. Program: Simplify Most Where-Object Filters   94
2.4. Program: Interactively Filter Lists of Objects   96
2.5. Work with Each Item in a List or Command Output   99
2.6. Automate Data-Intensive Tasks   101
2.7. Program: Simplify Most Foreach-Object Pipelines   105
2.8. Intercept Stages of the Pipeline   108
2.9. Automatically Capture Pipeline Output   109
2.10. Capture and Redirect Binary Process Output   111

**3. Variables and Objects.** . . . . . . . . . . . . . . . . . . . . . . . . . . . . . . . . . . . . . . . . . . **117**
3.1. Display the Properties of an Item as a List   118
3.2. Display the Properties of an Item as a Table   120
3.3. Store Information in Variables   122
3.4. Access Environment Variables   123
3.5. Program: Retain Changes to Environment Variables Set by a Batch File   126
3.6. Control Access and Scope of Variables and Other Items   128
3.7. Program: Create a Dynamic Variable   130
3.8. Work with .NET Objects   133
3.9. Create an Instance of a .NET Object   138
3.10. Create Instances of Generic Objects   140
3.11. Reduce Typing for Long Class Names   141
3.12. Use a COM Object   143
3.13. Learn About Types and Objects   143
3.14. Get Detailed Documentation About Types and Objects   145
3.15. Add Custom Methods and Properties to Objects   147
3.16. Create and Initialize Custom Objects   150

3.17. Add Custom Methods and Properties to Types      154
3.18. Define Custom Formatting for a Type      158

**4. Looping and Flow Control** . . . . . . . . . . . . . . . . . . . . . . . . . . . . . . . . . . . . . . . . **163**
4.1. Make Decisions with Comparison and Logical Operators      163
4.2. Adjust Script Flow Using Conditional Statements      165
4.3. Manage Large Conditional Statements with Switches      167
4.4. Repeat Operations with Loops      170
4.5. Add a Pause or Delay      172

**5. Strings and Unstructured Text** . . . . . . . . . . . . . . . . . . . . . . . . . . . . . . . . . . . . **175**
5.1. Create a String      175
5.2. Create a Multiline or Formatted String      177
5.3. Place Special Characters in a String      178
5.4. Insert Dynamic Information in a String      179
5.5. Prevent a String from Including Dynamic Information      180
5.6. Place Formatted Information in a String      181
5.7. Search a String for Text or a Pattern      183
5.8. Replace Text in a String      185
5.9. Split a String on Text or a Pattern      187
5.10. Combine Strings into a Larger String      190
5.11. Convert a String to Uppercase or Lowercase      191
5.12. Trim a String      193
5.13. Format a Date for Output      194
5.14. Program: Convert Text Streams to Objects      196
5.15. Generate Large Reports and Text Streams      200
5.16. Generate Source Code and Other Repetitive Text      202

**6. Calculations and Math** . . . . . . . . . . . . . . . . . . . . . . . . . . . . . . . . . . . . . . . . . . . **207**
6.1. Perform Simple Arithmetic      207
6.2. Perform Complex Arithmetic      209
6.3. Measure Statistical Properties of a List      213
6.4. Work with Numbers as Binary      214
6.5. Simplify Math with Administrative Constants      218
6.6. Convert Numbers Between Bases      219

**7. Lists, Arrays, and Hashtables** . . . . . . . . . . . . . . . . . . . . . . . . . . . . . . . . . . . . . **223**
7.1. Create an Array or List of Items      223
7.2. Create a Jagged or Multidimensional Array      225
7.3. Access Elements of an Array      226
7.4. Visit Each Element of an Array      228
7.5. Sort an Array or List of Items      229

7.6. Determine Whether an Array Contains an Item                      230
7.7. Combine Two Arrays                                               231
7.8. Find Items in an Array That Match a Value                        232
7.9. Compare Two Lists                                                233
7.10. Remove Elements from an Array                                   234
7.11. Find Items in an Array Greater or Less Than a Value             235
7.12. Use the ArrayList Class for Advanced Array Tasks                236
7.13. Create a Hashtable or Associative Array                         238
7.14. Sort a Hashtable by Key or Value                                239

8. Utility Tasks. . . . . . . . . . . . . . . . . . . . . . . . . . . . . . . . . . . . . . . . . . . . . . . . . .  243
8.1. Get the System Date and Time                                     243
8.2. Measure the Duration of a Command                                244
8.3. Read and Write from the Windows Clipboard                        246
8.4. Generate a Random Number or Object                               248
8.5. Program: Search the Windows Start Menu                           250
8.6. Program: Show Colorized Script Content                           251

## Part III.  Common Tasks

9. Simple Files. . . . . . . . . . . . . . . . . . . . . . . . . . . . . . . . . . . . . . . . . . . . . . . . . .  259
9.1. Get the Content of a File                                        259
9.2. Search a File for Text or a Pattern                              261
9.3. Parse and Manage Text-Based Logfiles                             264
9.4. Parse and Manage Binary Files                                    267
9.5. Create a Temporary File                                          270
9.6. Search and Replace Text in a File                                271
9.7. Program: Get the Encoding of a File                              275
9.8. Program: View the Hexadecimal Representation of Content          277

10. Structured Files. . . . . . . . . . . . . . . . . . . . . . . . . . . . . . . . . . . . . . . . . . . . . . .  281
10.1. Access Information in an XML File                               281
10.2. Perform an XPath Query Against XML                              284
10.3. Convert Objects to XML                                          286
10.4. Modify Data in an XML File                                      287
10.5. Easily Import and Export Your Structured Data                   289
10.6. Store the Output of a Command in a CSV or Delimited File        291
10.7. Import CSV and Delimited Data from a File                       292
10.8. Manage JSON Data Streams                                        294
10.9. Use Excel to Manage Command Output                              295

10.10. Parse and Interpret PowerShell Scripts 297

## 11. Code Reuse.......................................................... 303
11.1. Write a Script 303
11.2. Write a Function 306
11.3. Find a Verb Appropriate for a Command Name 308
11.4. Write a Script Block 309
11.5. Return Data from a Script, Function, or Script Block 311
11.6. Package Common Commands in a Module 314
11.7. Write Commands That Maintain State 317
11.8. Selectively Export Commands from a Module 320
11.9. Diagnose and Interact with Internal Module State 322
11.10. Handle Cleanup Tasks When a Module Is Removed 324
11.11. Access Arguments of a Script, Function, or Script Block 325
11.12. Add Validation to Parameters 330
11.13. Accept Script Block Parameters with Local Variables 334
11.14. Dynamically Compose Command Parameters 336
11.15. Provide -WhatIf, -Confirm, and Other Cmdlet Features 338
11.16. Add Help to Scripts or Functions 340
11.17. Add Custom Tags to a Function or Script Block 343
11.18. Access Pipeline Input 345
11.19. Write Pipeline-Oriented Scripts with Cmdlet Keywords 347
11.20. Write a Pipeline-Oriented Function 351
11.21. Organize Scripts for Improved Readability 352
11.22. Invoke Dynamically Named Commands 354
11.23. Program: Enhance or Extend an Existing Cmdlet 356

## 12. Internet-Enabled Scripts........................................... 365
12.1. Download a File from an FTP or Internet Site 365
12.2. Upload a File to an FTP Site 366
12.3. Download a Web Page from the Internet 368
12.4. Parse and Analyze a Web Page from the Internet 373
12.5. Script a Web Application Session 375
12.6. Program: Get-PageUrls 379
12.7. Interact with REST-Based Web APIs 383
12.8. Connect to a Web Service 385
12.9. Export Command Output as a Web Page 387
12.10. Send an Email 388
12.11. Program: Monitor Website Uptimes 389
12.12. Program: Interact with Internet Protocols 391

## 13. User Interaction.................................................... 397

13.1. Read a Line of User Input    397
13.2. Read a Key of User Input    398
13.3. Program: Display a Menu to the User    399
13.4. Display Messages and Output to the User    401
13.5. Provide Progress Updates on Long-Running Tasks    404
13.6. Write Culture-Aware Scripts    405
13.7. Support Other Languages in Script Output    409
13.8. Program: Invoke a Script Block with Alternate Culture Settings    412
13.9. Access Features of the Host's User Interface    414
13.10. Program: Add a Graphical User Interface to Your Script    415
13.11. Interact with MTA Objects    418

**14. Debugging**...................................................... **421**
14.1. Prevent Common Scripting Errors    422
14.2. Trace Script Execution    424
14.3. Set a Script Breakpoint    428
14.4. Debug a Script When It Encounters an Error    430
14.5. Create a Conditional Breakpoint    432
14.6. Investigate System State While Debugging    434
14.7. Program: Watch an Expression for Changes    437
14.8. Program: Get Script Code Coverage    440

**15. Tracing and Error Management**............................................ **443**
15.1. Determine the Status of the Last Command    443
15.2. View the Errors Generated by a Command    445
15.3. Manage the Error Output of Commands    447
15.4. Program: Resolve an Error    448
15.5. Configure Debug, Verbose, and Progress Output    450
15.6. Handle Warnings, Errors, and Terminating Errors    452
15.7. Output Warnings, Errors, and Terminating Errors    455
15.8. Program: Analyze a Script's Performance Profile    456

**16. Environmental Awareness**............................................. **463**
16.1. View and Modify Environment Variables    463
16.2. Modify the User or System Path    465
16.3. Access Information About Your Command's Invocation    466
16.4. Program: Investigate the InvocationInfo Variable    468
16.5. Find Your Script's Name    471
16.6. Find Your Script's Location    472
16.7. Find the Location of Common System Paths    473
16.8. Get the Current Location    476
16.9. Safely Build File Paths Out of Their Components    477

16.10. Interact with PowerShell's Global Environment    478
16.11. Determine PowerShell Version Information    479
16.12. Test for Administrative Privileges    480

**17. Extend the Reach of Windows PowerShell.** . . . . . . . . . . . . . . . . . . . . . . . . . . . . **483**
17.1. Automate Programs Using COM Scripting Interfaces    483
17.2. Program: Query a SQL Data Source    485
17.3. Access Windows Performance Counters    488
17.4. Access Windows API Functions    490
17.5. Program: Invoke Simple Windows API Calls    497
17.6. Define or Extend a .NET Class    500
17.7. Add Inline C# to Your PowerShell Script    503
17.8. Access a .NET SDK Library    505
17.9. Create Your Own PowerShell Cmdlet    507
17.10. Add PowerShell Scripting to Your Own Program    510

**18. Security and Script Signing.** . . . . . . . . . . . . . . . . . . . . . . . . . . . . . . . . . . . . . . **515**
18.1. Enable Scripting Through an Execution Policy    516
18.2. Disable Warnings for UNC Paths    519
18.3. Sign a PowerShell Script, Module, or Formatting File    520
18.4. Program: Create a Self-Signed Certificate    522
18.5. Manage PowerShell Security in an Enterprise    523
18.6. Block Scripts by Publisher, Path, or Hash    526
18.7. Verify the Digital Signature of a PowerShell Script    527
18.8. Securely Handle Sensitive Information    529
18.9. Securely Request Usernames and Passwords    531
18.10. Program: Start a Process as Another User    532
18.11. Program: Run a Temporarily Elevated Command    534
18.12. Securely Store Credentials on Disk    537
18.13. Access User and Machine Certificates    539
18.14. Program: Search the Certificate Store    540
18.15. Add and Remove Certificates    542
18.16. Manage Security Descriptors in SDDL Form    543

**19. Integrated Scripting Environment.** . . . . . . . . . . . . . . . . . . . . . . . . . . . . . . . . . **545**
19.1. Debug a Script    547
19.2. Customize Text and User Interface Colors    549
19.3. Connect to a Remote Computer    551
19.4. Extend ISE Functionality Through Its Object Model    552
19.5. Quickly Insert Script Snippets    553

## Part IV.    Administrator Tasks

**20. Files and Directories**. . . . . . . . . . . . . . . . . . . . . . . . . . . . . . . . . . . . . . . . . . . . . . . . .   **559**

20.1. Determine the Current Location                                           560
20.2. Get the Files in a Directory                                             561
20.3. Find All Files Modified Before a Certain Date                            563
20.4. Clear the Content of a File                                              564
20.5. Manage and Change the Attributes of a File                               565
20.6. Find Files That Match a Pattern                                          566
20.7. Manage Files That Include Special Characters                             569
20.8. Program: Get Disk Usage Information                                      570
20.9. Monitor a File for Changes                                               572
20.10. Get the Version of a DLL or Executable                                  573
20.11. Program: Get the MD5 or SHA1 Hash of a File                             574
20.12. Create a Directory                                                      576
20.13. Remove a File or Directory                                             577
20.14. Rename a File or Directory                                             578
20.15. Move a File or Directory                                              579
20.16. Create and Map PowerShell Drives                                       580
20.17. Access Long File and Directory Names                                   582
20.18. Unblock a File                                                         583
20.19. Interact with Alternate Data Streams                                   584
20.20. Program: Move or Remove a Locked File                                  586
20.21. Get the ACL of a File or Directory                                     587
20.22. Set the ACL of a File or Directory                                     589
20.23. Program: Add Extended File Properties to Files                         591
20.24. Program: Create a Filesystem Hard Link                                 593
20.25. Program: Create a ZIP Archive                                         595

**21. The Windows Registry**. . . . . . . . . . . . . . . . . . . . . . . . . . . . . . . . . . . . . . . . . . . . . . . . . .   **599**

21.1. Navigate the Registry                                                  599
21.2. View a Registry Key                                                    600
21.3. Modify or Remove a Registry Key Value                                  601
21.4. Create a Registry Key Value                                            602
21.5. Remove a Registry Key                                                  603
21.6. Safely Combine Related Registry Modifications                          604
21.7. Add a Site to an Internet Explorer Security Zone                       606
21.8. Modify Internet Explorer Settings                                      608
21.9. Program: Search the Windows Registry                                   609

21.10. Get the ACL of a Registry Key 611
21.11. Set the ACL of a Registry Key 612
21.12. Work with the Registry of a Remote Computer 614
21.13. Program: Get Registry Items from Remote Machines 616
21.14. Program: Get Properties of Remote Registry Keys 618
21.15. Program: Set Properties of Remote Registry Keys 620
21.16. Discover Registry Settings for Programs 622

22. **Comparing Data**. . . . . . . . . . . . . . . . . . . . . . . . . . . . . . . . . . . . . . . . . . . . **627**
22.1. Compare the Output of Two Commands 627
22.2. Determine the Differences Between Two Files 629
22.3. Verify Integrity of File Sets 630

23. **Event Logs**. . . . . . . . . . . . . . . . . . . . . . . . . . . . . . . . . . . . . . . . . . . . . . . . **633**
23.1. List All Event Logs 633
23.2. Get the Newest Entries from an Event Log 635
23.3. Find Event Log Entries with Specific Text 636
23.4. Retrieve and Filter Event Log Entries 638
23.5. Find Event Log Entries by Their Frequency 641
23.6. Back Up an Event Log 643
23.7. Create or Remove an Event Log 644
23.8. Write to an Event Log 646
23.9. Run a PowerShell Script for Windows Event Log Entries 646
23.10. Clear or Maintain an Event Log 648
23.11. Access Event Logs of a Remote Machine 650

24. **Processes**. . . . . . . . . . . . . . . . . . . . . . . . . . . . . . . . . . . . . . . . . . . . . . . . . **653**
24.1. List Currently Running Processes 654
24.2. Launch the Application Associated with a Document 655
24.3. Launch a Process 656
24.4. Stop a Process 658
24.5. Get the Owner of a Process 659
24.6. Get the Parent Process of a Process 660
24.7. Debug a Process 661

25. **System Services**. . . . . . . . . . . . . . . . . . . . . . . . . . . . . . . . . . . . . . . . . . . . **663**
25.1. List All Running Services 663
25.2. Manage a Running Service 665
25.3. Configure a Service 666

26. **Active Directory**. . . . . . . . . . . . . . . . . . . . . . . . . . . . . . . . . . . . . . . . . . . . **669**
26.1. Test Active Directory Scripts on a Local Installation 670

26.2. Create an Organizational Unit     673
26.3. Get the Properties of an Organizational Unit     674
26.4. Modify Properties of an Organizational Unit     675
26.5. Delete an Organizational Unit     675
26.6. Get the Children of an Active Directory Container     676
26.7. Create a User Account     677
26.8. Program: Import Users in Bulk to Active Directory     678
26.9. Search for a User Account     680
26.10. Get and List the Properties of a User Account     681
26.11. Modify Properties of a User Account     682
26.12. Change a User Password     683
26.13. Create a Security or Distribution Group     683
26.14. Search for a Security or Distribution Group     685
26.15. Get the Properties of a Group     686
26.16. Find the Owner of a Group     687
26.17. Modify Properties of a Security or Distribution Group     688
26.18. Add a User to a Security or Distribution Group     688
26.19. Remove a User from a Security or Distribution Group     689
26.20. List a User's Group Membership     690
26.21. List the Members of a Group     691
26.22. List the Users in an Organizational Unit     691
26.23. Search for a Computer Account     692
26.24. Get and List the Properties of a Computer Account     694

**27. Enterprise Computer Management.**     **695**
27.1. Join a Computer to a Domain or Workgroup     695
27.2. Remove a Computer from a Domain     696
27.3. Rename a Computer     697
27.4. Program: List Logon or Logoff Scripts for a User     698
27.5. Program: List Startup or Shutdown Scripts for a Machine     699
27.6. Deploy PowerShell-Based Logon Scripts     701
27.7. Enable or Disable the Windows Firewall     702
27.8. Open or Close Ports in the Windows Firewall     702
27.9. Program: List All Installed Software     704
27.10. Uninstall an Application     705
27.11. Manage Computer Restore Points     706
27.12. Reboot or Shut Down a Computer     708
27.13. Determine Whether a Hotfix Is Installed     710
27.14. Manage Scheduled Tasks on a Computer     710
27.15. Retrieve Printer Information     714
27.16. Retrieve Printer Queue Statistics     715
27.17. Manage Printers and Print Queues     717

27.18. Program: Summarize System Information                            718
27.19. Renew a DHCP Lease                                               720
27.20. Assign a Static IP Address                                       721
27.21. List All IP Addresses for a Computer                             723
27.22. List Network Adapter Properties                                  724

**28. Windows Management Instrumentation.** . . . . . . . . . . . . . . . . . . . . . . . . . . . . . . . . . **727**
28.1. Access Windows Management Instrumentation and CIM Data            730
28.2. Modify the Properties of a WMI or CIM Instance                    732
28.3. Invoke a Method on a WMI Instance or Class                        734
28.4. Program: Determine Properties Available to WMI and CIM Filters    736
28.5. Program: Search for WMI Classes                                   737
28.6. Use .NET to Perform Advanced WMI Tasks                            740
28.7. Improve the Performance of Large-Scale WMI Operations             742
28.8. Convert a VBScript WMI Script to PowerShell                       743

**29. Remoting.** . . . . . . . . . . . . . . . . . . . . . . . . . . . . . . . . . . . . . . . . . . . . . . . . . . . . . . . **749**
29.1. Find Commands That Support Their Own Remoting                     750
29.2. Enable PowerShell Remoting on a Computer                          752
29.3. Interactively Manage a Remote Computer                            754
29.4. Invoke a Command on a Remote Computer                             756
29.5. Disconnect and Reconnect PowerShell Sessions                      760
29.6. Program: Remotely Enable PowerShell Remoting                      763
29.7. Program: Invoke a PowerShell Expression on a Remote Machine       765
29.8. Test Connectivity Between Two Computers                           768
29.9. Limit Networking Scripts to Hosts That Respond                    771
29.10. Enable Remote Desktop on a Computer                              772
29.11. Configure User Permissions for Remoting                          772
29.12. Enable Remoting to Workgroup Computers                           774
29.13. Implicitly Invoke Commands from a Remote Computer                776
29.14. Create Sessions with Full Network Access                         779
29.15. Pass Variables to Remote Sessions                                783
29.16. Configure Advanced Remoting Quotas and Options                   785
29.17. Invoke a Command on Many Computers                               787
29.18. Run a Local Script on a Remote Computer                          789
29.19. Program: Transfer a File to a Remote Computer                    790
29.20. Determine Whether a Script Is Running on a Remote Computer       793
29.21. Create a Task-Specific Remoting Endpoint                         794

**30. Workflows.** . . . . . . . . . . . . . . . . . . . . . . . . . . . . . . . . . . . . . . . . . . . . . . . . . . . . . . **801**
30.1. Write a Workflow                                                  802
30.2. Run a Workflow                                                    808

30.3. Suspend and Resume a Workflow                                         811
30.4. Invoke Islands of Traditional PowerShell Script                       814
30.5. Invoke Workflow Actions in Parallel                                   816
30.6. Customize an Activity's Connection Parameters                         819
30.7. Write a Workflow That Requires Human Intervention                     825
30.8. Add Raw XAML to a Workflow                                            827
30.9. Reference Custom Activities in a Workflow                             828
30.10. Debug or Troubleshoot a Workflow                                     830
30.11. Use PowerShell Activities from a Traditional Windows Workflow
Application                                                                 834

31. Transactions. . . . . . . . . . . . . . . . . . . . . . . . . . . . . . . . . . . . . . . . . . . . . . . . . . . . . . . . . . . 837
31.1. Safely Experiment with Transactions                                   839
31.2. Change Error Recovery Behavior in Transactions                        841

32. Event Handling. . . . . . . . . . . . . . . . . . . . . . . . . . . . . . . . . . . . . . . . . . . . . . . . . . . . . . . 845
32.1. Respond to Automatically Generated Events                             846
32.2. Create and Respond to Custom Events                                   849
32.3. Create a Temporary Event Subscription                                 852
32.4. Forward Events from a Remote Computer                                 853
32.5. Investigate Internal Event Action State                               854
32.6. Use a Script Block as a .NET Delegate or Event Handler                856

## Part V.    References

A. PowerShell Language and Environment. . . . . . . . . . . . . . . . . . . . . . . . . . . . . . . . . . . . 861

B. Regular Expression Reference. . . . . . . . . . . . . . . . . . . . . . . . . . . . . . . . . . . . . . . . . . 919

C. XPath Quick Reference. . . . . . . . . . . . . . . . . . . . . . . . . . . . . . . . . . . . . . . . . . . . . . . . 929

D. .NET String Formatting. . . . . . . . . . . . . . . . . . . . . . . . . . . . . . . . . . . . . . . . . . . . . . . 933

E. .NET DateTime Formatting. . . . . . . . . . . . . . . . . . . . . . . . . . . . . . . . . . . . . . . . . . . . 937

F. Selected .NET Classes and Their Uses. . . . . . . . . . . . . . . . . . . . . . . . . . . . . . . . . . . 943

G. WMI Reference. . . . . . . . . . . . . . . . . . . . . . . . . . . . . . . . . . . . . . . . . . . . . . . . . . . . . . 951

H. Selected COM Objects and Their Uses. . . . . . . . . . . . . . . . . . . . . . . . . . . . . . . . . . . 959

I. Selected Events and Their Uses. . . . . . . . . . . . . . . . . . . . . . . . . . . . . . . . . . . . . . . 963

J. Standard PowerShell Verbs. . . . . . . . . . . . . . . . . . . . . . . . . . . . . . . . . . . . . . . . . 971

Index. . . . . . . . . . . . . . . . . . . . . . . . . . . . . . . . . . . . . . . . . . . . . . . . . . . . . . . . . . 975

# Foreword

When Lee Holmes asked me to write the introduction to the third edition of his *Windows PowerShell Cookbook*, I was deeply honored. I have known Lee for a long time, and we meet in real life every time I am out in Redmond, or when we happen to be speaking at the same conference. If you are like me, you already own the first two editions of this great book. You may even be asking yourself why you need a third edition of the same book, and I will tell you: this is not the same book. It is a completely revised book that takes advantage of the significant changes we have made to both Windows PowerShell 3.0 and to the underlying operating system.

Consider this: Windows PowerShell 1.0 had 129 cmdlets, but Windows PowerShell 3.0 on Windows 8 has over 2,000 cmdlets and functions. Because Lee's book is so practical in nature—it is, after all, a cookbook—this means that with so many more ingredients to add to the recipes, the recipes will necessarily change. In addition, with the new functionality comes additional opportunities for new recipes.

More than just a cookbook, however, the third edition of the Windows PowerShell Cookbook is also a textbook of how to write great Windows PowerShell scripts. Just as a budding saxophonist benefits from watching a legend such as Charlie Parker ply his ax, so too does a budding scripter benefit from watching one of the guys who *literally wrote* Windows PowerShell write scripts. Each of these recipes is a perfectly crafted example of a Windows PowerShell script—your task is to study these scripts so you can go and do likewise.

—Ed Wilson
*Microsoft Scripting Guy and author of* Windows Powershell 3.0
*and* Windows PowerShell 2.0 Best Practices

# Preface

In late 2002, Slashdot posted a story about a "next-generation shell" rumored to be in development at Microsoft. As a longtime fan of the power unlocked by shells and their scripting languages, the post immediately captured my interest. Could this shell provide the command-line power and productivity I'd long loved on Unix systems?

Since I had just joined Microsoft six months earlier, I jumped at the chance to finally get to the bottom of a Slashdot-sourced Microsoft Mystery. The post talked about strong integration with the .NET Framework, so I posted a query to an internal C# mailing list. I got a response that the project was called "Monad," which I then used to track down an internal prototype build.

Prototype was a generous term. In its early stages, the build was primarily a proof of concept. Want to clear the screen? No problem! Just lean on the Enter key until your previous commands and output scroll out of view! But even at these early stages, it was immediately clear that Monad marked a revolution in command-line shells. As with many things of this magnitude, its beauty was self-evident. Monad passed full-fidelity .NET objects between its commands. For even the most complex commands, Monad abolished the (until now, standard) need for fragile text-based parsing. Simple and powerful data manipulation tools supported this new model, creating a shell both powerful and easy to use.

I joined the Monad development team shortly after that to help do my part to bring this masterpiece of technology to the rest of the world. Since then, Monad has grown to become a real, tangible product—now called Windows PowerShell.

So why write a book about it? And why *this* book?

Many users have picked up PowerShell for the sake of learning PowerShell. Any tangible benefits come by way of side effect. Others, though, might prefer to opportunistically learn a new technology as it solves their needs. How do you use PowerShell to navigate the filesystem? How can you manage files and folders? Retrieve a web page?

This book focuses squarely on helping you learn PowerShell through task-based solutions to your most pressing problems. Read a recipe, read a chapter, or read the entire book—regardless, you're bound to learn something.

## Who This Book Is For

This book helps you use PowerShell to *get things done*. It contains hundreds of solutions to specific, real-world problems. For systems management, you'll find plenty of examples that show how to manage the filesystem, the Windows Registry, event logs, processes, and more. For enterprise administration, you'll find two entire chapters devoted to WMI, Active Directory, and other enterprise-focused tasks.

Along the way, you'll also learn an enormous amount about PowerShell: its features, its commands, and its scripting language—but most importantly you'll solve problems.

## How This Book Is Organized

This book consists of five main sections: a guided tour of PowerShell, PowerShell fundamentals, common tasks, administrator tasks, and a detailed reference.

### Part I: Tour

A Guided Tour of Windows PowerShell breezes through PowerShell at a high level. It introduces PowerShell's core features:

- An interactive shell
- A new command model
- An object-based pipeline
- A razor-sharp focus on administrators
- A consistent model for learning and discovery
- Ubiquitous scripting
- Integration with critical management technologies
- A consistent model for interacting with data stores

The tour helps you become familiar with PowerShell as a whole. This familiarity will create a mental framework for you to understand the solutions from the rest of the book.

## Part II: Fundamentals

Chapters 1 through 8 cover the fundamentals that underpin the solutions in this book. This section introduces you to the PowerShell interactive shell, fundamental pipeline and object concepts, and many features of the PowerShell scripting language.

## Part III: Common Tasks

Chapters 9 through 19 cover the tasks you will run into most commonly when starting to tackle more complex problems in PowerShell. This includes working with simple and structured files, Internet-connected scripts, code reuse, user interaction, and more.

## Part IV: Administrator Tasks

Chapters 20 through 32 focus on the most common tasks in systems and enterprise management. Chapters 20 through 25 focus on individual systems: the filesystem, the registry, event logs, processes, services, and more. Chapters 26 and 27 focus on Active Directory, as well as the typical tasks most common in managing networked or domain-joined systems. Chapters 28 through 30 focus on the three crucial facets of robust multi-machine management: WMI, PowerShell Remoting, and PowerShell Workflows.

## Part V: References

Many books belch useless information into their appendixes simply to increase page count. In this book, however, the detailed references underpin an integral and essential resource for learning and using PowerShell. The appendixes cover:

- The PowerShell language and environment
- Regular expression syntax and PowerShell-focused examples
- XPath quick reference
- .NET string formatting syntax and PowerShell-focused examples
- .NET DateTime formatting syntax and PowerShell-focused examples
- Administrator-friendly .NET classes and their uses
- Administrator-friendly WMI classes and their uses
- Administrator-friendly COM objects and their uses
- Selected events and their uses
- PowerShell's standard verbs

# What You Need to Use This Book

The majority of this book requires only a working installation of Windows PowerShell. Windows 7, Windows 8, Windows Server 2008 R2, and Windows Server 2012 include Windows PowerShell by default. If you do not yet have PowerShell installed, you may obtain it by following the download link here (*http://www.microsoft.com/PowerShell*). This link provides download instructions for PowerShell on Windows XP, Windows Server 2003, and Windows Vista. For Windows Server 2008, PowerShell comes installed as an optional component that you can enable through the Control Panel like other optional components.

The Active Directory scripts given in Chapter 26 are most useful when applied to an enterprise environment, but Recipe 26.1, "Test Active Directory Scripts on a Local Installation" shows how to install additional software (Active Directory Lightweight Directory Services, or Active Directory Application Mode) that lets you run these scripts against a local installation.

# Conventions Used in This Book

The following typographical conventions are used in this book:

Plain text
> Indicates menu titles, menu options, menu buttons, and keyboard accelerators

*Italic*
> Indicates new terms, URLs, email addresses, filenames, file extensions, pathnames, directories, and Unix utilities

`Constant width`
> Indicates commands, options, switches, variables, attributes, keys, functions, types, classes, namespaces, methods, modules, properties, parameters, values, objects, events, event handlers, tags, macros, or the output from commands

**`Constant width bold`**
> Shows commands or other text that should be typed literally by the user

*`Constant width italic`*
> Shows text that should be replaced with user-supplied values

 This icon signifies a tip, suggestion, or general note.

This icon indicates a warning or caution.

# Code Examples

## Obtaining Code Examples

To obtain electronic versions of the programs and examples given in this book, visit the *Examples* link here (*http://oreil.ly/powershell-cookbook*).

## Using Code Examples

This book is here to help you get your job done. In general, you may use the code in this book in your programs and documentation. You do not need to contact us for permission unless you're reproducing a significant portion of the code. For example, writing a program that uses several chunks of code from this book does not require permission. Selling or distributing a CD-ROM of examples from O'Reilly books *does* require permission. Answering a question by citing this book and quoting example code does not require permission. Incorporating a significant amount of example code from this book into your product's documentation *does* require permission.

We appreciate, but do not require, attribution. An attribution usually includes the title, author, publisher, and ISBN. For example: "*Windows PowerShell Cookbook, Third Edition,* by Lee Holmes (O'Reilly). Copyright 2013 Lee Holmes, 978-1-449-32068-3."

If you feel your use of code examples falls outside fair use or the permission given, feel free to contact us at *permissions@oreilly.com*.

# Safari® Books Online

 Safari Books Online (*www.safaribooksonline.com*) is an on-demand digital library that delivers expert content in both book and video form from the world's leading authors in technology and business.

Technology professionals, software developers, web designers, and business and creative professionals use Safari Books Online as their primary resource for research, problem solving, learning, and certification training.

Safari Books Online offers a range of product mixes and pricing programs for organizations, government agencies, and individuals. Subscribers have access to thousands of books, training videos, and prepublication manuscripts in one fully searchable database from publishers like O'Reilly Media, Prentice Hall Professional, Addison-Wesley Professional, Microsoft Press, Sams, Que, Peachpit Press, Focal Press, Cisco Press, John

Wiley & Sons, Syngress, Morgan Kaufmann, IBM Redbooks, Packt, Adobe Press, FT Press, Apress, Manning, New Riders, McGraw-Hill, Jones & Bartlett, Course Technology, and dozens more. For more information about Safari Books Online, please visit us online.

## How to Contact Us

Please address comments and questions concerning this book to the publisher:

O'Reilly Media, Inc.
1005 Gravenstein Highway North
Sebastopol, CA 95472
800-998-9938 (in the United States or Canada)
707-829-0515 (international or local)
707-829-0104 (fax)

We have a web page for this book, where we list errata, examples, and any additional information. You can access this page at *http://oreil.ly/powershell-cookbook*.

To comment or ask technical questions about this book, send email to *bookques tions@oreilly.com*.

For more information about our books, courses, conferences, and news, see our website at *http://www.oreilly.com*.

Find us on Facebook: *http://facebook.com/oreilly*

Follow us on Twitter: *http://twitter.com/oreillymedia*

Watch us on YouTube: *http://www.youtube.com/oreillymedia*

## Acknowledgments

Writing is the task of crafting icebergs. The heft of the book you hold in your hands is just a hint of the multiyear, multirelease effort it took to get it there. And by a cast much larger than me.

The groundwork started decades ago. My parents nurtured my interest in computers and software, supported an evening-only bulletin board service, put up with "viruses" that told them to buy a new computer for Christmas, and even listened to me blather about batch files or how PowerShell compares to Excel. Without their support, who knows where I'd be.

My family and friends have helped keep me sane for two editions of the book now. Ariel: you are the light of my life. Robin: thinking of you reminds me each day that serendipity is still alive and well in this busy world. Thank you to all of my friends and family for being there for me. You can have me back now. :)

I would not have written either edition of this book without the tremendous influence of Guy Allen, visionary of the University of Toronto's Professional Writing program. Guy: your mentoring forever changed me, just as it molds thousands of others from English hackers into writers.

Of course, members of the PowerShell team (both new and old) are the ones that made this a book about PowerShell. Building this product with you has been a unique challenge and experience—but most of all, a distinct pleasure. In addition to the PowerShell team, the entire PowerShell community defined this book's focus. From MVPs to early adopters to newsgroup lurkers: your support, questions, and feedback have been the inspiration behind each page.

Converting thoughts into print always involves a cast of unsung heroes, even though each author tries his best to convince the world how important these heroes are.

Thank you to the many technical reviewers who participated in O'Reilly's Open Feedback Publishing System, especially Aleksandar Nikolic and Shay Levy. I truly appreciate you donating your nights and weekends to help craft something of which we can all be proud.

To the awesome staff at O'Reilly—Rachel Roumeliotis, Kara Ebrahim, Mike Hendrickson, Genevieve d'Entremont, Teresa Elsey, Laurel Ruma, the O'Reilly Tools Monks, and the production team—your patience and persistence helped craft a book that holds true to its original vision. You also ensured that the book didn't just knock around in my head but actually got out the door.

This book would not have been possible without the support from each and every one of you.

# PART I

# Tour

# A Guided Tour of Windows PowerShell

## Introduction

Windows PowerShell promises to revolutionize the world of system management and command-line shells. From its object-based pipelines to its administrator focus to its enormous reach into other Microsoft management technologies, PowerShell drastically improves the productivity of administrators and power users alike.

When you're learning a new technology, it is natural to feel bewildered at first by all the unfamiliar features and functionality. This perhaps rings especially true for users new to Windows PowerShell because it may be their first experience with a fully featured command-line shell. Or worse, they've heard stories of PowerShell's fantastic integrated scripting capabilities and fear being forced into a world of programming that they've actively avoided until now.

Fortunately, these fears are entirely misguided; PowerShell is a shell that both grows with you and grows on you. Let's take a tour to see what it is capable of:

- PowerShell works with standard Windows commands and applications. You don't have to throw away what you already know and use.

- PowerShell introduces a powerful new type of command. PowerShell commands (called *cmdlets*) share a common *Verb-Noun* syntax and offer many usability improvements over standard commands.

- PowerShell understands objects. Working directly with richly structured objects makes working with (and combining) PowerShell commands immensely easier than working in the plain-text world of traditional shells.

- PowerShell caters to administrators. Even with all its advances, PowerShell focuses strongly on its use as an interactive shell: the experience of entering commands in a running PowerShell application.

- PowerShell supports discovery. Using three simple commands, you can learn and discover almost anything PowerShell has to offer.

- PowerShell enables ubiquitous scripting. With a fully fledged scripting language that works directly from the command line, PowerShell lets you automate tasks with ease.

- PowerShell bridges many technologies. By letting you work with .NET, COM, WMI, XML, and Active Directory, PowerShell makes working with these previously isolated technologies easier than ever before.

- PowerShell simplifies management of data stores. Through its provider model, PowerShell lets you manage data stores using the same techniques you already use to manage files and folders.

We'll explore each of these pillars in this introductory tour of PowerShell. If you are running Windows 7 (or later) or Windows 2008 R2 (or later), PowerShell is already installed. If not, visit the download link here (*http://www.microsoft.com/PowerShell*) to install it. PowerShell and its supporting technologies are together referred to as the *Windows Management Framework*.

# An Interactive Shell

At its core, PowerShell is first and foremost an interactive shell. While it supports scripting and other powerful features, its focus as a shell underpins everything.

Getting started in PowerShell is a simple matter of launching *PowerShell.exe* rather than *cmd.exe*—the shells begin to diverge as you explore the intermediate and advanced functionality, but you can be productive in PowerShell immediately.

To launch Windows PowerShell, do one of the following:

- Click Start→All Programs→Accessories→Windows PowerShell.

- Click Start→Run, and then type **PowerShell**.

A PowerShell prompt window opens that's nearly identical to the traditional command prompt window of Windows XP, Windows Server 2003, and their many ancestors. The `PS C:\Users\Lee>` prompt indicates that PowerShell is ready for input, as shown in Figure I-1.

*Figure I-1. Windows PowerShell, ready for input*

Once you've launched your PowerShell prompt, you can enter DOS-style and Unix-style commands to navigate around the filesystem just as you would with any Windows or Unix command prompt—as in the interactive session shown in Example I-1. In this example, we use the pushd, cd, dir, pwd, and popd commands to store the current location, navigate around the filesystem, list items in the current directory, and then return to the original location. Try it!

*Example I-1. Entering many standard DOS- and Unix-style file manipulation commands produces the same results you get when you use them with any other Windows shell*

```
PS C:\Documents and Settings\Lee> function Prompt { "PS > " }
PS > pushd .
PS > cd \
PS > dir


    Directory: C:\


Mode                LastWriteTime     Length Name
----                -------------     ------ ----
d----        11/2/2006    4:36 AM            $WINDOWS.~BT
d----         5/8/2007    8:37 PM            Blurpark
d----       11/29/2006    2:47 PM            Boot
d----       11/28/2006    2:10 PM            DECCHECK
d----        10/7/2006    4:30 PM            Documents and Settings
```

```
d----        5/21/2007    6:02 PM              F&SC-demo
d----         4/2/2007    7:21 PM              Inetpub
d----        5/20/2007    4:59 PM              Program Files
d----        5/21/2007    7:26 PM              temp
d----        5/21/2007    8:55 PM              Windows
-a---         1/7/2006   10:37 PM          0  autoexec.bat
-ar-s       11/29/2006    1:39 PM       8192  BOOTSECT.BAK
-a---         1/7/2006   10:37 PM          0  config.sys
-a---         5/1/2007    8:43 PM      33057  RUU.log
-a---         4/2/2007    7:46 PM       2487  secedit.INTEG.RAW

PS > popd
PS > pwd

Path
----
C:\Users\Lee
```

In this example, our first command customizes the prompt. In *cmd.exe*, customizing the prompt looks like `prompt $P$G`. In bash, it looks like `PS1="[\h] \w> "`. In Power-Shell, you define a function that returns whatever you want displayed. Recipe 11.2, "Write a Function" introduces functions and how to write them.

The `pushd` command is an alternative name (alias) to the much more descriptively named PowerShell command `Push-Location`. Likewise, the `cd`, `dir`, `popd`, and `pwd` commands all have more memorable counterparts.

Although navigating around the filesystem is helpful, so is running the tools you know and love, such as `ipconfig` and `notepad`. Type the command name and you'll see results like those shown in Example I-2.

*Example I-2. Windows tools and applications such as ipconfig run in PowerShell just as they do in cmd.exe*

```
PS > ipconfig

Windows IP Configuration


Ethernet adapter Wireless Network Connection 4:

        Connection-specific DNS Suffix  . : hsd1.wa.comcast.net.
        IP Address. . . . . . . . . . . . : 192.168.1.100
        Subnet Mask . . . . . . . . . . . : 255.255.255.0
        Default Gateway . . . . . . . . . : 192.168.1.1
PS > notepad
(notepad launches)
```

Entering `ipconfig` displays the IP addresses of your current network connections. Entering `notepad` runs—as you'd expect—the Notepad editor that ships with Windows. Try them both on your own machine.

## Structured Commands (Cmdlets)

In addition to supporting traditional Windows executables, PowerShell introduces a powerful new type of command called a *cmdlet* (pronounced "command-let"). All cmdlets are named in a *Verb-Noun* pattern, such as `Get-Process`, `Get-Content`, and `Stop-Process`.

```
PS > Get-Process -Name lsass

Handles  NPM(K)    PM(K)    WS(K) VM(M)   CPU(s)     Id ProcessName
-------  ------    -----    ----- -----   ------     -- -----------
    668      13     6228     1660    46            932 lsass
```

In this example, you provide a value to the `ProcessName` parameter to get a specific process by name.

 Once you know the handful of common verbs in PowerShell, learning how to work with new nouns becomes much easier. While you may never have worked with a certain object before (such as a Service), the standard `Get`, `Set`, `Start`, and `Stop` actions still apply. For a list of these common verbs, see Table J-1 in Appendix J.

You don't always have to type these full cmdlet names, however. PowerShell lets you use the `Tab` key to autocomplete cmdlet names and parameter names:

```
PS > Get-Pr<TAB> -N<TAB> lsass
```

For quick interactive use, even that may be too much typing. To help improve your efficiency, PowerShell defines aliases for all common commands and lets you define your own. In addition to alias names, PowerShell requires only that you type enough of the parameter name to disambiguate it from the rest of the parameters in that cmdlet. PowerShell is also case-insensitive. Using the built-in `gps` alias (which represents the `Get-Process` cmdlet) along with parameter shortening, you can instead type:

```
PS > gps -n lsass
```

Going even further, PowerShell supports *positional parameters* on cmdlets. Positional parameters let you provide parameter values in a certain position on the command line, rather than having to specify them by name. The `Get-Process` cmdlet takes a process name as its first positional parameter. This parameter even supports wildcards:

```
PS > gps l*s
```

## Deep Integration of Objects

PowerShell begins to flex more of its muscle as you explore the way it handles structured data and richly functional objects. For example, the following command generates a simple text string. Since nothing captures that output, PowerShell displays it to you:

```
PS > "Hello World"
Hello World
```

The string you just generated is, in fact, a fully functional object from the .NET Framework. For example, you can access its Length property, which tells you how many characters are in the string. To access a property, you place a dot between the object and its property name:

```
PS > "Hello World".Length
11
```

All PowerShell commands that produce output generate that output as objects as well. For example, the Get-Process cmdlet generates a System.Diagnostics.Process object, which you can store in a variable. In PowerShell, variable names start with a $ character. If you have an instance of Notepad running, the following command stores a reference to it:

```
$process = Get-Process notepad
```

Since this is a fully functional Process object from the .NET Framework, you can call methods on that object to perform actions on it. This command calls the Kill() method, which stops a process. To access a method, you place a dot between the object and its method name:

```
$process.Kill()
```

PowerShell supports this functionality more directly through the Stop-Process cmdlet, but this example demonstrates an important point about your ability to interact with these rich objects.

## Administrators as First-Class Users

While PowerShell's support for objects from the .NET Framework quickens the pulse of most users, PowerShell continues to focus strongly on administrative tasks. For example, PowerShell supports MB (for megabyte) and GB (for gigabyte) as some of its standard administrative constants. For example, how many disks will it take to back up a 40 GB hard drive to CD-ROM?

```
PS > 40GB / 650MB
63.0153846153846
```

Although the .NET Framework is traditionally a development platform, it contains a wealth of functionality useful for administrators too! In fact, it makes PowerShell a great calendar. For example, is 2008 a leap year? PowerShell can tell you:

```
PS > [DateTime]::IsLeapYear(2008)
True
```

Going further, how might you determine how much time remains until summer? The following command converts "06/21/2011" (the start of summer) to a date, and then subtracts the current date from that. It stores the result in the $result variable, and then accesses the TotalDays property.

```
PS > $result = [DateTime] "06/21/2011" - [DateTime]::Now
PS > $result.TotalDays
283.0549285662616
```

# Composable Commands

Whenever a command generates output, you can use a *pipeline character* (|) to pass that output directly to another command as input. If the second command understands the objects produced by the first command, it can operate on the results. You can chain together many commands this way, creating powerful compositions out of a few simple operations. For example, the following command gets all items in the *Path1* directory and moves them to the *Path2* directory:

```
Get-Item Path1\* | Move-Item -Destination Path2
```

You can create even more complex commands by adding additional cmdlets to the pipeline. In Example I-3, the first command gets all processes running on the system. It passes those to the Where-Object cmdlet, which runs a comparison against each incoming item. In this case, the comparison is $_.Handles -ge 500, which checks whether the Handles property of the current object (represented by the $_ variable) is greater than or equal to 500. For each object in which this comparison holds true, you pass the results to the Sort-Object cmdlet, asking it to sort items by their Handles property. Finally, you pass the objects to the Format-Table cmdlet to generate a table that contains the Handles, Name, and Description of the process.

*Example I-3. You can build more complex PowerShell commands by using pipelines to link cmdlets, as shown here with Get-Process, Where-Object, Sort-Object, and Format-Table*

```
PS > Get-Process |
    Where-Object { $_.Handles -ge 500 } |
    Sort-Object Handles |
    Format-Table Handles,Name,Description -Auto
```

```
Handles Name        Description
------- ----        -----------
    588 winlogon
    592 svchost
    667 lsass
    725 csrss
    742 System
    964 WINWORD     Microsoft Office Word
   1112 OUTLOOK     Microsoft Office Outlook
   2063 svchost
```

## Techniques to Protect You from Yourself

While aliases, wildcards, and composable pipelines are powerful, their use in commands that modify system information can easily be nerve-racking. After all, what does this command do? Think about it, but don't try it just yet:

```
PS > gps [b-t]*[c-r] | Stop-Process
```

It appears to stop all processes that begin with the letters b through t and end with the letters c through r. How can you be sure? Let PowerShell tell you. For commands that modify data, PowerShell supports -WhatIf and -Confirm parameters that let you see what a command *would* do:

```
PS > gps [b-t]*[c-r] | Stop-Process -whatif
What if: Performing operation "Stop-Process" on Target "ctfmon (812)".
What if: Performing operation "Stop-Process" on Target "Ditto (1916)".
What if: Performing operation "Stop-Process" on Target "dsamain (316)".
What if: Performing operation "Stop-Process" on Target "ehrecvr (1832)".
What if: Performing operation "Stop-Process" on Target "ehSched (1852)".
What if: Performing operation "Stop-Process" on Target "EXCEL (2092)".
What if: Performing operation "Stop-Process" on Target "explorer (1900)".
(...)
```

In this interaction, using the -WhatIf parameter with the Stop-Process pipelined command lets you preview which processes on your system will be stopped before you actually carry out the operation.

Note that this example is not a dare! In the words of one reviewer:

> Not only did it stop everything, but on Vista, it forced a shutdown with only one minute warning!
>
> It was very funny though...At least I had enough time to save everything first!

# Common Discovery Commands

While reading through a guided tour is helpful, I find that most learning happens in an ad hoc fashion. To find all commands that match a given wildcard, use the Get-Command cmdlet. For example, by entering the following, you can find out which PowerShell commands (and Windows applications) contain the word *process*.

```
PS > Get-Command *process*

CommandType     Name              Definition
-----------     ----              ----------
Cmdlet          Get-Process       Get-Process [[-Name] <Str...
Application     qprocess.exe      c:\windows\system32\qproc...
Cmdlet          Stop-Process      Stop-Process [-Id] <Int32...
```

To see what a command such as Get-Process does, use the Get-Help cmdlet, like this:

```
PS > Get-Help Get-Process
```

Since PowerShell lets you work with objects from the .NET Framework, it provides the Get-Member cmdlet to retrieve information about the properties and methods that an object, such as a .NET System.String, supports. Piping a string to the Get-Member command displays its type name and its members:

```
PS > "Hello World" | Get-Member


    TypeName: System.String

Name              MemberType            Definition
----              ----------            ----------
(...)
PadLeft           Method                System.String PadLeft(Int32 tota...
PadRight          Method                System.String PadRight(Int32 tot...
Remove            Method                System.String Remove(Int32 start...
Replace           Method                System.String Replace(Char oldCh...
Split             Method                System.String[] Split(Params Cha...
StartsWith        Method                System.Boolean StartsWith(String...
Substring         Method                System.String Substring(Int32 st...
ToCharArray       Method                System.Char[] ToCharArray(), Sys...
ToLower           Method                System.String ToLower(), System....
ToLowerInvariant  Method                System.String ToLowerInvariant()
ToString          Method                System.String ToString(), System...
ToUpper           Method                System.String ToUpper(), System....
ToUpperInvariant  Method                System.String ToUpperInvariant()
Trim              Method                System.String Trim(Params Char[]...
TrimEnd           Method                System.String TrimEnd(Params Cha...
TrimStart         Method                System.String TrimStart(Params C...
Chars             ParameterizedProperty System.Char Chars(Int32 index) {...
Length            Property              System.Int32 Length {get;}
```

# Ubiquitous Scripting

PowerShell makes no distinction between the commands typed at the command line and the commands written in a script. Your favorite cmdlets work in scripts and your favorite scripting techniques (e.g., the foreach statement) work directly on the command line. For example, to add up the handle count for all running processes:

```
PS > $handleCount = 0
PS > foreach($process in Get-Process) { $handleCount += $process.Handles }
PS > $handleCount
19403
```

While PowerShell provides a command (Measure-Object) to measure statistics about collections, this short example shows how PowerShell lets you apply techniques that normally require a separate scripting or programming language.

In addition to using PowerShell scripting keywords, you can also create and work directly with objects from the .NET Framework that you may be familiar with. PowerShell becomes almost like the C# immediate mode in Visual Studio. Example I-4 shows how PowerShell lets you easily interact with the .NET Framework.

*Example I-4. Using objects from the .NET Framework to retrieve a web page and process its content*

```
PS > $webClient = New-Object System.Net.WebClient
PS > $content = $webClient.DownloadString(
                "http://blogs.msdn.com/PowerShell/rss.aspx")
PS > $content.Substring(0,1000)
<?xml version="1.0" encoding="UTF-8" ?>
<?xml-stylesheet type="text/xsl" href="http://blogs.msdn.com/utility/FeedS
tylesheets/rss.xsl" media="screen"?><rss version="2.0" xmlns:dc="http://pu
rl.org/dc/elements/1.1/" xmlns:slash="http://purl.org/rss/1.0/modules/slas
h/" xmlns:wfw="http://wellformedweb.org/CommentAPI/"><channel><title>Windo
(...)
```

# Ad Hoc Development

By blurring the lines between interactive administration and writing scripts, the history buffers of PowerShell sessions quickly become the basis for ad hoc script development. In this example, you call the Get-History cmdlet to retrieve the history of your session. For each item, you get its CommandLine property (the thing you typed) and send the output to a new script file.

```
PS > Get-History | Foreach-Object { $_.CommandLine } > c:\temp\script.ps1
PS > notepad c:\temp\script.ps1
(save the content you want to keep)
PS > c:\temp\script.ps1
```

If this is the first time you've run a script in PowerShell, you will need to configure your execution policy. For more information about selecting an execution policy, see Recipe 18.1, "Enable Scripting Through an Execution Policy".

For more detail about saving your session history into a script, see Recipe 1.21, "Program: Create Scripts from Your Session History".

# Bridging Technologies

We've seen how PowerShell lets you fully leverage the .NET Framework in your tasks, but its support for common technologies stretches even further. As Example I-5 (continued from Example I-4) shows, PowerShell supports XML.

*Example I-5. Working with XML content in PowerShell*

```
PS > $xmlContent = [xml] $content
PS > $xmlContent

xml                     xml-stylesheet          rss
---                     --------------          ---
version="1.0" encoding... type="text/xsl" href="... rss

PS > $xmlContent.rss

version : 2.0
dc      : http://purl.org/dc/elements/1.1/
slash   : http://purl.org/rss/1.0/modules/slash/
wfw     : http://wellformedweb.org/CommentAPI/
channel : channel

PS > $xmlContent.rss.channel.item | select Title

title
-----
CMD.exe compatibility
Time Stamping Log Files
Microsoft Compute Cluster now has a PowerShell Provider and Cmdlets
The Virtuous Cycle: .NET Developers using PowerShell
(...)
```

PowerShell also lets you work with Windows Management Instrumentation (WMI) and CIM:

```
PS > Get-CimInstance Win32_Bios

SMBIOSBIOSVersion : ASUS A7N8X Deluxe ACPI BIOS Rev 1009
```

```
Manufacturer      : Phoenix Technologies, LTD
Name              : Phoenix - AwardBIOS v6.00PG
SerialNumber      : xxxxxxxxxxx
Version           : Nvidia - 42302e31
```

Or, as Example I-6 shows, you can work with Active Directory Service Interfaces (ADSI).

*Example I-6. Working with Active Directory in PowerShell*

```
PS > [ADSI] "WinNT://./Administrator" | Format-List *
```

```
UserFlags                    : {66113}
MaxStorage                   : {-1}
PasswordAge                  : {19550795}
PasswordExpired              : {0}
LoginHours                   : {255 255 255 255 255 255 255 255 255 255 255
                               255 255 255 255 255 255 255 255 255 255}
FullName                     : {}
Description                  : {Built-in account for administering the compu
                               ter/domain}
BadPasswordAttempts          : {0}
LastLogin                    : {5/21/2007 3:00:00 AM}
HomeDirectory                : {}
LoginScript                  : {}
Profile                      : {}
HomeDirDrive                 : {}
Parameters                   : {}
PrimaryGroupID               : {513}
Name                         : {Administrator}
MinPasswordLength            : {0}
MaxPasswordAge               : {3710851}
MinPasswordAge               : {0}
PasswordHistoryLength        : {0}
AutoUnlockInterval           : {1800}
LockoutObservationInterval   : {1800}
MaxBadPasswordsAllowed       : {0}
RasPermissions               : {1}
objectSid                    : {1 5 0 0 0 0 0 5 21 0 0 0 121 227 252 83 122
                               130 50 34 67 23 10 50 244 1 0 0}
```

Or, as Example I-7 shows, you can even use PowerShell for scripting traditional COM objects.

*Example I-7. Working with COM objects in PowerShell*

```
PS > $firewall = New-Object -com HNetCfg.FwMgr
PS > $firewall.LocalPolicy.CurrentProfile
```

```
Type                                               : 1
FirewallEnabled                                    : True
ExceptionsNotAllowed                               : False
NotificationsDisabled                              : False
UnicastResponsesToMulticastBroadcastDisabled       : False
```

---

```
RemoteAdminSettings                        : System.__ComObject
IcmpSettings                               : System.__ComObject
GloballyOpenPorts                          : {Media Center Extender Serv
                                             ice, Remote Media Center Ex
                                             perience, Adam Test Instanc
                                             e, QWAVE...}
Services                                   : {File and Printer Sharing,
                                             UPnP Framework, Remote Desk
                                             top}
AuthorizedApplications                     : {Remote Assistance, Windows
                                             Messenger, Media Center, T
                                             rillian...}
```

# Namespace Navigation Through Providers

Another avenue PowerShell offers for working with the system is *providers*. PowerShell providers let you navigate and manage data stores using the same techniques you already use to work with the filesystem, as illustrated in Example I-8.

*Example I-8. Navigating the filesystem*

```
PS > Set-Location c:\
PS > Get-ChildItem


    Directory: C:\


Mode                LastWriteTime     Length Name
----                -------------     ------ ----
d----         11/2/2006    4:36 AM           $WINDOWS.~BT
d----          5/8/2007    8:37 PM           Blurpark
d----         11/29/2006   2:47 PM           Boot
d----         11/28/2006   2:10 PM           DECCHECK
d----         10/7/2006    4:30 PM           Documents and Settings
d----          5/21/2007   6:02 PM           F&SC-demo
d----          4/2/2007    7:21 PM           Inetpub
d----          5/20/2007   4:59 PM           Program Files
d----          5/21/2007  11:47 PM           temp
d----          5/21/2007   8:55 PM           Windows
-a---          1/7/2006   10:37 PM        0 autoexec.bat
-ar-s         11/29/2006   1:39 PM     8192 BOOTSECT.BAK
-a---          1/7/2006   10:37 PM        0 config.sys
-a---          5/1/2007    8:43 PM    33057 RUU.log
-a---          4/2/2007    7:46 PM     2487 secedit.INTEG.RAW
```

This also works on the registry, as shown in Example I-9.

*Example I-9. Navigating the registry*

```
PS > Set-Location HKCU:\Software\Microsoft\Windows\
PS > Get-ChildItem


    Hive: HKEY_CURRENT_USER\Software\Microsoft\Windows
```

```
SKC VC Name                          Property
--- -- ----                          --------
 30  1 CurrentVersion                {ISC}
  3  1 Shell                         {BagMRU Size}
  4  2 ShellNoRoam                   {(default), BagMRU Size}

PS > Set-Location CurrentVersion\Run
PS > Get-ItemProperty .

(...)
FolderShare              : "C:\Program Files\FolderShare\FolderShare.exe" /
                           background
TaskSwitchXP             : d:\lee\tools\TaskSwitchXP.exe
ctfmon.exe               : C:\WINDOWS\system32\ctfmon.exe
Ditto                    : C:\Program Files\Ditto\Ditto.exe
(...)
```

And it even works on the machine's certificate store, as Example I-10 illustrates.

*Example I-10. Navigating the certificate store*

```
PS > Set-Location cert:\CurrentUser\Root
PS > Get-ChildItem

    Directory: Microsoft.PowerShell.Security\Certificate::CurrentUser\Root


Thumbprint                                Subject
----------                                -------
CDD4EEAE6000AC7F40C3802C171E30148030C072  CN=Microsoft Root Certificate...
BE36A4562FB2EE05DBB3D32323ADF445084ED656  CN=Thawte Timestamping CA, OU...
A43489159A520F0D93D032CCAF37E7FE20A8B419  CN=Microsoft Root Authority, ...
9FE47B4D05D46E8066BAB1D1BFC9E48F1DBE6B26  CN=PowerShell Local Certifica...
7F88CD7223F3C813818C994614A89C99FA3B5247  CN=Microsoft Authenticode(tm)...
245C97DF7514E7CF2DF8BE72AE957B9E04741E85  OU=Copyright (c) 1997 Microso...
(...)
```

# Much, Much More

As exciting as this guided tour was, it barely scratches the surface of how you can use PowerShell to improve your productivity and systems management skills. For more information about getting started in PowerShell, see Chapter 1.

# PART II
# Fundamentals

Chapter 1, *The Windows PowerShell Interactive Shell*
Chapter 2, *Pipelines*
Chapter 3, *Variables and Objects*
Chapter 4, *Looping and Flow Control*
Chapter 5, *Strings and Unstructured Text*
Chapter 6, *Calculations and Math*
Chapter 7, *Lists, Arrays, and Hashtables*
Chapter 8, *Utility Tasks*

# The Windows PowerShell Interactive Shell

## 1.0. Introduction

Above all else, the design of Windows PowerShell places priority on its use as an efficient and powerful interactive shell. Even its scripting language plays a critical role in this effort, as it too heavily favors interactive use.

What surprises most people when they first launch PowerShell is its similarity to the command prompt that has long existed as part of Windows. Familiar tools continue to run. Familiar commands continue to run. Even familiar hotkeys are the same. Supporting this familiar user interface, though, is a powerful engine that lets you accomplish once cumbersome administrative and scripting tasks with ease.

This chapter introduces PowerShell from the perspective of its interactive shell.

## 1.1. Run Programs, Scripts, and Existing Tools

### Problem

You rely on a lot of effort invested in your current tools. You have traditional executables, Perl scripts, VBScript, and of course, a legacy build system that has organically grown into a tangled mess of batch files. You want to use PowerShell, but you don't want to give up everything you already have.

### Solution

To run a program, script, batch file, or other executable command in the system's path, enter its filename. For these executable types, the extension is optional:

```
Program.exe arguments
ScriptName.ps1 arguments
BatchFile.cmd arguments
```

To run a command that contains a space in its name, enclose its filename in single-quotes (') and precede the command with an ampersand (&), known in PowerShell as the *invoke operator*:

```
& 'C:\Program Files\Program\Program.exe' arguments
```

To run a command in the current directory, place .\ in front of its filename:

```
.\Program.exe arguments
```

To run a command with spaces in its name from the current directory, precede it with both an ampersand and .\:

```
& '.\Program With Spaces.exe' arguments
```

## Discussion

In this case, the solution is mainly to use your current tools as you always have. The only difference is that you run them in the PowerShell interactive shell rather than *cmd.exe*.

### Specifying the command name

The final three tips in the Solution merit special attention. They are the features of PowerShell that many new users stumble on when it comes to running programs. The first is running commands that contain spaces. In *cmd.exe*, the way to run a command that contains spaces is to surround it with quotes:

```
"C:\Program Files\Program\Program.exe"
```

In PowerShell, though, placing text inside quotes is part of a feature that lets you evaluate complex expressions at the prompt, as shown in Example 1-1.

*Example 1-1. Evaluating expressions at the PowerShell prompt*

```
PS > 1 + 1
2
PS > 26 * 1.15
29.9
PS > "Hello" + " World"
Hello World
PS > "Hello World"
Hello World
PS > "C:\Program Files\Program\Program.exe"
C:\Program Files\Program\Program.exe
PS >
```

So, a program name in quotes is no different from any other string in quotes. It's just an expression. As shown previously, the way to run a command in a string is to precede that string with the invoke operator (&). If the command you want to run is a batch file that modifies its environment, see Recipe 3.5, "Program: Retain Changes to Environment Variables Set by a Batch File".

 By default, PowerShell's security policies prevent scripts from running. Once you begin writing or using scripts, though, you should configure this policy to something less restrictive. For information on how to configure your execution policy, see Recipe 18.1, "Enable Scripting Through an Execution Policy".

The second command that new users (and seasoned veterans before coffee!) sometimes stumble on is running commands from the current directory. In *cmd.exe*, the current directory is considered part of the *path*: the list of directories that Windows searches to find the program name you typed. If you are in the *C:\Programs* directory, *cmd.exe* looks in *C:\Programs* (among other places) for applications to run.

PowerShell, like most Unix shells, requires that you explicitly state your desire to run a program from the current directory. To do that, you use the .\Program.exe syntax, as shown previously. This prevents malicious users on your system from littering your hard drive with evil programs that have names similar to (or the same as) commands you might run while visiting that directory.

To save themselves from having to type the location of commonly used scripts and programs, many users put commonly used utilities along with their PowerShell scripts in a "tools" directory, which they add to their system's path. If PowerShell can find a script or utility in your system's path, you do not need to explicitly specify its location.

If you want PowerShell to automatically look in your current working directory for scripts, you can add a period (.) to your PATH environment variable.

For more information about updating your system path, see Recipe 16.2, "Modify the User or System Path".

If you want to capture the output of a command, you can either save the results into a variable, or save the results into a file. To save the results into a variable, see Recipe 3.3, "Store Information in Variables". To save the results into a file, see Recipe 1.26, "Store the Output of a Command into a File".

### Specifying command arguments

To specify arguments to a command, you can again type them just as you would in other shells. For example, to make a specified file read-only (two arguments to attrib.exe), simply type:

```
attrib +R c:\path\to\file.txt
```

Where many scripters get misled when it comes to command arguments is how to change them within your scripts. For example, how do you get the filename from a PowerShell variable? The answer is to define a variable to hold the argument value, and just use that in the place you used to write the command argument:

```
$filename = "c:\path\to\other\file.txt"
attrib +R $filename
```

You can use the same technique when you call a PowerShell cmdlet, script, or function:

```
$filename = "c:\path\to\other\file.txt"
Get-Acl -Path $filename
```

If you see a solution that uses the Invoke-Expression cmdlet to compose command arguments, it is almost certainly incorrect. The Invoke-Expression cmdlet takes the string that you give it and treats it like a full PowerShell script. As just one example of the problems this can cause, consider the following: filenames are allowed to contain the semicolon (;) character, but when Invoke-Expression sees a semicolon, it assumes that it is a new line of PowerShell script. For example, try running this:

```
$filename = "c:\file.txt; Write-Warning 'This could be bad'"
Invoke-Expression "Get-Acl -Path $filename"
```

Given that these dynamic arguments often come from user input, using Invoke-Expression to compose commands can (at best) cause unpredictable script results. Worse, it could result in damage to your system or a security vulnerability.

In addition to letting you supply arguments through variables one at a time, PowerShell also lets you supply several of them at once through a technique known as *splatting*. For more information about splatting, see Recipe 11.14, "Dynamically Compose Command Parameters".

## See Also

Recipe 3.3, "Store Information in Variables"

Recipe 3.5, "Program: Retain Changes to Environment Variables Set by a Batch File"

Recipe 11.14, "Dynamically Compose Command Parameters"

Recipe 16.2, "Modify the User or System Path"

Recipe 18.1, "Enable Scripting Through an Execution Policy"

# 1.2. Run a PowerShell Command

## Problem

You want to run a PowerShell command.

## Solution

To run a PowerShell command, type its name at the command prompt. For example:

```
PS > Get-Process

Handles  NPM(K)    PM(K)    WS(K)   VM(M)   CPU(s)     Id ProcessName
-------  ------    -----    -----   -----   ------     -- -----------
    133       5    11760     7668      46           1112 audiodg
    184       5    33248      508      93           1692 avgamsvr
    143       7    31852      984      97           1788 avgemc
```

## Discussion

The `Get-Process` command is an example of a native PowerShell command, called a *cmdlet*. As compared to traditional commands, cmdlets provide significant benefits to both administrators and developers:

- They share a common and regular command-line syntax.
- They support rich pipeline scenarios (using the output of one command as the input of another).
- They produce easily manageable object-based output, rather than error-prone plain-text output.

Because the `Get-Process` cmdlet generates rich object-based output, you can use its output for many process-related tasks.

Every PowerShell command lets you provide input to the command through its *parameters*. For more information on providing input to commands, see "Running Commands" (page 899).

The `Get-Process` cmdlet is just one of the many that PowerShell supports. See Recipe 1.11, "Find a Command to Accomplish a Task" to learn techniques for finding additional commands that PowerShell supports.

For more information about working with classes from the .NET Framework, see Recipe 3.8, "Work with .NET Objects".

## See Also

Recipe 1.11, "Find a Command to Accomplish a Task"

Recipe 3.8, "Work with .NET Objects"

"Running Commands" (page 899)

# 1.3. Resolve Errors Calling Native Executables

## Problem

You have a command line that works from *cmd.exe*, and want to resolve errors that occur from running that command in PowerShell.

## Solution

Enclose any affected command arguments in single quotes to prevent them from being interpreted by PowerShell, and replace any single quotes in the command with two single quotes.

```
PS > cmd /c echo '!"#$%&''()*+,-./09:;<=>?@AZ[\]^_`az{|}~'
!"#$%&'()*+,-./09:;<=>?@AZ[\]^_`az{|}~
```

For complicated commands where this does not work, use the verbatim argument (--%) syntax.

```
PS > cmd /c echo 'quotes' "and" $variables @{ etc = $true }
quotes and System.Collections.Hashtable

PS > cmd --% /c echo 'quotes' "and" $variables @{ etc = $true }
'quotes' "and" $variables @{ etc = $true }
```

## Discussion

One of PowerShell's primary goals has always been command consistency. Because of this, cmdlets are very regular in the way that they accept parameters. Native executables write their own parameter parsing, so you never know what to expect when working with them. In addition, PowerShell offers many features that make you more efficient at the command line: command substitution, variable expansion, and more. Since many native executables were written before PowerShell was developed, they may use special characters that conflict with these features.

As an example, the command given in the Solution uses all the special characters available on a typical keyboard. Without the quotes, PowerShell treats some of them as language features, as shown in Table 1-1.

*Table 1-1. Sample of special characters*

| Special character | Meaning |
| --- | --- |
| " | The beginning (or end) of quoted text |
| # | The beginning of a comment |
| $ | The beginning of a variable |
| & | Reserved for future use |
| ( ) | Parentheses used for subexpressions |
| ; | Statement separator |
| { } | Script block |
| \| | Pipeline separator |
| ` | Escape character |

When surrounded by single quotes, PowerShell accepts these characters as written, without the special meaning.

Despite these precautions, you may still sometimes run into a command that doesn't seem to work when called from PowerShell. For the most part, these can be resolved by reviewing what PowerShell passes to the command and escaping the special characters.

To see *exactly* what PowerShell passes to that command, you can view the output of the trace source called `NativeCommandParameterBinder`:

```
PS > Trace-Command NativeCommandParameterBinder {
    cmd /c echo '!"#$%&''()*+,-./09:;<=>?@AZ[\]^_`az{|}~'
} -PsHost

DEBUG: NativeCommandParameterBinder Information: 0 :  WriteLine
Argument 0: /c
DEBUG: NativeCommandParameterBinder Information: 0 :  WriteLine
Argument 1: echo
DEBUG: NativeCommandParameterBinder Information: 0 :  WriteLine
Argument 2: !#$%&'()*+,-./09:;<=>?@AZ[\]^_`az{|}~
!"#$%&'()*+,-./09:;<=>?@AZ[\]^_`az{|}~
```

If the command arguments shown in this output don't match the arguments you expect, they have special meaning to PowerShell and should be escaped.

For a complex enough command that "just used to work," though, escaping special characters is tiresome. To escape the whole command invocation, use the verbatim argument marker (- -%) to prevent PowerShell from interpreting any of the remaining characters on the line. You can place this marker anywhere in the command's arguments, letting you benefit from PowerShell constructs where appropriate. The following example uses a PowerShell variable for some of the command arguments, but then uses verbatim arguments for the rest:

```
PS > $username = "Lee"
PS > cmd /c echo Hello $username with 'quotes' "and" $variables @{ etc = $true }
Hello Lee with quotes and System.Collections.Hashtable
PS > cmd /c echo Hello $username `
    --% with 'quotes' "and" $variables @{ etc = $true }
Hello Lee with 'quotes' "and" $variables @{ etc = $true }
```

While in this mode, PowerShell also accepts *cmd.exe*-style environment variables—as these are frequently used in commands that "just used to work":

```
PS > $env:host = "myhost"
PS > ping %host%
Ping request could not find host %host%. Please check the name and try again.
PS > ping --% %host%

Pinging myhost [127.0.1.1] with 32 bytes of data:
(...)
```

### See Also

Appendix A, *PowerShell Language and Environment*

# 1.4. Supply Default Values for Parameters

## Problem

You want to define a default value for a parameter in a PowerShell command.

## Solution

Add an entry to the PSDefaultParameterValues hashtable.

```
PS > Get-Process

Handles  NPM(K)    PM(K)      WS(K) VM(M)   CPU(s)     Id ProcessName
-------  ------    -----      ----- -----   ------     -- -----------
    150      13     9692       9612    39    21.43    996 audiodg
   1013      84    45572      42716   315     1.67   4596 WWAHost
(...)

PS > $PSDefaultParameterValues["Get-Process:ID"] = $pid
PS > Get-Process

Handles  NPM(K)    PM(K)      WS(K) VM(M)   CPU(s)     Id ProcessName
-------  ------    -----      ----- -----   ------     -- -----------
    584      62   132776     157940   985    13.15   9104 powershell_ise

PS > Get-Process -Id 0
```

```
Handles  NPM(K)    PM(K)      WS(K) VM(M)   CPU(s)     Id ProcessName
-------  ------    -----      ----- -----   ------     -- -----------
      0       0        0         20     0                0 Idle
```

## Discussion

In PowerShell, many commands (cmdlets and advanced functions) have parameters
that let you configure their behavior. For a full description of how to provide input to
commands, see "Running Commands" (page 899). Sometimes, though, supplying values
for those parameters at each invocation becomes awkward or repetitive.

Until PowerShell version 3, it was the responsibility of each cmdlet author to recognize
awkward or repetitive configuration properties and build support for "preference variables" into the cmdlet itself. For example, the Send-MailMessage cmdlet looks for the
$PSEmailServer variable if you do not supply a value for its -SmtpServer parameter.

To make this support more consistent and configurable, PowerShell version 3 introduces
the PSDefaultParameterValues preference variable. This preference variable is a hashtable. Like all other PowerShell hashtables, entries come in two parts: the key and the
value.

Keys in the PSDefaultParameterValues hashtable must match the pattern *cmdlet:pa
rameter*—that is, a cmdlet name and parameter name, separated by a colon. Either (or
both) may use wildcards, and spaces between the command name, colon, and parameter
are ignored.

Values for the cmdlet/parameter pairs can be either a simple parameter value (a string,
boolean value, integer, etc.) or a script block. Simple parameter values are what you will
use most often.

If you need the default value to dynamically change based on what parameter values are
provided so far, you can use a script block as the default. When you do so, PowerShell
evaluates the script block and uses its result as the default value. If your script block
doesn't return a result, PowerShell doesn't apply a default value.

When PowerShell invokes your script block, $args[0] contains information about any
parameters bound so far: BoundDefaultParameters, BoundParameters, and BoundPo
sitionalParameters. As one example of this, consider providing default values to the
-Credential parameter based on the computer being connected to. Here is a function
that simply outputs the credential being used:

```
function RemoteConnector
{
    param(
        [Parameter()]
        $ComputerName,
```

```
        [Parameter(Mandatory = $true)]
        $Credential)

    "Connecting as " + $Credential.UserName
}
```

Now, you can define a credential map:

```
PS > $credmap = @{}
PS > $credmap["RemoteComputer1"] = Get-Credential
PS > $credmap["RemoteComputer2"] = Get-Credential
```

Then, create a parameter default for all `Credential` parameters that looks at the `Com
puterName` bound parameter:

```
$PSDefaultParameterValues["*:Credential"] = {
    if($args[0].BoundParameters -contains "ComputerName")
    {
        $cred = $credmap[$PSBoundParameters["ComputerName"]]
        if($cred) { $cred }
    }
}
```

Here is an example of this in use:

```
PS > RemoteConnector -ComputerName RemoteComputer1
Connecting as UserForRemoteComputer1
PS > RemoteConnector -ComputerName RemoteComputer2
Connecting as UserForRemoteComputer2
PS > RemoteConnector -ComputerName RemoteComputer3

cmdlet RemoteConnector at command pipeline position 1
Supply values for the following parameters:
Credential: (...)
```

For more information about working with hashtables in PowerShell, see "Hashtables
(Associative Arrays)" (page 872).

## See Also

"Hashtables (Associative Arrays)" (page 872)

"Running Commands" (page 899)

# 1.5. Invoke a Long-Running or Background Command

## Problem

You want to invoke a long-running command on a local or remote computer.

## Solution

Invoke the command as a Job to have PowerShell run it in the background:

```
PS > Start-Job { while($true) { Get-Random; Start-Sleep 5 } } -Name Sleeper

Id          Name          State     HasMoreData   Location
--          ----          -----     -----------   --------
1           Sleeper       Running   True          localhost

PS > Receive-Job Sleeper
671032665
1862308704
PS > Stop-Job Sleeper
```

## Discussion

PowerShell's job cmdlets provide a consistent way to create and interact with background tasks. In the Solution, we use the Start-Job cmdlet to launch a background job on the local computer. We give it the name of Sleeper, but otherwise we don't customize much of its execution environment.

In addition to allowing you to customize the job name, the Start-Job cmdlet also lets you launch the job under alternate user credentials or as a 32-bit process (if run originally from a 64-bit process).

Once you have launched a job, you can use the other Job cmdlets to interact with it:

Get-Job
: Gets all jobs associated with the current session. In addition, the -Before, -After, -Newest, and -State parameters let you filter jobs based on their state or completion time.

Wait-Job
: Waits for a job until it has output ready to be retrieved.

Receive-Job
: Retrieves any output the job has generated since the last call to Receive-Job.

Stop-Job
: Stops a job.

Remove-Job
: Removes a job from the list of active jobs.

In addition to the Start-Job cmdlet, you can also use the -AsJob parameter in many cmdlets to have them perform their tasks in the background. Two of the most useful examples are the Invoke-Command cmdlet (when operating against remote computers) and the set of WMI-related cmdlets.

If your job generates an error, the Receive-Job cmdlet will display it to you when you receive the results, as shown in Example 1-2. If you want to investigate these errors further, the object returned by Get-Job exposes them through the Error property.

*Example 1-2. Retrieving errors from a Job*

```
PS > Start-Job -Name ErrorJob { Write-Error Error! }

Id           Name           State    HasMoreData    Location
--           ----           -----    -----------    --------
1            ErrorJob       Running  True           localhost


PS > Receive-Job ErrorJob
Error!
    + CategoryInfo          : NotSpecified: (:) [Write-Error], WriteError
    Exception
    + FullyQualifiedErrorId : Microsoft.PowerShell.Commands.WriteErrorExc
    eption,Microsoft.PowerShell.Commands.WriteErrorCommand

PS > $job = Get-Job ErrorJob
PS > $job | Format-List *

State        : Completed
HasMoreData  : False
StatusMessage :
Location     : localhost
Command      :  Write-Error Error!
JobStateInfo : Completed
Finished     : System.Threading.ManualResetEvent
InstanceId   : 801e932c-5580-4c8b-af06-ddd1024840b7
Id           : 1
Name         : ErrorJob
ChildJobs    : {Job2}
Output       : {}
Error        : {}
Progress     : {}
Verbose      : {}
Debug        : {}
Warning      : {}

PS > $job.ChildJobs[0] | Format-List *
```

```
State            : Completed
StatusMessage    :
HasMoreData      : False
Location         : localhost
Runspace         : System.Management.Automation.RemoteRunspace
Command          :  Write-Error Error!
JobStateInfo     : Completed
Finished         : System.Threading.ManualResetEvent
InstanceId       : 60fa85da-448b-49ff-8116-6eae6c3f5006
Id               : 2
Name             : Job2
ChildJobs        : {}
Output           : {}
Error            : {Microsoft.PowerShell.Commands.WriteErrorException,Microso
                   ft.PowerShell.Commands.WriteErrorCommand}
Progress         : {}
Verbose          : {}
Debug            : {}
Warning          : {}


PS > $job.ChildJobs[0].Error
Error!
    + CategoryInfo          : NotSpecified: (:) [Write-Error], WriteError
    Exception
    + FullyQualifiedErrorId : Microsoft.PowerShell.Commands.WriteErrorExc
    eption,Microsoft.PowerShell.Commands.WriteErrorCommand

PS >
```

As this example shows, jobs are sometimes containers for other jobs, called *child jobs*. Jobs created through the Start-Job cmdlet will always be child jobs attached to a generic container. To access the errors returned by these jobs, you instead access the errors in its first child job (called child job number zero).

In addition to long-running jobs that execute under control of the current PowerShell session, you might want to register and control jobs that run on a schedule, or independently of the current PowerShell session. PowerShell has a handful of commands to let you work with scheduled jobs like this; for more information, see Recipe 27.14, "Manage Scheduled Tasks on a Computer".

## See Also

Recipe 27.14, "Manage Scheduled Tasks on a Computer"

Recipe 28.7, "Improve the Performance of Large-Scale WMI Operations"

Recipe 29.4, "Invoke a Command on a Remote Computer"

# 1.6. Program: Monitor a Command for Changes

As thrilling as our lives are, some days are reduced to running a command over and over and over. Did the files finish copying yet? Is the build finished? Is the site still up?

Usually, the answer to these questions comes from running a command, looking at its output, and then deciding whether it meets your criteria. And usually this means just waiting for the output to change, waiting for some text to appear, or waiting for some text to disappear.

Fortunately, Example 1-3 automates this tedious process for you.

*Example 1-3. Watch-Command.ps1*

```
##############################################################################
##
## Watch-Command
##
## From Windows PowerShell Cookbook (O'Reilly)
## by Lee Holmes (http://www.leeholmes.com/guide)
##
##############################################################################

<#

.SYNOPSIS

Watches the result of a command invocation, alerting you when the output
either matches a specified string, lacks a specified string, or has simply
changed.

.EXAMPLE

PS > Watch-Command { Get-Process -Name Notepad | Measure } -UntilChanged
Monitors Notepad processes until you start or stop one.

.EXAMPLE

PS > Watch-Command { Get-Process -Name Notepad | Measure } -Until "Count     : 1"
Monitors Notepad processes until there is exactly one open.

.EXAMPLE

PS > Watch-Command {
    Get-Process -Name Notepad | Measure } -While 'Count    : \d\s*\n'
Monitors Notepad processes while there are between 0 and 9 open
(once number after the colon).

#>


[CmdletBinding(DefaultParameterSetName = "Forever")]
```

```
param(
    ## The script block to invoke while monitoring
    [Parameter(Mandatory = $true, Position = 0)]
    [ScriptBlock] $ScriptBlock,

    ## The delay, in seconds, between monitoring attempts
    [Parameter()]
    [Double] $DelaySeconds = 1,

    ## Specifies that the alert sound should not be played
    [Parameter()]
    [Switch] $Quiet,

    ## Monitoring continues only while the output of the
    ## command remains the same.
    [Parameter(ParameterSetName = "UntilChanged", Mandatory = $false)]
    [Switch] $UntilChanged,

    ## The regular expression to search for. Monitoring continues
    ## until this expression is found.
    [Parameter(ParameterSetName = "Until", Mandatory = $false)]
    [String] $Until,

    ## The regular expression to search for. Monitoring continues
    ## until this expression is not found.
    [Parameter(ParameterSetName = "While", Mandatory = $false)]
    [String] $While
)

Set-StrictMode -Version 3

$initialOutput = ""

## Start a continuous loop
while($true)
{
    ## Run the provided script block
    $r = & $ScriptBlock

    ## Clear the screen and display the results
    Clear-Host
    $ScriptBlock.ToString().Trim()
    ""
    $textOutput = $r | Out-String
    $textOutput

    ## Remember the initial output, if we haven't
    ## stored it yet
    if(-not $initialOutput)
    {
        $initialOutput = $textOutput
    }
```

```
## If we are just looking for any change,
## see if the text has changed.
if($UntilChanged)
{
    if($initialOutput -ne $textOutput)
    {
        break
    }
}

## If we need to ensure some text is found,
## break if we didn't find it.
if($While)
{
    if($textOutput -notmatch $While)
    {
        break
    }
}

## If we need to wait for some text to be found,
## break if we find it.
if($Until)
{
    if($textOutput -match $Until)
    {
        break
    }
}

## Delay
Start-Sleep -Seconds $DelaySeconds
}

## Notify the user
if(-not $Quiet)
{
    [Console]::Beep(1000, 1000)
}
```

For more information about running scripts, see Recipe 1.1, "Run Programs, Scripts, and Existing Tools".

## See Also

Recipe 1.1, "Run Programs, Scripts, and Existing Tools"

# 1.7. Notify Yourself of Job Completion

## Problem

You want to notify yourself when a long-running job completes.

## Solution

Use the `Register-TemporaryEvent` command given in Recipe 32.3, "Create a Temporary Event Subscription" to register for the event's `StateChanged` event:

```
PS > $job = Start-Job -Name TenSecondSleep { Start-Sleep 10 }
PS > Register-TemporaryEvent $job StateChanged -Action {
    [Console]::Beep(100,100)
    Write-Host "Job #$($sender.Id) ($($sender.Name)) complete."
}

PS > Job #6 (TenSecondSleep) complete.
PS >
```

## Discussion

When a job completes, it raises a `StateChanged` event to notify subscribers that its state has changed. We can use PowerShell's event handling cmdlets to register for notifications about this event, but they are not geared toward this type of one-time event handling. To solve that, we use the `Register-TemporaryEvent` command given in Recipe 32.3, "Create a Temporary Event Subscription".

In our example action block in the Solution, we simply emit a beep and write a message saying that the job is complete.

As another option, you can also update your `prompt` function to highlight jobs that are complete but still have output you haven't processed:

```
$psJobs = @(Get-Job -State Completed | ? { $_.HasMoreData })
if($psJobs.Count -gt 0) {
    ($psJobs | Out-String).Trim() | Write-Host -Fore Yellow }
```

For more information about events and this type of automatic event handling, see Chapter 32.

## See Also

Recipe 1.1, "Run Programs, Scripts, and Existing Tools"

Chapter 32, *Event Handling*

# 1.8. Customize Your Shell, Profile, and Prompt

## Problem

You want to customize PowerShell's interactive experience with a personalized prompt, aliases, and more.

## Solution

When you want to customize aspects of PowerShell, place those customizations in your personal profile script. PowerShell provides easy access to this profile script by storing its location in the $profile variable.

 By default, PowerShell's security policies prevent scripts (including your profile) from running. Once you begin writing scripts, though, you should configure this policy to something less restrictive. For information on how to configure your execution policy, see Recipe 18.1, "Enable Scripting Through an Execution Policy".

To create a new profile (and overwrite one if it already exists):

```
New-Item -type file -force $profile
```

To edit your profile (in the Integrated Scripting Environment):

```
ise $profile
```

To see your profile file:

```
Get-ChildItem $profile
```

Once you create a profile script, you can add a function called prompt that returns a string. PowerShell displays the output of this function as your command-line prompt.

```
function prompt
{
    "PS [$env:COMPUTERNAME] >"
}
```

This example prompt displays your computer name, and looks like PS [LEE-DESK] >.

You may also find it helpful to add aliases to your profile. Aliases let you refer to common commands by a name that you choose. Personal profile scripts let you automatically define aliases, functions, variables, or any other customizations that you might set interactively from the PowerShell prompt. Aliases are among the most common customizations, as they let you refer to PowerShell commands (and your own scripts) by a name that is easier to type.

If you want to define an alias for a command but also need to modify the parameters to that command, then define a function instead. For more information, see Recipe 11.14, "Dynamically Compose Command Parameters".

For example:

```
Set-Alias new New-Object
Set-Alias iexplore 'C:\Program Files\Internet Explorer\iexplore.exe'
```

Your changes will become effective once you save your profile and restart PowerShell. Alternatively, you can reload your profile immediately by running this command:

```
. $profile
```

Functions are also very common customizations, with the most popular being the prompt function.

## Discussion

The Solution discusses three techniques to make useful customizations to your PowerShell environment: aliases, functions, and a hand-tailored prompt. You can (and will often) apply these techniques at any time during your PowerShell session, but your profile script is the standard place to put customizations that you want to apply to every session.

To remove an alias or function, use the Remove-Item cmdlet:

```
Remove-Item function:\MyCustomFunction
Remove-Item alias:\new
```

Although the Prompt function returns a simple string, you can also use the function for more complex tasks. For example, many users update their console window title (by changing the $host.UI.RawUI.WindowTitle variable) or use the Write-Host cmdlet to output the prompt in color. If your prompt function handles the screen output itself, it still needs to return a string (for example, a single space) to prevent PowerShell from using its default. If you don't want this extra space to appear in your prompt, add an extra space at the end of your Write-Host command and return the backspace ("`b") character, as shown in Example 1-4.

*Example 1-4. An example PowerShell prompt*

```
##############################################################################
##
## From Windows PowerShell Cookbook (O'Reilly)
## by Lee Holmes (http://www.leeholmes.com/guide)
```

```
    ##
    ##############################################################################

    Set-StrictMode -Version 3

    function Prompt
    {
        $id = 1
        $historyItem = Get-History -Count 1
        if($historyItem)
        {
            $id = $historyItem.Id + 1
        }

        Write-Host -ForegroundColor DarkGray "`n[$(Get-Location)]"
        Write-Host -NoNewLine "PS:$id > "
        $host.UI.RawUI.WindowTitle = "$(Get-Location)"

        "`b"
    }
```

In addition to showing the current location, this prompt also shows the ID for that command in your history. This lets you locate and invoke past commands with relative ease:

```
[c:\]
PS:73 >5 * 5
25

[c:\]
PS:74 >1 + 1
2

[c:\]
PS:75 >Invoke-History 73
5 * 5
25

[c:\]
PS:76 >
```

Although the profile referenced by $profile is the one you will almost always want to use, PowerShell actually supports four separate profile scripts. For further details on these scripts (along with other shell customization options), see "Common Customization Points" (page 914).

## See Also

Recipe 18.1, "Enable Scripting Through an Execution Policy"

"Common Customization Points" (page 914)

# 1.9. Customize PowerShell's User Input Behavior

## Problem

You want to override the way that PowerShell reads input at the prompt.

## Solution

Create a `PSConsoleHostReadLine` function. In that function, process the user input and return the resulting command. Example 1-5 implements a somewhat ridiculous Notepad-based user input mechanism:

*Example 1-5. A Notepad-based user input mechanism*

```
function PSConsoleHostReadLine
{
    $inputFile = Join-Path $env:TEMP PSConsoleHostReadLine
    Set-Content $inputFile "PS > "

    ## Notepad opens. Enter your command in it, save the file,
    ## and then exit.
    notepad $inputFile | Out-Null
    $userInput = Get-Content $inputFile
    $resultingCommand = $userInput.Replace("PS >", "")
    $resultingCommand
}
```

## Discussion

When PowerShell first came on the scene, Unix folks were among the first to notice. They'd enjoyed a powerful shell and a vigorous heritage of automation for years—and "when I'm forced to use Windows, PowerShell rocks" is a phrase we've heard many times.

This natural uptake was no mistake. There are many on the team who come from a deep Unix background, and similarities to traditional Unix shells were intentional. When coming from a Unix background, though, we still hear the occasional grumble that tab completion feels weird. Ctrl-R doesn't invoke history search? Tab cycles through matches, rather than lists them? Abhorrent!

In PowerShell versions 1 or 2, there was nothing you could reasonably do to address this. PowerShell reads its input from the console in what is known as *Cooked Mode*—where the Windows console subsystem handles all the keypresses, fancy F7 menus, and more. When you press Enter or Tab, PowerShell gets the text of what you have typed so far, but that's it. There is no way for it to know that you had pressed the (Unix-like) Ctrl-R, Ctrl-A, Ctrl-E, or any other keys.

This issue has been resolved in PowerShell version 3 through the `PSConsoleHostRead Line` function. When you define this method in the PowerShell console host, PowerShell calls that function instead of the Cooked Mode input functionality. And that's it—the rest is up to you. If you'd like to implement a custom input method, the freedom (and responsibility) is all yours.

 A community implementation of a Bash-like `PSConsoleHostRead Line` function is available here (*http://bit.ly/T4GE9f*).

For more information about handling keypresses and other forms of user input, see Chapter 13.

## See Also

Chapter 13, *User Interaction*

# 1.10. Customize PowerShell's Command Resolution Behavior

## Problem

You want to override or customize the command that PowerShell invokes before it is invoked.

## Solution

Assign a script block to one or all of the `PreCommandLookupAction`, `PostCommand LookupAction`, or `CommandNotFoundAction` properties of `$executionContext.Ses sionState.InvokeCommand`. Example 1-6 enables easy parent directory navigation when you type multiple dots.

*Example 1-6. Enabling easy parent path navigation through CommandNotFoundAction*

```
$executionContext.SessionState.InvokeCommand.CommandNotFoundAction = {
    param($CommandName, $CommandLookupEventArgs)

    ## If the command is only dots
    if($CommandName -match '^\.+$')
    {
        ## Associate a new command that should be invoked instead
        $CommandLookupEventArgs.CommandScriptBlock = {

            ## Count the number of dots, and run "Set-Location .." one
            ## less time.
```

```
        for($counter = 0; $counter -lt $CommandName.Length - 1; $counter++)
        {
            Set-Location ..
        }

    ## We call GetNewClosure() so that the reference to $CommandName can
    ## be used in the new command.
    }.GetNewClosure()
    }
}

PS C:\Users\Lee> cd $pshome
PS C:\Windows\System32\WindowsPowerShell\v1.0> ....
PS C:\Windows>
```

## Discussion

When you invoke a command in PowerShell, the engine goes through three distinct phases:

1. Retrieve the text of the command.
2. Find the command for that text.
3. Invoke the command that was found.

In PowerShell version 3, the $executionContext.SessionState.InvokeCommand property now lets you override any of these stages with script blocks to intercept any or all of the PreCommandLookupAction, PostCommandLookupAction, or CommandNotFound Action stages.

Each script block receives two parameters: the command name, and an object (Com mandLookupEventArgs) to control the command lookup behavior. If your handler assigns a script block to the CommandScriptBlock property of the CommandLookup EventArgs or assigns a CommandInfo to the Command property of the CommandLookup EventArgs, PowerShell will use that script block or command, respectively. If your script block sets the StopSearch property to true, PowerShell will do no further command resolution.

PowerShell invokes the PreCommandLookupAction script block when it knows the name of a command (i.e., Get-Process) but hasn't yet looked for the command itself. You can override this action if you want to react primarily based on the text of the command name or want to preempt PowerShell's regular command or alias resolution. For example, Example 1-7 demonstrates a PreCommandLookupAction that looks for commands with an asterisk before their name. When it sees one, it enables the -Verbose parameter.

*Example 1-7. Customizing the PreCommandLookupAction*

```
$executionContext.SessionState.InvokeCommand.PreCommandLookupAction = {
    param($CommandName, $CommandLookupEventArgs)
```

```
## If the command name starts with an asterisk, then
## enable its Verbose parameter
if($CommandName -match "\*")
{
    ## Remove the leading asterisk
    $NewCommandName = $CommandName -replace '\*',''

    ## Create a new script block that invokes the actual command,
    ## passes along all original arguments, and adds in the -Verbose
    ## parameter
    $CommandLookupEventArgs.CommandScriptBlock = {
        & $NewCommandName @args -Verbose

    ## We call GetNewClosure() so that the reference to $NewCommandName
    ## can be used in the new command.
    }.GetNewClosure()
}
}

PS > dir > 1.txt
PS > dir > 2.txt
PS > del 1.txt
PS > *del 2.txt
VERBOSE: Performing operation "Remove file" on Target "C:\temp\tempfolder\2.txt".
```

After PowerShell executes the PreCommandLookupAction (if one exists and doesn't return a command), it goes through its regular command resolution. If it finds a command, it invokes the script block associated with the PostCommandLookupAction. You can override this action if you want to react primarily to a command that is just about to be invoked. Example 1-8 demonstrates a PostCommandLookupAction that tallies the commands you use most frequently.

*Example 1-8. Customizing the PostCommandLookupAction*

```
$executionContext.SessionState.InvokeCommand.PostCommandLookupAction = {
    param($CommandName, $CommandLookupEventArgs)

    ## Stores a hashtable of the commands we use most frequently
    if(-not (Test-Path variable:\CommandCount))
    {
        $global:CommandCount = @{}
    }

    ## If it was launched by us (rather than as an internal helper
    ## command), record its invocation.
    if($CommandLookupEventArgs.CommandOrigin -eq "Runspace")
    {
        $commandCount[$CommandName] = 1 + $commandCount[$CommandName]
    }
}
```

```
PS > Get-Variable commandCount
PS > Get-Process -id $pid
PS > Get-Process -id $pid
PS > $commandCount

Name                      Value
----                      -----
Out-Default               4
Get-Variable              1
prompt                    4
Get-Process               2
```

If command resolution is unsuccessful, PowerShell invokes the `CommandNotFoundAc` `tion` script block if one exists. At its simplest, you can override this action if you want to recover from or override PowerShell's error behavior when it cannot find a command.

As a more advanced application, the `CommandNotFoundAction` lets you write PowerShell extensions that alter their behavior based on the *form* of the name, rather than the arguments passed to it. For example, you might want to automatically launch URLs just by typing them or navigate around providers just by typing relative path locations.

The Solution gives an example of implementing this type of handler. While dynamic relative path navigation is not a built-in feature of PowerShell, it is possible to get a very reasonable alternative by intercepting the `CommandNotFoundAction`. If we see a missing command that has a pattern we want to handle (a series of dots), we return a script block that does the appropriate relative path navigation.

# 1.11. Find a Command to Accomplish a Task

## Problem

You want to accomplish a task in PowerShell but don't know the command or cmdlet to accomplish that task.

## Solution

Use the `Get-Command` cmdlet to search for and investigate commands.

To get the summary information about a specific command, specify the command name as an argument:

```
Get-Command CommandName
```

To get the detailed information about a specific command, pipe the output of `Get-Command` to the `Format-List` cmdlet:

```
Get-Command CommandName | Format-List
```

To search for all commands with a name that contains *text*, surround the text with asterisk characters:

```
Get-Command *text*
```

To search for all commands that use the Get verb, supply Get to the -Verb parameter:

```
Get-Command -Verb Get
```

To search for all commands that act on a service, use Service as the value of the -Noun parameter:

```
Get-Command -Noun Service
```

## Discussion

One of the benefits that PowerShell provides administrators is the consistency of its command names. All PowerShell commands (called *cmdlets*) follow a regular *Verb-Noun* pattern—for example, Get-Process, Get-EventLog, and Set-Location. The verbs come from a relatively small set of standard verbs (as listed in Appendix J) and describe what action the cmdlet takes. The nouns are specific to the cmdlet and describe what the cmdlet acts on.

Knowing this philosophy, you can easily learn to work with groups of cmdlets. If you want to start a service on the local machine, the standard verb for that is Start. A good guess would be to first try Start-Service (which in this case would be correct), but typing Get-Command -Verb Start would also be an effective way to see what things you can start. Going the other way, you can see what actions are supported on services by typing Get-Command -Noun Service.

When you use the Get-Command cmdlet, PowerShell returns results from the list of all commands available on your system. If you'd instead like to search just commands from modules that you've loaded either explicitly or through autoloading, use the -List Imported parameter. For more information about PowerShell's autoloading of commands, see Recipe 1.29, "Extend Your Shell with Additional Commands".

See Recipe 1.12, "Get Help on a Command" for a way to list all commands along with a brief description of what they do.

The Get-Command cmdlet is one of the three commands you will use most commonly as you explore Windows PowerShell. The other two commands are Get-Help and Get-Member.

There is one important point to keep in mind when it comes to looking for a PowerShell command to accomplish a particular task. Many times, that PowerShell command does not exist, because the task is best accomplished the same way it always was—for example, ipconfig.exe to get IP configuration information, netstat.exe to list protocol statistics and current TCP/IP network connections, and many more.

For more information about the Get-Command cmdlet, type **Get-Help Get-Command**.

## See Also

Recipe 1.12, "Get Help on a Command"

# 1.12. Get Help on a Command

## Problem

You want to learn how a specific command works and how to use it.

## Solution

The command that provides help and usage information about a command is called Get-Help. It supports several different views of the help information, depending on your needs.

To get the summary of help information for a specific command, provide the command's name as an argument to the Get-Help cmdlet. This primarily includes its synopsis, syntax, and detailed description:

```
Get-Help CommandName
```

or:

```
CommandName -?
```

To get the detailed help information for a specific command, supply the -Detailed flag to the Get-Help cmdlet. In addition to the summary view, this also includes its parameter descriptions and examples:

```
Get-Help CommandName -Detailed
```

To get the full help information for a specific command, supply the -Full flag to the Get-Help cmdlet. In addition to the detailed view, this also includes its full parameter descriptions and additional notes:

```
Get-Help CommandName -Full
```

To get only the examples for a specific command, supply the -Examples flag to the Get-Help cmdlet:

```
Get-Help CommandName -Examples
```

To retrieve the most up-to-date online version of a command's help topic, supply the -Online flag to the Get-Help cmdlet:

```
Get-Help CommandName -Online
```

To view a searchable, graphical view of a help topic, use the -ShowWindow parameter:

```
Get-Help CommandName -ShowWindow
```

To find all help topics that contain a given keyword, provide that keyword as an argument to the Get-Help cmdlet. If the keyword isn't also the name of a specific help topic, this returns all help topics that contain the keyword, including its name, category, and synopsis:

```
Get-Help Keyword
```

## Discussion

The Get-Help cmdlet is the primary way to interact with the help system in PowerShell. Like the Get-Command cmdlet, the Get-Help cmdlet supports wildcards. If you want to list all commands that have help content that matches a certain pattern (for example, *process*), you can simply type **Get-Help \*process\***.

If the pattern matches only a single command, PowerShell displays the help for that command. Although command wildcarding and keyword searching is a helpful way to search PowerShell help, see Recipe 1.14, "Program: Search Help for Text" for a script that lets you search the help content for a specified pattern.

While there are thousands of pages of custom-written help content at your disposal, PowerShell by default includes only information that it can automatically generate from the information contained in the commands themselves: names, parameters, syntax, and parameter defaults. You need to update your help content to retrieve the rest. The first time you run Get-Help as an administrator on a system, PowerShell offers to download this updated help content:

```
PS > Get-Help Get-Process

Do you want to run Update-Help?
The Update-Help cmdlet downloads the newest Help files for Windows
PowerShell modules and installs them on your computer. For more details,
see the help topic at http://go.microsoft.com/fwlink/?LinkId=210614.

[Y] Yes  [N] No  [S] Suspend  [?] Help (default is "Y"):
```

Answer Y to this prompt, and PowerShell automatically downloads and installs the most recent help content for all modules on your system. For more information on updatable help, see Recipe 1.13, "Update System Help Content".

If you'd like to generate a list of all cmdlets and aliases (along with their brief synopses), run the following command:

```
Get-Help * -Category Cmdlet | Select-Object Name,Synopsis | Format-Table -Auto
```

In addition to console-based help, PowerShell also offers online access to its help content. The Solution demonstrates how to quickly access online help content.

---

The Get-Help cmdlet is one of the three commands you will use most commonly as you explore Windows PowerShell. The other two commands are Get-Command and Get-Member.

For more information about the Get-Help cmdlet, type **Get-Help Get-Help**.

## See Also

Recipe 1.14, "Program: Search Help for Text"

# 1.13. Update System Help Content

## Problem

You want to update your system's help content to the latest available.

## Solution

Run the Update-Help command. To retrieve help from a local path, use the -Source Path cmdlet parameter:

```
Update-Help
```

or:

```
Update-Help -SourcePath \\helpserver\help
```

## Discussion

One of PowerShell's greatest strengths is the incredible detail of its help content. Counting only the help content and about_* topics that describe core functionality, Power-Shell's help includes approximately half a million words and would span 1,200 pages if printed.

The challenge that every version of PowerShell has been forced to deal with is that this help content is written at the same time as PowerShell itself. Given that its goal is to *help the user*, the content that's ready by the time a version of PowerShell releases is a best-effort estimate of what users will need help with.

As users get their hands on PowerShell, they start to have questions. Some of these are addressed by the help topics, while some of them aren't. Sometimes the help is simply incorrect due to a product change during the release. Before PowerShell version 3, re-solving these issues meant waiting for the next release of Windows or relying solely on Get-Help's -Online parameter. To address this, PowerShell version 3 introduces up-datable help.

It's not only possible to update help, but in fact the `Update-Help` command is the *only* way to get help on your system. Out of the box, PowerShell provides an experience derived solely from what is built into the commands themselves: name, syntax, parameters, and default values.

The first time you run `Get-Help` as an administrator on a system, PowerShell offers to download updated help content:

```
PS > Get-Help Get-Process

Do you want to run Update-Help?
The Update-Help cmdlet downloads the newest Help files for Windows
PowerShell modules and installs them on your computer. For more details,
see the help topic at http://go.microsoft.com/fwlink/?LinkId=210614.

[Y] Yes  [N] No  [S] Suspend  [?] Help (default is "Y"):
```

Answer Y to this prompt, and PowerShell automatically downloads and installs the most recent help content for all modules on your system.

 If you are building a system image and want to prevent this prompt from ever appearing, set the registry key `HKLM:\Software\Microsoft\PowerShell\DisablePromptToUpdateHelp` to 1.

In addition to the prompt-driven experience, you can call the `Update-Help` cmdlet directly.

Both experiences look at each module on your system, comparing the help you have for that module with the latest version online. For in-box modules, PowerShell uses `download.microsoft.com` to retrieve updated help content. Other modules that you download from the Internet can use the `HelpInfoUri` module key to support their own updatable help.

By default, the `Update-Help` command retrieves its content from the Internet. If you want to update help on a machine not connected to the Internet, you can use the `-SourcePath` parameter of the `Update-Help` cmdlet. This path represents a directory or UNC path where PowerShell should look for updated help content. To populate this content, first use the `Save-Help` cmdlet to download the files, and then copy them to the source location.

For more information about PowerShell help, see Recipe 1.12, "Get Help on a Command".

## See Also

Recipe 1.12, "Get Help on a Command"

# 1.14. Program: Search Help for Text

Both the `Get-Command` and `Get-Help` cmdlets let you search for command names that match a given pattern. However, when you don't know exactly what portions of a command name you are looking for, you will more often have success searching through the help *content* for an answer. On Unix systems, this command is called `Apropos`.

The `Get-Help` cmdlet automatically searches the help database for keyword references when it can't find a help topic for the argument you supply. In addition to that, you might want to extend this even further to search for text *patterns* or even help topics that talk *about* existing help topics. PowerShell's help facilities support a version of wildcarded content searches, but don't support full regular expressions.

That doesn't need to stop us, though, as we can write the functionality ourselves.

To run this program, supply a search string to the `Search-Help` script (given in Example 1-9). The search string can be either simple text or a regular expression. The script then displays the name and synopsis of all help topics that match. To see the help content for that topic, use the `Get-Help` cmdlet.

*Example 1-9. Search-Help.ps1*

```
##############################################################################
##
## Search-Help
##
## From Windows PowerShell Cookbook (O'Reilly)
## by Lee Holmes (http://www.leeholmes.com/guide)
##
##############################################################################

<#

.SYNOPSIS

Search the PowerShell help documentation for a given keyword or regular
expression. For simple keyword searches in PowerShell version two or three,
simply use "Get-Help <keyword>"

.EXAMPLE

PS > Search-Help hashtable
Searches help for the term 'hashtable'

.EXAMPLE

PS > Search-Help "(datetime|ticks)"
Searches help for the term datetime or ticks, using the regular expression
syntax.
```

```
#>

param(
    ## The pattern to search for
    [Parameter(Mandatory = $true)]
    $Pattern
)

$helpNames = $(Get-Help * | Where-Object { $_.Category -ne "Alias" })

## Go through all of the help topics
foreach($helpTopic in $helpNames)
{
    ## Get their text content, and
    $content = Get-Help -Full $helpTopic.Name | Out-String
    if($content -match "(.{0,30}$pattern.{0,30})")
    {
        $helpTopic | Add-Member NoteProperty Match $matches[0].Trim()
        $helpTopic | Select-Object Name,Match
    }
}
```

For more information about running scripts, see Recipe 1.1, "Run Programs, Scripts, and Existing Tools".

## See Also

Recipe 1.1, "Run Programs, Scripts, and Existing Tools"

# 1.15. Launch PowerShell at a Specific Location

## Problem

You want to launch a PowerShell session in a specific location.

## Solution

Both Windows and PowerShell offer several ways to launch PowerShell in a specific location:

- Explorer's address bar
- PowerShell's command-line arguments
- Community extensions

# Discussion

If you are browsing the filesystem with Windows Explorer, typing PowerShell into the address bar launches PowerShell in that location (as shown in Figure 1-1).

*Figure 1-1. Launching PowerShell from Windows Explorer*

Additionally, Windows 8 offers an Open Windows PowerShell option directly from the File menu, as shown in Figure 1-2).

For another way to launch PowerShell from Windows Explorer, several members of the PowerShell community have written power toys and Windows Explorer extensions that provide a "Launch PowerShell Here" option when you right-click on a folder from Windows Explorer. An Internet search for "PowerShell Here" turns up several.

If you aren't browsing the desired folder with Windows Explorer, you can use Start→Run (or any other means of launching an application) to launch PowerShell at a specific location. For that, use PowerShell's -NoExit parameter, along with the implied -Command parameter. In the -Command parameter, call the Set-Location cmdlet to initially move to your desired location.

```
PowerShell -NoExit Set-Location 'C:\Program Files'
```

*Figure 1-2. Launching PowerShell in Windows 8*

## 1.16. Invoke a PowerShell Command or Script from Outside PowerShell

### Problem

You want to invoke a PowerShell command or script from a batch file, a logon script, a scheduled task, or any other non-PowerShell application.

### Solution

To invoke a PowerShell command, use the -Command parameter:

```
PowerShell -Command Get-Process; Read-Host
```

To launch a PowerShell script, use the -File parameter:

```
PowerShell -File 'full path to script' arguments
```

For example:

```
PowerShell -File 'c:\shared scripts\Get-Report.ps1' Hello World
```

## Discussion

By default, any arguments to *PowerShell.exe* get interpreted as commands to run. PowerShell runs the command as though you had typed it in the interactive shell, and then exits. You can customize this behavior by supplying other parameters to *PowerShell.exe*, such as -NoExit, -NoProfile, and more.

 If you are the author of a program that needs to run PowerShell scripts or commands, PowerShell lets you call these scripts and commands much more easily than calling its command-line interface. For more information about this approach, see Recipe 17.10, "Add PowerShell Scripting to Your Own Program".

Since launching a script is so common, PowerShell provides the -File parameter to eliminate the complexities that arise from having to invoke a script from the -Command parameter. This technique lets you invoke a PowerShell script as the target of a logon script, advanced file association, scheduled task, and more.

 When PowerShell detects that its input or output streams have been redirected, it suppresses any prompts that it might normally display. If you want to host an interactive PowerShell prompt inside another application (such as Emacs), use - as the argument for the -File parameter. In PowerShell (as with traditional Unix shells), this implies "taken from standard input."

```
powershell -File -
```

If the script is for background automation or a scheduled task, these scripts can sometimes interfere with (or become influenced by) the user's environment. For these situations, three parameters come in handy:

-NoProfile
Runs the command or script without loading user profile scripts. This makes the script launch faster, but it primarily prevents user preferences (e.g., aliases and preference variables) from interfering with the script's working environment.

-WindowStyle
Runs the command or script with the specified window style—most commonly Hidden. When run with a window style of Hidden, PowerShell hides its main window immediately. For more ways to control the window style from *within* PowerShell, see Recipe 24.3, "Launch a Process".

`-ExecutionPolicy`

Runs the command or script with a specified execution policy applied only to this instance of PowerShell. This lets you write PowerShell scripts to manage a system without having to change the system-wide execution policy. For more information about scoped execution policies, see Recipe 18.1, "Enable Scripting Through an Execution Policy".

If the arguments to the `-Command` parameter become complex, special character handling in the application calling PowerShell (such as *cmd.exe*) might interfere with the command you want to send to PowerShell. For this situation, PowerShell supports an `EncodedCommand` parameter: a Base64-encoded representation of the Unicode string you want to run. Example 1-10 demonstrates how to convert a string containing PowerShell commands to a Base64-encoded form.

*Example 1-10. Converting PowerShell commands into a Base64-encoded form*

```
$commands = '1..10 | % { "PowerShell Rocks" }'
$bytes = [System.Text.Encoding]::Unicode.GetBytes($commands)
$encodedString = [Convert]::ToBase64String($bytes)
```

Once you have the encoded string, you can use it as the value of the `EncodedCommand` parameter, as shown in Example 1-11.

*Example 1-11. Launching PowerShell with an encoded command from cmd.exe*

```
Microsoft Windows [Version 6.0.6000]
Copyright (c) 2006 Microsoft Corporation. All rights reserved.

C:\Users\Lee>PowerShell -EncodedCommand MQAuAC4AMQAwACAAfAAgACUAIAB7ACAAIgBQAG8A
   dwBlAHIAUwBoAGUAbABsACAAUgBvAGMAawBzACIAIAB9AA==
PowerShell Rocks
PowerShell Rocks
PowerShell Rocks
PowerShell Rocks
PowerShell Rocks
PowerShell Rocks
PowerShell Rocks
PowerShell Rocks
PowerShell Rocks
PowerShell Rocks
```

For more information about running scripts, see Recipe 1.1, "Run Programs, Scripts, and Existing Tools".

## See Also

Recipe 1.1, "Run Programs, Scripts, and Existing Tools"

Recipe 17.10, "Add PowerShell Scripting to Your Own Program"

# 1.17. Understand and Customize PowerShell's Tab Completion

## Problem

You want to customize how PowerShell reacts to presses of the Tab key (and additionally, Ctrl-Space in the case of IntelliSense in the Integrated Scripting Environment).

## Solution

Create a custom function called `TabExpansion2`. PowerShell invokes this function when you press Tab, or when it invokes IntelliSense in the Integrated Scripting Environment.

## Discussion

When you press Tab, PowerShell invokes a facility known as *tab expansion*: replacing what you've typed so far with an expanded version of that (if any apply.) For example, if you type `Set-Location C:\` and then press Tab, PowerShell starts cycling through directories under `C:\` for you to navigate into.

The features offered by PowerShell's built-in tab expansion are quite rich, as shown in Table 1-2.

*Table 1-2. Tab expansion features in Windows PowerShell*

| Description | Example |
| --- | --- |
| *Command completion*. Completes command names when current text appears to represent a command invocation. | `Get-Ch <Tab>` |
| *Parameter completion*. Completes command parameters for the current command. | `Get-ChildItem -Pat <Tab>` |
| *Argument completion*. Completes command arguments for the current command parameter. This applies to any command argument that takes a fixed set of values (enumerations or parameters that define a `ValidateSet` attribute). In addition, PowerShell contains extended argument completion for module names, help topics, CIM / WMI classes, event log names, job IDs and names, process IDs and names, provider names, drive names, service names and display names, and trace source names. | `Set-ExecutionPolicy -ExecutionPolicy <Tab>` |
| *History text completion*. Replaces the current input with items from the command history that match the text after the # character. | `# Process <Tab>` |
| *History ID completion*. Replaces the current input with the command line from item number *ID* in your command history. | `# 12 <Tab>` |

| Description | Example |
|---|---|
| *Filename completion.* Replaces the current parameter value with file names that match what you've typed so far. When applied to the Set-Location cmdlet, PowerShell further filters results to only directories. | `Set-Location C:\Windows\S<Tab>` |
| *Operator completion.* Replaces the current text with a matching operator. This includes flags supplied to the switch statement. | `"Hello World" -rep <Tab>`<br>`switch - c <Tab>` |
| *Variable completion.* Replaces the current text with available PowerShell variables. In the Integrated Scripting Environment, PowerShell incorporates variables even from script content that has never been invoked. | `$myGreeting = "Hello World";`<br>`$myGr <Tab>` |
| *Member completion.* Replaces member names for the currently referenced variable or type. When PowerShell can infer the members from previous commands in the pipeline, it even supports member completion within script blocks. | `[Console]::Ba<TAB>`<br>`Get-Process | Where-Object`<br>`{ $_.Ha <Tab>` |
| *Type completion.* Replaces abbreviated type names with their namespace-qualified name. | `[PSSer<TAB>`<br>`$l = New-Object List[Stri <Tab>` |

If you want to extend PowerShell's tab expansion capabilities, define a function called TabExpansion2. You can add this to your PowerShell profile directly, or dot-source it from your profile. Example 1-12 demonstrates an example custom tab expansion function that extends the functionality already built into PowerShell.

*Example 1-12. A sample implementation of TabExpansion2*

```
##############################################################################
##
## TabExpansion2
##
## From Windows PowerShell Cookbook (O'Reilly)
## by Lee Holmes (http://www.leeholmes.com/guide)
##
##############################################################################

function TabExpansion2
{
    [CmdletBinding(DefaultParameterSetName = 'ScriptInputSet')]
    Param(
        [Parameter(ParameterSetName = 'ScriptInputSet', Mandatory = $true,
            Position = 0)]
        [string] $inputScript,

        [Parameter(ParameterSetName = 'ScriptInputSet', Mandatory = $true,
            Position = 1)]
        [int] $cursorColumn,

        [Parameter(ParameterSetName = 'AstInputSet', Mandatory = $true,
            Position = 0)]
        [System.Management.Automation.Language.Ast] $ast,
```

```
    [Parameter(ParameterSetName = 'AstInputSet', Mandatory = $true,
        Position = 1)]
    [System.Management.Automation.Language.Token[]] $tokens,

    [Parameter(ParameterSetName = 'AstInputSet', Mandatory = $true,
        Position = 2)]
    [System.Management.Automation.Language.IScriptPosition] $positionOfCursor,

    [Parameter(ParameterSetName = 'ScriptInputSet', Position = 2)]
    [Parameter(ParameterSetName = 'AstInputSet', Position = 3)]
    [Hashtable] $options = $null
)

End
{
    ## Create a new 'Options' hashtable if one has not been supplied.
    ## In this hashtable, you can add keys for the following options, using
    ## $true or $false for their values:
    ##
    ## IgnoreHiddenShares - Ignore hidden UNC shares (such as \\COMPUTER\ADMIN$)
    ## RelativePaths - When expanding filenames and paths, $true forces PowerShell
    ## to replace paths with relative paths. When $false, forces PowerShell to
    ## replace them with absolute paths. By default, PowerShell makes this
    ## decision based on what you had typed so far before invoking tab completion.
    ## LiteralPaths - Prevents PowerShell from replacing special file characters
    ## (such as square brackets and back-ticks) with their escaped equivalent.
    if(-not $options) { $options = @{} }

    ## Demonstrate some custom tab expansion completers for parameters.
    ## This is a hashtable of parameter names (and optionally cmdlet names)
    ## that we add to the $options hashtable.
    ##
    ## When PowerShell evaluates the script block, $args gets the
    ## following: command name, parameter, word being completed,
    ## AST of the command being completed, and currently bound arguments.
    $options["CustomArgumentCompleters"] = @{
        "Get-ChildItem:Filter" = { "*.ps1","*.txt","*.doc" }
        "ComputerName" = { "ComputerName1","ComputerName2","ComputerName3" }
    }

    ## Also define a completer for a native executable.
    ## When PowerShell evaluates the script block, $args gets the
    ## word being completed, and AST of the command being completed.
    $options["NativeArgumentCompleters"] = @{
        "attrib" = { "+R","+H","+S" }
    }

    ## Define a "quick completions" list that we'll cycle through
    ## when the user types '!!' followed by TAB.
    $quickCompletions = @(
        'Get-Process -Name PowerShell | ? Id -ne $pid | Stop-Process',
```

```
            'Set-Location $pshome',
            ('$errors = $error | % { $_.InvocationInfo.Line }; Get-History | ' +
                ' ? { $_.CommandLine -notin $errors }')
    )

    ## First, check the built-in tab completion results
    $result = $null
    if ($psCmdlet.ParameterSetName -eq 'ScriptInputSet')
    {
        $result = [Management.Automation.CommandCompletion]::CompleteInput(
            <#inputScript#> $inputScript,
            <#cursorColumn#> $cursorColumn,
            <#options#>     $options)
    }
    else
    {
        $result = [Management.Automation.CommandCompletion]::CompleteInput(
            <#ast#>              $ast,
            <#tokens#>           $tokens,
            <#positionOfCursor#> $positionOfCursor,
            <#options#>          $options)
    }

    ## If we didn't get a result
    if($result.CompletionMatches.Count -eq 0)
    {
        ## If this was done at the command-line or in a remote session,
        ## create an AST out of the input
        if ($psCmdlet.ParameterSetName -eq 'ScriptInputSet')
        {
            $ast = [System.Management.Automation.Language.Parser]::ParseInput(
                $inputScript, [ref]$tokens, [ref]$null)
        }

        ## In this simple example, look at the text being supplied.
        ## We could do advanced analysis of the AST here if we wanted,
        ## but in this case just use its text. We use a regular expression
        ## to check if the text started with two exclamations, and then
        ## use a match group to retain the rest.
        $text = $ast.Extent.Text
        if($text -match '^!!(.*)')
        {
            ## Extract the rest of the text from the regular expression
            ## match group.
            $currentCompletionText = $matches[1].Trim()

            ## Go through each of our quick completions and add them to
            ## our completion results. The arguments to the completion results
            ## are the text to be used in tab completion, a potentially shorter
            ## version to use for display (i.e., IntelliSense in the ISE),
            ## the type of match, and a potentially more verbose description to
            ## be used as a tool tip.
```

```
        $quickCompletions |
            Where-Object { $_ -match $currentCompletionText } |
            Foreach-Object { $result.CompletionMatches.Add(
            (New-Object Management.Automation.CompletionResult $_,$_,"Text",$_) )
            }
        }
    }

    return $result
    }
}
```

## See Also

Recipe 10.10, "Parse and Interpret PowerShell Scripts"

"Common Customization Points" (page 914)

# 1.18. Program: Learn Aliases for Common Commands

In interactive use, full cmdlet names (such as Get-ChildItem) are cumbersome and slow to type. Although aliases are much more efficient, it takes a while to discover them. To learn aliases more easily, you can modify your prompt to remind you of the shorter version of any aliased commands that you use.

This involves two steps:

1. Add the program Get-AliasSuggestion.ps1, shown in Example 1-13, to your *tools* directory or another directory.

   *Example 1-13. Get-AliasSuggestion.ps1*

   ```
   ##############################################################################
   ##
   ## Get-AliasSuggestion
   ##
   ## From Windows PowerShell Cookbook (O'Reilly)
   ## by Lee Holmes (http://www.leeholmes.com/guide)
   ##
   ##############################################################################

   <#

   .SYNOPSIS

   Get an alias suggestion from the full text of the last command. Intended to
   be added to your prompt function to help learn aliases for commands.

   .EXAMPLE

   PS > Get-AliasSuggestion Remove-ItemProperty
   ```

```
Suggestion: An alias for Remove-ItemProperty is rp

#>

param(
    ## The full text of the last command
    $LastCommand
)

Set-StrictMode -Version 3

$helpMatches = @()

## Find all of the commands in their last input
$tokens = [Management.Automation.PSParser]::Tokenize(
    $lastCommand, [ref] $null)
$commands = $tokens | Where-Object { $_.Type -eq "Command" }

## Go through each command
foreach($command in $commands)
{
    ## Get the alias suggestions
    foreach($alias in Get-Alias -Definition $command.Content)
    {
        $helpMatches += "Suggestion: An alias for " +
            "$($alias.Definition) is $($alias.Name)"
    }
}

$helpMatches
```

2. Add the text from Example 1-14 to the Prompt function in your profile. If you do
   not yet have a Prompt function, see Recipe 1.8, "Customize Your Shell, Profile, and
   Prompt" to learn how to add one.

   *Example 1-14. A useful prompt to teach you aliases for common commands*

```
function Prompt
{
    ## Get the last item from the history
    $historyItem = Get-History -Count 1

    ## If there were any history items
    if($historyItem)
    {
        ## Get the training suggestion for that item
        $suggestions = @(Get-AliasSuggestion $historyItem.CommandLine)
        ## If there were any suggestions
        if($suggestions)
        {
            ## For each suggestion, write it to the screen
            foreach($aliasSuggestion in $suggestions)
```

```
                {
                    Write-Host "$aliasSuggestion"
                }
                Write-Host ""

            }
        }

        ## Rest of prompt goes here
        "PS [$env:COMPUTERNAME] >"
    }
```

For more information about running scripts, see Recipe 1.1, "Run Programs, Scripts, and Existing Tools".

## See Also

Recipe 1.1, "Run Programs, Scripts, and Existing Tools"

Recipe 1.8, "Customize Your Shell, Profile, and Prompt"

# 1.19. Program: Learn Aliases for Common Parameters

## Problem

You want to learn aliases defined for command parameters.

## Solution

Use the Get-ParameterAlias script, as shown in Example 1-15, to return all aliases for parameters used by the previous command in your session history.

*Example 1-15. Get-ParameterAlias.ps1*

```
##############################################################################
##
## Get-ParameterAlias
##
## From Windows PowerShell Cookbook (O'Reilly)
## by Lee Holmes (http://www.leeholmes.com/guide)
##
##############################################################################

<#

.SYNOPSIS

Looks in the session history, and returns any aliases that apply to
parameters of commands that were used.
```

```
.EXAMPLE

PS > dir -ErrorAction SilentlyContinue
PS > Get-ParameterAlias
An alias for the 'ErrorAction' parameter of 'dir' is ea

#>

Set-StrictMode -Version 3

## Get the last item from their session history
$history = Get-History -Count 1
if(-not $history)
{
    return
}

## And extract the actual command line they typed
$lastCommand = $history.CommandLine

## Use the Tokenizer API to determine which portions represent
## commands and parameters to those commands
$tokens = [System.Management.Automation.PsParser]::Tokenize(
    $lastCommand, [ref] $null)
$currentCommand = $null

## Now go through each resulting token
foreach($token in $tokens)
{
    ## If we've found a new command, store that.
    if($token.Type -eq "Command")
    {
        $currentCommand = $token.Content
    }

    ## If we've found a command parameter, start looking for aliases
    if(($token.Type -eq "CommandParameter") -and ($currentCommand))
    {
        ## Remove the leading "-" from the parameter
        $currentParameter = $token.Content.TrimStart("-")

        ## Determine all of the parameters for the current command.
        (Get-Command $currentCommand).Parameters.GetEnumerator() |

            ## For parameters that start with the current parameter name,
            Where-Object { $_.Key -like "$currentParameter*" } |

            ## return all of the aliases that apply. We use "starts with"
            ## because the user might have typed a shortened form of
            ## the parameter name.
            Foreach-Object {
```

```
        $_.Value.Aliases | Foreach-Object {
            "Suggestion: An alias for the '$currentParameter' " +
            "parameter of '$currentCommand' is '$_'"
        }
    }
}
}
```

# Discussion

To make it easy to type command parameters, PowerShell lets you type only as much of
the command parameter as is required to disambiguate it from other parameters of that
command. In addition to shortening implicitly supported by the shell, cmdlet authors
can also define explicit aliases for their parameters—for example, CN as a short form for
ComputerName.

While helpful, these aliases are difficult to discover.

If you want to see the aliases for a specific command, you can access its Parameters
collection:

```
PS > (Get-Command New-TimeSpan).Parameters.Values | Select Name,Aliases

Name                               Aliases
----                               -------
Start                              {LastWriteTime}
End                                {}
Days                               {}
Hours                              {}
Minutes                            {}
Seconds                            {}
Verbose                            {vb}
Debug                              {db}
ErrorAction                        {ea}
WarningAction                      {wa}
ErrorVariable                      {ev}
WarningVariable                    {wv}
OutVariable                        {ov}
OutBuffer                          {ob}
```

If you want to learn any aliases for parameters in your previous command, simply run
Get-ParameterAlias.ps1. To make PowerShell do this automatically, add a call to Get-
ParameterAlias.ps1 in your prompt.

This script builds on two main features: PowerShell's *Tokenizer API*, and the rich information returned by the Get-Command cmdlet. PowerShell's Tokenizer API examines its
input and returns PowerShell's interpretation of the input: commands, parameters, parameter values, operators, and more. Like the rich output produced by most of
PowerShell's commands, Get-Command returns information about a command's parameters, parameter sets, output type (if specified), and more.

For more information about the Tokenizer API, see Recipe 10.10, "Parse and Interpret PowerShell Scripts".

## See Also

Recipe 1.1, "Run Programs, Scripts, and Existing Tools"

Recipe 10.10, "Parse and Interpret PowerShell Scripts"

"Structured Commands (Cmdlets)" (page vii)

# 1.20. Access and Manage Your Console History

## Problem

After working in the shell for a while, you want to invoke commands from your history, view your command history, and save your command history.

## Solution

The shortcuts given in Recipe 1.8, "Customize Your Shell, Profile, and Prompt" let you manage your history, but PowerShell offers several features to help you work with your console in even more detail.

To get the most recent commands from your session, use the `Get-History` cmdlet (or its alias of h):

```
Get-History
```

To rerun a specific command from your session history, provide its ID to the `Invoke-History` cmdlet (or its alias of ihy):

```
Invoke-History ID
```

To increase (or limit) the number of commands stored in your session history, assign a new value to the `$MaximumHistoryCount` variable:

```
$MaximumHistoryCount = Count
```

To save your command history to a file, pipe the output of `Get-History` to the `Export-CliXml` cmdlet:

```
Get-History | Export-CliXml Filename
```

To add a previously saved command history to your current session history, call the `Import-CliXml` cmdlet and then pipe that output to the `Add-History` cmdlet:

```
Import-CliXml Filename | Add-History
```

To clear all commands from your session history, use the `Clear-History` cmdlet:

```
Clear-History
```

## Discussion

Unlike the console history hotkeys discussed in Recipe 1.8, "Customize Your Shell, Profile, and Prompt", the `Get-History` cmdlet produces rich objects that represent information about items in your history. Each object contains that item's ID, command line, start of execution time, and end of execution time.

Once you know the ID of a history item (as shown in the output of `Get-History`), you can pass it to `Invoke-History` to execute that command again. The example prompt function shown in Recipe 1.8, "Customize Your Shell, Profile, and Prompt" makes working with prior history items easy, as the prompt for each command includes the history ID that will represent it.

 You can easily see how long a series of commands took to invoke by looking at the `StartExecutionTime` and `EndExecutionTime` properties. This is a great way to get a handle on exactly how little time it took to come up with the commands that just saved you hours of manual work:

```
PS C:\> Get-History 65,66 | Format-Table *

Id CommandLine          StartExecutionTime      EndExecutionTime
-- -----------          ------------------      ----------------
65 dir                  10/13/2012 2:06:05 PM 10/13/2012 2:06:05 PM
66 Start-Sleep -Seconds 45 10/13/2012 2:06:15 PM 10/13/2012 2:07:00 PM
```

IDs provided by the `Get-History` cmdlet differ from the IDs given by the Windows console common history hotkeys (such as F7), because their history management techniques differ.

By default, PowerShell stores the last 4,096 entries of your command history. If you want to raise or lower this amount, set the `$MaximumHistoryCount` variable to the size you desire. To make this change permanent, set the variable in your PowerShell profile script.

By far, the most useful feature of PowerShell's command history is for reviewing ad hoc experimentation and capturing it in a script that you can then use over and over. For an overview of that process (and a script that helps to automate it), see Recipe 1.21, "Program: Create Scripts from Your Session History".

## See Also

Recipe 1.8, "Customize Your Shell, Profile, and Prompt"

Recipe 1.21, "Program: Create Scripts from Your Session History"

Recipe 1.22, "Invoke a Command from Your Session History"

# 1.21. Program: Create Scripts from Your Session History

After interactively experimenting at the command line for a while to solve a multistep task, you'll often want to keep or share the exact steps you used to eventually solve the problem. The script smiles at you from your history buffer, but it is unfortunately surrounded by many more commands that you *don't* want to keep.

 For an example of using the `Out-GridView` cmdlet to do this graphically, see Recipe 2.4, "Program: Interactively Filter Lists of Objects".

To solve this problem, use the `Get-History` cmdlet to view the recent commands that you've typed. Then, call `Copy-History` with the IDs of the commands you want to keep, as shown in Example 1-16.

*Example 1-16. Copy-History.ps1*

```
##############################################################################
##
## Copy-History
##
## From Windows PowerShell Cookbook (O'Reilly)
## by Lee Holmes (http://www.leeholmes.com/guide)
##
##############################################################################

<#

.SYNOPSIS

Copies selected commands from the history buffer into the clipboard as a script.

.EXAMPLE

PS > Copy-History
Copies the entire contents of the history buffer into the clipboard.

.EXAMPLE

PS > Copy-History -5
```

Copies the last five commands into the clipboard.

.EXAMPLE

```
PS > Copy-History 2,5,8,4
Copies commands 2,5,8, and 4.
```

.EXAMPLE

```
PS > Copy-History (1..10+5+6)
Copies commands 1 through 10, then 5, then 6, using PowerShell's array
slicing syntax.

#>

param(
    ## The range of history IDs to copy
    [int[]] $Range
)

Set-StrictMode -Version 3

$history = @()

## If they haven't specified a range, assume it's everything
if((-not $range) -or ($range.Count -eq 0))
{
    $history = @(Get-History -Count ([Int16]::MaxValue))
}
## If it's a negative number, copy only that many
elseif(($range.Count -eq 1) -and ($range[0] -lt 0))
{
    $count = [Math]::Abs($range[0])
    $history = (Get-History -Count $count)
}
## Otherwise, go through each history ID in the given range
## and add it to our history list.
else
{
    foreach($commandId in $range)
    {
        if($commandId -eq -1) { $history += Get-History -Count 1 }
        else { $history += Get-History -Id $commandId }
    }
}

## Finally, export the history to the clipboard.
$history | Foreach-Object { $_.CommandLine } | clip.exe
```

For more information about running scripts, see Recipe 1.1, "Run Programs, Scripts, and Existing Tools".

## See Also

Recipe 1.1, "Run Programs, Scripts, and Existing Tools"

Recipe 2.4, "Program: Interactively Filter Lists of Objects"

# 1.22. Invoke a Command from Your Session History

## Problem

You want to run a command from the history of your current session.

## Solution

Use the `Invoke-History` cmdlet (or its `ihy` alias) to invoke a specific command by its *ID*:

```
Invoke-History ID
```

To search through your history for a command containing *text*:

```
PS > #text<Tab>
```

To repopulate your command with the text of a previous command by its *ID*:

```
PS > #ID<Tab>
```

## Discussion

Once you've had your shell open for a while, your history buffer quickly fills with useful commands. The history management hotkeys described in Recipe 1.8, "Customize Your Shell, Profile, and Prompt" show one way to navigate your history, but this type of history navigation works only for command lines you've typed in that specific session. If you keep a persistent command history (as shown in Recipe 1.31, "Save State Between Sessions"), these shortcuts do not apply.

The `Invoke-History` cmdlet illustrates the simplest example of working with your command history. Given a specific history ID (perhaps shown in your prompt function), calling `Invoke-History` with that ID will run that command again. For more information about this technique, see Recipe 1.8, "Customize Your Shell, Profile, and Prompt".

As part of its tab-completion support, PowerShell gives you easy access to previous commands as well. If you prefix your command with the # character, tab completion takes one of two approaches:

*ID completion*

If you type a number, tab completion finds the entry in your command history with that ID, and then replaces your command line with the text of that history entry. This is especially useful when you want to slightly modify a previous history entry, since `Invoke-History` by itself doesn't support that.

*Pattern completion*

> If you type anything else, tab completion searches for entries in your command history that contain that text. Under the hood, PowerShell uses the -like operator to match your command entries, so you can use all of the wildcard characters supported by that operator. For more information on searching text for patterns, see Recipe 5.7, "Search a String for Text or a Pattern".

PowerShell's tab completion is largely driven by the fully customizable TabExpansion2 function. You can easily change this function to include more advanced functionality, or even just customize specific behaviors to suit your personal preferences. For more information, see Recipe 1.17, "Understand and Customize PowerShell's Tab Completion".

## See Also

Recipe 1.8, "Customize Your Shell, Profile, and Prompt"

Recipe 5.7, "Search a String for Text or a Pattern"

Recipe 1.17, "Understand and Customize PowerShell's Tab Completion"

Recipe 1.31, "Save State Between Sessions"

# 1.23. Program: Search Formatted Output for a Pattern

While PowerShell's built-in filtering facilities are incredibly flexible (for example, the Where-Object cmdlet), they generally operate against specific properties of the incoming object. If you are searching for text in the object's formatted output, or don't know which property contains the text you are looking for, simple text-based filtering is sometimes helpful.

To solve this problem, you can pipe the output into the Out-String cmdlet before passing it to the Select-String cmdlet:

```
Get-Service | Out-String -Stream | Select-String audio
```

Or, using built-in aliases:

```
Get-Service | oss | sls audio
```

In script form, Select-TextOutput (shown in Example 1-17) does exactly this, and it lets you search for a pattern in the visual representation of command output.

*Example 1-17. Select-TextOutput.ps1*

```
##############################################################################
##
## Select-TextOutput
##
## From Windows PowerShell Cookbook (O'Reilly)
```

```
## by Lee Holmes (http://www.leeholmes.com/guide)
##
##############################################################################

<#

.SYNOPSIS

Searches the textual output of a command for a pattern.

.EXAMPLE

PS > Get-Service | Select-TextOutput audio
Finds all references to "Audio" in the output of Get-Service

#>

param(
    ## The pattern to search for
    $Pattern
)

Set-StrictMode -Version 3
$input | Out-String -Stream | Select-String $pattern
```

For more information about running scripts, see Recipe 1.1, "Run Programs, Scripts, and Existing Tools".

## See Also

Recipe 1.1, "Run Programs, Scripts, and Existing Tools"

# 1.24. Interactively View and Process Command Output

## Problem

You want to graphically explore and analyze the output of a command.

## Solution

Use the Out-GridView cmdlet to interactively explore the output of a command.

# Discussion

The Out-GridView cmdlet is one of the rare PowerShell cmdlets that displays a graphical user interface. While the Where-Object and Sort-Object cmdlets are the most common way to sort and filter lists of items, the Out-GridView cmdlet is very effective at the style of repeated refinement that sometimes helps you develop complex queries. Figure 1-3 shows the Out-GridView cmdlet in action.

*Figure 1-3. Out-GridView, ready to filter*

Out-GridView lets you primarily filter your command output in two ways: a *quick filter* expression and a *criteria filter*.

*Quick filters* are fairly simple. As you type text in the topmost "Filter" window, Out-GridView filters the list to contain only items that match that text. If you want to restrict this text filtering to specific columns, simply provide a column name before your search string and separate the two with a colon. You can provide multiple search strings, in which case Out-GridView returns only rows that match all of the required strings.

 Unlike most filtering cmdlets in PowerShell, the quick filters in the Out-GridView cmdlet do not support wildcards or regular expressions. For this type of advanced query, criteria-based filtering can help.

*Criteria filters* give fine-grained control over the filtering used by the Out-GridView cmdlet. To apply a criteria filter, click the "Add criteria" button and select a property to filter on. Out-GridView adds a row below the quick filter field and lets you pick one of several operations to apply to this property:

- Less than or equal to
- Greater than or equal to
- Between
- Equals
- Does not equal
- Contains
- Does not contain

In addition to these filtering options, Out-GridView also lets you click and rearrange the header columns to sort by them.

### Processing output

Once you've sliced and diced your command output, you can select any rows you want to keep and press Ctrl-C to copy them to the clipboard. Out-GridView copies the items to the clipboard as tab-separated data, so you can easily paste the information into a spreadsheet or other file for further processing.

In addition to supporting clipboard output, the Out-GridView cmdlet supports full-fidelity object filtering if you use its -PassThru parameter. For an example of this full-fidelity filtering, see Recipe 2.4, "Program: Interactively Filter Lists of Objects".

## See Also

Recipe 2.4, "Program: Interactively Filter Lists of Objects"

# 1.25. Program: Interactively View and Explore Objects

When working with unfamiliar objects in PowerShell, much of your time is spent with the Get-Member and Format-List commands—navigating through properties, reviewing members, and more.

For ad hoc investigation, a graphical interface is often useful.

To solve this problem, Example 1-18 provides an interactive tree view that you can use to explore and navigate objects. For example, to examine the structure of a script as PowerShell sees it (its *abstract syntax tree*):

```
$ps = { Get-Process -ID $pid }.Ast
Show-Object $ps
```

For more information about parsing and analyzing the structure of PowerShell scripts, see Recipe 10.10, "Parse and Interpret PowerShell Scripts".

*Example 1-18. Show-Object.ps1*

```
#############################################################################
##
## Show-Object
##
## From Windows PowerShell Cookbook (O'Reilly)
## by Lee Holmes (http://www.leeholmes.com/guide)
##
#############################################################################

<#

.SYNOPSIS

Provides a graphical interface to let you explore and navigate an object.


.EXAMPLE

PS > $ps = { Get-Process -ID $pid }.Ast
PS > Show-Object $ps

#>

param(
    ## The object to examine
    [Parameter(ValueFromPipeline = $true)]
    $InputObject
)

Set-StrictMode -Version 3

Add-Type -Assembly System.Windows.Forms

## Figure out the variable name to use when displaying the
## object navigation syntax. To do this, we look through all
## of the variables for the one with the same object identifier.
$rootVariableName = dir variable:\* -Exclude InputObject,Args |
    Where-Object {
        $_.Value -and
        ($_.Value.GetType() -eq $InputObject.GetType()) -and
        ($_.Value.GetHashCode() -eq $InputObject.GetHashCode())
}

## If we got multiple, pick the first
$rootVariableName = $rootVariableName| % Name | Select -First 1
```

```
## If we didn't find one, use a default name
if(-not $rootVariableName)
{
    $rootVariableName = "InputObject"
}

## A function to add an object to the display tree
function PopulateNode($node, $object)
{
    ## If we've been asked to add a NULL object, just return
    if(-not $object) { return }

    ## If the object is a collection, then we need to add multiple
    ## children to the node
    if([System.Management.Automation.LanguagePrimitives]::GetEnumerator($object))
    {
        ## Some very rare collections don't support indexing (i.e.: $foo[0]).
        ## In this situation, PowerShell returns the parent object back when you
        ## try to access the [0] property.
        $isOnlyEnumerable = $object.GetHashCode() -eq $object[0].GetHashCode()

        ## Go through all the items
        $count = 0
        foreach($childObjectValue in $object)
        {
            ## Create the new node to add, with the node text of the item and
            ## value, along with its type
            $newChildNode = New-Object Windows.Forms.TreeNode
            $newChildNode.Text = "$($node.Name)[$count] = $childObjectValue : " +
                $childObjectValue.GetType()

            ## Use the node name to keep track of the actual property name
            ## and syntax to access that property.
            ## If we can't use the index operator to access children, add
            ## a special tag that we'll handle specially when displaying
            ## the node names.
            if($isOnlyEnumerable)
            {
                $newChildNode.Name = "@"
            }

            $newChildNode.Name += "[$count]"
            $null = $node.Nodes.Add($newChildNode)

            ## If this node has children or properties, add a placeholder
            ## node underneath so that the node shows a '+' sign to be
            ## expanded.
            AddPlaceholderIfRequired $newChildNode $childObjectValue

            $count++
        }
    }
```

```
        }
        else
        {
            ## If the item was not a collection, then go through its
            ## properties
            foreach($child in $object.PSObject.Properties)
            {
                ## Figure out the value of the property, along with
                ## its type.
                $childObject = $child.Value
                $childObjectType = $null
                if($childObject)
                {
                    $childObjectType = $childObject.GetType()
                }

                ## Create the new node to add, with the node text of the item and
                ## value, along with its type
                $childNode = New-Object Windows.Forms.TreeNode
                $childNode.Text = $child.Name + " = $childObject : $childObjectType"
                $childNode.Name = $child.Name
                $null = $node.Nodes.Add($childNode)

                ## If this node has children or properties, add a placeholder
                ## node underneath so that the node shows a '+' sign to be
                ## expanded.
                AddPlaceholderIfRequired $childNode $childObject
            }
        }
    }

## A function to add a placeholder if required to a node.
## If there are any properties or children for this object, make a temporary
## node with the text "..." so that the node shows a '+' sign to be
## expanded.
function AddPlaceholderIfRequired($node, $object)
{
    if(-not $object) { return }

    if([System.Management.Automation.LanguagePrimitives]::GetEnumerator($object) -or
        @($object.PSObject.Properties))
    {
        $null = $node.Nodes.Add( (New-Object Windows.Forms.TreeNode "...") )
    }
}

## A function invoked when a node is selected.
function OnAfterSelect
{
    param($Sender, $TreeViewEventArgs)

    ## Determine the selected node
```

```
    $nodeSelected = $Sender.SelectedNode

    ## Walk through its parents, creating the virtual
    ## PowerShell syntax to access this property.
    $nodePath = GetPathForNode $nodeSelected

    ## Now, invoke that PowerShell syntax to retrieve
    ## the value of the property.
    $resultObject = Invoke-Expression $nodePath
    $outputPane.Text = $nodePath

    ## If we got some output, put the object's member
    ## information in the text box.
    if($resultObject)
    {
        $members = Get-Member -InputObject $resultObject | Out-String
        $outputPane.Text += "`n" + $members
    }
}

## A function invoked when the user is about to expand a node
function OnBeforeExpand
{
    param($Sender, $TreeViewCancelEventArgs)

    ## Determine the selected node
    $selectedNode = $TreeViewCancelEventArgs.Node

    ## If it has a child node that is the placeholder, clear
    ## the placeholder node.
    if($selectedNode.FirstNode -and
        ($selectedNode.FirstNode.Text -eq "..."))
    {
        $selectedNode.Nodes.Clear()
    }
    else
    {
        return
    }

    ## Walk through its parents, creating the virtual
    ## PowerShell syntax to access this property.
    $nodePath = GetPathForNode $selectedNode

    ## Now, invoke that PowerShell syntax to retrieve
    ## the value of the property.
    Invoke-Expression "`$resultObject = $nodePath"

    ## And populate the node with the result object.
    PopulateNode $selectedNode $resultObject
}
```

```
## A function to handle keypresses on the form.
## In this case, we capture ^C to copy the path of
## the object property that we're currently viewing.
function OnKeyPress
{
    param($Sender, $KeyPressEventArgs)

    ## [Char] 3 = Control-C
    if($KeyPressEventArgs.KeyChar -eq 3)
    {
        $KeyPressEventArgs.Handled = $true

        ## Get the object path, and set it on the clipboard
        $node = $Sender.SelectedNode
        $nodePath = GetPathForNode $node
        [System.Windows.Forms.Clipboard]::SetText($nodePath)

        $form.Close()
    }
}

## A function to walk through the parents of a node,
## creating virtual PowerShell syntax to access this property.
function GetPathForNode
{
    param($Node)

    $nodeElements = @()

    ## Go through all the parents, adding them so that
    ## $nodeElements is in order.
    while($Node)
    {
        $nodeElements = ,$Node + $nodeElements
        $Node = $Node.Parent
    }

    ## Now go through the node elements
    $nodePath = ""
    foreach($Node in $nodeElements)
    {
        $nodeName = $Node.Name

        ## If it was a node that PowerShell is able to enumerate
        ## (but not index), wrap it in the array cast operator.
        if($nodeName.StartsWith('@'))
        {
            $nodeName = $nodeName.Substring(1)
            $nodePath = "@(" + $nodePath + ")"
        }
        elseif($nodeName.StartsWith('['))
        {
```

```
                    ## If it's a child index, we don't need to
                    ## add the dot for property access
            }
        elseif($nodePath)
        {
                    ## Otherwise, we're accessing a property. Add a dot.
                    $nodePath += "."
        }

            ## Append the node name to the path
            $nodePath += $nodeName
    }

    ## And return the result
    $nodePath
}

## Create the TreeView, which will hold our object navigation
## area.
$treeView = New-Object Windows.Forms.TreeView
$treeView.Dock = "Top"
$treeView.Height = 500
$treeView.PathSeparator = "."
$treeView.Add_AfterSelect( { OnAfterSelect @args } )
$treeView.Add_BeforeExpand( { OnBeforeExpand @args } )
$treeView.Add_KeyPress( { OnKeyPress @args } )

## Create the output pane, which will hold our object
## member information.
$outputPane = New-Object System.Windows.Forms.TextBox
$outputPane.Multiline = $true
$outputPane.ScrollBars = "Vertical"
$outputPane.Font = "Consolas"
$outputPane.Dock = "Top"
$outputPane.Height = 300

## Create the root node, which represents the object
## we are trying to show.
$root = New-Object Windows.Forms.TreeNode
$root.Text = "$InputObject : " + $InputObject.GetType()
$root.Name = '$' + $rootVariableName
$root.Expand()
$null = $treeView.Nodes.Add($root)

## And populate the initial information into the tree
## view.
PopulateNode $root $InputObject

## Finally, create the main form and show it.
$form = New-Object Windows.Forms.Form
$form.Text = "Browsing " + $root.Text
$form.Width = 1000
```

```
$form.Height = 800
$form.Controls.Add($outputPane)
$form.Controls.Add($treeView)
$null = $form.ShowDialog()
$form.Dispose()
```

For more information about running scripts, see Recipe 1.1, "Run Programs, Scripts, and Existing Tools".

## See Also

Recipe 1.1, "Run Programs, Scripts, and Existing Tools"

Recipe 10.10, "Parse and Interpret PowerShell Scripts"

# 1.26. Store the Output of a Command into a File

## Problem

You want to redirect the output of a command or pipeline into a file.

## Solution

To redirect the output of a command into a file, use either the Out-File cmdlet or one of the redirection operators.

Out-File:

```
Get-ChildItem | Out-File unicodeFile.txt
Get-Content filename.cs | Out-File -Encoding ASCII file.txt
Get-ChildItem | Out-File -Width 120 unicodeFile.cs
```

Redirection operators:

```
Get-ChildItem > files.txt
Get-ChildItem 2> errors.txt
Get-ChildItem n> otherStreams.txt
```

## Discussion

The Out-File cmdlet and redirection operators share a lot in common. For the most part, you can use either. The redirection operators are unique because they give the greatest amount of control over redirecting individual streams. The Out-File cmdlet is unique primarily because it lets you easily configure the formatting width and encoding.

If you want to save the objects from a command into a file (rather than the text-based representation that you see on screen), see Recipe 10.5, "Easily Import and Export Your Structured Data".

The default formatting width and the default output encoding are two aspects of output redirection that can sometimes cause difficulty.

The default formatting width sometimes causes problems because redirecting PowerShell-formatted output into a file is designed to mimic what you see on the screen. If your screen is 80 characters wide, the file will be 80 characters wide as well. Examples of PowerShell-formatted output include directory listings (that are implicitly formatted as a table) as well as any commands that you explicitly format using one of the *Format-** set of cmdlets. If this causes problems, you can customize the width of the file with the -Width parameter on the Out-File cmdlet.

The default output encoding sometimes causes unexpected results because PowerShell creates all files using the UTF-16 Unicode encoding by default. This allows PowerShell to fully support the entire range of international characters, cmdlets, and output. Although this is a great improvement on traditional shells, it may cause an unwanted surprise when running large search-and-replace operations on ASCII source code files, for example. To force PowerShell to send its output to a file in the ASCII encoding, use the -Encoding parameter on the Out-File cmdlet.

For more information about the Out-File cmdlet, type **Get-Help Out-File**. For a full list of supported redirection operators, see "Capturing Output" (page 913).

## See Also

Recipe 10.5, "Easily Import and Export Your Structured Data"

"Capturing Output" (page 913)

# 1.27. Add Information to the End of a File

## Problem

You want to redirect the output of a pipeline into a file but add the information to the end of that file.

## Solution

To redirect the output of a command into a file, use either the -Append parameter of the Out-File cmdlet or one of the appending redirection operators described in "Capturing Output" (page 913). Both support options to append text to the end of a file.

---

Out-File:

```
Get-ChildItem | Out-File -Append files.txt
```

Redirection operators:

```
Get-ChildItem >> files.txt
```

## Discussion

The Out-File cmdlet and redirection operators share a lot in common. For the most part, you can use either. See the discussion in Recipe 1.26, "Store the Output of a Command into a File" for a more detailed comparison of the two approaches, including reasons that you would pick one over the other.

## See Also

Recipe 1.26, "Store the Output of a Command into a File"

"Capturing Output" (page 913)

# 1.28. Record a Transcript of Your Shell Session

## Problem

You want to record a log or transcript of your shell session.

## Solution

To record a transcript of your shell session, run the command Start-Transcript. It has an optional -Path parameter that defaults to a filename based on the current system time. By default, PowerShell places this file in the *My Documents* directory. To stop recording the transcript of your shell system, run the command Stop-Transcript.

## Discussion

Although the Get-History cmdlet is helpful, it does not record the output produced during your PowerShell session. To accomplish that, use the Start-Transcript cmdlet. In addition to the Path parameter described previously, the Start-Transcript cmdlet also supports parameters that let you control how PowerShell interacts with the output file.

# 1.29. Extend Your Shell with Additional Commands

## Problem

You want to use PowerShell cmdlets, providers, or script-based extensions written by a third party.

## Solution

If the module is part of the standard PowerShell module path, simply run the command you want.

```
Invoke-NewCommand
```

If it is not, use the `Import-Module` command to import third-party commands into your PowerShell session.

To import a module from a specific directory:

```
Import-Module c:\path\to\module
```

To import a module from a specific file (module, script, or assembly):

```
Import-Module c:\path\to\module\file.ext
```

## Discussion

PowerShell supports two sets of commands that enable additional cmdlets and providers: `*-Module` and `*-PsSnapin`. Snapins were the packages for extensions in version 1 of PowerShell, and are rarely used. Snapins supported only compiled extensions and had onerous installation requirements.

Version 2 of PowerShell introduced *modules* that support everything that snapins support (and more) without the associated installation pain. That said, PowerShell version 2 also required that you remember which modules contained which commands and manually load those modules before using them. Windows 8 and Windows Server 2012 include thousands of commands in over 50 modules—quickly making reliance on one's memory an unsustainable approach.

PowerShell version 3 significantly improves the situation by autoloading modules for you. Internally, it maintains a mapping of command names to the module that contains them. Simply start using a command (which the `Get-Command` cmdlet can help you discover), and PowerShell loads the appropriate module automatically. If you wish to customize this autoloading behavior, you can use the `$PSModuleAutoLoadingPrefer ence` preference variable.

When PowerShell imports a module with a given name, it searches through every directory listed in the `PSModulePath` environment variable, looking for the first module that contains the subdirectories that match the name you specify. Inside those directories, it looks for the module (`*.psd1`, `*.psm1`, and `*.dll`) with the same name and loads it.

 When autoloading modules, PowerShell prefers modules in the system's module directory over those in your personal module path. This prevents user modules from accidentally overriding core functionality. If you want a module to override core functionality, you can still use the `Import-Module` cmdlet to load the module explicitly.

When you install a module on your own system, the most common place to put it is in the *WindowsPowerShell\Modules* directory in your *My Documents* directory. To have PowerShell look in another directory for modules, add it to your personal `PSModule Path` environment variable, just as you would add a *Tools* directory to your personal path.

For more information about managing system paths, see Recipe 16.2, "Modify the User or System Path".

If you want to load a module from a directory not in `PSModulePath`, you can provide the entire directory name and module name to the `Import-Module` command. For example, for a module named `Test`, use `Import-Module c:\path\to\Test`. As with loading modules by name, PowerShell looks in `c:\temp\path\to` for a module (*\*.psd1*, *\*.psm1*, or *\*.dll*) named `Test` and loads it.

If you know the specific module file you want to load, you can also specify the full path to that module.

If you want to find additional commands, there are several useful resources available.

*PowerShell Community Extensions*
> Located here (*http://pscx.codeplex.com*), the PowerShell Community Extensions project contains a curated collection of useful and powerful commands. It has been written by a handful of volunteers, many of them Microsoft MVPs.

*The Technet Script Center Gallery*
> Located here (*http://gallery.technet.microsoft.com/ScriptCenter/*), the TechNet Script Center Gallery offers a well-indexed and well-organized collection of PowerShell scripts.

*PoshCode*
> Located here (*http://poshcode.org*), PoshCode contains thousands of scripts and script snippets—of both high and low quality.

## See Also

Recipe 1.8, "Customize Your Shell, Profile, and Prompt"

Recipe 11.6, "Package Common Commands in a Module"

Recipe 16.2, "Modify the User or System Path"

# 1.30. Use Commands from Customized Shells

## Problem

You want to use the commands from a PowerShell-based product that launches a customized version of the PowerShell console, but in a regular PowerShell session.

## Solution

Launch the customized version of the PowerShell console, and then use the `Get-Module` and `Get-PsSnapin` commands to see what additional modules and/or snapins it loaded.

## Discussion

As described in Recipe 1.29, "Extend Your Shell with Additional Commands", PowerShell modules and snapins are the two ways that third parties can distribute and add additional PowerShell commands. Products that provide customized versions of the PowerShell console do this by calling *PowerShell.exe* with one of three parameters:

- `-PSConsoleFile`, to load a console file that provides a list of snapins to load.
- `-Command`, to specify an initial startup command (that then loads a snapin or module)
- `-File`, to specify an initial startup script (that then loads a snapin or module)

Regardless of which one it used, you can examine the resulting set of loaded extensions to see which ones you can import into your other PowerShell sessions.

### Detecting loaded snapins

The `Get-PsSnapin` command returns all snapins loaded in the current session. It always returns the set of core PowerShell snapins, but it will also return any additional snapins loaded by the customized environment. For example, if the name of a snapin you recognize is *Product.Feature.Commands*, you can load that into future PowerShell sessions by typing `Add-PsSnapin` *Product.Feature.Commands*. To automate this, add the command into your PowerShell profile.

If you are uncertain of which snapin to load, you can also use the Get-Command command to discover which snapin defines a specific command:

```
PS > Get-Command Get-Counter | Select PsSnapin

PSSnapIn
--------
Microsoft.PowerShell.Diagnostics
```

### Detecting loaded modules

Like the Get-PsSnapin command, the Get-Module command returns all modules loaded in the current session. It returns any modules you've added so far into that session, but it will also return any additional modules loaded by the customized environment. For example, if the name of a module you recognize is *ProductModule*, you can load that into future PowerShell sessions by typing Import-Module *ProductModule*. To automate this, add the command into your PowerShell profile.

If you are uncertain of which module to load, you can also use the Get-Command command to discover which module defines a specific command:

```
PS > Get-Command Start-BitsTransfer | Select Module

Module
------
BitsTransfer
```

## See Also

Recipe 1.29, "Extend Your Shell with Additional Commands"

# 1.31. Save State Between Sessions

## Problem

You want to save state or history between PowerShell sessions.

## Solution

Subscribe to the PowerShell.Exiting engine event to have PowerShell invoke a script or script block that saves any state you need.

To have PowerShell save your command history, place a call to Enable-History Persistence in your profile, as in Example 1-19.

*Example 1-19. Enable-HistoryPersistence.ps1*

```
##############################################################################
##
```

```
## Enable-HistoryPersistence
##
## From Windows PowerShell Cookbook (O'Reilly)
## by Lee Holmes (http://www.leeholmes.com/guide)
##
################################################################################

<#

.SYNOPSIS

Reloads any previously saved command history, and registers for the
PowerShell.Exiting engine event to save new history when the shell
exits.

#>

Set-StrictMode -Version 3

## Load our previous history
$GLOBAL:maximumHistoryCount = 32767
$historyFile = (Join-Path (Split-Path $profile) "commandHistory.clixml")
if(Test-Path $historyFile)
{
    Import-CliXml $historyFile | Add-History
}

## Register for the engine shutdown event
$null = Register-EngineEvent -SourceIdentifier `
    ([System.Management.Automation.PsEngineEvent]::Exiting) -Action {

    ## Save our history
    $historyFile = (Join-Path (Split-Path $profile) "commandHistory.clixml")
    $maximumHistoryCount = 1kb

    ## Get the previous history items
    $oldEntries = @()
    if(Test-Path $historyFile)
    {
        $oldEntries = Import-CliXml $historyFile -ErrorAction SilentlyContinue
    }

    ## And merge them with our changes
    $currentEntries = Get-History -Count $maximumHistoryCount
    $additions = Compare-Object $oldEntries $currentEntries `
        -Property CommandLine | Where-Object { $_.SideIndicator -eq "=>" } |
        Foreach-Object { $_.CommandLine }

    $newEntries = $currentEntries | ? { $additions -contains $_.CommandLine }

    ## Keep only unique command lines. First sort by CommandLine in
    ## descending order (so that we keep the newest entries,) and then
```

```
## re-sort by StartExecutionTime.
$history = @($oldEntries + $newEntries) |
    Sort -Unique -Descending CommandLine | Sort StartExecutionTime

## Finally, keep the last 100
Remove-Item $historyFile
$history | Select -Last 100 | Export-CliXml $historyFile
}
```

## Discussion

PowerShell provides easy script-based access to a broad variety of system, engine, and other events. You can register for notification of these events and even automatically process any of those events. In this example, we subscribe to the only one currently available, which is called PowerShell.Exiting. PowerShell generates this event when you close a session.

This script could do anything, but in this example we have it save our command history and restore it when we launch PowerShell. Why would we want to do this? Well, with a rich history buffer, we can more easily find and reuse commands we've previously run. For two examples of doing this, see Examples 1.20 and 1.22.

Example 1-19 takes two main actions. First, we load our stored command history (if any exists). Then, we register an automatic action to be processed whenever the engine generates its PowerShell.Exiting event. The action itself is relatively straightforward, although exporting our new history does take a little finesse. If you have several sessions open at the same time, each will update the saved history file when it exits. Since we don't want to overwrite the history saved by the other shells, we first reload the history from disk and combine it with the history from the current shell.

Once we have the combined list of command lines, we sort them and pick out the unique ones before storing them back in the file.

For more information about working with PowerShell engine events, see Recipe 32.2, "Create and Respond to Custom Events".

## See Also

Recipe 1.1, "Run Programs, Scripts, and Existing Tools"

Recipe 1.20, "Access and Manage Your Console History"

Recipe 32.2, "Create and Respond to Custom Events"

# CHAPTER 2

# Pipelines

## 2.0. Introduction

One of the fundamental concepts in a shell is called the *pipeline*. It also forms the basis of one of PowerShell's most significant advances. A pipeline is a big name for a simple concept—a series of commands where the output of one becomes the input of the next. A pipeline in a shell is much like an assembly line in a factory: it successively refines something as it passes between the stages, as shown in Example 2-1.

*Example 2-1. A PowerShell pipeline*

```
Get-Process | Where-Object WorkingSet -gt 500kb | Sort-Object -Descending Name
```

In PowerShell, you separate each stage in the pipeline with the pipe (|) character.

In Example 2-1, the `Get-Process` cmdlet generates objects that represent actual processes on the system. These process objects contain information about the process's name, memory usage, process ID, and more. As the `Get-Process` cmdlet generates output, it passes it along. Simultaneously, the `Where-Object` cmdlet gets to work directly with those processes, testing easily for those that use more than 500 KB of memory. It passes those along immediately as it processes them, allowing the `Sort-Object` cmdlet to also work directly with those processes and sort them by name in descending order.

This brief example illustrates a significant advancement in the power of pipelines: PowerShell passes full-fidelity objects along the pipeline, not their text representations.

In contrast, all other shells pass data as plain text between the stages. Extracting meaningful information from plain-text output turns the authoring of pipelines into a black art. Expressing the previous example in a traditional Unix-based shell is exceedingly difficult, and it is nearly impossible in *cmd.exe*.

Traditional text-based shells make writing pipelines so difficult because they require you to deeply understand the peculiarities of output formatting for each command in the pipeline, as shown in Example 2-2.

*Example 2-2. A traditional text-based pipeline*

```
lee@trinity:~$ ps -F | awk '{ if($5 > 500) print }' | sort -r -k 64,70
UID        PID  PPID  C    SZ   RSS PSR STIME TTY          TIME CMD
lee       8175  7967  0   965  1036   0 21:51 pts/0     00:00:00 ps -F
lee       7967  7966  0  1173  2104   0 21:38 pts/0     00:00:00 -bash
```

In this example, you have to know that, for every line, group number five represents the memory usage. You have to know another language (that of the awk tool) to filter by that column. Finally, you have to know the column range that contains the process name (columns 64 to 70 on this system) and then provide that to the sort command. And that's just a simple example.

An object-based pipeline opens up enormous possibilities, making system administration both immensely more simple and more powerful.

# 2.1. Filter Items in a List or Command Output

## Problem

You want to filter the items in a list or command output.

## Solution

Use the Where-Object cmdlet to select items in a list (or command output) that match a condition you provide. The Where-Object cmdlet has the standard aliases where and ?.

To list all running processes that have "search" in their name, use the -like operator to compare against the process's Name property:

```
Get-Process | Where-Object { $_.Name -like "*Search*" }
```

To list all processes not responding, test the Responding property:

```
Get-Process | Where-Object { -not $_.Responding }
```

To list all stopped services, use the -eq operator to compare against the service's Status property:

```
Get-Service | Where-Object { $_.Status -eq "Stopped" }
```

For simple comparisons on properties, you can omit the script block syntax and use the comparison parameters of Where-Object directly:

```
Get-Process | Where-Object Name -like "*Search*"
```

## Discussion

For each item in its input (which is the output of the previous command), the `Where-Object` cmdlet evaluates that input against the script block that you specify. If the script block returns `True`, then the `Where-Object` cmdlet passes the object along. Otherwise, it does not. A script block is a series of PowerShell commands enclosed by the { and } characters. You can write any PowerShell commands inside the script block. In the script block, the `$_` (or `$PSItem`) variable represents the current input object. For each item in the incoming set of objects, PowerShell assigns that item to the `$_` (or `$PSItem`) variable and then runs your script block. In the preceding examples, this incoming object represents the process, file, or service that the previous cmdlet generated.

This script block can contain a great deal of functionality, if desired. It can combine multiple tests, comparisons, and much more. For more information about script blocks, see Recipe 11.4, "Write a Script Block". For more information about the type of comparisons available to you, see "Comparison Operators" (page 879).

For simple filtering, the syntax of the `Where-Object` cmdlet may sometimes seem overbearing. Recipe 2.3, "Program: Simplify Most Where-Object Filters" shows two alternatives that can make simple filtering (such as the previous examples) easier to work with.

For complex filtering (for example, the type you would normally rely on a mouse to do with files in an Explorer window), writing the script block to express your intent may be difficult or even infeasible. If this is the case, Recipe 2.4, "Program: Interactively Filter Lists of Objects" shows a script that can make manual filtering easier to accomplish.

For more information about the `Where-Object` cmdlet, type **Get-Help Where-Object**.

## See Also

Recipe 2.3, "Program: Simplify Most Where-Object Filters"

Recipe 2.4, "Program: Interactively Filter Lists of Objects"

Recipe 11.4, "Write a Script Block"

"Comparison Operators" (page 879)

# 2.2. Group and Pivot Data by Name

## Problem

You want to easily access items in a list by a property name.

## Solution

Use the `Group-Object` cmdlet (which has the standard alias group) with the `-AsHash` and `-AsString` parameters. This creates a hashtable with the selected property (or expression) used as keys in that hashtable:

```
PS > $h = dir | group -AsHash -AsString Length
PS > $h

Name                           Value
----                           -----
746                            {ReplaceTest.ps1}
499                            {Format-String.ps1}
20494                          {test.dll}

PS > $h["499"]

    Directory: C:\temp

Mode                LastWriteTime     Length Name
----                -------------     ------ ----
-a---        10/18/2009   9:57 PM        499 Format-String.ps1


PS > $h["746"]

    Directory: C:\temp

Mode                LastWriteTime     Length Name
----                -------------     ------ ----
-a---        10/18/2009   9:51 PM        746 ReplaceTest.ps1
```

## Discussion

In some situations, you might find yourself repeatedly calling the `Where-Object` cmdlet to interact with the same list or output:

```
PS > $processes = Get-Process
PS > $processes | Where-Object { $_.Id -eq 1216 }

Handles  NPM(K)    PM(K)      WS(K) VM(M)   CPU(s)     Id ProcessName
-------  ------    -----      ----- -----   ------     -- -----------
     62       3     1012       3132    50     0.20   1216 dwm


PS > $processes | Where-Object { $_.Id -eq 212 }

Handles  NPM(K)    PM(K)      WS(K) VM(M)   CPU(s)     Id ProcessName
-------  ------    -----      ----- -----   ------     -- -----------
    614      10    28444       5484   117     1.27    212 SearchIndexer
```

In these situations, you can instead use the -AsHash parameter of the Group-Object cmdlet. When you use this parameter, PowerShell creates a hashtable to hold your results. This creates a map between the property you are interested in and the object it represents:

```
PS > $processes = Get-Process | Group-Object -AsHash Id
PS > $processes[1216]

Handles  NPM(K)    PM(K)     WS(K) VM(M)   CPU(s)     Id ProcessName
-------  ------    -----     ----- -----   ------     -- -----------
     62       3     1012      3132    50     0.20   1216 dwm

PS > $processes[212]

Handles  NPM(K)    PM(K)     WS(K) VM(M)   CPU(s)     Id ProcessName
-------  ------    -----     ----- -----   ------     -- -----------
    610      10    28444      5488   117     1.27    212 SearchIndexer
```

For simple types of data, this approach works well. Depending on your data, though, using the -AsHash parameter alone can create difficulties.

The first issue you might run into arises when the value of a property is $null. Hashtables in PowerShell (and the .NET Framework that provides the underlying support) do not support $null as a value, so you get a misleading error message:

```
PS > "Hello",(Get-Process -id $pid) | Group-Object -AsHash Id
Group-Object : The objects grouped by this property cannot be expanded
since there is a duplication of the key. Please give a valid property and try
again.
```

A second issue crops up when more complex data gets stored within the hashtable. This can unfortunately be true even of data that *appears* to be simple:

```
PS > $result = dir | Group-Object -AsHash Length
PS > $result

Name                       Value
----                       -----
746                        {ReplaceTest.ps1}
499                        {Format-String.ps1}
20494                      {test.dll}

PS > $result[746]
(Nothing appears)
```

This missing result is caused by an incompatibility between the information in the hashtable and the information you typed. This is normally not an issue in hashtables that you create yourself, because you provided all of the information to populate them. In this case, though, the Length values stored in the hashtable come from the directory listing and are of the type Int64. An explicit cast resolves the issue but takes a great deal of trial and error to discover:

```
PS > $result[ [int64] 746 ]

    Directory: C:\temp

Mode                LastWriteTime      Length Name
----                -------------      ------ ----
-a---        10/18/2009   9:51 PM        746 ReplaceTest.ps1
```

It is difficult to avoid both of these issues, so the Group-Object cmdlet also offers an
-AsString parameter to convert all of the values to their string equivalents. With that
parameter, you can always assume that the values will be treated as (and accessible by)
strings:

```
PS > $result = dir | Group-Object -AsHash -AsString Length
PS > $result["746"]

    Directory: C:\temp

Mode                LastWriteTime      Length Name
----                -------------      ------ ----
-a---        10/18/2009   9:51 PM        746 ReplaceTest.ps1
```

For more information about the Group-Object cmdlet, type **Get-Help Group-Object**.
For more information about PowerShell hashtables, see Recipe 7.13, "Create a Hashtable
or Associative Array".

### See Also

Recipe 7.13, "Create a Hashtable or Associative Array"

"Hashtables (Associative Arrays)" (page 872)

# 2.3. Program: Simplify Most Where-Object Filters

The Where-Object cmdlet is incredibly powerful, in that it allows you to filter your
output based on arbitrary criteria. For extremely simple filters (such as filtering based
only on a comparison to a single property), though, the script-block-based syntax can
get a little ungainly:

```
Get-Process | Where-Object { $_.Handles -gt 1000 }
```

In PowerShell version 3, the Where-Object cmdlet (and by extension its ? alias) was
extended to simplify most filters dramatically:

```
Get-Process | Where-Object Handles -gt 1000
Get-Process | ? HasExited
```

If you don't have access to PowerShell version 3, it is possible to write a similar script
(as shown in Example 2-3) to offload all the syntax to the script itself:

---

```
Get-Process | Compare-Property Handles gt 1000
Get-Process | Compare-Property HasExited
```

With a shorter alias, this becomes even easier to type:

```
PS > Set-Alias wheres Compare-Property
PS > Get-ChildItem | wheres Length gt 100
```

Example 2-3 implements this "simple where" functionality. Note that supplying a non-existing operator as the $operator parameter will generate an error message.

*Example 2-3. Compare-Property.ps1*

```
##############################################################################
##
## Compare-Property
##
## From Windows PowerShell Cookbook (O'Reilly)
## by Lee Holmes (http://www.leeholmes.com/guide)
##
##############################################################################

<#

.SYNOPSIS

Compare the property you provide against the input supplied to the script.
This provides the functionality of simple Where-Object comparisons without
the syntax required for that cmdlet.

.EXAMPLE

PS Get-Process | Compare-Property Handles gt 1000

.EXAMPLE

PS > Set-Alias ?? Compare-Property
PS > dir | ?? PsIsContainer

#>

param(
    ## The property to compare
    $Property,

    ## The operator to use in the comparison
    $Operator = "eq",

    ## The value to compare with
    $MatchText = "$true"
```

```
)

Begin { $expression = "`$_.$property -$operator `"$matchText`"" }
Process { if(Invoke-Expression $expression) { $_ } }
```

For more information about running scripts, see Recipe 1.1, "Run Programs, Scripts, and Existing Tools".

## See Also

Recipe 1.1, "Run Programs, Scripts, and Existing Tools"

# 2.4. Program: Interactively Filter Lists of Objects

There are times when the `Where-Object` cmdlet is too powerful. In those situations, the `Compare-Property` script shown in Recipe 2.3, "Program: Simplify Most Where-Object Filters" provides a much simpler alternative. There are also times when the `Where-Object` cmdlet is too simple—when expressing your selection logic as code is more cumbersome than selecting it manually. In those situations, an interactive filter can be much more effective.

PowerShell version 3 makes this interactive filtering incredibly easy through the `-PassThru` parameter of the `Out-GridView` cmdlet. For example, you can use this parameter after experimenting with commands for a while to create a simple script. Simply highlight the lines you want to keep, and press OK:

```
PS > $script = Get-History | Foreach-Object CommandLine | Out-GridView -PassThru
PS > $script | Set-Content c:\temp\script.ps1
```

By default, the `Out-GridView` cmdlet lets you select multiple items at once before pressing OK. If you'd rather constrain the selection to a single element, use `Single` as the value of the `-OutputMode` parameter.

If you have access only to PowerShell version 2, Example 2-4 implements a simple version of this interactive filter. It uses several concepts not yet covered in this book, so feel free to just consider it a neat script for now. To learn more about a part that you don't yet understand, look it up in the table of contents or the index.

*Example 2-4. Select-FilteredObject.ps1*

```
##############################################################################
##
## Select-FilteredObject
##
## From Windows PowerShell Cookbook (O'Reilly)
## by Lee Holmes (http://www.leeholmes.com/guide)
##
##############################################################################
```

```
<#

.SYNOPSIS

Provides an inteactive window to help you select complex sets of objects.
To do this, it takes all the input from the pipeline, and presents it in a
Notepad window.  Keep any lines that represent objects you want to retain,
delete the rest, then save the file and exit Notepad.

The script then passes the original objects that you kept along the
pipeline.

.EXAMPLE

PS > Get-Process | Select-FilteredObject | Stop-Process -WhatIf
Gets all of the processes running on the system, and displays them to you.
After you've selected the ones you want to stop, it pipes those into the
Stop-Process cmdlet.

#>

## PowerShell runs your "begin" script block before it passes you any of the
## items in the pipeline.
begin
{
    Set-StrictMode -Version 3

    ## Create a temporary file
    $filename = [System.IO.Path]::GetTempFileName()

    ## Define a header in a "here-string" that explains how to interact with
    ## the file
    $header = @"
############################################################
## Keep any lines that represent objects you want to retain,
## and delete the rest.
##
## Once you finish selecting objects, save this file and
## exit.
############################################################

"@

    ## Place the instructions into the file
    $header > $filename

    ## Initialize the variables that will hold our list of objects, and
    ## a counter to help us keep track of the objects coming down the
    ## pipeline
    $objectList = @()
    $counter = 0
}
```

```
## PowerShell runs your "process" script block for each item it passes down
## the pipeline. In this block, the "$_" variable represents the current
## pipeline object
process
{
    ## Add a line to the file, using PowerShell's format (-f) operator.
    ## When provided the ouput of Get-Process, for example, these lines look
    ## like:
    ## 30: System.Diagnostics.Process (powershell)
    "{0}: {1}" -f $counter,$_.ToString() >> $filename

    ## Add the object to the list of objects, and increment our counter.
    $objectList += $_
    $counter++
}

## PowerShell runs your "end" script block once it completes passing all
## objects down the pipeline.
end
{
    ## Start Notepad, then call the process's WaitForExit() method to
    ## pause the script until the user exits Notepad.
    $process = Start-Process Notepad -Args $filename -PassThru
    $process.WaitForExit()

    ## Go over each line of the file
    foreach($line in (Get-Content $filename))
    {
        ## Check if the line is of the special format: numbers, followed by
        ## a colon, followed by extra text.
        if($line -match "^(\d+?):.*")
        {
            ## If it did match the format, then $matches[1] represents the
            ## number -- a counter into the list of objects we saved during
            ## the "process" section.
            ## So, we output that object from our list of saved objects.
            $objectList[$matches[1]]
        }
    }

    ## Finally, clean up the temporary file.
    Remove-Item $filename
}
```

For more information about running scripts, see Recipe 1.1, "Run Programs, Scripts, and Existing Tools".

## See Also

Recipe 1.1, "Run Programs, Scripts, and Existing Tools"

Recipe 2.3, "Program: Simplify Most Where-Object Filters"

# 2.5. Work with Each Item in a List or Command Output

## Problem

You have a list of items and want to work with each item in that list.

## Solution

Use the `Foreach-Object` cmdlet (which has the standard aliases `foreach` and `%`) to work with each item in a list.

To apply a calculation to each item in a list, use the `$_` (or `$PSItem`) variable as part of a calculation in the script block parameter:

```
PS > 1..10 | Foreach-Object { $_ * 2 }
2
4
6
8
10
12
14
16
18
20
```

To run a program on each file in a directory, use the `$_` (or `$PSItem`) variable as a parameter to the program in the script block parameter:

```
Get-ChildItem *.txt | Foreach-Object { attrib -r $_ }
```

To access a method or property for each object in a list, access that method or property on the `$_` (or `$PSItem`) variable in the script block parameter. In this example, you get the list of running processes called `notepad`, and then wait for each of them to exit:

```
$notepadProcesses = Get-Process notepad
$notepadProcesses | Foreach-Object { $_.WaitForExit() }
```

## Discussion

Like the `Where-Object` cmdlet, the `Foreach-Object` cmdlet runs the script block that you specify for each item in the input. A script block is a series of PowerShell commands enclosed by the { and } characters. For each item in the set of incoming objects, PowerShell assigns that item to the $_ (or $PSItem) variable, one element at a time. In the examples given by the Solution, the $_ (or $PSItem) variable represents each file or process that the previous cmdlet generated.

This script block can contain a great deal of functionality, if desired. You can combine multiple tests, comparisons, and much more. For more information about script blocks, see Recipe 11.4, "Write a Script Block". For more information about the type of comparisons available to you, see "Comparison Operators" (page 879).

In addition to the script block supported by the Foreach-Object cmdlet to process each element of the pipeline, it also supports script blocks to be executed at the beginning and end of the pipeline. For example, consider the following code to measure the sum of elements in an array:

```
$myArray = 1,2,3,4,5
$sum = 0
$myArray | Foreach-Object { $sum += $_ }
$sum
```

You can simplify this to:

```
$myArray | Foreach-Object -Begin {
    $sum = 0 } -Process { $sum += $_ } -End { $sum }
```

Since you can also specify the -Begin, -Process, and -End parameters by position, this can simplify even further to:

```
$myArray | Foreach-Object { $sum = 0 } { $sum += $_ } { $sum }
```

For simple property or member access, the syntax of the Foreach-Object cmdlet may sometimes seem overbearing. Recipe 2.7, "Program: Simplify Most Foreach-Object Pipelines" shows several alternatives that can make simple member access easier to work with.

 The first example in the Solution demonstrates a neat way to generate ranges of numbers: 1..10

This is PowerShell's array range syntax, which you can learn more about in Recipe 7.3, "Access Elements of an Array".

The Foreach-Object cmdlet isn't the only way to perform actions on items in a list. The PowerShell scripting language supports several other keywords, such as for, (a different) foreach, do, and while. For information on how to use those keywords, see Recipe 4.4, "Repeat Operations with Loops".

For more information about the Foreach-Object cmdlet, type **Get-Help Foreach-Object**.

For more information about dealing with pipeline input in your own scripts, functions, and script blocks, see Recipe 11.18, "Access Pipeline Input".

## See Also

Recipe 4.4, "Repeat Operations with Loops"

Recipe 7.3, "Access Elements of an Array"

Recipe 11.4, "Write a Script Block"

Recipe 11.18, "Access Pipeline Input"

"Comparison Operators" (page 879)

# 2.6. Automate Data-Intensive Tasks

## Problem

You want to invoke a simple task on large amounts of data.

## Solution

If only one piece of data changes (such as a server name or username), store the data in a text file. Use the Get-Content cmdlet to retrieve the items, and then use the Foreach-Object cmdlet (which has the standard aliases foreach and %) to work with each item in that list. Example 2-5 illustrates this technique.

*Example 2-5. Using information from a text file to automate data-intensive tasks*

```
PS > Get-Content servers.txt
SERVER1
SERVER2
PS > $computers = Get-Content servers.txt
PS > $computers | Foreach-Object {
    Get-CimInstance Win32_OperatingSystem -Computer $_ }

SystemDirectory : C:\WINDOWS\system32
Organization    :
BuildNumber     : 2600
Version         : 5.1.2600

SystemDirectory : C:\WINDOWS\system32
Organization    :
BuildNumber     : 2600
Version         : 5.1.2600
```

If it becomes cumbersome (or unclear) to include the actions in the Foreach-Object cmdlet, you can also use the foreach scripting keyword, as illustrated in Example 2-6.

*Example 2-6. Using the foreach scripting keyword to make a looping statement easier to read*

```
$computers = Get-Content servers.txt

foreach($computer in $computers)
{
    ## Get the information about the operating system from WMI
    $system = Get-CimInstance Win32_OperatingSystem -Computer $computer

    ## Determine if it is running Windows XP
    if($system.Version -eq "5.1.2600")
    {
        "$computer is running Windows XP"
    }
}
```

If several aspects of the data change per task (for example, both the CIM class and the computer name for computers in a large report), create a CSV file with a row for each task. Use the Import-Csv cmdlet to import that data into PowerShell, and then use properties of the resulting objects as multiple sources of related data. Example 2-7 illustrates this technique.

*Example 2-7. Using information from a CSV to automate data-intensive tasks*

```
PS > Get-Content WmiReport.csv
ComputerName,Class
LEE-DESK,Win32_OperatingSystem
LEE-DESK,Win32_Bios
PS > $data = Import-Csv WmiReport.csv
PS > $data

ComputerName                       Class
------------                       -----
LEE-DESK                           Win32_OperatingSystem
LEE-DESK                           Win32_Bios

PS > $data |
    Foreach-Object { Get-CimInstance $_.Class -Computer $_.ComputerName }

SystemDirectory : C:\WINDOWS\system32
Organization    :
BuildNumber     : 2600
Version         : 5.1.2600

SMBIOSBIOSVersion : ASUS A7N8X Deluxe ACPI BIOS Rev 1009
Manufacturer      : Phoenix Technologies, LTD
Name              : Phoenix - AwardBIOS v6.00PG
SerialNumber      : xxxxxxxxxxx
Version           : Nvidia - 42302e31
```

# Discussion

One of the major benefits of PowerShell is its capability to automate repetitive tasks. Sometimes these repetitive tasks are action-intensive (such as system maintenance through registry and file cleanup) and consist of complex sequences of commands that will always be invoked together. In those situations, you can write a script to combine these operations to save time and reduce errors.

Other times, you need only to accomplish a single task (for example, retrieving the results of a WMI query) but need to invoke that task repeatedly for a large amount of data. In those situations, PowerShell's scripting statements, pipeline support, and data management cmdlets help automate those tasks.

One of the options given by the Solution is the `Import-Csv` cmdlet. The `Import-Csv` cmdlet reads a CSV file and, for each row, automatically creates an object with properties that correspond to the names of the columns. Example 2-8 shows the results of a CSV that contains a `ComputerName` and `Class` header.

*Example 2-8. The Import-Csv cmdlet creating objects with ComputerName and Class properties*

```
PS > $data = Import-Csv WmiReport.csv
PS > $data

ComputerName                            Class
------------                            -----
LEE-DESK                                Win32_OperatingSystem
LEE-DESK                                Win32_Bios

PS > $data[0].ComputerName
LEE-DESK
```

As the Solution illustrates, you can use the `Foreach-Object` cmdlet to provide data from these objects to repetitive cmdlet calls. It does this by specifying each parameter name, followed by the data (taken from a property of the current CSV object) that applies to it.

 If you already have the comma-separated values in a variable (rather than a file), you can use the `ConvertFrom-Csv` cmdlet to convert these values to objects.

While this is the most general solution, many cmdlet parameters can automatically retrieve their value from incoming objects if any property of that object has the same name. This enables you to omit the `Foreach-Object` and property mapping steps altogether. Parameters that support this feature are said to support *value from pipeline by property name*. The `Move-Item` cmdlet is one example of a cmdlet with parameters that support this, as shown by the `Accept pipeline input?` rows in Example 2-9.

*Example 2-9. Help content of the Move-Item cmdlet showing a parameter that accepts value from pipeline by property name*

```
PS > Get-Help Move-Item -Full
(...)
PARAMETERS

    -path <string[]>
        Specifies the path to the current location of the items. The default
        is the current directory. Wildcards are permitted.

        Required?                       true
        Position?                       1
        Default value                   <current location>
        Accept pipeline input?          true (ByValue, ByPropertyName)
        Accept wildcard characters?     true

    -destination <string>
        Specifies the path to the location where the items are being moved.
        The default is the current directory. Wildcards are permitted, but
        the result must specify a single location.

        To rename the item being moved, specify a new name in the value of
        Destination.

        Required?                       false
        Position?                       2
        Default value                   <current location>
        Accept pipeline input?          true (ByPropertyName)
        Accept wildcard characters?     True
        (...)
```

If you purposefully name the columns in the CSV to correspond to parameters that take their value from pipeline by property name, PowerShell can do some (or all) of the parameter mapping for you. Example 2-10 demonstrates a CSV file that moves items in bulk.

*Example 2-10. Using the Import-Csv cmdlet to automate a cmdlet that accepts value from pipeline by property name*

```
PS > Get-Content ItemMoves.csv
Path,Destination
test.txt,Test1Directory
test2.txt,Test2Directory
PS > dir test.txt,test2.txt | Select Name
```

```
Name
----
test.txt
test2.txt

PS > Import-Csv ItemMoves.csv | Move-Item
PS > dir Test1Directory | Select Name

Name
----
test.txt

PS > dir Test2Directory | Select Name
Name
----
test2.txt
```

For more information about the `Foreach-Object` cmdlet and `foreach` scripting key-word, see Recipe 2.5, "Work with Each Item in a List or Command Output". For more information about working with CSV files, see Recipe 10.7, "Import CSV and Delimited Data from a File". For more information about working with Windows Management Instrumentation (WMI), see Chapter 28.

## See Also

Recipe 2.5, "Work with Each Item in a List or Command Output"

Recipe 10.7, "Import CSV and Delimited Data from a File"

Chapter 28, *Windows Management Instrumentation*

# 2.7. Program: Simplify Most Foreach-Object Pipelines

The `Foreach-Object` cmdlet is incredibly powerful, in that it allows you to access meth-ods and properties of arbitrary pipeline objects. For simple scenarios (such as retrieving only a single property), though, the script-block-based syntax can get a little ungainly:

```
Get-Process | Foreach-Object { $_.Name }
```

In PowerShell version 3, the `Foreach-Object` cmdlet (and by extension its % alias) was extended to simplify property and method access dramatically:

```
Get-Process | Foreach-Object Name
Get-Process | % Name | % ToUpper
```

In addition to using the `Foreach-Object` cmdlet to support full member invocation, the PowerShell language has a quick way to easily enumerate properties. Just as you are able to access a property on a single element, PowerShell lets you use a similar syntax to access that property on each item of a collection:

```
PS > Start-Process PowerShell
PS > Start-Process PowerShell
PS > $processes = Get-Process -Name PowerShell
PS > $processes[0].Id
7928

PS > $processes.Id
7928
13120
```

If you don't have access to PowerShell version 3, it is possible to write a similar script (as shown in Example 2-11) to offload all the syntax to the script itself:

```
"Hello","World" | Invoke-Member Length
"Hello","World" | Invoke-Member -m ToUpper
```

With a shorter alias, this becomes even easier to type:

```
PS > Set-Alias :: Invoke-Member
PS > Get-ChildItem | :: Length
```

Example 2-11 implements this "simple foreach" functionality.

*Example 2-11. Invoke-Member.ps1*

```
##############################################################################
##
## Invoke-Member
##
## From Windows PowerShell Cookbook (O'Reilly)
## by Lee Holmes (http://www.leeholmes.com/guide)
##
##############################################################################

<#

.SYNOPSIS

Enables easy access to methods and properties of pipeline objects.

.EXAMPLE

PS > "Hello","World" | .\Invoke-Member Length
5
5

.EXAMPLE

PS > "Hello","World" | .\Invoke-Member -m ToUpper
HELLO
WORLD

.EXAMPLE
```

```
PS > "Hello","World" | .\Invoke-Member Replace l w
Hewwo
Worwd

#>

[CmdletBinding(DefaultParameterSetName= "Member")]
param(

    ## A switch parameter to identify the requested member as a method.
    ## Only required for methods that take no arguments.
    [Parameter(ParameterSetName = "Method")]
    [Alias("M","Me")]
    [switch] $Method,

    ## The name of the member to retrieve
    [Parameter(ParameterSetName = "Method", Position = 0)]
    [Parameter(ParameterSetName = "Member", Position = 0)]
    [string] $Member,

    ## Arguments for the method, if any
    [Parameter(
        ParameterSetName = "Method", Position = 1,
        Mandatory = $false, ValueFromRemainingArguments = $true)]
    [object[]] $ArgumentList = @(),

    ## The object from which to retrieve the member
    [Parameter(ValueFromPipeline = $true)]
    $InputObject
    )

process
{
    ## If the user specified a method, invoke it
    ## with any required arguments.
    if($psCmdlet.ParameterSetName -eq "Method")
    {
        $inputObject.$member.Invoke(@($argumentList))
    }
    ## Otherwise, retrieve the property
    else
    {
        $inputObject.$member
    }
}
```

## See Also

Recipe 1.1, "Run Programs, Scripts, and Existing Tools"

Recipe 2.3, "Program: Simplify Most Where-Object Filters"

# 2.8. Intercept Stages of the Pipeline

## Problem

You want to intercept or take some action at different stages of the PowerShell pipeline.

## Solution

Use the `New-CommandWrapper` script given in Recipe 11.23, "Program: Enhance or Extend an Existing Cmdlet" to wrap the `Out-Default` command, and place your custom functionality in that.

## Discussion

For any pipeline, PowerShell adds an implicit call to the `Out-Default` cmdlet at the end. By adding a command wrapper over this function we can heavily customize the pipeline processing behavior.

When PowerShell creates a pipeline, it first calls the `BeginProcessing()` method of each command in the pipeline. For advanced functions (the type created by the `New-CommandWrapper` script), PowerShell invokes the `Begin` block. If you want to do anything at the beginning of the pipeline, then put your customizations in that block.

For each object emitted by the pipeline, PowerShell sends that object to the `Process Record()` method of the next command in the pipeline. For advanced functions (the type created by the `New-CommandWrapper` script), PowerShell invokes the `Process` block. If you want to do anything for each element in the pipeline, put your customizations in that block.

Finally, when PowerShell has processed all items in the pipeline, it calls the `End Processing()` method of each command in the pipeline. For advanced functions (the type created by the `New-CommandWrapper` script), PowerShell invokes the `End` block. If you want to do anything at the end of the pipeline, then put your customizations in that block.

For two examples of this approach, see Recipe 2.9, "Automatically Capture Pipeline Output" and Recipe 11.22, "Invoke Dynamically Named Commands".

For more information about running scripts, see Recipe 1.1, "Run Programs, Scripts, and Existing Tools".

## See Also

Recipe 1.1, "Run Programs, Scripts, and Existing Tools"

Recipe 2.9, "Automatically Capture Pipeline Output"

Recipe 11.22, "Invoke Dynamically Named Commands"

Recipe 11.23, "Program: Enhance or Extend an Existing Cmdlet"

# 2.9. Automatically Capture Pipeline Output

## Problem

You want to automatically capture the output of the last command without explicitly storing its output in a variable.

## Solution

Invoke the Add-ObjectCollector script (shown in Example 2-12), which in turn builds upon the New-CommandWrapper script.

*Example 2-12. Add-ObjectCollector.ps1*

```
##############################################################################
##
## Add-ObjectCollector
##
## From Windows PowerShell Cookbook (O'Reilly)
## by Lee Holmes (http://www.leeholmes.com/guide)
##
##############################################################################

<#

.SYNOPSIS

Adds a new Out-Default command wrapper to store up to 500 elements from
the previous command. This wrapper stores output in the $ll variable.

.EXAMPLE

PS > Get-Command $pshome\powershell.exe

CommandType     Name                           Definition
-----------     ----                           ----------
Application     powershell.exe                 C:\Windows\System32\Windo...

PS > $ll.Definition
C:\Windows\System32\WindowsPowerShell\v1.0\powershell.exe

.NOTES

This command builds on New-CommandWrapper, also included in the Windows
PowerShell Cookbook.
```

```
#>

Set-StrictMode -Version 3

New-CommandWrapper Out-Default `
    -Begin {
        $cachedOutput = New-Object System.Collections.ArrayList
    } `
    -Process {
        ## If we get an input object, add it to our list of objects
        if($_ -ne $null) { $null = $cachedOutput.Add($_) }
        while($cachedOutput.Count -gt 500) { $cachedOutput.RemoveAt(0) }
    } `
    -End {
        ## Be sure we got objects that were not just errors (
        ## so that we don't wipe out the saved output when we get errors
        ## trying to work with it.)
        ## Also don't capture formatting information, as those objects
        ## can't be worked with.
        $uniqueOutput = $cachedOutput | Foreach-Object {
            $_.GetType().FullName } | Select -Unique
        $containsInterestingTypes = ($uniqueOutput -notcontains `
            "System.Management.Automation.ErrorRecord") -and
            ($uniqueOutput -notlike `
                "Microsoft.PowerShell.Commands.Internal.Format.*")

        ## If we actually had output, and it was interesting information,
        ## save the output into the $ll variable
        if(($cachedOutput.Count -gt 0) -and $containsInterestingTypes)
        {
            $GLOBAL:ll = $cachedOutput | % { $_ }
        }
    }
}
```

## Discussion

The example in the Solution builds a command wrapper over the Out-Default command by first creating an ArrayList during the Begin stage of the pipeline.

As each object passes down the pipeline (and is processed by the Process block of Out-Default), the wrapper created by Add-ObjectCollector adds the object to the Array List.

Once the pipeline completes, the Add-ObjectCollector wrapper stores the saved items in the $ll variable, making them always available at the next prompt.

## See Also

Recipe 1.1, "Run Programs, Scripts, and Existing Tools"

Recipe 2.8, "Intercept Stages of the Pipeline"

Recipe 11.23, "Program: Enhance or Extend an Existing Cmdlet"

# 2.10. Capture and Redirect Binary Process Output

## Problem

You want to run programs that transfer complex binary data between themselves.

## Solution

Use the `Invoke-BinaryProcess` script to invoke the program, as shown in Example 2-13. If it is the source of binary data, use the `-RedirectOutput` parameter. If it consumes binary data, use the `-RedirectInput` parameter.

*Example 2-13. Invoke-BinaryProcess.ps1*

```
##############################################################################
##
## Invoke-BinaryProcess
##
## From Windows PowerShell Cookbook (O'Reilly)
## by Lee Holmes (http://www.leeholmes.com/guide)
##
##############################################################################

<#

.SYNOPSIS

Invokes a process that emits or consumes binary data.

.EXAMPLE

PS > Invoke-BinaryProcess binaryProcess.exe -RedirectOutput -ArgumentList "-Emit" |
        Invoke-BinaryProcess binaryProcess.exe -RedirectInput -ArgumentList "-Consume"

#>

param(
    ## The name of the process to invoke
    [string] $ProcessName,
```

```
    ## Specifies that input to the process should be treated as
    ## binary
    [Alias("Input")]
    [switch] $RedirectInput,

    ## Specifies that the output of the process should be treated
    ## as binary
    [Alias("Output")]
    [switch] $RedirectOutput,

    ## Specifies the arguments for the process
    [string] $ArgumentList
)

Set-StrictMode -Version 3

## Prepare to invoke the process
$processStartInfo = New-Object System.Diagnostics.ProcessStartInfo
$processStartInfo.FileName = (Get-Command $processname).Definition
$processStartInfo.WorkingDirectory = (Get-Location).Path
if($argumentList) { $processStartInfo.Arguments = $argumentList }
$processStartInfo.UseShellExecute = $false

## Always redirect the input and output of the process.
## Sometimes we will capture it as binary, other times we will
## just treat it as strings.
$processStartInfo.RedirectStandardOutput = $true
$processStartInfo.RedirectStandardInput = $true

$process = [System.Diagnostics.Process]::Start($processStartInfo)

## If we've been asked to redirect the input, treat it as bytes.
## Otherwise, write any input to the process as strings.
if($redirectInput)
{
    $inputBytes = @($input)
    $process.StandardInput.BaseStream.Write($inputBytes, 0, $inputBytes.Count)
    $process.StandardInput.Close()
}
else
{
    $input | % { $process.StandardInput.WriteLine($_) }
    $process.StandardInput.Close()
}

## If we've been asked to redirect the output, treat it as bytes.
## Otherwise, read any input from the process as strings.
if($redirectOutput)
{
    $byteRead = -1
    do
```

```
    {
        $byteRead = $process.StandardOutput.BaseStream.ReadByte()
        if($byteRead -ge 0) { $byteRead }
    } while($byteRead -ge 0)
}
else
{
    $process.StandardOutput.ReadToEnd()
}
```

## Discussion

When PowerShell launches a native application, one of the benefits it provides is allowing you to use PowerShell commands to work with the output. For example:

```
PS > (ipconfig)[7]
   Link-local IPv6 Address . . . . . : fe80::20f9:871:8365:f368%8
PS > (ipconfig)[8]
   IPv4 Address. . . . . . . . . . : 10.211.55.3
```

PowerShell enables this by splitting the output of the program on its newline characters, and then passing each line independently down the pipeline. This includes programs that use the Unix newline (\n) as well as the Windows newline (\r\n).

If the program outputs binary data, however, that reinterpretation can corrupt data as it gets redirected to another process or file. For example, some programs communicate between themselves through complicated binary data structures that cannot be modified along the way. This is common in some image editing utilities and other non-PowerShell tools designed for pipelined data manipulation.

We can see this through an example *BinaryProcess.exe* application that either emits binary data or consumes it. Here is the C# source code to the *BinaryProcess.exe* application:

```
using System;
using System.IO;

public class BinaryProcess
{
    public static void Main(string[] args)
    {
        if(args[0] == "-consume")
        {
            using(Stream inputStream = Console.OpenStandardInput())
            {
                for(byte counter = 0; counter < 255; counter++)
                {
                    byte received = (byte) inputStream.ReadByte();
                    if(received != counter)
                    {
                        Console.WriteLine(
```

```
                    "Got an invalid byte: {0}, expected {1}.",
                    received, counter);
                return;
            }
            else
            {
                Console.WriteLine(
                    "Properly received byte: {0}.", received, counter);
            }
        }
    }
}

if(args[0] == "-emit")
{
    using(Stream outputStream = Console.OpenStandardOutput())
    {
        for(byte counter = 0; counter < 255; counter++)
        {
            outputStream.WriteByte(counter);
        }
    }
}
}
}
```

When we run it with the -emit parameter, PowerShell breaks the output into three objects:

```
PS > $output = .\binaryprocess.exe -emit
PS > $output.Count
3
```

We would expect this output to contain the numbers 0 through 254, but we see that it does not:

```
PS > $output | Foreach-Object { "------------";
    $_.ToCharArray() | Foreach-Object { [int] $_ } }
------------
0
1
2
3
4
5
6
7
8
9
------------
11
12
------------
```

```
14
15
16
17
18
19
20
21
22
(...)
255
214
220
162
163
165
8359
402
225
```

At number 10, PowerShell interprets that byte as the end of the line, and uses that to split the output into a new element. It does the same for number 13. Things appear to get even stranger when we get to the higher numbers and PowerShell starts to interpret combinations of bytes as Unicode characters from another language.

The Solution resolves this behavior by managing the output of the binary process directly. If you supply the -RedirectInput parameter, the script assumes an incoming stream of binary data and passes it to the program directly. If you supply the -RedirectOutput parameter, the script assumes that the output is binary data, and likewise reads it from the process directly.

## See Also

Recipe 1.1, "Run Programs, Scripts, and Existing Tools"

# CHAPTER 3

# Variables and Objects

## 3.0. Introduction

As touched on in Chapter 2, PowerShell makes life immensely easier by keeping information in its native form: *objects*. Users expend most of their effort in traditional shells just trying to resuscitate information that the shell converted from its native form to plain text. Tools have evolved that ease the burden of working with plain text, but that job is still significantly more difficult than it needs to be.

Since PowerShell builds on Microsoft's .NET Framework, native information comes in the form of .NET *objects*—packages of information and functionality closely related to that information.

Let's say that you want to get a list of running processes on your system. In other shells, your command (such as `tlist.exe` or `/bin/ps`) generates a plain-text report of the running processes on your system. To work with that output, you send it through a bevy of text processing tools—if you are lucky enough to have them available.

PowerShell's `Get-Process` cmdlet generates a list of the running processes on your system. In contrast to other shells, though, these are full-fidelity `System.Diagnostics.Process` objects straight out of the .NET Framework. The .NET Framework documentation describes them as objects that "[provide] access to local and remote processes, and [enable] you to start and stop local system processes." With those objects in hand, PowerShell makes it trivial for you to access properties of objects (such as their process name or memory usage) and to access functionality on these objects (such as stopping them, starting them, or waiting for them to exit).

# 3.1. Display the Properties of an Item as a List

## Problem

You have an item (for example, an error record, directory item, or .NET object), and you want to display detailed information about that object in a list format.

## Solution

To display detailed information about an item, pass that item to the `Format-List` cmdlet. For example, to display an error in list format, type the following commands:

```
$currentError = $error[0]
$currentError | Format-List -Force
```

## Discussion

Many commands by default display a summarized view of their output in a table format, for example, the `Get-Process` cmdlet:

```
PS > Get-Process PowerShell
```

| Handles | NPM(K) | PM(K) | WS(K) | VM(M) | CPU(s) | Id | ProcessName |
|---------|--------|-------|-------|-------|--------|------|-------------|
| 920 | 10 | 43808 | 48424 | 183 | 4.69 | 1928 | powershell |
| 149 | 6 | 18228 | 8660 | 146 | 0.48 | 1940 | powershell |
| 431 | 11 | 33308 | 19072 | 172 | | 2816 | powershell |

In most cases, the output actually contains a great deal more information. You can use the `Format-List` cmdlet to view it:

```
PS > Get-Process PowerShell | Format-List *
```

```
__NounName          : Process
Name                : powershell
Handles             : 443
VM                  : 192176128
WS                  : 52363264
PM                  : 47308800
NPM                 : 9996
Path                : C:\WINDOWS\system32\WindowsPowerShell\v1.0\power
                      shell.exe
Company             : Microsoft Corporation
CPU                 : 4.921875
FileVersion         : 6.0.6002.18139 (vistasp2_gdr_win7ip_winman(wmbla
                      ).090902-1426)
ProductVersion      : 6.0.6002.18139
Description         : Windows PowerShell
(...)
```

The `Format-List` cmdlet is one of the four PowerShell formatting cmdlets. These cmdlets are `Format-Table`, `Format-List`, `Format-Wide`, and `Format-Custom`. The `Format-List` cmdlet takes input and displays information about that input as a list.

By default, PowerShell takes the list of properties to display from the *\*.format.ps1xml* files in PowerShell's installation directory. In many situations, you'll only get a small set of the properties:

```
PS > Get-Process PowerShell | Format-List

Id      : 2816
Handles : 431
CPU     :
Name    : powershell

Id      : 5244
Handles : 665
CPU     : 10.296875
Name    : powershell
```

To display all properties of the item, type **Format-List \***. If you type `Format-List *` but still do not get a list of the item's properties, then the item is defined in the *\*.format.ps1xml* files, but does not define anything to be displayed for the list command. In that case, type **Format-List -Force**.

One common stumbling block in PowerShell's formatting cmdlets comes from putting them in the middle of a script or pipeline:

```
PS > Get-Process PowerShell | Format-List | Sort Name
out-lineoutput : The object of type "Microsoft.PowerShell.Commands.Internal.
Format.FormatEntryData" is not valid or not in the correct sequence. This is
likely caused by a user-specified "format-*" command which is conflicting with
the default formatting.
```

Internally, PowerShell's formatting commands generate a new type of object: `Microsoft.PowerShell.Commands.Internal.Format.*`. When these objects make it to the end of the pipeline, PowerShell automatically sends them to an output cmdlet: by default, `Out-Default`. These `Out-*` cmdlets assume that the objects arrive in a certain order, so doing anything with the output of the formatting commands causes an error in the output system.

To resolve this problem, try to avoid calling the formatting cmdlets in the middle of a script or pipeline. When you do this, the output of your script no longer lends itself to the object-based manipulation so synonymous with PowerShell.

If you want to use the formatted output directly, send the output through the `Out-String` cmdlet as described in Recipe 1.23, "Program: Search Formatted Output for a Pattern".

For more information about the `Format-List` cmdlet, type **Get-Help Format-List**.

# 3.2. Display the Properties of an Item as a Table

## Problem

You have a set of items (for example, error records, directory items, or .NET objects), and you want to display summary information about them in a table format.

## Solution

To display summary information about a set of items, pass those items to the `Format-Table` cmdlet. This is the default type of formatting for sets of items in PowerShell and provides several useful features.

To use PowerShell's default formatting, pipe the output of a cmdlet (such as the `Get-Process` cmdlet) to the `Format-Table` cmdlet:

```
Get-Process | Format-Table
```

To display specific properties (such as `Name` and `WorkingSet`) in the table formatting, supply those property names as parameters to the `Format-Table` cmdlet:

```
Get-Process | Format-Table Name,WS
```

To instruct PowerShell to format the table in the most readable manner, supply the `-Auto` flag to the `Format-Table` cmdlet. PowerShell defines `WS` as an alias of the `WorkingSet` property for processes:

```
Get-Process | Format-Table Name,WS -Auto
```

To define a custom column definition (such as a process's `WorkingSet` in megabytes), supply a custom formatting expression to the `Format-Table` cmdlet:

```
$fields = "Name",@{
    Label = "WS (MB)"; Expression = {$_.WS / 1mb}; Align = "Right"}
Get-Process | Format-Table $fields -Auto
```

## Discussion

The `Format-Table` cmdlet is one of the four PowerShell formatting cmdlets. These cmdlets are `Format-Table`, `Format-List`, `Format-Wide`, and `Format-Custom`. The `Format-Table` cmdlet takes input and displays information about that input as a table. By default, PowerShell takes the list of properties to display from the *\*.format.ps1xml* files in PowerShell's installation directory. You can display all properties of the items if you type **Format-Table \***, although this is rarely a useful view.

The `-Auto` parameter to `Format-Table` is a helpful way to automatically format the table in the most readable way possible. It does come at a cost, however. To figure out the best table layout, PowerShell needs to examine each item in the incoming set of items. For small sets of items, this doesn't make much difference, but for large sets (such as a recursive directory listing) it does. Without the -Auto parameter, the Format-Table cmdlet can display items as soon as it receives them. With the -Auto flag, the cmdlet displays results only after it receives all the input.

Perhaps the most interesting feature of the Format-Table cmdlet is illustrated by the last example: the ability to define completely custom table columns. You define a custom table column similarly to the way that you define a custom column list. Rather than specify an existing property of the items, you provide a hashtable. That hashtable includes up to three keys: the column's label, a formatting expression, and alignment. The Format-Table cmdlet shows the label as the column header and uses your expression to generate data for that column. The label must be a string, the expression must be a script block, and the alignment must be either "Left", "Center", or "Right". In the expression script block, the $_ (or $PSItem) variable represents the current item being formatted.

The Select-Object cmdlet supports a similar hashtable to add calculated properties, but uses Name (rather than Label) as the key to identify the property. After realizing how confusing this was, version 2 of PowerShell updated both cmdlets to accept both Name and Label.

The expression shown in the last example takes the working set of the current item and divides it by 1 megabyte (1 MB).

One common stumbling block in PowerShell's formatting cmdlets comes from putting them in the middle of a script or pipeline:

```
PS > Get-Process | Format-Table | Sort Name
out-lineoutput : The object of type "Microsoft.PowerShell.Commands.Internal.
Format.FormatEntryData" is not valid or not in the correct sequence. This is
likely caused by a user-specified "format-*" command which is conflicting with
the default formatting.
```

Internally, PowerShell's formatting commands generate a new type of object: Microsoft.PowerShell.Commands.Internal.Format.*. When these objects make it to the end of the pipeline, PowerShell then automatically sends them to an output cmdlet: by default, Out-Default. These Out-* cmdlets assume that the objects arrive in a certain order, so doing anything with the output of the formatting commands causes an error in the output system.

To resolve this problem, try to avoid calling the formatting cmdlets in the middle of a script or pipeline. When you do this, the output of your script no longer lends itself to the object-based manipulation so synonymous with PowerShell.

If you want to use the formatted output directly, send the output through the Out-String cmdlet as described in Recipe 1.23, "Program: Search Formatted Output for a Pattern".

For more information about the Format-Table cmdlet, type **Get-Help Format-Table**. For more information about hashtables, see Recipe 7.13, "Create a Hashtable or Associative Array". For more information about script blocks, see Recipe 11.4, "Write a Script Block".

## See Also

Recipe 1.23, "Program: Search Formatted Output for a Pattern"

Recipe 7.13, "Create a Hashtable or Associative Array"

Recipe 11.4, "Write a Script Block"

# 3.3. Store Information in Variables

## Problem

You want to store the output of a pipeline or command for later use or to work with it in more detail.

## Solution

To store output for later use, store the output of the command in a variable. You can access this information later, or even pass it down the pipeline as though it were the output of the original command:

```
PS > $result = 2 + 2
PS > $result
4

PS > $output = ipconfig
PS > $output | Select-String "Default Gateway" | Select -First 1

    Default Gateway . . . . . . . . . : 192.168.11.1

PS > $processes = Get-Process
PS > $processes.Count
85
PS > $processes | Where-Object { $_.ID -eq 0 }

Handles  NPM(K)    PM(K)      WS(K) VM(M)   CPU(s)     Id ProcessName
-------  ------    -----      ----- -----   -----      -- -----------
      0       0        0         16     0                0 Idle
```

## Discussion

Variables in PowerShell (and all other scripting and programming languages) let you store the output of something so that you can use it later. A variable name starts with a dollar sign ($) and can be followed by nearly any character. A small set of characters have special meaning to PowerShell, so PowerShell provides a way to make variable names that include even these.

For more information about the syntax and types of PowerShell variables, see "Variables" (page 864).

You can store the result of any pipeline or command in a variable to use it later. If that command generates simple data (such as a number or string), then the variable contains simple data. If the command generates rich data (such as the objects that represent system processes from the Get-Process cmdlet), then the variable contains that list of rich data. If the command (such as a traditional executable) generates plain text (such as the output of traditional executable), then the variable contains plain text.

 If you've stored a large amount of data into a variable but no longer need that data, assign a new value (such as $null) to that variable. That will allow PowerShell to release the memory it was using to store that data.

In addition to variables that you create, PowerShell automatically defines several variables that represent things such as the location of your profile file, the process ID of PowerShell, and more. For a full list of these automatic variables, type **Get-Help about_automatic_variables**.

## See Also

"Variables" (page 864)

# 3.4. Access Environment Variables

## Problem

You want to use an environment variable (such as the system path or the current user's name) in your script or interactive session.

## Solution

PowerShell offers several ways to access environment variables.

To list all environment variables, list the children of the env drive:

```
Get-ChildItem env:
```

To get an environment variable using a more concise syntax, precede its name with $env:

```
$env:variablename
```

(For example, $env:username.)

To get an environment variable using its provider path, supply env: or Environ
ment:: to the Get-ChildItem cmdlet:

```
Get-ChildItem env:variablename
Get-ChildItem Environment::variablename
```

## Discussion

PowerShell provides access to environment variables through its *environment provider*.
Providers let you work with data stores (such as the registry, environment variables, and
aliases) much as you would access the filesystem.

By default, PowerShell creates a drive (called env) that works with the *environment
provider* to let you access environment variables. The environment provider lets you
access items in the env: drive as you would any other drive: dir env:\variablename or
dir env:variablename. If you want to access the provider directly (rather than go
through its drive), you can also type **dir Environment::variablename**.

However, the most common (and easiest) way to work with environment variables is by
typing **$env:variablename**. This works with any provider but is most typically used
with environment variables.

This is because the environment provider shares something in common with several
other providers—namely, support for the *-Content set of core cmdlets (see
Example 3-1).

*Example 3-1. Working with content on different providers*

```
PS > "hello world" > test
PS > Get-Content test
hello world
PS > Get-Content c:test
hello world
PS > Get-Content variable:ErrorActionPreference
Continue
PS > Get-Content function:more
param([string[]]$paths)
$OutputEncoding = [System.Console]::OutputEncoding

if($paths)
{
    foreach ($file in $paths)
    {
        Get-Content $file | more.com
```

```
        }
}
else
{
    $input | more.com
}
PS > Get-Content env:systemroot
C:\WINDOWS
```

For providers that support the content cmdlets, PowerShell lets you interact with this content through a special variable syntax (see Example 3-2).

*Example 3-2. Using PowerShell's special variable syntax to access content*

```
PS > $function:more
param([string[]]$paths); if(($paths -ne $null) -and ($paths.length -ne 0)) { ...
      Get-Content $local:file | Out-Host -p } else { $input | Out-Host ...
PS > $variable:ErrorActionPreference
Continue
PS > $c:test
hello world
PS > $env:systemroot
C:\WINDOWS
```

This variable syntax for content management lets you both get and set content:

```
PS > $function:more = { $input | less.exe }
PS > $function:more
$input | less.exe
```

Now, when it comes to accessing complex provider paths using this method, you'll quickly run into naming issues (even if the underlying file exists):

```
PS > $c:\temp\test.txt
Unexpected token '\temp\test.txt' in expression or statement.
At line:1 char:17
+ $c:\temp\test.txt <<<<
```

The solution to that lies in PowerShell's escaping support for complex variable names. To define a complex variable name, enclose it in braces:

```
PS > ${1234123!@#$!@#$12$!@#$@!} = "Crazy Variable!"
PS > ${1234123!@#$!@#$12$!@#$@!}
Crazy Variable!
PS > dir variable:\1*
```

```
Name                            Value
----                            -----
1234123!@#$!@#$12$!@#$@!         Crazy Variable!
```

The following is the content equivalent (assuming that the file exists):

```
PS > ${c:\temp\test.txt}
hello world
```

Since environment variable names do not contain special characters, this `Get-Content` variable syntax is the best (and easiest) way to access environment variables.

For more information about working with PowerShell variables, see "Variables" (page 864). For more information about working with environment variables, type `Get-Help About_Environment_Variable`.

### See Also

"Variables" (page 864)

## 3.5. Program: Retain Changes to Environment Variables Set by a Batch File

When a batch file modifies an environment variable, *cmd.exe* retains this change even after the script exits. This often causes problems, as one batch file can accidentally pollute the environment of another. That said, batch file authors sometimes intentionally change the global environment to customize the path and other aspects of the environment to suit a specific task.

However, environment variables are private details of a process and disappear when that process exits. This makes the environment customization scripts mentioned earlier stop working when you run them from PowerShell—just as they fail to work when you run them from another *cmd.exe* (for example, `cmd.exe /c MyEnvironmentCustomiz er.cmd`).

The script in Example 3-3 lets you run batch files that modify the environment and retain their changes even after *cmd.exe* exits. It accomplishes this by storing the environment variables in a text file once the batch file completes, and then setting all those environment variables again in your PowerShell session.

To run this script, type **Invoke-CmdScript *Scriptname.cmd*** or **Invoke-CmdScript *Scriptname.bat***—whichever extension the batch files uses.

 If this is the first time you've run a script in PowerShell, you will need to configure your Execution Policy. For more information about selecting an execution policy, see Recipe 18.1, "Enable Scripting Through an Execution Policy".

Notice that this script uses the full names for cmdlets: `Get-Content`, `Foreach-Object`, `Set-Content`, and `Remove-Item`. This makes the script readable and is ideal for scripts that somebody else will read. It is by no means required, though. For quick scripts and interactive use, shorter aliases (such as `gc`, `%`, `sc`, and `ri`) can make you more productive.

---

*Example 3-3. Invoke-CmdScript.ps1*

```
###########################################################################
##
## Invoke-CmdScript
##
## From Windows PowerShell Cookbook (O'Reilly)
## by Lee Holmes (http://www.leeholmes.com/guide)
##
###########################################################################

<#

.SYNOPSIS

Invoke the specified batch file (and parameters), but also propagate any
environment variable changes back to the PowerShell environment that
called it.

.EXAMPLE

PS > type foo-that-sets-the-FOO-env-variable.cmd
@set FOO=%*
echo FOO set to %FOO%.

PS > $env:FOO
PS > Invoke-CmdScript "foo-that-sets-the-FOO-env-variable.cmd" Test

C:\Temp>echo FOO set to Test.
FOO set to Test.

PS > $env:FOO
Test

#>

param(
    ## The path to the script to run
    [Parameter(Mandatory = $true)]
    [string] $Path,

    ## The arguments to the script
    [string] $ArgumentList
)

Set-StrictMode -Version 3

$tempFile = [IO.Path]::GetTempFileName()

## Store the output of cmd.exe.  We also ask cmd.exe to output
## the environment table after the batch file completes
cmd /c " `"$Path`" " $argumentList && set > `"$tempFile`" "
```

```
## Go through the environment variables in the temp file.
## For each of them, set the variable in our local environment.
Get-Content $tempFile | Foreach-Object {
    if($_ -match "^(.*?)=(.*)$")
    {
        Set-Content "env:\$($matches[1])" $matches[2]
    }
}

Remove-Item $tempFile
```

For more information about running scripts, see Recipe 1.1, "Run Programs, Scripts, and Existing Tools".

### See Also

Recipe 1.1, "Run Programs, Scripts, and Existing Tools"

Recipe 18.1, "Enable Scripting Through an Execution Policy"

# 3.6. Control Access and Scope of Variables and Other Items

## Problem

You want to control how you define (or interact with) the visibility of variables, aliases, functions, and drives.

## Solution

PowerShell offers several ways to access variables.

To create a variable with a specific scope, supply that scope before the variable name:

```
$SCOPE:variable = value
```

To access a variable at a specific scope, supply that scope before the variable name:

```
$SCOPE:variable
```

To create a variable that remains even after the script exits, create it in the GLOBAL scope:

```
$GLOBAL:variable = value
```

To change a scriptwide variable from within a function, supply SCRIPT as its scope name:

```
$SCRIPT:variable = value
```

# Discussion

PowerShell controls access to variables, functions, aliases, and drives through a mechanism known as *scoping*. The *scope* of an item is another term for its visibility. You are always in a scope (called the *current* or *local* scope), but some actions change what that means.

When your code enters a nested prompt, script, function, or script block, PowerShell creates a new scope. That scope then becomes the local scope. When it does this, PowerShell remembers the relationship between your old scope and your new scope. From the view of the new scope, the old scope is called the *parent scope*. From the view of the old scope, the new scope is called a *child scope*. Child scopes get access to all the variables in the parent scope, but changing those variables in the child scope doesn't change the version in the parent scope.

 Trying to change a scriptwide variable from a function is often a "gotcha" because a function is a new scope. As mentioned previously, changing something in a child scope (the function) doesn't affect the parent scope (the script). The rest of this discussion describes ways to change the value for the entire script.

When your code exits a nested prompt, script, function, or script block, the opposite happens. PowerShell removes the old scope, then changes the local scope to be the scope that originally created it—the parent of that old scope.

Some scopes are so common that PowerShell gives them special names:

*Global*
> The outermost scope. Items in the global scope are visible from all other scopes.

*Script*
> The scope that represents the current script. Items in the script scope are visible from all other scopes in the script.

*Local*
> The current scope.

When you define the scope of an item, PowerShell supports two additional scope names that act more like options: `Private` and `AllScope`. When you define an item to have a `Private` scope, PowerShell does not make that item directly available to child scopes. PowerShell does not *hide* it from child scopes, though, as child scopes can still use the `-Scope` parameter of the `Get-Variable` cmdlet to get variables from parent scopes. When you specify the `AllScope` option for an item (through one of the `*-Variable`, `*-Alias`, or `*-Drive` cmdlets), child scopes that change the item also affect the value in parent scopes.

With this background, PowerShell provides several ways for you to control access and scope of variables and other items.

### Variables

To define a variable at a specific scope (or access a variable at a specific scope), use its scope name in the variable reference. For example:

```
$SCRIPT:myVariable = value
```

As illustrated in "Variables" (page 864), the *-Variable set of cmdlets also lets you specify scope names through their -Scope parameter.

### Functions

To define a function at a specific scope (or access a function at a specific scope), use its scope name when creating the function. For example:

```
function GLOBAL:MyFunction { ... }
GLOBAL:MyFunction args
```

### Aliases and drives

To define an alias or drive at a specific scope, use the Option parameter of the *-Alias and *-Drive cmdlets. To access an alias or drive at a specific scope, use the Scope parameter of the *-Alias and *-Drive cmdlets.

For more information about scopes, type **Get-Help About-Scope**.

## See Also

"Variables" (page 864)

# 3.7. Program: Create a Dynamic Variable

When working with variables and commands, some concepts feel too minor to deserve an entire new command or function, but the readability of your script suffers without them.

A few examples where this becomes evident are date math (*yesterday* becomes (Get-Date).AddDays(-1)) and deeply nested variables (*windowTitle* becomes $host.UI.RawUI.WindowTitle).

There are innovative solutions on the Internet that use PowerShell's debugging facilities to create a breakpoint that changes a variable's value whenever you attempt to read from it. While unique, this solution causes PowerShell to think that any scripts that rely on the variable are in debugging mode. This, unfortunately, prevents PowerShell from enabling some important performance optimizations in those scripts.

Although we could write our own extensions to make these easier to access, Get-Yesterday, Get-WindowTitle, and Set-WindowTitle feel too insignificant to deserve their own commands.

PowerShell lets you define your own types of variables by extending its PSVariable class, but that functionality is largely designed for developer scenarios, and not for scripting scenarios. Example 3-4 resolves this quandary by creating a new variable type (DynamicVariable) that supports dynamic script actions when you get or set the variable's value.

*Example 3-4. New-DynamicVariable.ps1*

```
##############################################################################
##
## New-DynamicVariable
##
## From Windows PowerShell Cookbook (O'Reilly)
## by Lee Holmes (http://www.leeholmes.com/guide)
##
##############################################################################

<#

.SYNOPSIS

Creates a variable that supports scripted actions for its getter and setter

.EXAMPLE

PS > .\New-DynamicVariable GLOBAL:WindowTitle `
    -Getter { $host.UI.RawUI.WindowTitle } `
    -Setter { $host.UI.RawUI.WindowTitle = $args[0] }

PS > $windowTitle
Administrator: C:\Windows\System32\WindowsPowerShell\v1.0\powershell.exe
PS > $windowTitle = "Test"
PS > $windowTitle
Test

#>

param(
```

```
    ## The name for the dynamic variable
    [Parameter(Mandatory = $true)]
    $Name,

    ## The script block to invoke when getting the value of the variable
    [Parameter(Mandatory = $true)]
    [ScriptBlock] $Getter,

    ## The script block to invoke when setting the value of the variable
    [ScriptBlock] $Setter
)

Set-StrictMode -Version 3

Add-Type @"
using System;
using System.Collections.ObjectModel;
using System.Management.Automation;

namespace Lee.Holmes
{
    public class DynamicVariable : PSVariable
    {
        public DynamicVariable(
            string name,
            ScriptBlock scriptGetter,
            ScriptBlock scriptSetter)
                : base(name, null, ScopedItemOptions.AllScope)
        {
            getter = scriptGetter;
            setter = scriptSetter;
        }
        private ScriptBlock getter;
        private ScriptBlock setter;

        public override object Value
        {
            get
            {
                if(getter != null)
                {
                    Collection<PSObject> results = getter.Invoke();
                    if(results.Count == 1)
                    {
                        return results[0];
                    }
                    else
                    {
                        PSObject[] returnResults =
                            new PSObject[results.Count];
                        results.CopyTo(returnResults, 0);
                        return returnResults;
```

```
                }
            }
            else { return null; }
        }
        set
        {
            if(setter != null) { setter.Invoke(value); }
        }
    }
}
}
"@

## If we've already defined the variable, remove it.
if(Test-Path variable:\$name)
{
    Remove-Item variable:\$name -Force
}

## Set the new variable, along with its getter and setter.
$executioncontext.SessionState.PSVariable.Set(
    (New-Object Lee.Holmes.DynamicVariable $name,$getter,$setter))
```

# 3.8. Work with .NET Objects

## Problem

You want to use and interact with one of the features that makes PowerShell so powerful: its intrinsic support for .NET objects.

## Solution

PowerShell offers ways to access methods (both static and instance) and properties.

To call a static method on a class, place the type name in square brackets, and then
separate the class name from the method name with two colons:

```
[ClassName]::MethodName(parameter list)
```

To call a method on an object, place a dot between the variable that represents that object
and the method name:

```
$objectReference.MethodName(parameter list)
```

To access a static property on a class, place the type name in square brackets, and then
separate the class name from the property name with two colons:

```
[ClassName]::PropertyName
```

To access a property on an object, place a dot between the variable that represents that object and the property name:

```
$objectReference.PropertyName
```

## Discussion

One feature that gives PowerShell its incredible reach into both system administration and application development is its capability to leverage Microsoft's enormous and broad .NET Framework. The .NET Framework is a large collection of classes. Each class embodies a specific concept and groups closely related functionality and information. Working with the .NET Framework is one aspect of PowerShell that introduces a revolution to the world of management shells.

An example of a class from the .NET Framework is `System.Diagnostics.Process`— the grouping of functionality that "provides access to local and remote processes, and enables you to start and stop local system processes."

 The terms *type* and *class* are often used interchangeably.

Classes contain *methods* (which let you perform operations) and *properties* (which let you access information).

For example, the `Get-Process` cmdlet generates `System.Diagnostics.Process` objects, not a plain-text report like traditional shells. Managing these processes becomes incredibly easy, as they contain a rich mix of information (properties) and operations (methods). You no longer have to parse a stream of text for the ID of a process; you can just ask the object directly!

```
PS > $process = Get-Process Notepad
PS > $process.Id
3872
```

### Static methods

```
[ClassName]::MethodName(parameter list)
```

Some methods apply only to the concept the class represents. For example, retrieving all running processes on a system relates to the general concept of processes instead of a specific process. Methods that apply to the class/type as a whole are called *static methods*.

For example:

```
PS > [System.Diagnostics.Process]::GetProcessById(0)
```

This specific task is better handled by the `Get-Process` cmdlet, but it demonstrates PowerShell's capability to call methods on .NET classes. It calls the static `GetProcess ById` method on the `System.Diagnostics.Process` class to get the process with the ID of 0. This generates the following output:

```
Handles NPM(K) PM(K) WS(K) VM(M) CPU(s) Id ProcessName
------- ------ ----- ----- ----- ------ -- -----------
      0      0     0    16     0         0 Idle
```

### Instance methods

> `$objectReference.MethodName(parameter list)`

Some methods relate only to specific, tangible realizations (called instances) of a class. An example of this would be stopping a process actually running on the system, as opposed to the general concept of processes. If `$objectReference` refers to a specific `System.Diagnostics.Process` (as output by the `Get-Process` cmdlet, for example), you may call methods to start it, stop it, or wait for it to exit. Methods that act on instances of a class are called *instance methods*.

 The term *object* is often used interchangeably with the term *instance*.

For example:

```
PS > $process = Get-Process Notepad
PS > $process.WaitForExit()
```

stores the Notepad process into the `$process` variable. It then calls the `WaitForEx it()` instance method on that specific process to pause PowerShell until the process exits. To learn about the different sets of parameters (overloads) that a given method supports, type that method name without any parameters:

```
PS > $now = Get-Date
PS > $now.ToString

OverloadDefinitions
-------------------
string ToString()
string ToString(string format)
string ToString(System.IFormatProvider provider)
string ToString(string format, System.IFormatProvider provider)
string IFormattable.ToString(string format, System.IFormatProvider formatProvider)
string IConvertible.ToString(System.IFormatProvider provider)
```

For both static methods and instance methods, you may sometimes run into situations where PowerShell either generates an error or fails to invoke the method you expected. In this case, review the output of the Trace-Command cmdlet, with MemberResolution as the trace type (see Example 3-5).

*Example 3-5. Investigating PowerShell's method resolution*

```
PS > Trace-Command MemberResolution -PsHost {
    [System.Diagnostics.Process]::GetProcessById(0) }

DEBUG: MemberResolution Information: 0 : cache hit, Calling Method: static
 System.Diagnostics.Process GetProcessById(int processId)
DEBUG: MemberResolution Information: 0 : Method argument conversion.
DEBUG: MemberResolution Information: 0 :     Converting parameter "0" to
"System.Int32".
DEBUG: MemberResolution Information: 0 : Checking for possible references.

Handles  NPM(K)    PM(K)      WS(K) VM(M)   CPU(s)     Id ProcessName
-------  ------    -----      ----- -----   ------     -- -----------
      0       0        0         12     0                0 Idle
```

If you are adapting a C# example from the Internet and PowerShell can't find a method used in the example, the method may have been added through a relatively rare technique called *explicit interface implementation*. If this is the case, you can cast the object to that interface before calling the method:

```
$sourceObject = 123
$result = ([IConvertible] $sourceObject).ToUint16($null)
```

## Static properties

```
[ClassName]::PropertyName
```

or:

```
[ClassName]::PropertyName = value
```

Like static methods, some properties relate only to information about the concept that the class represents. For example, the System.DateTime class "represents an instant in time, typically expressed as a date and time of day." It provides a Now static property that returns the current time:

```
PS > [System.DateTime]::Now
Saturday, June 2, 2010 4:57:20 PM
```

This specific task is better handled by the Get-Date cmdlet, but it demonstrates PowerShell's capability to access properties on .NET objects.

Although they are relatively rare, some types let you set the value of some static properties as well: for example, the [System.Environment]::CurrentDirectory property. This property represents the process's current directory—which represents PowerShell's startup directory, as opposed to the path you see in your prompt.

### Instance properties

```
$objectReference.PropertyName
```

or:

```
$objectReference.PropertyName = value
```

Like instance methods, some properties relate only to specific, tangible realizations (called *instances*) of a class. An example of this would be the day of an actual instant in time, as opposed to the general concept of dates and times. If *$objectReference* refers to a specific System.DateTime (as output by the Get-Date cmdlet or [System.DateTime]::Now, for example), you may want to retrieve its day of week, day, or month. Properties that return information about instances of a class are called *instance properties*.

For example:

```
PS > $today = Get-Date
PS > $today.DayOfWeek
Saturday
```

This example stores the current date in the $today variable. It then calls the DayOfWeek instance property to retrieve the day of the week for that specific date.

With this knowledge, the next questions are: "How do I learn about the functionality available in the .NET Framework?" and "How do I learn what an object does?"

For an answer to the first question, see Appendix F for a hand-picked list of the classes in the .NET Framework most useful to system administrators. For an answer to the second, see Recipe 3.13, "Learn About Types and Objects" and Recipe 3.14, "Get Detailed Documentation About Types and Objects".

## See Also

Recipe 3.13, "Learn About Types and Objects"

Recipe 3.14, "Get Detailed Documentation About Types and Objects"

Appendix F, *Selected .NET Classes and Their Uses*

# 3.9. Create an Instance of a .NET Object

## Problem

You want to create an instance of a .NET object to interact with its methods and properties.

## Solution

Use the `New-Object` cmdlet to create an instance of an object.

To create an instance of an object using its default constructor, use the `New-Object` cmdlet with the class name as its only parameter:

```
PS > $generator = New-Object System.Random
PS > $generator.NextDouble()
0.853699042859347
```

To create an instance of an object that takes parameters for its constructor, supply those parameters to the `New-Object` cmdlet. In some instances, the class may exist in a separate library not loaded in PowerShell by default, such as the `System.Windows.Forms` assembly. In that case, you must first load the assembly that contains the class:

```
Add-Type -Assembly System.Windows.Forms
$image = New-Object System.Drawing.Bitmap source.gif
$image.Save("source_converted.jpg", "JPEG")
```

To create an object and use it at the same time (without saving it for later), wrap the call to `New-Object` in parentheses:

```
PS > (New-Object Net.WebClient).DownloadString("http://live.com")
```

## Discussion

Many cmdlets (such as `Get-Process` and `Get-ChildItem`) generate live .NET objects that represent tangible processes, files, and directories. However, PowerShell supports much more of the .NET Framework than just the objects that its cmdlets produce. These additional areas of the .NET Framework supply a huge amount of functionality that you can use in your scripts and general system administration tasks.

 To create an instance of a generic object, see Example 3-6.

When it comes to using most of these classes, the first step is often to create an instance of the class, store that instance in a variable, and then work with the methods and properties on that instance. To create an instance of a class, you use the `New-Object` cmdlet. The first parameter to the `New-Object` cmdlet is the type name, and the second parameter is the list of arguments to the constructor, if it takes any. The `New-Object` cmdlet supports PowerShell's *type shortcuts*, so you never have to use the fully qualified type name. For more information about type shortcuts, see "Type Shortcuts" (page 893).

A common pattern when working with .NET objects is to create them, set a few properties, and then use them. The `-Property` parameter of the `New-Object` cmdlet lets you combine these steps:

```
$startInfo = New-Object Diagnostics.ProcessStartInfo -Property @{
    'Filename' = "powershell.exe";
    'WorkingDirectory' = $pshome;
    'Verb' = "RunAs"
}
[Diagnostics.Process]::Start($startInfo)
```

Or even more simply through PowerShell's built-in type conversion:

```
$startInfo = [Diagnostics.ProcessStartInfo] @{
    'Filename' = "powershell.exe";
    'WorkingDirectory' = $pshome;
    'Verb' = "RunAs"
}
```

When calling the `New-Object` cmdlet directly, you might encounter difficulty when trying to specify a parameter that itself is a list. Assuming `$byte` is an array of bytes:

```
PS > $memoryStream = New-Object System.IO.MemoryStream $bytes
New-Object : Cannot find an overload for ".ctor" and the argument count: "11".
At line:1 char:27
+ $memoryStream = New-Object <<<< System.IO.MemoryStream $bytes
```

To solve this, provide an array that contains an array:

```
PS > $parameters = ,$bytes
PS > $memoryStream = New-Object System.IO.MemoryStream $parameters
```

or:

```
PS > $memoryStream = New-Object System.IO.MemoryStream @(,$bytes)
```

### Load types from another assembly

PowerShell makes most common types available by default. However, many are available only after you load the library (called the assembly) that defines them. The MSDN documentation for a class includes the assembly that defines it. For more information about loading types from another assembly, please see Recipe 17.8, "Access a .NET SDK Library".

For a hand-picked list of the classes in the .NET Framework most useful to system administrators, see Appendix F. To learn more about the functionality that a class supports, see Recipe 3.13, "Learn About Types and Objects".

For more information about the New-Object cmdlet, type **Get-Help New-Object**. For more information about the Add-Type cmdlet, type **Get-Help Add-Type**.

### See Also

Recipe 3.8, "Work with .NET Objects"

Recipe 3.13, "Learn About Types and Objects"

Recipe 17.8, "Access a .NET SDK Library"

Appendix F, *Selected .NET Classes and Their Uses*

Example 3-6

# 3.10. Create Instances of Generic Objects

When you work with the .NET Framework, you'll often run across classes that have the primary responsibility of managing other objects. For example, the System. Collections.ArrayList class lets you manage a dynamic list of objects. You can add objects to an ArrayList, remove objects from it, sort the objects inside, and more. These objects can be any type of object: String objects, integers, DateTime objects, and many others. However, working with classes that support arbitrary objects can sometimes be a little awkward. One example is *type safety*. If you accidentally add a String to a list of integers, you might not find out until your program fails.

Although the issue becomes largely moot when you're working only inside PowerShell, a more common complaint in strongly typed languages (such as C#) is that you have to remind the environment (through explicit casts) about the type of your object when you work with it again:

```
// This is C# code
System.Collections.ArrayList list =
    new System.Collections.ArrayList();
list.Add("Hello World");

string result = (String) list[0];
```

To address these problems, the .NET Framework includes a feature called *generic types*: classes that support arbitrary types of objects but let you specify *which type* of object. In this case, a collection of strings:

```
// This is C# code
System.Collections.ObjectModel.Collection<String> list =
```

```
    new System.Collections.ObjectModel.Collection<String>();
list.Add("Hello World");

string result = list[0];
```

PowerShell version 2 and on support generic parameters by placing them between square brackets, as demonstrated in Example 3-6. If you are using PowerShell version 1, see `New-GenericObject` included in the book's sample downloads.

*Example 3-6. Creating a generic object*

```
PS > $coll = New-Object System.Collections.ObjectModel.Collection[Int]
PS > $coll.Add(15)
PS > $coll.Add("Test")
Cannot convert argument "0", with value: "Test", for "Add" to type "System
.Int32": "Cannot convert value "Test" to type "System.Int32". Error: "Input
string was not in a correct format.""
At line:1 char:10
+ $coll.Add <<<< ("Test")
    + CategoryInfo          : NotSpecified: (:) [], MethodException
    + FullyQualifiedErrorId : MethodArgumentConversionInvalidCastArgument
```

For a generic type that takes two or more parameters, provide a comma-separated list of types, enclosed in quotes (see Example 3-7).

*Example 3-7. Creating a multiparameter generic object*

```
PS > $map = New-Object "System.Collections.Generic.Dictionary[String,Int]"
PS > $map.Add("Test", 15)
PS > $map.Add("Test2", "Hello")
Cannot convert argument "1", with value: "Hello", for "Add" to type "System
.Int32": "Cannot convert value "Hello" to type "System.Int32". Error:
"Input string was not in a correct format.""
At line:1 char:9
+ $map.Add <<<< ("Test2", "Hello")
    + CategoryInfo          : NotSpecified: (:) [], MethodException
    + FullyQualifiedErrorId : MethodArgumentConversionInvalidCastArgument
```

# 3.11. Reduce Typing for Long Class Names

## Problem

You want to reduce the amount of redundant information in your script when you interact with classes that have long type names.

## Solution

To reduce typing for static methods, store the type name in a variable:

```
$math = [System.Math]
$math::Min(1,10)
$math::Max(1,10)
```

To reduce typing for multiple objects in a namespace, use the -f operator:

```
$namespace = "System.Collections.{0}"
$arrayList = New-Object ($namespace -f "ArrayList")
$queue = New-Object ($namespace -f "Queue")
```

To reduce typing for static methods of multiple types in a namespace, use the -f operator along with a cast:

```
$namespace = "System.Diagnostics.{0}"
([Type] ($namespace -f "EventLog"))::GetEventLogs()
([Type] ($namespace -f "Process"))::GetCurrentProcess()
```

## Discussion

One thing you will notice when working with some .NET classes (or classes from a third-party SDK) is that it quickly becomes tiresome to specify their fully qualified type names. For example, many useful collection classes in the .NET Framework start with Sys tem.Collections. This is called the *namespace* of that class. Most programming languages solve this problem with a using directive that lets you specify a list of namespaces for that language to search when you type a plain class name such as ArrayList. PowerShell lacks a using directive, but there are several options to get the benefits of one.

If you are repeatedly working with static methods on a specific type, you can store that type in a variable to reduce typing, as shown in the Solution:

```
$math = [System.Math]
$math::Min(1,10)
$math::Max(1,10)
```

If you are creating instances of different classes from a namespace, you can store the namespace in a variable and then use the PowerShell -f *(format)* operator to specify the unique class name:

```
$namespace = "System.Collections.{0}"
$arrayList = New-Object ($namespace -f "ArrayList")
$queue = New-Object ($namespace -f "Queue")
```

If you are working with static methods from several types in a namespace, you can store the namespace in a variable, use the -f operator to specify the unique class name, and then finally cast that into a type:

```
$namespace = "System.Diagnostics.{0}"
([Type] ($namespace -f "EventLog"))::GetEventLogs()
([Type] ($namespace -f "Process"))::GetCurrentProcess()
```

For more information about PowerShell's format operator, see Recipe 5.6, "Place Formatted Information in a String".

## See Also

Recipe 5.6, "Place Formatted Information in a String"

# 3.12. Use a COM Object

## Problem

You want to create a COM object to interact with its methods and properties.

## Solution

Use the `New-Object` cmdlet (with the `-ComObject` parameter) to create a COM object from its *ProgID*. You can then interact with the methods and properties of the COM object as you would any other object in PowerShell.

```
$object = New-Object -ComObject ProgId
```

For example:

```
PS > $sapi = New-Object -Com Sapi.SpVoice
PS > $sapi.Speak("Hello World")
```

## Discussion

Historically, many applications have exposed their scripting and administration interfaces as COM objects. While .NET APIs (and PowerShell cmdlets) are by far the most common, interacting with COM objects is still a routine administrative task.

As with classes in the .NET Framework, it is difficult to know what COM objects you can use to help you accomplish your system administration tasks. For a hand-picked list of the COM objects most useful to system administrators, see Appendix H.

For more information about the `New-Object` cmdlet, type **Get-Help New-Object**.

## See Also

Appendix H, *Selected COM Objects and Their Uses*

# 3.13. Learn About Types and Objects

## Problem

You have an instance of an object and want to know what methods and properties it supports.

## Solution

The most common way to explore the methods and properties supported by an object is through the Get-Member cmdlet.

To get the instance members of an object you've stored in the $object variable, pipe it to the Get-Member cmdlet:

```
$object | Get-Member
Get-Member -InputObject $object
```

To get the static members of an object you've stored in the $object variable, supply the -Static flag to the Get-Member cmdlet:

```
$object | Get-Member -Static
Get-Member -Static -InputObject $object
```

To get the static members of a specific type, pipe that type to the Get-Member cmdlet, and also specify the -Static flag:

```
[Type] | Get-Member -Static
Get-Member -InputObject [Type]
```

To get members of the specified member type (for example, Method or Property) from an object you have stored in the $object variable, supply that member type to the -MemberType parameter:

```
$object | Get-Member -MemberType MemberType
Get-Member -MemberType MemberType -InputObject $object
```

## Discussion

The Get-Member cmdlet is one of the three commands you will use most commonly as you explore Windows PowerShell. The other two commands are Get-Command and Get-Help.

 To interactively explore an object's methods and properties, see Recipe 1.25, "Program: Interactively View and Explore Objects".

If you pass the Get-Member cmdlet a collection of objects (such as an Array or Array List) through the pipeline, PowerShell extracts each item from the collection and then passes them to the Get-Member cmdlet one by one. The Get-Member cmdlet then returns the members of each unique type that it receives. Although helpful the vast majority of the time, this sometimes causes difficulty when you want to learn about the members or properties of the collection class itself.

If you want to see the properties of a collection (as opposed to the elements it contains), provide the collection to the -InputObject parameter instead. Alternatively, you can wrap the collection in an array (using PowerShell's *unary comma operator*) so that the collection class remains when the Get-Member cmdlet unravels the outer array:

```
PS > $files = Get-ChildItem
PS > ,$files | Get-Member

    TypeName: System.Object[]

Name          MemberType      Definition
----          ----------      ----------
Count         AliasProperty   Count = Length
Address       Method          System.Object& Address(Int32 )
(...)
```

For another way to learn detailed information about types and objects, see Recipe 3.14, "Get Detailed Documentation About Types and Objects".

For more information about the Get-Member cmdlet, type **Get-Help Get-Member**.

## See Also

Recipe 1.25, "Program: Interactively View and Explore Objects"

Recipe 3.14, "Get Detailed Documentation About Types and Objects"

# 3.14. Get Detailed Documentation About Types and Objects

## Problem

You have a type of object and want to know detailed information about the methods and properties it supports.

## Solution

The documentation for the .NET Framework [available here (*http://msdn.micro soft.com*)] is the best way to get detailed documentation about the methods and properties supported by an object. That exploration generally comes in two stages:

1. Find the type of the object.

   To determine the type of an object, you can either use the type name shown by the Get-Member cmdlet (as described in Recipe 3.13, "Learn About Types and Objects") or call the GetType() method of an object (if you have an instance of it):

```
PS > $date = Get-Date
PS > $date.GetType().ToString()
System.DateTime
```

2. Enter that type name into the search box here (*http://msdn.microsoft.com*).

## Discussion

When the Get-Member cmdlet does not provide the information you need, the MSDN documentation for a type is a great alternative. It provides much more detailed information than the help offered by the Get-Member cmdlet—usually including detailed descriptions, related information, and even code samples. MSDN documentation focuses on developers using these types through a language such as C#, though, so you may find interpreting the information for use in PowerShell to be a little difficult at first.

Typically, the documentation for a class first starts with a general overview, and then provides a hyperlink to the members of the class—the list of methods and properties it supports.

 To get to the documentation for the members quickly, search for them more explicitly by adding the term "members" to your MSDN search term: "*typename* members."

Documentation for the members of a class lists the class's methods and properties, as does the output of the Get-Member cmdlet. The S icon represents static methods and properties. Click the member name for more information about that method or property.

### Public constructors

This section lists the constructors of the type. You use a constructor when you create the type through the New-Object cmdlet. When you click on a constructor, the documentation provides all the different ways that you can create that object, including the parameter list that you will use with the New-Object cmdlet.

### Public fields/public properties

This section lists the names of the fields and properties of an object. The S icon represents a static field or property. When you click on a field or property, the documentation also provides the type returned by this field or property.

For example, you might see the following in the definition for System.DateTime.Now:

```
C#
public static DateTime Now { get; }
```

`Public` means that the `Now` property is public—that you can access it from PowerShell. `Static` means that the property is static (as described in Recipe 3.8, "Work with .NET Objects"). `DateTime` means that the property returns a `DateTime` object when you call it. `get;` means that you can get information from this property but cannot set the information. Many properties support a `set;` as well (such as the `IsReadOnly` property on `System.IO.FileInfo`), which means that you can change its value.

### Public methods

This section lists the names of the methods of an object. The S icon represents a static method. When you click on a method, the documentation provides all the different ways that you can call that method, including the parameter list that you will use to call that method in PowerShell.

For example, you might see the following in the definition for `System.DateTime.Add Days()`:

```
C#
public DateTime AddDays (
    double value
)
```

`Public` means that the `AddDays` method is public—that you can access it from Power-Shell. `DateTime` means that the method returns a `DateTime` object when you call it. The text `double value` means that this method requires a parameter (of type `double`). In this case, that parameter determines the number of days to add to the `DateTime` object on which you call the method.

## See Also

Recipe 3.8, "Work with .NET Objects"

Recipe 3.13, "Learn About Types and Objects"

# 3.15. Add Custom Methods and Properties to Objects

## Problem

You have an object and want to add your own custom properties or methods (*members*) to that object.

## Solution

Use the `Add-Member` cmdlet to add custom members to an object.

## Discussion

The `Add-Member` cmdlet is extremely useful in helping you add custom members to individual objects. For example, imagine that you want to create a report from the files in the current directory, and that report should include each file's owner. The `Owner` property is not standard on the objects that `Get-ChildItem` produces, but you could write a small script to add them, as shown in Example 3-8.

*Example 3-8. A script that adds custom properties to its output of file objects*

```
###############################################################################
##
## Get-OwnerReport
##
## From Windows PowerShell Cookbook (O'Reilly)
## by Lee Holmes (http://www.leeholmes.com/guide)
##
###############################################################################

<#

.SYNOPSIS

Gets a list of files in the current directory, but with their owner added
to the resulting objects.

.EXAMPLE

PS > Get-OwnerReport | Format-Table Name,LastWriteTime,Owner
Retrieves all files in the current directory, and displays the
Name, LastWriteTime, and Owner

#>

Set-StrictMode -Version 3

$files = Get-ChildItem
foreach($file in $files)
{
    $owner = (Get-Acl $file).Owner
    $file | Add-Member NoteProperty Owner $owner
    $file
}
```

For more information about running scripts, see Recipe 1.1, "Run Programs, Scripts, and Existing Tools".

The most common type of information to add to an object is static information in a `NoteProperty`. `Add-Member` even uses this as the default if you omit it:

```
PS > $item = Get-Item C:\
PS > $item | Add-Member VolumeName "Operating System"
PS > $item.VolumeName
Operating System
```

In addition to note properties, the `Add-Member` cmdlet supports several other property and method types, including `AliasProperty`, `ScriptProperty`, `CodeProperty`, `CodeMethod`, and `ScriptMethod`. For a more detailed description of these other property types, see "Working with the .NET Framework" (page 891), as well as the help documentation for the `Add-Member` cmdlet.

 To create entirely new objects (instead of adding information to existing ones), see Recipe 3.16, "Create and Initialize Custom Objects".

Although the `Add-Member` cmdlet lets you customize specific objects, it does not let you customize all objects of that type. For information on how to do that, see Recipe 3.17, "Add Custom Methods and Properties to Types".

### Calculated properties

*Calculated* properties are another useful way to add information to output objects. If your script or command uses a `Format-Table` or `Select-Object` command to generate its output, you can create additional properties by providing an expression that generates their value. For example:

```
Get-ChildItem |
   Select-Object Name,
        @{Name="Size (MB)"; Expression={ "{0,8:0.00}" -f ($_.Length / 1MB) } }
```

In this command, we get the list of files in the directory. We use the `Select-Object` command to retrieve its name and a calculated property called `Size (MB)`. This calculated property returns the size of the file in megabytes, rather than the default (bytes).

 The `Format-Table` cmdlet supports a similar hashtable to add calculated properties, but uses `Label` (rather than `Name`) as the key to identify the property. To eliminate the confusion this produced, version 2 of PowerShell updated the two cmdlets to accept both `Name` and `Label`.

For more information about the `Add-Member` cmdlet, type **Get-Help Add-Member**.

For more information about adding calculated properties, type **Get-Help Select-Object** or **Get-Help Format-Table**.

## See Also

Recipe 1.1, "Run Programs, Scripts, and Existing Tools"

Recipe 3.16, "Create and Initialize Custom Objects"

Recipe 3.17, "Add Custom Methods and Properties to Types"

"Working with the .NET Framework" (page 891)

# 3.16. Create and Initialize Custom Objects

## Problem

You want to return structured results from a command so that users can easily sort, group, and filter them.

## Solution

Use the [PSCustomObject] type cast to a new PSCustomObject, supplying a hashtable with the custom information as its value, as shown in Example 3-9.

*Example 3-9. Creating a custom object*

```
$output = [PSCustomObject] @{
    'User' = 'DOMAIN\User';
    'Quota' = 100MB;
    'ReportDate' = Get-Date;
}
```

If you want to create a custom object with associated functionality, place the function-ality in a module, and load that module with the -AsCustomObject parameter:

```
$obj = Import-Module PlottingObject -AsCustomObject
$obj.Move(10,10)

$obj.Points = SineWave
while($true) { $obj.Rotate(10); $obj.Draw(); Sleep -m 20 }
```

## Discussion

When your script outputs information to the user, always prefer richly structured data over hand-formatted reports. By emitting custom objects, you give the end user as much control over your script's output as PowerShell gives you over the output of its own commands.

Despite the power afforded by the output of custom objects, user-written scripts have frequently continued to generate plain-text output. This can be partly blamed on PowerShell's previously cumbersome support for the creation and initialization of custom objects, as shown in Example 3-10.

*Example 3-10. Creating a custom object in PowerShell version 1*

```
$output = New-Object PsObject
Add-Member -InputObject $output NoteProperty User 'DOMAIN\user'
Add-Member -InputObject $output NoteProperty Quota 100MB
Add-Member -InputObject $output NoteProperty ReportDate (Get-Date)

$output
```

In PowerShell version 1, creating a custom object required creating a new object (of the type PsObject), and then calling the Add-Member cmdlet multiple times to add the desired properties. PowerShell version 2 made this immensely easier by adding the -Property parameter to the New-Object cmdlet, which applied to the PSObject type as well. PowerShell version 3 made this as simple as possible by directly supporting the [PSCustomObject] type cast.

While creating a PSCustomObject makes it easy to create data-centric objects (often called *property bags*), it does not let you add functionality to those objects. When you need functionality as well, the next step is to create a module and import that module with the -AsCustomObject parameter (see Example 3-11). Any variables exported by that module become properties on the resulting object, and any functions exported by that module become methods on the resulting object.

 An important point about importing a module as a custom object is that variables defined in that custom object are shared by all versions of that object. If you import the module again as a custom object (but store the result in another variable), the two objects will share their internal state.

*Example 3-11. Creating a module designed to be used as a custom object*

```
##############################################################################
##
## PlottingObject.psm1
##
## From Windows PowerShell Cookbook (O'Reilly)
## by Lee Holmes (http://www.leeholmes.com/guide)
##
##############################################################################

<#

.SYNOPSIS
```

Demonstrates a module designed to be imported as a custom object

.EXAMPLE

```
Remove-Module PlottingObject
function SineWave { -15..15 | % { ,($_,(10 * [Math]::Sin($_ / 3))) } }
function Box { -5..5 | % { ($_,-5),($_,5),(-5,$_),(5,$_) } }

$obj = Import-Module PlottingObject -AsCustomObject
$obj.Move(10,10)

$obj.Points = SineWave
while($true) { $obj.Rotate(10); $obj.Draw(); Sleep -m 20 }

$obj.Points = Box
while($true) { $obj.Rotate(10); $obj.Draw(); Sleep -m 20 }

#>

## Declare some internal variables
$SCRIPT:x = 0
$SCRIPT:y = 0
$SCRIPT:angle = 0
$SCRIPT:xScale = -50,50
$SCRIPT:yScale = -50,50

## And a variable that we will later export
$SCRIPT:Points = @()
Export-ModuleMember -Variable Points

## A function to rotate the points by a certain amount
function Rotate($angle)
{
    $SCRIPT:angle += $angle
}
Export-ModuleMember -Function Rotate

## A function to move the points by a certain amount
function Move($xDelta, $yDelta)
{
    $SCRIPT:x += $xDelta
    $SCRIPT:y += $yDelta
}
Export-ModuleMember -Function Move

## A function to draw the given points
function Draw
{
    $degToRad = 180 * [Math]::Pi
    Clear-Host
```

```
    ## Draw the origin
    PutPixel 0 0 +

    ## Go through each of the supplied points,
    ## move them the amount specified, and then rotate them
    ## by the angle specified
    foreach($point in $points)
    {
        $pointX,$pointY = $point
        $pointX = $pointX + $SCRIPT:x
        $pointY = $pointY + $SCRIPT:y

        $newX = $pointX * [Math]::Cos($SCRIPT:angle / $degToRad ) -
            $pointY * [Math]::Sin($SCRIPT:angle / $degToRad )
        $newY = $pointY * [Math]::Cos($SCRIPT:angle / $degToRad ) +
            $pointX * [Math]::Sin($SCRIPT:angle / $degToRad )

        PutPixel $newX $newY O
    }

    [Console]::WriteLine()
}
Export-ModuleMember -Function Draw

## A helper function to draw a pixel on the screen
function PutPixel($x, $y, $character)
{
    $scaledX = ($x - $xScale[0]) / ($xScale[1] - $xScale[0])
    $scaledX *= [Console]::WindowWidth

    $scaledY = (($y * 4 / 3) - $yScale[0]) / ($yScale[1] - $yScale[0])
    $scaledY *= [Console]::WindowHeight

    try
    {
        [Console]::SetCursorPosition($scaledX,
            [Console]::WindowHeight - $scaledY)
        [Console]::Write($character)
    }
    catch
    {
        ## Take no action on error. We probably just rotated a point
        ## out of the screen boundary.
    }
}
```

For more information about creating modules, see Recipe 11.6, "Package Common Commands in a Module".

If neither of these options suits your requirements (or if you need to create an object that can be consumed by other .NET libraries), use the Add-Type cmdlet. For more information about this approach, see Recipe 17.6, "Define or Extend a .NET Class".

## See Also

Recipe 7.13, "Create a Hashtable or Associative Array"

Recipe 11.6, "Package Common Commands in a Module"

Recipe 17.6, "Define or Extend a .NET Class"

# 3.17. Add Custom Methods and Properties to Types

## Problem

You want to add your own custom properties or methods to all objects of a certain type.

## Solution

Use the `Update-TypeData` cmdlet to add custom members to all objects of a type.

```
Update-TypeData -TypeName AddressRecord `
    -MemberType AliasProperty -Membername Cell -Value Phone
```

Alternatively, use custom type extension files.

## Discussion

Although the `Add-Member` cmdlet is extremely useful in helping you add custom members to individual objects, it requires that you add the members to each object that you want to interact with. It does not let you automatically add them to all objects of that type. For that purpose, PowerShell supports another mechanism—*custom type extensions*.

The simplest and most common way to add members to all instances of a type is through the `Update-TypeData` cmdlet. This cmdlet supports aliases, notes, script methods, and more:

```
$r = [PSCustomObject] @{
    Name = "Lee";
    Phone = "555-1212";
    SSN = "123-12-1212"
}
$r.PSTypeNames.Add("AddressRecord")
Update-TypeData -TypeName AddressRecord `
    -MemberType AliasProperty -Membername Cell -Value Phone
```

Custom type extensions let you easily add your own features to any type exposed by the system. If you write code (for example, a script or function) that primarily interacts with a single type of object, then that code might be better suited as an extension to the type instead.

For example, imagine a script that returns the free disk space on a given drive. That might be helpful as a script, but instead you might find it easier to make PowerShell's PSDrive objects themselves tell you how much free space they have left.

In addition to the Update-TypeData approach, PowerShell supports type extensions through XML-based type extension files. Since type extension files are XML files, make sure that your customizations properly encode the characters that have special meaning in XML files, such as <, >, and &.

For more information about the features supported by these formatting XML files, type **Get-Help about_format.ps1xml**.

### Getting started

If you haven't done so already, the first step in creating a type extension file is to create an empty one. The best location for this is probably in the same directory as your custom profile, with the filename *Types.Custom.ps1xml*, as shown in Example 3-12.

*Example 3-12. Sample Types.Custom.ps1xml file*

```
<?xml version="1.0" encoding="utf-8" ?>
<Types>
</Types>
```

Next, add a few lines to your PowerShell profile so that PowerShell loads your type extensions during startup:

```
$typeFile = (Join-Path (Split-Path $profile) "Types.Custom.ps1xml")
Update-TypeData -PrependPath $typeFile
```

By default, PowerShell loads several type extensions from the *Types.ps1xml* file in PowerShell's installation directory. The Update-TypeData cmdlet tells PowerShell to also look in your *Types.Custom.ps1xml* file for extensions. The -PrependPath parameter makes PowerShell favor your extensions over the built-in ones in case of conflict.

Once you have a custom types file to work with, adding functionality becomes relatively straightforward. As a theme, these examples do exactly what we alluded to earlier: add functionality to PowerShell's PSDrive type.

PowerShell version 2 does this automatically. Type **Get-PSDrive** to see the result.

To support this, you need to extend your custom types file so that it defines additions to the System.Management.Automation.PSDriveInfo type, shown in Example 3-13. System.Management.Automation.PSDriveInfo is the type that the Get-PSDrive cmdlet generates.

*Example 3-13. A template for changes to a custom types file*

```xml
<?xml version="1.0" encoding="utf-8" ?>
<Types>
  <Type>
    <Name>System.Management.Automation.PSDriveInfo</Name>
    <Members>
        add members such as <ScriptProperty> here
    <Members>
  </Type>
</Types>
```

## Add a ScriptProperty

A ScriptProperty lets you add properties (that get and set information) to types, using PowerShell script as the extension language. It consists of three child elements: the Name of the property, the *getter* of the property (via the GetScriptBlock child), and the *setter* of the property (via the SetScriptBlock child).

In both the GetScriptBlock and SetScriptBlock sections, the $this variable refers to the current object being extended. In the SetScriptBlock section, the $args[0] variable represents the value that the user supplied as the righthand side of the assignment.

Example 3-14 adds an AvailableFreeSpace ScriptProperty to PSDriveInfo, and should be placed within the members section of the template given in Example 3-13. When you access the property, it returns the amount of free space remaining on the drive. When you set the property, it outputs what changes you must make to obtain that amount of free space.

*Example 3-14. A ScriptProperty for the PSDriveInfo type*

```
<ScriptProperty>
  <Name>AvailableFreeSpace</Name>
  <GetScriptBlock>
    ## Ensure that this is a FileSystem drive
    if($this.Provider.ImplementingType -eq
      [Microsoft.PowerShell.Commands.FileSystemProvider])
    {
        ## Also ensure that it is a local drive
        $driveRoot = $this.Root
        $fileZone = [System.Security.Policy.Zone]::CreateFromUrl(`
                $driveRoot).SecurityZone
        if($fileZone -eq "MyComputer")
        {
            $drive = New-Object System.IO.DriveInfo $driveRoot
            $drive.AvailableFreeSpace
        }
    }
  </GetScriptBlock>
  <SetScriptBlock>
```

```
## Get the available free space
$availableFreeSpace = $this.AvailableFreeSpace

## Find out the difference between what is available, and what they
## asked for.
$spaceDifference = ((([long] $args[0]) - $availableFreeSpace) / 1MB

## If they want more free space than they have, give that message
if($spaceDifference -gt 0)
{
    $message = "To obtain $args bytes of free space, " +
        " free $spaceDifference megabytes."
    Write-Host $message
}
## If they want less free space than they have, give that message
else
{
    $spaceDifference = $spaceDifference * -1
    $message = "To obtain $args bytes of free space, " +
        " use up $spaceDifference more megabytes."
    Write-Host $message
}
</SetScriptBlock>
</ScriptProperty>
```

## Add an AliasProperty

An `AliasProperty` gives an alternative name (alias) for a property. The referenced property does not need to exist when PowerShell processes your type extension file, since you (or another script) might later add the property through mechanisms such as the `Add-Member` cmdlet.

Example 3-15 adds a `Free AliasProperty` to `PSDriveInfo`, and it should also be placed within the members section of the template given in Example 3-13. When you access the property, it returns the value of the `AvailableFreeSpace` property. When you set the property, it sets the value of the `AvailableFreeSpace` property.

*Example 3-15. An AliasProperty for the PSDriveInfo type*

```
<AliasProperty>
  <Name>Free</Name>
  <ReferencedMemberName>AvailableFreeSpace</ReferencedMemberName>
</AliasProperty>
```

## Add a ScriptMethod

A `ScriptMethod` lets you define an action on an object, using PowerShell script as the extension language. It consists of two child elements: the `Name` of the property and the `Script`.

In the script element, the $this variable refers to the current object you are extending. Like a standalone script, the $args variable represents the arguments to the method. Unlike standalone scripts, ScriptMethods do not support the param statement for parameters.

Example 3-16 adds a Remove ScriptMethod to PSDriveInfo. Like the other additions, place these customizations within the members section of the template given in Example 3-13. When you call this method with no arguments, the method simulates removing the drive (through the -WhatIf option to Remove-PSDrive). If you call this method with $true as the first argument, it actually removes the drive from the PowerShell session.

*Example 3-16. A ScriptMethod for the PSDriveInfo type*

```
<ScriptMethod>
  <Name>Remove</Name>
  <Script>
    $force = [bool] $args[0]
    ## Remove the drive if they use $true as the first parameter
    if($force)
    {
        $this | Remove-PSDrive
    }
    ## Otherwise, simulate the drive removal
    else
    {
        $this | Remove-PSDrive -WhatIf
    }
  </Script>
</ScriptMethod>
```

### Add other extension points

PowerShell supports several additional features in the types extension file, including CodeProperty, NoteProperty, CodeMethod, and MemberSet. Although not generally useful to end users, developers of PowerShell providers and cmdlets will find these features helpful. For more information about these additional features, see the Windows PowerShell SDK or the MSDN documentation.

# 3.18. Define Custom Formatting for a Type

## Problem

You want to emit custom objects from a script and have them formatted in a specific way.

## Solution

Use a custom format extension file to define the formatting for that type, followed by a call to the `Update-FormatData` cmdlet to load them into your session:

```
$formatFile = Join-Path (Split-Path $profile) "Format.Custom.Ps1Xml"
Update-FormatData -PrependPath $typesFile
```

If a file-based approach is not an option, use the `Formats` property of the `[Run space]::DefaultRunspace.InitialSessionState` type to add new formatting definitions for the custom type.

## Discussion

When PowerShell commands produce output, this output comes in the form of richly structured objects rather than basic streams of text. These richly structured objects stop being of any use once they make it to the screen, though, so PowerShell guides them through one last stage before showing them on screen: *formatting* and *output*.

The formatting and output system is based on the concept of *views*. Views can take several forms: table views, list views, complex views, and more. The most common view type is a table view. This is the form you see when you use `Format-Table` in a command, or when an object has four or fewer properties.

As with the custom type extensions described in Recipe 3.17, "Add Custom Methods and Properties to Types", PowerShell supports both file-based and in-memory updates of type formatting definitions.

The simplest and most common way to define formatting for a type is through the `Update-FormatData` cmdlet, as shown in the Solution. The `Update-FormatData` cmdlet takes paths to *Format.ps1xml* files as input. There are many examples of formatting definitions in the PowerShell installation directory that you can use. To create your own formatting customizations, use these files as a source of examples, but do not modify them directly. Instead, create a new file and use the `Update-FormatData` cmdlet to load your customizations.

For more information about the features supported by these formatting XML files, type **Get-Help about_format.ps1xml**.

In addition to file-based formatting, PowerShell makes it possible (although not easy) to create formatting definitions from scratch. Example 3-17 provides a script to simplify this process.

*Example 3-17. Add-FormatData.ps1*

```
##############################################################################
##
## Add-FormatData
##
```

```
## From Windows PowerShell Cookbook (O'Reilly)
## by Lee Holmes (http://www.leeholmes.com/guide)
##
#############################################################################

<#

.SYNOPSIS

Adds a table formatting definition for the specified type name.

.EXAMPLE

PS > $r = [PSCustomObject] @{
    Name = "Lee";
    Phone = "555-1212";
    SSN = "123-12-1212"
}
PS > $r.PSTypeNames.Add("AddressRecord")
PS > Add-FormatData -TypeName AddressRecord -TableColumns Name, Phone
PS > $r

Name Phone
---- -----
Lee  555-1212

#>

param(
    ## The type name (or PSTypeName) that the table definition should
    ## apply to.
    $TypeName,

    ## The columns to be displayed by default
    [string[]] $TableColumns
)

Set-StrictMode -Version 3

## Define the columns within a table control row
$rowDefinition = New-Object Management.Automation.TableControlRow

## Create left-aligned columns for each provided column name
foreach($column in $TableColumns)
{
    $rowDefinition.Columns.Add(
            (New-Object Management.Automation.TableControlColumn "Left",
            (New-Object Management.Automation.DisplayEntry $column,"Property")))
}

$tableControl = New-Object Management.Automation.TableControl
$tableControl.Rows.Add($rowDefinition)
```

```
## And then assign the table control to a new format view,
## which we then add to an extended type definition. Define this view for the
## supplied custom type name.
$formatViewDefinition =
    New-Object Management.Automation.FormatViewDefinition "TableView",$tableControl
$extendedTypeDefinition =
    New-Object Management.Automation.ExtendedTypeDefinition $TypeName
$extendedTypeDefinition.FormatViewDefinition.Add($formatViewDefinition)

## Add the definition to the session, and refresh the format data
[Runspace]::DefaultRunspace.InitialSessionState.Formats.Add($extendedTypeDefinition)
Update-FormatData
```

# CHAPTER 4

# Looping and Flow Control

## 4.0. Introduction

As you begin to write scripts or commands that interact with unknown data, the concepts of looping and flow control become increasingly important.

PowerShell's looping statements and commands let you perform an operation (or set of operations) without having to repeat the commands themselves. This includes, for example, doing something a specified number of times, processing each item in a collection, or working until a certain condition comes to pass.

PowerShell's flow control and comparison statements let you adapt your script or command to unknown data. They let you execute commands based on the value of that data, skip commands based on the value of that data, and more.

Together, looping and flow control statements add significant versatility to your PowerShell toolbox.

## 4.1. Make Decisions with Comparison and Logical Operators

### Problem

You want to compare some data with other data and make a decision based on that comparison.

### Solution

Use PowerShell's logical operators to compare pieces of data and make decisions based on them.

*Comparison operators*

```
-eq, -ne, -ge, -gt, -in, -notin, -lt, -le, -like, -notlike, -match, -notmatch,
-contains, -notcontains, -is, -isnot
```

*Logical operators*

```
-and, -or, -xor, -not
```

For a detailed description (and examples) of these operators, see "Comparison Operators" (page 879).

## Discussion

PowerShell's logical and comparison operators let you compare pieces of data or test data for some condition. An operator either compares two pieces of data (a *binary* operator) or tests one piece of data (a *unary* operator). All comparison operators are binary operators (they compare two pieces of data), as are most of the logical operators. The only unary logical operator is the `-not` operator, which returns the `true/false` opposite of the data that it tests.

Comparison operators compare two pieces of data and return a result that depends on the specific comparison operator. For example, you might want to check whether a collection has at least a certain number of elements:

```
PS > (dir).Count -ge 4
True
```

or check whether a string matches a given regular expression:

```
PS > "Hello World" -match "H.*World"
True
```

Most comparison operators also adapt to the type of their input. For example, when you apply them to simple data such as a string, the `-like` and `-match` comparison operators determine whether the string matches the specified pattern. When you apply them to a collection of simple data, those same comparison operators return all elements in that collection that match the pattern you provide.

 The `-match` operator takes a regular expression as its argument. One of the more common regular expression symbols is the $ character, which represents the end of line. The $ character also represents the start of a PowerShell variable, though! To prevent PowerShell from interpreting characters as language terms or escape sequences, place the string in single quotes rather than double quotes:

```
PS > "Hello World" -match "Hello"
True
PS > "Hello World" -match 'Hello$'
False
```

By default, PowerShell's comparison operators are case-insensitive. To use the case-sensitive versions, prefix them with the character c:

```
-ceq, -cne, -cge, -cgt, -cin, -clt, -cle, -clike, -cnotlike,
-cmatch, -cnotmatch, -ccontains, -cnotcontains
```

For a detailed description of the comparison operators, their case-sensitive counterparts, and how they adapt to their input, see "Comparison Operators" (page 879).

Logical operators combine `true` or `false` statements and return a result that depends on the specific logical operator. For example, you might want to check whether a string matches the wildcard pattern you supply *and* that it is longer than a certain number of characters:

```
PS > $data = "Hello World"
PS > ($data -like "*llo W*") -and ($data.Length -gt 10)
True
PS > ($data -like "*llo W*") -and ($data.Length -gt 20)
False
```

Some of the comparison operators actually incorporate aspects of the logical operators. Since using the opposite of a comparison (such as `-like`) is so common, PowerShell provides comparison operators (such as `-notlike`) that save you from having to use the `-not` operator explicitly.

For a detailed description of the individual logical operators, see "Comparison Operators" (page 879).

Comparison operators and logical operators (when combined with flow control statements) form the core of how we write a script or command that adapts to its data and input.

See also "Conditional Statements" (page 882) for detailed information about these statements.

For more information about PowerShell's operators, type `Get-Help About_Operators`.

## See Also

"Comparison Operators" (page 879)

"Conditional Statements" (page 882)

# 4.2. Adjust Script Flow Using Conditional Statements

## Problem

You want to control the conditions under which PowerShell executes commands or portions of your script.

## Solution

Use PowerShell's `if`, `elseif`, and `else` conditional statements to control the flow of execution in your script.

For example:

```
$temperature = 90

if($temperature -le 0)
{
    "Balmy Canadian Summer"
}
elseif($temperature -le 32)
{
    "Freezing"
}
elseif($temperature -le 50)
{
    "Cold"
}
elseif($temperature -le 70)
{
    "Warm"
}
else
{
    "Hot"
}
```

## Discussion

Conditional statements include the following:

`if` *statement*
> Executes the script block that follows it if its *condition* evaluates to `true`

`elseif` *statement*
> Executes the script block that follows it if its *condition* evaluates to `true` and none of the conditions in the `if` or `elseif` statements before it evaluate to `true`

`else` *statement*
> Executes the script block that follows it if none of the conditions in the `if` or `elseif` statements before it evaluate to `true`

In addition to being useful for script control flow, conditional statements are often a useful way to assign data to a variable. PowerShell makes this very easy by letting you assign the results of a conditional statement directly to a variable:

```
$result = if(Get-Process -Name notepad) { "Running" } else { "Not running" }
```

This technique is the equivalent of a ternary operator in other programming languages, or can form the basis of one if you'd like a more compact syntax.

For more information about these flow control statements, type **Get-Help About_Flow_Control**.

# 4.3. Manage Large Conditional Statements with Switches

## Problem

You want to find an easier or more compact way to represent a large if ... elseif ... else conditional statement.

## Solution

Use PowerShell's switch statement to more easily represent a large if ... elseif ... else conditional statement.

For example:

```
$temperature = 20

switch($temperature)
{
    { $_ -lt 32 }    { "Below Freezing"; break }
    32               { "Exactly Freezing"; break }
    { $_ -le 50 }    { "Cold"; break }
    { $_ -le 70 }    { "Warm"; break }
    default          { "Hot" }
}
```

## Discussion

PowerShell's switch statement lets you easily test its input against a large number of comparisons. The switch statement supports several options that allow you to configure how PowerShell compares the input against the conditions—such as with a wildcard, regular expression, or even an arbitrary script block. Since scanning through the text in a file is such a common task, PowerShell's switch statement supports that directly. These additions make PowerShell switch statements a great deal more powerful than those in C and C++.

As another example of the switch statement in action, consider how to determine the SKU of the current operating system. For example, is the script running on Windows 7 Ultimate? Windows Server Cluster Edition? The Get-CimInstance cmdlet lets you determine the operating system SKU, but unfortunately returns its result as a simple number. A switch statement lets you map these numbers to their English equivalents based on the official documentation listed at this site (*http://bit.ly/ZfOMtC*):

```
##############################################################################
##
## Get-OperatingSystemSku
##
## From Windows PowerShell Cookbook (O'Reilly)
## by Lee Holmes (http://www.leeholmes.com/guide)
##
##############################################################################

<#

.SYNOPSIS

Gets the sku information for the current operating system

.EXAMPLE

PS > Get-OperatingSystemSku
Professional with Media Center

#>

param($Sku =
    (Get-CimInstance Win32_OperatingSystem).OperatingSystemSku)

Set-StrictMode -Version 3

switch ($Sku)
{
    0   { "An unknown product"; break; }
    1   { "Ultimate"; break; }
    2   { "Home Basic"; break; }
    3   { "Home Premium"; break; }
    4   { "Enterprise"; break; }
    5   { "Home Basic N"; break; }
    6   { "Business"; break; }
    7   { "Server Standard"; break; }
    8   { "Server Datacenter (full installation)"; break; }
    9   { "Windows Small Business Server"; break; }
    10  { "Server Enterprise (full installation)"; break; }
    11  { "Starter"; break; }
    12  { "Server Datacenter (core installation)"; break; }
    13  { "Server Standard (core installation)"; break; }
    14  { "Server Enterprise (core installation)"; break; }
    15  { "Server Enterprise for Itanium-based Systems"; break; }
    16  { "Business N"; break; }
    17  { "Web Server (full installation)"; break; }
    18  { "HPC Edition"; break; }
    19  { "Windows Storage Server 2008 R2 Essentials"; break; }
    20  { "Storage Server Express"; break; }
    21  { "Storage Server Standard"; break; }
    22  { "Storage Server Workgroup"; break; }
```

```
23  { "Storage Server Enterprise"; break; }
24  { "Windows Server 2008 for Windows Essential Server Solutions"; break; }
25  { "Small Business Server Premium"; break; }
26  { "Home Premium N"; break; }
27  { "Enterprise N"; break; }
28  { "Ultimate N"; break; }
29  { "Web Server (core installation)"; break; }
30  { "Windows Essential Business Server Management Server"; break; }
31  { "Windows Essential Business Server Security Server"; break; }
32  { "Windows Essential Business Server Messaging Server"; break; }
33  { "Server Foundation"; break; }
34  { "Windows Home Server 2011"; break; }
35  { "Windows Server 2008 without Hyper-V for Windows Essential Server
        Solutions"; break; }
36  { "Server Standard without Hyper-V"; break; }
37  { "Server Datacenter without Hyper-V (full installation)"; break; }
38  { "Server Enterprise without Hyper-V (full installation)"; break; }
39  { "Server Datacenter without Hyper-V (core installation)"; break; }
40  { "Server Standard without Hyper-V (core installation)"; break; }
41  { "Server Enterprise without Hyper-V (core installation)"; break; }
42  { "Microsoft Hyper-V Server"; break; }
43  { "Storage Server Express (core installation)"; break; }
44  { "Storage Server Standard (core installation)"; break; }
45  { "Storage Server Workgroup (core installation)"; break; }
46  { "Storage Server Enterprise (core installation)"; break; }
46  { "Storage Server Enterprise (core installation)"; break; }
47  { "Starter N"; break; }
48  { "Professional"; break; }
49  { "Professional N"; break; }
50  { "Windows Small Business Server 2011 Essentials"; break; }
51  { "Server For SB Solutions"; break; }
52  { "Server Solutions Premium"; break; }
53  { "Server Solutions Premium (core installation)"; break; }
54  { "Server For SB Solutions EM"; break; }
55  { "Server For SB Solutions EM"; break; }
56  { "Windows MultiPoint Server"; break; }
59  { "Windows Essential Server Solution Management"; break; }
60  { "Windows Essential Server Solution Additional"; break; }
61  { "Windows Essential Server Solution Management SVC"; break; }
62  { "Windows Essential Server Solution Additional SVC"; break; }
63  { "Small Business Server Premium (core installation)"; break; }
64  { "Server Hyper Core V"; break; }
72  { "Server Enterprise (evaluation installation)"; break; }
76  { "Windows MultiPoint Server Standard (full installation)"; break; }
77  { "Windows MultiPoint Server Premium (full installation)"; break; }
79  { "Server Standard (evaluation installation)"; break; }
80  { "Server Datacenter (evaluation installation)"; break; }
84  { "Enterprise N (evaluation installation)"; break; }
95  { "Storage Server Workgroup (evaluation installation)"; break; }
96  { "Storage Server Standard (evaluation installation)"; break; }
98  { "Windows 8 N"; break; }
99  { "Windows 8 China"; break; }
```

```
100 { "Windows 8 Single Language"; break; }
101 { "Windows 8"; break; }
103 { "Professional with Media Center"; break; }

default {"UNKNOWN: " + $SKU }
}
```

Although used as a way to express large conditional statements more cleanly, a `switch` statement operates much like a large sequence of `if` statements, as opposed to a large sequence of `if … elseif … elseif … else` statements. Given the input that you provide, PowerShell evaluates that input against *each* of the comparisons in the `switch` statement. If the comparison evaluates to `true`, PowerShell then executes the script block that follows it. Unless that script block contains a `break` statement, PowerShell continues to evaluate the following comparisons.

For more information about PowerShell's `switch` statement, see "Conditional Statements" (page 882) or type **Get-Help About_Switch**.

## See Also

"Conditional Statements" (page 882)

# 4.4. Repeat Operations with Loops

## Problem

You want to execute the same block of code more than once.

## Solution

Use one of PowerShell's looping statements (`for`, `foreach`, `while`, and `do`) or PowerShell's `Foreach-Object` cmdlet to run a command or script block more than once. For a detailed description of these looping statements, see "Looping Statements" (page 885). For example:

for *loop*

```
for($counter = 1; $counter -le 10; $counter++)
{
   "Loop number $counter"
}
```

foreach *loop*

```
foreach($file in dir)
{
   "File length: " + $file.Length
}
```

Foreach-Object *cmdlet*

```
Get-ChildItem | Foreach-Object { "File length: " + $_.Length }
```

while *loop*

```
$response = ""
while($response -ne "QUIT")
{
  $response = Read-Host "Type something"
}
```

do..while *loop*

```
$response = ""
do
{
  $response = Read-Host "Type something"
} while($response -ne "QUIT")
```

do..until *loop*

```
$response = ""
do
{
  $response = Read-Host "Type something"
} until($response -eq "QUIT")
```

## Discussion

Although any of the looping statements can be written to be functionally equivalent to any of the others, each lends itself to certain problems.

You usually use a for loop when you need to perform an operation an exact number of times. Because using it this way is so common, it is often called a *counted* for *loop*.

You usually use a foreach loop when you have a collection of objects and want to visit each item in that collection. If you do not yet have that entire collection in memory (as in the dir collection from the foreach example shown earlier), the Foreach-Object cmdlet is usually a more efficient alternative.

Unlike the foreach loop, the Foreach-Object cmdlet lets you process each element in the collection *as PowerShell generates it.* This is an important distinction; asking PowerShell to collect the entire output of a large command (such as Get-Content *huge file.txt*) in a foreach loop can easily drag down your system.

A handy shortcut to repeat an operation on the command line is:

```
PS > 1..10 | foreach { "Working" }
Working
Working
Working
Working
Working
Working
Working
Working
Working
Working
```

Like pipeline-oriented functions, the Foreach-Object cmdlet lets you define commands to execute before the looping begins, during the looping, and after the looping completes:

```
PS > "a","b","c" | Foreach-Object `
    -Begin { "Starting"; $counter = 0 } `
    -Process { "Processing $_"; $counter++ } `
    -End { "Finishing: $counter" }

Starting
Processing a
Processing b
Processing c
Finishing: 3
```

The while and do..while loops are similar, in that they continue to execute the loop as long as its condition evaluates to true. A while loop checks for this before running your script block, whereas a do..while loop checks the condition after running your script block. A do..until loop is exactly like a do..while loop, except that it exits when its condition returns $true, rather than when its condition returns $false.

For a detailed description of these looping statements, see "Looping Statements" (page 885) or type Get-Help About_For, Get-Help About_Foreach, Get-Help about_While, or Get-Help about_Do.

## See Also

"Looping Statements" (page 885)

# 4.5. Add a Pause or Delay

## Problem

You want to pause or delay your script or command.

---

## Solution

To pause until the user presses the Enter key, use the pause command :

```
PS > pause
Press Enter to continue...:
```

To pause until the user presses any key, use the ReadKey() method on the $host object:

```
PS > $host.UI.RawUI.ReadKey()
```

To pause a script for a given amount of time, use the Start-Sleep cmdlet:

```
PS > Start-Sleep 5
PS > Start-Sleep -Milliseconds 300
```

## Discussion

When you want to pause your script until the user presses a key or for a set amount of time, pause and Start-Sleep are the two cmdlets you are most likely to use.

 If you want to retrieve user input rather than just pause, the Read-Host cmdlet lets you read input from the user. For more information, see Recipe 13.1, "Read a Line of User Input".

In other situations, you may sometimes want to write a loop in your script that runs at a constant speed—such as once per minute or 30 times per second. That is typically a difficult task, as the commands in the loop might take up a significant amount of time, or even an inconsistent amount of time.

In the past, many computer games suffered from solving this problem incorrectly. To control their game speed, game developers added commands to slow down their game. For example, after much tweaking and fiddling, the developers might realize that the game plays correctly on a typical machine if they make the computer count to 1 million every time it updates the screen. Unfortunately, the speed of these commands (such as counting) depends heavily on the speed of the computer. Since a fast computer can count to 1 million much more quickly than a slow computer, the game ends up running much more quickly (often to the point of incomprehensibility) on faster computers!

To make your loop run at a regular speed, you can measure how long the commands in a loop take to complete, and then delay for whatever time is left, as shown in Example 4-1.

*Example 4-1. Running a loop at a constant speed*

```
$loopDelayMilliseconds = 650
while($true)
{
```

```
    $startTime = Get-Date

    ## Do commands here
    "Executing"

    $endTime = Get-Date
    $loopLength = ($endTime - $startTime).TotalMilliseconds
    $timeRemaining = $loopDelayMilliseconds - $loopLength

    if($timeRemaining -gt 0)
    {
        Start-Sleep -Milliseconds $timeRemaining
    }
}
```

For more information about the Start-Sleep cmdlet, type **Get-Help Start-Sleep**.

## See Also

Recipe 13.1, "Read a Line of User Input"

# CHAPTER 5

# Strings and Unstructured Text

## 5.0. Introduction

Creating and manipulating text has long been one of the primary tasks of scripting languages and traditional shells. In fact, Perl (the language) started as a simple (but useful) tool designed for text processing. It has grown well beyond those humble roots, but its popularity provides strong evidence of the need it fills.

In text-based shells, this strong focus continues. When most of your interaction with the system happens by manipulating the text-based output of programs, powerful text processing utilities become crucial. These text parsing tools, such as `awk`, `sed`, and `grep`, form the keystones of text-based systems management.

In PowerShell's object-based environment, this traditional tool chain plays a less critical role. You can accomplish most of the tasks that previously required these tools much more effectively through other PowerShell commands. However, being an object-based shell does not mean that PowerShell drops all support for text processing. Dealing with strings and unstructured text continues to play an important part in a system administrator's life. Since PowerShell lets you manage the majority of your system in its full fidelity (using cmdlets and objects), the text processing tools can once again focus primarily on actual text processing tasks.

## 5.1. Create a String

### Problem

You want to create a variable that holds text.

## Solution

Use PowerShell string variables as a way to store and work with text.

To define a string that supports variable expansion and escape characters in its definition, surround it with double quotes:

```
$myString = "Hello World"
```

To define a literal string (one that does not interpret variable expansion or escape characters), surround it with single quotes:

```
$myString = 'Hello World'
```

## Discussion

String literals come in two varieties: *literal* (*nonexpanding*) and *expanding* strings. To create a literal string, place single quotes ($myString = 'Hello World') around the text. To create an expanding string, place double quotes ($myString = "Hello World") around the text.

In a literal string, all the text between the single quotes becomes part of your string. In an expanding string, PowerShell expands variable names (such as $replacement String) and escape sequences (such as `n) with their values (such as the content of $replacementString and the newline character, respectively).

For a detailed explanation of the escape sequences and replacement rules inside PowerShell strings, see "Strings" (page 865).

One exception to the "all text in a literal string is literal" rule comes from the quote characters themselves. In either type of string, PowerShell lets you place two of that string's quote characters together to add the quote character itself:

```
$myString = "This string includes ""double quotes"" because it combined quote
characters."
$myString = 'This string includes ''single quotes'' because it combined quote
characters.'
```

This helps prevent escaping atrocities that would arise when you try to include a single quote in a single-quoted string. For example:

```
$myString = 'This string includes ' + "'" + 'single quotes' + "'"
```

This example shows how easy PowerShell makes it to create new strings by adding other strings together. This is an attractive way to build a formatted report in a script but should be used with caution. Because of the way that the .NET Framework (and therefore PowerShell) manages strings, adding information to the end of a large string this way causes noticeable performance problems. If you intend to create large reports, see Recipe 5.15, "Generate Large Reports and Text Streams".

## See Also

Recipe 5.15, "Generate Large Reports and Text Streams"

"Strings" (page 865)

# 5.2. Create a Multiline or Formatted String

## Problem

You want to create a variable that holds text with newlines or other explicit formatting.

## Solution

Use a PowerShell *here string* to store and work with text that includes newlines and other formatting information.

```
$myString = @"
This is the first line
of a very long string. A "here string"
lets you create blocks of text
that span several lines.
"@
```

## Discussion

PowerShell begins a here string when it sees the characters @" followed by a newline. It ends the string when it sees the characters "@ on their own line. These seemingly odd restrictions let you create strings that include quote characters, newlines, and other symbols that you commonly use when you create large blocks of preformatted text.

These restrictions, while useful, can sometimes cause problems when you copy and paste PowerShell examples from the Internet. Web pages often add spaces at the end of lines, which can interfere with the strict requirements of the beginning of a here string. If PowerShell produces an error when your script defines a here string, check that the here string does not include an errant space after its first quote character.

Like string literals, here strings may be literal (and use single quotes) or expanding (and use double quotes).

# 5.3. Place Special Characters in a String

## Problem

You want to place special characters (such as tab and newline) in a string variable.

## Solution

In an expanding string, use PowerShell's escape sequences to include special characters such as tab and newline.

```
PS > $myString = "Report for Today`n---------------"
PS > $myString
Report for Today
---------------
```

## Discussion

As discussed in Recipe 5.1, "Create a String", PowerShell strings come in two varieties: literal (or nonexpanding) and expanding strings. A literal string uses single quotes around its text, whereas an expanding string uses double quotes around its text.

In a literal string, all the text between the single quotes becomes part of your string. In an expanding string, PowerShell expands variable names (such as $ENV:SystemRoot) and escape sequences (such as `n) with their values (such as the SystemRoot environment variable and the newline character).

Unlike many languages that use a backslash character (\) for escape sequences, PowerShell uses a backtick (`) character. This stems from its focus on system administration, where backslashes are ubiquitous in pathnames.

For a detailed explanation of the escape sequences and replacement rules inside PowerShell strings, see "Strings" (page 865).

## See Also

Recipe 5.1, "Create a String"

"Strings" (page 865)

# 5.4. Insert Dynamic Information in a String

## Problem

You want to place dynamic information (such as the value of another variable) in a string.

## Solution

In an expanding string, include the name of a variable in the string to insert the value of that variable:

```
PS > $header = "Report for Today"
PS > $myString = "$header`n---------------"
PS > $myString
Report for Today
---------------
```

To include information more complex than just the value of a variable, enclose it in a subexpression:

```
PS > $header = "Report for Today"
PS > $myString = "$header`n$('-' * $header.Length)"
PS > $myString
Report for Today
---------------
```

## Discussion

Variable substitution in an expanding string is a simple enough concept, but subexpressions deserve a little clarification.

A *subexpression* is the dollar sign character, followed by a PowerShell command (or set of commands) contained in parentheses:

```
$(subexpression)
```

When PowerShell sees a subexpression in an expanding string, it evaluates the subexpression and places the result in the expanding string. In the Solution, the expression `'-' * $header.Length` tells PowerShell to make a line of dashes `$header.Length` long.

Another way to place dynamic information inside a string is to use PowerShell's string formatting operator, which uses the same rules that .NET string formatting does:

```
PS > $header = "Report for Today"
PS > $myString = "{0}`n{1}" -f $header,('-' * $header.Length)
PS > $myString
Report for Today
----------------
```

For an explanation of PowerShell's formatting operator, see Recipe 5.6, "Place Formatted Information in a String". For more information about PowerShell's escape characters, type **Get-Help About_Escape_Characters** or type **Get-Help About_Special_ Characters**.

### See Also

Recipe 5.6, "Place Formatted Information in a String"

# 5.5. Prevent a String from Including Dynamic Information

## Problem

You want to prevent PowerShell from interpreting special characters or variable names inside a string.

## Solution

Use a nonexpanding string to have PowerShell interpret your string exactly as entered. A nonexpanding string uses the single quote character around its text.

```
PS > $myString = 'Useful PowerShell characters include: $, `, " and { }'
PS > $myString
Useful PowerShell characters include: $, `, " and { }
```

If you want to include newline characters as well, use a nonexpanding *here string*, as in Example 5-1.

*Example 5-1. A nonexpanding here string that includes newline characters*

```
PS > $myString = @'
Tip of the Day
-------------
Useful PowerShell characters include: $, `, ', " and { }
'@
```

```
PS > $myString
Tip of the Day
Useful PowerShell characters include: $, `, ', " and { }
```

## Discussion

In a literal string, all the text between the single quotes becomes part of your string. This is in contrast to an expanding string, where PowerShell expands variable names (such as $myString) and escape sequences (such as `n) with their values (such as the content of $myString and the newline character).

 Nonexpanding strings are a useful way to manage files and folders containing special characters that might otherwise be interpreted as escape sequences. For more information about managing files with special characters in their name, see Recipe 20.7, "Manage Files That Include Special Characters".

As discussed in Recipe 5.1, "Create a String", one exception to the "all text in a literal string is literal" rule comes from the quote characters themselves. In either type of string, PowerShell lets you place two of that string's quote characters together to include the quote character itself:

```
$myString = "This string includes ""double quotes"" because it combined quote
characters."
$myString = 'This string includes ''single quotes'' because it combined quote
characters.'
```

## See Also

Recipe 5.1, "Create a String"

Recipe 20.7, "Manage Files That Include Special Characters"

# 5.6. Place Formatted Information in a String

## Problem

You want to place formatted information (such as right-aligned text or numbers rounded to a specific number of decimal places) in a string.

## Solution

Use PowerShell's formatting operator to place formatted information inside a string:

```
PS > $formatString = "{0,8:D4} {1:C}`n"
PS > $report = "Quantity Price`n"
PS > $report += "---------------`n"
PS > $report += $formatString -f 50,2.5677
PS > $report += $formatString -f 3,9
PS > $report
Quantity Price
---------------
    0050 $2.57
    0003 $9.00
```

## Discussion

PowerShell's string formatting operator (-f) uses the same string formatting rules as the String.Format() method in the .NET Framework. It takes a format string on its left side and the items you want to format on its right side.

In the Solution, you format two numbers: a quantity and a price. The first number ({0}) represents the quantity and is right-aligned in a box of eight characters (,8). It is formatted as a decimal number with four digits (:D4). The second number ({1}) represents the price, which you format as currency (:C).

 If you find yourself hand-crafting text-based reports, STOP! Let PowerShell's built-in commands do all the work for you. Instead, emit custom objects so that your users can work with your script as easily as they work with regular PowerShell commands. For more information, see Recipe 3.16, "Create and Initialize Custom Objects".

For a detailed explanation of PowerShell's formatting operator, see "Simple Operators" (page 873). For a detailed list of the formatting rules, see Appendix D.

Although primarily used to control the layout of information, the string-formatting operator is also a readable replacement for what is normally accomplished with string concatenation:

```
PS > $number1 = 10
PS > $number2 = 32
PS > "$number2 divided by $number1 is " + $number2 / $number1
32 divided by 10 is 3.2
```

The string formatting operator makes this much easier to read:

```
PS > "{0} divided by {1} is {2}" -f $number2, $number1, ($number2 / $number1)
32 divided by 10 is 3.2
```

If you want to support named replacements (rather than index-based replacements), you can use the Format-String script given in Recipe 5.16, "Generate Source Code and Other Repetitive Text".

In addition to the string formatting operator, PowerShell provides three formatting commands (`Format-Table`, `Format-Wide`, and `Format-List`) that let you easily generate formatted reports. For detailed information about those cmdlets, see "Custom Formatting Files" (page 913).

## See Also

Recipe 3.16, "Create and Initialize Custom Objects"

"Simple Operators" (page 873)

"Custom Formatting Files" (page 913)

Appendix D, *.NET String Formatting*

# 5.7. Search a String for Text or a Pattern

## Problem

You want to determine whether a string contains another string, or you want to find the position of a string within another string.

## Solution

PowerShell provides several options to help you search a string for text.

Use the `-like` operator to determine whether a string matches a given DOS-like wildcard:

```
PS > "Hello World" -like "*llo W*"
True
```

Use the `-match` operator to determine whether a string matches a given regular expression:

```
PS > "Hello World" -match '.*l[l-z]o W.*$'
True
```

Use the `Contains()` method to determine whether a string contains a specific string:

```
PS > "Hello World".Contains("World")
True
```

Use the `IndexOf()` method to determine the location of one string within another:

```
PS > "Hello World".IndexOf("World")
6
```

## Discussion

Since PowerShell strings are fully featured .NET objects, they support many string-oriented operations directly. The `Contains()` and `IndexOf()` methods are two examples of the many features that the `String` class supports. To learn what other functionality the `String` class supports, see Recipe 3.13, "Learn About Types and Objects".

 To search entire files for text or a pattern, see Recipe 9.2, "Search a File for Text or a Pattern".

Although they use similar characters, simple wildcards and regular expressions serve significantly different purposes. Wildcards are much simpler than regular expressions, and because of that, more constrained. While you can summarize the rules for wildcards in just four bullet points, entire books have been written to help teach and illuminate the use of regular expressions.

 A common use of regular expressions is to search for a string that spans multiple lines. By default, regular expressions do not search across lines, but you can use the *singleline* (`?s`) option to instruct them to do so:

```
PS > "Hello `n World" -match "Hello.*World"
False
PS > "Hello `n World" -match "(?s)Hello.*World"
True
```

Wildcards lend themselves to simple text searches, whereas regular expressions lend themselves to more complex text searches.

For a detailed description of the `-like` operator, see "Comparison Operators" (page 879). For a detailed description of the `-match` operator, see "Simple Operators" (page 873). For a detailed list of the regular expression rules and syntax, see Appendix B.

One difficulty sometimes arises when you try to store the result of a PowerShell command in a string, as shown in Example 5-2.

*Example 5-2. Attempting to store output of a PowerShell command in a string*

```
PS > Get-Help Get-ChildItem

NAME
    Get-ChildItem

SYNOPSIS
    Gets the items and child items in one or more specified locations.
```

(...)

```
PS > $helpContent = Get-Help Get-ChildItem
PS > $helpContent -match "location"
False
```

The -match operator searches a string for the pattern you specify but seems to fail in this case. This is because all PowerShell commands generate objects. If you don't store that output in another variable or pass it to another command, PowerShell converts the output to a text representation before it displays it to you. In Example 5-2, $helpCon tent is a fully featured object, not just its string representation:

```
PS > $helpContent.Name
Get-ChildItem
```

To work with the text-based representation of a PowerShell command, you can explicitly send it through the Out-String cmdlet. The Out-String cmdlet converts its input into the text-based form you are used to seeing on the screen:

```
PS > $helpContent = Get-Help Get-ChildItem | Out-String -Stream
PS > $helpContent -match "location"
True
```

For a script that makes searching textual command output easier, see Recipe 1.23, "Program: Search Formatted Output for a Pattern".

## See Also

Recipe 1.23, "Program: Search Formatted Output for a Pattern"

Recipe 3.13, "Learn About Types and Objects"

"Simple Operators" (page 873)

"Comparison Operators" (page 879)

Appendix B, *Regular Expression Reference*

# 5.8. Replace Text in a String

## Problem

You want to replace a portion of a string with another string.

## Solution

PowerShell provides several options to help you replace text in a string with other text.

Use the Replace() method on the string itself to perform simple replacements:

```
PS > "Hello World".Replace("World", "PowerShell")
Hello PowerShell
```

Use PowerShell's regular expression -replace operator to perform more advanced regular expression replacements:

```
PS > "Hello World" -replace '(.*) (.*)','$2 $1'
World Hello
```

## Discussion

The Replace() method and the -replace operator both provide useful ways to replace text in a string. The Replace() method is the quickest but also the most constrained. It replaces every occurrence of the exact string you specify with the exact replacement string that you provide. The -replace operator provides much more flexibility because its arguments are regular expressions that can match and replace complex patterns.

Given the power of the regular expressions it uses, the -replace operator carries with it some pitfalls of regular expressions as well.

First, the regular expressions that you use with the -replace operator often contain characters (such as the dollar sign, which represents a group number) that PowerShell normally interprets as variable names or escape characters. To prevent PowerShell from interpreting these characters, use a nonexpanding string (single quotes) as shown in the Solution.

Another, less common pitfall is wanting to use characters that have special meaning to regular expressions as part of your replacement text. For example:

```
PS > "Power[Shell]" -replace "[Shell]","ful"
Powfulr[fulfulfulfulful]
```

That's clearly not what we intended. In regular expressions, square brackets around a set of characters means "match any of the characters inside of the square brackets." In our example, this translates to "Replace the characters S, h, e, and l with 'ful.'"

To avoid this, we can use the regular expression escape character to escape the square brackets:

```
PS > "Power[Shell]" -replace "\[Shell\]","ful"
Powerful
```

However, this means knowing all of the regular expression special characters and modifying the input string. Sometimes we don't control that, so the [Regex]::Escape() method comes in handy:

```
PS > "Power[Shell]" -replace ([Regex]::Escape("[Shell]")),"ful"
Powerful
```

For extremely advanced regular expression replacement needs, you can use a script block to accomplish your replacement tasks, as described in Recipe 32.6, "Use a Script Block as a .NET Delegate or Event Handler". For example, to capitalize the first character (\w) after a word boundary (\b):

```
PS > [Regex]::Replace("hello world", '\b(\w)', { $args[0].Value.ToUpper() })
Hello World
```

For more information about the -replace operator, see "Simple Operators" (page 873) and Appendix B.

## See Also

"Simple Operators" (page 873)

Appendix B, *Regular Expression Reference*

# 5.9. Split a String on Text or a Pattern

## Problem

You want to split a string based on some literal text or a regular expression pattern.

## Solution

Use PowerShell's -split operator to split on a sequence of characters or specific string:

```
PS > "a-b-c-d-e-f" -split "-c-"
a-b
d-e-f
```

To split on a pattern, supply a regular expression as the first argument:

```
PS > "a-b-c-d-e-f" -split "b|[d-e]"
a-
-c-

-f
```

## Discussion

To split a string, many beginning scripters already comfortable with C# use the String.Split() and [Regex]::Split() methods from the .NET Framework. While still available in PowerShell, PowerShell's -split operator provides a more natural way to split a string into smaller strings. When used with no arguments (the *unary* split operator), it splits a string on whitespace characters, as in Example 5-3.

*Example 5-3. PowerShell's unary split operator*

```
PS > -split "Hello World `t How `n are you?"
Hello
World
How
are
you?
```

When used with an argument, it treats the argument as a regular expression and then splits based on that pattern.

```
PS > "a-b-c-d-e-f" -split 'b|[d-e]'
a-
-c-
-
-f
```

If the replacement pattern avoids characters that have special meaning in a regular expression, you can use it to split a string based on another string.

```
PS > "a-b-c-d-e-f" -split '-c-'
a-b
d-e-f
```

If the replacement pattern has characters that have special meaning in a regular expression (such as the . character, which represents "any character"), use the -split operator's SimpleMatch option, as in Example 5-4.

*Example 5-4. PowerShell's SimpleMatch split option*

```
PS > "a.b.c" -split '.'
(A bunch of newlines. Something went wrong!)




PS > "a.b.c" -split '.',0,"SimpleMatch"
a
b
c
```

For more information about the -split operator's options, type **Get-Help about_split**.

While regular expressions offer an enormous amount of flexibility, the -split operator gives you ultimate flexibility by letting you supply a script block for a split operation. For each character, it invokes the script block and splits the string based on the result. In the script block, $_ (or $PSItem) represents the current character. For example, Example 5-5 splits a string on even numbers.

---

*Example 5-5. Using a script block to split a string*

```
PS > "1234567890" -split { ($_ % 2) -eq 0 }
1
3
5
7
9
```

When you're using a script block to split a string, $_ represents the current character. For arguments, $args[0] represents the entire string, and $args[1] represents the index of the string currently being examined.

To split an entire file by a pattern, use the -Delimiter parameter of the Get-Content cmdlet:

```
PS > Get-Content test.txt
Hello
World
PS > (Get-Content test.txt)[0]
Hello
PS > Get-Content test.txt -Delimiter l
Hel
l
o
Worl
d
PS > (Get-Content test.txt -Delimiter l)[0]
Hel
PS > (Get-Content test.txt -Delimiter l)[1]
l
PS > (Get-Content test.txt -Delimiter l)[2]
o
Worl
PS > (Get-Content test.txt -Delimiter l)[3]
d
```

For more information about the -split operator, see "Simple Operators" (page 873) or type Get-Help about_split.

## See Also

"Simple Operators" (page 873)

Appendix B, *Regular Expression Reference*

# 5.10. Combine Strings into a Larger String

## Problem

You want to combine several separate strings into a single string.

## Solution

Use PowerShell's *unary* -join operator to combine separate strings into a larger string using the default empty separator:

```
PS > -join ("A","B","C")
ABC
```

If you want to define the operator that PowerShell uses to combine the strings, use PowerShell's *binary* -join operator:

```
PS > ("A","B","C") -join "`r`n"
A
B
C
```

## Discussion

In PowerShell version 1, the [String]::Join() method was the primary option available for joining strings. While these methods are still available in PowerShell, the -join operator provides a more natural way to combine strings. When used with no arguments (the *unary* join operator), it joins the list using the default empty separator. When used between a list and a separator (the *binary* join operator), it joins the strings using the provided separator.

Aside from its performance benefit, the -join operator solves an extremely common difficulty that arises from trying to combine strings by hand.

When first writing the code to join a list with a separator (for example, a comma and a space), you usually end up leaving a lonely separator at the beginning or end of the output:

```
PS > $list = "Hello","World"
PS > $output = ""
PS >
PS > foreach($item in $list)
{
    $output += $item + ", "
}

PS > $output
Hello, World,
```

You can resolve this by adding some extra logic to the foreach loop:

```
PS > $list = "Hello","World"
PS > $output = ""
PS >
PS > foreach($item in $list)
{
    if($output -ne "") { $output += ", " }
    $output += $item
}

PS > $output
Hello, World
```

Or, save yourself the trouble and use the -join operator directly:

```
PS > $list = "Hello","World"
PS > $list -join ", "
Hello, World
```

For a more structured way to join strings into larger strings or reports, see Recipe 5.6, "Place Formatted Information in a String".

### See Also

Recipe 5.6, "Place Formatted Information in a String"

# 5.11. Convert a String to Uppercase or Lowercase

## Problem

You want to convert a string to uppercase or lowercase.

## Solution

Use the ToUpper() or ToLower() methods of the string to convert it to uppercase or lowercase, respectively.

To convert a string to uppercase, use the ToUpper() method:

```
PS > "Hello World".ToUpper()
HELLO WORLD
```

To convert a string to lowercase, use the ToLower() method:

```
PS > "Hello World".ToLower()
hello world
```

## Discussion

Since PowerShell strings are fully featured .NET objects, they support many string-oriented operations directly. The `ToUpper()` and `ToLower()` methods are two examples of the many features that the `String` class supports. To learn what other functionality the `String` class supports, see Recipe 3.13, "Learn About Types and Objects".

Neither PowerShell nor the methods of the .NET `String` class directly support capitalizing only the first letter of a word. If you want to capitalize only the first character of a word or sentence, try the following commands:

```
PS > $text = "hello"
PS > $newText = $text.Substring(0,1).ToUpper() +
    $text.Substring(1)
$newText

Hello
```

You can also use an advanced regular expression replacement, as described in Recipe 32.6, "Use a Script Block as a .NET Delegate or Event Handler":

```
[Regex]::Replace("hello world", '\b(\w)', { $args[0].Value.ToUpper() })
```

One thing to keep in mind as you convert a string to uppercase or lowercase is your motivation for doing it. One of the most common reasons is for comparing strings, as shown in Example 5-6.

*Example 5-6. Using the ToUpper() method to normalize strings*

```
## $text comes from the user, and contains the value "quit"
if($text.ToUpper() -eq "QUIT") { ... }
```

Unfortunately, explicitly changing the capitalization of strings fails in subtle ways when your script runs in different cultures. Many cultures follow different capitalization and comparison rules than you may be used to. For example, the Turkish language includes two types of the letter *I*: one with a dot and one without. The uppercase version of the lowercase letter *i* corresponds to the version of the capital *I* with a dot, not the capital *I* used in `QUIT`. Those capitalization rules cause the string comparison code in Example 5-6 to fail in the Turkish culture.

Recipe 13.8, "Program: Invoke a Script Block with Alternate Culture Settings" shows us this quite clearly:

```
PS > Use-Culture tr-TR { "quit".ToUpper() -eq "QUIT" }
False
PS > Use-Culture tr-TR { "quIt".ToUpper() -eq "QUIT" }
True
PS > Use-Culture tr-TR { "quit".ToUpper() }
QUİT
```

For comparing some input against a hardcoded string in a case-insensitive manner, the better solution is to use PowerShell's -eq operator without changing any of the casing yourself. The -eq operator is case-insensitive and culture-neutral by default:

```
PS > $text1 = "Hello"
PS > $text2 = "HELLO"
PS > $text1 -eq $text2
True

PS > Use-Culture tr-TR { "quit" -eq "QUIT" }
True
```

For more information about writing culture-aware scripts, see Recipe 13.6, "Write Culture-Aware Scripts".

## See Also

Recipe 3.13, "Learn About Types and Objects"

Recipe 13.6, "Write Culture-Aware Scripts"

Recipe 32.6, "Use a Script Block as a .NET Delegate or Event Handler"

# 5.12. Trim a String

## Problem

You want to remove leading or trailing spaces from a string or user input.

## Solution

Use the Trim() method of the string to remove all leading and trailing whitespace characters from that string.

```
PS > $text = " `t Test String`t `t"
PS > "|" + $text.Trim() + "|"
|Test String|
```

## Discussion

The Trim() method cleans all whitespace from the beginning *and* end of a string. If you want just one or the other, you can call the TrimStart() or TrimEnd() method to remove whitespace from the beginning or the end of the string, respectively. If you want to remove specific characters from the beginning or end of a string, the Trim(), Trim Start(), and TrimEnd() methods provide options to support that. To trim a list of specific characters from the end of a string, provide that list to the method, as shown in Example 5-7.

*Example 5-7. Trimming a list of characters from the end of a string*

```
PS > "Hello World".TrimEnd('d','l','r','o','W',' ')
He
```

 At first blush, the following command that attempts to trim the text "World" from the end of a string appears to work incorrectly:

```
PS > "Hello World".TrimEnd(" World")
He
```

This happens because the TrimEnd() method takes a list of characters to remove from the end of a string. PowerShell automatically converts a string to a list of characters if required, and in this case converts your string to the characters W, o, r, l, d, and a space. These are in fact the same characters as were used in Example 5-7, so it has the same effect.

If you want to replace text anywhere in a string (and not just from the beginning or end), see Recipe 5.8, "Replace Text in a String".

## See Also

Recipe 5.8, "Replace Text in a String"

# 5.13. Format a Date for Output

## Problem

You want to control the way that PowerShell displays or formats a date.

## Solution

To control the format of a date, use one of the following options:

- The Get-Date cmdlet's -Format parameter:

```
PS > Get-Date -Date "05/09/1998 1:23 PM" -Format "dd-MM-yyyy @ hh:mm:ss"
09-05-1998 @ 01:23:00
```

- PowerShell's string formatting (-f) operator:

```
PS > $date = [DateTime] "05/09/1998 1:23 PM"
PS > "{0:dd-MM-yyyy @ hh:mm:ss}" -f $date
09-05-1998 @ 01:23:00
```

- The object's ToString() method:

```
PS > $date = [DateTime] "05/09/1998 1:23 PM"
PS > $date.ToString("dd-MM-yyyy @ hh:mm:ss")
09-05-1998 @ 01:23:00
```

- The `Get-Date` cmdlet's `-UFormat` parameter, which supports Unix date format strings:

```
PS > Get-Date -Date "05/09/1998 1:23 PM" -UFormat "%d-%m-%Y @ %I:%M:%S"
09-05-1998 @ 01:23:00
```

## Discussion

Except for the `-UFormat` parameter of the `Get-Date` cmdlet, all date formatting in PowerShell uses the standard .NET `DateTime` format strings. These format strings enable you to display dates in one of many standard formats (such as your system's short or long date patterns), or in a completely custom manner. For more information on how to specify standard .NET `DateTime` format strings, see Appendix E.

If you are already used to the Unix-style date formatting strings (or are converting an existing script that uses a complex one), the `-UFormat` parameter of the `Get-Date` cmdlet may be helpful. It accepts the format strings accepted by the Unix `date` command, but does not provide any functionality that standard .NET date formatting strings cannot.

When working with the string version of dates and times, be aware that they are the most common source of *internationalization* issues—problems that arise from running a script on a machine with a different culture than the one it was written on. In North America, "05/09/1998" means "May 9, 1998." In many other cultures, though, it means "September 5, 1998." Whenever possible, use and compare `DateTime` objects (rather than strings) to other `DateTime` objects, as that avoids these cultural differences. Example 5-8 demonstrates this approach.

*Example 5-8. Comparing DateTime objects with the -gt operator*

```
PS > $dueDate = [DateTime] "01/01/2006"
PS > if([DateTime]::Now -gt $dueDate)
{
    "Account is now due"
}

Account is now due
```

 PowerShell *always* assumes the North American date format when it interprets a `DateTime` constant such as `[DateTime] "05/09/1998"`. This is for the same reason that all languages interpret numeric constants (such as `12.34`) in the North American format. If it did otherwise, nearly every script that dealt with dates and times would fail on international systems.

For more information about the Get-Date cmdlet, type **Get-Help Get-Date**. For more information about dealing with dates and times in a culture-aware manner, see Recipe 13.6, "Write Culture-Aware Scripts".

## See Also

Recipe 13.6, "Write Culture-Aware Scripts"

Appendix E, *.NET DateTime Formatting*

# 5.14. Program: Convert Text Streams to Objects

One of the strongest features of PowerShell is its object-based pipeline. You don't waste your energy creating, destroying, and recreating the object representation of your data. In other shells, you lose the full-fidelity representation of data when the pipeline converts it to pure text. You can regain some of it through excessive text parsing, but not all of it.

However, you still often have to interact with low-fidelity input that originates from outside PowerShell. Text-based data files and legacy programs are two examples.

PowerShell offers great support for two of the three text-parsing staples:

*Sed*
> Replaces text. For that functionality, PowerShell offers the -replace operator.

*Grep*
> Searches text. For that functionality, PowerShell offers the Select-String cmdlet, among others.

The third traditional text-parsing tool, *Awk*, lets you chop a line of text into more intuitive groupings. PowerShell offers the -split operator for strings, but that lacks some of the power you usually need to break a string into groups.

The Convert-TextObject script presented in Example 5-9 lets you convert text streams into a set of objects that represent those text elements according to the rules you specify. From there, you can use all of PowerShell's object-based tools, which gives you even more power than you would get with the text-based equivalents.

*Example 5-9. Convert-TextObject.ps1*

```
###############################################################################
##
## Convert-TextObject
##
## From Windows PowerShell Cookbook (O'Reilly)
## by Lee Holmes (http://www.leeholmes.com/guide)
##
###############################################################################
```

```
<#

.SYNOPSIS

Convert a simple string into a custom PowerShell object.

.EXAMPLE

PS > "Hello World" | Convert-TextObject
Generates an Object with "P1=Hello" and "P2=World"

.EXAMPLE

PS > "Hello World" | Convert-TextObject -Delimiter "ll"
Generates an Object with "P1=He" and "P2=o World"

.EXAMPLE

PS > "Hello World" | Convert-TextObject -Pattern "He(ll.*o)r(ld)"
Generates an Object with "P1=llo Wo" and "P2=ld"

.EXAMPLE

PS > "Hello World" | Convert-TextObject -PropertyName FirstWord,SecondWord
Generates an Object with "FirstWord=Hello" and "SecondWord=World

.EXAMPLE

PS > "123 456" | Convert-TextObject -PropertyType $([string],[int])
Generates an Object with "Property1=123" and "Property2=456"
The second property is an integer, as opposed to a string

.EXAMPLE

PS > $ipAddress = (ipconfig | Convert-TextObject -Delim ": ")[2].P2
PS > $ipAddress
192.168.1.104

#>

[CmdletBinding(DefaultParameterSetName = "ByDelimiter")]
param(
    ## If specified, gives the .NET regular expression with which to
    ## split the string. The script generates properties for the
    ## resulting object out of the elements resulting from this split.
    ## If not specified, defaults to splitting on the maximum amount
    ## of whitespace: "\s+", as long as Pattern is not
    ## specified either.
    [Parameter(ParameterSetName = "ByDelimiter", Position = 0)]
    [string] $Delimiter = "\s+",
```

```
## If specified, gives the .NET regular expression with which to
## parse the string. The script generates properties for the
## resulting object out of the groups captured by this regular
## expression.
[Parameter(Mandatory = $true,
    ParameterSetName = "ByPattern",
    Position = 0)]
[string] $Pattern,

## If specified, the script will pair the names from this object
## definition with the elements from the parsed string.  If not
## specified (or the generated object contains more properties
## than you specify,) the script uses property names in the
## pattern of P1,P2,...,PN
[Parameter(Position = 1)]
[Alias("PN")]
[string[]] $PropertyName = @(),

## If specified, the script will pair the types from this list with
## the properties from the parsed string.  If not specified (or the
## generated object contains more properties than you specify,) the
## script sets the properties to be of type [string]
[Parameter(Position = 2)]
[Alias("PT")]
[type[]] $PropertyType = @(),

## The input object to process
[Parameter(ValueFromPipeline = $true)]
[string] $InputObject
)

begin {
    Set-StrictMode -Version 3
}

process {
    $returnObject = New-Object PSObject

    $matches = $null
    $matchCount = 0

    if($PSBoundParameters["Pattern"])
    {
        ## Verify that the input contains the pattern
        ## Populates the matches variable by default
        if(-not ($InputObject -match $pattern))
        {
            return
        }

        $matchCount = $matches.Count
```

```
    $startIndex = 1
}
else
{
    ## Verify that the input contains the delimiter
    if(-not ($InputObject -match $delimiter))
    {
        return
    }

    ## If so, split the input on that delimiter
    $matches = $InputObject -split $delimiter
    $matchCount = $matches.Length
    $startIndex = 0
}

## Go through all of the matches, and add them as notes to the output
## object.
for($counter = $startIndex; $counter -lt $matchCount; $counter++)
{
    $currentPropertyName = "P$($counter - $startIndex + 1)"
    $currentPropertyType = [string]

    ## Get the property name
    if($counter -lt $propertyName.Length)
    {
        if($propertyName[$counter])
        {
            $currentPropertyName = $propertyName[$counter - 1]
        }
    }

    ## Get the property value
    if($counter -lt $propertyType.Length)
    {
        if($propertyType[$counter])
        {
            $currentPropertyType = $propertyType[$counter - 1]
        }
    }

    Add-Member -InputObject $returnObject NoteProperty `
        -Name $currentPropertyName `
        -Value ($matches[$counter].Trim() -as $currentPropertyType)
}

$returnObject
}
```

## See Also

Recipe 1.1, "Run Programs, Scripts, and Existing Tools"

---

# 5.15. Generate Large Reports and Text Streams

## Problem

You want to write a script that generates a large report or large amount of data.

## Solution

The best approach to generating a large amount of data is to take advantage of PowerShell's streaming behavior whenever possible. Opt for solutions that pipeline data between commands:

```
Get-ChildItem C:\*.txt -Recurse | Out-File c:\temp\AllTextFiles.txt
```

rather than collect the output at each stage:

```
$files = Get-ChildItem C:\*.txt -Recurse
$files | Out-File c:\temp\AllTextFiles.txt
```

If your script generates a large text report (and streaming is not an option), use the `StringBuilder` class:

```
$output = New-Object System.Text.StringBuilder
Get-ChildItem C:\*.txt -Recurse |
    Foreach-Object { [void] $output.AppendLine($_.FullName) }
$output.ToString()
```

rather than simple text concatenation:

```
$output = ""
Get-ChildItem C:\*.txt -Recurse | Foreach-Object { $output += $_.FullName }
$output
```

## Discussion

In PowerShell, combining commands in a pipeline is a fundamental concept. As scripts and cmdlets generate output, PowerShell passes that output to the next command in the pipeline as soon as it can. In the Solution, the `Get-ChildItem` commands that retrieve all text files on the *C:* drive take a very long time to complete. However, since they *begin* to generate data almost immediately, PowerShell can pass that data on to the next command as soon as the `Get-ChildItem` cmdlet produces it. This is true of any commands that generate or consume data and is called *streaming*. The pipeline completes almost as soon as the `Get-ChildItem` cmdlet finishes producing its data and uses memory very efficiently as it does so.

The second Get-ChildItem example (which collects its data) prevents PowerShell from taking advantage of this streaming opportunity. It first stores all the files in an array, which, because of the amount of data, takes a long time and an enormous amount of memory. Then, it sends all those objects into the output file, which takes a long time as well.

However, most commands can consume data produced by the pipeline directly, as illustrated by the Out-File cmdlet. For those commands, PowerShell provides streaming behavior as long as you combine the commands into a pipeline. For commands that do not support data coming from the pipeline directly, the Foreach-Object cmdlet (with the aliases of foreach and %) lets you work with each piece of data as the previous command produces it, as shown in the StringBuilder example.

### Creating large text reports

When you generate large reports, it is common to store the entire report into a string, and then write that string out to a file once the script completes. You can usually accomplish this most effectively by streaming the text directly to its destination (a file or the screen), but sometimes this is not possible.

Since PowerShell makes it so easy to add more text to the end of a string (as in $out put += $_.FullName), many initially opt for that approach. This works great for small-to-medium strings, but it causes significant performance problems for large strings.

 As an example of this performance difference, compare the following:

```
PS > Measure-Command {
    $output = New-Object Text.StringBuilder
    1..10000 |
        Foreach-Object { $output.Append("Hello World") }
}

(...)
TotalSeconds : 2.3471592

PS > Measure-Command {
    $output = ""
    1..10000 | Foreach-Object { $output += "Hello World" }
}

(...)
TotalSeconds    : 4.9884882
```

In the .NET Framework (and therefore PowerShell), strings never change after you create them. When you add more text to the end of a string, PowerShell has to build a *new* string by combining the two smaller strings. This operation takes a long time for large strings, which is why the .NET Framework includes the System.Text.String Builder class. Unlike normal strings, the StringBuilder class assumes that you will modify its data—an assumption that allows it to adapt to change much more efficiently.

# 5.16. Generate Source Code and Other Repetitive Text

## Problem

You want to simplify the creation of large amounts of repetitive source code or other text.

## Solution

Use PowerShell's string formatting operator (-f) to place dynamic information inside of a preformatted string, and then repeat that replacement for each piece of dynamic information.

## Discussion

Code generation is a useful technique in nearly any technology that produces output from some text-based input. For example, imagine having to create an HTML report to show all of the processes running on your system at that time. In this case, "code" is the HTML code understood by a web browser.

HTML pages start with some standard text (<html>, <head>, <body>), and then you would likely include the processes in an HTML <table>. Each row would include columns for each of the properties in the process you're working with.

Generating this by hand would be mind-numbing and error-prone. Instead, you can write a function to generate the code for the row:

```
function Get-HtmlRow($process)
{
    $template = "<TR> <TD>{0}</TD> <TD>{1}</TD> </TR>"
    $template -f $process.Name,$process.ID
}
```

and then generate the report in milliseconds, rather than hours:

```
"<HTML><BODY><TABLE>" > report.html
Get-Process | Foreach-Object { Get-HtmlRow $_ } >> report.html
"</TABLE></BODY></HTML>" >> report.html
Invoke-Item .\report.html
```

In addition to the formatting operator, you can sometimes use the String.Replace method:

```
$string = @'
Name is __NAME__
Id is __ID__
'@

$string = $string.Replace("__NAME__", $process.Name)
$string = $string.Replace("__ID__", $process.Id)
```

This works well (and is very readable) if you have tight control over the data you'll be using as replacement text. If it is at all possible for the replacement text to contain one of the special tags (__NAME__ or __ID__, for example), then they will *also* get replaced by further replacements and corrupt your final output.

To avoid this issue, you can use the Format-String script shown in Example 5-10.

*Example 5-10. Format-String.ps1*

```
###########################################################################
##
## Format-String
##
## From Windows PowerShell Cookbook (O'Reilly)
## by Lee Holmes (http://www.leeholmes.com/guide)
##
###########################################################################

<#

.SYNOPSIS

Replaces text in a string based on named replacement tags

.EXAMPLE

PS > Format-String "Hello {NAME}" @{ NAME = 'PowerShell' }
Hello PowerShell

.EXAMPLE

PS > Format-String "Your score is {SCORE:P}" @{ SCORE = 0.85 }
Your score is 85.00 %

#>

param(
    ## The string to format. Any portions in the form of {NAME}
    ## will be automatically replaced by the corresponding value
    ## from  the supplied hashtable.
    $String,

    ## The named replacements to use in the string
    [hashtable] $Replacements
)
```

```
Set-StrictMode -Version 3

$currentIndex = 0
$replacementList = @()

if($String -match "{{|}}")
{
    throw "Escaping of replacement terms are not supported."
}

## Go through each key in the hashtable
foreach($key in $replacements.Keys)
{
    ## Convert the key into a number, so that it can be used by
    ## String.Format
    $inputPattern = '{(.*)' + $key + '(.*)}'
    $replacementPattern = '{${1}' + $currentIndex + '${2}}'
    $string = $string -replace $inputPattern,$replacementPattern
    $replacementList += $replacements[$key]

    $currentIndex++
}

## Now use String.Format to replace the numbers in the
## format string.
$string -f $replacementList
```

PowerShell includes several commands for code generation that you've probably used without recognizing their "code generation" aspect. The ConvertTo-Html cmdlet applies code generation of incoming objects to HTML reports. The ConvertTo-Csv cmdlet applies code generation to CSV files. The ConvertTo-Xml cmdlet applies code generation to XML files.

Code generation techniques seem to come up naturally when you realize you are writing a report, but they are often missed when writing source code of another programming or scripting language. For example, imagine you need to write a C# function that outputs all of the details of a process. The System.Diagnostics.Process class has a lot of properties, so that's going to be a long function. Writing it by hand is going to be difficult, so you can have PowerShell do most of it for you.

For any object (for example, a process that you've retrieved from the Get-Process command), you can access its PsObject.Properties property to get a list of all of its properties. Each of those has a Name property, so you can use that to generate the C# code:

```
$process.PsObject.Properties |
    Foreach-Object {
        'Console.WriteLine("{0}: " + process.{0});' -f $_.Name }
```

This generates more than 60 lines of C# source code, rather than having you do it by hand:

```
Console.WriteLine("Name: " + process.Name);
Console.WriteLine("Handles: " + process.Handles);
Console.WriteLine("VM: " + process.VM);
Console.WriteLine("WS: " + process.WS);
Console.WriteLine("PM: " + process.PM);
Console.WriteLine("NPM: " + process.NPM);
Console.WriteLine("Path: " + process.Path);
Console.WriteLine("Company: " + process.Company);
Console.WriteLine("CPU: " + process.CPU);
Console.WriteLine("FileVersion: " + process.FileVersion);
Console.WriteLine("ProductVersion: " + process.ProductVersion);
(...)
```

Similar benefits come from generating bulk SQL statements, repetitive data structures, and more.

PowerShell code generation can still help you with large-scale administration tasks, even when PowerShell is not available. Given a large list of input (for example, a complex list of files to copy), you can easily generate a *cmd.exe* batch file or Unix shell script to automate the task. Generate the script in PowerShell, and then invoke it on the system of your choice!

# Calculations and Math

## 6.0. Introduction

Math is an important feature in any scripting language. Math support in a language includes addition, subtraction, multiplication, and division, of course, but extends into more advanced mathematical operations. So it should not surprise you that PowerShell provides a strong suite of mathematical and calculation-oriented features.

Since PowerShell provides full access to its scripting language from the command line, this keeps a powerful and useful command-line calculator always at your fingertips! In addition to its support for traditional mathematical operations, PowerShell also caters to system administrators by working natively with concepts such as megabytes and gigabytes, simple statistics (such as sum and average), and conversions between bases.

## 6.1. Perform Simple Arithmetic

### Problem

You want to use PowerShell to calculate simple mathematical results.

### Solution

Use PowerShell's arithmetic operators:

| | |
|---|---|
| + | Addition |
| - | Subtraction |
| * | Multiplication |
| / | Division |
| % | Modulus |

| +=, -=, *=, /=, and %= | Assignment variations of the previously listed operators |
|---|---|
| () | Precedence/order of operations |

For a detailed description of these mathematical operators, see "Simple Operators" (page 873).

## Discussion

One difficulty in many programming languages comes from the way that they handle data in variables. For example, this C# snippet stores the value of 1 in the result variable, when the user probably wanted the result to hold the floating-point value of 1.5:

```
double result = 0;
result = 3/2;
```

This is because C# (along with many other languages) determines the result of the division from the type of data being used in the division. In the previous example, it decides that you want the answer to be an integer because you used two integers in the division.

PowerShell, on the other hand, avoids this problem. Even if you use two integers in a division, PowerShell returns the result as a floating-point number if required. This is called *widening*.

```
PS > $result = 0
PS > $result = 3/2
PS > $result
1.5
```

One exception to this automatic widening is when you explicitly tell PowerShell the type of result you want. For example, you might use an integer cast ([int]) to say that you want the result to be an integer after all:

```
PS > $result = [int] (3/2)
PS > $result
2
```

Many programming languages drop the portion after the decimal point when they convert them from floating-point numbers to integers. This is called *truncation*. PowerShell, on the other hand, uses *banker's rounding* for this conversion. It converts floating-point numbers to their nearest integer, rounding to the nearest even number in case of a tie.

Several programming techniques use truncation, though, so it is still important that a scripting language somehow support it. PowerShell does not have a built-in operator that performs truncation-style division, but it does support it through the [Math]::Truncate() method in the .NET Framework:

```
PS > $result = 3/2
PS > [Math]::Truncate($result)
1
```

If that syntax seems burdensome, the following example defines a `trunc` function that truncates its input:

```
PS > function trunc($number) { [Math]::Truncate($number) }
PS > $result = 3/2
PS > trunc $result
1
```

## See Also

"Simple Operators" (page 873)

# 6.2. Perform Complex Arithmetic

## Problem

You want to use PowerShell to calculate more complex or advanced mathematical results.

## Solution

PowerShell supports more advanced mathematical tasks primarily through its support for the `System.Math` class in the .NET Framework.

To find the absolute value of a number, use the `[Math]::Abs()` method:

```
PS > [Math]::Abs(-10.6)
10.6
```

To find the power (such as the square or the cube) of a number, use the `[Math]::Pow()` method. In this case, the method is finding 123 squared:

```
PS > [Math]::Pow(123, 2)
15129
```

To find the square root of a number, use the `[Math]::Sqrt()` method:

```
PS > [Math]::Sqrt(100)
10
```

To find the sine, cosine, or tangent of an angle (given in radians), use the `[Math]::Sin()`, `[Math]::Cos()`, or `[Math]::Tan()` method:

```
PS > [Math]::Sin( [Math]::PI / 2 )
1
```

To find the angle (given in radians) of a sine, cosine, or tangent value, use the `[Math]::ASin()`, `[Math]::ACos()`, or `[Math]::ATan()` method:

```
PS > [Math]::ASin(1)
1.5707963267949
```

See Recipe 3.13, "Learn About Types and Objects" to learn how to find out what other features the System.Math class provides.

## Discussion

Once you start working with the System.Math class, it may seem as though its designers left out significant pieces of functionality. The class supports the square root of a number, but doesn't support other roots (such as the cube root). It supports sine, cosine, and tangent (and their inverses) in radians, but not in the more commonly used measure of degrees.

### Working with any root

To determine any root (such as the cube root) of a number, you can use the function given in Example 6-1.

*Example 6-1. A root function and some example calculations*

```
PS > function root($number, $root) { [Math]::Pow($number, 1 / $root) }
PS > root 64 3
4
PS > root 25 5
1.90365393871588
PS > [Math]::Pow(1.90365393871588, 5)
25.0000000000001
PS > [Math]::Pow( $(root 25 5), 5)
25
```

This function applies the mathematical fact that the square root of a number is the same as raising that number to the power of 1/2, the cube of a number is the same as raising it to the power of 1/3, etc.

The example also illustrates a very important point about math on computers. When you use this function (or anything else that manipulates floating-point numbers), always be aware that the results of floating-point answers are only ever approximations of the actual result. If you combine multiple calculations in the same statement (or store intermediate results into variables), programming and scripting languages can sometimes keep an accurate answer (such as in the second [Math]::Pow() attempt), but that exception is rare.

Some mathematical systems avoid this problem by working with equations and calculations as symbols (and not numbers). Like humans, these systems know that taking the square of a number that you just took the square root of gives you the original number right back—so they don't actually have to do either of those operations. These systems, however, are extremely specialized and usually very expensive.

## Working with degrees instead of radians

Converting radians (the way that mathematicians commonly measure angles) to degrees (the way that most people commonly measure angles) is much more straightforward than the root function. A circle has 2 * Pi radians if you measure in radians, and 360 degrees if you measure in degrees. That gives the following two functions:

```
function Convert-RadiansToDegrees($angle) { $angle / (2 * [Math]::Pi) * 360 }
function Convert-DegreesToRadians($angle) { $angle / 360 * (2 * [Math]::Pi) }
```

and their usage:

```
PS > Convert-RadiansToDegrees ([Math]::Pi)
180
PS > Convert-RadiansToDegrees ([Math]::Pi / 2)
90
PS > Convert-DegreesToRadians 360
6.28318530717959
PS > Convert-DegreesToRadians 45
0.785398163397448
PS > [Math]::Tan( (Convert-DegreesToRadians 45) )
1
```

## Working with large numbers

In addition to its support for all of the standard .NET data types (bytes, integers, floats, and decimals), PowerShell also lets you work with extremely large numbers that these standard data types cannot handle:

```
PS > [Math]::Pow(12345, 123)
Infinity

PS > [BigInt]::Pow(12345, 123)
17922747853679707527695216231943419712992696443062340535140391466684
40953031931423861053031289352606613314821666096691426463815891552569
61299625923906846736377224598990446854741893321648522851663303862851
16587975372427272838604280411617304001701448802369380754772495091658
80584554994292720483269340987503673640044881128194397555564034430275
23561951313385041616743787240003466700321402142800004483416756392021
35945746171990585436418152506177298295938033884123488041067995268917
9117442108690738677978515625
```

In addition to the static methods offered by the BigInt class, you can do standard mathematical operations (addition, subtraction, multiplication, division) with big integers directly:

```
PS > $num1 = [BigInt] "96282208839921398410851090293377372323"
PS > $num2 = [BigInt] "98651648681681681768716871671106806788"
PS > $num1 * $num2
9498398640772225936470872065833701475115972299172612052721422766167885899728524
```

As an important note, be sure to always enclose `BigInt` numbers in strings, and then cast them to the `BigInt` type. If you don't, PowerShell thinks that you are trying to provide a number of type `Double` (which loses data for extremely large numbers), and then converts that number to the big integer.

```
PS > $r = 96282208839921398410851090293377372323
PS > $r
9.62822088399214E+38

PS > [BigInt] $r
96282208839921391210961894499716327014

PS > [BigInt] 96282208839921398410851090293377372323
96282208839921391210961894499716327014

PS > [BigInt] "96282208839921398410851090293377372323"
96282208839921398410851090293377372323
```

### Working with imaginary and complex numbers

When you need to work with calculations that involve the square root of −1, the `System.Numerics.Complex` class provides a great deal of support:

```
PS > [System.Numerics.Complex]::ImaginaryOne | Format-List

Real      : 0
Imaginary : 1
Magnitude : 1
Phase     : 1.5707963267949
```

In addition to the static methods offered by the `Complex` class, you can do standard mathematical operations (addition, subtraction, multiplication, division) with complex numbers directly:

```
PS > [System.Numerics.Complex]::ImaginaryOne *
    [System.Numerics.Complex]::ImaginaryOne | Format-List

Real      : -1
Imaginary : 0
Magnitude : 1
Phase     : 3.14159265358979
```

## See Also

Recipe 3.13, "Learn About Types and Objects"

# 6.3. Measure Statistical Properties of a List

## Problem

You want to measure the numeric (minimum, maximum, sum, average) or textual (characters, words, lines) features of a list of objects.

## Solution

Use the `Measure-Object` cmdlet to measure these statistical properties of a list.

To measure the numeric features of a stream of objects, pipe those objects to the `Measure-Object` cmdlet:

```
PS > 1..10 | Measure-Object -Average -Sum


Count    : 10
Average  : 5.5
Sum      : 55
Maximum  :
Minimum  :
Property :
```

To measure the numeric features of a specific property in a stream of objects, supply that property name to the `-Property` parameter of the `Measure-Object` cmdlet. For example, in a directory with files:

```
PS > Get-ChildItem | Measure-Object -Property Length -Max -Min -Average -Sum

Count    : 427
Average  : 10617025.4918033
Sum      : 4533469885
Maximum  : 647129088
Minimum  : 0
Property : Length
```

To measure the textual features of a stream of objects, use the `-Character`, `-Word`, and `-Line` parameters of the `Measure-Object` cmdlet:

```
PS > Get-ChildItem > output.txt
PS > Get-Content output.txt | Measure-Object -Character -Word -Line
```

| Lines | Words | Characters Property |
| ----- | ----- | ---------- -------- |
| 964 | 6083 | 33484 |

## Discussion

By default, the `Measure-Object` cmdlet counts only the number of objects it receives. If you want to measure additional properties (such as the maximum, minimum, average, sum, characters, words, or lines) of those objects, then you need to specify them as options to the cmdlet.

For the numeric properties, though, you usually don't want to measure the objects themselves. Instead, you probably want to measure a specific property from the list—such as the `Length` property of a file. For that purpose, the `Measure-Object` cmdlet supports the `-Property` parameter to which you provide the property you want to measure.

Sometimes you might want to measure a property that isn't a simple number—such as the `LastWriteTime` property of a file. Since the `LastWriteTime` property is a `Date Time`, you can't determine its average immediately. However, if any property allows you to convert it to a number and back in a meaningful way (such as the `Ticks` property of a `DateTime`), then you can still compute its statistical properties. Example 6-2 shows how to get the average `LastWriteTime` from a list of files.

*Example 6-2. Using the Ticks property of the DateTime class to determine the average LastWriteTime of a list of files*

```
PS > ## Get the LastWriteTime from each file
PS > $times = dir | Foreach-Object { $_.LastWriteTime }

PS > ## Measure the average Ticks property of those LastWriteTime
PS > $results = $times | Measure-Object Ticks -Average

PS > ## Create a new DateTime out of the average Ticks
PS > New-Object DateTime $results.Average

Sunday, June 11, 2006 6:45:01 AM
```

For more information about the `Measure-Object` cmdlet, type **Get-Help Measure-Object**.

# 6.4. Work with Numbers as Binary

## Problem

You want to work with the individual bits of a number or work with a number built by combining a series of flags.

## Solution

To directly enter a hexadecimal number, use the `0x` prefix:

```
PS > $hexNumber = 0x1234
PS > $hexNumber
4660
```

To convert a number to its binary representation, supply a base of 2 to the
[Convert]::ToString() method:

```
PS > [Convert]::ToString(1234, 2)
10011010010
```

To convert a binary number into its decimal representation, supply a base of 2 to the
[Convert]::ToInt32() method:

```
PS > [Convert]::ToInt32("10011010010", 2)
1234
```

To manage the individual bits of a number, use PowerShell's binary operators. In this
case, the Archive flag is just one of the many possible attributes that may be true of a
given file:

```
PS > $archive = [System.IO.FileAttributes] "Archive"
PS > attrib +a test.txt
PS > Get-ChildItem | Where { $_.Attributes -band $archive } | Select Name

Name
----
test.txt
PS > attrib -a test.txt
PS > Get-ChildItem | Where { $_.Attributes -band $archive } | Select Name
PS >
```

## Discussion

In some system administration tasks, it is common to come across numbers that seem
to mean nothing by themselves. The attributes of a file are a perfect example:

```
PS > (Get-Item test.txt).Encrypt()
PS > (Get-Item test.txt).IsReadOnly = $true
PS > [int] (Get-Item test.txt -force).Attributes
16417
PS > (Get-Item test.txt -force).IsReadOnly = $false
PS > (Get-Item test.txt).Decrypt()
PS > [int] (Get-Item test.txt).Attributes
32
```

What can the numbers 16417 and 32 possibly tell us about the file?

The answer to this comes from looking at the attributes in another light—as a set of
features that can be either true or false. Take, for example, the possible attributes for an
item in a directory shown by Example 6-3.

*Example 6-3. Possible attributes of a file*

```
PS > [Enum]::GetNames([System.IO.FileAttributes])
ReadOnly
Hidden
System
Directory
Archive
Device
Normal
Temporary
SparseFile
ReparsePoint
Compressed
Offline
NotContentIndexedEncrypted
```

If a file is `ReadOnly`, `Archive`, and `Encrypted`, then you might consider the following as a succinct description of the attributes on that file:

```
ReadOnly = True
Archive = True
Encrypted = True
```

It just so happens that computers have an extremely concise way of representing sets of true and false values—a representation known as *binary*. To represent the attributes of a directory item as binary, you simply put them in a table. We give the item a 1 if the attribute applies to the item and a 0 otherwise (see Table 6-1).

*Table 6-1. Attributes of a directory item*

| Attribute | True (1) or false (0) |
|---|---|
| Encrypted | 1 |
| NotContentIndexed | 0 |
| Offline | 0 |
| Compressed | 0 |
| ReparsePoint | 0 |
| SparseFile | 0 |
| Temporary | 0 |
| Normal | 0 |
| Device | 0 |
| Archive | 1 |
| Directory | 0 |
| <Unused> | 0 |
| System | 0 |
| Hidden | 0 |

| Attribute | True (1) or false (0) |
|---|---|
| ReadOnly | 1 |

If we treat those features as the individual binary digits in a number, that gives us the number 100000000100001. If we convert that number to its decimal form, it becomes clear where the number 16417 came from:

```
PS > [Convert]::ToInt32("100000000100001", 2)
16417
```

This technique sits at the core of many properties that you can express as a combination of features or flags. Rather than list the features in a table, though, the documentation usually describes the number that would result from that feature being the only one active—such as FILE_ATTRIBUTE_REPARSEPOINT = 0x400. Example 6-4 shows the various representations of these file attributes.

*Example 6-4. Integer, hexadecimal, and binary representations of possible file attributes*

```
PS > $attributes = [Enum]::GetValues([System.IO.FileAttributes])
PS > $attributes | Select-Object `
    @{"Name"="Property";
        "Expression"= { $_ } },
    @{"Name"="Integer";
        "Expression"= { [int] $_ } },
    @{"Name"="Hexadecimal";
        "Expression"= { [Convert]::ToString([int] $_, 16) } },
    @{"Name"="Binary";
        "Expression"= { [Convert]::ToString([int] $_, 2) } } |
    Format-Table -auto


            Property Integer Hexadecimal Binary
            -------- ------- ----------- ------
            ReadOnly       1 1           1
              Hidden       2 2           10
              System       4 4           100
           Directory      16 10          10000
             Archive      32 20          100000
              Device      64 40          1000000
              Normal     128 80          10000000
           Temporary     256 100         100000000
          SparseFile     512 200         1000000000
         ReparsePoint    1024 400        10000000000
          Compressed    2048 800         100000000000
             Offline    4096 1000        1000000000000
    NotContentIndexed    8192 2000       10000000000000
           Encrypted   16384 4000        100000000000000
```

Knowing how that 16417 number was formed, you can now use the properties in meaningful ways. For example, PowerShell's -band operator allows you to check whether a certain bit has been set:

```
PS > $encrypted = 16384
PS > $attributes = (Get-Item test.txt -force).Attributes
PS > ($attributes -band $encrypted) -eq $encrypted
True
PS > $compressed = 2048
PS > ($attributes -band $compressed) -eq $compressed
False
PS >
```

Although that example uses the numeric values explicitly, it would be more common to enter the number by its name:

```
PS > $archive = [System.IO.FileAttributes] "Archive"
PS > ($attributes -band $archive) -eq $archive
True
```

For more information about PowerShell's binary operators, see "Simple Operators" (page 873).

## See Also

"Simple Operators" (page 873)

# 6.5. Simplify Math with Administrative Constants

## Problem

You want to work with common administrative numbers (that is, kilobytes, megabytes, gigabytes, terabytes, and petabytes) without having to remember or calculate those numbers.

## Solution

Use PowerShell's administrative constants (KB, MB, GB, TB, and PB) to help work with these common numbers.

For example, we can calculate the download time (in seconds) of a 10.18 megabyte file over a connection that gets 215 kilobytes per second:

```
PS > 10.18mb / 215kb
48.4852093023256
```

## Discussion

PowerShell's administrative constants are based on powers of two, since they are the type most commonly used when working with computers. Each is 1,024 times bigger than the one before it:

```
1kb = 1024
1mb = 1024 * 1 kb
1gb = 1024 * 1 mb
1tb = 1024 * 1 gb
1pb = 1024 * 1 tb
```

Some people (such as hard drive manufacturers) prefer to call numbers based on powers of two "kibibytes," "mebibytes," and "gibibytes." They use the terms "kilobytes," "megabytes," and "gigabytes" to mean numbers that are 1,000 times bigger than the ones before them—numbers based on powers of 10.

Although not represented by administrative constants, PowerShell still makes it easy to work with these numbers in powers of 10—for example, to figure out how big a "300 GB" hard drive is when reported by Windows. To do this, use scientific (exponential) notation:

```
PS > $kilobyte = 1e3
PS > $kilobyte
1000
PS > $megabyte = 1e6
PS > $megabyte
1000000
PS > $gigabyte = 1e9
PS > $gigabyte
1000000000
PS > (300 * $gigabyte) / 1GB
279.396772384644
```

## See Also

"Simple Assignment" (page 867)

# 6.6. Convert Numbers Between Bases

## Problem

You want to convert a number to a different base.

## Solution

The PowerShell scripting language allows you to enter both decimal and hexadecimal numbers directly. It does not natively support other number bases, but its support for interaction with the .NET Framework enables conversion both to and from binary, octal, decimal, and hexadecimal.

To convert a hexadecimal number into its decimal representation, prefix the number with 0x to enter the number as hexadecimal:

```
PS > $myErrorCode = 0xFE4A
PS > $myErrorCode
65098
```

To convert a binary number into its decimal representation, supply a base of 2 to the [Convert]::ToInt32() method:

```
PS > [Convert]::ToInt32("10011010010", 2)
1234
```

To convert an octal number into its decimal representation, supply a base of 8 to the [Convert]::ToInt32() method:

```
PS > [Convert]::ToInt32("1234", 8)
668
```

To convert a number into its hexadecimal representation, use either the [Convert] class or PowerShell's format operator:

```
PS > ## Use the [Convert] class
PS > [Convert]::ToString(1234, 16)
4d2

PS > ## Use the formatting operator
PS > "{0:X4}" -f 1234
04D2
```

To convert a number into its binary representation, supply a base of 2 to the [Convert]::ToString() method:

```
PS > [Convert]::ToString(1234, 2)
10011010010
```

To convert a number into its octal representation, supply a base of 8 to the [Convert]::ToString() method:

```
PS > [Convert]::ToString(1234, 8)
2322
```

## Discussion

It is most common to want to convert numbers between bases when you are dealing with numbers that represent binary combinations of data, such as the attributes of a file. For more information on how to work with binary data like this, see Recipe 6.4, "Work with Numbers as Binary".

## See Also

Recipe 6.4, "Work with Numbers as Binary"

# Lists, Arrays, and Hashtables

## 7.0. Introduction

Most scripts deal with more than one thing—lists of servers, lists of files, lookup codes, and more. To enable this, PowerShell supports many features to help you through both its language features and utility cmdlets.

PowerShell makes working with arrays and lists much like working with other data types: you can easily create an array or list and then add or remove elements from it. You can just as easily sort it, search it, or combine it with another array. When you want to store a mapping between one piece of data and another, a hashtable fulfills that need perfectly.

## 7.1. Create an Array or List of Items

### Problem

You want to create an array or list of items.

### Solution

To create an array that holds a given set of items, separate those items with commas:

```
PS > $myArray = 1,2,"Hello World"
PS > $myArray
1
2
Hello World
```

To create an array of a specific size, use the New-Object cmdlet:

```
PS > $myArray = New-Object string[] 10
PS > $myArray[5] = "Hello"
PS > $myArray[5]
Hello
```

To create an array of a specific type, use a strongly typed collection:

```
PS > $list = New-Object Collections.Generic.List[Int]
PS > $list.Add(10)
PS > $list.Add("Hello")
Cannot convert argument "0", with value: "Hello", for "Add" to type "System
.Int32": "Cannot convert value "Hello" to type "System.Int32". Error:
"Input string was not in a correct format.""
```

To store the output of a command that generates a list, use variable assignment:

```
PS > $myArray = Get-Process
PS > $myArray
```

| Handles | NPM(K) | PM(K) | WS(K) | VM(M) | CPU(s) | Id | ProcessName |
|---------|--------|-------|-------|-------|--------|------|-------------|
| 274 | 6 | 1316 | 3908 | 33 | | 3164 | alg |
| 983 | 7 | 3636 | 7472 | 30 | | 688 | csrss |
| 69 | 4 | 924 | 3332 | 30 | 0.69 | 2232 | ctfmon |
| 180 | 5 | 2220 | 6116 | 37 | | 2816 | dllhost |
| (...) | | | | | | | |

To create an array that you plan to modify frequently, use an ArrayList, as shown by Example 7-1.

*Example 7-1. Using an ArrayList to manage a dynamic collection of items*

```
PS > $myArray = New-Object System.Collections.ArrayList
PS > [void] $myArray.Add("Hello")
PS > [void] $myArray.AddRange( ("World","How","Are","You") )
PS > $myArray
Hello
World
How
Are
You
PS > $myArray.RemoveAt(1)
PS > $myArray
Hello
How
Are
You
```

## Discussion

Aside from the primitive data types (such as strings, integers, and decimals), lists of items are a common concept in the scripts and commands that you write. Most commands generate lists of data: the Get-Content cmdlet generates a list of strings in a file, the Get-Process cmdlet generates a list of processes running on the system, and the Get-Command cmdlet generates a list of commands, just to name a few.

 The Solution shows how to store the output of a command that generates a list. If a command outputs only one item (such as a single line from a file, a single process, or a single command), then that output is no longer a list. If you want to treat that output as a list even when it is not, use the list evaluation syntax, @( ), to force PowerShell to interpret it as an array:

```
$myArray = @(Get-Process Explorer)
```

When you want to create a list of a specific type, the Solution demonstrates how to use the System.Collections.Generic.List collection to do that. After the type name, you define the type of the list in square brackets, such as [Int], [String], or whichever type you want to restrict your collection to. These types of specialized objects are called *generic objects*. For more information about creating generic objects, see "Creating Instances of Types" (page 894).

For more information on lists and arrays in PowerShell, see "Arrays and Lists" (page 869).

## See Also

"Arrays and Lists" (page 869)

"Creating Instances of Types" (page 894)

# 7.2. Create a Jagged or Multidimensional Array

## Problem

You want to create an array of arrays or an array of multiple dimensions.

## Solution

To create an array of arrays (a *jagged* array), use the @( ) array syntax:

```
PS > $jagged = @(
    (1,2,3,4),
    (5,6,7,8)
```

```
        )
PS > $jagged[0][1]
2
PS > $jagged[1][3]
8
```

To create a (nonjagged) multidimensional array, use the New-Object cmdlet:

```
PS > $multidimensional = New-Object "int32[,]" 2,4
PS > $multidimensional[0,1] = 2
PS > $multidimensional[1,3] = 8
PS >
PS > $multidimensional[0,1]
2
PS > $multidimensional[1,3]
8
```

## Discussion

Jagged and multidimensional arrays are useful for holding lists of lists and arrays of arrays. Jagged arrays are arrays of arrays, where each array has only as many elements as it needs. A nonjagged array is more like a grid or matrix, where every array needs to be the same size. Jagged arrays are much easier to work with (and use less memory), but nonjagged multidimensional arrays are sometimes useful for dealing with large grids of data.

Since a jagged array is an array of arrays, creating an item in a jagged array follows the same rules as creating an item in a regular array. If any of the arrays are single-element arrays, use the unary comma operator. For example, to create a jagged array with one nested array of one element:

```
PS > $oneByOneJagged = @(
 ,(,1)

PS > $oneByOneJagged[0][0]
```

For more information on lists and arrays in PowerShell, see "Arrays and Lists" (page 869).

## See Also

"Arrays and Lists" (page 869)

# 7.3. Access Elements of an Array

## Problem

You want to access the elements of an array.

## Solution

To access a specific element of an array, use PowerShell's array access mechanism:

```
PS > $myArray = 1,2,"Hello World"
PS > $myArray[1]
2
```

To access a range of array elements, use array ranges and array slicing:

```
PS > $myArray = 1,2,"Hello World"
PS > $myArray[1..2 + 0]
2
Hello World
1
```

## Discussion

PowerShell's array access mechanisms provide a convenient way to access either specific elements of an array or more complex combinations of elements in that array. In PowerShell (as with most other scripting and programming languages), the item at index 0 represents the first item in the array.

For long lists of items, knowing the index of an element can sometimes pose a problem. For a solution to this, see the Add-FormatTableIndexParameter script included with this book's code examples. This script adds a new -IncludeIndex parameter to the Format-Table cmdlet:

```
PS > $items = Get-Process outlook,powershell,emacs,notepad
PS > $items

Handles  NPM(K)    PM(K)     WS(K) VM(M)   CPU(s)     Id ProcessName
-------  ------    -----     ----- -----   ------     -- -----------
    163       6    17660     24136   576     7.63   7136 emacs
     74       4     1252      6184    56     0.19  11820 notepad
   3262      48    46664     88280   376    20.98   8572 OUTLOOK
    285      11    31328     21952   171   613.71   4716 powershell
    767      14    56568     66032   227   104.10  11368 powershell


PS > $items | Format-Table -IncludeIndex

PSIndex Handles  NPM(K)    PM(K)     WS(K) VM(M)   CPU(s)     Id ProcessName
------- -------  ------    -----     ----- -----   ------     -- -----------
0           163       6    17660     24136   576     7.63   7136 emacs
1            74       4     1252      6184    56     0.19  11820 notepad
2          3262      48    46664     88280   376    20.98   8572 OUTLOOK
3           285      11    31328     21952   171   613.71   4716 powershell
4           767      14    56568     66032   227   104.15  11368 powershell


PS > $items[2]
```

```
Handles  NPM(K)    PM(K)      WS(K) VM(M)   CPU(s)     Id ProcessName
-------  ------    -----      ----- -----   ------     -- -----------
   3262      48    46664      88280   376    20.98   8572 OUTLOOK
```

Although working with the elements of an array by their numerical index is helpful, you may find it useful to refer to them by something else—such as their name, or even a custom label. This type of array is known as an *associative array* (or *hashtable*). For more information about working with hashtables and associative arrays, see Recipe 7.13, "Create a Hashtable or Associative Array".

For more information on lists and arrays in PowerShell (including the array ranges and slicing syntax), see "Arrays and Lists" (page 869). For more information about obtaining the code examples for this book, see "Code Examples" (page xxiii).

### See Also

Recipe 7.13, "Create a Hashtable or Associative Array"

"Arrays and Lists" (page 869)

# 7.4. Visit Each Element of an Array

## Problem

You want to work with each element of an array.

## Solution

To access each item in an array one by one, use the `Foreach-Object` cmdlet:

```
PS > $myArray = 1,2,3
PS > $sum = 0
PS > $myArray | Foreach-Object { $sum += $_ }
PS > $sum
6
```

To access each item in an array in a more script-like fashion, use the `foreach` scripting keyword:

```
PS > $myArray = 1,2,3
PS > $sum = 0
PS > foreach($element in $myArray) { $sum += $element }
PS > $sum
6
```

To access items in an array by position, use a `for` loop:

```
PS > $myArray = 1,2,3
PS > $sum = 0
```

```
PS > for($counter = 0; $counter -lt $myArray.Count; $counter++) {
    $sum += $myArray[$counter]
}

PS > $sum
6
```

## Discussion

PowerShell provides three main alternatives to working with elements in an array. The Foreach-Object cmdlet and foreach scripting keyword techniques visit the items in an array one element at a time, whereas the for loop (and related looping constructs) lets you work with the items in an array in a less structured way.

For more information about the Foreach-Object cmdlet, see Recipe 2.5, "Work with Each Item in a List or Command Output".

For more information about the foreach scripting keyword, the for keyword, and other looping constructs, see Recipe 4.4, "Repeat Operations with Loops".

## See Also

Recipe 2.5, "Work with Each Item in a List or Command Output"

Recipe 4.4, "Repeat Operations with Loops"

# 7.5. Sort an Array or List of Items

## Problem

You want to sort the elements of an array or list.

## Solution

To sort a list of items, use the Sort-Object cmdlet:

```
PS > Get-ChildItem | Sort-Object -Descending Length | Select Name,Length

Name                                                              Length
----                                                              ------
Convert-TextObject.ps1                                              6868
Select-FilteredObject.ps1                                          3252
Get-PageUrls.ps1                                                   2878
Get-Characteristics.ps1                                            2515
Get-Answer.ps1                                                     1890
New-GenericObject.ps1                                              1490
Invoke-CmdScript.ps1                                               1313
```

## Discussion

The Sort-Object cmdlet provides a convenient way for you to sort items by a property that you specify. If you don't specify a property, the Sort-Object cmdlet follows the sorting rules of those items if they define any.

The Sort-Object cmdlet also supports custom sort expressions, rather than just sorting on existing properties. To sort by your own logic, use a script block as the sort expression. This example sorts by the second character:

```
PS > "Hello","World","And","PowerShell" | Sort-Object { $_.Substring(1,1) }
Hello
And
PowerShell
World
```

If you want to sort a list that you've saved in a variable, you can either store the results back in that variable or use the [Array]::Sort() method from the .NET Framework:

```
PS > $list = "Hello","World","And","PowerShell"
PS > $list = $list | Sort-Object
PS > $list
And
Hello
PowerShell
World
PS > $list = "Hello","World","And","PowerShell"
PS > [Array]::Sort($list)
PS > $list
And
Hello
PowerShell
World
```

In addition to sorting by a property or expression in ascending or descending order, the Sort-Object cmdlet's -Unique switch also allows you to remove duplicates from the sorted collection.

For more information about the Sort-Object cmdlet, type **Get-Help Sort-Object**.

# 7.6. Determine Whether an Array Contains an Item

## Problem

You want to determine whether an array or list contains a specific item.

## Solution

To determine whether a list contains a specific item, use the -contains operator:

```
PS > "Hello","World" -contains "Hello"
True
PS > "Hello","World" -contains "There"
False
```

Alternatively, use the -in operator, which acts like the -contains operator with its operands reversed:

```
PS > "Hello" -in "Hello","World"
True
PS > "There" -in "Hello","World"
False
```

## Discussion

The -contains and -in operators are useful ways to quickly determine whether a list contains a specific element. To search a list for items that instead match a pattern, use the -match or -like operators.

For more information about the -contains, -in, -match, and -like operators, see "Comparison Operators" (page 879).

## See Also

"Comparison Operators" (page 879)

# 7.7. Combine Two Arrays

## Problem

You have two arrays and want to combine them into one.

## Solution

To combine PowerShell arrays, use the addition operator (+):

```
PS > $firstArray = "Element 1","Element 2","Element 3","Element 4"
PS > $secondArray = 1,2,3,4
PS >
PS > $result = $firstArray + $secondArray
PS > $result
Element 1
Element 2
Element 3
Element 4
1
2
3
4
```

## Discussion

One common reason to combine two arrays is when you want to add data to the end of one of the arrays. For example:

```
PS > $array = 1,2
PS > $array = $array + 3,4
PS > $array
1
2
3
4
```

You can write this more clearly as:

```
PS > $array = 1,2
PS > $array += 3,4
PS > $array
1
2
3
4
```

When this is written in the second form, however, you might think that PowerShell simply adds the items to the end of the array while keeping the array itself intact. This is not true, since arrays in PowerShell (like most other languages) stay the same length once you create them. To combine two arrays, PowerShell creates a new array large enough to hold the contents of both arrays and then copies both arrays into the destination array.

If you plan to add and remove data from an array frequently, the System. Collections.ArrayList class provides a more dynamic alternative. For more information about using the ArrayList class, see Recipe 7.12, "Use the ArrayList Class for Advanced Array Tasks".

### See Also

Recipe 7.12, "Use the ArrayList Class for Advanced Array Tasks"

# 7.8. Find Items in an Array That Match a Value

## Problem

You have an array and want to find all elements that match a given item or term—either exactly, by pattern, or by regular expression.

## Solution

To find all elements that match an item, use the `-eq`, `-like`, and `-match` comparison operators:

```
PS > $array = "Item 1","Item 2","Item 3","Item 1","Item 12"
PS > $array -eq "Item 1"
Item 1
Item 1
PS > $array -like "*1*"
Item 1
Item 1
Item 12
PS > $array -match "Item .."
Item 12
```

## Discussion

The `-eq`, `-like`, and `-match` operators are useful ways to find elements in a collection that match your given term. The `-eq` operator returns all elements that are equal to your term, the `-like` operator returns all elements that match the wildcard given in your pattern, and the `-match` operator returns all elements that match the regular expression given in your pattern.

For more complex comparison conditions, the `Where-Object` cmdlet lets you find elements in a list that satisfy much more complex conditions:

```
PS > $array = "Item 1","Item 2","Item 3","Item 1","Item 12"
PS > $array | Where-Object { $_.Length -gt 6 }
Item 12
```

For more information, see Recipe 2.1, "Filter Items in a List or Command Output".

For more information about the `-eq`, `-like`, and `-match` operators, see "Comparison Operators" (page 879).

## See Also

Recipe 2.1, "Filter Items in a List or Command Output"

"Comparison Operators" (page 879)

# 7.9. Compare Two Lists

## Problem

You have two lists and want to find items that exist in only one or the other list.

## Solution

To compare two lists, use the `Compare-Object` cmdlet:

```
PS > $array1 = "Item 1","Item 2","Item 3","Item 1","Item 12"
PS > $array2 = "Item 1","Item 8","Item 3","Item 9","Item 12"
PS > Compare-Object $array1 $array2

InputObject                   SideIndicator
-----------                   -------------
Item 8                        =>
Item 9                        =>
Item 2                        <=
Item 1                        <=
```

## Discussion

The `Compare-Object` cmdlet lets you compare two lists. By default, it shows only the items that exist exclusively in one of the lists, although its `-IncludeEqual` parameter lets you include items that exist in both. If it returns no results, the two lists are equal.

For more information, see Chapter 22.

## See Also

Chapter 22, *Comparing Data*

# 7.10. Remove Elements from an Array

## Problem

You want to remove all elements from an array that match a given item or term—either exactly, by pattern, or by regular expression.

## Solution

To remove all elements from an array that match a pattern, use the `-ne`, `-notlike`, and `-notmatch` comparison operators, as shown in Example 7-2.

*Example 7-2. Removing elements from an array using the -ne, -notlike, and -notmatch operators*

```
PS > $array = "Item 1","Item 2","Item 3","Item 1","Item 12"
PS > $array -ne "Item 1"
Item 2
Item 3
Item 12
PS > $array -notlike "*1*"
Item 2
```

```
Item 3
PS > $array -notmatch "Item .."
Item 1
Item 2
Item 3
Item 1
```

To actually remove the items from the array, store the results back in the array:

```
PS > $array = "Item 1","Item 2","Item 3","Item 1","Item 12"
PS > $array = $array -ne "Item 1"
PS > $array
Item 2
Item 3
Item 12
```

## Discussion

The -eq, -like, and -match operators are useful ways to find elements in a collection that match your given term. Their opposites, the -ne, -notlike, and -notmatch operators, return all elements that do not match that given term.

To remove all elements from an array that match a given pattern, you can then save all elements that *do not* match that pattern.

For more information about the -ne, -notlike, and -notmatch operators, see "Comparison Operators" (page 879).

## See Also

"Comparison Operators" (page 879)

# 7.11. Find Items in an Array Greater or Less Than a Value

## Problem

You have an array and want to find all elements greater or less than a given item or value.

## Solution

To find all elements greater or less than a given value, use the -gt, -ge, -lt, and -le comparison operators:

```
PS > $array = "Item 1","Item 2","Item 3","Item 1","Item 12"
PS > $array -ge "Item 3"
Item 3
PS > $array -lt "Item 3"
```

```
Item 1
Item 2
Item 1
Item 12
```

## Discussion

The -gt, -ge, -lt, and -le operators are useful ways to find elements in a collection that are greater or less than a given value. Like all other PowerShell comparison operators, these use the comparison rules of the items in the collection. Since the array in the Solution is an array of strings, this result can easily surprise you:

```
PS > $array -lt "Item 2"
Item 1
Item 1
Item 12
```

The reason for this becomes clear when you look at the sorted array—Item 12 comes before Item 2 *alphabetically*, which is the way that PowerShell compares arrays of strings:

```
PS > $array | Sort-Object
Item 1
Item 1
Item 12
Item 2
Item 3
```

For more information about the -gt, -ge, -lt, and -le operators, see "Comparison Operators" (page 879).

## See Also

"Comparison Operators" (page 879)

# 7.12. Use the ArrayList Class for Advanced Array Tasks

## Problem

You have an array that you want to frequently add elements to, remove elements from, search, and modify.

## Solution

To work with an array frequently after you define it, use the System.Collections .ArrayList class:

```
PS > $myArray = New-Object System.Collections.ArrayList
PS > [void] $myArray.Add("Hello")
```

```
PS > [void] $myArray.AddRange( ("World","How","Are","You") )
PS > $myArray
Hello
World
How
Are
You
PS > $myArray.RemoveAt(1)
PS > $myArray
Hello
How
Are
You
```

## Discussion

Like in most other languages, arrays in PowerShell stay the same length once you create them. PowerShell allows you to add items, remove items, and search for items in an array, but these operations may be time-consuming when you are dealing with large amounts of data. For example, to combine two arrays, PowerShell creates a new array large enough to hold the contents of both arrays and then copies both arrays into the destination array.

In comparison, the ArrayList class is designed to let you easily add, remove, and search for items in a collection.

PowerShell passes along any data that your script generates, unless you capture it or cast it to [void]. Since it is designed primarily to be used from programming languages, the System.Collections.ArrayList class produces output, even though you may not expect it to. To prevent it from sending data to the output pipeline, either capture the data or cast it to [void]:

```
PS > $collection = New-Object System.Collections.ArrayList
PS > $collection.Add("Hello")
0
PS > [void] $collection.Add("World")
```

If you plan to add and remove data to and from an array frequently, the System.Collections.ArrayList class provides a more dynamic alternative.

For more information about working with classes from the .NET Framework, see Recipe 3.8, "Work with .NET Objects".

## See Also

Recipe 3.8, "Work with .NET Objects"

# 7.13. Create a Hashtable or Associative Array

## Problem

You have a collection of items that you want to access through a label that you provide.

## Solution

To define a mapping between labels and items, use a hashtable (associative array):

```
PS > $myHashtable = @{ Key1 = "Value1"; "Key 2" = 1,2,3 }
PS > $myHashtable["New Item"] = 5
PS >
PS > $myHashTable

Name                          Value
----                          -----
Key 2                         {1, 2, 3}
New Item                      5
Key1                          Value1
```

## Discussion

Hashtables are much like arrays that let you access items by whatever label you want—not just through their index in the array. Because of that freedom, they form the keystone of a huge number of scripting techniques. Since they let you map names to values, they form the natural basis for lookup tables such as those for zip codes and area codes. Since they let you map names to fully featured objects and script blocks, they can often take the place of custom objects. And since you can map rich objects to other rich objects, they can even form the basis of more advanced data structures such as caches and object graphs.

The Solution demonstrates how to create and initialize a hashtable at the same time, but you can also create one and work with it incrementally:

```
PS > $myHashtable = @{}
PS > $myHashtable["Hello"] = "World"
PS > $myHashtable.AnotherHello = "AnotherWorld"
PS > $myHashtable

Name                          Value
----                          -----
AnotherHello                  AnotherWorld
Hello                         World
```

When working with hashtables, you might notice that they usually list their elements out of order—or at least, in a different order than how you inserted them. To create a hashtable that retains its insertion order, use the [ordered] type cast as described in Recipe 7.14, "Sort a Hashtable by Key or Value".

This ability to map labels to structured values also proves helpful in interacting with cmdlets that support advanced configuration parameters, such as the calculated property parameters available on the Format-Table and Select-Object cmdlets. For an example of this use, see Recipe 3.2, "Display the Properties of an Item as a Table".

For more information about working with hashtables, see "Hashtables (Associative Arrays)" (page 872).

## See Also

Recipe 3.2, "Display the Properties of an Item as a Table"

Recipe 7.14, "Sort a Hashtable by Key or Value"

"Hashtables (Associative Arrays)" (page 872)

# 7.14. Sort a Hashtable by Key or Value

## Problem

You have a hashtable of keys and values, and you want to get the list of values that result from sorting the keys in order.

## Solution

To sort a hashtable, use the GetEnumerator() method on the hashtable to gain access to its individual elements. Then, use the Sort-Object cmdlet to sort by Name or Value.

```
foreach($item in $myHashtable.GetEnumerator() | Sort Name)
{
    $item.Value
}
```

If you control the definition of the hashtable, use the [Ordered] type cast while defining the hashtable to have it retain the order supplied in the definition.

```
$orderedHashtable = [Ordered] @{ Item1 = "Hello"; Item2 = "World" }
```

## Discussion

Since the primary focus of a hashtable is to simply map keys to values, it does not usually retain any ordering whatsoever—such as the order you added the items, the sorted order of the keys, or the sorted order of the values.

This becomes clear in Example 7-3.

*Example 7-3. A demonstration of hashtable items not retaining their order*

```
PS > $myHashtable = @{}
PS > $myHashtable["Hello"] = 3
PS > $myHashtable["Ali"] = 2
PS > $myHashtable["Alien"] = 4
PS > $myHashtable["Duck"] = 1
PS > $myHashtable["Hectic"] = 11
PS > $myHashtable

Name                          Value
----                          -----
Hectic                        11
Duck                          1
Alien                         4
Hello                         3
Ali                           2
```

However, the hashtable object supports a `GetEnumerator()` method that lets you deal with the individual hashtable entries—all of which have a `Name` and `Value` property. Once you have those, we can sort by them as easily as we can sort any other PowerShell data. Example 7-4 demonstrates this technique.

*Example 7-4. Sorting a hashtable by name and value*

```
PS > $myHashtable.GetEnumerator() | Sort Name

Name                          Value
----                          -----
Ali                           2
Alien                         4
Duck                          1
Hectic                        11
Hello                         3


PS > $myHashtable.GetEnumerator() | Sort Value

Name                          Value
----                          -----
Duck                          1
Ali                           2
Hello                         3
Alien                         4
Hectic                        11
```

By using the [Ordered] type cast, you can create a hashtable that retains the order in which you define and add items:

```
PS > $myHashtable = [Ordered] @{
    Duck = 1;
    Ali = 2;
    Hectic = 11;
```

---

```
    Alien = 4;
  }

PS > $myHashtable["Hello"] = 3
PS > $myHashtable

Name                     Value
----                     -----
Duck                     1
Ali                      2
Hectic                   11
Alien                    4
Hello                    3
```

For more information about working with hashtables, see "Hashtables (Associative Arrays)" (page 872).

## See Also

"Hashtables (Associative Arrays)" (page 872)

# Utility Tasks

## 8.0. Introduction

When you are scripting or just using the interactive shell, a handful of needs arise that are simple but useful: measuring commands, getting random numbers, and more.

## 8.1. Get the System Date and Time

### Problem

You want to get the system date.

### Solution

To get the system date, run the command `Get-Date`.

### Discussion

The `Get-Date` command generates rich object-based output, so you can use its result for many date-related tasks. For example, to determine the current day of the week:

```
PS > $date = Get-Date
PS > $date.DayOfWeek
Sunday
```

If you want to format the date for output (for example, as a logfile stamp), see Recipe 5.13, "Format a Date for Output".

For more information about the `Get-Date` cmdlet, type **Get-Help Get-Date**.

For more information about working with classes from the .NET Framework, see Recipe 3.8, "Work with .NET Objects".

## See Also

Recipe 3.8, "Work with .NET Objects"

Recipe 5.13, "Format a Date for Output"

# 8.2. Measure the Duration of a Command

## Problem

You want to know how long a command takes to execute.

## Solution

To measure the duration of a command, use the Measure-Command cmdlet:

```
PS > Measure-Command { Start-Sleep -Milliseconds 337 }

Days              : 0
Hours             : 0
Minutes           : 0
Seconds           : 0
Milliseconds      : 339
Ticks             : 3392297
TotalDays         : 3.92626967592593E-06
TotalHours        : 9.42304722222222E-05
TotalMinutes      : 0.00565382833333333
TotalSeconds      : 0.3392297
TotalMilliseconds : 339.2297
```

## Discussion

In interactive use, it is common to want to measure the duration of a command. An example of this might be running a performance benchmark on an application you've developed. The Measure-Command cmdlet makes this easy to do. Because the command generates rich object-based output, you can use its output for many date-related tasks. See Recipe 3.8, "Work with .NET Objects" for more information.

If the accuracy of a command measurement is important, general system activity can easily influence the timing of the result. A common technique for improving accuracy is to repeat the measurement many times, ignore the outliers (the top and bottom 10 percent), and then average the remaining results. Example 8-1 implements this technique.

*Example 8-1. Measure-CommandPerformance.ps1*

```
##############################################################################
##
## Measure-CommandPerformance
```

```
##
## From Windows PowerShell Cookbook (O'Reilly)
## by Lee Holmes (http://www.leeholmes.com/guide)
##
###########################################################################

<#

.SYNOPSIS

Measures the average time of a command, accounting for natural variability by
automatically ignoring the top and bottom ten percent.

.EXAMPLE

PS > Measure-CommandPerformance.ps1 { Start-Sleep -m 300 }

Count    : 30
Average  : 312.10155
(...)

#>

param(
    ## The command to measure
    [Scriptblock] $Scriptblock,

    ## The number of times to measure the command's performance
    [int] $Iterations = 30
)

Set-StrictMode -Version 3

## Figure out how many extra iterations we need to account for the outliers
$buffer = [int] ($iterations * 0.1)
$totalIterations = $iterations + (2 * $buffer)

## Get the results
$results = 1..$totalIterations |
    Foreach-Object { Measure-Command $scriptblock }

## Sort the results, and skip the outliers
$middleResults = $results | Sort TotalMilliseconds |
    Select -Skip $buffer -First $iterations

## Show the average
$middleResults | Measure-Object -Average TotalMilliseconds
```

For more information about the Measure-Command cmdlet, type **Get-Help Measure-Command.**

## See Also

Recipe 3.8, "Work with .NET Objects"

# 8.3. Read and Write from the Windows Clipboard

## Problem

You want to interact with the Windows clipboard.

## Solution

Use the `Get-Clipboard` and `Set-Clipboard` scripts, as shown in Examples 8-2 and 8-3.

*Example 8-2. Get-Clipboard.ps1*

```
##############################################################################
##
## Get-Clipboard
##
## From Windows PowerShell Cookbook (O'Reilly)
## by Lee Holmes (http://www.leeholmes.com/guide)
##
##############################################################################

<#

.SYNOPSIS

Retrieve the text contents of the Windows Clipboard.

.EXAMPLE

PS > Get-Clipboard
Hello World

#>

Set-StrictMode -Version 3

Add-Type -Assembly PresentationCore
[Windows.Clipboard]::GetText()
```

*Example 8-3. Set-Clipboard.ps1*

```
##############################################################################
##
## Set-Clipboard
##
## From Windows PowerShell Cookbook (O'Reilly)
## by Lee Holmes (http://www.leeholmes.com/guide)
```

```
##
##############################################################################

<#

.SYNOPSIS

Sends the given input to the Windows clipboard.

.EXAMPLE

PS > dir | Set-Clipboard
This example sends the view of a directory listing to the clipboard

.EXAMPLE

PS > Set-Clipboard "Hello World"
This example sets the clipboard to the string, "Hello World".

#>

param(
    ## The input to send to the clipboard
    [Parameter(ValueFromPipeline = $true)]
    [object[]] $InputObject
)

begin
{
    Set-StrictMode -Version 3
    $objectsToProcess = @()
}

process
{
    ## Collect everything sent to the script either through
    ## pipeline input, or direct input.
    $objectsToProcess += $inputObject
}

end
{
    ## Convert the input objects to text
    $clipText = ($objectsToProcess | Out-String -Stream) -join "`r`n"

    ## And finally set the clipboard text
    Add-Type -Assembly PresentationCore
    [Windows.Clipboard]::SetText($clipText)
}
```

## Discussion

While Windows includes a command-line utility (clip.exe) to place text in the Windows clipboard, it doesn't support direct input (e.g., clip.exe "Hello World"), and it doesn't have a corresponding utility to retrieve the contents from the Windows clipboard.

The Set-Clipboard and Get-Clipboard scripts given in the Solution resolve both of these issues.

Both rely on the System.Windows.Clipboard class, which has a special requirement that it must be run from an application in single-threaded apartment (STA) mode. This is PowerShell's default, but if you launch PowerShell with its -MTA parameter, these scripts will not work.

For more information about working with classes from the .NET Framework, see Recipe 3.8, "Work with .NET Objects".

## See Also

Recipe 3.8, "Work with .NET Objects"

# 8.4. Generate a Random Number or Object

## Problem

You want to generate a random number or pick a random element from a set of objects.

## Solution

Call the Get-Random cmdlet to generate a random positive integer:

```
Get-Random
```

Use the -Minimum and -Maximum parameters to generate a number between Minimum and up to (but not including) Maximum:

```
Get-Random -Minimum 1 -Maximum 21
```

Use simple pipeline input to pick a random element from a list:

```
PS > $suits = "Hearts","Clubs","Spades","Diamonds"
PS > $faces = (2..10)+"A","J","Q","K"
PS > $cards = foreach($suit in $suits) {
    foreach($face in $faces) { "$face of $suit" } }
PS > $cards | Get-Random
A of Spades
PS > $cards | Get-Random
2 of Clubs
```

## Discussion

The `Get-Random` cmdlet solves the problems usually associated with picking random numbers or random elements from a collection: *scaling* and *seeding*.

Most random number generators only generate numbers between 0 and 1. If you need a number from a different range, you have to go through a separate scaling step to map those numbers to the appropriate range. Although not terribly difficult, it's a usability hurdle that requires more than trivial knowledge to do properly.

Ensuring that the random number generator picks *good* random numbers is a different problem entirely. All general-purpose random number generators use mathematical equations to generate their values. They make new values by incorporating the number they generated just before that—a feedback process that guarantees evenly distributed sequences of numbers. Maintaining this internal state is critical, as restarting from a specific point will always generate the same number, which is not very random at all! You lose this internal state every time you create a new random number generator.

To create their first value, generators need a random number *seed*. You can supply a seed directly (for example, through the `-SetSeed` parameter of the `Get-Random` cmdlet) for testing purposes, but it is usually derived from the system time.

Unless you reuse the same random number generator, this last point usually leads to the downfall of realistically random numbers. When you generate them quickly, you create new random number generators that are likely to have the same seed. This tends to create runs of duplicate random numbers:

```
PS > 1..10 | Foreach-Object { (New-Object System.Random).Next(1, 21) }
20
7
7
15
15
11
11
18
18
18
```

The `Get-Random` cmdlet saves you from this issue by internally maintaining a random number generator and its state:

```
PS > 1..10 | Foreach-Object { Get-Random -Min 1 -Max 21 }
20
18
7
12
16
10
```

```
9
13
16
14
```

For more information about working with classes from the .NET Framework, see Recipe 3.8, "Work with .NET Objects".

## See Also

Recipe 3.8, "Work with .NET Objects"

# 8.5. Program: Search the Windows Start Menu

When working at the command line, you might want to launch a program that is normally found only on your Start menu. While you could certainly click through the Start menu to find it, you could also search the Start menu with a script, as shown in Example 8-4.

*Example 8-4. Search-StartMenu.ps1*

```
##############################################################################
##
## Search-StartMenu
##
## From Windows PowerShell Cookbook (O'Reilly)
## by Lee Holmes (http://www.leeholmes.com/blog)
##
##############################################################################

<#

.SYNOPSIS

Search the Start Menu for items that match the provided text. This script
searches both the name (as displayed on the Start Menu itself,) and the
destination of the link.

.EXAMPLE

PS > Search-StartMenu "Character Map" | Invoke-Item
Searches for the "Character Map" appication, and then runs it

PS > Search-StartMenu PowerShell | Select-FilteredObject | Invoke-Item
Searches for anything with "PowerShell" in the application name, lets you
pick which one to launch, and then launches it.

#>

param(
    ## The pattern to match
```

```
        [Parameter(Mandatory = $true)]
        $Pattern
    )

    Set-StrictMode -Version 3

    ## Get the locations of the start menu paths
    $myStartMenu = [Environment]::GetFolderPath("StartMenu")
    $shell = New-Object -Com WScript.Shell
    $allStartMenu = $shell.SpecialFolders.Item("AllUsersStartMenu")

    ## Escape their search term, so that any regular expression
    ## characters don't affect the search
    $escapedMatch = [Regex]::Escape($pattern)

    ## Search in "my start menu" for text in the link name or link destination
    dir $myStartMenu *.lnk -rec | Where-Object {
        ($_.Name -match "$escapedMatch") -or
        ($_ | Select-String "\\[^\\]*$escapedMatch\." -Quiet)
    }

    ## Search in "all start menu" for text in the link name or link destination
    dir $allStartMenu *.lnk -rec | Where-Object {
        ($_.Name -match "$escapedMatch") -or
        ($_ | Select-String "\\[^\\]*$escapedMatch\." -Quiet)
    }
```

For more information about running scripts, see Recipe 1.1, "Run Programs, Scripts, and Existing Tools".

## See Also

Recipe 1.1, "Run Programs, Scripts, and Existing Tools"

# 8.6. Program: Show Colorized Script Content

## Discussion

When viewing or demonstrating scripts, syntax highlighting makes the information immensely easier to read. Viewing the scripts in the PowerShell Integrated Scripting Environment (ISE) is the most natural (and powerful) option, but you might want to view them in the console as well.

In addition to basic syntax highlighting, other useful features during script review are line numbers and highlighting ranges of lines. Range highlighting is especially useful when discussing portions of a script in a larger context.

Example 8-5 enables all of these scenarios by providing syntax highlighting of scripts in a console session. Figure 8-1 shows a sample of the colorized content.

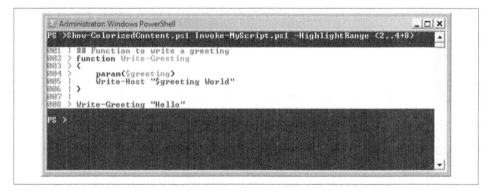

*Figure 8-1. Sample colorized content*

In addition to having utility all on its own, Show-ColorizedContent.ps1 demonstrates how to use PowerShell's Tokenizer API, as introduced in Recipe 10.10, "Parse and Interpret PowerShell Scripts". While many of the techniques in this example are specific to syntax highlighting in a PowerShell console, many more apply to all forms of script manipulation.

*Example 8-5. Show-ColorizedContent.ps1*

```
##############################################################################
##
## Show-ColorizedContent
##
## From Windows PowerShell Cookbook (O'Reilly)
## by Lee Holmes (http://www.leeholmes.com/guide)
##
##############################################################################

<#

.SYNOPSIS

Displays syntax highlighting, line numbering, and range highlighting for
PowerShell scripts.

.EXAMPLE

PS > Show-ColorizedContent Invoke-MyScript.ps1

001 | function Write-Greeting
002 | {
003 |     param($greeting)
004 |     Write-Host "$greeting World"
005 | }
006 |
007 | Write-Greeting "Hello"
```

```
.EXAMPLE

PS > Show-ColorizedContent Invoke-MyScript.ps1 -highlightRange (1..3+7)

001 > function Write-Greeting
002 > {
003 >     param($greeting)
004 |     Write-Host "$greeting World"
005 | }
006 |
007 > Write-Greeting "Hello"

#>

param(
    ## The path to colorize
    [Parameter(Mandatory = $true)]
    $Path,

    ## The range of lines to highlight
    $HighlightRange = @(),

    ## Switch to exclude line numbers
    [Switch] $ExcludeLineNumbers
)

Set-StrictMode -Version 3

## Colors to use for the different script tokens.
## To pick your own colors:
## [Enum]::GetValues($host.UI.RawUI.ForegroundColor.GetType()) |
##     Foreach-Object { Write-Host -Fore $_ "$_" }
$replacementColours = @{
    'Attribute' = 'DarkCyan'
    'Command' = 'Blue'
    'CommandArgument' = 'Magenta'
    'CommandParameter' = 'DarkBlue'
    'Comment' = 'DarkGreen'
    'GroupEnd' = 'Black'
    'GroupStart' = 'Black'
    'Keyword' = 'DarkBlue'
    'LineContinuation' = 'Black'
    'LoopLabel' = 'DarkBlue'
    'Member' = 'Black'
    'NewLine' = 'Black'
    'Number' = 'Magenta'
    'Operator' = 'DarkGray'
    'Position' = 'Black'
    'StatementSeparator' = 'Black'
    'String' = 'DarkRed'
    'Type' = 'DarkCyan'
```

```
    'Unknown' = 'Black'
    'Variable' = 'Red'
}

$highlightColor = "Red"
$highlightCharacter = ">"
$highlightWidth = 6
if($excludeLineNumbers) { $highlightWidth = 0 }

## Read the text of the file, and tokenize it
$content = Get-Content $Path -Raw
$parsed = [System.Management.Automation.PsParser]::Tokenize(
    $content, [ref] $null) | Sort StartLine,StartColumn

## Write a formatted line -- in the format of:
## <Line Number> <Separator Character> <Text>
function WriteFormattedLine($formatString, [int] $line)
{
    if($excludeLineNumbers) { return }

    ## By default, write the line number in gray, and use
    ## a simple pipe as the separator
    $hColor = "DarkGray"
    $separator = "|"

    ## If we need to highlight the line, use the highlight
    ## color and highlight separator as the separator
    if($highlightRange -contains $line)
    {
        $hColor = $highlightColor
        $separator = $highlightCharacter
    }

    ## Write the formatted line
    $text = $formatString -f $line,$separator
    Write-Host -NoNewLine -Fore $hColor -Back White $text
}

## Complete the current line with filler cells
function CompleteLine($column)
{
    ## Figure how much space is remaining
    $lineRemaining = $host.UI.RawUI.WindowSize.Width -
        $column - $highlightWidth + 1

    ## If we have less than 0 remaining, we've wrapped onto the
    ## next line. Add another buffer width worth of filler
    if($lineRemaining -lt 0)
    {
        $lineRemaining += $host.UI.RawUI.WindowSize.Width
    }
```

```
    Write-Host -NoNewLine -Back White (" " * $lineRemaining)
}

## Write the first line of context information (line number,
## highlight character.)
Write-Host
WriteFormattedLine "{0:D3} {1} " 1

## Now, go through each of the tokens in the input
## script
$column = 1
foreach($token in $parsed)
{
    $color = "Gray"

    ## Determine the highlighting color for that token by looking
    ## in the hashtable that maps token types to their color
    $color = $replacementColours[[string]$token.Type]
    if(-not $color) { $color = "Gray" }

    ## If it's a newline token, write the next line of context
    ## information
    if(($token.Type -eq "NewLine") -or ($token.Type -eq "LineContinuation"))
    {
        CompleteLine $column
        WriteFormattedLine "{0:D3} {1} " ($token.StartLine + 1)
        $column = 1
    }
    else
    {
        ## Do any indenting
        if($column -lt $token.StartColumn)
        {
            $text = " " * ($token.StartColumn - $column)
            Write-Host -Back White -NoNewLine $text
            $column = $token.StartColumn
        }

        ## See where the token ends
        $tokenEnd = $token.Start + $token.Length - 1

        ## Handle the line numbering for multi-line strings and comments
        if(
            (($token.Type -eq "String") -or
            ($token.Type -eq "Comment")) -and
            ($token.EndLine -gt $token.StartLine))
        {
            ## Store which line we've started at
            $lineCounter = $token.StartLine

            ## Split the content of this token into its lines
            ## We use the start and end of the tokens to determine
```

```
## the position of the content, but use the content
## itself (rather than the token values) for manipulation.
$stringLines = $(
    -join $content[$token.Start..$tokenEnd] -split "`n")

## Go through each of the lines in the content
foreach($stringLine in $stringLines)
{
    $stringLine = $stringLine.Trim()

    ## If we're on a new line, fill the right hand
    ## side of the line with spaces, and write the header
    ## for the new line.
    if($lineCounter -gt $token.StartLine)
    {
        CompleteLine $column
        WriteFormattedLine "{0:D3} {1} " $lineCounter
        $column = 1
    }

    ## Now write the text of the current line
    Write-Host -NoNewLine -Fore $color -Back White $stringLine
    $column += $stringLine.Length
    $lineCounter++

    }
}
## Write out a regular token
else
{
    ## We use the start and end of the tokens to determine
    ## the position of the content, but use the content
    ## itself (rather than the token values) for manipulation.
    $text = (-join $content[$token.Start..$tokenEnd])
    Write-Host -NoNewLine -Fore $color -Back White $text
}
## Update our position in the column
$column = $token.EndColumn
    }
}

CompleteLine $column
Write-Host
```

For more information about running scripts, see Recipe 1.1, "Run Programs, Scripts, and Existing Tools".

## See Also

Recipe 1.1, "Run Programs, Scripts, and Existing Tools"

Recipe 10.10, "Parse and Interpret PowerShell Scripts"

# PART III
# Common Tasks

Chapter 9, *Simple Files*
Chapter 10, *Structured Files*
Chapter 11, *Code Reuse*
Chapter 12, *Internet-Enabled Scripts*
Chapter 13, *User Interaction*
Chapter 14, *Debugging*
Chapter 15, *Tracing and Error Management*
Chapter 16, *Environmental Awareness*
Chapter 17, *Extend the Reach of Windows PowerShell*
Chapter 18, *Security and Script Signing*
Chapter 19, *Integrated Scripting Environment*

# Simple Files

## 9.0. Introduction

When administering a system, you naturally spend a significant amount of time working with the files on that system. Many of the things you want to do with these files are simple: get their content, search them for a pattern, or replace text inside them.

For even these simple operations, PowerShell's object-oriented flavor adds several unique and powerful twists.

## 9.1. Get the Content of a File

### Problem

You want to get the content of a file.

### Solution

Provide the filename as an argument to the Get-Content cmdlet:

```
PS > $content = Get-Content c:\temp\file.txt
```

Place the filename in a ${} section to use the cmdlet Get-Content variable syntax:

```
PS > $content = ${c:\temp\file.txt}
```

Provide the filename as an argument to the ReadAllLines() or ReadAllText() methods to use the System.IO.File class from the .NET Framework:

```
PS > $content = Get-Content c:\temp\file.txt -Raw
PS > $contentLines = [System.IO.File]::ReadAllLines("c:\temp\file.txt")
```

# Discussion

PowerShell offers three primary ways to get the content of a file. The first is the Get-Content cmdlet—the cmdlet designed for this purpose. In fact, the Get-Content cmdlet works on any PowerShell drive that supports the concept of items with content. This includes Alias:, Function:, and more. The second and third ways are the Get-Content variable syntax and the ReadAllText() method.

When working against files, the Get-Content cmdlet returns the content of the file line by line. When it does this, PowerShell supplies additional information about that output line. This information, which PowerShell attaches as properties to each output line, includes the drive and path from where that line originated, among other things.

 If you want PowerShell to split the file content based on a string that you choose (rather than the default of newlines), the Get-Content cmdlet's -Delimiter parameter lets you provide one.

While useful, having PowerShell attach this extra information when you are not using it can sometimes slow down scripts that operate on large files. If you need to process a large file more quickly, the Get-Content cmdlet's ReadCount parameter lets you control how many lines PowerShell reads from the file at once. With a ReadCount of 1 (which is the default), PowerShell returns each line one by one. With a ReadCount of 2, PowerShell returns two lines at a time. With a ReadCount of less than 1, PowerShell returns all lines from the file at once.

 Beware of using a ReadCount of less than 1 for extremely large files. One of the benefits of the Get-Content cmdlet is its streaming behavior. No matter how large the file, you will still be able to process each line of the file without using up all your system's memory. Since a ReadCount of less than 1 reads the entire file before returning any results, large files have the potential to use up your system's memory. For more information about how to effectively take advantage of PowerShell's streaming capabilities, see Recipe 5.15, "Generate Large Reports and Text Streams".

If performance is a primary concern, the [System.IO.File]::ReadAllLines() method from the .NET Framework returns all of the lines of a file, but doesn't attach the additional (sometimes useful) properties to each line. This method also loads the entire file into memory before giving you access to it, so may be unsuitable for extremely large files.

When you want to deal with the entire content of a file at once (and not split it into lines), use the -Raw parameter of the Get-Content cmdlet.

```
$rawContent = Get-Content c:\temp\file.txt -Raw
```

The -Raw parameter was introduced in PowerShell version 3. If you have access only to PowerShell version 2, you can use the [System.IO.File]::ReadAllText() method from the .NET Framework. Both of these options load the entire file into memory before giving you access to it, so may be unsuitable for extremely large files.

For more information about the Get-Content cmdlet, type **Get-Help Get-Content**. For information on how to work with more structured files (such as XML and CSV), see Chapter 10. For more information on how to work with binary files, see Recipe 9.4, "Parse and Manage Binary Files".

## See Also

Recipe 5.15, "Generate Large Reports and Text Streams"

Recipe 9.4, "Parse and Manage Binary Files"

Chapter 10, *Structured Files*

# 9.2. Search a File for Text or a Pattern

## Problem

You want to find a string or regular expression in a file.

## Solution

To search a file for an exact (but case-insensitive) match, use the -Simple parameter of the Select-String cmdlet:

```
PS > Select-String -Simple SearchText file.txt
```

To search a file for a regular expression, provide that pattern to the Select-String cmdlet:

```
PS > Select-String "\(...\) ...-...." phone.txt
```

To recursively search all *.txt files for a regular expression, pipe the results of Get-ChildItem to the Select-String cmdlet:

```
PS > Get-ChildItem *.txt -Recurse | Select-String pattern
```

Or, using built-in aliases:

```
PS > dir *.txt -rec | sls pattern
```

## Discussion

The `Select-String` cmdlet is the easiest way to search files for a pattern or specific string. In contrast to the traditional text-matching utilities (such as `grep`) that support the same type of functionality, the matches returned by the `Select-String` cmdlet include detailed information about the match itself.

```
PS > $matches = Select-String "output file" transcript.txt
PS > $matches | Select LineNumber,Line

          LineNumber Line
          ---------- ----
                   7 Transcript started, output file...
```

With a regular expression match, you'll often want to find out exactly what text was matched by the regular expression. PowerShell captures this in the `Matches` property of the result. For each match, the `Value` property represents the text matched by your pattern.

```
PS > Select-String "\(...\) ...-...." phone.txt | Select -Expand Matches

...
Value      : (425) 555-1212

...
Value      : (416) 556-1213
```

If your regular expression defines groups (portions of the pattern enclosed in parentheses), you can access the text matched by those groups through the `Groups` property. The first group (`Group[0]`) represents all of the text matched by your pattern. Additional groups (1 and on) represent the groups you defined. In this case, we add additional parentheses around the area code to capture it.

```
PS > Select-String "\((...)\) ...-...." phone.txt |
    Select -Expand Matches | Foreach { $_.Groups[1] }

Success   : True
Captures  : {425}
Index     : 1
Length    : 3
Value     : 425

Success   : True
Captures  : {416}
Index     : 1
Length    : 3
Value     : 416
```

If your regular expression defines a *named capture* (with the text *?<Name>* at the beginning of a group), the `Groups` collection lets you access those by name. In this example, we capture the area code using `AreaCode` as the capture name.

```
PS > Select-String "\((?<AreaCode>...)\) ...-...." phone.txt |
    Select -Expand Matches | Foreach { $_.Groups["AreaCode"] }

Success   : True
Captures  : {425}
Index     : 1
Length    : 3
Value     : 425

Success   : True
Captures  : {416}
Index     : 1
Length    : 3
Value     : 416
```

By default, the Select-String cmdlet captures only the first match per line of input. If the input can have multiple matches per line, use the -AllMatches parameter.

```
PS > Get-Content phone.txt
(425) 555-1212
(416) 556-1213 (416) 557-1214

PS > Select-String "\((...)\) ...-...." phone.txt |
    Select -Expand Matches | Select -Expand Value

(425) 555-1212
(416) 556-1213

PS > Select-String "\((...)\) ...-...." phone.txt -AllMatches |
    Select -Expand Matches | Select -Expand Value

(425) 555-1212
(416) 556-1213
(416) 557-1214
```

For more information about captures, named captures, and other aspects of regular expressions, see Appendix B.

 If the information you need is on a different line than the line that has the match, use the -Context parameter to have that line included in Select-String's output. PowerShell places the result in the Context.PreContext and Context.PostContext properties of Select-String's output.

If you want to search multiple files of a specific extension, the Select-String cmdlet lets you use wildcards (such as *.txt) on the filename. For more complicated lists of files (which includes searching all files in the directory), it is usually better to use the Get-ChildItem cmdlet to generate the list of files as shown previously in the Solution.

Since the `Select-String` cmdlet outputs the filename, line number, and matching line for every match it finds, this output may sometimes include too much detail. A perfect example is when you are searching for a binary file that contains a specific string. A binary file (such as a DLL or EXE) rarely makes sense when displayed as text, so your screen quickly fills with apparent garbage.

The solution to this problem comes from `Select-String`'s `-Quiet` switch. It simply returns `true` or `false`, depending on whether the file contains the string. So, to find the DLL or EXE in the current directory that contains the text "Debug":

```
Get-ChildItem | Where { $_ | Select-String "Debug" -Quiet }
```

Two other common tools used to search files for text are the `-match` operator and the `switch` statement with the `-file` option. For more information about those, see Recipe 5.7, "Search a String for Text or a Pattern" and Recipe 4.3, "Manage Large Conditional Statements with Switches". For more information about the `Select-String` cmdlet, type **Get-Help Select-String**.

### See Also

Recipe 4.3, "Manage Large Conditional Statements with Switches"

Recipe 5.7, "Search a String for Text or a Pattern"

Appendix B, *Regular Expression Reference*

# 9.3. Parse and Manage Text-Based Logfiles

## Problem

You want to parse and analyze a text-based logfile using PowerShell's standard object management commands.

## Solution

Use the `Convert-TextObject` script given in Recipe 5.14, "Program: Convert Text Streams to Objects" to work with text-based logfiles. With your assistance, it converts streams of text into streams of objects, which you can then easily work with using PowerShell's standard commands.

The `Convert-TextObject` script primarily takes two arguments:

- A regular expression that describes how to break the incoming text into groups
- A list of property names that the script then assigns to those text groups

As an example, you can use patch logs from the Windows directory. These logs track the patch installation details from updates applied to the machine (except for Windows Vista). One detail included in these logfiles is the names and versions of the files modified by that specific patch, as shown in Example 9-1.

*Example 9-1. Getting a list of files modified by hotfixes*

```
PS > cd $env:WINDIR
PS > $parseExpression = "(.*): Destination:(.*) \((.*)\)"
PS > $files = dir kb*.log -Exclude *uninst.log
PS > $logContent = $files | Get-Content | Select-String $parseExpression
PS > $logContent

(...)
0.734: Destination:C:\WINNT\system32\shell32.dll (6.0.3790.205)
0.734: Destination:C:\WINNT\system32\wininet.dll (6.0.3790.218)
0.734: Destination:C:\WINNT\system32\urlmon.dll (6.0.3790.218)
0.734: Destination:C:\WINNT\system32\shlwapi.dll (6.0.3790.212)
0.734: Destination:C:\WINNT\system32\shdocvw.dll (6.0.3790.214)
0.734: Destination:C:\WINNT\system32\digest.dll (6.0.3790.0)
0.734: Destination:C:\WINNT\system32\browseui.dll (6.0.3790.218)
(...)
```

Like most logfiles, the format of the text is very regular but hard to manage. In this example, you have:

- A number (the number of seconds since the patch started)
- The text "`: Destination:`"
- The file being patched
- An open parenthesis
- The version of the file being patched
- A close parenthesis

You don't care about any of the text, but the time, file, and file version are useful properties to track:

```
$properties = "Time","File","FileVersion"
```

So now, you use the `Convert-TextObject` script to convert the text output into a stream of objects:

```
PS > $logObjects = $logContent |
    Convert-TextObject -ParseExpression $parseExpression -PropertyName $properties
```

We can now easily query those objects using PowerShell's built-in commands. For example, you can find the files most commonly affected by patches and service packs, as shown by Example 9-2.

*Example 9-2. Finding files most commonly affected by hotfixes*

```
PS > $logObjects | Group-Object file | Sort-Object -Descending Count |
    Select-Object Count,Name | Format-Table -Auto


Count Name
----- ----
  152 C:\WINNT\system32\shdocvw.dll
  147 C:\WINNT\system32\shlwapi.dll

  128 C:\WINNT\system32\wininet.dll
  116 C:\WINNT\system32\shell32.dll
   92 C:\WINNT\system32\rpcss.dll
   92 C:\WINNT\system32\olecli32.dll
   92 C:\WINNT\system32\ole32.dll
   84 C:\WINNT\system32\urlmon.dll
(...)
```

Using this technique, you can work with most text-based logfiles.

## Discussion

In Example 9-2, you got all the information you needed by splitting the input text into groups of simple strings. The time offset, file, and version information served their purposes as is. In addition to the features used by Example 9-2, however, the Convert-TextObject script also supports a parameter that lets you control the data types of those properties. If one of the properties should be treated as a number or a DateTime, you may get incorrect results if you work with that property as a string. For more information about this functionality, see the description of the -PropertyType parameter in the Convert-TextObject script.

Although most logfiles have entries designed to fit within a single line, some span multiple lines. When a logfile contains entries that span multiple lines, it includes some sort of special marker to separate log entries from each other. Look at this example:

```
PS > Get-Content AddressBook.txt
Name: Chrissy
Phone: 555-1212
----
Name: John
Phone: 555-1213
```

The key to working with this type of logfile comes from two places. The first is the -Delimiter parameter of the Get-Content cmdlet, which makes it split the file based on that delimiter instead of newlines. The second is to write a ParseExpression regular expression that ignores the newline characters that remain in each record:

```
PS > $records = gc AddressBook.txt -Delimiter "----"
PS > $parseExpression = "(?s)Name: (\S*).*Phone: (\S*).*"
```

```
PS > $records | Convert-TextObject -ParseExpression $parseExpression

Property1                                    Property2
---------                                    ---------
Chrissy                                      555-1212
John                                         555-1213
```

The parse expression in this example uses the *single line* option (?s) so that the (.*) portion of the regular expression accepts newline characters as well. For more information about these (and other) regular expression options, see Appendix B.

For extremely large logfiles, handwritten parsing tools may not meet your needs. In those situations, specialized log management tools can prove helpful. One example is Microsoft's free Log Parser (*http://www.logparser.com*). Another common alternative is to import the log entries to a SQL database, and then perform ad hoc queries on database tables instead.

## See Also

Recipe 5.14, "Program: Convert Text Streams to Objects"

Appendix B, *Regular Expression Reference*

# 9.4. Parse and Manage Binary Files

## Problem

You want to work with binary data in a file.

## Solution

There are two main techniques when working with binary data in a file. The first is to read the file using the Byte encoding, so that PowerShell does not treat the content as text. The second is to use the BitConverter class to translate these bytes back and forth into numbers that you more commonly care about.

Example 9-3 displays the "characteristics" of a Windows executable. The beginning section of any executable (a .dll, .exe, or any of several others) starts with a binary section known as the *portable executable (PE) header*. Part of this header includes characteristics about that file, such as whether the file is a DLL.

For more information about the PE header format, see this site (*http://bit.ly/T7j4sl*).

*Example 9-3. Get-Characteristics.ps1*

```
###########################################################################
##
## Get-Characteristics
```

```
##
## From Windows PowerShell Cookbook (O'Reilly)
## by Lee Holmes (http://www.leeholmes.com/guide)
##
################################################################################

<#

.SYNOPSIS

Get the file characteristics of a file in the PE Executable File Format.

.EXAMPLE

PS > Get-Characteristics $env:WINDIR\notepad.exe
IMAGE_FILE_LOCAL_SYMS_STRIPPED
IMAGE_FILE_RELOCS_STRIPPED
IMAGE_FILE_EXECUTABLE_IMAGE
IMAGE_FILE_32BIT_MACHINE
IMAGE_FILE_LINE_NUMS_STRIPPED

#>

param(
    ## The path to the file to check
    [Parameter(Mandatory = $true)]
    [string] $Path
)

Set-StrictMode -Version 3

## Define the characteristics used in the PE file header.
## Taken from:
## http://www.microsoft.com/whdc/system/platform/firmware/PECOFF.mspx
$characteristics = @{}
$characteristics["IMAGE_FILE_RELOCS_STRIPPED"] = 0x0001
$characteristics["IMAGE_FILE_EXECUTABLE_IMAGE"] = 0x0002
$characteristics["IMAGE_FILE_LINE_NUMS_STRIPPED"] = 0x0004
$characteristics["IMAGE_FILE_LOCAL_SYMS_STRIPPED"] = 0x0008
$characteristics["IMAGE_FILE_AGGRESSIVE_WS_TRIM"] = 0x0010
$characteristics["IMAGE_FILE_LARGE_ADDRESS_AWARE"] = 0x0020
$characteristics["RESERVED"] = 0x0040
$characteristics["IMAGE_FILE_BYTES_REVERSED_LO"] = 0x0080
$characteristics["IMAGE_FILE_32BIT_MACHINE"] = 0x0100
$characteristics["IMAGE_FILE_DEBUG_STRIPPED"] = 0x0200
$characteristics["IMAGE_FILE_REMOVABLE_RUN_FROM_SWAP"] = 0x0400
$characteristics["IMAGE_FILE_NET_RUN_FROM_SWAP"] = 0x0800
$characteristics["IMAGE_FILE_SYSTEM"] = 0x1000
$characteristics["IMAGE_FILE_DLL"] = 0x2000
$characteristics["IMAGE_FILE_UP_SYSTEM_ONLY"] = 0x4000
$characteristics["IMAGE_FILE_BYTES_REVERSED_HI"] = 0x8000
```

```
## Get the content of the file, as an array of bytes
$fileBytes = Get-Content $path -ReadCount 0 -Encoding byte

## The offset of the signature in the file is stored at location 0x3c.
$signatureOffset = $fileBytes[0x3c]

## Ensure it is a PE file
$signature = [char[]] $fileBytes[$signatureOffset..($signatureOffset + 3)]
if(($signature -join '') -ne "PE`0`0")
{
    throw "This file does not conform to the PE specification."
}

## The location of the COFF header is 4 bytes into the signature
$coffHeader = $signatureOffset + 4

## The characteristics data are 18 bytes into the COFF header. The
## BitConverter class manages the conversion of the 4 bytes into an integer.
$characteristicsData = [BitConverter]::ToInt32($fileBytes, $coffHeader + 18)

## Go through each of the characteristics. If the data from the file has that
## flag set, then output that characteristic.
foreach($key in $characteristics.Keys)
{
    $flag = $characteristics[$key]
    if(($characteristicsData -band $flag) -eq $flag)
    {
        $key
    }
}
```

## Discussion

For most files, this technique is the easiest way to work with binary data. If you actually modify the binary data, then you will also want to use the Byte encoding when you send it back to disk:

```
$fileBytes | Set-Content modified.exe -Encoding Byte
```

For extremely large files, though, it may be unacceptably slow to load the entire file into memory when you work with it. If you begin to run against this limit, the solution is to use file management classes from the .NET Framework. These classes include BinaryR eader, StreamReader, and others. For more information about working with classes from the .NET Framework, see Recipe 3.8, "Work with .NET Objects". For more information about running scripts, see Recipe 1.1, "Run Programs, Scripts, and Existing Tools".

## See Also

Recipe 1.1, "Run Programs, Scripts, and Existing Tools"

Recipe 3.8, "Work with .NET Objects"

# 9.5. Create a Temporary File

## Problem

You want to create a file for temporary purposes and want to be sure that the file does not already exist.

## Solution

Use the [System.IO.Path]::GetTempFilename() method from the .NET Framework to create a temporary file:

```
$filename = [System.IO.Path]::GetTempFileName()
(... use the file ...)
Remove-Item -Force $filename
```

## Discussion

It is common to want to create a file for temporary purposes. For example, you might want to search and replace text inside a file. Doing this to a large file requires a temporary file (see Recipe 9.6, "Search and Replace Text in a File"). Another example is the temporary file used by Recipe 2.4, "Program: Interactively Filter Lists of Objects".

Often, people create this temporary file wherever they can think of: in *C:\*, the script's current location, or any number of other places. Although this may work on the author's system, it rarely works well elsewhere. For example, if the user does not use her Administrator account for day-to-day tasks, your script will not have access to *C:\* and will fail.

Another difficulty comes from trying to create a unique name for the temporary file. If your script just hardcodes a name (no matter how many random characters it has), it will fail if you run two copies at the same time. You might even craft a script smart enough to search for a filename that does not exist, create it, and then use it. Unfortunately, this could still break if another copy of your script creates that file after you see that it is missing but before you actually create the file.

Finally, there are several security vulnerabilities that your script might introduce should it write its temporary files to a location that other users can read or write.

---

Luckily, the authors of the .NET Framework provided the [System.IO.Path]::Get TempFilename() method to resolve these problems for you. It creates a unique filename in a reliable location and in a secure manner. The method returns a filename, which you can then use as you want.

 Remember to delete this file when your script no longer needs it; otherwise, your script will waste disk space and cause needless clutter on your users' systems. Remember: your scripts should solve the administrator's problems, not cause them!

By default, the GetTempFilename() method returns a file with a *.tmp* extension. For most purposes, the file extension does not matter, and this works well. In the rare instances when you need to create a file with a specific extension, the [System .IO.Path]::ChangeExtension() method lets you change the extension of that temporary file. The following example creates a new temporary file that uses the *.cs* file extension:

```
$filename = [System.IO.Path]::GetTempFileName()
$newname = [System.IO.Path]::ChangeExtension($filename, ".cs")
Move-Item $filename $newname
(... use the file ...)
Remove-Item $newname
```

### See Also

Recipe 2.4, "Program: Interactively Filter Lists of Objects"

Recipe 9.6, "Search and Replace Text in a File"

# 9.6. Search and Replace Text in a File

## Problem

You want to search for text in a file and replace that text with something new.

## Solution

To search and replace text in a file, first store the content of the file in a variable, and then store the replaced text back in that file, as shown in Example 9-4.

*Example 9-4. Replacing text in a file*

```
PS > $filename = "file.txt"
PS > $match = "source text"
PS > $replacement = "replacement text"
PS >
```

```
PS > $content = Get-Content $filename
PS > $content
This is some source text that we want
to replace. One of the things you may need
to be careful about with Source
Text is when it spans multiple lines,
and may have different Source Text
capitalization.
PS >
PS > $content = $content -creplace $match,$replacement
PS > $content
This is some replacement text that we want
to replace. One of the things you may need
to be careful about with Source
Text is when it spans multiple lines,
and may have different Source Text
capitalization.
PS > $content | Set-Content $filename
```

## Discussion

Using PowerShell to search and replace text in a file (or many files!) is one of the best examples of using a tool to automate a repetitive task. What could literally take months by hand can be shortened to a few minutes (or hours, at most).

> Notice that the Solution uses the `-creplace` operator to replace text in a case-sensitive manner. This is almost always what you will want to do, as the replacement text uses the exact capitalization that you provide. If the text you want to replace is capitalized in several different ways (as in the term `Source Text` from the Solution), then search and replace several times with the different possible capitalizations.

Example 9-4 illustrates what is perhaps the simplest (but actually most common) scenario:

- You work with an ASCII text file.
- You replace some literal text with a literal text replacement.
- You don't worry that the text match might span multiple lines.
- Your text file is relatively small.

If some of those assumptions don't hold true, then this discussion shows you how to tailor the way you search and replace within this file.

### Work with files encoded in Unicode or another (OEM) code page

By default, the Set-Content cmdlet assumes that you want the output file to contain plain ASCII text. If you work with a file in another encoding (for example, Unicode or an OEM code page such as Cyrillic), use the -Encoding parameter of the Out-File cmdlet to specify that:

```
$content | Out-File -Encoding Unicode $filename
$content | Out-File -Encoding OEM $filename
```

### Replace text using a pattern instead of plain text

Although it is most common to replace one literal string with another literal string, you might want to replace text according to a pattern in some advanced scenarios. One example might be swapping first name and last name. PowerShell supports this type of replacement through its support of regular expressions in its replacement operator:

```
PS > $content = Get-Content names.txt
PS > $content
John Doe
Mary Smith
PS > $content -replace '(.*) (.*)','$2, $1'
Doe, John
Smith, Mary
```

### Replace text that spans multiple lines

The Get-Content cmdlet used in the Solution retrieves a list of lines from the file. When you use the -replace operator against this array, it replaces your text in each of those lines individually. If your match spans multiple lines, as shown between lines 3 and 4 in Example 9-4, the -replace operator will be unaware of the match and will not perform the replacement.

If you want to replace text that spans multiple lines, then it becomes necessary to stop treating the input text as a collection of lines. Once you stop treating the input as a collection of lines, it is also important to use a replacement expression that can ignore line breaks, as shown in Example 9-5.

*Example 9-5. Replacing text across multiple lines in a file*

```
$singleLine = Get-Content file.txt -Raw
$content = $singleLine -creplace "(?s)Source(\s*)Text",'Replacement$1Text'
```

The first and second lines of Example 9-5 read the entire content of the file as a single string. They do this by using the -Raw parameter of the Get-Content cmdlet, since the Get-Content cmdlet by default splits the content of the file into individual lines.

The third line of this solution replaces the text by using a regular expression pattern. The section Source(\s*)Text scans for the word Source, followed optionally by some whitespace, followed by the word Text. Since the whitespace portion of the regular expression has parentheses around it, we want to remember exactly what that whitespace was. By default, regular expressions do not let newline characters count as whitespace, so the first portion of the regular expression uses the *single-line option* (?s) to allow newline characters to count as whitespace. The replacement portion of the -replace operator replaces that match with Replacement, followed by the exact whitespace from the match that we captured ($1), followed by Text. For more information, see "Simple Operators" (page 873).

### Replace text in large files

The approaches used so far store the entire contents of the file in memory as they replace the text in them. Once we've made the replacements in memory, we write the updated content back to disk. This works well when replacing text in small, medium, and even moderately large files. For extremely large files (for example, more than several hundred megabytes), using this much memory may burden your system and slow down your script. To solve that problem, you can work on the files line by line, rather than with the entire file at once.

Since you're working with the file line by line, it will still be in use when you try to write replacement text back into it. You can avoid this problem if you write the replacement text into a temporary file until you've finished working with the main file. Once you've finished scanning through your file, you can delete it and replace it with the temporary file.

```
$filename = "file.txt"
$temporaryFile = [System.IO.Path]::GetTempFileName()

$match = "source text"
$replacement = "replacement text"

Get-Content $filename |
    Foreach-Object { $_ -creplace $match,$replacement } |
    Add-Content $temporaryFile

Remove-Item $filename
Move-Item $temporaryFile $filename
```

## See Also

"Simple Operators" (page 873)

# 9.7. Program: Get the Encoding of a File

Both PowerShell and the .NET Framework do a lot of work to hide from you the complexities of file encodings. The `Get-Content` cmdlet automatically detects the encoding of a file, and then handles all encoding issues before returning the content to you. When you do need to know the encoding of a file, though, the solution requires a bit of work.

Example 9-6 resolves this by doing the hard work for you. Files with unusual encodings are supposed to (and almost always do) have a *byte order mark* to identify the encoding. After the byte order mark, they have the actual content. If a file lacks the byte order mark (no matter how the content is encoded), `Get-FileEncoding` assumes the .NET Framework's default encoding of UTF-7. If the content is not actually encoded as defined by the byte order mark, `Get-FileEncoding` still outputs the declared encoding.

*Example 9-6. Get-FileEncoding.ps1*

```
##############################################################################
##
## Get-FileEncoding
##
## From Windows PowerShell Cookbook (O'Reilly)
## by Lee Holmes (http://www.leeholmes.com/guide)
##
##############################################################################

<#

.SYNOPSIS

Gets the encoding of a file

.EXAMPLE

Get-FileEncoding.ps1 .\UnicodeScript.ps1

BodyName            : unicodeFFFE
EncodingName        : Unicode (Big-Endian)
HeaderName          : unicodeFFFE
WebName             : unicodeFFFE
WindowsCodePage     : 1200
IsBrowserDisplay    : False
IsBrowserSave       : False
IsMailNewsDisplay   : False
IsMailNewsSave      : False
IsSingleByte        : False
EncoderFallback     : System.Text.EncoderReplacementFallback
DecoderFallback     : System.Text.DecoderReplacementFallback
IsReadOnly          : True
CodePage            : 1201

#>
```

```
param(
    ## The path of the file to get the encoding of.
    $Path
)

Set-StrictMode -Version 3

## First, check if the file is binary. That is, if the first
## 5 lines contain any non-printable characters.
$nonPrintable = [char[]] (0..8 + 10..31 + 127 + 129 + 141 + 143 + 144 + 157)
$lines = Get-Content $Path -ErrorAction Ignore -TotalCount 5
$result = @($lines | Where-Object { $_.IndexOfAny($nonPrintable) -ge 0 })
if($result.Count -gt 0)
{
    "Binary"
    return
}

## Next, check if it matches a well-known encoding.

## The hashtable used to store our mapping of encoding bytes to their
## name. For example, "255-254 = Unicode"
$encodings = @{}

## Find all of the encodings understood by the .NET Framework. For each,
## determine the bytes at the start of the file (the preamble) that the .NET
## Framework uses to identify that encoding.
foreach($encoding in [System.Text.Encoding]::GetEncodings())
{
    $preamble = $encoding.GetEncoding().GetPreamble()
    if($preamble)
    {
        $encodingBytes = $preamble -join '-'
        $encodings[$encodingBytes] = $encoding.GetEncoding()
    }
}

## Find out the lengths of all of the preambles.
$encodingLengths = $encodings.Keys | Where-Object { $_ } |
    Foreach-Object { ($_ -split "-").Count }

## Assume the encoding is UTF7 by default
$result = [System.Text.Encoding]::UTF7

## Go through each of the possible preamble lengths, read that many
## bytes from the file, and then see if it matches one of the encodings
## we know about.
foreach($encodingLength in $encodingLengths | Sort -Descending)
{
    $bytes = Get-Content -encoding byte -readcount $encodingLength $path |
            Select -First 1
```

```
$encoding = $encodings[$bytes -join '-']

## If we found an encoding that had the same preamble bytes,
## save that output and break.
if($encoding)
{
    $result = $encoding
    break
}
}

## Finally, output the encoding.
$result
```

For more information about running scripts, see Recipe 1.1, "Run Programs, Scripts, and Existing Tools".

## See Also

Recipe 1.1, "Run Programs, Scripts, and Existing Tools"

# 9.8. Program: View the Hexadecimal Representation of Content

When dealing with binary data, it is often useful to see the value of the actual bytes being used in that binary data. In addition to the value of the data, finding its offset in the file or content is usually important as well.

Example 9-7 enables both scenarios by displaying content in a report that shows all of this information. The leftmost column displays the offset into the content, increasing by 16 bytes at a time. The middle 16 columns display the hexadecimal representation of the byte at that position in the content. The header of each column shows how far into the 16-byte chunk that character is. The far-right column displays the ASCII representation of the characters in that row.

To determine the position of a byte within the input, add the number at the far left of the row to the number at the top of the column for that character. For example, 0000230 (shown at the far left) + C (shown at the top of the column) = 000023C. Therefore, the byte in this example is at offset 23C in the content.

*Example 9-7. Format-Hex.ps1*

```
#############################################################################
##
## Format-Hex
##
## From Windows PowerShell Cookbook (O'Reilly)
## by Lee Holmes (http://www.leeholmes.com/guide)
```

```
##
##############################################################################

<#

.SYNOPSIS

Outputs a file or pipelined input as a hexadecimal display. To determine the
offset of a character in the input, add the number at the far left of the row
with the number at the top of the column for that character.

.EXAMPLE

PS > "Hello World" | Format-Hex

            0  1  2  3  4  5  6  7  8  9  A  B  C  D  E  F

00000000    48 00 65 00 6C 00 6C 00 6F 00 20 00 57 00 6F 00    H.e.l.l.o. .W.o.
00000010    72 00 6C 00 64 00                                  r.l.d.

.EXAMPLE

PS > Format-Hex c:\temp\example.bmp

#>

[CmdletBinding(DefaultParameterSetName = "ByPath")]
param(
    ## The file to read the content from
    [Parameter(ParameterSetName = "ByPath", Position = 0)]
    [string] $Path,

    ## The input (bytes or strings) to format as hexadecimal
    [Parameter(
        ParameterSetName = "ByInput", Position = 0,
        ValueFromPipeline = $true)]
    [Object] $InputObject
)

begin
{
    Set-StrictMode -Version 3

    ## Create the array to hold the content. If the user specified the
    ## -Path parameter, read the bytes from the path.
    [byte[]] $inputBytes = $null
    if($Path) { $inputBytes = Get-Content $Path -Encoding Byte -Raw }

    ## Store our header, and formatting information
    $counter = 0
    $header = "            0  1  2  3  4  5  6  7  8  9  A  B  C  D  E  F"
    $nextLine = "{0}    " -f [Convert]::ToString(
```

```
            $counter, 16).ToUpper().PadLeft(8, '0')
        $asciiEnd = ""

        ## Output the header
        "`r`n$header`r`n"
}

process
{
    ## If they specified the -InputObject parameter, retrieve the bytes
    ## from that input
    if($PSCmdlet.ParameterSetName -eq "ByInput")
    {
        ## If it's an actual byte, add it to the inputBytes array.
        if($InputObject -is [Byte])
        {
            $inputBytes = $InputObject
        }
        else
        {
            ## Otherwise, convert it to a string and extract the bytes
            ## from that.
            $inputString = [string] $InputObject
            $inputBytes = [Text.Encoding]::Unicode.GetBytes($inputString)
        }
    }

    ## Now go through the input bytes
    foreach($byte in $inputBytes)
    {
        ## Display each byte, in 2-digit hexadecimal, and add that to the
        ## lefthand side.
        $nextLine += "{0:X2} " -f $byte

        ## If the character is printable, add its ascii representation to
        ## the righthand side.  Otherwise, add a dot to the righthand side.
        if(($byte -ge 0x20) -and ($byte -le 0xFE))
        {
            $asciiEnd += [char] $byte
        }
        else
        {
            $asciiEnd += "."
        }

        $counter++;

        ## If we've hit the end of a line, combine the right half with the
        ## left half, and start a new line.
        if(($counter % 16) -eq 0)
        {
```

```
        "$nextLine $asciiEnd"
        $nextLine = "{0}   " -f [Convert]::ToString(
            $counter, 16).ToUpper().PadLeft(8, '0')
        $asciiEnd = "";
    }
  }
}

end
{
    ## At the end of the file, we might not have had the chance to output
    ## the end of the line yet.  Only do this if we didn't exit on the 16-byte
    ## boundary, though.
    if(($counter % 16) -ne 0)
    {
        while(($counter % 16) -ne 0)
        {
            $nextLine += "   "
            $asciiEnd += " "
            $counter++;
        }
        "$nextLine $asciiEnd"
    }

    ""
}
```

For more information about running scripts, see Recipe 1.1, "Run Programs, Scripts, and Existing Tools".

## See Also

Recipe 1.1, "Run Programs, Scripts, and Existing Tools"

# Structured Files

## 10.0. Introduction

In the world of text-only system administration, managing structured files is often a pain. For example, working with (or editing) an XML file means either loading it into an editor to modify by hand or writing a custom tool that can do that for you. Even worse, it may mean modifying the file as though it were plain text while hoping to not break the structure of the XML itself.

In that same world, working with a file in comma-separated values (CSV) format means going through the file yourself, splitting each line by the commas in it. It's a seemingly great approach, until you find yourself faced with anything but the simplest of data.

Structure and structured files don't come only from other programs, either. When you're writing scripts, one common goal is to save structured data so that you can use it later. In most scripting (and programming) languages, this requires that you design a data structure to hold that data, design a way to store and retrieve it from disk, and bring it back to a usable form when you want to work with it again.

Fortunately, working with XML, CSV, and even your own structured files becomes much easier with PowerShell at your side.

## 10.1. Access Information in an XML File

### Problem

You want to work with and access information in an XML file.

## Solution

Use PowerShell's XML cast to convert the plain-text XML into a form that you can more easily work with. In this case, we use the RSS feed downloaded from the Windows PowerShell blog:

```
PS > $xml = [xml] (Get-Content powershell_blog.xml)
```

 See Recipe 12.1, "Download a File from an FTP or Internet Site" for more detail about how to use PowerShell to download this file:

```
Invoke-WebRequest blogs.msdn.com/b/powershell/rss.aspx `
    -OutFile powershell_blog.xml
```

Like other rich objects, PowerShell displays the properties of the XML as you explore. These properties are child nodes and attributes in the XML, as shown by Example 10-1.

*Example 10-1. Accessing properties of an XML document*

```
PS > $xml
xml                          xml-stylesheet                rss
---                          --------------                ---
                                                           rss


PS > $xml.rss


version : 2.0
dc      : http://purl.org/dc/elements/1.1/
slash   : http://purl.org/rss/1.0/modules/slash/
wfw     : http://wellformedweb.org/CommentAPI/
channel : channel
```

If more than one node shares the same name (as in the item nodes of an RSS feed), then the property name represents a collection of nodes:

```
PS > ($xml.rss.channel.item).Count
15
```

You can access those items individually, like you would normally work with an array, as shown in Example 10-2.

*Example 10-2. Accessing individual items in an XML document*

```
PS > ($xml.rss.channel.item)[0]


title    : Windows Management Framework is here!
link     : http://blogs.msdn.com/powershell/archive/2009/10/27/windows-
           management-framework-is-here.aspx
pubDate  : Tue, 27 Oct 2009 18:25:13 GMT
guid     : guid
creator  : PowerShellTeam
```

```
comments     : {15, http://blogs.msdn.com/powershell/comments/9913618.aspx}
commentRss   : http://blogs.msdn.com/powershell/commentrss.aspx?PostID=9913
               618
comment      : http://blogs.msdn.com/powershell/rsscomments.aspx?PostID=991
               3618
description  : <p>Windows Management Framework, which includes Windows Power
               Shell 2.0, WinRM 2.0, and BITS 4.0, was officially released
               to the world this morning.
(...)
```

You can access properties of those elements the same way you would normally work with an object:

```
PS > ($xml.rss.channel.item)[0].title
Windows Management Framework is here!
```

Since these are rich PowerShell objects, Example 10-3 demonstrates how you can use PowerShell's advanced object-based cmdlets for further work, such as sorting and filtering.

*Example 10-3. Sorting and filtering items in an XML document*

```
PS > $xml.rss.channel.item | Sort-Object title | Select-Object title


title
-----
Analyzing Weblog Data Using the Admin Development Model
Announcing: Open Source PowerShell Cmdlet and Help Designer
Help Us Improve Microsoft Windows Management Framework
Introducing the Windows 7 Resource Kit PowerShell Pack
New and Improved PowerShell Connect Site
PowerShell V2 Virtual Launch Party
Remoting for non-Admins
Select -ExpandProperty <PropertyName>
The Glory of Quick and Dirty Scripting
Tonight is the Virtual Launch Party @ PowerScripting Podcast
Understanding the Feedback Process
What's New in PowerShell V2 -  By Joel "Jaykul" Bennett
What's Up With Command Prefixes?
Windows Management Framework is here!
XP and W2K3 Release Candidate Versions of PowerShell Are Now Available ...
```

## Discussion

PowerShell's native XML support provides an excellent way to easily navigate and access XML files. By exposing the XML hierarchy as properties, you can perform most tasks without having to resort to text-only processing or custom tools.

In fact, PowerShell's support for interaction with XML goes beyond just presenting your data in an object-friendly way. The objects created by the [xml] cast in fact represent fully featured `System.Xml.XmlDocument` objects from the .NET Framework. Each property of the resulting objects represents a `System.Xml.XmlElement` object from the .NET Framework as well. The underlying objects provide a great deal of additional functionality that you can use to perform both common and complex tasks on XML files.

The underlying `System.Xml.XmlDocument` and `System.Xml.XmlElement` objects that support your XML also provide useful properties in their own right: `Attributes`, `Name`, `OuterXml`, and more.

```
PS > $xml.rss.Attributes

#text
-----
2.0
http://purl.org/dc/elements/1.1/
http://purl.org/rss/1.0/modules/slash/
http://wellformedweb.org/CommentAPI/
```

For more information about using the underlying .NET objects for more advanced tasks, see Recipe 10.2, "Perform an XPath Query Against XML" and Recipe 10.4, "Modify Data in an XML File".

For more information about working with XML in PowerShell, see Table F-11 in Appendix F.

## See Also

Recipe 10.2, "Perform an XPath Query Against XML"

Recipe 10.4, "Modify Data in an XML File"

Recipe 12.1, "Download a File from an FTP or Internet Site"

Table F-11

# 10.2. Perform an XPath Query Against XML

## Problem

You want to perform an advanced query against an XML file, using XML's standard *XPath syntax*.

## Solution

Use PowerShell's `Select-Xml` cmdlet to perform an XPath query against a file.

For example, to find all post titles shorter than 30 characters in an RSS feed:

```
PS > $query = "/rss/channel/item[string-length(title) < 30]/title"
PS > Select-Xml -XPath $query -Path .\powershell_blog.xml | Select -Expand Node

#text
-----
Remoting for non-Admins
```

## Discussion

Although a language all of its own, the XPath query syntax provides a powerful, XML-centric way to write advanced queries for XML files. The Select-Xml cmdlet lets you apply these concepts to files, XML nodes, or simply plain text.

 The XPath queries supported by the Select-Xml cmdlet are a popular industry standard. Beware, though. Unlike those in the rest of Power-Shell, these queries are case-sensitive!

The Select-Xml cmdlet generates a SelectXmlInfo object. This lets you chain separate XPath queries together. To retrieve the actual result of the selection, access the Node property.

```
PS > Get-Content page.html
<HTML>
    <HEAD>
        <TITLE>Welcome to my Website</TITLE>
    </HEAD>
    <BODY>
        <P>...</P>
    </BODY>
</HTML>
PS > $content = [xml] (Get-Content page.html)
PS > $result = $content | Select-Xml "/HTML/HEAD" | Select-Xml "TITLE"
PS > $result
```

| Node  | Path        | Pattern |
| ----  | ----        | ------- |
| TITLE | InputStream | TITLE   |

```
PS > $result.Node

#text
-----
Welcome to my Website
```

This works even for content accessed through PowerShell's XML support, as in this case, which uses the RSS feed downloaded from the Windows PowerShell blog:

---

```
PS > $xml = [xml] (Get-Content powershell_blog.xml)
PS > $xml | Select-Xml $query | Select -Expand Node

#text
-----
Remoting for non-Admins
```

For simpler queries, you may find PowerShell's object-based XML navigation concepts easier to work with. For more information about working with XML through Power-Shell's XML type, see Table F-11 in Appendix F. For more information about XPath syntax, see Appendix C.

## See Also

Appendix C, *XPath Quick Reference*

Table F-11

# 10.3. Convert Objects to XML

## Problem

You want to convert command output to XML for further processing or viewing.

## Solution

Use PowerShell's ConvertTo-Xml cmdlet to save the output of a command as XML:

```
$xml = Get-Process | ConvertTo-Xml
```

You can then use PowerShell's XML support (XML navigation, Select-Xml, and more) to work with the content.

## Discussion

Although it is usually easiest to work with objects in their full fidelity, you may sometimes want to convert them to XML for further processing by other programs. The solution is the ConvertTo-Xml cmdlet.

> PowerShell includes another similar-sounding cmdlet called Export-CliXml. Unlike the ConvertTo-Xml cmdlet, which is intended to produce useful output for humans and programs alike, the Export-CliXml cmdlet is designed for PowerShell-centric data interchange. For more information, see Recipe 10.5, "Easily Import and Export Your Structured Data".

The `ConvertTo-Xml` cmdlet gives you two main targets for this conversion. The default is an XML document, which is the same type of object created by the `[xml]` cast in PowerShell. This is also the format supported by the `Select-Xml` cmdlet, so you can pipe the output of `ConvertTo-Xml` directly into it.

```
PS > $xml = Get-Process | ConvertTo-Xml
PS > $xml | Select-Xml '//Property[@Name = "Name"]' | Select -Expand Node

Name                     Type                    #text
----                     ----                    -----
Name                     System.String          audiodg
Name                     System.String          csrss
Name                     System.String          dwm
(...)
```

The second format is a simple string, and it is suitable for redirection into a file. To save the XML into a file, use the `-As` parameter with `String` as the argument, and then use the file redirection operator:

```
Get-Process | ConvertTo-Xml -As String > c:\temp\processes.xml
```

If you already have an XML document that you obtained from `ConvertTo-Xml` or PowerShell's `[xml]` cast, you can still save it into a file by calling its `Save()` method:

```
$xml = Get-Process | ConvertTo-Xml
$xml.Save("c:\temp\output.xml")
```

For more information on how to work with XML data in PowerShell, see Recipe 10.1, "Access Information in an XML File".

## See Also

Recipe 10.1, "Access Information in an XML File"

Recipe 10.5, "Easily Import and Export Your Structured Data"

# 10.4. Modify Data in an XML File

## Problem

You want to use PowerShell to modify the data in an XML file.

## Solution

To modify data in an XML file, load the file into PowerShell's XML data type, change the content you want, and then save the file back to disk. Example 10-4 demonstrates this approach.

*Example 10-4. Modifying an XML file from PowerShell*

```
PS > ## Store the filename
PS > $filename = (Get-Item phone.xml).FullName
PS >
PS > ## Get the content of the file, and load it
PS > ## as XML
PS > Get-Content $filename
<AddressBook>
  <Person contactType="Personal">
    <Name>Lee</Name>
    <Phone type="home">555-1212</Phone>
    <Phone type="work">555-1213</Phone>
  </Person>
  <Person contactType="Business">
    <Name>Ariel</Name>
    <Phone>555-1234</Phone>
  </Person>
</AddressBook>
PS > $phoneBook = [xml] (Get-Content $filename)
PS >
PS > ## Get the part with data we want to change
PS > $person = $phoneBook.AddressBook.Person[0]
PS >
PS > ## Change the text part of the information,
PS > ## and the type (which was an attribute)
PS > $person.Phone[0]."#text" = "555-1214"
PS > $person.Phone[0].type = "mobile"
PS >
PS > ## Add a new phone entry
PS > $newNumber = [xml] '<Phone type="home">555-1215</Phone>'
PS > $newNode = $phoneBook.ImportNode($newNumber.Phone, $true)
PS > [void] $person.AppendChild($newNode)
PS >
PS > ## Save the file to disk
PS > $phoneBook.Save($filename)
PS > Get-Content $filename
<AddressBook>
  <Person contactType="Personal">
    <Name>Lee</Name>
    <Phone type="mobile">555-1214</Phone>
    <Phone type="work">555-1213</Phone>
    <Phone type="home">555-1215</Phone>
  </Person>
  <Person contactType="Business">
    <Name>Ariel</Name>
    <Phone>555-1234</Phone>
  </Person>
</AddressBook>
```

## Discussion

In the preceding Solution, you change Lee's phone number (which was the "text" portion of the XML's original first Phone node) from 555-1212 to 555-1214. You also change the type of the phone number (which was an attribute of the Phone node) from "home" to "mobile".

Adding new information to the XML is nearly as easy. To add information to an XML file, you need to add it as a *child node* to another node in the file. The easiest way to get that child node is to write the string that represents the XML and then create a temporary PowerShell XML document from that. From that temporary document, you use the main XML document's ImportNode() function to import the node you care about—specifically, the Phone node in this example.

Once we have the child node, you need to decide where to put it. Since we want this Phone node to be a child of the Person node for Lee, we will place it there. To add a child node ($newNode in Example 10-4) to a destination node ($person in the example), use the AppendChild() method from the destination node.

> The Save() method on the XML document allows you to save to more than just files. For a quick way to convert XML into a "beautified" form, save it to the console:
>
> ```
> $phoneBook.Save([Console]::Out)
> ```

Finally, we save the XML back to the file from which it came.

# 10.5. Easily Import and Export Your Structured Data

## Problem

You have a set of data (such as a hashtable or array) and want to save it to disk so that you can use it later. Conversely, you have saved structured data to a file and want to import it so that you can use it.

## Solution

Use PowerShell's Export-CliXml cmdlet to save structured data to disk, and the Import-CliXml cmdlet to import it again from disk.

For example, imagine storing a list of your favorite directories in a hashtable, so that you can easily navigate your system with a "Favorite CD" function. Example 10-5 shows this function.

*Example 10-5. A function that requires persistent structured data*

```
PS > $favorites = @{}
PS > $favorites["temp"] = "c:\temp"
PS > $favorites["music"] = "h:\lee\my music"
PS > function fcd {
    param([string] $location) Set-Location $favorites[$location]
}

PS > Get-Location

Path
----
HKLM:\software

PS > fcd temp
PS > Get-Location

Path
----
C:\temp
```

Unfortunately, the $favorites variable vanishes whenever you close PowerShell.

To get around this, you could recreate the $favorites variable in your profile, but another approach is to export it directly to a file. This command assumes that you have already created a profile, and it places the file in the same location as that profile:

```
PS > $filename = Join-Path (Split-Path $profile) favorites.clixml
PS > $favorites | Export-CliXml $filename
PS > $favorites = $null
PS > $favorites
PS >
```

Once the file is on disk, you can reload it using the Import-CliXml cmdlet, as shown in Example 10-6.

*Example 10-6. Restoring structured data from disk*

```
PS > $favorites = Import-CliXml $filename
PS > $favorites

Name                    Value
----                    -----
music                   h:\lee\my music
temp                    c:\temp

PS > fcd music
PS > Get-Location

Path
----
H:\lee\My Music
```

## Discussion

PowerShell provides the `Export-CliXml` and `Import-CliXml` cmdlets to let you easily move structured data into and out of files. These cmdlets accomplish this in a very data-centric and future-proof way—by storing only the names, values, and basic data types for the properties of that data.

 By default, PowerShell stores one level of data: all directly accessible simple properties (such as the `WorkingSet` of a process) but a plain-text representation for anything deeper (such as a process's `Threads` collection). For information on how to control the depth of this export, type **`Get-Help Export-CliXml`** and see the explanation of the `-Depth` parameter.

After you import data saved by `Export-CliXml`, you again have access to the properties and values from the original data. PowerShell converts some objects back to their fully featured objects (such as `System.DateTime` objects), but for the most part does not retain functionality (for example, methods) from the original objects.

# 10.6. Store the Output of a Command in a CSV or Delimited File

## Problem

You want to store the output of a command in a CSV file for later processing. This is helpful when you want to export the data for later processing outside PowerShell.

## Solution

Use PowerShell's `Export-Csv` cmdlet to save the output of a command into a CSV file. For example, to create an inventory of the processes running on a system:

```
Get-Process | Export-Csv c:\temp\processes.csv
```

You can then review this output in a tool such as Excel, mail it to others, or do whatever else you might want to do with a CSV file.

## Discussion

The CSV file format is one of the most common formats for exchanging semistructured data between programs and systems.

---

PowerShell's `Export-Csv` cmdlet provides an easy way to export data from the Power-Shell environment while still allowing you to keep a fair amount of your data's structure. When PowerShell exports your data to the CSV, it creates a row for each object that you provide. For each row, PowerShell creates columns in the CSV that represent the values of your object's properties.

 If you want to use the CSV-structured data as input to another tool that supports direct CSV pipeline input, you can use the `ConvertTo-Csv` cmdlet to bypass the step of storing it in a file.

If you want to separate the data with a character *other than* a comma, use the `-Delimiter` parameter. If you want to append to a CSV file rather than create a new one, use the `-Append` parameter.

One thing to keep in mind is that the CSV file format supports only plain strings for property values. If a property on your object isn't actually a string, PowerShell converts it to a string for you. Having PowerShell convert rich property values (such as integers) to strings, however, does mean that a certain amount of information is not preserved. If your ultimate goal is to load this unmodified data again in PowerShell, the `Export-CliXml` cmdlet provides a much better alternative. For more information about the `Export-CliXml` cmdlet, see Recipe 10.5, "Easily Import and Export Your Structured Data".

For more information on how to import data from a CSV file into PowerShell, see Recipe 10.7, "Import CSV and Delimited Data from a File".

## See Also

Recipe 10.5, "Easily Import and Export Your Structured Data"

Recipe 10.7, "Import CSV and Delimited Data from a File"

# 10.7. Import CSV and Delimited Data from a File

## Problem

You want to import structured data that has been stored in a CSV file or a file that uses some other character as its delimiter.

## Solution

Use PowerShell's `Import-Csv` cmdlet to import structured data from a CSV file. Use the `-Delimiter` parameter if fields are separated by a character other than a comma.

For example, to load the (tab-separated) Windows Update log:

```
$header = "Date","Time","PID","TID","Component","Text"
$log = Import-Csv $env:WINDIR\WindowsUpdate.log -Delimiter "`t" -Header $header
```

Then, manage the log as you manage other rich PowerShell output:

```
$log | Group-Object Component
```

## Discussion

As mentioned in Recipe 10.6, "Store the Output of a Command in a CSV or Delimited File", the CSV file format is one of the most common formats for exchanging semi-structured data between programs and systems.

PowerShell's `Import-Csv` cmdlet provides an easy way to import this data into the PowerShell environment from other programs. When PowerShell imports your data from the CSV, it creates a new object for each row in the CSV. For each object, PowerShell creates properties on the object from the values of the columns in the CSV.

If the names of the CSV columns match parameter names, many commands let you pipe this output to automatically set the values of parameters.

For more information about this feature, see Recipe 2.6, "Automate Data-Intensive Tasks".

If you are dealing with data in a CSV format that is the output of another tool or command, the `Import-Csv` cmdlet's file-based behavior won't be of much help. In this case, use the `ConvertFrom-Csv` cmdlet.

One thing to keep in mind is that the CSV file format supports only plain strings for property values. When you import data from a CSV, properties that look like dates will still only be strings. Properties that look like numbers will only be strings. Properties that look like any sort of rich data type will only be strings. This means that sorting on any property will always be an *alphabetical* sort, which is usually not the same as the sorting rules for the rich data types that the property might look like.

If your ultimate goal is to load rich unmodified data from something that you've previously exported from PowerShell, the `Import-CliXml` cmdlet provides a much better alternative. For more information about the `Import-CliXml` cmdlet, see Recipe 10.5, "Easily Import and Export Your Structured Data".

For more information on how to export data from PowerShell to a CSV file, see Recipe 10.6, "Store the Output of a Command in a CSV or Delimited File".

## See Also

Recipe 2.6, "Automate Data-Intensive Tasks"

Recipe 10.5, "Easily Import and Export Your Structured Data"

Recipe 10.6, "Store the Output of a Command in a CSV or Delimited File"

# 10.8. Manage JSON Data Streams

## Problem

You want to work with sources that produce or consume JSON-formatted data.

## Solution

Use PowerShell's `ConvertTo-Json` and `ConvertFrom-Json` commands to convert data to and from JSON formatting, respectively:

```
PS > $object = [PSCustomObject] @{
    Name = "Lee";
    Phone = "555-1212"
}

PS > $json = ConvertTo-Json $object
PS > $json
{
    "Name":  "Lee",
    "Phone":  "555-1212"
}

PS > $newObject = ConvertFrom-Json $json
PS > $newObject

Name        Phone
----        -----
Lee         555-1212
```

## Discussion

When you're writing scripts to interact with web APIs and web services, the JSON data format is one of the most common that you'll find. JSON stands for *JavaScript Object Notation*, and gained prominence with JavaScript-heavy websites and web APIs as an easy way to transfer structured data.

If you use PowerShell's `Invoke-RestMethod` cmdlet to interact with these web APIs, PowerShell automatically converts objects to and from JSON if required. If you use the `Invoke-WebRequest` cmdlet to retrieve data from a web page (or simply need JSON in another scenario), these cmdlets can prove extremely useful.

Since the JSON encoding format uses very little markup, it is an excellent way to visualize complex objects—especially properties and nested properties:

```
$s = Get-Service -Name winrm
$s | ConvertTo-Json -Depth 2
```

One common reason for encoding JSON is to use it in a web application. In that case, it is common to compress the resulting JSON to remove any spaces and newlines that are not required. The `ConvertTo-Json` cmdlet supports this through its `-Compress` parameter:

```
PS > ConvertTo-Json $object -Compress
{"Name":"Lee","Phone":"555-1212"}
```

For more information about working with JSON-based web APIs, see Recipe 12.7, "Interact with REST-Based Web APIs".

## See Also

Recipe 12.7, "Interact with REST-Based Web APIs"

# 10.9. Use Excel to Manage Command Output

## Problem

You want to use Excel to manipulate or visualize the output of a command.

## Solution

Use PowerShell's `Export-Csv` cmdlet to save the output of a command in a CSV file, and then load that CSV in Excel. If you have Excel associated with *.csv* files, the `Invoke-Item` cmdlet launches Excel when you provide it with a *.csv* file as an argument.

Example 10-7 demonstrates how to generate a CSV file containing the disk usage for subdirectories of the current directory.

*Example 10-7. Using Excel to visualize disk usage on the system*

```
PS > $filename = "c:\temp\diskusage.csv"
PS >
PS > $output = Get-ChildItem -Attributes Directory |
    Select-Object Name,
        @{ Name="Size";
            Expression={ ($_ | Get-ChildItem -Recurse |
                Measure-Object -Sum Length).Sum + 0 } }
```

```
PS > $output | Export-Csv $filename
PS >
PS > Invoke-Item $filename
```

In Excel, you can manipulate or format the data as you wish. As Figure 10-1 shows, we can manually create a pie chart.

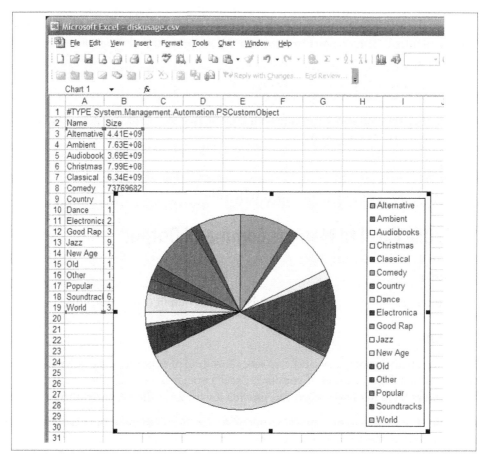

*Figure 10-1. Visualizing data in Excel*

## Discussion

Although used only as a demonstration, Example 10-7 packs quite a bit into just a few lines.

The first `Get-ChildItem` line uses the `-Directory` parameter to list all of the directories in the current directory. For each of those directories, you use the `Select-Object` cmdlet to pick out its `Name` and `Size`.

Directories don't have a `Size` property, though. To get that, we use `Select-Object`'s hashtable syntax to generate a *calculated property*. This calculated property (as defined by the `Expression` script block) uses the `Get-ChildItem` and `Measure-Object` cmdlets to add up the `Length` of all files in the given directory.

For more information about creating and working with calculated properties, see Recipe 3.15, "Add Custom Methods and Properties to Objects".

## See Also

Recipe 3.15, "Add Custom Methods and Properties to Objects"

# 10.10. Parse and Interpret PowerShell Scripts

## Problem

You want to access detailed structural and language-specific information about the content of a PowerShell script.

## Solution

For simple analysis of the script's textual representation, use PowerShell's Tokenizer API to convert the script into the same internal representation that PowerShell uses to understand the script's elements.

```
PS > $script = '$myVariable = 10'
PS > $errors = [System.Management.Automation.PSParseError[]] @()
PS > [Management.Automation.PsParser]::Tokenize($script, [ref] $errors) |
    Format-Table -Auto

Content       Type     Start Length StartLine StartColumn EndLine EndColumn
-------       ----     ----- ------ --------- ----------- ------- ---------
myVariable Variable     0      11       1           1        1        12
=          Operator    12       1       1          13        1        14
10         Number      14       2       1          15        1        17
```

For detailed analysis of the script's structure, use PowerShell's Abstract Syntax Tree (AST) API to convert the script into the same internal representation that PowerShell uses to understand the script's structure.

```
PS > $script = { $myVariable = 10 }
PS > $script.Ast.EndBlock.Statements[0].GetType()
```

```
IsPublic IsSerial Name
-------- -------- ----
True     False    AssignmentStatementAst

PS > $script.Ast.EndBlock.Statements[0]

Left          : $myVariable
Operator      : Equals
Right         : 10
ErrorPosition : =
Extent        : $myVariable = 10
Parent        : $myVariable = 10
```

## Discussion

When PowerShell loads a script, it goes through two primary steps in order to interpret it: tokenization and AST generation.

### Tokenization

When PowerShell loads a script, the first step is to *tokenize* that script. Tokenization is based on the textual representation of a script, and determines which portions of the script represent variables, numbers, operators, commands, parameters, aliases, and more.

While this is a fairly advanced concept, the Tokenizer API exposes the results of this step. This lets you work with the rich visual structure of PowerShell scripts the same way that the PowerShell engine does.

Without the support of a Tokenizer API, tool authors are usually required to build complicated regular expressions that attempt to emulate the PowerShell engine. Although these regular expressions are helpful for many situations, they tend to fall apart on more complex scripts.

As an example of this problem, consider the first line of Figure 10-2. "Write-Host" is an argument to the Write-Host cmdlet, but gets parsed as a string. The second line, while still providing an argument to the Write-Host cmdlet, does not treat the argument the same way. In fact, since it matches a cmdlet name, the argument gets colored like another call to the Write-Host cmdlet. In the here string that follows, the Write-Host cmdlet name gets highlighted again, even though it is really just part of a string.

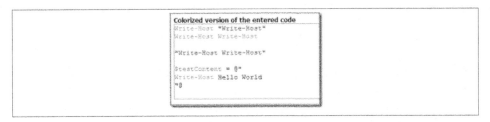

*Figure 10-2. Tokenization errors in a complex script*

Since the Tokenizer API follows the same rules as the PowerShell engine, it avoids the pitfalls of the regular-expression-based approach while producing output that is much easier to consume. When run on the same input, it produces the output shown in Example 10-8.

*Example 10-8. Successfully tokenizing a complex script*

```
PS > [Management.Automation.PsParser]::Tokenize($content, [ref] $errors) | ft -auto
```

| Content | Type | StartLine | StartColumn | EndLine | EndColumn |
| ------- | ---- | --------- | ----------- | ------- | --------- |
| Write-Host | Command | 1 | 1 | 1 | 11 |
| Write-Host | String | 1 | 12 | 1 | 24 |
| ... | NewLine | 1 | 24 | 2 | 1 |
| Write-Host | Command | 2 | 1 | 2 | 11 |
| Write-Host | CommandArgument | 2 | 12 | 2 | 22 |
| ... | NewLine | 2 | 22 | 3 | 1 |
| ... | NewLine | 3 | 1 | 4 | 1 |
| Write-Host Write-Host | String | 4 | 1 | 4 | 24 |
| ... | NewLine | 4 | 24 | 5 | 1 |
| ... | NewLine | 5 | 1 | 6 | 1 |
| testContent | Variable | 6 | 1 | 6 | 13 |
| = | Operator | 6 | 14 | 6 | 15 |
| Write-Host Hello World | String | 6 | 16 | 8 | 3 |
| ... | NewLine | 8 | 3 | 9 | 1 |

This adds a whole new dimension to the way you can interact with PowerShell scripts. Some natural outcomes are:

- Syntax highlighting
- Automated script editing (for example, replacing aliased commands with their expanded equivalents)
- Script style and form verification

If the script contains any errors, PowerShell captures those in the $errors collection you are required to supply. If you don't want to keep track of errors, you can supply [ref] $null as the value for that parameter.

For an example of the Tokenizer API in action, see Recipe 8.6, "Program: Show Colorized Script Content".

## AST generation

After PowerShell parses the textual tokens from your script, it generates a tree structure to represent the actual structure of your script. For example, scripts don't just have loose collections of tokens—they have Begin, Process and End blocks. Those blocks may have Statements, which themselves can contain PipelineElements with Commands. For example:

```
PS > $ast = { Get-Process -Id $pid }.Ast
PS > $ast.EndBlock.Statements[0].PipelineElements[0].CommandElements[0].Value
Get-Process
```

As the Solution demonstrates, the easiest way to retrieve the AST for a command is to access the AST property on its script block. For example:

```
PS C:\Users\Lee> function prompt { "PS > " }
PS > $ast = (Get-Command prompt).ScriptBlock.Ast
PS > $ast

IsFilter   : False
IsWorkflow : False
Name       : prompt
Parameters :
Body       : { "PS > " }
Extent     : function prompt { "PS > " }
Parent     : function prompt { "PS > " }
```

If you want to create an AST from text content, use the [ScriptBlock]::Create() method:

```
PS > $scriptBlock = [ScriptBlock]::Create('Get-Process -ID $pid')
PS > $scriptBlock.Ast


ParamBlock         :
BeginBlock         :
ProcessBlock       :
EndBlock           : Get-Process -ID $pid
DynamicParamBlock  :
ScriptRequirements :
Extent             : Get-Process -ID $pid
Parent             :
```

With the PowerShell AST at your disposal, advanced script analysis is easier than it's ever been. To learn more about the methods and properties exposed by the PowerShell AST, see Recipe 3.13, "Learn About Types and Objects".

## See Also

Recipe 8.6, "Program: Show Colorized Script Content"

Recipe 3.13, "Learn About Types and Objects"

# Code Reuse

## 11.0. Introduction

One thing that surprises many people is how much you can accomplish in PowerShell from the interactive prompt alone. Since PowerShell makes it so easy to join its powerful commands together into even more powerful combinations, enthusiasts grow to relish this brevity. In fact, there is a special place in the heart of most scripting enthusiasts set aside entirely for the most compact expressions of power: the *one-liner*.

Despite its interactive efficiency, you obviously don't want to retype all your brilliant ideas anew each time you need them. When you want to save or reuse the commands that you've written, PowerShell provides many avenues to support you: scripts, modules, functions, script blocks, and more.

## 11.1. Write a Script

### Problem

You want to store your commands in a script so that you can share them or reuse them later.

### Solution

To write a PowerShell script, create a plain-text file with your editor of choice. Add your PowerShell commands to that script (the same PowerShell commands you use from the interactive shell), and then save it with a *.ps1* extension.

# Discussion

One of the most important things to remember about PowerShell is that running scripts and working at the command line are essentially equivalent operations. If you see it in a script, you can type it or paste it at the command line. If you typed it on the command line, you can paste it into a text file and call it a script.

Once you write your script, PowerShell lets you call it in the same way that you call other programs and existing tools. Running a script does the same thing as running all the commands in that script.

 PowerShell introduces a few features related to running scripts and tools that may at first confuse you if you aren't aware of them. For more information about how to call scripts and existing tools, see Recipe 1.1, "Run Programs, Scripts, and Existing Tools".

The first time you try to run a script in PowerShell, you'll likely see the following error message:

```
File c:\tools\myFirstScript.ps1 cannot be loaded because the execution of
scripts is disabled on this system. Please see "get-help about_signing" for
more details.
At line:1 char:12
+ myFirstScript <<<<
```

Since relatively few computer users write scripts, PowerShell's default security policies prevent scripts from running. Once you begin writing scripts, though, you should configure this policy to something less restrictive. For information on how to configure your execution policy, see Recipe 18.1, "Enable Scripting Through an Execution Policy".

When it comes to the filename of your script, picking a descriptive name is the best way to guarantee that you will always remember what that script does—or at least have a good idea. This is an issue that PowerShell tackles elegantly, by naming every cmdlet in the *Verb-Noun* pattern: a command that performs an action (*verb*) on an item (*noun*). As a demonstration of the usefulness of this philosophy, consider the names of typical Windows commands given in Example 11-1.

*Example 11-1. The names of some standard Windows commands*

```
PS > dir $env:WINDIR\System32\*.exe | Select-Object Name

Name
----
accwiz.exe
actmovie.exe
ahui.exe
alg.exe
```

```
append.exe
arp.exe
asr_fmt.exe
asr_ldm.exe
asr_pfu.exe
at.exe
atmadm.exe
attrib.exe
(...)
```

Compare this to the names of some standard Windows PowerShell cmdlets, given in Example 11-2.

*Example 11-2. The names of some standard Windows PowerShell cmdlets*

```
PS > Get-Command | Select-Object Name

Name
----
Add-Content
Add-History
Add-Member
Add-PSSnapin
Clear-Content
Clear-Item
Clear-ItemProperty
Clear-Variable
Compare-Object
ConvertFrom-SecureString
Convert-Path
ConvertTo-Html
(...)
```

As an additional way to improve discovery, PowerShell takes this even further with the philosophy (and explicit goal) that "you can manage 80 percent of your system with less than 50 verbs." As you learn the standard verbs for a concept, such as Get (which represents the standard concepts of read, open, and so on), you can often guess the verb of a command as the first step in discovering it.

When you name your script (*especially* if you intend to share it), make every effort to pick a name that follows these conventions. Recipe 11.3, "Find a Verb Appropriate for a Command Name" shows a useful cmdlet to help you find a verb to name your scripts properly. As evidence of its utility for scripts, consider some of the scripts included in this book:

```
PS > dir | select Name

Name
----
Compare-Property.ps1
Convert-TextObject.ps1
```

```
Get-AliasSuggestion.ps1
Get-Answer.ps1
Get-Characteristics.ps1
Get-OwnerReport.ps1
Get-PageUrls.ps1
Invoke-CmdScript.ps1
New-GenericObject.ps1
Select-FilteredObject.ps1
(...)
```

Like the PowerShell cmdlets, the names of these scripts are clear, are easy to understand, and use verbs from PowerShell's standard verb list.

## See Also

Recipe 1.1, "Run Programs, Scripts, and Existing Tools"

Recipe 11.3, "Find a Verb Appropriate for a Command Name"

Appendix J, *Standard PowerShell Verbs*

# 11.2. Write a Function

## Problem

You have commands in your script that you want to call multiple times or a section of your script that you consider to be a "helper" for the main purpose of your script.

## Solution

Place this common code in a function, and then call that function instead. For example, this Celsius conversion code in a script:

```
param([double] $fahrenheit)

## Convert it to Celsius
$celsius = $fahrenheit - 32
$celsius = $celsius / 1.8

## Output the answer
"$fahrenheit degrees Fahrenheit is $celsius degrees Celsius."
```

could be placed in a function (itself placed in a script):

```
param([double] $fahrenheit)

## Convert Fahrenheit to Celsius
function ConvertFahrenheitToCelsius([double] $fahrenheit)
{
    $celsius = $fahrenheit - 32
```

```
    $celsius = $celsius / 1.8
    $celsius
}

$celsius = ConvertFahrenheitToCelsius $fahrenheit

## Output the answer
"$fahrenheit degrees Fahrenheit is $celsius degrees Celsius."
```

Although using a function arguably makes this specific script longer and more difficult to understand, the technique is extremely valuable (and used) in almost all nontrivial scripts.

## Discussion

Once you define a function, any command after that definition can use it. This means that you must define your function *before* any part of your script that uses it. You might find this unwieldy if your script defines many functions, as the function definitions obscure the main logic portion of your script. If this is the case, you can put your main logic in a Main function, as described in Recipe 11.21, "Organize Scripts for Improved Readability".

 A common question that comes from those accustomed to batch scripting in *cmd.exe* is, "What is the PowerShell equivalent of a GOTO?" In situations where the GOTO is used to call subroutines or other isolated helper parts of the batch file, use a PowerShell function to accomplish that task. If the GOTO is used as a way to loop over something, PowerShell's looping mechanisms are more appropriate.

In PowerShell, calling a function is designed to feel just like calling a cmdlet or a script. As a user, you should not have to know whether a little helper routine was written as a cmdlet, script, or function. When you call a function, simply add the parameters after the function name, with spaces separating each one (as shown in the Solution). This is in contrast to the way that you call functions in many programming languages (such as C#), where you use parentheses after the function name and commas between each parameter:

```
## Correct
ConvertFahrenheitToCelsius $fahrenheit

## Incorrect
ConvertFahrenheitToCelsius($fahrenheit)
```

Also, notice that the return value from a function is anything that the function writes to the output pipeline (such as $celsius in the Solution). You can write return $celsius if you want, but it is unnecessary.

For more information about writing functions, see "Writing Scripts, Reusing Functionality" (page 897). For more information about PowerShell's looping statements, see Recipe 4.4, "Repeat Operations with Loops".

## See Also

Recipe 4.4, "Repeat Operations with Loops"

"Writing Scripts, Reusing Functionality" (page 897)

# 11.3. Find a Verb Appropriate for a Command Name

## Problem

You are writing a new script or function and want to select an appropriate verb for that command.

## Solution

Review the output of the `Get-Verb` command to find a verb appropriate for your command:

```
PS > Get-Verb In* | Format-Table -Auto

Verb       Group
----       -----
Initialize Data
Install    Lifecycle
Invoke     Lifecycle
```

## Discussion

Consistency of command names is one of PowerShell's most beneficial features, largely due to its standard set of verbs. While descriptive command names (such as `Stop-Process`) make it clear what a command does, standard verbs make commands easier to discover.

For example, many technologies have their own words for creating something: *new, create, instantiate, build,* and more. When a user looks for a command (without the benefit of standard verbs), the user has to know the domain-specific terminology for that action. If the user doesn't know the domain-specific verb, she is forced to page through long lists of commands in the hope that something rings a bell.

When commands use PowerShell's standard verbs, however, discovery becomes much easier. Once users learn the *standard verb* for an action, they don't need to search for its domain-specific alternatives. Most importantly, the time they invest (actively or otherwise) learning the standard PowerShell verbs improves their efficiency with *all* commands, not just commands from a specific domain.

 This discoverability issue is so important that PowerShell generates a warning message when a module defines a command with a nonstandard verb. To support domain-specific names for your commands *in addition* to the standard names, simply define an alias. For more information, see Recipe 11.8, "Selectively Export Commands from a Module".

To make it easier to select a standard verb while writing a script or function, PowerShell provides a `Get-Verb` function. You can review the output of that function to find a verb suitable for your command. For an even more detailed description of the standard verbs, see Appendix J.

## See Also

Recipe 11.8, "Selectively Export Commands from a Module"

Appendix J, *Standard PowerShell Verbs*

# 11.4. Write a Script Block

## Problem

You have a section of your script that works nearly the same for all input, aside from a minor change in logic.

## Solution

As shown in Example 11-3, place the minor logic differences in a script block, and then pass that script block as a parameter to the code that requires it. Use the invoke operator (&) to execute the script block.

*Example 11-3. A script that applies a script block to each element in the pipeline*

```
##############################################################################
##
## Invoke-ScriptBlock
##
## From Windows PowerShell Cookbook (O'Reilly)
## by Lee Holmes (http://www.leeholmes.com/guide)
```

```
##
################################################################################

<#

.SYNOPSIS

Apply the given mapping command to each element of the input. (Note that
PowerShell includes this command natively, and calls it Foreach-Object)

.EXAMPLE

PS > 1,2,3 | Invoke-ScriptBlock { $_ * 2 }

#>

param(
    ## The script block to apply to each incoming element
    [ScriptBlock] $MapCommand
)

begin
{
    Set-StrictMode -Version 3
}
process
{
    & $mapCommand
}
```

## Discussion

Imagine a script that needs to multiply all the elements in a list by two:

```
function MultiplyInputByTwo
{
    process
    {
        $_ * 2
    }
}
```

but it also needs to perform a more complex calculation:

```
function MultiplyInputComplex
{
    process
    {
        ($_ + 2) * 3
    }
}
```

These two functions are strikingly similar, except for the single line that actually performs the calculation. As we add more calculations, this quickly becomes more evident. Adding each new seven-line function gives us only one unique line of value!

```
PS > 1,2,3 | MultiplyInputByTwo
2
4
6
PS > 1,2,3 | MultiplyInputComplex
9
12
15
```

If we instead use a script block to hold this "unknown" calculation, we don't need to keep on adding new functions:

```
PS > 1,2,3 | Invoke-ScriptBlock { $_ * 2 }
2
4
6
PS > 1,2,3 | Invoke-ScriptBlock { ($_ + 2) * 3 }
9
12
15
PS > 1,2,3 | Invoke-ScriptBlock { ($_ + 3) * $_ }
4
10
18
```

In fact, the functionality provided by `Invoke-ScriptBlock` is so helpful that it is a standard PowerShell cmdlet—called `Foreach-Object`. For more information about script blocks, see "Writing Scripts, Reusing Functionality" (page 897). For more information about running scripts, see Recipe 1.1, "Run Programs, Scripts, and Existing Tools".

## See Also

Recipe 1.1, "Run Programs, Scripts, and Existing Tools"

"Writing Scripts, Reusing Functionality" (page 897)

# 11.5. Return Data from a Script, Function, or Script Block

## Problem

You want your script or function to return data to whatever called it.

## Solution

To return data from a script or function, write that data to the output pipeline:

```
##############################################################################
## Get-Tomorrow
##
## Get the date that represents tomorrow
##
## From Windows PowerShell Cookbook (O'Reilly)
## by Lee Holmes (http://www.leeholmes.com/guide)
##
##############################################################################

Set-StrictMode -Version 3

function GetDate
{
    Get-Date
}

$tomorrow = (GetDate).AddDays(1)
$tomorrow
```

## Discussion

In PowerShell, any data that your function or script generates gets sent to the output pipeline, unless something captures that output. The GetDate function generates data (a date) and does not capture it, so that becomes the output of the function. The portion of the script that calls the GetDate function captures that output and then manipulates it.

Finally, the script writes the $tomorrow variable to the pipeline without capturing it, so that becomes the return value of the script itself.

> Some .NET methods—such as the System.Collections.ArrayList class—produce output, even though you may not expect them to. To prevent these methods from sending data to the output pipeline, either capture the data or cast it to [void]:
>
> ```
> PS > $collection = New-Object System.Collections.ArrayList
> PS > $collection.Add("Hello")
> 0
> PS > [void] $collection.Add("Hello")
> ```

Even with this "pipeline output becomes the return value" philosophy, PowerShell continues to support the traditional return keyword as a way to return from a function or script. If you specify anything after the keyword (such as return "Hello"), PowerShell treats that as a "Hello" statement followed by a return statement.

If you want to make your intention clear to other readers of your script, you can use the Write-Output cmdlet to explicitly send data down the pipeline. Both produce the same result, so this is only a matter of preference.

If you write a collection (such as an array or ArrayList) to the output pipeline, Power-Shell in fact writes each element of that collection to the pipeline. To keep the collection intact as it travels down the pipeline, prefix it with a comma when you return it. This returns a collection (that will be unraveled) with one element: the collection you wanted to keep intact.

```
function WritesObjects
{
    $arrayList = New-Object System.Collections.ArrayList
    [void] $arrayList.Add("Hello")
    [void] $arrayList.Add("World")

    $arrayList
}

function WritesArrayList
{
    $arrayList = New-Object System.Collections.ArrayList
    [void] $arrayList.Add("Hello")
    [void] $arrayList.Add("World")

    ,$arrayList
}

$objectOutput = WritesObjects

# The following command would generate an error
# $objectOutput.Add("Extra")

$arrayListOutput = WritesArrayList
$arrayListOutput.Add("Extra")
```

Although relatively uncommon in PowerShell's world of fully structured data, you may sometimes want to use an exit code to indicate the success or failure of your script. For this, PowerShell offers the exit keyword.

For more information about the return and exit statements, please see "Writing Scripts, Reusing Functionality" (page 897) and Recipe 15.1, "Determine the Status of the Last Command".

## See Also

Recipe 15.1, "Determine the Status of the Last Command"

"Writing Scripts, Reusing Functionality" (page 897)

# 11.6. Package Common Commands in a Module

## Problem

You've developed a useful set of commands or functions. You want to offer them to the user or share them between multiple scripts.

## Solution

First, place these common function definitions by themselves in a file with the extension *.psm1*, as shown in Example 11-4.

*Example 11-4. A module of temperature commands*

```
##############################################################################
##
## Temperature.psm1
## Commands that manipulate and convert temperatures
##
## From Windows PowerShell Cookbook (O'Reilly)
## by Lee Holmes (http://www.leeholmes.com/guide)
##
##############################################################################

## Convert Fahrenheit to Celcius
function Convert-FahrenheitToCelcius([double] $fahrenheit)
{
    $celcius = $fahrenheit - 32
    $celcius = $celcius / 1.8
    $celcius
}

## Convert Celcius to Fahrenheit
function Convert-CelciusToFahrenheit([double] $celcius)
{
    $fahrenheit = $celcius * 1.8
    $fahrenheit = $fahrenheit + 32
    $fahrenheit
}
```

Next, place that file in your *Modules* directory (as defined in the `PSModulePath` environment variable), in a subdirectory with the same name. For example, place *Temperature.psm1* in *<My Documents>\WindowsPowerShell\Modules\Temperature*. Call the `Import-Module` command to import the module (and its commands) into your session, as shown by Example 11-5.

*Example 11-5. Importing a module*

```
PS > Import-Module Temperature
PS > Convert-FahrenheitToCelsius 81
27.2222222222222
```

## Discussion

PowerShell modules give you an easy way to package related commands and functionality. As the Solution demonstrates, writing a module is as simple as adding functions to a file.

As with the naming of core commands, the naming of commands packaged in a module plays a critical role in giving users a consistent and discoverable PowerShell experience. When you name the commands in your module, ensure that they follow a `Verb-Noun` syntax and that you select verbs from PowerShell's standard set of verbs. If your module does not follow these standards, your users will receive a warning message when they load your module. For information about how to make your module commands discoverable (and as domain-specific as required), see Recipe 11.8, "Selectively Export Commands from a Module".

In addition to creating the *.psm1* file that contains your module's commands, you should also create a *module manifest* to describe its contents and system requirements. Module manifests let you define the module's author, company, copyright information, and more. For more information, see the `New-ModuleManifest` cmdlet.

After writing a module, the last step is making it available to the system. When you call `Import-Module <module name>` to load a module, PowerShell looks through each directory listed in the `PSModulePath` environment variable.

> The `PSModulePath` variable is an environment variable, just like the system's `PATH` environment variable. For more information on how to view and modify environment variables, see Recipe 16.1, "View and Modify Environment Variables".

If PowerShell finds a directory named *<module name>*, it looks in that directory for a *psm1* file with that name as well. Once it finds the *psm1* file, it loads that module into your session. In addition to *psm1* files, PowerShell also supports *module manifest* (*psd1*) files that let you define a great deal of information *about* the module: its author, description, nested modules, version requirements, and much more. For more information, type **Get-Help New-ModuleManifest**.

If you want to make your module available to just yourself (or the "current user" if you're installing your module as part of a setup process), place it in the per-user modules folder: *<My Documents>\WindowsPowerShell\Modules\<module name>*. If you want to make the module available to all users of the system, place your module in its own directory under the *Program Files* directory, and then add that directory to the systemwide PSMo dulePath environment variable.

If you don't want to permanently install your module, you can instead specify the complete path to the *psm1* file when you load the module. For example:

```
Import-Module c:\tools\Temperature.psm1
```

If you want to load a module from the same directory that your script is in, see Recipe 16.6, "Find Your Script's Location".

When you load a module from a script, PowerShell makes the commands from that module available to the entire session. If your script loads the Temperature module, for example, the functions in that module will still be available after your script exits. To ensure that your script doesn't accidentally influence the user's session after it exits, you should remove any modules that you load:

```
$moduleToRemove = $null
if(-not (Get-Module <Module Name>))
{
    $moduleToRemove = Import-Module <Module Name> -Passthru
}


#####################
##
## script goes here
##
#####################

if($moduleToRemove)
{
    $moduleToRemove | Remove-Module
}
```

If you have a *module* that loads a helper module (as opposed to a *script* that loads a helper module), this step is not required. Modules loaded by a module impact only the module that loads them.

If you want to let users configure your module when they load it, you can define a parameter block at the beginning of your module. These parameters then get filled through the `-ArgumentList` parameter of the `Import-Module` command. For example, a module that takes a "retry count" and website as parameters:

```
param(
    [int] $RetryCount,
    [URI] $Website
)

function Get-Page
{
    ....
```

The user would load the module with the following command line:

```
Import-Module <module name> -ArgumentList 10,"http://www.example.com"
Get-Page "/index.html"
```

One important point when it comes to the `-ArgumentList` parameter is that its support for user input is much more limited than support offered for most scripts, functions, and script blocks. PowerShell lets you access the parameters in most `param()` statements by name, by alias, and in or out of order. Arguments supplied to the `Import-Module` command, on the other hand, must be supplied as values only, and in the exact order the module defines them.

For more information about accessing arguments of a command, see Recipe 11.11, "Access Arguments of a Script, Function, or Script Block". For more information about importing a module (and the different types of modules available), see Recipe 1.29, "Extend Your Shell with Additional Commands". For more information about modules, type **Get-Help about_Modules**.

## See Also

Recipe 1.29, "Extend Your Shell with Additional Commands"

Recipe 11.8, "Selectively Export Commands from a Module"

Recipe 11.11, "Access Arguments of a Script, Function, or Script Block"

Recipe 16.1, "View and Modify Environment Variables"

# 11.7. Write Commands That Maintain State

## Problem

You have a function or script that needs to maintain state between invocations.

## Solution

Place those commands in a *module*. Store any information you want to retain in a variable, and give that variable a SCRIPT scope. See Example 11-6.

*Example 11-6. A module that maintains state*

```
##############################################################################
##
## PersistentState.psm1
## Demonstrates persistent state through module-scoped variables
##
## From Windows PowerShell Cookbook (O'Reilly)
## by Lee Holmes (http://www.leeholmes.com/guide)
##
##############################################################################

$SCRIPT:memory = $null

function Set-Memory
{
    param(
        [Parameter(ValueFromPipeline = $true)]
        $item
    )

    begin { $SCRIPT:memory = New-Object System.Collections.ArrayList }
    process { $null = $memory.Add($item) }
}

function Get-Memory
{
    $memory.ToArray()
}

Set-Alias remember Set-Memory
Set-Alias recall Get-Memory

Export-ModuleMember -Function Set-Memory,Get-Memory
Export-ModuleMember -Alias remember,recall
```

## Discussion

When writing scripts or commands, you'll frequently need to maintain state between the invocation of those commands. For example, your commands might remember user preferences, cache configuration data, or store other types of module state. See Example 11-7.

*Example 11-7. Working with commands that maintain state*

```
PS > Import-Module PersistentState
PS > Get-Process -Name PowerShell | remember
```

```
PS > recall

Handles  NPM(K)    PM(K)    WS(K) VM(M)   CPU(s)     Id ProcessName
-------  ------    -----    ----- -----   ------     -- -----------
    527       6    32704    44140   172     2.13   2644 powershell
    517       7    23080    33328   154     1.81   2812 powershell
    357       6    31848    33760   165     1.42   3576 powershell
```

In basic scripts, the only way to maintain state across invocations is to store the information in a global variable. This introduces two problems, though.

The first problem is that global variables impact much more than just the script that defines them. Once your script stores information in a global variable, it pollutes the user's session. If the user has a variable with the same name, your script overwrites its contents. The second problem is the natural counterpart to this pollution. When your script stores information in a global variable, both the user and other scripts have access to it. Due to accident or curiosity, it is quite easy for these "internal" global variables to be damaged or corrupted.

You can resolve this issue through the use of modules. By placing your commands in a module, PowerShell makes variables with a *script* scope available to all commands in that module. In addition to making script-scoped variables available to all of your commands, PowerShell maintains their value between invocations of those commands.

 Like variables, PowerShell drives obey the concept of scope. When you use the New-PSDrive cmdlet from within a module, that drive stays private to that module. To create a new drive that is visible from outside your module as well, create it with a *global* scope:

```
New-PSDrive -Name Temp FileSystem -Root C:\Temp -Scope Global
```

For more information about variables and their scopes, see Recipe 3.6, "Control Access and Scope of Variables and Other Items". For more information about defining a module, see Recipe 11.6, "Package Common Commands in a Module".

## See Also

Recipe 3.6, "Control Access and Scope of Variables and Other Items"

Recipe 11.6, "Package Common Commands in a Module"

# 11.8. Selectively Export Commands from a Module

## Problem

You have a module and want to export only certain commands from that module.

## Solution

Use the Export-ModuleMember cmdlet to declare the specific commands you want exported. All other commands then remain internal to your module. See Example 11-8.

*Example 11-8. Exporting specific commands from a module*

```
##############################################################################
##
## SelectiveCommands.psm1
## Demonstrates the selective export of module commands
##
## From Windows PowerShell Cookbook (O'Reilly)
## by Lee Holmes (http://www.leeholmes.com/guide)
##
##############################################################################

## An internal helper function
function MyInternalHelperFunction
{
    "Result from my internal helper function"
}

## A command exported from the module
function Get-SelectiveCommandInfo
{
    "Getting information from the SelectiveCommands module"
    MyInternalHelperFunction
}

## Alternate names for our standard command
Set-Alias gsci Get-SelectiveCommandInfo
Set-Alias DomainSpecificVerb-Info Get-SelectiveCommandInfo

## Export specific commands
Export-ModuleMember -Function Get-SelectiveCommandInfo
Export-ModuleMember -Alias gsci,DomainSpecificVerb-Info
```

## Discussion

When PowerShell imports a module, it imports all functions defined in that module by default. This makes it incredibly simple (for you as a module author) to create a library of related commands.

Once your module commands get more complex, you'll often write helper functions and support routines. Since these commands aren't intended to be exposed directly to users, you'll instead need to selectively export commands from your module. The `Export-ModuleMember` command allows exactly that.

Once your module includes a call to `Export-ModuleMember`, PowerShell no longer exports all functions in your module. Instead, it exports only the commands that you define. The first call to `Export-ModuleMember` in Example 11-8 demonstrates how to selectively export a function from a module.

Since consistency of command names is one of PowerShell's most beneficial features, PowerShell generates a warning message if your module exports functions (either explicitly or by default) that use nonstandard verbs. For example, imagine that you have a technology that uses *regenerate configuration* as a highly specific phrase for a task. In addition, it already has a `regen` command to accomplish this task.

You might naturally consider `Regenerate-Configuration` and `regen` as function names to export from your module, but doing that would alienate users who don't have a strong background in your technology. Without your same technical expertise, they wouldn't know the name of the command, and instead would instinctively look for `Reset-Configuration`, `Restore-Configuration`, or `Initialize-Configuration` based on their existing PowerShell knowledge. In this situation, the solution is to name your functions with a standard verb and *also* use command aliases to support your domain-specific experts.

The `Export-ModuleMember` cmdlet supports this situation as well. In addition to letting you selectively export commands from your module, it also lets you export alternative names (*aliases*) for your module commands. The second call to `Export-ModuleMember` in Example 11-8 (along with the alias definitions that precede it) demonstrates how to export aliases from a module.

For more information about command naming, see Recipe 11.3, "Find a Verb Appropriate for a Command Name". For more information about writing a module, see Recipe 11.6, "Package Common Commands in a Module".

## See Also

Recipe 3.6, "Control Access and Scope of Variables and Other Items"

Recipe 11.3, "Find a Verb Appropriate for a Command Name"

Recipe 11.6, "Package Common Commands in a Module"

# 11.9. Diagnose and Interact with Internal Module State

## Problem

You have a module and want to examine its internal variables and functions.

## Solution

Use the Enter-Module script (Example 11-9) to temporarily enter the module and invoke commands within its scope.

*Example 11-9. Invoking commands from within the scope of a module*

```
##############################################################################
##
## Enter-Module
##
## From Windows PowerShell Cookbook (O'Reilly)
## by Lee Holmes (http://www.leeholmes.com/guide)
##
##############################################################################

<#

.SYNOPSIS

Lets you examine internal module state and functions by executing user
input in the scope of the supplied module.

.EXAMPLE

PS > Import-Module PersistentState
PS > Get-Module PersistentState

ModuleType Name                         ExportedCommands
---------- ----                         ----------------
Script     PersistentState              {Set-Memory, Get-Memory}


PS > "Hello World" | Set-Memory
PS > $m = Get-Module PersistentState
PS > Enter-Module $m
PersistentState: dir variable:\mem*

Name                         Value
----                         -----
memory                       {Hello World}

PersistentState: exit
PS >
```

```
#>

param(
    ## The module to examine
    [System.Management.Automation.PSModuleInfo] $Module
)

Set-StrictMode -Version 3

$userInput = Read-Host $($module.Name)
while($userInput -ne "exit")
{
    $scriptblock = [ScriptBlock]::Create($userInput)
    & $module $scriptblock

    $userInput = Read-Host $($module.Name)
}
```

## Discussion

PowerShell modules are an effective way to create sets of related commands that share private state. While commands in a module can share private state between themselves, PowerShell prevents that state from accidentally impacting the rest of your PowerShell session.

When you are developing a module, though, you might sometimes need to interact with this internal state for diagnostic purposes. To support this, PowerShell lets you target a specific module with the invocation (&) operator:

```
PS > $m = Get-Module PersistentState
PS > & $m { dir variable:\mem* }

Name                          Value
----                          -----
memory                        {Hello World}
```

This syntax gets cumbersome for more detailed investigation tasks, so Enter-Module automates the prompting and invocation for you.

For more information about writing a module, see Recipe 11.6, "Package Common Commands in a Module".

## See Also

Recipe 11.6, "Package Common Commands in a Module"

# 11.10. Handle Cleanup Tasks When a Module Is Removed

## Problem

You have a module and want to perform some action (such as cleanup tasks) when that module is removed.

## Solution

Assign a script block to the $MyInvocation.MyCommand.ScriptBlock.Module.OnRemove event. Place any cleanup commands in that script block. See Example 11-10.

*Example 11-10. Handling cleanup tasks from within a module*

```
##############################################################################
##
## TidyModule.psm1
##
## From Windows PowerShell Cookbook (O'Reilly)
## by Lee Holmes (http://www.leeholmes.com/guide)
##
##############################################################################

<#

.SYNOPSIS
Demonstrates how to handle cleanup tasks when a module is removed

.EXAMPLE

PS > Import-Module TidyModule
PS > $TidyModuleStatus
Initialized
PS > Remove-Module TidyModule
PS > $TidyModuleStatus
Cleaned Up

#>

## Perform some initialization tasks
$GLOBAL:TidyModuleStatus = "Initialized"

## Register for cleanup
$MyInvocation.MyCommand.ScriptBlock.Module.OnRemove = {
    $GLOBAL:TidyModuleStatus = "Cleaned Up"
}
```

## Discussion

PowerShell modules have a natural way to define initialization requirements (any script written in the body of the module), but cleanup requirements are not as simple.

During module creation, you can access your module through the $MyInvo cation.MyCommand.ScriptBlock.Module property. Each module has an OnRemove event, which you can then subscribe to by assigning it a script block. When PowerShell unloads your module, it invokes that script block.

Beware of using this technique for extremely sensitive cleanup requirements. If the user simply exits the PowerShell window, the OnRemove event is not processed. If this is a concern, register for the PowerShell.Exiting engine event and remove your module from there:

```
Register-EngineEvent PowerShell.Exiting { Remove-Module TidyModule }
```

This saves the user from having to remember to call Remove-Module.

For more information about writing a module, see Recipe 11.6, "Package Common Commands in a Module". For more information about PowerShell events, see Recipe 32.2, "Create and Respond to Custom Events".

## See Also

Recipe 11.6, "Package Common Commands in a Module"

Recipe 32.2, "Create and Respond to Custom Events"

# 11.11. Access Arguments of a Script, Function, or Script Block

## Problem

You want to access the arguments provided to a script, function, or script block.

## Solution

To access arguments by name, use a param statement:

```
param($firstNamedArgument, [int] $secondNamedArgument = 0)

"First named argument is: $firstNamedArgument"
"Second named argument is: $secondNamedArgument"
```

To access unnamed arguments by position, use the $args array:

```
"First positional argument is: " + $args[0]
"Second positional argument is: " + $args[1]
```

You can use these techniques in exactly the same way with scripts, functions, and script blocks, as illustrated by Example 11-11.

*Example 11-11. Working with arguments in scripts, functions, and script blocks*

```
##############################################################################
##
## Get-Arguments
##
## From Windows PowerShell Cookbook (O'Reilly)
## by Lee Holmes (http://www.leeholmes.com/guide)
##
##############################################################################

<#

.SYNOPSIS

Uses command-line arguments

#>

param(
    ## The first named argument
    $FirstNamedArgument,

    ## The second named argument
    [int] $SecondNamedArgument = 0
)

Set-StrictMode -Version 3

## Display the arguments by name
"First named argument is: $firstNamedArgument"
"Second named argument is: $secondNamedArgument"

function GetArgumentsFunction
{
    ## We could use a param statement here, as well
    ## param($firstNamedArgument, [int] $secondNamedArgument = 0)

    ## Display the arguments by position
    "First positional function argument is: " + $args[0]
    "Second positional function argument is: " + $args[1]
}

GetArgumentsFunction One Two

$scriptBlock =
{
    param($firstNamedArgument, [int] $secondNamedArgument = 0)
```

```
## We could use $args here, as well
"First named scriptblock argument is: $firstNamedArgument"
"Second named scriptblock argument is: $secondNamedArgument"
}

& $scriptBlock -First One -Second 4.5
```

Example 11-11 produces the following output:

```
PS > Get-Arguments First 2
First named argument is: First
Second named argument is: 2
First positional function argument is: One
Second positional function argument is: Two
First named scriptblock argument is: One
Second named scriptblock argument is: 4
```

# Discussion

Although PowerShell supports both the param keyword and the $args array, you will most commonly want to use the param keyword to define and access script, function, and script block parameters.

> In most languages, the most common reason to access parameters through an $args array is to determine the name of the currently running script. For information about how to do this in PowerShell, see Recipe 16.3, "Access Information About Your Command's Invocation".

When you use the param keyword to define your parameters, PowerShell provides your script or function with many useful features that allow users to work with your script much as they work with cmdlets:

- Users need to specify only enough of the parameter name to disambiguate it from other parameters.
- Users can understand the meaning of your parameters much more clearly.
- You can specify the type of your parameters, which PowerShell uses to convert input if required.
- You can specify default values for your parameters.

### Supporting PowerShell's common parameters

In addition to the parameters you define, you might also want to support PowerShell's standard parameters: -Verbose, -Debug, -ErrorAction, -WarningAction, -Error Variable, -WarningVariable, -OutVariable, and -OutBuffer.

To get these additional parameters, add the [CmdletBinding()] attribute inside your function, or declare it at the top of your script. The param() statement is required, even if your function or script declares no parameters. These (and other associated) additional features now make your function an *advanced function*. See Example 11-12.

*Example 11-12. Declaring an advanced function*

```
function Invoke-MyAdvancedFunction
{
    [CmdletBinding()]
    param()

    Write-Verbose "Verbose Message"
}
```

If your function defines a parameter with advanced *validation*, you don't need to explicitly add the [CmdletBinding()] attribute. In that case, PowerShell already knows to treat your command as an advanced function.

 During PowerShell's beta phases, *advanced functions* were known as *script cmdlets*. We decided to change the name because the term *script cmdlets* caused a sense of fear of the great unknown. Users would be comfortable writing functions, but "didn't have the time to learn those new script cmdlet things." Because script cmdlets were just regular functions with additional power, the new name made a lot more sense.

Although PowerShell adds all of its common parameters to your function, you don't actually need to implement the code to support them. For example, calls to Write-Verbose usually generate no output. When the user specifies the -Verbose parameter to your function, PowerShell then automatically displays the output of the Write-Verbose cmdlet.

```
PS > Invoke-MyAdvancedFunction
PS > Invoke-MyAdvancedFunction -Verbose
VERBOSE: Verbose Message
```

If your cmdlet modifies system state, it is extremely helpful to support the standard -WhatIf and -Confirm parameters. For information on how to accomplish this, see Recipe 11.15, "Provide -WhatIf, -Confirm, and Other Cmdlet Features".

### Using the $args array

Despite all of the power exposed by named parameters, common parameters, and advanced functions, the $args array is still sometimes helpful. For example, it provides a clean way to deal with all arguments at once:

```
function Reverse
{
    $argsEnd = $args.Length - 1
    $args[$argsEnd..0]
}
```

This produces:

```
PS > Reverse 1 2 3 4
4
3
2
1
```

If you have defined parameters in your script, the $args array represents any arguments not captured by those parameters:

```
PS > function MyParamsAndArgs {
    param($MyArgument)

    "Got MyArgument: $MyArgument"
    "Got Args: $args"
}

PS > MyParamsAndArgs -MyArgument One Two Three
Got MyArgument: One
Got Args: Two Three
```

For more information about the param statement, see "Writing Scripts, Reusing Functionality" (page 897). For more information about running scripts, see Recipe 1.1, "Run Programs, Scripts, and Existing Tools". For more information about functionality (such as -Whatif and -Confirm) exposed by the PowerShell engine, see Recipe 11.15, "Provide -WhatIf, -Confirm, and Other Cmdlet Features".

For information about how to declare parameters with rich validation and behavior, see Recipe 11.12, "Add Validation to Parameters".

## See Also

Recipe 1.1, "Run Programs, Scripts, and Existing Tools"

Recipe 11.12, "Add Validation to Parameters"

Recipe 11.15, "Provide -WhatIf, -Confirm, and Other Cmdlet Features"

Recipe 16.3, "Access Information About Your Command's Invocation"

"Writing Scripts, Reusing Functionality" (page 897)

# 11.12. Add Validation to Parameters

## Problem

You want to ensure that user input to a parameter satisfies certain restrictions or constraints.

## Solution

Use the [`Parameter()`] attribute to declare the parameter as mandatory, positional, part of a mutually exclusive set of parameters, or able to receive its input from the pipeline.

```
param(
    [Parameter(
        Mandatory = $true,
        Position = 0,
        ValueFromPipeline = $true,
        ValueFromPipelineByPropertyName = $true)]
    [string[]] $Name
)
```

Use additional validation attributes to define aliases, support for null or empty values, count restrictions (for collections), length restrictions (for strings), regular expression requirements, range requirements (for numbers), permissible value requirements, or even arbitrary script requirements.

```
param(
    [ValidateLength(5,10)]
    [string] $Name
)

"Hello $Name"
```

## Discussion

Traditional shells require extensions (scripts and commands) to write their parameter support by hand, resulting in a wide range of behavior. Some implement a bare, confusing minimum of support. Others implement more complex features, but differently than any other command. The bare, confusing minimum is by far the most common, as writing fully featured parameter support is a complex endeavor.

Luckily, the PowerShell engine already wrote all of the complex parameter handling support and manages all of this detail for you. Rather than write the code to enforce it, you can simply mark parameters as mandatory or positional or state their validation requirements. This built-in support for parameter behavior and validation forms a centerpiece of PowerShell's unique consistency.

Parameter validation is one of the main distinctions between scripts that are well be-haved and those that are not. When running a new script (or one you wrote distantly in the past), reviewing the parameter definitions and validation requirements is one of the quickest ways to familiarize yourself with how that script behaves.

From the script author's perspective, validation requirements save you from writing verification code that you'll need to write anyway.

### Defining parameter behavior

The elements of the `[Parameter()]` attribute mainly define how your parameter be-haves in relation to other parameters. All elements are optional.

You can omit the `'= $true'` assignment for any element that simply takes a `$true` or `$false` value.

`Mandatory = $true`
> Defines the parameter as mandatory. If the user doesn't supply a value to this pa-rameter, PowerShell automatically prompts the user for it. When not specified, the parameter is optional.

`Position = position`
> Defines the position of this parameter. This applies when the user provides param-eter values without specifying the parameter they apply to (for example, *Argu ment2* in `Invoke-MyFunction -Param1 Argument1 Argument2`). PowerShell sup-plies these values to parameters that have defined a `Position`, from lowest to high-est. When not specified, the name of this parameter must be supplied by the user.

`ParameterSetName = name`
> Defines this parameter as a member of a set of other related parameters. Parameter behavior for this parameter is then specific to this related set of parameters, and the parameter exists only in parameter sets in which it is defined. This feature is used, for example, when the user may supply only a `Name` *or* `ID`. To include a parameter in two or more specific parameter sets, use two or more `[Parameter()]` attributes. When not specified, this parameter is a member of all parameter sets. To define the default parameter set name of your cmdlet, supply it in the `CmdletBinding` attribute: `[CmdletBinding(DefaultParameterSetName = "Name")]`.

`ValueFromPipeline = $true`
> Declares this parameter as one that directly accepts pipeline input. If the user pipes data into your script or function, PowerShell assigns this input to your parameter in your command's `process {}` block. For more information about accepting pipe-line input, see Recipe 11.18, "Access Pipeline Input". Beware of applying this pa-rameter to `String` parameters, as almost all input can be converted to strings—often producing a result that doesn't make much sense. When not specified, this parameter does not accept pipeline input directly.

**ValueFromPipelineByPropertyName = $true**

Declares this parameter as one that accepts pipeline input if a property of an incoming object matches its name. If this is true, PowerShell assigns the value of that property to your parameter in your command's process {} block. For more information about accepting pipeline input, see Recipe 11.18, "Access Pipeline Input". When not specified, this parameter does not accept pipeline input by property name.

**ValueFromRemainingArguments = $true**

Declares this parameter as one that accepts all remaining input that has not otherwise been assigned to positional or named parameters. Only one parameter can have this element. If no parameter declares support for this capability, PowerShell generates an error for arguments that cannot be assigned.

## Defining parameter validation

In addition to the [Parameter()] attribute, PowerShell lets you apply other attributes that add further behavior or validation constraints to your parameters. All validation attributes are optional.

**[Alias("name")]**

Defines an alternate name for this parameter. This is especially helpful for long parameter names that are descriptive but have a more common colloquial term. When not specified, the parameter can be referred to only by the name you originally declared. You can supply many aliases to a parameter. To learn about aliases for command parameters, see Recipe 1.19, "Program: Learn Aliases for Common Parameters".

**[AllowNull()]**

Allows this parameter to receive $null as its value. This is required only for mandatory parameters. When not specified, mandatory parameters cannot receive $null as their value, although optional parameters can.

**[AllowEmptyString()]**

Allows this string parameter to receive an empty string as its value. This is required only for mandatory parameters. When not specified, mandatory string parameters cannot receive an empty string as their value, although optional string parameters can. You can apply this to parameters that are not strings, but it has no impact.

**[AllowEmptyCollection()]**

Allows this collection parameter to receive an empty collection as its value. This is required only for mandatory parameters. When not specified, mandatory collection parameters cannot receive an empty collection as their value, although optional collection parameters can. You can apply this to parameters that are not collections, but it has no impact.

`[ValidateCount(`*`lower limit, upper limit`*`)]`
> Restricts the number of elements that can be in a collection supplied to this parameter. When not specified, mandatory parameters have a lower limit of one element. Optional parameters have no restrictions. You can apply this to parameters that are not collections, but it has no impact.

`[ValidateLength(`*`lower limit, upper limit`*`)]`
> Restricts the length of strings that this parameter can accept. When not specified, mandatory parameters have a lower limit of one character. Optional parameters have no restrictions. You can apply this to parameters that are not strings, but it has no impact.

`[ValidatePattern("`*`regular expression`*`")]`
> Enforces a pattern that input to this string parameter must match. When not specified, string inputs have no pattern requirements. You can apply this to parameters that are not strings, but it has no impact.
>
> If your parameter has a pattern requirement, though, it may be more effective to validate the parameter in the body of your script or function instead. The error message that PowerShell generates when a parameter fails to match this pattern is not very user-friendly ("The argument…does not match the *<pattern>* pattern"). Instead, you can generate a message to explain the *intent* of the pattern:
>
> ```
> if($EmailAddress -notmatch Pattern)
> {
>     throw "Please specify a valid email address."
> }
> ```

`[ValidateRange(`*`lower limit, upper limit`*`)]`
> Restricts the upper and lower limit of numerical arguments that this parameter can accept. When not specified, parameters have no range limit. You can apply this to parameters that are not numbers, but it has no impact.

`[ValidateScript( {` *`script block`* `} )]`
> Ensures that input supplied to this parameter satisfies the condition that you supply in the script block. PowerShell assigns the proposed input to the `$_` (or `$PSItem`) variable, and then invokes your script block. If the script block returns `$true` (or anything that can be converted to `$true`, such as nonempty strings), PowerShell considers the validation to have been successful.

`[ValidateSet("`*`First Option`*`", "`*`Second Option`*`", ..., "`*`Last Option`*`")]`
> Ensures that input supplied to this parameter is equal to one of the options in the set. PowerShell uses its standard meaning of equality during this comparison (the same rules used by the `-eq` operator). If your validation requires nonstandard rules (such as case-sensitive comparison of strings), you can instead write the validation in the body of the script or function.

```
[ValidateNotNull()]
```
Ensures that input supplied to this parameter is not null. This is the default behavior of mandatory parameters, and this attribute is useful only for optional parameters. When applied to string parameters, a $null parameter value instead gets converted to an empty string.

```
[ValidateNotNullOrEmpty()]
```
Ensures that input supplied to this parameter is neither null nor empty. This is the default behavior of mandatory parameters, and this attribute is useful only for optional parameters. When applied to string parameters, the input must be a string with a length greater than 1. When applied to collection parameters, the collection must have at least one element. When applied to other types of parameters, this attribute is equivalent to the [ValidateNotNull()] attribute.

For more information, type **Get-Help about_functions_advanced_parameters**.

## See Also

Recipe 1.19, "Program: Learn Aliases for Common Parameters"

Recipe 11.18, "Access Pipeline Input"

"Providing Input to Commands" (page 902)

# 11.13. Accept Script Block Parameters with Local Variables

## Problem

Your command takes a script block as a parameter. When you invoke that script block, you want variables to refer to variables from the user's session, not your script.

## Solution

Call the GetNewClosure() method on the supplied script block before either defining any of your own variables or invoking the script block. See Example 11-13.

*Example 11-13. A command that supports variables from the user's session*

```
##############################################################################
##
## Invoke-ScriptBlockClosure
##
## From Windows PowerShell Cookbook (O'Reilly)
## by Lee Holmes (http://www.leeholmes.com/guide)
##
##############################################################################

<#
```

```
.SYNOPSIS

Demonstrates the GetNewClosure() method on a script block that pulls variables
in from the user's session (if they are defined).

.EXAMPLE

PS > $name = "Hello There"
PS > Invoke-ScriptBlockClosure { $name }
Hello There
Hello World
Hello There

#>

param(
    ## The script block to invoke
    [ScriptBlock] $ScriptBlock
)

Set-StrictMode -Version 3

## Create a new script block that pulls variables
## from the user's scope (if defined).
$closedScriptBlock = $scriptBlock.GetNewClosure()

## Invoke the script block normally. The contents of
## the $name variable will be from the user's session.
& $scriptBlock

## Define a new variable
$name = "Hello World"

## Invoke the script block normally. The contents of
## the $name variable will be "Hello World", now from
## our scope.
& $scriptBlock

## Invoke the "closed" script block. The contents of
## the $name variable will still be whatever was in the user's session
## (if it was defined).
& $closedScriptBlock
```

## Discussion

Whenever you invoke a script block (for example, one passed by the user as a parameter value), PowerShell treats variables in that script block as though you had typed them yourself. For example, if a variable referenced by the script block is defined in your script or module, PowerShell will use that value when it evaluates the variable.

This is often desirable behavior, although its use ultimately depends on your script. For example, Recipe 11.4, "Write a Script Block" accepts a script block parameter that is intended to refer to variables defined *within* the script: $_ (or $PSItem), specifically.

Alternatively, this might not always be what you want. Sometimes, you might prefer that variable names refer to variables from the *user's session*, rather than potentially from your script.

The solution, in this case, is to call the GetNewClosure() method. This method makes the script block self-contained, or *closed*. Variables maintain the value they had when the GetNewClosure() method was called, even if a new variable with that name is created.

### See Also

Recipe 3.6, "Control Access and Scope of Variables and Other Items"

Recipe 11.4, "Write a Script Block"

# 11.14. Dynamically Compose Command Parameters

## Problem

You want to specify the parameters of a command you are about to invoke but don't know beforehand what those parameters will be.

## Solution

Define the parameters and their values as elements of a hashtable, and then use the @ character to pass that hashtable to a command:

```
PS > $parameters = @{
    Name = "PowerShell";
    WhatIf = $true
}

PS > Stop-Process @parameters
What if: Performing operation "Stop-Process" on Target "powershell (2380)".
What if: Performing operation "Stop-Process" on Target "powershell (2792)".
```

## Discussion

When you're writing commands that call other commands, a common problem is not knowing the exact parameter values that you'll pass to a target command. The solution to this is simple, and comes by storing the parameter values in variables:

```
PS > function Stop-ProcessWhatIf($name)
{
```

```
    Stop-Process -Name $name -Whatif
}

PS > Stop-ProcessWhatIf PowerShell
What if: Performing operation "Stop-Process" on Target "powershell (2380)".
What if: Performing operation "Stop-Process" on Target "powershell (2792)".
```

When you're using this approach, things seem to get much more difficult if you don't know beforehand which parameter *names* you want to pass along. PowerShell significantly improves the situation through a technique called *splatting* that lets you pass along parameter values *and* names.

The first step is to define a variable—for example, `parameters`. In that variable, store a hashtable of parameter names and their values. When you call a command, you can pass the hashtable of parameter names and values with the @ character and the variable name that stores them. Note that you use the @ character to represent the variable, instead of the usual $ character:

```
Stop-Process @parameters
```

This is a common need when you're writing commands that are designed to enhance or extend existing commands. In that situation, you simply want to pass all of the user's input (parameter values *and* names) on to the existing command, even though you don't know exactly what they supplied.

To simplify this situation even further, *advanced functions* have access to an automatic variable called `PSBoundParameters`. This automatic variable is a hashtable that stores all parameters passed to the current command, and it is suitable for both tweaking and splatting. For an example of this approach, see Recipe 11.23, "Program: Enhance or Extend an Existing Cmdlet".

In addition to supporting splatting of the `PSBoundParameters` automatic variable, PowerShell also supports splatting of the `$args` array for extremely lightweight command wrappers:

```
PS > function rsls { dir -rec | Select-String @args }
PS > rsls -SimpleMatch '["Pattern"]'
```

For more information about advanced functions, see Recipe 11.11, "Access Arguments of a Script, Function, or Script Block".

## See Also

Recipe 11.11, "Access Arguments of a Script, Function, or Script Block"

Recipe 11.23, "Program: Enhance or Extend an Existing Cmdlet"

# 11.15. Provide -WhatIf, -Confirm, and Other Cmdlet Features

## Problem

You want to support the standard -WhatIf and -Confirm parameters, and access cmdlet-centric support in the PowerShell engine.

## Solution

Ensure your script or function declares the [CmdletBinding()] attribute, and then access engine features through the $psCmdlet automatic variable.

```
function Invoke-MyAdvancedFunction
{
    [CmdletBinding(SupportsShouldProcess = $true)]
    param()

    if($psCmdlet.ShouldProcess("test.txt", "Remove Item"))
    {
        "Removing test.txt"
    }

    Write-Verbose "Verbose Message"
}
```

## Discussion

When a script or function progresses to an *advanced function*, PowerShell defines an additional $psCmdlet automatic variable. This automatic variable exposes support for the -WhatIf and -Confirm automatic parameters. If your command defined parameter sets, it also exposes the parameter set name that PowerShell selected based on the user's choice of parameters. For more information about advanced functions, see Recipe 11.11, "Access Arguments of a Script, Function, or Script Block".

To support the -WhatIf and -Confirm parameters, add the [CmdletBinding(Supports ShouldProcess = $true)] attribute inside of your script or function. You should support this on any scripts or functions that modify system state, as they let your users investigate what your script will do before actually doing it. Then, you simply surround the portion of your script that changes the system with an if($psCmdlet.Should Process(...) ) { } block. Example 11-14 demonstrates this approach.

*Example 11-14. Adding support for -WhatIf and -Confirm*

```
function Invoke-MyAdvancedFunction
{
    [CmdletBinding(SupportsShouldProcess = $true)]
    param()
```

```
    if($psCmdlet.ShouldProcess("test.txt", "Remove Item"))
    {
        "Removing test.txt"
    }

    Write-Verbose "Verbose Message"
}
```

Now your advanced function is as well behaved as built-in PowerShell cmdlets!

```
PS > Invoke-MyAdvancedFunction -WhatIf
What if: Performing operation "Remove Item" on Target "test.txt".
```

If your command causes a high-impact result that should be evaluated with caution, call the $psCmdlet.ShouldContinue() method. This generates a warning for users—but be sure to support a -Force parameter that lets them bypass this message.

```
function Invoke-MyDangerousFunction
{
    [CmdletBinding()]
    param(
        [Switch] $Force
    )

    if($Force -or $psCmdlet.ShouldContinue(
        "Do you wish to invoke this dangerous operation?
         Changes can not be undone.",
        "Invoke dangerous action?"))
    {
        "Invoking dangerous action"
    }
}
```

This generates a standard PowerShell confirmation message:

```
PS > Invoke-MyDangerousFunction

Invoke dangerous action?
Do you wish to invoke this dangerous operation? Changes can not be undone.
[Y] Yes  [N] No  [S] Suspend  [?] Help (default is "Y"):
Invoking dangerous action

PS > Invoke-MyDangerousFunction -Force
Invoking dangerous action
```

To explore the $psCmdlet automatic variable further, you can use Example 11-15. This command creates the bare minimum of advanced functions, and then invokes whatever script block you supply within it.

*Example 11-15. Invoke-AdvancedFunction.ps1*

```
param(
    [Parameter(Mandatory = $true)]
    [ScriptBlock] $Scriptblock
    )

## Invoke the script block supplied by the user.
& $scriptblock
```

For open-ended exploration, use `$host.EnterNestedPrompt()` as the script block:

```
PS > Invoke-AdvancedFunction { $host.EnterNestedPrompt() }
PS > $psCmdlet | Get-Member


    TypeName: System.Management.Automation.PSScriptCmdlet

Name                       MemberType Definition
----                       ---------- ----------
(...)
WriteDebug                 Method     System.Void WriteDebug(s...
WriteError                 Method     System.Void WriteError(S...
WriteObject                Method     System.Void WriteObject(...
WriteProgress              Method     System.Void WriteProgres...
WriteVerbose               Method     System.Void WriteVerbose...
WriteWarning               Method     System.Void WriteWarning...
(...)
ParameterSetName           Property   System.String ParameterS...

PS >> exit
PS >
```

For more about cmdlet support in the PowerShell engine, see the developer's reference here (*http://msdn.microsoft.com/en-us/library/dd878294%28VS.85%29.aspx*).

## See Also

Recipe 11.11, "Access Arguments of a Script, Function, or Script Block"

# 11.16. Add Help to Scripts or Functions

## Problem

You want to make your command and usage information available to the `Get-Help` command.

## Solution

Add descriptive help comments at the beginning of your script for its synopsis, description, examples, notes, and more. Add descriptive help comments before parameters to describe their meaning and behavior:

```
#############################################################################
##
## Measure-CommandPerformance
##
## From Windows PowerShell Cookbook (O'Reilly)
## by Lee Holmes (http://www.leeholmes.com/guide)
##
#############################################################################

<#

.SYNOPSIS

Measures the average time of a command, accounting for natural variability by
automatically ignoring the top and bottom ten percent.

.EXAMPLE

PS > Measure-CommandPerformance.ps1 { Start-Sleep -m 300 }

Count    : 30
Average  : 312.10155
(...)

#>

param(
    ## The command to measure
    [Scriptblock] $Scriptblock,

    ## The number of times to measure the command's performance
    [int] $Iterations = 30
)

Set-StrictMode -Version 3

## Figure out how many extra iterations we need to account for the outliers
$buffer = [int] ($iterations * 0.1)
$totalIterations = $iterations + (2 * $buffer)

## Get the results
$results = 1..$totalIterations |
    Foreach-Object { Measure-Command $scriptblock }
```

```
## Sort the results, and skip the outliers
$middleResults = $results | Sort TotalMilliseconds |
    Select -Skip $buffer -First $iterations

## Show the average
$middleResults | Measure-Object -Average TotalMilliseconds
```

## Discussion

Like parameter validation, discussed in Recipe 11.12, "Add Validation to Parameters", rich help is something traditionally supported in only the most high-end commands. For most commands, you're lucky if you can figure out how to get some form of usage message.

As with PowerShell's easy-to-define support for advanced parameter validation, adding help to commands and functions is extremely simple. Despite its simplicity, comment-based help provides all the power you've come to expect of fully featured PowerShell commands: overview, description, examples, parameter-specific details, and more.

PowerShell creates help for your script or function by looking at its comments. If the comments include any supported help tags, PowerShell adds those to the help for your command.

To speed up processing of these help comments, PowerShell places restrictions on where they may appear. In addition, if it encounters a comment that is *not* a help-based comment, it stops searching that block of comments for help tags. This may come as a surprise if you are used to placing headers or copyright information at the beginning of your script. The Solution demonstrates how to avoid this problem by putting the header and comment-based help in separate comment blocks. For more information about these guidelines, type **Get-Help about_Comment_Based_Help**.

You can place your help tags in either single-line comments or multiline (block) comments. You may find multiline comments easier to work with, as you can write them in editors that support spelling and grammar checks and then simply paste them into your script. Also, adjusting the word-wrapping of your comment is easier when you don't have to repair comment markers at the beginning of the line. From the user's perspective, multiline comments offer a significant benefit for the *.EXAMPLES* section because they require much less modification before being tried.

For a list of the most common help tags, see "Help Comments" (page 863).

## See Also

Recipe 11.12, "Add Validation to Parameters"

"Help Comments" (page 863)

# 11.17. Add Custom Tags to a Function or Script Block

## Problem

You want to tag or add your own custom information to a function or script block.

## Solution

If you want the custom information to always be associated with the function or script block, declare a `System.ComponentModel.Description` attribute inside that function:

```
function TestFunction
{
    [System.ComponentModel.Description("Information I care about")]
    param()

    "Some function with metadata"
}
```

If you don't control the source code of the function, create a new `System.ComponentModel.Description` attribute, and add it to the script block's `Attributes` collection manually:

```
$testFunction = Get-Command TestFunction
$newAttribute =
  New-Object ComponentModel.DescriptionAttribute "More information I care about"
$testFunction.ScriptBlock.Attributes.Add($newAttribute)
```

To retrieve any attributes associated with a function or script block, access the `ScriptBlock.Attributes` property:

```
PS > $testFunction = Get-Command TestFunction
PS > $testFunction.ScriptBlock.Attributes

Description                      TypeId
-----------                      ------
Information I care about         System.ComponentModel.Description...
```

## Discussion

Although a specialized need for sure, it is sometimes helpful to add your own custom information to functions or script blocks. For example, once you've built up a large set of functions, many are really useful only in a specific context. Some functions might apply to only one of your clients, whereas others are written for a custom website you're developing. If you forget the name of a function, you might have difficulty going through all of your functions to find the ones that apply to your current context.

You might find it helpful to write a new function, Get-CommandForContext, that takes a context (for example, *website*) and returns only commands that apply to that context.

```
function Get-CommandForContext($context)
{
    Get-Command -CommandType Function |
        Where-Object { $_.ScriptBlock.Attributes |
            Where-Object { $_.Description -eq "Context=$context" } }
}
```

Then write some functions that apply to specific contexts:

```
function WebsiteFunction
{
    [System.ComponentModel.Description("Context=Website")]
    param()

    "Some function I use with my website"
}

function ExchangeFunction
{
    [System.ComponentModel.Description("Context=Exchange")]
    param()

    "Some function I use with Exchange"
}
```

Then, by building on these two, we have a context-sensitive equivalent to Get-Command:

```
PS > Get-CommandForContext Website

CommandType     Name                    Definition
-----------     ----                    ----------
Function        WebsiteFunction         ...


PS > Get-CommandForContext Exchange

CommandType     Name                    Definition
-----------     ----                    ----------
Function        ExchangeFunction        ...
```

While the System.ComponentModel.Description attribute is the most generically useful, PowerShell lets you place any attribute in a function. You can define your own (by deriving from the `System.Attribute` class in the .NET Framework) or use any of the other attributes included in the .NET Framework. Example 11-16 shows the PowerShell commands to find all attributes that have a constructor that takes a single string as its argument. These attributes are likely to be generally useful.

*Example 11-16. Finding all useful attributes*

```
$types = [Appdomain]::CurrentDomain.GetAssemblies() |
    Foreach-Object { $_.GetTypes() }

foreach($type in $types)
{
    if($type.BaseType -eq [System.Attribute])
    {
        foreach($constructor in $type.GetConstructors())
        {
            if($constructor.ToString() -match "\(System.String\)")
            {
                $type
            }
        }
    }
}
```

For more information about working with .NET objects, see Recipe 3.8, "Work with .NET Objects".

## See Also

Recipe 3.8, "Work with .NET Objects"

# 11.18. Access Pipeline Input

## Problem

You want to interact with input that a user sends to your function, script, or script block via the pipeline.

## Solution

To access pipeline input, use the `$input` variable, as shown in Example 11-17.

*Example 11-17. Accessing pipeline input*

```
function InputCounter
{
    $count = 0
```

```
## Go through each element in the pipeline, and add up
## how many elements there were.
foreach($element in $input)
{
    $count++
}

$count
}
```

This function produces the following (or similar) output when run against your Windows system directory:

```
PS > dir $env:WINDIR | InputCounter
295
```

## Discussion

In your scripts, functions, and script blocks, the $input variable represents an *enumerator* (as opposed to a simple array) for the pipeline input the user provides. An enumerator lets you use a foreach statement to efficiently scan over the elements of the input (as shown in Example 11-17) but does not let you directly access specific items (such as the fifth element in the input).

 An enumerator only lets you scan forward through its contents. Once you access an element, PowerShell automatically moves on to the next one. If you need to access an item that you've already accessed, you must either call $input.Reset() to scan through the list again from the beginning or store the input in an array.

If you need to access specific elements in the input (or access items multiple times), the best approach is to store the input in an array. This prevents your script from taking advantage of the $input enumerator's streaming behavior, but is sometimes the only alternative. To store the input in an array, use PowerShell's list evaluation syntax ( @( ) ) to force PowerShell to interpret it as an array:

```
function ReverseInput
{
    $inputArray = @($input)
    $inputEnd = $inputArray.Count - 1

    $inputArray[$inputEnd..0]
}
```

This produces:

```
PS > 1,2,3,4 | ReverseInput
4
3
2
1
```

If dealing with pipeline input plays a major role in your script, function, or script block, PowerShell provides an alternative means of dealing with pipeline input that may make your script easier to write and understand. For more information, see Recipe 11.19, "Write Pipeline-Oriented Scripts with Cmdlet Keywords".

## See Also

Recipe 11.19, "Write Pipeline-Oriented Scripts with Cmdlet Keywords"

# 11.19. Write Pipeline-Oriented Scripts with Cmdlet Keywords

## Problem

Your script, function, or script block primarily takes input from the pipeline, and you want to write it in a way that makes this intention both easy to implement and easy to read.

## Solution

To cleanly separate your script into regions that deal with the initialization, per-record processing, and cleanup portions, use the begin, process, and end keywords, respectively. For example, a pipeline-oriented conversion of the Solution in Recipe 11.18, "Access Pipeline Input" looks like Example 11-18.

*Example 11-18. A pipeline-oriented script that uses cmdlet keywords*

```
function InputCounter
{
    begin
    {
        $count = 0
    }

    ## Go through each element in the pipeline, and add up
    ## how many elements there were.
    process
    {
        Write-Debug "Processing element $_"
        $count++
    }
```

```
    end
    {
        $count
    }
}
```

This produces the following output:

```
PS > $debugPreference = "Continue"
PS > dir | InputCounter
DEBUG: Processing element Compare-Property.ps1
DEBUG: Processing element Convert-TextObject.ps1
DEBUG: Processing element ConvertFrom-FahrenheitWithFunction.ps1
DEBUG: Processing element ConvertFrom-FahrenheitWithoutFunction.ps1
DEBUG: Processing element Get-AliasSuggestion.ps1
(...)
DEBUG: Processing element Select-FilteredObject.ps1
DEBUG: Processing element Set-ConsoleProperties.ps1
20
```

## Discussion

If your script, function, or script block deals primarily with input from the pipeline, the begin, process, and end keywords let you express your solution most clearly. Readers of your script (including you!) can easily see which portions of your script deal with initialization, per-record processing, and cleanup. In addition, separating your code into these blocks lets your script consume elements from the pipeline as soon as the previous script produces them.

Take, for example, the Get-InputWithForeach and Get-InputWithKeyword functions shown in Example 11-19. The first function visits each element in the pipeline with a foreach statement over its input, whereas the second uses the begin, process, and end keywords.

*Example 11-19. Two functions that take different approaches to processing pipeline input*

```
## From Windows PowerShell Cookbook (O'Reilly)
## by Lee Holmes (http://www.leeholmes.com/guide)

Set-StrictMode -Version 3

## Process each element in the pipeline, using a
## foreach statement to visit each element in $input
function Get-InputWithForeach($identifier)
{
    Write-Host "Beginning InputWithForeach (ID: $identifier)"

    foreach($element in $input)
    {
        Write-Host "Processing element $element (ID: $identifier)"
        $element
```

```
    }

    Write-Host "Ending InputWithForeach (ID: $identifier)"
}

## Process each element in the pipeline, using the
## cmdlet-style keywords to visit each element in $input
function Get-InputWithKeyword($identifier)
{
    begin
    {
        Write-Host "Beginning InputWithKeyword (ID: $identifier)"
    }

    process
    {
        Write-Host "Processing element $_ (ID: $identifier)"
        $_
    }

    end
    {
        Write-Host "Ending InputWithKeyword (ID: $identifier)"
    }
}
```

Both of these functions act the same when run individually, but the difference becomes clear when we combine them with other scripts or functions that take pipeline input. When a script uses the $input variable, it must wait until the previous script finishes producing output before it can start. If the previous script takes a long time to produce all its records (for example, a large directory listing), then your user must wait until the entire directory listing completes to see any results, rather than seeing results for each item as the script generates it.

 If a script, function, or script block uses the cmdlet-style keywords, it must place all its code (aside from comments or its param statement if it uses one) inside one of the three blocks. If your code needs to define and initialize variables or define functions, place them in the begin block. Unlike most blocks of code contained within curly braces, the code in the begin, process, and end blocks has access to variables and functions defined within the blocks before it.

When we chain together two scripts that process their input with the begin, process, and end keywords, the second script gets to process input as soon as the first script produces it.

```
PS > 1,2,3 | Get-InputWithKeyword 1 | Get-InputWithKeyword 2
Starting InputWithKeyword (ID: 1)
Starting InputWithKeyword (ID: 2)
Processing element 1 (ID: 1)
Processing element 1 (ID: 2)
1
Processing element 2 (ID: 1)
Processing element 2 (ID: 2)
2
Processing element 3 (ID: 1)
Processing element 3 (ID: 2)
3
Stopping InputWithKeyword (ID: 1)
Stopping InputWithKeyword (ID: 2)
```

When we chain together two scripts that process their input with the $input variable, the second script can't start until the first completes.

```
PS > 1,2,3 | Get-InputWithForeach 1 | Get-InputWithForeach 2
Starting InputWithForeach (ID: 1)
Processing element 1 (ID: 1)
Processing element 2 (ID: 1)
Processing element 3 (ID: 1)
Stopping InputWithForeach (ID: 1)
Starting InputWithForeach (ID: 2)
Processing element 1 (ID: 2)
1
Processing element 2 (ID: 2)
2
Processing element 3 (ID: 2)
3
Stopping InputWithForeach (ID: 2)
```

When the first script uses the cmdlet-style keywords, and the second script uses the $input variable, the second script can't start until the first completes.

```
PS > 1,2,3 | Get-InputWithKeyword 1 | Get-InputWithForeach 2
Starting InputWithKeyword (ID: 1)
Processing element 1 (ID: 1)
Processing element 2 (ID: 1)
Processing element 3 (ID: 1)
Stopping InputWithKeyword (ID: 1)
Starting InputWithForeach (ID: 2)
Processing element 1 (ID: 2)
1
Processing element 2 (ID: 2)
2
Processing element 3 (ID: 2)
3
Stopping InputWithForeach (ID: 2)
```

When the first script uses the $input variable and the second script uses the cmdlet-style keywords, the second script gets to process input as soon as the first script produces it. Notice, however, that InputWithKeyword starts before InputWithForeach. This is because functions with no explicit begin, process, or end blocks have all of their code placed in an end block by default.

```
PS > 1,2,3 | Get-InputWithForeach 1 | Get-InputWithKeyword 2
Starting InputWithKeyword (ID: 2)
Starting InputWithForeach (ID: 1)
Processing element 1 (ID: 1)
Processing element 1 (ID: 2)
1
Processing element 2 (ID: 1)
Processing element 2 (ID: 2)
2
Processing element 3 (ID: 1)
Processing element 3 (ID: 2)
3
Stopping InputWithForeach (ID: 1)
Stopping InputWithKeyword (ID: 2)
```

For more information about dealing with pipeline input, see "Writing Scripts, Reusing Functionality" (page 897).

## See Also

Recipe 11.18, "Access Pipeline Input"

"Writing Scripts, Reusing Functionality" (page 897)

# 11.20. Write a Pipeline-Oriented Function

## Problem

Your function primarily takes its input from the pipeline, and you want it to perform the same steps for each element of that input.

## Solution

To write a pipeline-oriented function, define your function using the filter keyword, rather than the function keyword. PowerShell makes the current pipeline object available as the $_ (or $PSItem) variable:

```
filter Get-PropertyValue($property)
{
    $_.$property
}
```

## Discussion

A filter is the equivalent of a function that uses the cmdlet-style keywords and has all its code inside the `process` section.

The Solution demonstrates an extremely useful filter: one that returns the value of a property for each item in a pipeline:

```
PS > Get-Process | Get-PropertyValue Name
audiodg
avgamsvr
avgemc
avgrssvc
avgrssvc
avgupsvc
(...)
```

For a more complete example of this approach, see Recipe 2.7, "Program: Simplify Most Foreach-Object Pipelines". For more information about the cmdlet-style keywords, see Recipe 11.19, "Write Pipeline-Oriented Scripts with Cmdlet Keywords".

## See Also

Recipe 2.7, "Program: Simplify Most Foreach-Object Pipelines"

Recipe 11.19, "Write Pipeline-Oriented Scripts with Cmdlet Keywords"

# 11.21. Organize Scripts for Improved Readability

## Problem

You have a long script that includes helper functions, but those helper functions obscure the main intent of the script.

## Solution

Place the main logic of your script in a function called `Main`, and place that function at the top of your script. At the bottom of your script (after all the helper functions have also been defined), dot-source the `Main` function:

```
## LongScript.ps1

function Main
{
    "Invoking the main logic of the script"
    CallHelperFunction1
    CallHelperFunction2
}
```

```
function CallHelperFunction1
{
    "Calling the first helper function"
}

function CallHelperFunction2
{
    "Calling the second helper function"
}

. Main
```

## Discussion

When PowerShell invokes a script, it executes it in order from the beginning to the end. Just as when you type commands in the console, PowerShell generates an error if you try to call a function that you haven't yet defined.

When writing a long script with lots of helper functions, this usually results in those helper functions migrating to the top of the script so that they are all defined by the time your main logic finally executes them. When reading the script, then, you are forced to wade through pages of seemingly unrelated helper functions just to reach the main logic of the script.

You might wonder why PowerShell requires this strict ordering of function definitions and when they are called. After all, a script is self-contained, and it would be possible for PowerShell to process all of the function definitions before invoking the script.

The reason is parity with the interactive environment. Pasting a script into the console window is a common diagnostic or experimental technique, as is highlighting portions of a script in the Integrated Scripting Environment and selecting "Run Selection." If PowerShell did something special in an imaginary *script mode*, these techniques would not be possible.

To resolve this problem, you can place the main script logic in a function of its own. The name doesn't matter, but Main is a traditional name. If you place this function at the top of the script, your main logic is visible immediately.

Functions aren't automatically executed, so the final step is to invoke the Main function. Place this call at the end of your script, and you can be sure that all the required helper functions have been defined. Dot-sourcing this function ensures that it is processed in the *script scope*, rather than the isolated function scope that would normally be created for it.

For more information about dot sourcing and script scopes, see Recipe 3.6, "Control Access and Scope of Variables and Other Items".

## See Also

Recipe 3.6, "Control Access and Scope of Variables and Other Items"

# 11.22. Invoke Dynamically Named Commands

## Problem

You want to take an action based on the *pattern* of a command name, as opposed to the name of the command itself.

## Solution

Add a `$executionContext.SessionState.InvokeCommand.CommandNotFoundAction` that intercepts PowerShell's `CommandNotFound` error and takes action based on the `CommandName` that was not found.

Example 11-20 illustrates this technique by supporting relative path navigation without an explicit call to `Set-Location`.

*Example 11-20. Add-RelativePathCapture.ps1*

```
##############################################################################
##
## Add-RelativePathCapture
##
## From Windows PowerShell Cookbook (O'Reilly)
## by Lee Holmes (http://www.leeholmes.com/guide)
##
##############################################################################

<#

.SYNOPSIS

Adds a new CommandNotFound handler that captures relative path
navigation without having to explicitly call 'Set-Location'

.EXAMPLE

PS C:\Users\Lee\Documents>..
PS C:\Users\Lee>...
PS C:\>

#>
```

```
Set-StrictMode -Version 3

$executionContext.SessionState.InvokeCommand.CommandNotFoundAction = {
    param($CommandName, $CommandLookupEventArgs)

    ## If the command is only dots
    if($CommandName -match '^\.+$')
    {
        ## Associate a new command that should be invoked instead
        $CommandLookupEventArgs.CommandScriptBlock = {

            ## Count the number of dots, and run "Set-Location .." one
            ## less time.
            for($counter = 0; $counter -lt $CommandName.Length - 1; $counter++)
            {
                Set-Location ..
            }

        ## We call GetNewClosure() so that the reference to $CommandName can
        ## be used in the new command.
        }.GetNewClosure()

        ## Stop going through the command resolution process. This isn't
        ## strictly required in the CommandNotFoundAction.
        $CommandLookupEventArgs.StopSearch = $true
    }
}
```

## Discussion

PowerShell supports several useful forms of named commands (cmdlets, functions, and aliases), but you may find yourself wanting to write extensions that alter their behavior based on the *form* of the name, rather than the arguments passed to it. For example, you might want to automatically launch URLs just by typing them or navigate around providers just by typing relative path locations.

While relative path navigation is not a built-in feature of PowerShell, it is possible to get a very reasonable alternative by customizing PowerShell's CommandNotFoundAction. For more information on customizing PowerShell's command resolution behavior, see Recipe 1.10, "Customize PowerShell's Command Resolution Behavior".

## See Also

Recipe 1.10, "Customize PowerShell's Command Resolution Behavior"

# 11.23. Program: Enhance or Extend an Existing Cmdlet

While PowerShell's built-in commands are useful, you may sometimes wish they included an additional parameter or supported a minor change to their functionality. This is usually a difficult proposition: in addition to the complexity of parsing parameters and passing only the correct ones along, wrapped commands should also be able to benefit from the streaming nature of PowerShell's pipeline.

PowerShell significantly improves the situation by combining three features:

*Steppable pipelines*

> Given a script block that contains a single pipeline, the `GetSteppablePipeline()` method returns a `SteppablePipeline` object that gives you control over the `Begin`, `Process`, and `End` stages of the pipeline.

*Argument splatting*

> Given a hashtable of names and values, PowerShell lets you pass the entire hashtable to a command. If you use the `@` symbol to identify the hashtable variable name (rather than the `$` symbol), PowerShell then treats each element of the hashtable as though it were a parameter to the command.

*Proxy command APIs*

> With enough knowledge of steppable pipelines, splatting, and parameter validation, you can write your own function that can effectively wrap another command. The proxy command APIs make this significantly easier by autogenerating large chunks of the required boilerplate script.

These three features finally enable the possibility of powerful command extensions, but putting them together still requires a fair bit of technical expertise. To make things easier, use the `New-CommandWrapper` script (Example 11-21) to easily create commands that wrap (and extend) existing commands.

*Example 11-21. New-CommandWrapper.ps1*

```
##############################################################################
##
## New-CommandWrapper
##
## From Windows PowerShell Cookbook (O'Reilly)
## by Lee Holmes (http://www.leeholmes.com/guide)
##
##############################################################################

<#

.SYNOPSIS

Adds parameters and functionality to existing cmdlets and functions.
```

```
.EXAMPLE

New-CommandWrapper Get-Process `
    -AddParameter @{
        SortBy = {
            $newPipeline = {
                __ORIGINAL_COMMAND__ | Sort-Object -Property $SortBy
            }
        }
    }
```

This example adds a 'SortBy' parameter to Get-Process. It accomplishes
this by adding a Sort-Object command to the pipeline.

```
.EXAMPLE

$parameterAttributes = @'
        [Parameter(Mandatory = $true)]
        [ValidateRange(50,75)]
        [Int]
'@

New-CommandWrapper Clear-Host `
    -AddParameter @{
        @{
            Name = 'MyMandatoryInt';
            Attributes = $parameterAttributes
        } = {
            Write-Host $MyMandatoryInt
            Read-Host "Press ENTER"
        }
    }
```

This example adds a new mandatory 'MyMandatoryInt' parameter to
Clear-Host. This parameter is also validated to fall within the range
of 50 to 75. It doesn't alter the pipeline, but does display some
information on the screen before processing the original pipeline.

```
#>

param(
    ## The name of the command to extend
    [Parameter(Mandatory = $true)]
    $Name,

    ## Script to invoke before the command begins
    [ScriptBlock] $Begin,

    ## Script to invoke for each input element
    [ScriptBlock] $Process,

    ## Script to invoke at the end of the command
```

```
    [ScriptBlock] $End,

    ## Parameters to add, and their functionality.
    ##
    ## The Key of the hashtable can be either a simple parameter name,
    ## or a more advanced parameter description.
    ##
    ## If you want to add additional parameter validation (such as a
    ## parameter type), then the key can itself be a hashtable with the keys
    ## 'Name' and 'Attributes'. 'Attributes' is the text you would use when
    ## defining this parameter as part of a function.
    ##
    ## The value of each hashtable entry is a script block to invoke
    ## when this parameter is selected. To customize the pipeline,
    ## assign a new script block to the $newPipeline variable. Use the
    ## special text, __ORIGINAL_COMMAND__, to represent the original
    ## command. The $targetParameters variable represents a hashtable
    ## containing the parameters that will be passed to the original
    ## command.
    [HashTable] $AddParameter
)

Set-StrictMode -Version 3

## Store the target command we are wrapping, and its command type
$target = $Name
$commandType = "Cmdlet"

## If a function already exists with this name (perhaps it's already been
## wrapped), rename the other function and chain to its new name.
if(Test-Path function:\$Name)
{
    $target = "$Name" + "-" + [Guid]::NewGuid().ToString().Replace("-","")
    Rename-Item function:\GLOBAL:$Name GLOBAL:$target
    $commandType = "Function"
}

## The template we use for generating a command proxy
$proxy = @'

__CMDLET_BINDING_ATTRIBUTE__
param(
__PARAMETERS__
)
begin
{
    try {
        __CUSTOM_BEGIN__

        ## Access the REAL Foreach-Object command, so that command
        ## wrappers do not interfere with this script
        $foreachObject = $executionContext.InvokeCommand.GetCmdlet(
```

```
        "Microsoft.PowerShell.Core\Foreach-Object")

    $wrappedCmd = $ExecutionContext.InvokeCommand.GetCommand(
        '__COMMAND_NAME__',
        [System.Management.Automation.CommandTypes]::__COMMAND_TYPE__)

    ## TargetParameters represents the hashtable of parameters that
    ## we will pass along to the wrapped command
    $targetParameters = @{}
    $PSBoundParameters.GetEnumerator() |
        & $foreachObject {
            if($command.Parameters.ContainsKey($_.Key))
            {
                $targetParameters.Add($_.Key, $_.Value)
            }
        }

    ## finalPipeline represents the pipeline we wil ultimately run
    $newPipeline = { & $wrappedCmd @targetParameters }
    $finalPipeline = $newPipeline.ToString()

    __CUSTOM_PARAMETER_PROCESSING__

    $steppablePipeline = [ScriptBlock]::Create(
        $finalPipeline).GetSteppablePipeline()
    $steppablePipeline.Begin($PSCmdlet)
    } catch {
        throw
    }
}

process
{
    try {
        __CUSTOM_PROCESS__
        $steppablePipeline.Process($_)
    } catch {
        throw
    }
}

end
{
    try {
        __CUSTOM_END__
        $steppablePipeline.End()
    } catch {
        throw
    }
}

dynamicparam
```

```
{
    ## Access the REAL Get-Command, Foreach-Object, and Where-Object
    ## commands, so that command wrappers do not interfere with this script
    $getCommand = $executionContext.InvokeCommand.GetCmdlet(
        "Microsoft.PowerShell.Core\Get-Command")
    $foreachObject = $executionContext.InvokeCommand.GetCmdlet(
        "Microsoft.PowerShell.Core\Foreach-Object")
    $whereObject = $executionContext.InvokeCommand.GetCmdlet(
        "Microsoft.PowerShell.Core\Where-Object")

    ## Find the parameters of the original command, and remove everything
    ## else from the bound parameter list so we hide parameters the wrapped
    ## command does not recognize.
    $command = & $getCommand __COMMAND_NAME__ -Type __COMMAND_TYPE__
    $targetParameters = @{}
    $PSBoundParameters.GetEnumerator() |
        & $foreachObject {
            if($command.Parameters.ContainsKey($_.Key))
            {
                $targetParameters.Add($_.Key, $_.Value)
            }
        }

    ## Get the argument list as it would be passed to the target command
    $argList = @($targetParameters.GetEnumerator() |
        Foreach-Object { "-$($_.Key)"; $_.Value })

    ## Get the dynamic parameters of the wrapped command, based on the
    ## arguments to this command
    $command = $null
    try
    {
        $command = & $getCommand __COMMAND_NAME__ -Type __COMMAND_TYPE__ `
            -ArgumentList $argList
    }
    catch
    {

    }

    $dynamicParams = @($command.Parameters.GetEnumerator() |
        & $whereObject { $_.Value.IsDynamic })

    ## For each of the dynamic parameters, add them to the dynamic
    ## parameters that we return.
    if ($dynamicParams.Length -gt 0)
    {
        $paramDictionary = `
            New-Object Management.Automation.RuntimeDefinedParameterDictionary
        foreach ($param in $dynamicParams)
        {
            $param = $param.Value
```

```
                $arguments = $param.Name, $param.ParameterType, $param.Attributes
                $newParameter = `
                    New-Object Management.Automation.RuntimeDefinedParameter `
                    $arguments
                $paramDictionary.Add($param.Name, $newParameter)
        }
        return $paramDictionary
    }
}

<#

.ForwardHelpTargetName __COMMAND_NAME__
.ForwardHelpCategory __COMMAND_TYPE__

#>

'@

## Get the information about the original command
$originalCommand = Get-Command $target
$metaData = New-Object System.Management.Automation.CommandMetaData `
    $originalCommand
$proxyCommandType = [System.Management.Automation.ProxyCommand]

## Generate the cmdlet binding attribute, and replace information
## about the target
$proxy = $proxy.Replace("__CMDLET_BINDING_ATTRIBUTE__",
    $proxyCommandType::GetCmdletBindingAttribute($metaData))
$proxy = $proxy.Replace("__COMMAND_NAME__", $target)
$proxy = $proxy.Replace("__COMMAND_TYPE__", $commandType)

## Stores new text we'll be putting in the param() block
$newParamBlockCode = ""

## Stores new text we'll be putting in the begin block
## (mostly due to parameter processing)
$beginAdditions = ""

## If the user wants to add a parameter
$currentParameter = $originalCommand.Parameters.Count
if($AddParameter)
{
    foreach($parameter in $AddParameter.Keys)
    {
        ## Get the code associated with this parameter
        $parameterCode = $AddParameter[$parameter]

        ## If it's an advanced parameter declaration, the hashtable
        ## holds the validation and/or type restrictions
        if($parameter -is [Hashtable])
        {
```

```
        ## Add their attributes and other information to
        ## the variable holding the parameter block additions
        if($currentParameter -gt 0)
        {
            $newParamBlockCode += ","
        }

        $newParamBlockCode += "`n`n    " +
            $parameter.Attributes + "`n" +
            '    $' + $parameter.Name

        $parameter = $parameter.Name
    }
    else
    {
        ## If this is a simple parameter name, add it to the list of
        ## parameters. The proxy generation APIs will take care of
        ## adding it to the param() block.
        $newParameter =
            New-Object System.Management.Automation.ParameterMetadata `
                $parameter
        $metaData.Parameters.Add($parameter, $newParameter)
    }

    $parameterCode = $parameterCode.ToString()

    ## Create the template code that invokes their parameter code if
    ## the parameter is selected.
    $templateCode = @"

if(`$PSBoundParameters['$parameter'])
{
    $parameterCode

    ## Replace the __ORIGINAL_COMMAND__ tag with the code
    ## that represents the original command
    `$alteredPipeline = `$newPipeline.ToString()
    `$finalPipeline = `$alteredPipeline.Replace(
        '__ORIGINAL_COMMAND__', `$finalPipeline)
}
"@

    ## Add the template code to the list of changes we're making
    ## to the begin() section.
    $beginAdditions += $templateCode
    $currentParameter++
    }
}

## Generate the param() block
$parameters = $proxyCommandType::GetParamBlock($metaData)
if($newParamBlockCode) { $parameters += $newParamBlockCode }
```

---

```
$proxy = $proxy.Replace('__PARAMETERS__', $parameters)

## Update the begin, process, and end sections
$proxy = $proxy.Replace('__CUSTOM_BEGIN__', $Begin)
$proxy = $proxy.Replace('__CUSTOM_PARAMETER_PROCESSING__', $beginAdditions)
$proxy = $proxy.Replace('__CUSTOM_PROCESS__', $Process)
$proxy = $proxy.Replace('__CUSTOM_END__', $End)

## Save the function wrapper
Write-Verbose $proxy
Set-Content function:\GLOBAL:$NAME $proxy

## If we were wrapping a cmdlet, hide it so that it doesn't conflict with
## Get-Help and Get-Command
if($commandType -eq "Cmdlet")
{
    $originalCommand.Visibility = "Private"
}
```

## See Also

Recipe 1.1, "Run Programs, Scripts, and Existing Tools"

# Internet-Enabled Scripts

## 12.0. Introduction

Although PowerShell provides an enormous benefit even when your scripts interact only with the local system, working with data sources from the Internet opens exciting and unique opportunities. For example, you might download files or information from the Internet, interact with a web service, store your output as HTML, or even send an email that reports the results of a long-running script.

Through its cmdlets and access to the networking support in the .NET Framework, PowerShell provides ample opportunities for Internet-enabled administration.

## 12.1. Download a File from an FTP or Internet Site

### Problem

You want to download a file from an FTP location or website on the Internet.

### Solution

Use the -OutFile parameter of the Invoke-WebRequest cmdlet:

```
PS > $source = "http://www.leeholmes.com/favicon.ico"
PS > $destination = "c:\temp\favicon.ico"
PS >
PS > Invoke-WebRequest $source -OutFile $destination
```

## Discussion

The Invoke-WebRequest cmdlet lets you easily upload and download data from remote web servers. It acts much like a web browser in that you can specify a user agent, a proxy (if your outgoing connection requires one), and even credentials.

 If you require a solution that works with PowerShell version 2, use the DownloadFile() method of the System.Net.WebClient class from the .NET Framework.

While the Solution demonstrates downloading a file from a web (HTTP) resource, the Invoke-WebRequest cmdlet also supports FTP locations. To specify an FTP location, use ftp:// at the beginning of the source, as shown in Example 12-1.

*Example 12-1. Downloading a file from an FTP site*

```
PS > $source = "ftp://site.com/users/user/backups/backup.zip"
PS > $destination = "c:\temp\backup.zip"
PS >
PS > Invoke-WebRequest $source -OutFile $destination -Credential myFtpUser
```

Unlike files downloaded from most Internet sites, FTP transfers usually require a username and password. To specify your username and password, use the -Credential parameter.

If the file you are downloading is ultimately a web page that you want to parse or read through, the Invoke-WebRequest cmdlet has other features designed more specifically for that scenario. For more information on how to download and parse web pages, see Recipe 12.3, "Download a Web Page from the Internet".

## See Also

Recipe 12.3, "Download a Web Page from the Internet"

# 12.2. Upload a File to an FTP Site

## Problem

You want to upload a file to an FTP site.

## Solution

To upload a file to an FTP site, use the System.Net.WebClient class from the .NET Framework:

```
PS > $source = "c:\temp\backup.zip"
PS > $destination = "ftp://site.com/users/user/backups/backup.zip"
PS > $cred = Get-Credential
PS > $wc = New-Object System.Net.WebClient
PS > $wc.Credentials = $cred
PS > $wc.UploadFile($destination, $source)
PS > $wc.Dispose()
```

## Discussion

For basic file uploads to a remote FTP site, the System.Net.WebClient class offers an extremely simple solution. For more advanced FTP scenarios (such as deleting files), the System.Net.WebRequest class offers much more fine-grained control, as shown in Example 12-2.

*Example 12-2. Deleting a file from an FTP site*

```
PS > $file = "ftp://site.com/users/user/backups/backup.zip"
PS > $request = [System.Net.WebRequest]::Create($file)
PS > $cred = Get-Credential
PS > $request.Credentials = $cred
PS > $request.Method = [System.Net.WebRequestMethods+Ftp]::DeleteFile
PS > $response = $request.GetResponse()
PS > $response
PS > $response.Close()
```

In addition to Delete, the WebRequest class supports many other FTP methods. You can see them all by getting the static properties of the [System.Net.WebRequestMethods +Ftp] class, as shown in Example 12-3.

*Example 12-3. Standard supported FTP methods*

```
PS > [System.Net.WebRequestMethods+Ftp] | Get-Member -Static -Type Property


    TypeName: System.Net.WebRequestMethods+Ftp

Name                       MemberType Definition
----                       ---------- ----------
AppendFile                 Property   static string AppendFile {get;}
DeleteFile                 Property   static string DeleteFile {get;}
DownloadFile               Property   static string DownloadFile {get;}
GetDateTimestamp           Property   static string GetDateTimestamp {get;}
GetFileSize                Property   static string GetFileSize {get;}
ListDirectory              Property   static string ListDirectory {get;}
ListDirectoryDetails       Property   static string ListDirectoryDetails {get;}
MakeDirectory              Property   static string MakeDirectory {get;}
PrintWorkingDirectory      Property   static string PrintWorkingDirectory {get;}
RemoveDirectory            Property   static string RemoveDirectory {get;}
Rename                     Property   static string Rename {get;}
UploadFile                 Property   static string UploadFile {get;}
UploadFileWithUniqueName   Property   static string UploadFileWithUniqueName {get;}
```

These properties are just strings that correspond to the standard FTP commands, so you can also just use their values directly if you know them:

```
$request.Method = "DELE"
```

If you want to download files from an FTP site, see Recipe 12.1, "Download a File from an FTP or Internet Site".

### See Also

Recipe 12.1, "Download a File from an FTP or Internet Site"

# 12.3. Download a Web Page from the Internet

## Problem

You want to download a web page from the Internet and work with the content directly.

## Solution

Use the `Invoke-WebRequest` cmdlet to download a web page, and then access the Content property (or cast the result to a `[string]`):

```
PS > $source = "http://www.bing.com/search?q=sqrt(2)"
PS > $result = [string] (Invoke-WebRequest $source)
```

If you require a solution that works with PowerShell version 2, use the `System.Net.WebClient` class from the .NET Framework:

```
PS > $source = "http://www.bing.com/search?q=sqrt(2)"
PS > $wc = New-Object System.Net.WebClient
PS > $result = $wc.DownloadString($source)
```

## Discussion

When writing automation in a web-connected world, we aren't always fortunate enough to have access to a web service that returns richly structured data. Because of this, re-trieving data from services on the Internet often comes by means of *screen scraping*: downloading the HTML of the web page and then carefully separating out the content you want from the vast majority of the content that you do not.

 If extracting structured data from a web page is your primary goal, the `Invoke-WebRequest` cmdlet offers options much more powerful than basic screen scraping. For more information, see Recipe 12.4, "Parse and Analyze a Web Page from the Internet".

---

The technique of screen scraping has been around much longer than the Internet! As long as computer systems have generated output designed primarily for humans, screen scraping tools have risen to make this output available to other computer programs.

Unfortunately, screen scraping is an error-prone way to extract content. And that's no exaggeration! As proof, Example 12-5 (shown later in this recipe) broke four or five times while the first edition of this book was being written, and then again after it was published. Then it broke several times during the second edition, and again after it was published. Such are the perils of screen scraping.

If the web page authors change the underlying HTML, your code will usually stop working correctly. If the site's HTML is written as valid XHTML, you may be able to use PowerShell's built-in XML support to more easily parse the content.

For more information about PowerShell's built-in XML support, see Recipe 10.1, "Access Information in an XML File".

Despite its fragility, pure screen scraping is often the only alternative. Since screen scraping is just text manipulation, you have the same options you do with other text reports. For some fairly structured web pages, you can get away with a single regular expression replacement (plus cleanup), as shown in Example 12-4.

*Example 12-4. Search-Bing.ps1*

```
##############################################################################
##
## Search-Bing
##
## From Windows PowerShell Cookbook (O'Reilly)
## by Lee Holmes (http://www.leeholmes.com/guide)
##
##############################################################################

<#

.SYNOPSIS

Search Bing for a given term

.EXAMPLE

PS > Search-Bing PowerShell
Searches Bing for the term "PowerShell"

#>

param(
    ## The term to search for
    $Pattern = "PowerShell"
)
```

```
Set-StrictMode -Version 3

## Create the URL that contains the Twitter search results
Add-Type -Assembly System.Web
$queryUrl = 'http://www.bing.com/search?q={0}'
$queryUrl = $queryUrl -f ([System.Web.HttpUtility]::UrlEncode($pattern))

## Download the web page
$results = [string] (Invoke-WebRequest $queryUrl)

## Extract the text of the results, which are contained in
## segments that look like "<div class="sb_tlst">...</div>"
$matches = $results |
    Select-String -Pattern '(?s)<div[^>]*sb_tlst[^>]*>.*?</div>' -AllMatches

foreach($match in $matches.Matches)
{
    ## Extract the URL, keeping only the text inside the quotes
    ## of the HREF
    $url = $match.Value -replace '.*href="(.*?)".*','$1'
    $url = [System.Web.HttpUtility]::UrlDecode($url)

    ## Extract the page name,  replace anything in angle
    ## brackets with an empty string.
    $item = $match.Value -replace '<[^>]*>', ''

    ## Output the item
    [PSCustomObject] @{ Item = $item; Url = $url }
}
```

Text parsing on less structured web pages, while possible to accomplish with complicated regular expressions, can often be made much simpler through more straightforward text manipulation. Example 12-5 uses this second approach to fetch "Instant Answers" from Bing.

*Example 12-5. Get-Answer.ps1*

```
##############################################################################
##
## Get-Answer
##
## From Windows PowerShell Cookbook (O'Reilly)
## by Lee Holmes (http://www.leeholmes.com/guide)
##
##############################################################################

<#

.SYNOPSIS

Uses Bing Answers to answer your question
```

---

```
.EXAMPLE

PS > Get-Answer "sqrt(2)"
sqrt(2) = 1.41421356

.EXAMPLE

PS > Get-Answer msft stock
Microsoft Corp (US:MSFT) NASDAQ
29.66  -0.35 (-1.17%)
After Hours: 30.02 +0.36 (1.21%)
Open: 30.09    Day's Range: 29.59 - 30.20
Volume: 55.60 M    52 Week Range: 17.27 - 31.50
P/E Ratio: 16.30    Market Cap: 260.13 B

.EXAMPLE

PS > Get-Answer "What is the time in Seattle, WA?"
Current time in Seattle, WA
01:12:41 PM
08/18/2012 ? Pacific Daylight Time

#>

Set-StrictMode -Version 3

$question = $args -join " "

function Main
{
    ## Load the System.Web.HttpUtility DLL, to let us URLEncode
    Add-Type -Assembly System.Web

    ## Get the web page into a single string with newlines between
    ## the lines.
    $encoded = [System.Web.HttpUtility]::UrlEncode($question)
    $url = "http://www.bing.com/search?q=$encoded"
    $text = [String] (Invoke-WebRequest $url)

    ## Find the start of the answers section
    $startIndex = $text.IndexOf('<div class="ans"')

    ## The end is either defined by an "attribution" div
    ## or the start of a "results" div
    $endIndex = $text.IndexOf('<div class="sn_att2"', $startIndex)
    if($endIndex -lt 0)
    {
        $endIndex = $text.IndexOf('<div id="results"', $startIndex) }

    ## If we found a result, then filter the result
    if(($startIndex -ge 0) -and ($endIndex -ge 0))
    {
```

```
        ## Pull out the text between the start and end portions
        $partialText = $text.Substring($startIndex, $endIndex - $startIndex)

        ## Very fragile screen scraping here. Replace a bunch of
        ## tags that get placed on new lines with the newline
        ## character, and a few others with spaces.
        $partialText = $partialText -replace '<div[^>]*>',"`n"
        $partialText = $partialText -replace '<tr[^>]*>',"`n"
        $partialText = $partialText -replace '<li[^>]*>',"`n"
        $partialText = $partialText -replace '<br[^>]*>',"`n"
        $partialText = $partialText -replace '<p [^>]*>',"`n"
        $partialText = $partialText -replace '<span[^>]*>'," "
        $partialText = $partialText -replace '<td[^>]*>',"    "

        $partialText = CleanHtml $partialText

        ## Now split the results on newlines, trim each line, and then
        ## join them back.
        $partialText = $partialText -split "`n" |
            Foreach-Object { $_.Trim() } | Where-Object { $_ }
        $partialText = $partialText -join "`n"

        [System.Web.HttpUtility]::HtmlDecode($partialText.Trim())
    }
    else
    {
        "No answer found."
    }
}


## Clean HTML from a text chunk
function CleanHtml ($htmlInput)
{
    $tempString = [Regex]::Replace($htmlInput, "(?s)<[^>]*>", "")
    $tempString.Replace("  ", "")
}
```

Main

When using the Invoke-WebRequest cmdlet, you might notice some web applications
acting oddly or returning an error that you're using an unsupported browser.

The reason for this is that all web browsers send a user agent identifier along with their
web request. This identifier tells the website what application is making the request—
such as Internet Explorer, Firefox, or an automated crawler from a search engine. Many
websites check this user agent identifier to determine how to display the page. Unfortunately, many fail entirely if they can't determine the user agent for the incoming request.

By default, PowerShell identifies itself with a brower-like user agent: `Mozilla/5.0+` `(Windows+NT;+Windows+NT+6.2;+en-US)+WindowsPowerShell/3.0`. If you need to customize the user agent string for a request, you can specify this with the `-User` `Agent` parameter. This parameter takes a simple string. Static properties of the `[Micro` `soft.PowerShell.Commands.PSUserAgent]` class provide some preconfigured defaults:

```
PS > $userAgent = [Microsoft.PowerShell.Commands.PSUserAgent]::Chrome
PS > $result = Invoke-WebRequest http://www.bing.com -UserAgent $userAgent
```

For more information about parsing web pages, see Recipe 12.4, "Parse and Analyze a Web Page from the Internet".

## See Also

Recipe 1.1, "Run Programs, Scripts, and Existing Tools"

Recipe 10.1, "Access Information in an XML File"

Recipe 12.4, "Parse and Analyze a Web Page from the Internet"

# 12.4. Parse and Analyze a Web Page from the Internet

## Problem

You want to parse and interact with content from a web page.

## Solution

Use the `Invoke-WebRequest` cmdlet to download a web page, and then access the `ParsedHtml` property:

```
PS > $source = "http://www.bing.com/search?q=sqrt(2)"
PS > $result = Invoke-WebRequest $source
PS > $resultContainer = $result.ParsedHtml.GetElementById("results_container")
PS > $answerElement = $resultContainer.getElementsByTagName("div") |
    Where-Object ClassName -eq "ans" | Select -First 1
PS > $answerElement.innerText
```

To retrieve just the images, links, or input fields, access those properties on the result of `Invoke-WebRequest`:

```
PS > $source = "http://www.bing.com/search?q=sqrt(2)"
PS > $result = Invoke-WebRequest $source
PS > $result.Links
```

## Discussion

When you're retrieving data from web pages on the Internet, the usual approach relies on text manipulation—regular expressions, string replacement, and formatting. If you are very lucky, the web page is written carefully in a way that makes it also an XML document—in which case, you can use PowerShell's XML support to extract information. Recipe 12.3, "Download a Web Page from the Internet" describes this approach.

> If you need to interact with an XML or REST-based Internet API, see Recipe 12.7, "Interact with REST-Based Web APIs".

The risk of these approaches is that a change of a few characters or spaces can easily break whatever text manipulation you've designed.

The solution usually comes from using toolkits that parse a web page the way a browser would. Most importantly, these toolkits need to account for poorly written HTML: unmatched quote characters, missing closing tags, character encodings, and anything else the sewers of the Internet can manage to throw at it.

Fortunately, PowerShell's `Invoke-WebRequest` cmdlet exposes an extremely powerful parsing engine: the one that ships in the operating system itself with Internet Explorer.

When you access the `ParsedHtml` property of the object returned by `Invoke-WebRequest`, you are given access directly to the Document Object Model (DOM) that Internet Explorer uses when it parses web pages. This property returns an HTML element that initially represents the entire HTML document. To access HTML elements, it supports useful methods and properties—the most useful being `getElementById` (to find elements with a specific ID), `getElementsByTagName` (to find all `DIV` elements, `IMG` elements, etc.), and `childNodes` (to retrieve child elements specifically by position).

> The Internet Explorer engine required by the `ParsedHtml` property is not supported on Server Core editions of Windows Server. If you want to do web page parsing on Server Core, be sure to supply the `-UseBa sicParsing` parameter of `Invoke-WebRequest`. This mode performs only limited parsing on the requested web page—images, input fields, links, and raw HTML content.

To see all of methods and properties available through the `ParsedHtml` property, use the `Get-Member` cmdlet:

```
PS > $result = Invoke-WebRequest $source
PS > $result.ParsedHtml | Get-Member
```

---

When you retrieve an item (such as a DIV or paragraph) using these methods and properties, you get back another element that supports the same properties. This makes iteration and refinement both possible and generally accurate. You'll typically have to review the HTML content itself to discover the element IDs, names, and class names that you can use to find the specific HTML elements that you need.

Given the amount of information in a web page, it is important to narrow down your search as quickly as possible so that Internet Explorer and PowerShell don't need to search though every element looking for the item that matches. The getElement ById() method is the quickest way to narrow down your search, followed by getEle mentsByTagName() and finally by using the Where-Object cmdlet.

 If you have to rely on the Where-Object cmdlet to filter your results, be sure to use the Select-Object cmdlet to pick only the first item as shown in the Solution. This prompts PowerShell to stop searching for HTML elements as soon as it finds the one you need. Otherwise, it will continue to look through all of the remaining document elements—a very slow process.

Once you've narrowed down the element you need, the InnerText and InnerHtml properties are very useful. If you still need to do additional text or HTML manipulation, they represent the plain-text content of your element and actual HTML text of your element, respectively.

In addition to parsing single HTML web pages, you may want to script multipage web sessions. For an example of this, see Recipe 12.5, "Script a Web Application Session".

## See Also

Recipe 10.1, "Access Information in an XML File"

Recipe 12.3, "Download a Web Page from the Internet"

Recipe 12.5, "Script a Web Application Session"

Recipe 12.7, "Interact with REST-Based Web APIs"

# 12.5. Script a Web Application Session

## Problem

You want to interact with a website or application that requires dynamic cookies, logins, or multiple requests.

## Solution

Use the `Invoke-WebRequest` cmdlet to download a web page, and access the `-Session Variable` and `-WebSession` parameters. For example, to retrieve the number of active Facebook notifications:

```
$cred = Get-Credential
$login = Invoke-WebRequest facebook.com/login.php -SessionVariable fb
$login.Forms[0].Fields.email = $cred.UserName
$login.Forms[0].Fields.pass = $cred.GetNetworkCredential().Password
$mainPage = Invoke-WebRequest $login.Forms[0].Action `
    -WebSession $fb -Body $login -Method Post
$mainPage.ParsedHtml.getElementById("notificationsCountValue").InnerText
```

## Discussion

While many pages on the Internet provide their information directly when you access a web page, many others are not so simple. For example, the site may be protected by a login page (which then sets cookies), followed by another form (which requires those cookies) that returns a search result.

Automating these scenarios almost always requires a fairly in-depth understanding of the web application in question, as well as how web applications work in general.

Even with that understanding, automating these scenarios usually requires a vast amount of scripting: parsing HTTP headers, sending them in subsequent requests, hand-crafting form POST responses, and more.

As an example of bare scripting of a Facebook login, consider the following example that merely determines the login cookie to be used in further page requests:

```
$Credential = Get-Credential

## Get initial cookies
$wc = New-Object System.Net.WebClient
$wc.Headers.Add("User-Agent", "User-Agent: Mozilla/4.0 (compatible; MSIE 7.0;)")

$result = $wc.DownloadString("http://www.facebook.com/")
$cookie = $wc.ResponseHeaders["Set-Cookie"]
$cookie = ($cookie.Split(',') -match '^\S+=\S+;' -replace ';.*',"") -join '; '

$wc = New-Object System.Net.WebClient
$wc.Headers.Add("User-Agent", "User-Agent: Mozilla/4.0 (compatible; MSIE 7.0;)")
$wc.Headers.Add("Cookie", $cookie)
$postValues = New-Object System.Collections.Specialized.NameValueCollection
$postValues.Add("email", $credential.GetNetworkCredential().Username)
$postValues.Add("pass", $credential.GetNetworkCredential().Password)

## Get the resulting cookie, and convert it into the form to be returned
## in the query string
$result = $wc.UploadValues(
```

```
        "https://login.facebook.com/login.php?login_attempt=1", $postValues)
$cookie = $wc.ResponseHeaders["Set-Cookie"]
$cookie = ($cookie.Split(',') -match '^\S+=\S+;' -replace ';.*',"") -join '; '
$cookie
```

This is just for the login. Scripting a full web session using this manual approach can easily take hundreds of lines of script.

The `-SessionVariable` and `-WebSession` parameters of the `Invoke-WebRequest` cmdlet don't remove the need to understand how your target web application works. They do, however, remove the drudgery and complexity of dealing with the bare HTTP requests and responses. This improved session support comes primarily through four features:

*Automated cookie management*

Most web applications store their state in cookies—session IDs and login information being the two most common things to store. When a web application requests that a cookie be stored or deleted, `Invoke-WebRequest` automatically records this information in the provided session variable. Subsequent requests that use this session variable automatically supply any cookies required by the web application. You can see the cookies in use by looking at the `Cookies` property of the session variable:

```
$fb.Cookies.GetCookies("http://www.facebook.com") | Select Name,Value
```

*Automatic redirection support*

After you submit a web form (especially a login form), many sites redirect through a series of intermediate pages before you finally land on the destination page. In basic HTTP scripting, this forces you to handle the many HTTP redirect status codes, parse the `Location` header, and resubmit all the appropriate values. The `Invoke-WebRequest` cmdlet handles this for you; the result it returns comes from the final page in any redirect sequences. If you wish to override this behavior, use the `-MaximumRedirection` parameter.

*Form detection*

Applications that require advanced session scripting tend to take most of their input data from fields in HTML forms, rather than items in the URL itself. `Invoke-WebRequest` exposes these forms through the `Forms` property of its result. This collection returns the form ID (useful if there are multiple forms), the form action (URL that should be used to submit the form), and fields defined by the form.

*Form submission*

In traditional HTTP scripting, submitting a form is a complicated process. You need to gather all the form fields, encode them properly, determine the resulting encoded length, and POST all of this data to the destination URL.

`Invoke-WebRequest` makes this very simple through the `-Body` parameter used as input when you select `POST` as the value of the `-Method` parameter. The `-Body` parameter accepts input in one of three formats:

- The result of a previous `Invoke-WebRequest` call, in which case values from the first form are used (if the response contains only one form).
- A specific form (as manually selected from the `Forms` property of a previous `Invoke-WebRequest` call), in which case values from that form are used.
- An `IDictionary` (hashtable), in which case names and values from that dictionary are used.
- An XML node, in which case the XML is encoded directly. This is used primarily for scripting REST APIs, and is unlikely to be used when scripting web application sessions.
- A byte array, in which case the bytes are used and encoded directly. This is used primarily for scripting data uploads.

Let's take a look at how these play a part in the script from the Solution, which detects how many notifications are pending on Facebook. Given how fast web applications change, it's unlikely that this example will continue to work for long. It does demonstrate the thought process, however.

When you first connect to Facebook, you need to log in. Facebook funnels this through a page called *login.php*:

```
$login = Invoke-WebRequest http://www.facebook.com/login.php -SessionVariable fb
```

If you look at the page that gets returned, there is a single form that includes `email` and `pass` fields:

```
PS > $login.Forms.Fields

Key                Value
---                -----
(...)
return_session     0
legacy_return      1
session_key_only   0
trynum             1
email
pass
persist_box        1
default_persistent 0
(...)
```

We fill these in:

```
$cred = Get-Credential
$login.Forms[0].Fields.email = $cred.UserName
$login.Forms[0].Fields.pass = $cred.GetNetworkCredential().Password
```

And submit the form. We use `$fb` for the `-WebSession` parameter, as that is what we used during the original request. We `POST` to the URL referred to in the `Action` field of the login form, and use the `$login` variable as the request body. The `$login` variable is the response that we got from the first request, where we customized the `email` and `pass` form fields. PowerShell recognizes that this was the result of a previous web request, and uses that single form as the `POST` body:

```
$mainPage = Invoke-WebRequest $login.Forms[0].Action -WebSession $fb `
    -Body $login -Method Post
```

If you look at the raw HTML returned by this response (the `Content` property), you can see that the notification count is contained in a `span` element with the ID of `notifica tionsCountValue`:

```
(...) <span id="notificationsCountValue">1</span> (...)
```

To retrieve this element, we use the `ParsedHtml` property of the response, call the `GetE lementById` method, and return the `InnerText` property:

```
$mainPage.ParsedHtml.getElementById("notificationsCountValue").InnerText
```

Using these techniques, we can unlock a great deal of functionality on the Internet previously hidden behind complicated HTTP scripting.

For more information about using the `ParsedHtml` property to parse and analyze web pages, see Recipe 12.4, "Parse and Analyze a Web Page from the Internet".

### See Also

Recipe 12.4, "Parse and Analyze a Web Page from the Internet"

# 12.6. Program: Get-PageUrls

When working with HTML, it is common to require advanced regular expressions that separate the content you care about from the content you don't. A perfect example of this is extracting all the HTML links from a web page.

In PowerShell version 3, the answer is easy: use the `Links` property returned by the `Invoke-WebRequest` cmdlet, as shown in Recipe 12.4, "Parse and Analyze a Web Page from the Internet".

In PowerShell version 2, we need to get more creative.

Links come in many forms, depending on how lenient you want to be. They may be well formed according to the various HTML standards. They may use relative paths or they may use absolute paths. They may place double quotes around the URL or they may place single quotes around the URL. If you're really unlucky, they may accidentally include quotes on only one side of the URL.

Example 12-6 demonstrates some approaches for dealing with this type of advanced parsing task. Given a web page that you've downloaded from the Internet, it extracts all links from the page and returns a list of the URLs on that page. It also fixes URLs that were originally written as relative URLs (for example, */file.zip*) to include the server from which they originated.

*Example 12-6. Get-PageUrls.ps1*

```
##############################################################################
##
## Get-PageUrls
##
## From Windows PowerShell Cookbook (O'Reilly)
## by Lee Holmes (http://www.leeholmes.com/guide)
##
##############################################################################

<#

.SYNOPSIS

Parse all of the URLs out of a given file.

.EXAMPLE

PS > Get-PageUrls microsoft.html http://www.microsoft.com
Gets all of the URLs from HTML stored in microsoft.html, and converts relative
URLs to the domain of http://www.microsoft.com

.EXAMPLE

PS > Get-PageUrls microsoft.html http://www.microsoft.com 'aspx$'
Gets all of the URLs from HTML stored in microsoft.html, converts relative
URLs to the domain of http://www.microsoft.com, and returns only URLs that end
in 'aspx'.

#>

param(
    ## The filename to parse
    [Parameter(Mandatory = $true)]
    [string] $Path,

    ## The URL from which you downloaded the page.
    ## For example, http://www.microsoft.com
    [Parameter(Mandatory = $true)]
    [string] $BaseUrl,

    [switch] $Images,

    ## The Regular Expression pattern with which to filter
    ## the returned URLs
```

```
        [string] $Pattern = ".*"
)

Set-StrictMode -Version 3

## Load the System.Web DLL so that we can decode URLs
Add-Type -Assembly System.Web

## Defines the regular expression that will parse a URL
## out of an anchor tag.
$regex = "<\s*a\s*[^>]*?href\s*=\s*[`'""']*([^`'"">]+)[^>]*?>"
if($Images)
{
    $regex = "<\s*img\s*[^>]*?src\s*=\s*[`'""']*([^`'"">]+)[^>]*?>"
}

## Parse the file for links
function Main
{
    ## Do some minimal source URL fixups, by switching backslashes to
    ## forward slashes
    $baseUrl = $baseUrl.Replace("\", "/")

    if($baseUrl.IndexOf("://") -lt 0)
    {
        throw "Please specify a base URL in the form of " +
            "http://server/path_to_file/file.html"
    }

    ## Determine the server from which the file originated.  This will
    ## help us resolve links such as "/somefile.zip"
    $baseUrl = $baseUrl.Substring(0, $baseUrl.LastIndexOf("/") + 1)
    $baseSlash = $baseUrl.IndexOf("/", $baseUrl.IndexOf("://") + 3)

    if($baseSlash -ge 0)
    {
        $domain = $baseUrl.Substring(0, $baseSlash)
    }
    else
    {
        $domain = $baseUrl
    }


    ## Put all of the file content into a big string, and
    ## get the regular expression matches
    $content = (Get-Content $path) -join ' '
    $contentMatches = @(GetMatches $content $regex)

    foreach($contentMatch in $contentMatches)
    {
        if(-not ($contentMatch -match $pattern)) { continue }
```

```
        if($contentMatch -match "javascript:") { continue }

        $contentMatch = $contentMatch.Replace("\", "/")

        ## Hrefs may look like:
        ## ./file
        ## file
        ## ../../../file
        ## /file
        ## url
        ## We'll keep all of the relative paths, as they will resolve.
        ## We only need to resolve the ones pointing to the root.
        if($contentMatch.IndexOf("://") -gt 0)
        {
            $url = $contentMatch
        }
        elseif($contentMatch[0] -eq "/")
        {
            $url = "$domain$contentMatch"
        }
        else
        {
            $url = "$baseUrl$contentMatch"
            $url = $url.Replace("/./", "/")
        }

        ## Return the URL, after first removing any HTML entities
        [System.Web.HttpUtility]::HtmlDecode($url)
    }
}

function GetMatches([string] $content, [string] $regex)
{
    $returnMatches = new-object System.Collections.ArrayList

    ## Match the regular expression against the content, and
    ## add all trimmed matches to our return list
    $resultingMatches = [Regex]::Matches($content, $regex, "IgnoreCase")
    foreach($match in $resultingMatches)
    {
        $cleanedMatch = $match.Groups[1].Value.Trim()
        [void] $returnMatches.Add($cleanedMatch)
    }

    $returnMatches
}

. Main
```

For more information about running scripts, see Recipe 1.1, "Run Programs, Scripts, and Existing Tools".

## See Also

Recipe 1.1, "Run Programs, Scripts, and Existing Tools"

# 12.7. Interact with REST-Based Web APIs

## Problem

You want to work with an XML or JSON REST-based API.

## Solution

Use the `Invoke-RestMethod` cmdlet to work with REST-based APIs. Example 12-7 demonstrates using the StackOverflow API to retrieve the 10 most recent unanswered quesions tagged "PowerShell."

*Example 12-7. Using Invoke-RestMethod with the StackOverflow API*

```
PS > $url = "https://api.stackexchange.com/2.0/questions/unanswered" +
    "?order=desc&sort=activity&tagged=powershell&pagesize=10&site=stackoverflow"
PS > $result = Invoke-RestMethod $url
PS > $result.Items | Foreach-Object { $_.Title; $_.Link; "" }

Can I have powershell scripts in file with no extension?
http://stackoverflow.com/questions/12230228/can-i-have-powershell-scripts...

Powershell: Replacing regex named groups with variables
http://stackoverflow.com/questions/12225415/powershell-replacing-regex-named...

(...)
```

## Discussion

Most web pages that return useful data provide this information with the intention that it will only ever be displayed by a web browser. Extracting this information is always difficult, although Recipe 12.4, "Parse and Analyze a Web Page from the Internet" usually makes the solution simpler than straight text manipulation.

When a web page is designed to be consumed by other programs or scripts, it is usually called a *web service* or *web API*. Web services are the more fully featured of the two. They rely on a technology called SOAP (Simple Object Access Protocol), and mimic traditional programming APIs that support rigid structures, standardized calling behavior, and strongly typed objects. Recipe 12.8, "Connect to a Web Service" demonstrates how to interact with web services from PowerShell.

While much less structured, web APIs tend to follow some similar basic design philosophies—primarily URL structures, standard HTTP methods (GET/POST), and data types (JSON/XML). These loosely defined design philosophies are usually grouped under the term *REST* (Representational State Transfer), making *REST API* the term most commonly used for non-SOAP web services.

While still designed to be consumed by programs or scripts, REST APIs have a much less rigid structure. Because of their simplicity, they have become the dominant form of web service on the Internet.

The `Invoke-RestMethod` cmdlet forms the basis of how you interact with REST APIs from PowerShell. It acts much like the `Invoke-WebRequest` cmdlet in that it lets you invoke standard HTTP operations against URLs: GET, PUT, POST, and more. Unlike `Invoke-WebRequest`, though, `Invoke-RestMethod` assumes that the data returned from the website is designed to be consumed by a program. Depending on the data returned by the web service (XML or JSON), it automatically interprets the returned data and converts it into PowerShell objects.

 If this interpretation is incorrect for a website or REST API, you can always use the `Invoke-WebRequest` cmdlet directly.

As another example of interacting with REST APIs, Example 12-8 demonstrates using the StackOverflow API to find the accepted answer for the PowerShell questions matching your search term.

*Example 12-8. Searching StackOverflow for answers to a PowerShell question*

```
##############################################################################
##
## Search-StackOverflow
##
## From Windows PowerShell Cookbook (O'Reilly)
## by Lee Holmes (http://www.leeholmes.com/guide)
##
##############################################################################

<#

.SYNOPSIS

Searches Stack Overflow for PowerShell questions that relate to your
search term, and provides the link to the accepted answer.


.EXAMPLE
```

```
PS > Search-StackOverflow upload ftp
Searches StackOverflow for questions about how to upload FTP files

.EXAMPLE

PS > $answers = Search-StackOverflow.ps1 upload ftp
PS > $answers | Out-GridView -PassThru | Foreach-Object { start $_ }

Launches Out-GridView with the answers from a search. Select the URLs
that you want to launch, and then press OK. PowerShell then launches
your default web brower for those URLs.

#>

Set-StrictMode -Off
Add-Type -Assembly System.Web

$query = ($args | Foreach-Object { '"' + $_ + '"' }) -join " "
$query = [System.Web.HttpUtility]::UrlEncode($query)

## Use the StackOverflow API to retrieve the answer for a question
$url = "https://api.stackexchange.com/2.0/search?order=desc&sort=relevance" +
    "&pagesize=5&tagged=powershell&intitle=$query&site=stackoverflow"
$question = Invoke-RestMethod $url

## Now go through and show the questions and answers
$question.Items | Where accepted_answer_id | Foreach-Object {
        "Question: " + $_.Title
        "http://www.stackoverflow.com/questions/$($_.accepted_answer_id)"
        ""
}
```

## See Also

Recipe 12.4, "Parse and Analyze a Web Page from the Internet"

# 12.8. Connect to a Web Service

## Problem

You want to connect to and interact with an Internet web service.

## Solution

Use the New-WebserviceProxy cmdlet to work with a web service.

```
PS > $url = "http://www.terraserver-usa.com/TerraService2.asmx"
PS > $terraServer = New-WebserviceProxy $url -Namespace Cookbook
PS > $place = New-Object Cookbook.Place
PS > $place.City = "Redmond"
```

```
PS > $place.State = "WA"
PS > $place.Country = "USA"
PS > $facts = $terraserver.GetPlaceFacts($place)
PS > $facts.Center
```

```
                      Lon                                Lat
                      ---                                ---
          -122.110000610352                  47.6699981689453
```

## Discussion

Although screen scraping (parsing the HTML of a web page) is the most common way to obtain data from the Internet, web services are becoming increasingly common. Web services provide a significant advantage over HTML parsing, as they are much less likely to break when the web designer changes minor features in a design.

 If you need to interact with an XML or REST-based Internet API, see Recipe 12.7, "Interact with REST-Based Web APIs".

The benefit of web services isn't just their more stable interface, however. When you're working with web services, the .NET Framework lets you generate *proxies* that enable you to interact with the web service as easily as you would work with a regular .NET object. That is because to you, the web service user, these proxies act almost exactly the same as any other .NET object. To call a method on the web service, simply call a method on the proxy.

The New-WebserviceProxy cmdlet simplifies all of the work required to connect to a web service, making it just as easy as a call to the New-Object cmdlet.

The primary differences you will notice when working with a web service proxy (as opposed to a regular .NET object) are the speed and Internet connectivity requirements. Depending on conditions, a method call on a web service proxy could easily take several seconds to complete. If your computer (or the remote computer) experiences network difficulties, the call might even return a network error message (such as a timeout) instead of the information you had hoped for.

If the web service requires authentication in a domain, specify the -UseDefault Credential parameter. If it requires explicit credentials, use the -Credential parameter.

When you create a new web service proxy, PowerShell creates a new .NET object on your behalf that connects to that web service. All .NET types live within a *namespace* to prevent them from conflicting with other types that have the same name, so PowerShell automatically generates the namespace name for you. You normally won't need to pay attention to this namespace. However, some web services require input objects that the web service also defines, such as the Place object in the Solution. For these web services, use the -Namespace parameter to place the web service (and its support objects) in a namespace of your choice.

 Support objects from one web service proxy cannot be consumed by a different web service proxy, even if they are two proxies to a web service at the same URL. If you need to work with two connections to a web service at the same URL, and your task requires creating support objects for that service, be sure to use two different namespaces for those proxies.

For more information about running scripts, see Recipe 1.1, "Run Programs, Scripts, and Existing Tools".

### See Also

Recipe 1.1, "Run Programs, Scripts, and Existing Tools"

Recipe 12.7, "Interact with REST-Based Web APIs"

# 12.9. Export Command Output as a Web Page

### Problem

You want to export the results of a command as a web page so that you can post it to a web server.

### Solution

Use PowerShell's ConvertTo-Html cmdlet to convert command output into a web page. For example, to create a quick HTML summary of PowerShell's commands:

```
PS > $filename = "c:\temp\help.html"
PS >
PS > $commands = Get-Command | Where { $_.CommandType -ne "Alias" }
PS > $summary = $commands | Get-Help | Select Name,Synopsis
PS > $summary | ConvertTo-Html | Set-Content $filename
```

## Discussion

When you use the ConvertTo-Html cmdlet to export command output to a file, PowerShell generates an HTML table that represents the command output. In the table, it creates a row for each object that you provide. For each row, PowerShell creates columns to represent the values of your object's properties.

If the table format makes the output difficult to read, ConvertTo-Html offers the -As parameter that lets you set the output style to either Table or List.

While the default output is useful, you can customize the structure and style of the resulting HTML as much as you see fit. For example, the -PreContent and -Post Content parameters let you include additional text before and after the resulting table or list. The -Head parameter lets you define the content of the head section of the HTML. Even if you want to generate most of the HTML from scratch, you can still use the -Fragment parameter to generate just the inner table or list.

For more information about the ConvertTo-Html cmdlet, type **Get-Help ConvertTo-Html**.

# 12.10. Send an Email

## Problem

You want to send an email.

## Solution

Use the Send-MailMessage cmdlet to send an email.

```
PS > Send-MailMessage -To guide@leeholmes.com `
    -From user@example.com `
    -Subject "Hello!" `
    -Body "Hello, from another satisfied Cookbook reader!" `
    -SmtpServer mail.example.com
```

## Discussion

The Send-MailMessage cmdlet supports everything you would expect an email-centric cmdlet to support: attachments, plain-text messages, HTML messages, priority, receipt requests, and more. The most difficult aspect usually is remembering the correct SMTP server to use.

The Send-MailMessage cmdlet helps solve this problem as well. If you don't specify the -SmtpServer parameter, it uses the server specified in the $PSEmailServer variable, if any.

---

For most of its functionality, the Send-MailMessage cmdlet leverages the System.Net.Mail.MailMessage class from the .NET Framework. If you need functionality not exposed by the Send-MailMessage cmdlet, working with that class directly may be an option.

# 12.11. Program: Monitor Website Uptimes

When managing a website (or even your own blog), it is useful to track the response times and availability of a URL. This can help detect site outages, or simply times of unexpected load.

The Invoke-WebRequest cmdlet makes this incredibly easy to implement:

```
PS > Test-Uri http://www.leeholmes.com/blog

Time              : 9/1/2012 8:10:22 PM
Uri               : http://www.leeholmes.com/blog
StatusCode        : 200
StatusDescription : OK
ResponseLength    : 126750
TimeTaken         : 1800.7406
```

If you combine this with a scheduled job that logs the results to a CSV, you can easily monitor the health of a site over time. For an example of this approach, see Recipe 27.14, "Manage Scheduled Tasks on a Computer".

Example 12-9 shows how to use the Invoke-WebRequest cmdlet as the basis of a website uptime monitor.

*Example 12-9. Testing a URI for its status and responsiveness*

```
##############################################################################
##
## Test-Uri
##
## From Windows PowerShell Cookbook (O'Reilly)
## by Lee Holmes (http://www.leeholmes.com/guide)
##
##############################################################################

<#

.SYNOPSIS

Connects to a given URI and returns status about it: URI, response code,
and time taken.

.EXAMPLE

PS > Test-Uri bing.com
```

```
Uri              : bing.com
StatusCode       : 200
StatusDescription : OK
ResponseLength   : 34001
TimeTaken        : 459.0009

#>

param(
    ## The URI to test
    $Uri
)

$request = $null
$time = try
{
    ## Request the URI, and measure how long the response took.
    $result = Measure-Command { $request = Invoke-WebRequest -Uri $uri }
    $result.TotalMilliseconds
}
catch
{
    ## If the request generated an exception (i.e.: 500 server
    ## error or 404 not found), we can pull the status code from the
    ## Exception.Response property
    $request = $_.Exception.Response
    $time = -1
}

$result = [PSCustomObject] @{
    Time = Get-Date;
    Uri = $uri;
    StatusCode = [int] $request.StatusCode;
    StatusDescription = $request.StatusDescription;
    ResponseLength = $request.RawContentLength;
    TimeTaken = $time;
}

$result
```

For more information about running scripts, see Recipe 1.1, "Run Programs, Scripts, and Existing Tools".

## See Also

Recipe 1.1, "Run Programs, Scripts, and Existing Tools"

# 12.12. Program: Interact with Internet Protocols

Although it is common to work at an abstract level with websites and web services, an entirely separate style of Internet-enabled scripting comes from interacting with the remote computer at a much lower level. This lower level (called the TCP level, for *Transmission Control Protocol*) forms the communication foundation of most Internet protocols—such as Telnet, SMTP (sending mail), POP3 (receiving mail), and HTTP (retrieving web content).

The .NET Framework provides classes that let you interact with many of the Internet protocols directly: the `System.Web.Mail.SmtpMail` class for SMTP, the `System.Net.Web Client` class for HTTP, and a few others. When the .NET Framework does not support an Internet protocol that you need, though, you can often script the application protocol directly if you know the details of how it works.

Example 12-10 shows how to receive information about mail waiting in a remote POP3 mailbox, using the `Send-TcpRequest` script given in Example 12-11.

*Example 12-10. Interacting with a remote POP3 mailbox*

```
## Get the user credential
if(-not (Test-Path Variable:\mailCredential))
{
    $mailCredential = Get-Credential
}
$address = $mailCredential.UserName
$password = $mailCredential.GetNetworkCredential().Password

## Connect to the remote computer, send the commands, and receive the output
$pop3Commands = "USER $address","PASS $password","STAT","QUIT"
$output = $pop3Commands | Send-TcpRequest mail.myserver.com 110
$inbox = $output.Split("`n")[3]

## Parse the output for the number of messages waiting and total bytes
$status = $inbox |
    Convert-TextObject -PropertyName "Response","Waiting","BytesTotal","Extra"
"{0} messages waiting, totaling {1} bytes." -f $status.Waiting, $status.BytesTotal
```

In Example 12-10, you connect to port 110 of the remote mail server. You then issue commands to request the status of the mailbox in a form that the mail server understands. The format of this network conversation is specified and required by the standard POP3 protocol. Example 12-10 uses the `Convert-TextObject` command, which is provided in Recipe 5.14, "Program: Convert Text Streams to Objects".

Example 12-11 supports the core functionality of Example 12-10. It lets you easily work with plain-text TCP protocols.

*Example 12-11. Send-TcpRequest.ps1*

```
#############################################################################
##
## Send-TcpRequest
##
## From Windows PowerShell Cookbook (O'Reilly)
## by Lee Holmes (http://www.leeholmes.com/guide)
##
#############################################################################

<#

.SYNOPSIS

Send a TCP request to a remote computer, and return the response.
If you do not supply input to this script (via either the pipeline, or the
-InputObject parameter,) the script operates in interactive mode.

.EXAMPLE

PS > $http = @"
  GET / HTTP/1.1
  Host:bing.com
  `n`n
"@

$http | Send-TcpRequest bing.com 80

#>

param(
    ## The computer to connect to
    [string] $ComputerName = "localhost",

    ## A switch to determine if you just want to test the connection
    [switch] $Test,

    ## The port to use
    [int] $Port = 80,

    ## A switch to determine if the connection should be made using SSL
    [switch] $UseSSL,

    ## The input string to send to the remote host
    [string] $InputObject,

    ## The delay, in milliseconds, to wait between commands
    [int] $Delay = 100
)

Set-StrictMode -Version 3
```

```
[string] $SCRIPT:output = ""

## Store the input into an array that we can scan over. If there was no input,
## then we will be in interactive mode.
$currentInput = $inputObject
if(-not $currentInput)
{
    $currentInput = @($input)
}
$scriptedMode = ([bool] $currentInput) -or $test

function Main
{
    ## Open the socket, and connect to the computer on the specified port
    if(-not $scriptedMode)
    {
        write-host "Connecting to $computerName on port $port"
    }

    try
    {
        $socket = New-Object Net.Sockets.TcpClient($computerName, $port)
    }
    catch
    {
        if($test) { $false }
        else { Write-Error "Could not connect to remote computer: $_" }

        return
    }

    ## If we're just testing the connection, we've made the connection
    ## successfully, so just return $true
    if($test) { $true; return }

    ## If this is interactive mode, supply the prompt
    if(-not $scriptedMode)
    {
        write-host "Connected.  Press ^D followed by [ENTER] to exit.`n"
    }

    $stream = $socket.GetStream()

    ## If we wanted to use SSL, set up that portion of the connection
    if($UseSSL)
    {
        $sslStream = New-Object System.Net.Security.SslStream $stream,$false
        $sslStream.AuthenticateAsClient($computerName)
        $stream = $sslStream
    }

    $writer = new-object System.IO.StreamWriter $stream
```

```
while($true)
{
    ## Receive the output that has buffered so far
    $SCRIPT:output += GetOutput

    ## If we're in scripted mode, send the commands,
    ## receive the output, and exit.
    if($scriptedMode)
    {
        foreach($line in $currentInput)
        {
            $writer.WriteLine($line)
            $writer.Flush()
            Start-Sleep -m $Delay
            $SCRIPT:output += GetOutput
        }

        break
    }
    ## If we're in interactive mode, write the buffered
    ## output, and respond to input.
    else
    {
        if($output)
        {
            foreach($line in $output.Split("`n"))
            {
                write-host $line
            }
            $SCRIPT:output = ""
        }

        ## Read the user's command, quitting if they hit ^D
        $command = read-host
        if($command -eq ([char] 4)) { break; }

        ## Otherwise, Write their command to the remote host
        $writer.WriteLine($command)
        $writer.Flush()
    }
}

## Close the streams
$writer.Close()
$stream.Close()

## If we're in scripted mode, return the output
if($scriptedMode)
{
    $output
}
```

```
}

## Read output from a remote host
function GetOutput
{
    ## Create a buffer to receive the response
    $buffer = new-object System.Byte[] 1024
    $encoding = new-object System.Text.AsciiEncoding

    $outputBuffer = ""
    $foundMore = $false

    ## Read all the data available from the stream, writing it to the
    ## output buffer when done.
    do
    {
        ## Allow data to buffer for a bit
        start-sleep -m 1000

        ## Read what data is available
        $foundmore = $false
        $stream.ReadTimeout = 1000

        do
        {
            try
            {
                $read = $stream.Read($buffer, 0, 1024)

                if($read -gt 0)
                {
                    $foundmore = $true
                    $outputBuffer += ($encoding.GetString($buffer, 0, $read))
                }
            } catch { $foundMore = $false; $read = 0 }
        } while($read -gt 0)
    } while($foundmore)

    $outputBuffer
}

. Main
```

For more information about running scripts, see Recipe 1.1, "Run Programs, Scripts, and Existing Tools".

## See Also

Recipe 1.1, "Run Programs, Scripts, and Existing Tools"

Recipe 5.14, "Program: Convert Text Streams to Objects"

# User Interaction

## 13.0. Introduction

Although most scripts are designed to run automatically, you will frequently find it useful to have your scripts interact with the user.

 The best way to get input from your user is through the arguments and parameters to your script or function. This lets your users run your script without having to be there as it runs!

If your script greatly benefits from (or requires) an interactive experience, PowerShell offers a range of possibilities. This might be simply waiting for a keypress, prompting for input, or displaying a richer choice-based prompt.

User input isn't the only aspect of interaction, though. In addition to its input facilities, PowerShell supports output as well—from displaying simple text strings to much more detailed progress reporting and interaction with UI frameworks.

## 13.1. Read a Line of User Input

### Problem

You want to use input from the user in your script.

## Solution

To obtain user input, use the Read-Host cmdlet:

```
PS > $directory = Read-Host "Enter a directory name"
Enter a directory name: C:\MyDirectory
PS > $directory
C:\MyDirectory
```

## Discussion

The Read-Host cmdlet reads a single line of input from the user. If the input contains sensitive data, the cmdlet supports an -AsSecureString parameter to read this input as a SecureString.

If the user input represents a date, time, or number, be aware that most cultures represent these data types differently. For more information about writing culture-aware scripts, see Recipe 13.6, "Write Culture-Aware Scripts".

For more information about the Read-Host cmdlet, type **Get-Help Read-Host**. For an example of reading user input through a graphical prompt, see the Read-InputBox script included in this book's code examples. For more information about obtaining these examples, see "Code Examples" (page xxiii).

## See Also

Recipe 13.6, "Write Culture-Aware Scripts"

# 13.2. Read a Key of User Input

## Problem

You want your script to get a single keypress from the user.

## Solution

For most purposes, use the [Console]::ReadKey() method to read a key:

```
PS > $key = [Console]::ReadKey($true)
PS > $key

KeyChar                     Key                 Modifiers
-------                     ---                 ---------
      h                       H                       Alt
```

For highly interactive use (for example, when you care about key down and key up), use:

```
PS > $key = $host.UI.RawUI.ReadKey("NoEcho,IncludeKeyDown")
PS > $key

    VirtualKeyCode        Character   ControlKeyState      KeyDown
    --------------        ---------   ---------------      -------
                16                    ...ssed, NumLockOn      True

PS > $key.ControlKeyState
ShiftPressed, NumLockOn
```

## Discussion

For most purposes, the [Console]::ReadKey() is the best way to get a keystroke from a user, as it accepts simple keypresses and more complex keypresses that might include the Ctrl, Alt, and Shift keys. We pass the $true parameter to tell the method to not display the character on the screen, and only to return it to us.

 If you want to read a key of user input as a way to pause your script, you can use PowerShell's built-in pause command.

If you need to capture individual key down and key up events (including those of the Ctrl, Alt, and Shift keys), use the $host.UI.RawUI.ReadKey() method.

# 13.3. Program: Display a Menu to the User

It is often useful to read input from the user but restrict input to a list of choices that you specify. The following script lets you access PowerShell's prompting functionality in a manner that is friendlier than what PowerShell exposes by default. It returns a number that represents the position of the user's choice from the list of options you provide.

PowerShell's prompting requires that you include an accelerator key (the & before a letter in the option description) to define the keypress that represents that option. Since you don't always control the list of options (for example, a list of possible directories), Example 13-1 automatically generates sensible accelerator characters for any descriptions that lack them.

*Example 13-1. Read-HostWithPrompt.ps1*

```
##############################################################################
##
## Read-HostWithPrompt
##
## From Windows PowerShell Cookbook (O'Reilly)
## by Lee Holmes (http://www.leeholmes.com/guide)
```

```
##
###############################################################################

<#

.SYNOPSIS

Read user input, with choices restricted to the list of options you
provide.

.EXAMPLE

PS > $caption = "Please specify a task"
PS > $message = "Specify a task to run"
PS > $option = "&Clean Temporary Files","&Defragment Hard Drive"
PS > $helptext = "Clean the temporary files from the computer",
>>              "Run the defragment task"
>>
PS > $default = 1
PS > Read-HostWithPrompt $caption $message $option $helptext $default

Please specify a task
Specify a task to run
[C] Clean Temporary Files  [D] Defragment Hard Drive  [?] Help
(default is "D"):?
C - Clean the temporary files from the computer
D - Run the defragment task
[C] Clean Temporary Files  [D] Defragment Hard Drive  [?] Help
(default is "D"):C
0

#>

param(
    ## The caption for the prompt
    $Caption = $null,

    ## The message to display in the prompt
    $Message = $null,

    ## Options to provide in the prompt
    [Parameter(Mandatory = $true)]
    $Option,

    ## Any help text to provide
    $HelpText = $null,

    ## The default choice
    $Default = 0
)

Set-StrictMode -Version 3
```

```
## Create the list of choices
$choices = New-Object `
    Collections.ObjectModel.Collection[Management.Automation.Host.ChoiceDescription]

## Go through each of the options, and add them to the choice collection
for($counter = 0; $counter -lt $option.Length; $counter++)
{
    $choice = New-Object Management.Automation.Host.ChoiceDescription `
        $option[$counter]

    if($helpText -and $helpText[$counter])
    {
        $choice.HelpMessage = $helpText[$counter]
    }

    $choices.Add($choice)
}

## Prompt for the choice, returning the item the user selected
$host.UI.PromptForChoice($caption, $message, $choices, $default)
```

For more information about running scripts, see Recipe 1.1, "Run Programs, Scripts, and Existing Tools".

## See Also

Recipe 1.1, "Run Programs, Scripts, and Existing Tools"

# 13.4. Display Messages and Output to the User

## Problem

You want to display messages and other information to the user.

## Solution

Simply have your script output the string information. If you like to be more explicit in your scripting, call the Write-Output cmdlet:

```
PS > function Get-Information
{
    "Hello World"
    Write-Output (1 + 1)
}

PS > Get-Information
Hello World
```

```
2
PS > $result = Get-Information
PS > $result[1]
2
```

## Discussion

Most scripts that you write should output richly structured data, such as the actual count of bytes in a directory (if you are writing a directory information script). That way, other scripts can use the output of that script as a building block for their functionality.

When you do want to provide output specifically to the user, use the Write-Host, Write-Debug, and Write-Verbose cmdlets:

```
PS > function Get-DirectorySize
{
    $size = (Get-ChildItem | Measure-Object -Sum Length).Sum
    Write-Host ("Directory size: {0:N0} bytes" -f $size)
}

PS > Get-DirectorySize
Directory size: 46,581 bytes
PS > $size = Get-DirectorySize
Directory size: 46,581 bytes
```

If you want a message to help you (or the user) diagnose and debug your script, use the Write-Debug cmdlet. If you want a message to provide detailed trace-type output, use the Write-Verbose cmdlet, as shown in Example 13-2.

*Example 13-2. A function that provides debug and verbose output*

```
PS > function Get-DirectorySize
{
    Write-Debug "Current Directory: $(Get-Location)"

    Write-Verbose "Getting size"
    $size = (Get-ChildItem | Measure-Object -Sum Length).Sum
    Write-Verbose "Got size: $size"

    Write-Host ("Directory size: {0:N0} bytes" -f $size)
}

PS > $DebugPreference = "Continue"
PS > Get-DirectorySize
DEBUG: Current Directory: D:\lee\OReilly\Scripts\Programs
Directory size: 46,581 bytes
PS > $DebugPreference = "SilentlyContinue"
PS > $VerbosePreference = "Continue"
PS > Get-DirectorySize
```

```
VERBOSE: Getting size
VERBOSE: Got size: 46581
Directory size: 46,581 bytes
PS > $VerbosePreference = "SilentlyContinue"
```

However, be aware that this type of output bypasses normal file redirection and is therefore difficult for the user to capture. In the case of the `Write-Host` cmdlet, use it only when your script already generates other structured data that the user would want to capture in a file or variable.

Most script authors eventually run into the problem illustrated by Example 13-3 when their script tries to output formatted data to the user.

*Example 13-3. An error message caused by formatting statements*

```
PS > ## Get the list of items in a directory, sorted by length
PS > function Get-ChildItemSortedByLength($path = (Get-Location))
{
    Get-ChildItem $path | Format-Table | Sort Length
}

PS > Get-ChildItemSortedByLength
out-lineoutput : Object of type "Microsoft.PowerShell.Commands.Internal.
Format.FormatEntryData" is not legal or not in the correct sequence. This is
likely caused by a user-specified "format-*" command which is conflicting
with the default formatting.
```

This happens because the `Format-*` cmdlets actually generate formatting information for the `Out-Host` cmdlet to consume. The `Out-Host` cmdlet (which PowerShell adds automatically to the end of your pipelines) then uses this information to generate formatted output. To resolve this problem, always ensure that formatting commands are the last commands in your pipeline, as shown in Example 13-4.

*Example 13-4. A function that does not generate formatting errors*

```
PS > ## Get the list of items in a directory, sorted by length
PS > function Get-ChildItemSortedByLength($path = (Get-Location))
{
    ## Problematic version
    ## Get-ChildItem $path | Format-Table | Sort Length

    ## Fixed version
    Get-ChildItem $path | Sort Length | Format-Table
}

PS > Get-ChildItemSortedByLength

(...)
```

```
Mode              LastWriteTime    Length Name
----              -------------    ------ ----
-a---      3/11/2007   3:21 PM         59 LibraryProperties.ps1
-a---      3/6/2007   10:27 AM        150 Get-Tomorrow.ps1
-a---      3/4/2007    3:10 PM        194 ConvertFrom-FahrenheitWithout
                                          Function.ps1
-a---      3/4/2007    4:40 PM        257 LibraryTemperature.ps1
-a---      3/4/2007    4:57 PM        281 ConvertFrom-FahrenheitWithLib
                                          rary.ps1
-a---      3/4/2007    3:14 PM        337 ConvertFrom-FahrenheitWithFunc
                                          tion.ps1
(...)
```

These examples are included as *LibraryDirectory.ps1* in this book's code examples. For more information about obtaining these examples, see "Code Examples" (page xxiii).

When it comes to producing output for the user, a common reason is to provide progress messages. PowerShell actually supports this in a much richer way, through its `Write-Progress` cmdlet. For more information about the `Write-Progress` cmdlet, see Recipe 13.5, "Provide Progress Updates on Long-Running Tasks".

## See Also

Recipe 13.5, "Provide Progress Updates on Long-Running Tasks"

# 13.5. Provide Progress Updates on Long-Running Tasks

## Problem

You want to display status information to the user for long-running tasks.

## Solution

To provide status updates, use the `Write-Progress` cmdlet shown in Example 13-5.

*Example 13-5. Using the Write-Progress cmdlet to display status updates*

```
##############################################################################
##
## Invoke-LongRunningOperation
##
## From Windows PowerShell Cookbook (O'Reilly)
## by Lee Holmes (http://www.leeholmes.com/guide)
##
##############################################################################

<#
```

```
.SYNOPSIS

Demonstrates the functionality of the Write-Progress cmdlet

#>

Set-StrictMode -Version 3

$activity = "A long running operation"
$status = "Initializing"

## Initialize the long-running operation
for($counter = 0; $counter -lt 100; $counter++)
{
    $currentOperation = "Initializing item $counter"
    Write-Progress $activity $status -PercentComplete $counter `
        -CurrentOperation $currentOperation
    Start-Sleep -m 20
}

$status = "Running"

## Initialize the long-running operation
for($counter = 0; $counter -lt 100; $counter++)
{
    $currentOperation = "Running task $counter"
    Write-Progress $activity $status -PercentComplete $counter `
        -CurrentOperation $currentOperation
    Start-Sleep -m 20
}
```

## Discussion

The Write-Progress cmdlet enables you to provide structured status information to the users of your script for long-running operations (see Figure 13-1).

Like the other detailed information channels (Write-Debug, Write-Verbose, and the other Write-* cmdlets), PowerShell lets users control how much of this information they see.

For more information about the Write-Progress cmdlet, type **Get-Help Write-Progress**.

# 13.6. Write Culture-Aware Scripts

## Problem

You want to ensure that your script works well on computers around the world.

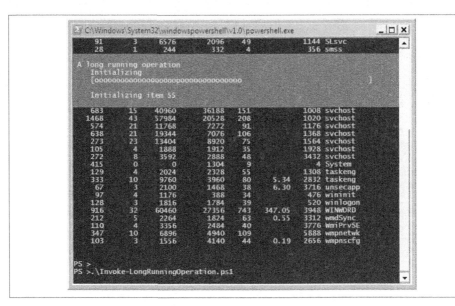

| 91 | 3 | 6576 | 2096 | 49 | | 1144 | SLsvc |
| 28 | 1 | 244 | 332 | 4 | | 356 | smss |

```
A long running operation
  Initializing
  [oooooooooooooooooooooooooooooooooooo                    ]

  Initializing item 55
```

| 683 | 15 | 40960 | 36188 | 151 | | 1008 | svchost |
| 1468 | 43 | 57984 | 20528 | 208 | | 1020 | svchost |
| 574 | 21 | 11768 | 7272 | 91 | | 1176 | svchost |
| 638 | 21 | 19344 | 7076 | 106 | | 1368 | svchost |
| 273 | 23 | 13404 | 8920 | 75 | | 1564 | svchost |
| 105 | 4 | 1888 | 1912 | 35 | | 1928 | svchost |
| 272 | 8 | 3592 | 2888 | 48 | | 3432 | svchost |
| 415 | 0 | 0 | 1304 | 9 | | 4 | System |
| 129 | 4 | 2024 | 2328 | 55 | | 1308 | taskeng |
| 333 | 10 | 9760 | 3960 | 80 | 5.34 | 2832 | taskeng |
| 67 | 3 | 2100 | 1468 | 38 | 6.30 | 3716 | unsecapp |
| 97 | 4 | 1176 | 388 | 34 | | 476 | wininit |
| 128 | 3 | 1816 | 1784 | 39 | | 520 | winlogon |
| 916 | 32 | 60460 | 27356 | 743 | 347.05 | 3948 | WINWORD |
| 212 | 5 | 2264 | 1824 | 63 | 0.55 | 3312 | wmdSync |
| 110 | 4 | 3356 | 2484 | 40 | | 3776 | WmiPrvSE |
| 347 | 10 | 6896 | 4940 | 109 | | 5888 | wmpnetwk |
| 103 | 3 | 1556 | 4140 | 44 | 0.19 | 2656 | wmpnscfg |

```
PS >
PS >.\Invoke-LongRunningOperation.ps1
```

*Figure 13-1. Example output from a long-running operation*

## Solution

To write culture-aware scripts, keep the following guidelines in mind as you develop your scripts:

- Create dates, times, and numbers using PowerShell's language primitives.
- Compare strings using PowerShell's built-in operators.
- Avoid treating user input as a collection of characters.
- Use `Parse()` methods to convert user input to dates, times, and numbers.

## Discussion

Writing culture-aware programs has long been isolated to the world of professional software developers. It's not that users of simple programs and scripts can't benefit from culture awareness, though. It has just frequently been too difficult for nonprofessional programmers to follow the best practices. However, PowerShell makes this much easier than traditional programming languages.

As your script travels between different cultures, several things change.

### Date, time, and number formats

Most cultures have unique date, time, and number formats. To guarantee that your script works in all cultures, PowerShell first ensures that its language primitives remain consistent no matter where your script runs. Even if your script runs on a machine in France (which uses a comma for its decimal separator), you can always rely on the statement `$myDouble = 3.5` to create a number halfway between three and four. Likewise, you can always count on the statement `$christmas = [DateTime]"12/25/2007"` to create a date that represents Christmas in 2007—even in cultures that write dates in the order of day, month, year.

Culture-aware programs always display dates, times, and numbers using the preferences of that culture. This doesn't break scripts as they travel between cultures and is an important aspect of writing culture-aware scripts. PowerShell handles this for you, as it uses the current culture's preferences whenever it displays data.

 If your script asks the user for a date, time, or number, make sure that you respect the format of the user's culture when you do so. To convert user input to a specific type of data, use the `Get-Date` cmdlet:

```
$userInput = Read-Host "Please enter a date"
$enteredDate = Get-Date -Date $userInput
```

So, to ensure that your script remains culture-aware with respect to dates, times, and number formats, simply use PowerShell's language primitives when you define them in your script. When you read them from the user, use `Parse()` methods when you convert them from strings.

### Complexity of user input and file content

English is a rare language in that its alphabet is so simple. This leads to all kinds of programming tricks that treat user input and file content as arrays of bytes or simple plain-text (ASCII) characters. In most international languages, these tricks fail. In fact, many international symbols take up two characters' worth of data in the string that contains them.

PowerShell uses the standard Unicode character set for all string-based operations: reading input from the user, displaying output to the user, sending data through the pipeline, and working with files.

Although PowerShell fully supports Unicode, the *powershell.exe* command-line host does not output some characters correctly, because of limitations in the Windows console system. Graphical PowerShell hosts (such as the Integrated Scripting Environment and the many third-party PowerShell IDEs) are not affected by these limitations, however.

If you use PowerShell's standard features when working with user input, you do not have to worry about its complexity. If you want to work with individual characters or words in the input, though, you will need to take special precautions. The System. Globalization.StringInfo class lets you do this in a culture-aware way. For more information about working with the StringInfo class, see this site (*http://msdn.micro soft.com/en-us/library/7h9tk6x8.aspx*).

So, to ensure that your script remains culture-aware with respect to user input, simply use PowerShell's support for string operations whenever possible.

### Capitalization rules

A common requirement in scripts is to compare user input against some predefined text (such as a menu selection). You normally want this comparison to be case insensitive, so that "QUIT" and "qUiT" mean the same thing.

A traditional way to accomplish this is to convert the user input to uppercase or lowercase:

```
## $text comes from the user, and contains the value "quit"
if($text.ToUpper() -eq "QUIT") { ... }
```

Unfortunately, explicitly changing the capitalization of strings fails in subtle ways when run in different cultures, as many cultures have different capitalization and comparison rules. For example, the Turkish language includes two types of the letter *I*: one with a dot and one without. The uppercase version of the lowercase letter *i* corresponds to the version of the capital *I* with a dot, not the capital *I* used in QUIT. That example causes the preceding string comparison to fail on a Turkish system.

Recipe 13.8, "Program: Invoke a Script Block with Alternate Culture Settings" lets us see this quite clearly:

```
PS > Use-Culture tr-TR { "quit".ToUpper() -eq "QUIT" }
False
PS > Use-Culture tr-TR { "quIt".ToUpper() -eq "QUIT" }
True
PS > Use-Culture tr-TR { "quit".ToUpper() }
QUİT
```

To compare some input against a hardcoded string in a case-insensitive manner, the better solution is to use PowerShell's -eq operator without changing any of the casing yourself. The -eq operator is case-insensitive and culture-neutral by default:

```
PS > $text1 = "Hello"
PS > $text2 = "HELLO"
PS > $text1 -eq $text2
True
```

So, to ensure that your script remains culture-aware with respect to capitalization rules, simply use PowerShell's case-insensitive comparison operators whenever it's possible.

### Sorting rules

Sorting rules frequently change between cultures. For example, compare English and Danish with the script given in Recipe 13.8, "Program: Invoke a Script Block with Alternate Culture Settings":

```
PS > Use-Culture en-US { "Apple","Æble" | Sort-Object }
Æble
Apple
PS > Use-Culture da-DK { "Apple","Æble" | Sort-Object }
Apple
Æble
```

To ensure that your script remains culture-aware with respect to sorting rules, assume that output is sorted correctly after you sort it—but don't depend on the actual order of sorted output.

### Other guidelines

For other resources on writing culture-aware programs, see here (*http://msdn.micro soft.com/en-us/library/h6270d0z.aspx*) and here (*http://msdn.microsoft.com/en-us/goglo bal/bb688110.aspx*).

## See Also

Recipe 13.8, "Program: Invoke a Script Block with Alternate Culture Settings"

# 13.7. Support Other Languages in Script Output

## Problem

You are displaying text messages to the user and want to support international languages.

## Solution

Use the `Import-LocalizedData` cmdlet, shown in Example 13-6.

*Example 13-6. Importing culture-specific strings for a script or module*

```
## Create some default messages for English cultures, and
## when culture-specific messages are not available.
$messages = DATA {
    @{
        Greeting = "Hello, {0}"
        Goodbye = "So long."
    }
}

## Import localized messages for the current culture.
Import-LocalizedData messages -ErrorAction SilentlyContinue

## Output the localized messages
$messages.Greeting -f "World"
$messages.Goodbye
```

## Discussion

The `Import-LocalizedData` cmdlet lets you easily write scripts that display different messages for different languages.

The core of this localization support comes from the concept of a *message table*: a simple mapping of message IDs (such as a `Greeting` or `Goodbye` message) to the actual message it represents. Instead of directly outputting a string to the user, you instead retrieve the string from the message table and output that. Localization of your script comes from replacing the message table with one that contains messages appropriate for the current language.

PowerShell uses standard hashtables to define message tables. Keys and values in the hashtable represent message IDs and their corresponding strings, respectively.

> The Solution defines the default message table within a DATA section. As with loading messages from *.psd1* files, this places PowerShell in a data-centric subset of the full PowerShell language. While not required, it is a useful practice for both error detection and consistency.

After defining a default message table in your script, the next step is to create localized versions and place them in language-specific directories alongside your script. The real magic of the `Import-LocalizedData` cmdlet comes from the intelligence it applies when loading the appropriate message file.

As a background, the standard way to refer to a culture (for localization purposes) is an identifier that combines the *culture* and *region*. For example, German as spoken in Germany is defined by the identifier de-DE. English as spoken in the United States is defined by the identifier en-US, whereas English as spoken in Canada is defined by the identifier en-CA. Most languages are spoken in many regions.

When you call the Import-LocalizedData cmdlet, PowerShell goes to the same directory as your script, and first tries to load your messages from a directory with a name that matches the full name of the current culture (for example, *en-CA* or *en-GB*). If that fails, it falls back to the region-neutral directory (such as *en* or *de*) and on to the other fallback languages defined by the operating system.

To make your efforts available to the broadest set of languages, place your localized messages in the most general directory that applies. For example, place French messages (first) in the *fr* directory so that all French-speaking regions can benefit. If you want to customize your messages to a specific region after that, place them in a region-specific directory.

Rather than define these message tables in script files (like your main script), place them in *.psd1* files that have the same name as your script. For example, Example 13-6 places its localized messages in *Import-LocalizedData.psd1*. PowerShell's *psd1* files represent a data-centric subset of the full PowerShell language and are ideally suited for localization. In the *.psd1* file, define a hashtable (Example 13-7)—but do not store it in a variable like you do for the default message table.

*Example 13-7. A localized .psd1 file that defines a message table*

```
@{
    Greeting = "Guten Tag, {0}"
    Goodbye = "Auf Wiedersehen."
}
```

If you already use a set of tools to help you manage the software localization process, they may not understand the PowerShell *.psd1* file format. Another standard message format is simple name-value mapping, so PowerShell supports that through the ConvertFrom-StringData cmdlet:

```
ConvertFrom-StringData @'
Greeting = Guten Tag, {0}
Goodbye = Auf Wiedersehen
'@
```

Notice that the Greeting message in Example 13-6 uses {0}-style placeholders (and PowerShell's string formatting operator) to output strings with replaceable text.

Using this technique is vastly preferable to using string concatenation (e.g., $messages.GreetingBeforeName + " World " + $messages.GreetingAftername) because it gives additional flexibility during localization of languages with different sentence structures.

To test your script under different languages, you can use Recipe 13.8, "Program: Invoke a Script Block with Alternate Culture Settings", as in this example:

```
PS > Use-Culture de-DE { Invoke-LocalizedScript }
Guten Tag, World
Auf Wiedersehen.
```

For more information about script internationalization, type **Get-Help about_Script_Internationalization**.

## See Also

Recipe 13.8, "Program: Invoke a Script Block with Alternate Culture Settings"

# 13.8. Program: Invoke a Script Block with Alternate Culture Settings

Given PowerShell's diverse user community, scripts that you share will often be run on a system set to a language other than English. To ensure that your script runs properly in other languages, it is helpful to give it a test run in that culture. Example 13-8 lets you run the script block you provide in a culture of your choosing.

*Example 13-8. Use-Culture.ps1*

```
###############################################################################
##
## Use-Culture
##
## From Windows PowerShell Cookbook (O'Reilly)
## by Lee Holmes (http://www.leeholmes.com/guide)
##
###############################################################################

<#

.SYNOPSIS

Invoke a script block under the given culture

.EXAMPLE

PS > Use-Culture fr-FR { Get-Date -Date "25/12/2007" }
mardi 25 decembre 2007 00:00:00
```

```
#>

param(
    ## The culture in which to evaluate the given script block
    [Parameter(Mandatory = $true)]
    [System.Globalization.CultureInfo] $Culture,

    ## The code to invoke in the context of the given culture
    [Parameter(Mandatory = $true)]
    [ScriptBlock] $ScriptBlock
)

Set-StrictMode -Version 3

## A helper function to set the current culture
function Set-Culture([System.Globalization.CultureInfo] $culture)
{
    [System.Threading.Thread]::CurrentThread.CurrentUICulture = $culture
    [System.Threading.Thread]::CurrentThread.CurrentCulture = $culture
}

## Remember the original culture information
$oldCulture = [System.Threading.Thread]::CurrentThread.CurrentUICulture

## Restore the original culture information if
## the user's script encounters errors.
trap { Set-Culture $oldCulture }

## Set the current culture to the user's provided
## culture.
Set-Culture $culture

## Invoke the user's script block
& $ScriptBlock

## Restore the original culture information.
Set-Culture $oldCulture
```

For more information about running scripts, see Recipe 1.1, "Run Programs, Scripts, and Existing Tools".

## See Also

Recipe 1.1, "Run Programs, Scripts, and Existing Tools"

# 13.9. Access Features of the Host's User Interface

## Problem

You want to interact with features in the user interface of the hosting application, but PowerShell doesn't directly provide cmdlets for them.

## Solution

To access features of the host's user interface, use the $host.UI.RawUI variable:

```
$host.UI.RawUI.WindowTitle = Get-Location
```

## Discussion

PowerShell itself consists of two main components. The first is an engine that interprets commands, executes pipelines, and performs other similar actions. The second is the hosting application—the way that users interact with the PowerShell engine.

The default shell, *PowerShell.exe*, is a user interface based on the traditional Windows console. The graphical Integrated Scripting Environment hosts PowerShell in a graphical user interface. In fact, PowerShell makes it relatively simple for developers to build their own hosting applications, or even to embed the PowerShell engine features into their own applications.

You (and your scripts) can always depend on the functionality available through the $host.UI variable, as that functionality remains the same for all hosts. Example 13-9 shows the features available to you in all hosts.

*Example 13-9. Functionality available through the $host.UI property*

```
PS > $host.UI | Get-Member | Select Name,MemberType | Format-Table -Auto

Name                    MemberType
----                    ----------
(...)
Prompt                  Method
PromptForChoice         Method
PromptForCredential     Method
ReadLine                Method
ReadLineAsSecureString  Method
Write                   Method
WriteDebugLine          Method
WriteErrorLine          Method
WriteLine               Method
WriteProgress           Method
WriteVerboseLine        Method
WriteWarningLine        Method
RawUI                   Property
```

If you (or your scripts) want to interact with portions of the user interface specific to the current host, PowerShell provides that access through the `$host.UI.RawUI` variable. Example 13-10 shows the features available to you in the PowerShell console host.

*Example 13-10. Functionality available through the default console host*

```
PS > $host.UI.RawUI | Get-Member |
    Select Name,MemberType | Format-Table -Auto

Name                     MemberType
----                     ----------
(...)
FlushInputBuffer            Method
GetBufferContents           Method
GetHashCode                 Method
GetType                     Method
LengthInBufferCells         Method
NewBufferCellArray          Method
ReadKey                     Method
ScrollBufferContents        Method
SetBufferContents           Method
BackgroundColor           Property
BufferSize                Property
CursorPosition            Property
CursorSize                Property
ForegroundColor           Property
KeyAvailable              Property
MaxPhysicalWindowSize     Property
MaxWindowSize             Property
WindowPosition            Property
WindowSize                Property
WindowTitle               Property
```

If you rely on the host-specific features from `$host.UI.RawUI`, be aware that your script will require modifications (perhaps major modifications) before it will run properly on other hosts.

# 13.10. Program: Add a Graphical User Interface to Your Script

Although the techniques provided in the rest of this chapter usually are all you need, it is sometimes helpful to provide a graphical user interface to interact with the user.

Since PowerShell fully supports traditional executables, simple programs usually can fill this need. If creating a simple program in an environment such as Visual Studio is inconvenient, you can often use PowerShell to create these applications directly.

In addition to creating Windows Forms applications through PowerShell scripts, the popular Show-UI community project lets you easily create rich WPF (Windows Presentation Foundation) interfaces for your PowerShell scripts. For more information, search the Internet for "PowerShell Show-UI."

Example 13-11 demonstrates the techniques you can use to develop a Windows Forms application using PowerShell scripting alone. The functionality itself is now covered in PowerShell version 3 by the Out-GridView cmdlet, but it demonstrates several useful techniques and is useful in PowerShell version 2!

For an example of using the Out-GridView cmdlet to do this in PowerShell version 3, see Recipe 2.4, "Program: Interactively Filter Lists of Objects".

*Example 13-11. Select-GraphicalFilteredObject.ps1*

```
##############################################################################
##
## Select-GraphicalFilteredObject
##
## From Windows PowerShell Cookbook (O'Reilly)
## by Lee Holmes (http://www.leeholmes.com/guide)
##
##############################################################################

<#

.SYNOPSIS

Display a Windows Form to help the user select a list of items piped in.
Any selected items get passed along the pipeline.

.EXAMPLE

PS > dir | Select-GraphicalFilteredObject

   Directory: C:\

Mode                LastWriteTime     Length Name
----                -------------     ------ ----
d----         10/7/2006   4:30 PM            Documents and Settings
d----         3/18/2007   7:56 PM            Windows

#>

Set-StrictMode -Version 2

$objectArray = @($input)

## Ensure that they've piped information into the script
if($objectArray.Count -eq 0)
{
```

```
    Write-Error "This script requires pipeline input."
    return
}

## Load the Windows Forms assembly
Add-Type -Assembly System.Windows.Forms

## Create the main form
$form = New-Object Windows.Forms.Form
$form.Size = New-Object Drawing.Size @(600,600)

## Create the listbox to hold the items from the pipeline
$listbox = New-Object Windows.Forms.CheckedListBox
$listbox.CheckOnClick = $true
$listbox.Dock = "Fill"
$form.Text = "Select the list of objects you wish to pass down the pipeline"
$listBox.Items.AddRange($objectArray)

## Create the button panel to hold the OK and Cancel buttons
$buttonPanel = New-Object Windows.Forms.Panel
$buttonPanel.Size = New-Object Drawing.Size @(600,30)
$buttonPanel.Dock = "Bottom"

## Create the Cancel button, which will anchor to the bottom right
$cancelButton = New-Object Windows.Forms.Button
$cancelButton.Text = "Cancel"
$cancelButton.DialogResult = "Cancel"
$cancelButton.Top = $buttonPanel.Height - $cancelButton.Height - 5
$cancelButton.Left = $buttonPanel.Width - $cancelButton.Width - 10
$cancelButton.Anchor = "Right"

## Create the OK button, which will anchor to the left of Cancel
$okButton = New-Object Windows.Forms.Button
$okButton.Text = "Ok"
$okButton.DialogResult = "Ok"
$okButton.Top = $cancelButton.Top
$okButton.Left = $cancelButton.Left - $okButton.Width - 5
$okButton.Anchor = "Right"

## Add the buttons to the button panel
$buttonPanel.Controls.Add($okButton)
$buttonPanel.Controls.Add($cancelButton)

## Add the button panel and list box to the form, and also set
## the actions for the buttons
$form.Controls.Add($listBox)
$form.Controls.Add($buttonPanel)
$form.AcceptButton = $okButton
$form.CancelButton = $cancelButton
$form.Add_Shown( { $form.Activate() } )
```

```
## Show the form, and wait for the response
$result = $form.ShowDialog()

## If they pressed OK (or Enter,) go through all the
## checked items and send the corresponding object down the pipeline
if($result -eq "OK")
{
    foreach($index in $listBox.CheckedIndices)
    {
        $objectArray[$index]
    }
}
```

For more information about running scripts, see Recipe 1.1, "Run Programs, Scripts, and Existing Tools".

## See Also

Recipe 1.1, "Run Programs, Scripts, and Existing Tools"

Recipe 2.4, "Program: Interactively Filter Lists of Objects"

# 13.11. Interact with MTA Objects

## Problem

You want to interact with an object that requires that the current thread be in multi-threaded apartment (MTA) mode.

## Solution

Launch PowerShell with the -MTA switch. If you do this as part of a script or helper command, you can also use the -NoProfile switch to avoid the performance impact and side effects of loading the user's profile:

```
PS > $output = PowerShell -NoProfile -MTA -Command {
    $myObject = New-Object SomeObjectThatRequiresMTA
    $myObject.SomeMethod()
}
```

## Discussion

Threading modes define an agreement between an application and how it interacts with some of its objects. Most objects in the .NET Framework (and thus, PowerShell and nearly everything it interacts with) ignore the threading mode and are not impacted by it.

Some objects do require a specific threading mode, though, called *multithreaded apartment*. PowerShell uses a threading mode called *single-threaded apartment* (STA) by default, so some rare objects will generate an error about their threading requirements when you're working with them.

If you frequently find that you need to use MTA mode, you can simply modify the PowerShell link on your Start menu to always load PowerShell with the -MTA parameter.

 PowerShell version 2 used MTA mode by default. This prevented many UI components used commonly in scripts, and most importantly was inconsistent with the PowerShell ISE (Integrated Scripting Environment) that uses STA mode by default. If you have an advanced threading scenario in a script that no longer works in PowerShell version 3, this may be the cause. In that case, loading PowerShell in MTA mode can resolve the issue.

If your entire script requires MTA mode, you have two primary options: detect the current threading mode or relaunch yourself under STA mode.

To detect the current threading mode, you can access the $host.Runspace.Apartment State variable. If its value is not STA, the current threading mode is MTA.

If your script has simple parameter requirements, you may be able to relaunch yourself automatically, as in Example 13-12.

*Example 13-12. A script that relaunches itself in MTA mode*

```
##############################################################################
##
## Invoke-ScriptThatRequiresMta
##
## From Windows PowerShell Cookbook (O'Reilly)
## by Lee Holmes (http://www.leeholmes.com/guide)
##
##############################################################################

<#

.SYNOPSIS

Demonstrates a technique to relaunch a script that requires MTA mode.
This is useful only for simple parameter definitions that can be
specified positionally.

#>

param(
    $Parameter1,
```

```
        $Parameter2
)

Set-StrictMode -Version 3

"Current threading mode: " + $host.Runspace.ApartmentState
"Parameter1 is: $parameter1"
"Parameter2 is: $parameter2"

if($host.Runspace.ApartmentState -eq "STA")
{
    "Relaunching"
    $file = $myInvocation.MyCommand.Path
    powershell -NoProfile -Mta -File $file $parameter1 $parameter2
    return
}

"After relaunch - current threading mode: " + $host.Runspace.ApartmentState
```

When you run this script, you get the following output:

```
PS > .\Invoke-ScriptThatRequiresMta.ps1 Test1 Test2
Current threading mode: STA
Parameter1 is: Test1
Parameter2 is: Test2
Relaunching
Current threading mode: Unknown
Parameter1 is: Test1
Parameter2 is: Test2
After relaunch - current threading mode: Unknown
```

For more information about PowerShell's command-line parameters, see Recipe 1.16, "Invoke a PowerShell Command or Script from Outside PowerShell". For more information about running scripts, see Recipe 1.1, "Run Programs, Scripts, and Existing Tools".

## See Also

Recipe 1.1, "Run Programs, Scripts, and Existing Tools"

Recipe 1.16, "Invoke a PowerShell Command or Script from Outside PowerShell"

# Debugging

## 14.0. Introduction

While developing scripts and functions, you'll often find yourself running into behavior that you didn't intend. This is a natural part of software development, and the path to diagnosing these issues is the fine art known as *debugging*.

For the simplest of problems, a well-placed call to `Write-Host` can answer many of your questions. Did your script get to the places you thought it should? Were the variables set to the values you thought they should be?

Once problems get more complex, print-style debugging quickly becomes cumbersome and unwieldy. Rather than continually modifying your script to diagnose its behavior, you can leverage PowerShell's much more extensive debugging facilities to help you get to the root of the problem.

```
PS > Set-PsBreakPoint .\Invoke-ComplexDebuggerScript.ps1 -Line 14

  ID Script          Line Command        Variable         Action
  -- ------          ---- -------        --------         ------
   0 Invoke-Comple...   14

PS > .\Invoke-ComplexDebuggerScript.ps1
Calculating lots of complex information
1225
89
Entering debug mode. Use h or ? for help.

Hit Line breakpoint on
'Z:\Documents\CookbookV2\chapters\current\PowerShellCookbook\Invoke-Complex
DebuggerScript.ps1:14'

Invoke-ComplexDebuggerScript.ps1:14        $dirCount = 0
```

```
PS > ?

s, stepInto            Single step (step into functions, scripts, etc.)
v, stepOver            Step to next statement (step over functions, scripts,
                       etc.)
o, stepOut             Step out of the current function, script, etc.

c, continue            Continue execution
q, quit                Stop execution and exit the debugger

k, Get-PSCallStack  Display call stack

l, list                List source code for the current script.
                       Use "list" to start from the current line, "list <m>"
                       to start from line <m>, and "list <m> <n>" to list <n>
                       lines starting from line <m>

<enter>                Repeat last command if it was stepInto, stepOver, or
                       list

?, h                   Displays this help message


For instructions about how to customize your debugger prompt, type "help
about_prompt".

PS > k

Command                      Arguments            Location
-------                      ---------            --------
HelperFunction               {}                   Invoke-ComplexDebugge...
Invoke-ComplexDebugge... {}                       Invoke-ComplexDebugge...
prompt                       {}                   prompt
```

By leveraging strict mode, you can often save yourself from writing bugs in the first place. Once you discover an issue, script tracing can help you get a quick overview of the execution flow taken by your script. For interactive diagnosis, PowerShell's Integrated Scripting Environment (ISE) offers full-featured graphical debugging support. From the command line, the *-PsBreakPoint cmdlets let you investigate your script when it hits a specific line, condition, or error.

# 14.1. Prevent Common Scripting Errors

## Problem

You want to have PowerShell warn you when your script contains an error likely to result in a bug.

## Solution

Use the `Set-StrictMode` cmdlet to place PowerShell in a mode that prevents many of the scripting errors that tend to introduce bugs.

```
PS > function BuggyFunction
{
    $testVariable = "Hello"
    if($testVariab1e -eq "Hello")
    {
        "Should get here"
    }
    else
    {
        "Should not get here"
    }
}

PS > BuggyFunction
Should not get here

PS > Set-StrictMode -Version Latest
PS > BuggyFunction
The variable '$testVariab1e' cannot be retrieved because it has not been set.
At line:4 char:21
+     if($testVariab1e <<<<  -eq "Hello")
    + CategoryInfo          : InvalidOperation: (testVariab1e:Token) []
    + FullyQualifiedErrorId : VariableIsUndefined
```

## Discussion

By default, PowerShell allows you to assign data to variables you haven't yet created (thereby creating those variables). It also allows you to retrieve data from variables that don't exist—which usually happens by accident and almost always causes bugs. The Solution demonstrates this trap, where the *l* in *variable* was accidentally replaced by the number 1.

To help save you from getting stung by this problem and others like it, PowerShell provides a *strict* mode that generates an error if you attempt to access a nonexisting variable. Example 14-1 demonstrates this mode.

*Example 14-1. PowerShell operating in strict mode*

```
PS > $testVariable = "Hello"
PS > $tsetVariable += " World"
PS > $testVariable
Hello
PS > Remove-Item Variable:\tsetvariable
PS > Set-StrictMode -Version Latest
PS > $testVariable = "Hello"
PS > $tsetVariable += " World"
```

```
The variable '$tsetVariable' cannot be retrieved because it has not been set.
At line:1 char:14
+ $tsetVariable <<<<  += "World"
    + CategoryInfo          : InvalidOperation: (tsetVariable:Token) []
    + FullyQualifiedErrorId : VariableIsUndefined
```

In addition to saving you from accessing nonexistent variables, strict mode also detects the following:

- Accessing nonexistent properties on an object
- Calling functions as though they were methods

One unique feature of the Set-StrictMode cmdlet is the -Version parameter. As PowerShell releases new versions of the Set-StrictMode cmdlet, the cmdlet will become more powerful and detect additional scripting errors. Because of this, a script that works with one version of strict mode might not work under a later version. Use -Version Latest if you can change your script in response to possible bugs it might discover. If you won't have the flexibility to modify your script to account for new strict mode rules, use -Version 3 (or whatever version of PowerShell you support) as the value of the -Version parameter.

 The Set-StrictMode cmdlet is *scoped*, meaning that the strict mode set in one script or function doesn't impact the scripts or functions that call it. To temporarily disable strict mode for a region of a script, do so in a new script block:

```
& { Set-StrictMode -Off; $tsetVariable }
```

For the sake of your script debugging health and sanity, strict mode should be one of the first additions you make to your PowerShell profile.

### See Also

Recipe 1.8, "Customize Your Shell, Profile, and Prompt"

# 14.2. Trace Script Execution

## Problem

You want to review the flow of execution taken by your script as PowerShell runs it.

## Solution

Use the `-Trace` parameter of the `Set-PsDebug` cmdlet to have PowerShell trace your script as it executes it:

```
PS > function BuggyFunction
{
    $testVariable = "Hello"
    if($testVariable -eq "Hello")
    {
        "Should get here"
    }
    else
    {
        "Should not get here"
    }
}

PS > Set-PsDebug -Trace 1
PS > BuggyFunction
DEBUG:    1+  <<<< BuggyFunction
DEBUG:    3+      $testVariable = <<<<  "Hello"
DEBUG:    4+      if <<<< ($testVariable -eq "Hello")
DEBUG:   10+          "Should not get here" <<<<
Should not get here
```

## Discussion

When it comes to simple interactive debugging (as opposed to bug prevention), PowerShell supports several of the most useful debugging features that you might be accustomed to. For the full experience, the Integrated Scripting Environment (ISE) offers a full-fledged graphical debugger. For more information about debugging in the ISE, see Recipe 19.1, "Debug a Script".

From the command line, though, you still have access to tracing (through the `Set-PsDebug -Trace` statement), stepping (through the `Set-PsDebug -Step` statement), and environment inspection (through the `$host.EnterNestedPrompt()` call). The `*-Ps Breakpoint` cmdlets support much more functionality in addition to these primitives, but the `Set-PsDebug` cmdlet is useful for some simple problems.

As a demonstration of these techniques, consider Example 14-2.

*Example 14-2. A complex script that interacts with PowerShell's debugging features*

```
##############################################################################
##
## Invoke-ComplexScript
##
## From Windows PowerShell Cookbook (O'Reilly)
## by Lee Holmes (http://www.leeholmes.com/guide)
##
```

```
##############################################################################

<#

.SYNOPSIS

Demonstrates the functionality of PowerShell's debugging support.

#>

Set-StrictMode -Version 3

Write-Host "Calculating lots of complex information"

$runningTotal = 0
$runningTotal += [Math]::Pow(5 * 5 + 10, 2)

Write-Debug "Current value: $runningTotal"

Set-PsDebug -Trace 1
$dirCount = @(Get-ChildItem $env:WINDIR).Count

Set-PsDebug -Trace 2
$runningTotal -= 10
$runningTotal /= 2

Set-PsDebug -Step
$runningTotal *= 3
$runningTotal /= 2

$host.EnterNestedPrompt()

Set-PsDebug -off
```

As you try to determine why this script isn't working as you expect, a debugging session might look like Example 14-3.

*Example 14-3. Debugging a complex script*

```
PS > $debugPreference = "Continue"
PS > Invoke-ComplexScript.ps1
Calculating lots of complex information
DEBUG: Current value: 1225
DEBUG:    17+ $dirCount = @(Get-ChildItem $env:WINDIR).Count
DEBUG:    17+ $dirCount = @(Get-ChildItem $env:WINDIR).Count
DEBUG:    19+ Set-PsDebug -Trace 2
DEBUG:    20+ $runningTotal -= 10
DEBUG:     ! SET $runningTotal = '1215'.
DEBUG:    21+ $runningTotal /= 2
DEBUG:     ! SET $runningTotal = '607.5'.
DEBUG:    23+ Set-PsDebug -Step
```

```
Continue with this operation?
  24+ $runningTotal *= 3
[Y] Yes  [A] Yes to All  [N] No  [L] No to All  [S] Suspend [?] Help
(default is "Y"):y
DEBUG:    24+ $runningTotal *= 3
DEBUG:    !  SET $runningTotal = '1822.5'.

Continue with this operation?
  25+ $runningTotal /= 2
[Y] Yes  [A] Yes to All  [N] No  [L] No to All  [S] Suspend [?] Help
(default is "Y"):y
DEBUG:    25+ $runningTotal /= 2
DEBUG:    !  SET $runningTotal = '911.25'.

Continue with this operation?
  27+ $host.EnterNestedPrompt()
[Y] Yes  [A] Yes to All  [N] No  [L] No to All  [S] Suspend [?] Help
(default is "Y"):y
DEBUG:    27+ $host.EnterNestedPrompt()
DEBUG:      ! CALL method 'System.Void EnterNestedPrompt()'
PS > $dirCount
296
PS > $dirCount + $runningTotal
1207.25
PS > exit

Continue with this operation?
  29+ Set-PsDebug -off
[Y] Yes  [A] Yes to All  [N] No  [L] No to All  [S] Suspend [?] Help
(default is "Y"):y
DEBUG:    29+ Set-PsDebug -off
```

Together, these interactive debugging features are bound to help you diagnose and resolve simple problems quickly. For more complex problems, PowerShell's graphical debugger (in the ISE) and the *-PsBreakpoint cmdlets are here to help.

For more information about the Set-PsDebug cmdlet, type **Get-Help Set-PsDebug**. For more information about setting script breakpoints, see Recipe 14.3, "Set a Script Breakpoint".

## See Also

Recipe 1.1, "Run Programs, Scripts, and Existing Tools"

Recipe 14.3, "Set a Script Breakpoint"

Recipe 19.1, "Debug a Script"

# 14.3. Set a Script Breakpoint

## Problem

You want PowerShell to enter debugging mode when it executes a specific command, executes a particular line in your script, or updates a variable.

## Solution

Use the `Set-PsBreakpoint` cmdlet to set a new breakpoint:

```
Set-PsBreakPoint .\Invoke-ComplexDebuggerScript.ps1 -Line 21
Set-PSBreakpoint -Command Get-ChildItem
Set-PsBreakPoint -Variable dirCount
```

## Discussion

A breakpoint is a location (or condition) that causes PowerShell to temporarily pause execution of a running script. When it does so, it enters debugging mode. Debugging mode lets you investigate the state of the script and also gives you fine-grained control over the script's execution.

For more information about interacting with PowerShell's debugging mode, see Recipe 14.6, "Investigate System State While Debugging".

The `Set-PsBreakpoint` cmdlet supports three primary types of breakpoints:

*Positional*

Positional breakpoints (lines and optionally columns) cause PowerShell to pause execution once it reaches the specified location in the script you identify.

```
PS > Set-PSBreakpoint -Script .\Invoke-ComplexDebuggerScript.ps1 -Line 21

ID Script                         Line Command Variable Action
-- ------                         ---- ------- -------- ------
 0 Invoke-ComplexDebuggerScript.ps1   21


PS > .\Invoke-ComplexDebuggerScript.ps1
Calculating lots of complex information
Entering debug mode. Use h or ? for help.

Hit Line breakpoint on
'(...)\Invoke-ComplexDebuggerScript.ps1:21'

Invoke-ComplexDebuggerScript.ps1:21  $runningTotal
```

When running the debugger from the command line, you can use Recipe 8.6, "Program: Show Colorized Script Content" to determine script line numbers.

---

*Command*

Command breakpoints cause PowerShell to pause execution before calling the specified command. This is especially helpful for diagnosing in-memory functions or for pausing before your script invokes a cmdlet. If you specify the `-Script` parameter, PowerShell pauses only when the command is either defined by that script (as in the case of dot-sourced functions) or called by that script. Although command breakpoints do not support the `-Line` parameter, you can get the same effect by setting a positional breakpoint on the script that defines them.

```
PS > Show-ColorizedContent $profile.CurrentUserAllHosts

(...)
084 | function grep(
085 |     [string] $text = $(throw "Specify a search string"),
086 |     [string] $filter = "*",
087 |     [switch] $rec,
088 |     [switch] $edit
089 |     )
090 | {
091 |     $results = & {
092 |         if($rec) { gci . $filter -rec | select-string $text }
093 |         else {gci $filter | select-string $text }
094 |     }
095 |     $results
096 | }
(...)

PS > Set-PsBreakpoint $profile.CurrentUserAllHosts -Line 92 -Column 18

  ID Script                    Line Command Variable
  -- ------                    ---- ------- --------
   0 profile.ps1                 92

PS > grep "function grep" *.ps1 -rec
Entering debug mode. Use h or ? for help.

Hit Line breakpoint on 'E:\Lee\WindowsPowerShell\profile.ps1:92, 18'

profile.ps1:92          if($rec) { gci . $filter -rec | select-string $text }

(...)
```

*Variable*

By default, variable breakpoints cause PowerShell to pause execution before changing the value of a variable.

```
PS > Set-PsBreakPoint -Variable dirCount

ID Script Line Command Variable Action
-- ------ ---- ------- -------- ------
 0                     dirCount
```

```
PS > .\Invoke-ComplexDebuggerScript.ps1
Calculating lots of complex information
1225
Entering debug mode. Use h or ? for help.

Hit Variable breakpoint on '$dirCount' (Write access)

Invoke-ComplexDebuggerScript.ps1:23
$dirCount = @(Get-ChildItem $env:WINDIR).Count
PS >
```

In addition to letting you break before it changes the value of a variable, PowerShell also lets you break before it accesses the value of a variable.

Once you have a breakpoint defined, you can use the `Disable-PsBreakpoint` and `Enable-PsBreakpoint` cmdlets to control how PowerShell reacts to those breakpoints. If a breakpoint is disabled, PowerShell does not pause execution when it reaches that breakpoint. To remove a breakpoint completely, use the `Remove-PsBreakpoint` cmdlet.

In addition to interactive debugging, PowerShell also lets you define actions to perform automatically when it reaches a breakpoint. For more information, see Recipe 14.5, "Create a Conditional Breakpoint".

For more information about PowerShell's debugging support, type **Get-Help about_De buggers**.

## See Also

Recipe 14.5, "Create a Conditional Breakpoint"

Recipe 14.6, "Investigate System State While Debugging"

# 14.4. Debug a Script When It Encounters an Error

## Problem

You want PowerShell to enter debugging mode as soon as it encounters an error.

## Solution

Run the `Enable-BreakOnError` script (as shown in Example 14-4) to have PowerShell automatically pause script execution when it encounters an error.

*Example 14-4. Enable-BreakOnError.ps1*

```
##############################################################################
##
## Enable-BreakOnError
```

```
##
## From Windows PowerShell Cookbook (O'Reilly)
## by Lee Holmes (http://www.leeholmes.com/guide)
##
################################################################################

<#

.SYNOPSIS

Creates a breakpoint that only fires when PowerShell encounters an error

.EXAMPLE

PS > Enable-BreakOnError

ID Script          Line Command        Variable       Action
-- ------          ---- -------        --------       ------
 0                      Out-Default                   ...

PS > 1/0
Entering debug mode. Use h or ? for help.

Hit Command breakpoint on 'Out-Default'


PS > $error
Attempted to divide by zero.

#>

Set-StrictMode -Version 3

## Store the current number of errors seen in the session so far
$GLOBAL:EnableBreakOnErrorLastErrorCount = $error.Count

Set-PSBreakpoint -Command Out-Default -Action {

    ## If we're generating output, and the error count has increased,
    ## break into the debugger.
    if($error.Count -ne $EnableBreakOnErrorLastErrorCount)
    {
        $GLOBAL:EnableBreakOnErrorLastErrorCount = $error.Count
        break
    }
}
```

## Discussion

When PowerShell generates an error, its final action is displaying that error to you. This goes through the Out-Default cmdlet, as does all other PowerShell output. Knowing this, Example 14-4 defines a conditional breakpoint. That breakpoint fires only when the number of errors in the global $error collection changes from the last time it checked.

If you don't want PowerShell to break on all errors, you might just want to set a breakpoint on the last error you encountered. For that, run Set-PsBreakpointLastError (Example 14-5) and then run your script again.

*Example 14-5. Set-PsBreakpointLastError.ps1*

```
Set-StrictMode -Version Latest

$lastError = $error[0]
Set-PsBreakpoint $lastError.InvocationInfo.ScriptName `
    $lastError.InvocationInfo.ScriptLineNumber
```

For more information about intercepting stages of the PowerShell pipeline via the Out-Default cmdlet, see Recipe 2.8, "Intercept Stages of the Pipeline". For more information about conditional breakpoints, see Recipe 14.5, "Create a Conditional Breakpoint".

For more information about PowerShell's debugging support, type **Get-Help about_De buggers**.

## See Also

Recipe 2.8, "Intercept Stages of the Pipeline"

Recipe 14.5, "Create a Conditional Breakpoint"

# 14.5. Create a Conditional Breakpoint

## Problem

You want PowerShell to enter debugging mode when it encounters a breakpoint, but only when certain other conditions hold true as well.

## Solution

Use the -Action parameter to define an action that PowerShell should take when it encounters the breakpoint. If the action includes a break statement, PowerShell pauses execution and enters debugging mode.

```
PS > Get-Content .\looper.ps1
for($count = 0; $count -lt 10; $count++)
```

```
{
    "Count is: $count"
}

PS > Set-PsBreakpoint .\looper.ps1 -Line 3 -Action {
    if($count -eq 4) { break }
}

   ID Script          Line Command        Variable       Action
   -- ------          ---- -------        --------       ------
    0 looper.ps1         3                               ...

PS > .\looper.ps1
Count is: 0
Count is: 1
Count is: 2
Count is: 3
Entering debug mode. Use h or ? for help.

Hit Line breakpoint on 'C:\temp\looper.ps1:3'

looper.ps1:3        "Count is: $count"
PS > $count
4
PS > c
Count is: 4
Count is: 5
Count is: 6
Count is: 7
Count is: 8
Count is: 9
```

## Discussion

Conditional breakpoints are a great way to automate repetitive interactive debugging. When you are debugging an often-executed portion of your script, the problematic behavior often doesn't occur until that portion of your script has been executed hundreds or thousands of times. By narrowing down the conditions under which the breakpoint should apply (such as the value of an interesting variable), you can drastically simplify your debugging experience.

The Solution demonstrates a conditional breakpoint that triggers only when the value of the $count variable is 4. When the -Action script block executes a break statement, PowerShell enters debug mode.

Inside the -Action script block, you have access to all variables that exist at that time. You can review them, or even change them if desired.

In addition to being useful for conditional breakpoints, the -Action script block also proves helpful for generalized logging or automatic debugging. For example, consider the following action that logs the text of a line whenever the script reaches that line:

```
PS > cd c:\temp
PS > Set-PsBreakpoint .\looper.ps1 -line 3 -Action {
    $debugPreference = "Continue"
    Write-Debug (Get-Content .\looper.ps1)[2]
}

   ID Script              Line Command          Variable        Action
   -- ------              ---- -------          --------        ------
    0 looper.ps1             3                                  ...

PS > .\looper.ps1
DEBUG:     "Count is: $count"
Count is: 0
DEBUG:     "Count is: $count"
Count is: 1
DEBUG:     "Count is: $count"
Count is: 2
DEBUG:     "Count is: $count"
(...)
```

When we create the breakpoint, we know which line we've set it on. When we hit the breakpoint, we can simply get the content of the script and return the appropriate line.

For an even more complete example of conditional breakpoints being used to perform code coverage analysis, see Recipe 14.8, "Program: Get Script Code Coverage".

For more information about PowerShell's debugging support, type **Get-Help about_De buggers**.

## See Also

Recipe 14.8, "Program: Get Script Code Coverage"

# 14.6. Investigate System State While Debugging

## Problem

PowerShell has paused execution after hitting a breakpoint, and you want to investigate the state of your script.

## Solution

Examine the $PSDebugContext variable to investigate information about the current breakpoint and script location. Examine other variables to investigate the internal state of your script. Use the debug mode commands (Get-PsCallstack, List, and others) for more information about how you got to the current breakpoint and what source code corresponds to the current location:

```
PS > Get-Content .\looper.ps1
param($userInput)

for($count = 0; $count -lt 10; $count++)
{
    "Count is: $count"
}

if($userInput -eq "One")
{
    "Got 'One'"
}

if($userInput -eq "Two")
{
    "Got 'Two'"
}

PS > Set-PsBreakpoint c:\temp\looper.ps1 -Line 5
```

| ID | Script | Line | Command | Variable | Action |
|----|--------|------|---------|----------|--------|
| 0 | looper.ps1 | 5 | | | |

```
PS > c:\temp\looper.ps1 -UserInput "Hello World"
Entering debug mode. Use h or ? for help.

Hit Line breakpoint on 'C:\temp\looper.ps1:5'

looper.ps1:5       "Count is: $count"
PS > $PSDebugContext.InvocationInfo.Line
    "Count is: $count"
PS > $PSDebugContext.InvocationInfo.ScriptLineNumber
5
PS > $count
0
PS > s
Count is: 0
looper.ps1:3    for($count = 0; $count -lt 10; $count++)
PS > s
looper.ps1:3    for($count = 0; $count -lt 10; $count++)
PS > s
Hit Line breakpoint on 'C:\temp\looper.ps1:5'
```

```
looper.ps1:5       "Count is: $count"
PS > s
Count is: 1
looper.ps1:3    for($count = 0; $count -lt 10; $count++)
PS > $count
1
PS > $userInput
Hello World
PS > Get-PsCallStack

Command                      Arguments                  Location
-------                      ---------                  --------
looper.ps1                   {userInput=Hello World}    looper.ps1: Line 3
prompt                       {}                         prompt


PS > l 3 3

    3:* for($count = 0; $count -lt 10; $count++)
    4:  {
    5:      "Count is: $count"

PS >
```

## Discussion

When PowerShell pauses your script as it hits a breakpoint, it enters a debugging mode very much like the regular console session you are used to. You can execute commands, get and set variables, and otherwise explore the state of the system.

What makes debugging mode unique, however, is its context. When you enter commands in the PowerShell debugger, you are investigating the live state of the script. If you pause in the middle of a loop, you can view and modify the counter variable that controls that loop. Commands that you enter, in essence, become temporary parts of the script itself.

In addition to the regular variables available to you, PowerShell creates a new $PSDebugContext automatic variable whenever it reaches a breakpoint. The $PSDebugContext.BreakPoints property holds the current breakpoint, whereas the $PSDebugContext.InvocationInfo property holds information about the current location in the script:

```
PS > $PSDebugContext.InvocationInfo

MyCommand        :
BoundParameters  : {}
UnboundArguments : {}
ScriptLineNumber : 3
OffsetInLine     : 40
```

```
HistoryId        : -1
ScriptName       : C:\temp\looper.ps1
Line             : for($count = 0; $count -lt 10; $count++)
PositionMessage  :
                   At C:\temp\looper.ps1:3 char:40
                   + for($count = 0; $count -lt 10; $count++ <<<< )
InvocationName   : ++
PipelineLength   : 0
PipelinePosition : 0
ExpectingInput   : False
CommandOrigin    : Internal
```

For information about the nesting of functions and commands that called each other to reach this point (the *call stack*), type **Get-PsCallStack**.

If you find yourself continually monitoring a specific variable (or set of variables) for changes, Recipe 14.7, "Program: Watch an Expression for Changes" shows a script that lets you automatically watch an expression of your choice.

After investigating the state of the script, you can analyze its flow of execution through the three stepping commands: *step into*, *step over*, and *step out*. These functions single-step through your script with three different behaviors: entering functions and scripts as you go, skipping over functions and scripts as you go, or popping out of the current function or script (while still executing its remainder.)

For more information about PowerShell's debugging support, type **Get-Help about_Debuggers**.

## See Also

Recipe 14.7, "Program: Watch an Expression for Changes"

# 14.7. Program: Watch an Expression for Changes

When debugging a script (or even just generally using the shell), you might find yourself monitoring the same expression very frequently. This gets tedious to type by hand, so Example 14-6 simplifies the task by automatically displaying the value of expressions that interest you as part of your prompt.

*Example 14-6. Watch-DebugExpression.ps1*

```
##############################################################################
##
## Watch-DebugExpression
##
## From Windows PowerShell Cookbook (O'Reilly)
## by Lee Holmes (http://www.leeholmes.com/guide)
##
##############################################################################
```

```
<#

.SYNOPSIS

Updates your prompt to display the values of information you want to track.

.EXAMPLE

PS > Watch-DebugExpression { (Get-History).Count }

Expression          Value
----------          -----
(Get-History).Count     3

PS > Watch-DebugExpression { $count }

Expression          Value
----------          -----
(Get-History).Count     4
$count

PS > $count = 100

Expression          Value
----------          -----
(Get-History).Count     5
$count                100

PS > Watch-DebugExpression -Reset
PS >

#>

param(
    ## The expression to track
    [ScriptBlock] $ScriptBlock,

    ## Switch to no longer watch an expression
    [Switch] $Reset
)

Set-StrictMode -Version 3

if($Reset)
{
    Set-Item function:\prompt ([ScriptBlock]::Create($oldPrompt))

    Remove-Item variable:\expressionWatch
    Remove-Item variable:\oldPrompt

    return
}
```

```
## Create the variableWatch variable if it doesn't yet exist
if(-not (Test-Path variable:\expressionWatch))
{
    $GLOBAL:expressionWatch = @()
}

## Add the current variable name to the watch list
$GLOBAL:expressionWatch += $scriptBlock

## Update the prompt to display the expression values,
## if needed.
if(-not (Test-Path variable:\oldPrompt))
{
    $GLOBAL:oldPrompt = Get-Content function:\prompt
}

if($oldPrompt -notlike '*$expressionWatch*')
{
    $newPrompt = @'
        $results = foreach($expression in $expressionWatch)
        {
            New-Object PSObject -Property @{
                Expression = $expression.ToString().Trim();
                Value = & $expression
            } | Select Expression,Value
        }
        Write-Host "`n"
        Write-Host ($results | Format-Table -Auto | Out-String).Trim()
        Write-Host "`n"

'@

    $newPrompt += $oldPrompt

    Set-Item function:\prompt ([ScriptBlock]::Create($newPrompt))
}
```

For more information about running scripts, see Recipe 1.1, "Run Programs, Scripts, and Existing Tools".

## See Also

Recipe 1.1, "Run Programs, Scripts, and Existing Tools"

# 14.8. Program: Get Script Code Coverage

When developing a script, testing it (either automatically or by hand) is a critical step in knowing how well it does the job you think it does. While you can spend enormous amounts of time testing new and interesting variations in your script, how do you know when you are done?

Code coverage is the standard technique to answer this question. You instrument your script so that the system knows what portions it executed, and then review the report at the end to see which portions were *not* executed. If a portion was not executed during your testing, you have untested code and can improve your confidence in its behavior by adding more tests.

In PowerShell, we can combine two powerful techniques to create a code coverage analysis tool: the Tokenizer API and conditional breakpoints.

First, we use the Tokenizer API to discover all of the unique elements of our script: its statements, variables, loops, and more. Each token tells us the line and column that holds it, so we then create breakpoints for all of those line and column combinations.

When we hit a breakpoint, we record that we hit it and then continue.

Once the script in Example 14-7 completes, we can compare the entire set of tokens against the ones we actually hit. Any tokens that were not hit by a breakpoint represent gaps in our tests.

*Example 14-7. Get-ScriptCoverage.ps1*

```
##############################################################################
##
## Get-ScriptCoverage
##
## From Windows PowerShell Cookbook (O'Reilly)
## by Lee Holmes (http://www.leeholmes.com/guide)
##
##############################################################################

<#

.SYNOPSIS

Uses conditional breakpoints to obtain information about what regions of
a script are executed when run.

.EXAMPLE

PS > Get-Content c:\temp\looper.ps1

param($userInput)
```

```
for($count = 0; $count -lt 10; $count++)
{
    "Count is: $count"
}

if($userInput -eq "One")
{
    "Got 'One'"
}

if($userInput -eq "Two")
{
    "Got 'Two'"
}

PS > $action = { c:\temp\looper.ps1 -UserInput 'One' }
PS > $coverage = Get-ScriptCoverage c:\temp\looper.ps1 -Action $action
PS > $coverage | Select Content,StartLine,StartColumn | Format-Table -Auto

Content    StartLine StartColumn
-------    --------- -----------
userInput          1           7
Got 'Two'         15           5
```

This example exercises a 'looper.ps1' script, and supplies it with some
user input. The output demonstrates that we didn't exercise the
"Got 'Two'" statement.

```
#>

param(
    ## The path of the script to monitor
    $Path,

    ## The command to exercise the script
    [ScriptBlock] $Action = { & $path }
)

Set-StrictMode -Version 3

## Determine all of the tokens in the script
$scriptContent = Get-Content $path
$ignoreTokens = "Comment","NewLine","StatementSeparator","Keyword",
    "GroupStart","GroupEnd"
$tokens = [System.Management.Automation.PsParser]::Tokenize(
    $scriptContent, [ref] $null) |
    Where-Object { $ignoreTokens -notcontains $_.Type }
$tokens = $tokens | Sort-Object StartLine,StartColumn

## Create a variable to hold the tokens that PowerShell actually hits
$visited = New-Object System.Collections.ArrayList
```

```
## Go through all of the tokens
$breakpoints = foreach($token in $tokens)
{
    ## Create a new action. This action logs the token that we
    ## hit. We call GetNewClosure() so that the $token variable
    ## gets the _current_ value of the $token variable, as opposed
    ## to the value it has when the breakpoints gets hit.
    $breakAction = { $null = $visited.Add($token) }.GetNewClosure()

    ## Set a breakpoint on the line and column of the current token.
    ## We use the action from above, which simply logs that we've hit
    ## that token.
    Set-PsBreakpoint $path -Line `
        $token.StartLine -Column $token.StartColumn -Action $breakAction
}

## Invoke the action that exercises the script
$null = . $action

## Remove the temporary breakpoints we set
$breakpoints | Remove-PsBreakpoint

## Sort the tokens that we hit, and compare them with all of the tokens
## in the script. Output the result of that comparison.
$visited = $visited | Sort-Object -Unique StartLine,StartColumn
Compare-Object $tokens $visited -Property StartLine,StartColumn -PassThru

## Clean up our temporary variable
Remove-Item variable:\visited
```

For more information about running scripts, see Recipe 1.1, "Run Programs, Scripts, and Existing Tools".

## See Also

Recipe 1.1, "Run Programs, Scripts, and Existing Tools"

Recipe 10.10, "Parse and Interpret PowerShell Scripts"

Recipe 14.5, "Create a Conditional Breakpoint"

# Tracing and Error Management

## 15.0. Introduction

What if it doesn't all go according to plan? This is the core question behind error management in any system and it plays a large part in writing PowerShell scripts as well.

Although this is a chief concern in many systems, PowerShell's support for error management provides several unique features designed to make your job easier. The primary benefit is a distinction between terminating and nonterminating errors.

When you're running a complex script or scenario, the last thing you want is for your world to come crashing down because a script can't open one of the 1,000 files it is operating on. Although the system should make you aware of the failure, the script should still continue to the next file. That is an example of a nonterminating error. But what if the script runs out of disk space while running a backup? That should absolutely be an error that causes the script to exit—also known as a terminating error.

Given this helpful distinction, PowerShell provides several features that let you manage errors generated by scripts and programs, and also allows you to generate errors yourself.

## 15.1. Determine the Status of the Last Command

### Problem

You want to get status information about the last command you executed, such as whether it succeeded.

## Solution

Use one of the two variables PowerShell provides to determine the status of the last command you executed: the $lastExitCode variable and the $? variable.

$lastExitCode
> A number that represents the exit code/error level of the last script or application that exited

$? *(pronounced "dollar hook")*
> A Boolean value that represents the success or failure of the last command

## Discussion

The $lastExitCode PowerShell variable is similar to the %errorlevel% variable in DOS. It holds the exit code of the last application to exit. This lets you continue to interact with traditional executables (such as ping, findstr, and choice) that use exit codes as a primary communication mechanism. PowerShell also extends the meaning of this variable to include the exit codes of scripts, which can set their status using the exit statement. Example 15-1 demonstrates this interaction.

*Example 15-1. Interacting with the $lastExitCode and $? variables*

```
PS > ping localhost

Pinging MyComputer [127.0.0.1] with 32 bytes of data:

Reply from 127.0.0.1: bytes=32 time<1ms TTL=128
Reply from 127.0.0.1: bytes=32 time<1ms TTL=128
Reply from 127.0.0.1: bytes=32 time<1ms TTL=128
Reply from 127.0.0.1: bytes=32 time<1ms TTL=128

Ping statistics for 127.0.0.1:
    Packets: Sent = 4, Received = 4, Lost = 0 (0% loss),
Approximate round trip times in milliseconds:
    Minimum = 0ms, Maximum = 0ms, Average = 0ms
PS > $?
True
PS > $lastExitCode
0
PS > ping missing-host
Ping request could not find host missing-host. Please check the name and try again.
PS > $?
False
PS > $lastExitCode
1
```

The $? variable describes the exit status of the last application in a more general manner. PowerShell sets this variable to False on error conditions such as the following:

- An application exits with a nonzero exit code.
- A cmdlet or script writes anything to its error stream.
- A cmdlet or script encounters a terminating error or exception.

For commands that do not indicate an error condition, PowerShell sets the $? variable to True.

# 15.2. View the Errors Generated by a Command

## Problem

You want to view the errors generated in the current session.

## Solution

To access the list of errors generated so far, use the $error variable, as shown by Example 15-2.

*Example 15-2. Viewing errors contained in the $error variable*

```
PS > 1/0
Attempted to divide by zero.
At line:1 char:3
+ 1/ <<<< 0
    + CategoryInfo         : NotSpecified: (:) [], ParentContainsError
    RecordException
    + FullyQualifiedErrorId : RuntimeException


PS > $error[0] | Format-List -Force

ErrorRecord              : Attempted to divide by zero.
StackTrace               :    at System.Management.Automation.Expressio
                             (...)
WasThrownFromThrowStatement : False
Message                  : Attempted to divide by zero.
Data                     : {}
InnerException           : System.DivideByZeroException: Attempted to
                             divide by zero.
                               at System.Management.Automation.ParserOps
                             .PolyDiv(ExecutionContext context, Token op
                             Token, Object lval, Object rval)
TargetSite               : System.Collections.ObjectModel.Collection`1[
                             System.Management.Automation.PSObject] Invoke
                             (System.Collections.IEnumerable)
HelpLink                 :
Source                   : System.Management.Automation
```

## Discussion

The PowerShell $error variable always holds the list of errors generated so far in the current shell session. This list includes both terminating and nonterminating errors.

PowerShell displays fairly detailed information when it encounters an error:

```
PS > Stop-Process -name IDoNotExist
Stop-Process : Cannot find a process with the name "IDoNotExist". Verify
the process name and call the cmdlet again.
At line:1 char:13
+ Stop-Process <<<<  -name IDoNotExist
    + CategoryInfo          : ObjectNotFound: (IDoNotExist:String) [Stop-
  Process], ProcessCommandException
    + FullyQualifiedErrorId : NoProcessFoundForGivenName,Microsoft.Power
  Shell.Commands.StopProcessCommand
```

One unique feature about these errors is that they benefit from a diverse and international community of PowerShell users. Notice the FullyQualifiedErrorId line: an error identifier that remains the same no matter which language the error occurs in. When a user pastes this error message on an Internet forum, newsgroup, or blog, this fully qualified error ID never changes. English-speaking users can then benefit from errors posted by non-English-speaking PowerShell users, and vice versa.

If you want to view an error in a table or list (through the Format-Table or Format-List cmdlets), you must also specify the -Force option to override this customized view.

 For extremely detailed information about an error, see Recipe 15.4, "Program: Resolve an Error".

If you want to display errors in a more compact manner, PowerShell supports an additional view called CategoryView that you set through the $errorView preference variable:

```
PS > Get-ChildItem IDoNotExist
Get-ChildItem : Cannot find path 'C:\IDoNotExist' because it does not exist.
At line:1 char:14
+ Get-ChildItem <<<<  IDoNotExist
    + CategoryInfo          : ObjectNotFound: (C:\IDoNotExist:String)
  [Get-ChildItem], ItemNotFoundException
    + FullyQualifiedErrorId : PathNotFound,Microsoft.PowerShell.Commands.
  GetChildItemCommand

PS > $errorView = "CategoryView"
PS > Get-ChildItem IDoNotExist
ObjectNotFound: (C:\IDoNotExist:String) [Get-ChildItem], ItemNotFound
Exception
```

To clear the list of errors, call the `Clear()` method on the `$error` list:

```
PS > $error.Count
2
PS > $error.Clear()
PS > $error.Count
0
```

For more information about PowerShell's preference variables, type **Get-Help about_preference_variables**. If you want to determine only the success or failure of the last command, see Recipe 15.1, "Determine the Status of the Last Command".

### See Also

Recipe 15.1, "Determine the Status of the Last Command"

Recipe 15.4, "Program: Resolve an Error"

# 15.3. Manage the Error Output of Commands

## Problem

You want to display detailed information about errors that come from commands.

## Solution

To list all errors (up to `$MaximumErrorCount`) that have occurred in this session, access the `$error` array:

```
$error
```

To list the last error that occurred in this session, access the first element in the `$error` array:

```
$error[0]
```

To list detailed information about an error, pipe the error into the `Format-List` cmdlet with the `-Force` parameter:

```
$currentError = $error[0]
$currentError | Format-List -Force
```

To list detailed information about the command that caused an error, access its `InvocationInfo` property:

```
$currentError = $error[0]
$currentError.InvocationInfo
```

To display errors in a more succinct category-based view, change the `$errorView` variable to `"CategoryView"`:

```
$errorView = "CategoryView"
```

To clear the list of errors collected by PowerShell so far, call the `Clear()` method on the `$error` variable:

```
$error.Clear()
```

## Discussion

Errors are a simple fact of life in the administrative world. Not all errors mean disaster, though. Because of this, PowerShell separates errors into two categories: *nonterminating* and *terminating*.

Nonterminating errors are the most common type of error. They indicate that the cmdlet, script, function, or pipeline encountered an error that it was able to recover from or was able to continue past. An example of a nonterminating error comes from the `Copy-Item` cmdlet. If it fails to copy a file from one location to another, it can still proceed with the rest of the files specified.

A terminating error, on the other hand, indicates a deeper, more fundamental error in the operation. An example of this can again come from the `Copy-Item` cmdlet when you specify invalid command-line parameters.

Digging into an error (and its nested errors) can be cumbersome, so for a script that automates this task, see Recipe 15.4, "Program: Resolve an Error".

## See Also

Recipe 15.4, "Program: Resolve an Error"

# 15.4. Program: Resolve an Error

Analyzing an error frequently requires several different investigative steps: displaying the error, exploring its context, and analyzing its inner exceptions.

Example 15-3 automates these mundane tasks for you.

*Example 15-3. Resolve-Error.ps1*

```
##############################################################################
##
## Resolve-Error
##
## From Windows PowerShell Cookbook (O'Reilly)
## by Lee Holmes (http://www.leeholmes.com/guide)
##
##############################################################################

<#
```

```
.SYNOPSIS

Displays detailed information about an error and its context.

#>

param(
    ## The error to resolve
    $ErrorRecord = ($error[0])
)

Set-StrictMode -Off

""
"If this is an error in a script you wrote, use the Set-PsBreakpoint cmdlet"
"to diagnose it."
""

'Error details ($error[0] | Format-List * -Force)'
"-"*80
$errorRecord | Format-List * -Force

'Information about the command that caused this error ' +
    '($error[0].InvocationInfo | Format-List *)'
"-"*80
$errorRecord.InvocationInfo | Format-List *

'Information about the error''s target ' +
    '($error[0].TargetObject | Format-List *)'
"-"*80
$errorRecord.TargetObject | Format-List *

'Exception details ($error[0].Exception | Format-List * -Force)'
"-"*80

$exception = $errorRecord.Exception

for ($i = 0; $exception; $i++, ($exception = $exception.InnerException))
{
    "$i" * 80
    $exception | Format-List * -Force
}
```

For more information about running scripts, see Recipe 1.1, "Run Programs, Scripts, and Existing Tools".

## See Also

Recipe 1.1, "Run Programs, Scripts, and Existing Tools"

# 15.5. Configure Debug, Verbose, and Progress Output

## Problem

You want to manage the detailed debug, verbose, and progress output generated by cmdlets and scripts.

## Solution

To enable debug output for scripts and cmdlets that generate it:

```
$debugPreference = "Continue"
Start-DebugCommand
```

To enable verbose mode for a cmdlet that checks for the -Verbose parameter:

```
Copy-Item c:\temp\*.txt c:\temp\backup\ -Verbose
```

To disable progress output from a script or cmdlet that generates it:

```
$progressPreference = "SilentlyContinue"
Get-Progress.ps1
```

## Discussion

In addition to error output (as described in Recipe 15.3, "Manage the Error Output of Commands"), many scripts and cmdlets generate several other types of output. These include the following types:

*Debug output*

Helps you diagnose problems that may arise and can provide a view into the inner workings of a command. You can use the Write-Debug cmdlet to produce this type of output in a script or the WriteDebug() method to produce this type of output in a cmdlet. PowerShell displays this output in yellow by default, but you can customize it through the $host.PrivateData.Debug* color configuration variables.

*Verbose output*

Helps you monitor the actions of commands at a finer level than the default. You can use the Write-Verbose cmdlet to produce this type of output in a script or the WriteVerbose() method to produce this type of output in a cmdlet. PowerShell displays this output in yellow by default, but you can customize it through the $host.PrivateData.Verbose* color configuration variables.

*Progress output*

Helps you monitor the status of long-running commands. You can use the Write-Progress cmdlet to produce this type of output in a script or the WritePro gress() method to produce this type of output in a cmdlet. PowerShell displays this output in yellow by default, but you can customize the color through the $host.PrivateData.Progress* color configuration variables.

Some cmdlets generate verbose and debug output only if you specify the -Verbose and -Debug parameters, respectively.

> Like PowerShell's *parameter disambiguation* support that lets you type only as much of a parameter as is required to disambiguate it from other parameters of the same cmdlet, PowerShell supports *enumeration disambiguation* when parameter values are limited to a specific set of values. This is perhaps most useful when interactively running a command that you know will generate errors:
>
> ```
> PS > Get-ChildItem c:\windows -Recurse -ErrorAction Ignore
> PS > dir c:\windows -rec -ea ig
> ```

To configure the debug, verbose, and progress output of a script or cmdlet, modify the $debugPreference, $verbosePreference, and $progressPreference shell variables. These variables can accept the following values:

Ignore

Do not display this output, and do not add it to the $error collection. Only supported when supplied to the ErrorAction parameter of a command.

SilentlyContinue

Do not display this output, but add it to the $error collection.

Stop

Treat this output as an error.

Continue

Display this output.

Inquire

Display a continuation prompt for this output.

## See Also

Recipe 15.3, "Manage the Error Output of Commands"

# 15.6. Handle Warnings, Errors, and Terminating Errors

## Problem

You want to handle warnings, errors, and terminating errors generated by scripts or other tools that you call.

## Solution

To control how your script responds to warning messages, set the $warningPrefer ence variable. In this example, to ignore them:

```
$warningPreference = "SilentlyContinue"
```

To control how your script responds to nonterminating errors, set the $errorAction Preference variable. In this example, to ignore them:

```
$errorActionPreference = "SilentlyContinue"
```

To control how your script responds to terminating errors, you can use either the try/catch/finally statements or the trap statement. In this example, we output a message and continue with the script:

```
try
{
    1 / $null
}
catch [DivideByZeroException]
{
    "Don't divide by zero: $_"
}
finally
{
    "Script that will be executed even if errors occur in the try statement"
}
```

Use the trap statement if you want its error handling to apply to the entire scope:

```
trap [DivideByZeroException] { "Don't divide by zero!"; continue }
1 / $null
```

## Discussion

PowerShell defines several preference variables that help you control how your script reacts to warnings, errors, and terminating errors. As an example of these error management techniques, consider the following script.

```
##############################################################################
##
## Get-WarningsAndErrors
##
```

```
## From Windows PowerShell Cookbook (O'Reilly)
## by Lee Holmes (http://www.leeholmes.com/guide)
##
##############################################################################

<#

.SYNOPSIS

Demonstrates the functionality of the Write-Warning, Write-Error, and throw
statements

#>

Set-StrictMode -Version 3

Write-Warning "Warning: About to generate an error"
Write-Error "Error: You are running this script"
throw "Could not complete operation."
```

For more information about running scripts, see Recipe 1.1, "Run Programs, Scripts, and Existing Tools".

You can now see how a script might manage those separate types of errors:

```
PS > $warningPreference = "Continue"
PS > Get-WarningsAndErrors
WARNING: Warning: About to generate an error
Get-WarningsAndErrors : Error: You are running this script
At line:1 char:22
+ Get-WarningsAndErrors <<<<
    + CategoryInfo          : NotSpecified: (:) [Write-Error], WriteError
    Exception
    + FullyQualifiedErrorId : Microsoft.PowerShell.Commands.WriteError
    Exception,Get-WarningsAndErrors

Could not complete operation.
At line:15 char:6
+ throw <<<<  "Could not complete operation."
    + CategoryInfo          : OperationStopped: (Could not complete
    operation.:String) [], RuntimeException
    + FullyQualifiedErrorId : Could not complete operation.
```

Once you modify the warning preference, the original warning message gets suppressed. A value of SilentlyContinue is useful when you are expecting an error of some sort.

```
PS > $warningPreference = "SilentlyContinue"
PS > Get-WarningsAndErrors
Get-WarningsAndErrors : Error: You are running this script
At line:1 char:22
+ Get-WarningsAndErrors <<<<
    + CategoryInfo          : NotSpecified: (:) [Write-Error], WriteError
    Exception
```

```
    + FullyQualifiedErrorId : Microsoft.PowerShell.Commands.WriteError
    Exception,Get-WarningsAndErrors

Could not complete operation.
At line:15 char:6
+ throw <<<<  "Could not complete operation."
    + CategoryInfo          : OperationStopped: (Could not complete
    operation.:String) [], RuntimeException
        + FullyQualifiedErrorId : Could not complete operation.
```

When you modify the error preference, you suppress errors and exceptions as well:

```
PS > $errorActionPreference = "SilentlyContinue"
PS > Get-WarningsAndErrors
PS >
```

In addition to the $errorActionPreference variable, all cmdlets let you specify your preference during an individual call. With an error action preference of SilentlyContinue, PowerShell doesn't display or react to errors. It does, however, still add the error to the $error collection for futher processing. If you want to suppress even that, use an error action preference of Ignore.

```
PS > $errorActionPreference = "Continue"
PS > Get-ChildItem IDoNotExist
Get-ChildItem : Cannot find path '...\IDoNotExist' because it does not exist.
At line:1 char:14
+ Get-ChildItem  <<<< IDoNotExist
PS > Get-ChildItem IDoNotExist -ErrorAction SilentlyContinue
PS >
```

If you reset the error preference back to Continue, you can see the impact of a try/catch/finally statement. The message from the Write-Error call makes it through, but the exception does not:

```
PS > $errorActionPreference = "Continue"
PS > try { Get-WarningsAndErrors } catch { "Caught an error" }
Get-WarningsAndErrors : Error: You are running this script
At line:1 char:28
+ try { Get-WarningsAndErrors <<<<  } catch { "Caught an error" }
    + CategoryInfo          : NotSpecified: (:) [Write-Error], WriteError
    Exception
        + FullyQualifiedErrorId : Microsoft.PowerShell.Commands.WriteError
    Exception,Get-WarningsAndErrors

Caught an error
```

The try/catch/finally statement acts like the similar statement in other programming languages. First, it executes the code inside of its script block. If it encounters a terminating error, it executes the code inside of the catch script block. It executes the code in the finally statement no matter what—an especially useful feature for cleanup or error-recovery code.

A similar technique is the `trap` statement:

```
PS > $errorActionPreference = "Continue"
PS > trap { "Caught an error"; continue }; Get-WarningsAndErrors
Get-WarningsAndErrors : Error: You are running this script
At line:1 char:60
+ trap { "Caught an error"; continue }; Get-WarningsAndErrors <<<<
    + CategoryInfo          : NotSpecified: (:) [Write-Error], WriteError
   Exception
    + FullyQualifiedErrorId : Microsoft.PowerShell.Commands.WriteError
   Exception,Get-WarningsAndErrors

Caught an error
```

Within a `catch` block or `trap` statement, the `$_` (or `$PSItem`) variable represents the current exception or error being processed.

Unlike the `try` statement, the `trap` statement handles terminating errors for anything in the scope that defines it. For more information about scopes, see Recipe 3.6, "Control Access and Scope of Variables and Other Items".

 After handling an error, you can also remove it from the system's error collection by typing `$error.RemoveAt(0)`.

For more information about PowerShelll's automatic variables, type **Get-Help about _automatic_variables**. For more information about error management in PowerShell, see "Managing Errors" (page 909). For more detailed information about the valid settings of these preference variables, see Appendix A.

## See Also

Recipe 1.1, "Run Programs, Scripts, and Existing Tools"

Recipe 3.6, "Control Access and Scope of Variables and Other Items"

"Managing Errors" (page 909)

Appendix A, *PowerShell Language and Environment*

# 15.7. Output Warnings, Errors, and Terminating Errors

## Problem

You want your script to notify its caller of a warning, error, or terminating error.

## Solution

To write warnings and errors, use the `Write-Warning` and `Write-Error` cmdlets, respectively. Use the `throw` statement to generate a terminating error.

## Discussion

When you need to notify the caller of your script about an unusual condition, the `Write-Warning`, `Write-Error`, and `throw` statements are the way to do it. If your user should consider the message as more of a warning, use the `Write-Warning` cmdlet. If your script encounters an error (but can reasonably continue past that error), use the `Write-Error` cmdlet. If the error is fatal and your script simply cannot continue, use a `throw` statement.

For more information on generating these errors and handling them when thrown by other scripts, see Recipe 15.6, "Handle Warnings, Errors, and Terminating Errors". For more information about error management in PowerShell, see "Managing Errors" (page 909). For more information about running scripts, see Recipe 1.1, "Run Programs, Scripts, and Existing Tools".

## See Also

Recipe 1.1, "Run Programs, Scripts, and Existing Tools"

Recipe 15.6, "Handle Warnings, Errors, and Terminating Errors"

"Managing Errors" (page 909)

# 15.8. Program: Analyze a Script's Performance Profile

When you write scripts that heavily interact with the user, you may sometimes feel that your script could benefit from better performance.

The first rule for tackling performance problems is to measure the problem. Unless you can guide your optimization efforts with hard performance data, you are almost certainly directing your efforts to the wrong spots. Random cute performance improvements will quickly turn your code into an unreadable mess, often with no appreciable performance gain! Low-level optimization has its place, but it should always be guided by hard data that supports it.

The way to obtain hard performance data is from a profiler. PowerShell doesn't ship with a script profiler, but Example 15-4 uses PowerShell features to implement one.

*Example 15-4. Get-ScriptPerformanceProfile.ps1*

```
##############################################################################
##
```

```
## Get-ScriptPerformanceProfile
##
## From Windows PowerShell Cookbook (O'Reilly)
## by Lee Holmes (http://www.leeholmes.com/guide)
##
##############################################################################

<#

.SYNOPSIS

Computes the performance characteristics of a script, based on the transcript
of it running at trace level 1.

.DESCRIPTION

To profile a script:

    1) Turn on script tracing in the window that will run the script:
       Set-PsDebug -trace 1
    2) Turn on the transcript for the window that will run the script:
       Start-Transcript
       (Note the filename that PowerShell provides as the logging destination.)
    3) Type in the script name, but don't actually start it.
    4) Open another PowerShell window, and navigate to the directory holding
       this script.  Type in '.\Get-ScriptPerformanceProfile <transcript>',
       replacing <transcript> with the path given in step 2.  Don't
       press <Enter> yet.
    5) Switch to the profiled script window, and start the script.
       Switch to the window containing this script, and press <Enter>
    6) Wait until your profiled script exits, or has run long enough to be
       representative of its work.  To be statistically accurate, your script
       should run for at least ten seconds.
    7) Switch to the window running this script, and press a key.
    8) Switch to the window holding your profiled script, and type:
       Stop-Transcript
    9) Delete the transcript.

.NOTES

You can profile regions of code (i.e., functions) rather than just lines
by placing the following call at the start of the region:
    Write-Debug "ENTER <region_name>"
and the following call and the end of the region:
    Write-Debug "EXIT"
This is implemented to account exclusively for the time spent in that
region, and does not include time spent in regions contained within the
region.  For example, if FunctionA calls FunctionB, and you've surrounded
each by region markers, the statistics for FunctionA will not include the
statistics for FunctionB.

#>
```

```
param(
    ## The path of the transcript logfile
    [Parameter(Mandatory = $true)]
    $Path
)

Set-StrictMode -Version 3

function Main
{
    ## Run the actual profiling of the script.  $uniqueLines gets
    ## the mapping of line number to actual script content.
    ## $samples gets a hashtable mapping line number to the number of times
    ## we observed the script running that line.
    $uniqueLines = @{}
    $samples = GetSamples $uniqueLines

    "Breakdown by line:"
    "---------------------------"

    ## Create a new hashtable that flips the $samples hashtable --
    ## one that maps the number of times sampled to the line sampled.
    ## Also, figure out how many samples we got altogether.
    $counts = @{}
    $totalSamples = 0;
    foreach($item in $samples.Keys)
    {
        $counts[$samples[$item]] = $item
        $totalSamples += $samples[$item]
    }

    ## Go through the flipped hashtable, in descending order of number of
    ## samples.  As we do so, output the number of samples as a percentage of
    ## the total samples.  This gives us the percentage of the time our
    ## script spent executing that line.
    foreach($count in ($counts.Keys | Sort-Object -Descending))
    {
        $line = $counts[$count]
        $percentage = "{0:#0}" -f ($count * 100 / $totalSamples)
        "{0,3}%: Line {1,4} -{2}" -f $percentage,$line,
            $uniqueLines[$line]
    }

    ## Go through the transcript log to figure out which lines are part of
    ## any marked regions.  This returns a hashtable that maps region names
    ## to the lines they contain.
    ""
    "Breakdown by marked regions:"
    "---------------------------"
    $functionMembers = GenerateFunctionMembers
```

```
## For each region name, cycle through the lines in the region.  As we
## cycle through the lines, sum up the time spent on those lines and
## output the total.
foreach($key in $functionMembers.Keys)
{
    $totalTime = 0
    foreach($line in $functionMembers[$key])
    {
        $totalTime += ($samples[$line] * 100 / $totalSamples)
    }

    $percentage = "{0:#0}" -f $totalTime
    "{0,3}%: {1}" -f $percentage,$key
}
}

## Run the actual profiling of the script.  $uniqueLines gets
## the mapping of line number to actual script content.
## Return a hashtable mapping line number to the number of times
## we observed the script running that line.
function GetSamples($uniqueLines)
{
    ## Open the logfile.  We use the .Net file I/O, so that we keep
    ## monitoring just the end of the file.  Otherwise, we would make our
    ## timing inaccurate as we scan the entire length of the file every time.
    $logStream = [System.IO.File]::Open($Path, "Open", "Read", "ReadWrite")
    $logReader = New-Object System.IO.StreamReader $logStream

    $random = New-Object Random
    $samples = @{}

    $lastCounted = $null

    ## Gather statistics until the user presses a key.
    while(-not $host.UI.RawUI.KeyAvailable)
    {
        ## We sleep a slightly random amount of time.  If we sleep a constant
        ## amount of time, we run the very real risk of improperly sampling
        ## scripts that exhibit periodic behavior.
        $sleepTime = [int] ($random.NextDouble() * 100.0)
        Start-Sleep -Milliseconds $sleepTime

        ## Get any content produced by the transcript since our last poll.
        ## From that poll, extract the last DEBUG statement (which is the last
        ## line executed.)
        $rest = $logReader.ReadToEnd()
        $lastEntryIndex = $rest.LastIndexOf("DEBUG: ")

        ## If we didn't get a new line, then the script is still working on
        ## the last line that we captured.
        if($lastEntryIndex -lt 0)
        {
```

```
            if($lastCounted) { $samples[$lastCounted] ++ }
            continue;
        }

        ## Extract the debug line.
        $lastEntryFinish = $rest.IndexOf("\n", $lastEntryIndex)
        if($lastEntryFinish -eq -1) { $lastEntryFinish = $rest.length }

        $scriptLine = $rest.Substring(
            $lastEntryIndex, ($lastEntryFinish - $lastEntryIndex)).Trim()
        if($scriptLine -match 'DEBUG:[ \t]*([0-9]*)\+(.*)')
        {
            ## Pull out the line number from the line
            $last = $matches[1]

            $lastCounted = $last
            $samples[$last] ++

            ## Pull out the actual script line that matches the line number
            $uniqueLines[$last] = $matches[2]
        }

        ## Discard anything that's buffered during this poll, and start
        ## waiting again
        $logReader.DiscardBufferedData()
    }

    ## Clean up
    $logStream.Close()
    $logReader.Close()

    $samples
}

## Go through the transcript log to figure out which lines are part of any
## marked regions.  This returns a hashtable that maps region names to
## the lines they contain.
function GenerateFunctionMembers
{
    ## Create a stack that represents the callstack.  That way, if a marked
    ## region contains another marked region, we attribute the statistics
    ## appropriately.
    $callstack = New-Object System.Collections.Stack
    $currentFunction = "Unmarked"
    $callstack.Push($currentFunction)

    $functionMembers = @{}

    ## Go through each line in the transcript file, from the beginning
    foreach($line in (Get-Content $Path))
    {
        ## Check if we're entering a monitor block
```

```
## If so, store that we're in that function, and push it onto
## the callstack.
if($line -match 'write-debug "ENTER (.*)"')
{
    $currentFunction = $matches[1]
    $callstack.Push($currentFunction)
}
## Check if we're exiting a monitor block
## If so, clear the "current function" from the callstack,
## and store the new "current function" onto the callstack.
elseif($line -match 'write-debug "EXIT"')
{
    [void] $callstack.Pop()
    $currentFunction = $callstack.Peek()
}
## Otherwise, this is just a line with some code.
## Add the line number as a member of the "current function"
else
{
    if($line -match 'DEBUG:[ \t]*([0-9]*)\+')
    {
        ## Create the arraylist if it's not initialized
        if(-not $functionMembers[$currentFunction])
        {
            $functionMembers[$currentFunction] =
                New-Object System.Collections.ArrayList
        }

        ## Add the current line to the ArrayList
        $hitLines = $functionMembers[$currentFunction]
        if(-not $hitLines.Contains($matches[1]))
        {
            [void] $hitLines.Add($matches[1])
        }
    }
}
    }
}

    $functionMembers
}

. Main
```

For more information about running scripts, see Recipe 1.1, "Run Programs, Scripts, and Existing Tools".

## See Also

Recipe 1.1, "Run Programs, Scripts, and Existing Tools"

# Environmental Awareness

## 16.0. Introduction

While many of your scripts will be designed to work in isolation, you will often find it helpful to give your script information about its execution environment: its name, current working directory, environment variables, common system paths, and more.

PowerShell offers several ways to get at this information—from its cmdlets and built-in variables to features that it offers from the .NET Framework.

## 16.1. View and Modify Environment Variables

### Problem

You want to interact with your system's environment variables.

### Solution

To interact with environment variables, access them in almost the same way that you access regular PowerShell variables. The only difference is that you place env: between the dollar sign ($) and the variable name:

```
PS > $env:Username
Lee
```

You can modify environment variables this way, too. For example, to temporarily add the current directory to the path:

```
PS > Invoke-DemonstrationScript
The term 'Invoke-DemonstrationScript' is not recognized as the name of a cmdlet,
function, script file, or operable program. Check the spelling of the name, or
if a path was included, verify that the path is correct and try again.
```

```
At line:1 char:27
+ Invoke-DemonstrationScript <<<<
    + CategoryInfo          : ObjectNotFound: (Invoke-DemonstrationScript
    :String) [], CommandNotFoundException
    + FullyQualifiedErrorId : CommandNotFoundException


Suggestion [3,General]: The command Invoke-DemonstrationScript was not
found, but does exist in the current location. Windows PowerShell doesn't load
commands from the current location by default. If you trust this command,
instead type ".\Invoke-DemonstrationScript". See "get-help about_Command_
Precedence" for more details.

PS > $env:PATH = $env:PATH + ".;"
PS > Invoke-DemonstrationScript
The script ran!
```

## Discussion

In batch files, environment variables are the primary way to store temporary information or to transfer information between batch files. PowerShell variables and script parameters are more effective ways to solve those problems, but environment variables continue to provide a useful way to access common system settings, such as the system's path, temporary directory, domain name, username, and more.

PowerShell surfaces environment variables through its *environment provider*: a container that lets you work with environment variables much as you would work with items in the filesystem or registry providers. By default, PowerShell defines an *env:* drive (much like *c:* or *d:*) that provides access to this information:

```
PS > dir env:

Name                           Value
----                           -----
Path                           c:\progra~1\ruby\bin;C:\WINDOWS\system32;C:\
TEMP                           C:\DOCUME~1\Lee\LOCALS~1\Temp
SESSIONNAME                    Console
PATHEXT                        .COM;.EXE;.BAT;.CMD;.VBS;.VBE;.JS;.JSE;.WSF;
(...)
```

Since it is a regular PowerShell drive, the full way to get the value of an environment variable looks like this:

```
PS > Get-Content Env:\Username
Lee
```

When it comes to environment variables, though, that is a syntax you will almost never need to use, because of PowerShell's support for the Get-Content and Set-Content variable syntax, which shortens that to:

```
PS > $env:Username
Lee
```

This syntax works for all drives but is used most commonly to access environment variables. For more information about this syntax, see Recipe 16.3, "Access Information About Your Command's Invocation".

Some environment variables actually get their values from a combination of two places: the machine-wide settings and the current-user settings. If you want to access environment variable values specifically configured at the machine or user level, use the [Environment]::GetEnvironmentVariable() method. For example, if you've defined a *tools* directory in your path, you might see:

```
PS > [Environment]::GetEnvironmentVariable("Path", "User")
d:\lee\tools
```

To set these machine- or user-specific environment variables permanently, use the [Environment]::SetEnvironmentVariable() method:

```
[Environment]::SetEnvironmentVariable(<name>, <value>, <target>)
```

The *target* parameter defines where this variable should be stored: User for the current user and Machine for all users on the machine. For example, to permanently add your *tools* directory to your path:

```
$pathElements = @([Environment]::GetEnvironmentVariable("Path", "User") -split ";")
$pathElements += "d:\tools"
$newPath = $pathElements -join ";"
[Environment]::SetEnvironmentVariable("Path", $newPath, "User")
```

For more information about modifying the system path, see Recipe 16.2, "Modify the User or System Path".

For more information about the Get-Content and Set-Content variable syntax, see "Variables" (page 864). For more information about the environment provider, type **Get-Help About_Environment**.

## See Also

Recipe 16.2, "Modify the User or System Path"

Recipe 16.3, "Access Information About Your Command's Invocation"

"Variables" (page 864)

# 16.2. Modify the User or System Path

## Problem

You want to update your (or the system's) PATH variable.

## Solution

Use the `[Environment]::SetEnvironmentVariable()` method to set the `PATH` environment variable.

```
$scope = "User"
$pathElements = @([Environment]::GetEnvironmentVariable("Path", $scope)
                -split ";")
$pathElements += "d:\tools"
$newPath = $pathElements -join ";"
[Environment]::SetEnvironmentVariable("Path", $newPath, $scope)
```

## Discussion

In Windows, the `PATH` environment variable describes the list of directories that applications should search when looking for executable commands. As a convention, items in the path are separated by the semicolon character.

As mentioned in Recipe 16.1, "View and Modify Environment Variables", environment variables have two scopes: systemwide variables, and per-user variables. The `PATH` variable that you see when you type `$env:PATH` is the result of combining these two.

When you want to modify the path, you need to decide if you want the path changes to apply to all users on the system, or just yourself. If you want the changes to apply to the entire system, use a scope of `Machine` in the example given by the Solution. If you want it to apply just to your user account, use a scope of `User`.

As mentioned, elements in the path are separated by the semicolon character. To update the path, the Solution first uses the `-split` operator to create a list of the individual directories that were separated by semicolons. It adds a new element to the path, and then uses the `-join` operator to recombine the elements with the semicolon character. This helps prevent doubled-up semicolons, missing semicolons, or having to worry whether the semicolons go before the path element or after.

For more information about working with environment variables, see Recipe 16.1, "View and Modify Environment Variables".

## See Also

Recipe 16.1, "View and Modify Environment Variables"

# 16.3. Access Information About Your Command's Invocation

## Problem

You want to learn about how the user invoked your script, function, or script block.

## Solution

To access information about how the user invoked your command, use the `$PSScriptRoot`, `$PSCommandPath`, and `$myInvocation` variables:

```
"Script's path: $PSCommandPath"
"Script's location: $PSScriptRoot"
"You invoked this script by typing: " + $myInvocation.Line
```

## Discussion

The `$PSScriptRoot` and `$PSCommandPath` variables provide quick access to the information a command most commonly needs about itself: its full path and location.

In addition, the `$myInvocation` variable provides a great deal of information about the current script, function, or script block—and the context in which it was invoked:

MyCommand
: Information about the command (script, function, or script block) itself.

ScriptLineNumber
: The line number in the script that called this command.

ScriptName
: In a function or script block, the name of the script that called this command.

Line
: The verbatim text used in the line of script (or command line) that called this command.

InvocationName
: The name that the user supplied to invoke this command. This will be different from the information given by MyCommand if the user has defined an alias for the command.

PipelineLength
: The number of commands in the pipeline that invoked this command.

PipelinePosition
: The position of this command in the pipeline that invoked this command.

One important point about working with the `$myInvocation` variable is that it changes depending on the type of command from which you call it. If you access this information from a function, it provides information specific to that function—not the script from which it was called. Since scripts, functions, and script blocks are fairly unique, information in the `$myInvocation.MyCommand` variable changes slightly between the different command types.

### Scripts

Definition *and* `Path`
> The full path to the currently running script

`Name`
> The name of the currently running script

`CommandType`
> Always `ExternalScript`

### Functions

Definition *and* `ScriptBlock`
> The source code of the currently running function

`Options`
> The options (`None`, `ReadOnly`, `Constant`, `Private`, `AllScope`) that apply to the currently running function

`Name`
> The name of the currently running function

`CommandType`
> Always `Function`

### Script blocks

Definition *and* `ScriptBlock`
> The source code of the currently running script block

`Name`
> Empty

`CommandType`
> Always `Script`

# 16.4. Program: Investigate the InvocationInfo Variable

When you're experimenting with the information available through the `$myInvocation` variable, it is helpful to see how this information changes between scripts, functions, and script blocks. For a useful deep dive into the resources provided by the `$myInvocation` variable, review the output of Example 16-1.

*Example 16-1. Get-InvocationInfo.ps1*

```
##############################################################################
##
## Get-InvocationInfo
##
```

```
## From Windows PowerShell Cookbook (O'Reilly)
## by Lee Holmes (http://www.leeholmes.com/guide)
##
###############################################################################

<#

.SYNOPSIS

Display the information provided by the $myInvocation variable

#>

param(
    ## Switch to no longer recursively call ourselves
    [switch] $PreventExpansion
)

Set-StrictMode -Version 3

## Define a helper function, so that we can see how $myInvocation changes
## when it is called, and when it is dot-sourced
function HelperFunction
{
    "      MyInvocation from function:"
    "-"*50
    $myInvocation

    "      Command from function:"
    "-"*50
    $myInvocation.MyCommand
}

## Define a script block, so that we can see how $myInvocation changes
## when it is called, and when it is dot-sourced
$myScriptBlock = {
    "      MyInvocation from script block:"
    "-"*50
    $myInvocation

    "      Command from script block:"
    "-"*50
    $myInvocation.MyCommand
}

## Define a helper alias
Set-Alias gii .\Get-InvocationInfo

## Illustrate how $myInvocation.Line returns the entire line that the
## user typed.
"You invoked this script by typing: " + $myInvocation.Line
```

```
## Show the information that $myInvocation returns from a script
"MyInvocation from script:"
"-"*50
$myInvocation

"Command from script:"
"-"*50
$myInvocation.MyCommand

## If we were called with the -PreventExpansion switch, don't go
## any further
if($preventExpansion)
{
    return
}

## Show the information that $myInvocation returns from a function
"Calling HelperFunction"
"-"*50
HelperFunction

## Show the information that $myInvocation returns from a dot-sourced
## function
"Dot-Sourcing HelperFunction"
"-"*50
. HelperFunction

## Show the information that $myInvocation returns from an aliased script
"Calling aliased script"
"-"*50
gii -PreventExpansion

## Show the information that $myInvocation returns from a script block
"Calling script block"
"-"*50
& $myScriptBlock

## Show the information that $myInvocation returns from a dot-sourced
## script block
"Dot-Sourcing script block"
"-"*50
. $myScriptBlock

## Show the information that $myInvocation returns from an aliased script
"Calling aliased script"
"-"*50
gii -PreventExpansion
```

For more information about running scripts, see Recipe 1.1, "Run Programs, Scripts, and Existing Tools".

## See Also

Recipe 1.1, "Run Programs, Scripts, and Existing Tools"

# 16.5. Find Your Script's Name

## Problem

You want to know the path and name of the currently running script.

## Solution

To determine the full path and filename of the currently executing script, use the `$PSCommandPath` variable. To determine the text that the user actually typed to invoke your script (for example, in a "Usage" message), use the `$myInvocation.Invocation Name` variable.

## Discussion

Because it is so commonly used, PowerShell provides access to the script's full path through the `$PSCommandPath` variable. If you want to know just the name of the script (rather than its full path), use the `Split-Path` cmdlet:

```
$scriptName = Split-Path -Leaf $PSCommandPath
```

However, the `$PSCommandPath` variable was introduced in PowerShell version 3. If you need to access this information in PowerShell version 2, use this function:

```
function Get-ScriptName
{
    $myInvocation.ScriptName
}
```

By placing the `$myInvocation.ScriptName` statement in a function, we drastically simplify the logic it takes to determine the name of the currently running script. If you don't want to use a function, you can invoke a script block directly, which also simplifies the logic required to determine the current script's name:

```
$scriptName = & { $myInvocation.ScriptName }
```

Although this is a fairly complex way to get access to the current script's name, the alternative is a bit more error-prone. If you are in the body of a script, you can directly get the name of the current script by typing:

```
$myInvocation.Path
```

If you are in a function or script block, though, you must use:

```
$myInvocation.ScriptName
```

Working with the $myInvocation.InvocationName variable is sometimes tricky, as it returns the script name when called directly in the script, but not when called from a function in that script. If you need this information from a function, pass it to the function as a parameter.

For more information about working with the $myInvocation variable, see Recipe 16.3, "Access Information About Your Command's Invocation".

## See Also

Recipe 16.3, "Access Information About Your Command's Invocation"

# 16.6. Find Your Script's Location

## Problem

You want to know the location of the currently running script.

## Solution

To determine the location of the currently executing script, use the $PSScriptRoot variable. For example, to load a data file from the same location as your script:

```
$dataPath = Join-Path $PSScriptRoot data.clixml
```

Or to run a command from the same location as your script:

```
$helperUtility = Join-Path $PSScriptRoot helper.exe
& $helperUtility
```

## Discussion

Because it is so commonly used, PowerShell provides access to the script's location through the $PSScriptRoot variable. However, this variable was introduced in Power-Shell version 3. If you need to access this information in PowerShell version 2, use this function:

```
function Get-ScriptPath
{
    Split-Path $myInvocation.ScriptName
}
```

Once we know the full path to a script, the Split-Path cmdlet makes it easy to determine its location. Its sibling, the Join-Path cmdlet, makes it easy to form new paths from their components as well.

By accessing the $myInvocation.ScriptName variable in a function, we drastically simplify the logic it takes to determine the location of the currently running script. For a discussion about alternatives to using a function for this purpose, see Recipe 16.5, "Find Your Script's Name".

For more information about working with the $myInvocation variable, see Recipe 16.3, "Access Information About Your Command's Invocation".

For more information about the Join-Path cmdlet, see Recipe 16.9, "Safely Build File Paths Out of Their Components".

## See Also

Recipe 16.3, "Access Information About Your Command's Invocation"

Recipe 16.5, "Find Your Script's Name"

Recipe 16.9, "Safely Build File Paths Out of Their Components"

# 16.7. Find the Location of Common System Paths

## Problem

You want to know the location of common system paths and special folders, such as *My Documents* and *Program Files*.

## Solution

To determine the location of common system paths and special folders, use the [Environment]::GetFolderPath() method:

```
PS > [Environment]::GetFolderPath("System")
C:\WINDOWS\system32
```

For paths not supported by this method (such as *All Users Start Menu*), use the WScript.Shell COM object:

```
$shell = New-Object -Com WScript.Shell
$allStartMenu = $shell.SpecialFolders.Item("AllUsersStartMenu")
```

## Discussion

The [Environment]::GetFolderPath() method lets you access the many common locations used in Windows. To use it, provide the short name for the location (such as System or Personal). Since you probably don't have all these short names memorized, one way to see all these values is to use the [Enum]::GetValues() method, as shown in Example 16-2.

*Example 16-2. Folders supported by the [Environment]::GetFolderPath() method*

```
PS > [Enum]::GetValues([Environment+SpecialFolder])
Desktop
Programs
Personal
Favorites
Startup
Recent
SendTo
StartMenu
MyMusic
DesktopDirectory
MyComputer
Templates
ApplicationData
LocalApplicationData
InternetCache
Cookies
History
CommonApplicationData
System
ProgramFiles
MyPictures
CommonProgramFiles
```

Since this is such a common task for all enumerated constants, though, PowerShell actually provides the possible values in the error message if it is unable to convert your input:

```
PS > [Environment]::GetFolderPath("aouaoue")
Cannot convert argument "0", with value: "aouaoue", for "GetFolderPath" to
type "System.Environment+SpecialFolder": "Cannot convert value "aouaoue"
to type "System.Environment+SpecialFolder" due to invalid enumeration values.
Specify one of the following enumeration values and try again. The possible
enumeration values are "Desktop, Programs, Personal, MyDocuments, Favorites,
Startup, Recent, SendTo, StartMenu, MyMusic, DesktopDirectory, MyComputer,
Templates, ApplicationData, LocalApplicationData, InternetCache, Cookies,
History, CommonApplicationData, System, ProgramFiles, MyPictures,
CommonProgramFiles"."
At line:1 char:29
+ [Environment]::GetFolderPath( <<<< "aouaoue")
```

Although this method provides access to the most-used common system paths, it does not provide access to all of them. For the paths that the [Environment]::GetFolder Path() method does not support, use the WScript.Shell COM object. The WScript.Shell COM object supports the following paths: *AllUsersDesktop, AllUsers-StartMenu, AllUsersPrograms, AllUsersStartup, Desktop, Favorites, Fonts, MyDocuments, NetHood, PrintHood, Programs, Recent, SendTo, StartMenu, Startup,* and *Templates.*

---

It would be nice if you could use either the [Environment]::GetFolderPath() method *or* the WScript.Shell COM object, but each of them supports a significant number of paths that the other does not, as Example 16-3 illustrates.

*Example 16-3. Differences between folders supported by [Environment]::GetFolder-Path() and the WScript.Shell COM object*

```
PS > $shell = New-Object -Com WScript.Shell
PS > $shellPaths = $shell.SpecialFolders | Sort-Object
PS >
PS > $netFolders = [Enum]::GetValues([Environment+SpecialFolder])
PS > $netPaths = $netFolders |
    Foreach-Object { [Environment]::GetFolderPath($_) } | Sort-Object

PS > ## See the shell-only paths
PS > Compare-Object $shellPaths $netPaths |
    Where-Object { $_.SideIndicator -eq "<=" }


InputObject                                              SideIndicator
-----------                                              -------------
C:\Documents and Settings\All Users\Desktop              <=
C:\Documents and Settings\All Users\Start Menu           <=
C:\Documents and Settings\All Users\Start Menu\Programs  <=
C:\Documents and Settings\All Users\Start Menu\Programs\... <=
C:\Documents and Settings\Lee\NetHood                    <=
C:\Documents and Settings\Lee\PrintHood                  <=
C:\Windows\Fonts                                         <=


PS > ## See the .NET-only paths
PS > Compare-Object $shellPaths $netPaths |
    Where-Object { $_.SideIndicator -eq "=>" }


InputObject                                              SideIndicator
-----------                                              -------------
                                                         =>
C:\Documents and Settings\All Users\Application Data     =>
C:\Documents and Settings\Lee\Cookies                    =>
C:\Documents and Settings\Lee\Local Settings\Application... =>
C:\Documents and Settings\Lee\Local Settings\History     =>
C:\Documents and Settings\Lee\Local Settings\Temporary I... =>
C:\Program Files                                         =>
C:\Program Files\Common Files                            =>
C:\WINDOWS\system32                                      =>
d:\lee                                                   =>
D:\Lee\My Music                                          =>
D:\Lee\My Pictures                                       =>
```

For more information about working with classes from the .NET Framework, see Recipe 3.8, "Work with .NET Objects".

---

## See Also

Recipe 3.8, "Work with .NET Objects"

# 16.8. Get the Current Location

## Problem

You want to determine the current location.

## Solution

To determine the current location, use the `Get-Location` cmdlet:

```
PS > Get-Location

Path
----
C:\temp

PS > $currentLocation = (Get-Location).Path
PS > $currentLocation
C:\temp
```

In addition, PowerShell also provides access to the current location through the $pwd automatic variable:

```
PS > $pwd

Path
----
C:\temp

PS > $currentLocation = $pwd.Path
PS > $currentLocation
C:\temp
```

## Discussion

One problem that sometimes impacts scripts that work with the .NET Framework is that PowerShell's concept of "current location" isn't always the same as the *Power-Shell.exe* process's "current directory." Take, for example:

```
PS > Get-Location

Path
----
C:\temp
```

```
PS > Get-Process | Export-CliXml processes.xml
PS > $reader = New-Object Xml.XmlTextReader processes.xml
PS > $reader.BaseURI
file:///C:/Documents and Settings/Lee/processes.xml
```

PowerShell keeps these concepts separate because it supports multiple pipelines of execution. The process-wide current directory affects the entire process, so you would risk corrupting the environment of all background tasks as you navigate around the shell if that changed the process's current directory.

When you use filenames in most .NET methods, the best practice is to use fully qualified pathnames. The `Resolve-Path` cmdlet makes this easy:

```
PS > Get-Location

Path
----
C:\temp

PS > Get-Process | Export-CliXml processes.xml
PS > $reader = New-Object Xml.XmlTextReader (Resolve-Path processes.xml)
PS > $reader.BaseURI
file:///C:/temp/processes.xml
```

If you want to access a path that doesn't already exist, use the `Join-Path` cmdlet in combination with the `Get-Location` cmdlet:

```
PS > Join-Path (Get-Location) newfile.txt
C:\temp\newfile.txt
```

For more information about the `Join-Path` cmdlet, see Recipe 16.9, "Safely Build File Paths Out of Their Components".

## See Also

Recipe 16.9, "Safely Build File Paths Out of Their Components"

# 16.9. Safely Build File Paths Out of Their Components

## Problem

You want to build a new path out of a combination of subpaths.

## Solution

To join elements of a path together, use the `Join-Path` cmdlet:

```
PS > Join-Path (Get-Location) newfile.txt
C:\temp\newfile.txt
```

## Discussion

The usual way to create new paths is by combining strings for each component, placing a path separator between them:

```
PS > "$(Get-Location)\newfile.txt"
C:\temp\newfile.txt
```

Unfortunately, this approach suffers from a handful of problems:

- What if the directory returned by Get-Location already has a slash at the end?
- What if the path contains forward slashes instead of backslashes?
- What if we are talking about registry paths instead of filesystem paths?

Fortunately, the Join-Path cmdlet resolves these issues and more.

For more information about the Join-Path cmdlet, type **Get-Help Join-Path**.

# 16.10. Interact with PowerShell's Global Environment

## Problem

You want to store information in the PowerShell environment so that other scripts have access to it.

## Solution

To make a variable available to the entire PowerShell session, use a $GLOBAL: prefix when you store information in that variable:

```
## Create the web service cache, if it doesn't already exist
if(-not (Test-Path Variable:\Lee.Holmes.WebServiceCache))
{
    ${GLOBAL:Lee.Holmes.WebServiceCache} = @{}
}
```

## Discussion

The primary guidance when it comes to storing information in the session's global environment is to avoid it when possible. Scripts that store information in the global scope are prone to breaking other scripts and prone to being broken by other scripts.

This is a common practice in batch file programming, but script parameters and return values usually provide a much cleaner alternative.

Most scripts that use global variables do that to maintain state between invocations. PowerShell handles this in a much cleaner way through the use of *modules*. For information about this technique, see Recipe 11.7, "Write Commands That Maintain State".

If you do need to write variables to the global scope, make sure that you create them with a name unique enough to prevent collisions with other scripts, as illustrated in the Solution. Good options for naming prefixes are the script name, author's name, or company name.

For more information about setting variables at the global scope (and others), see Recipe 3.6, "Control Access and Scope of Variables and Other Items".

### See Also

Recipe 3.6, "Control Access and Scope of Variables and Other Items"

Recipe 11.7, "Write Commands That Maintain State"

# 16.11. Determine PowerShell Version Information

## Problem

You want information about the current PowerShell version, CLR version, compatible PowerShell versions, and more.

## Solution

Access the $PSVersionTable automatic variable:

```
PS > $psVersionTable

Name                           Value
----                           -----
PSVersion                      3.0
WSManStackVersion              3.0
SerializationVersion           1.1.0.1
CLRVersion                     4.0.30319.18010
BuildVersion                   6.2.9200.16384
PSCompatibleVersions           {1.0, 2.0, 3.0}
PSRemotingProtocolVersion      2.2
```

## Discussion

The $PSVersionTable automatic variable holds version information for all of Power-Shell's components: the PowerShell version, its build information, Common Language Runtime (CLR) version, and more.

This automatic variable was introduced in version 2 of PowerShell, so if your script might be launched in PowerShell version 1, you should use the `Test-Path` cmdlet to test for the existence of the `$PSVersionTable` automatic variable if your script needs to change its behavior:

```
if(Test-Path variable:\PSVersionTable)
{
    ...
}
```

This technique isn't completely sufficient for writing scripts that work in all versions of PowerShell, however. If your script uses language features introduced by newer versions of PowerShell (such as new keywords), the script will fail to load in earlier versions.

If the ability to run your script in multiple versions of PowerShell is a strong requirement, the best approach is to simply write a script that works in the oldest version of PowerShell that you need to support. It will automatically work in newer versions.

# 16.12. Test for Administrative Privileges

## Problem

You have a script that will fail if not run from an administrative session and want to detect this as soon as the script starts.

## Solution

Use the `IsInRole()` method of the `System.Security.Principal.WindowsPrincipal` class:

```
$identity = [System.Security.Principal.WindowsIdentity]::GetCurrent()
$principal = [System.Security.Principal.WindowsPrincipal] $identity
$role = [System.Security.Principal.WindowsBuiltInRole] "Administrator"

if(-not $principal.IsInRole($role))
{
    throw "This script must be run from an elevated shell."
}
```

## Discussion

Testing for administrative rights, while seemingly simple, is a much trickier task than might be expected.

Before PowerShell, many batch files tried to simply write a file into the operating system's installation directory. If that worked, you're an administrator so you can clean up and move on. If not, generate an error. But if you use `C:\Windows` as the path, your script will fail when somebody installs the operating system on a different drive. If you use the `%SYSTEMROOT%` environment variable, you still might trigger suspicion from antivirus programs.

As an improvement to that technique, some batch files try to parse the output of the `NET LOCALGROUP Administrators` command. Unfortunately, this fails on non-English machines, where the group name might be `NET LOCALGROUP Administratoren`. Most importantly, it detects only if the user is part of the Administrators group, not if his current shell is elevated and he can act as one.

Given that PowerShell has full access to the .NET Framework, the command becomes much simpler. The `System.Security.Principal.WindowsPrincipal` class provides a method to let you detect if the current session is acting in its administrative capacity.

This method isn't without its faults, though. Most examples that you'll find on the Internet are simply wrong. The most common example of applying this API uses this as the command: `$principal.IsInRole("Administrators")`. If you examine the method definitions, though, you'll see that the common example ends up calling the first overload definition that takes a string:

```
PS > $principal.IsInRole

OverloadDefinitions
-------------------
bool IsInRole(string role)
bool IsInRole(System.Security.Principal.WindowsBuiltInRole role)
bool IsInRole(int rid)
bool IsInRole(System.Security.Principal.SecurityIdentifier sid)
bool IPrincipal.IsInRole(string role)
```

If you look up the documentation, this string-based overload suffers from the same flaw that the `NET LOCALGROUP Administrators` command does: it relies on group names that change when the operating system language changes.

Fortunately, the API offers an overload that takes a `System.Security.Principal.Win dowsBuiltInRole` enumeration, and those values don't change between languages. This is the approach that the Solution relies upon.

For more information about dealing with .NET objects, see Recipe 3.8, "Work with .NET Objects".

## See Also

Recipe 3.8, "Work with .NET Objects"

# Extend the Reach of Windows PowerShell

## 17.0. Introduction

The PowerShell environment is phenomenally comprehensive. It provides a great surface of cmdlets to help you manage your system, a great scripting language to let you automate those tasks, and direct access to all the utilities and tools you already know.

The cmdlets, scripting language, and preexisting tools are just part of what makes PowerShell so comprehensive, however. In addition to these features, PowerShell provides access to a handful of technologies that drastically increase its capabilities: the .NET Framework, Windows Management Instrumentation (WMI), COM automation objects, native Windows API calls, and more.

Not only does PowerShell give you access to these technologies, but it also gives you access to them in a consistent way. The techniques you use to interact with properties and methods of PowerShell objects are the same techniques that you use to interact with properties and methods of .NET objects. In turn, those are the same techniques that you use to work with WMI and COM objects.

Working with these techniques and technologies provides another huge benefit—knowledge that easily transfers to working in .NET programming languages such as C#.

## 17.1. Automate Programs Using COM Scripting Interfaces

### Problem

You want to automate a program or system task through its COM automation interface.

## Solution

To instantiate and work with COM objects, use the New-Object cmdlet's -ComObject parameter.

```
$shell = New-Object -ComObject "Shell.Application"
$shell.Windows() | Format-Table LocationName,LocationUrl
```

## Discussion

Like WMI, COM automation interfaces have long been a standard tool for scripting and system administration. When an application exposes management or automation tasks, COM objects are the second most common interface (right after custom command-line tools).

PowerShell exposes COM objects like it exposes most other management objects in the system. Once you have access to a COM object, you work with its properties and methods in the same way that you work with methods and properties of other objects in PowerShell.

> Some COM objects require a special interaction mode called *multi-threaded apartment* (MTA) to work correctly. For information about how to interact with components that require MTA interaction, see Recipe 13.11, "Interact with MTA Objects".

In addition to automation tasks, many COM objects exist entirely to improve the scripting experience in languages such as VBScript. Two examples are working with files and sorting an array.

Most of these COM objects become obsolete in PowerShell, as PowerShell often provides better alternatives to them! In many cases, PowerShell's cmdlets, scripting language, or access to the .NET Framework provide the same or similar functionality to a COM object that you might be used to.

For more information about working with COM objects, see Recipe 3.12, "Use a COM Object". For a list of the most useful COM objects, see Appendix H.

## See Also

Recipe 3.12, "Use a COM Object"

Appendix H, *Selected COM Objects and Their Uses*

# 17.2. Program: Query a SQL Data Source

It is often helpful to perform ad hoc queries and commands against a data source such as a SQL server, Access database, or even an Excel spreadsheet. This is especially true when you want to take data from one system and put it in another, or when you want to bring the data into your PowerShell environment for detailed interactive manipulation or processing.

Although you can directly access each of these data sources in PowerShell (through its support of the .NET Framework), each data source requires a unique and hard-to-remember syntax. Example 17-1 makes working with these SQL-based data sources both consistent and powerful.

*Example 17-1. Invoke-SqlCommand.ps1*

```
##############################################################################
##
## Invoke-SqlCommand
##
## From Windows PowerShell Cookbook (O'Reilly)
## by Lee Holmes (http://www.leeholmes.com/guide)
##
##############################################################################

<#

.SYNOPSIS

Return the results of a SQL query or operation

.EXAMPLE

Invoke-SqlCommand.ps1 -Sql "SELECT TOP 10 * FROM Orders"
Invokes a command using Windows authentication

.EXAMPLE

PS > $cred = Get-Credential
PS > Invoke-SqlCommand.ps1 -Sql "SELECT TOP 10 * FROM Orders" -Cred $cred
Invokes a command using SQL Authentication

.EXAMPLE

PS > $server = "MYSERVER"
PS > $database = "Master"
PS > $sql = "UPDATE Orders SET EmployeeID = 6 WHERE OrderID = 10248"
PS > Invoke-SqlCommand $server $database $sql
Invokes a command that performs an update

.EXAMPLE
```

```
PS > $sql = "EXEC SalesByCategory 'Beverages'"
PS > Invoke-SqlCommand -Sql $sql
Invokes a stored procedure

.EXAMPLE

PS > Invoke-SqlCommand (Resolve-Path access_test.mdb) -Sql "SELECT * FROM Users"
Access an Access database

.EXAMPLE

PS > Invoke-SqlCommand (Resolve-Path xls_test.xls) -Sql 'SELECT * FROM [Sheet1$]'
Access an Excel file

#>

param(
    ## The data source to use in the connection
    [string] $DataSource = ".\SQLEXPRESS",

    ## The database within the data source
    [string] $Database = "Northwind",

    ## The SQL statement(s) to invoke against the database
    [Parameter(Mandatory = $true)]
    [string[]] $SqlCommand,

    ## The timeout, in seconds, to wait for the query to complete
    [int] $Timeout = 60,

    ## The credential to use in the connection, if any.
    $Credential
)


Set-StrictMode -Version 3

## Prepare the authentication information. By default, we pick
## Windows authentication
$authentication = "Integrated Security=SSPI;"

## If the user supplies a credential, then they want SQL
## authentication
if($credential)
{
    $credential = Get-Credential $credential
    $plainCred = $credential.GetNetworkCredential()
    $authentication =
        ("uid={0};pwd={1};" -f $plainCred.Username,$plainCred.Password)
}

## Prepare the connection string out of the information they provide
```

```
$connectionString = "Provider=sqloledb; " +
                    "Data Source=$dataSource; " +
                    "Initial Catalog=$database; " +
                    "$authentication; "

## If they specify an Access database or Excel file as the connection
## source, modify the connection string to connect to that data source
if($dataSource -match '\.xls$|\.mdb$')
{
    $connectionString = "Provider=Microsoft.Jet.OLEDB.4.0; " +
        "Data Source=$dataSource; "

    if($dataSource -match '\.xls$')
    {
        $connectionString += 'Extended Properties="Excel 8.0;"; '

        ## Generate an error if they didn't specify the sheet name properly
        if($sqlCommand -notmatch '\[.+\$\]')
        {
            $error = 'Sheet names should be surrounded by square brackets, ' +
                'and have a dollar sign at the end: [Sheet1$]'
            Write-Error $error
            return
        }
    }
}

## Connect to the data source and open it
$connection = New-Object System.Data.OleDb.OleDbConnection $connectionString
$connection.Open()

foreach($commandString in $sqlCommand)
{
    $command = New-Object Data.OleDb.OleDbCommand $commandString,$connection
    $command.CommandTimeout = $timeout

    ## Fetch the results, and close the connection
    $adapter = New-Object System.Data.OleDb.OleDbDataAdapter $command
    $dataset = New-Object System.Data.DataSet
    [void] $adapter.Fill($dataSet)

    ## Return all of the rows from their query
    $dataSet.Tables | Select-Object -Expand Rows
}

$connection.Close()
```

For more information about running scripts, see Recipe 1.1, "Run Programs, Scripts, and Existing Tools".

## See Also

Recipe 1.1, "Run Programs, Scripts, and Existing Tools"

# 17.3. Access Windows Performance Counters

## Problem

You want to access system performance counter information from PowerShell.

## Solution

To retrieve information about a specific performance counter, use the Get-Counter cmdlet, as shown in Example 17-2.

*Example 17-2. Accessing performance counter data through the Get-Counter cmdlet*

```
PS > $counter = Get-Counter "\System\System Up Time"
PS > $uptime = $counter.CounterSamples[0].CookedValue
PS > New-TimeSpan -Seconds $uptime


Days              : 8
Hours             : 1
Minutes           : 38
Seconds           : 58
Milliseconds      : 0
Ticks             : 6971380000000
TotalDays         : 8.06872685185185
TotalHours        : 193.649444444444
TotalMinutes      : 11618.9666666667
TotalSeconds      : 697138
TotalMilliseconds : 697138000
```

Alternatively, WMI's Win32_Perf* set of classes supports many of the most common performance counters:

```
Get-CimInstance Win32_PerfFormattedData_Tcpip_NetworkInterface
```

## Discussion

The Get-Counter cmdlet provides handy access to all Windows performance counters. With no parameters, it summarizes system activity:

```
PS > Get-Counter -Continuous

Timestamp                CounterSamples
---------                --------------
1/9/2010 7:26:49 PM      \\...\network interface(ethernet
                         adapter)\bytes total/sec :
```

---

```
102739.3921377

\\...\processor(_total)\% processor
time :
35.6164383561644

\\...\memory\% committed bytes in use
:
29.4531607006855

\\...\memory\cache faults/sec :
98.1952324093294

\\...\physicaldisk(_total)\% disk time
:
144.227945205479

\\...\physicaldisk(_total)\current disk
queue length :
0
```

(...)

When you supply a path to a specific counter, the Get-Counter cmdlet retrieves only the samples for that path. The -Computer parameter lets you target a specific remote computer, if desired:

```
PS > $computer = $ENV:Computername
PS > Get-Counter -Computer $computer "processor(_total)\% processor time"

Timestamp               CounterSamples
---------               --------------
1/9/2010 7:31:58 PM     \\...\processor(_total)\% processor time :
                        15.8710351576814
```

If you don't know the path to the performance counter you want, you can use the -ListSet parameter to search for a counter or set of counters. To see all counter sets, use * as the parameter value:

```
PS > Get-Counter -List * | Format-List CounterSetName,Description


CounterSetName : TBS counters
Description    : Performance counters for the TPM Base Services component.

CounterSetName : WSMan Quota Statistics
Description    : Displays quota usage and violation information for WS-
                 Management processes.

CounterSetName : Netlogon
Description    : Counters for measuring the performance of Netlogon.
```

(...)

If you want to find a specific counter, use the `Where-Object` cmdlet to compare against the `Description` or `Paths` property:

```
Get-Counter -ListSet * | Where-Object { $_.Description -match "garbage" }
Get-Counter -ListSet * | Where-Object { $_.Paths -match "Gen 2 heap" }
```

```
CounterSetName      : .NET CLR Memory
MachineName         : .
CounterSetType      : MultiInstance
Description         : Counters for CLR Garbage Collected heap.
Paths              : {\.NET CLR Memory(*)\# Gen 0 Collections, \.NET CLR
                     Memory(*)\# Gen 1 Collections, \.NET CLR Memory(*)\#
                     Gen 2 Collections, \.NET CLR Memory(*)\Promoted Memory
                     from Gen 0...}
PathsWithInstances : {\.NET CLR Memory(_Global_)\# Gen 0 Collections, \.NET
                     CLR Memory(powershell)\# Gen 0 Collections, \.NET CLR
                     Memory(powershell_ise)\# Gen 0 Collections, \.NET
                     CLR Memory(PresentationFontCache)\# Gen 0 Collections
                     ...}
Counter            : {\.NET CLR Memory(*)\# Gen 0 Collections, \.NET CLR
                     Memory(*)\# Gen 1 Collections, \.NET CLR Memory(*)\#
                     Gen 2 Collections, \.NET CLR Memory(*)\Promoted Memory
                     from Gen 0...}
```

Once you've retrieved a set of counters, you can use the `Export-Counter` cmdlet to save them in a format supported by other tools, such as the *.blg* files supported by the Windows Performance Monitor application.

If you already have a set of performance counters saved in a *.blg* file or *.tsv* file that were exported from Windows Performance Monitor, you can use the `Import-Counter` cmdlet to work with those samples in PowerShell.

# 17.4. Access Windows API Functions

## Problem

You want to access functions from the Windows API, as you would access them through a Platform Invoke (P/Invoke) in a .NET language such as C#.

## Solution

As shown in Example 17-3, obtain (or create) the signature of the Windows API function, and then pass that to the `-MemberDefinition` parameter of the `Add-Type` cmdlet. Store the output object in a variable, and then use the method on that variable to invoke the Windows API function.

*Example 17-3. Get-PrivateProfileString.ps1*

```
###############################################################################
##
## Get-PrivateProfileString
##
## From Windows PowerShell Cookbook (O'Reilly)
## by Lee Holmes (http://www.leeholmes.com/guide)
##
###############################################################################

<#

.SYNOPSIS

Retrieves an element from a standard .INI file

.EXAMPLE

PS > Get-PrivateProfileString c:\windows\system32\tcpmon.ini `
    "<Generic Network Card>" Name
Generic Network Card

#>

param(
    ## The INI file to retrieve
    $Path,

    ## The section to retrieve from
    $Category,

    ## The item to retrieve
    $Key
)

Set-StrictMode -Version 3

## The signature of the Windows API that retrieves INI
## settings
$signature = @'
[DllImport("kernel32.dll")]
public static extern uint GetPrivateProfileString(
    string lpAppName,
    string lpKeyName,
    string lpDefault,
    StringBuilder lpReturnedString,
    uint nSize,
    string lpFileName);
'@
```

```
## Create a new type that lets us access the Windows API function
$type = Add-Type -MemberDefinition $signature `
    -Name Win32Utils -Namespace GetPrivateProfileString `
    -Using System.Text -PassThru

## The GetPrivateProfileString function needs a StringBuilder to hold
## its output. Create one, and then invoke the method
$builder = New-Object System.Text.StringBuilder 1024
$null = $type::GetPrivateProfileString($category,
    $key, "", $builder, $builder.Capacity, $path)

## Return the output
$builder.ToString()
```

## Discussion

You can access many simple Windows APIs using the script given in Recipe 17.5, "Program: Invoke Simple Windows API Calls". This approach is difficult for more complex APIs, however.

To support interacting with Windows APIs, use PowerShell's Add-Type cmdlet.

Add-Type offers four basic modes of operation:

```
PS > Get-Command Add-Type | Select -Expand ParameterSets | Select Name

Name
----
FromSource
FromMember
FromPath
FromAssemblyName
```

These modes of operation are:

FromSource

Compile some C# (or other language) code that completely defines a type. This is useful when you want to define an entire class, its methods, namespace, etc. You supply the actual code as the value to the -TypeDefinition parameter, usually through a variable. For more information about this technique, see Recipe 17.6, "Define or Extend a .NET Class".

FromPath

Compile from a file on disk, or load the types from an assembly at that location. For more information about this technique, see Recipe 17.8, "Access a .NET SDK Library".

FromAssemblyName

Load an assembly from the .NET Global Assembly Cache (GAC) by its shorter name. This is not the same as the [Reflection.Assembly]::LoadWithPartial Name method, since that method introduces your script to many subtle breaking changes. Instead, PowerShell maintains a large mapping table that converts the shorter name you type into a strongly named assembly reference. For more information about this technique, see Recipe 17.8, "Access a .NET SDK Library".

FromMember

Generates a type out of a member definition (or a set of them). For example, if you specify only a method definition, PowerShell automatically generates the wrapper class for you. This parameter set is explicitly designed to easily support P/Invoke calls.

Now, how do you use the FromMember parameter set to call a Windows API? The Solution shows the end result of this process, but let's take it step by step. First, imagine that you want to access sections of an INI file.

PowerShell doesn't have a native way to manage INI files, and neither does the .NET Framework. However, the Windows API does, through a call to the function called GetPrivateProfileString. The .NET Framework lets you access Windows functions through a technique called *P/Invoke* (Platform Invocation Services). Most calls boil down to a simple *P/Invoke definition*, which usually takes a lot of trial and error. However, a great community has grown around these definitions, resulting in an enormous resource called P/Invoke .NET (*http://www.pinvoke.net/*). The .NET Framework team also supports a tool called the P/Invoke Interop Assistant that generates these definitions as well, but we won't consider that for now.

First, we'll create a script called *Get-PrivateProfileString.ps1*. It's a template for now:

```
## Get-PrivateProfileString.ps1
param(
    $Path,
    $Category,
    $Key)

$null
```

To start fleshing this out, we visit P/Invoke .NET and search for GetPrivateProfile String, as shown in Figure 17-1.

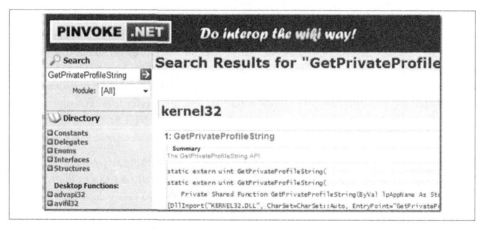

Figure 17-1. Visiting P/Invoke .NET

Click into the definition, and we see the C# signature, as shown in Figure 17-2.

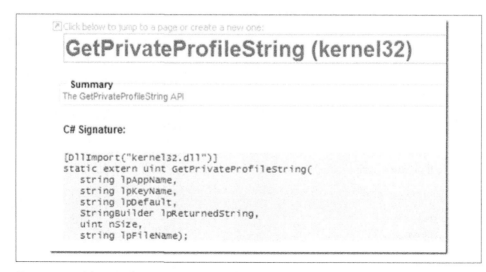

Figure 17-2. The Windows API signature for GetPrivateProfileString

Next, we copy that signature as a here string into our script. Notice in the following code example that we've added public to the declaration. The signatures on P/Invoke .NET assume that you'll call the method from within the C# class that defines it. We'll be calling it from scripts (which are outside of the C# class that defines it), so we need to change its visibility.

```
## Get-PrivateProfileString.ps1
param(
    $Path,
```

```
        $Category,
        $Key)

$signature = @'
[DllImport("kernel32.dll")]
public static extern uint GetPrivateProfileString(
    string lpAppName,
    string lpKeyName,
    string lpDefault,
    StringBuilder lpReturnedString,
    uint nSize,
    string lpFileName);
'@

$null
```

Now we add the call to Add-Type. This signature becomes the building block for a new class, so we only need to give it a name. To prevent its name from colliding with other classes with the same name, we also put it in a namespace. The name of our script is a good choice:

```
## Get-PrivateProfileString.ps1
param(
    $Path,
    $Category,
    $Key)

$signature = @'
[DllImport("kernel32.dll")]
public static extern uint GetPrivateProfileString(
    string lpAppName,
    string lpKeyName,
    string lpDefault,
    StringBuilder lpReturnedString,
    uint nSize,
    string lpFileName);
'@

$type = Add-Type -MemberDefinition $signature `
    -Name Win32Utils -Namespace GetPrivateProfileString `
    -PassThru

$null
```

When we try to run this script, though, we get an error:

```
The type or namespace name 'StringBuilder' could not be found (are you missing a
using directive or an assembly reference?)
c:\Temp\obozeqo1.0.cs(12) :    string lpDefault,
c:\Temp\obozeqo1.0.cs(13) : >>>    StringBuilder lpReturnedString,
c:\Temp\obozeqo1.0.cs(14) :    uint nSize,
```

Indeed we are missing something. The `StringBuilder` class is defined in the `System.Text` namespace, which requires a `using` directive to be placed at the top of the program by the class definition. Since we're letting PowerShell define the type for us, we can either rename `StringBuilder` to `System.Text.StringBuilder` or add a `-Using Namespace` parameter to have PowerShell add the using statement for us.

 PowerShell adds references to the `System` and `System.Runtime.Inter opServices` namespaces by default.

Let's do the latter:

```
## Get-PrivateProfileString.ps1
param(
    $Path,
    $Category,
    $Key)

$signature = @'
[DllImport("kernel32.dll")]
public static extern uint GetPrivateProfileString(
    string lpAppName,
    string lpKeyName,
    string lpDefault,
    StringBuilder lpReturnedString,
    uint nSize,
    string lpFileName);
'@

$type = Add-Type -MemberDefinition $signature `
    -Name Win32Utils -Namespace GetPrivateProfileString `
    -Using System.Text -PassThru

$builder = New-Object System.Text.StringBuilder 1024
$null = $type::GetPrivateProfileString($category,
    $key, "", $builder, $builder.Capacity, $path)

$builder.ToString()
```

Now we can plug in all of the necessary parameters. The `GetPrivateProfileString` function puts its output in a `StringBuilder`, so we'll have to feed it one and return its contents. This gives us the script shown in Example 17-3.

```
PS > Get-PrivateProfileString c:\windows\system32\tcpmon.ini `
    "<Generic Network Card>" Name
Generic Network Card
```

So now we have it. With just a few lines of code, we've defined and invoked a Win32 API call.

---

For more information about working with classes from the .NET Framework, see Recipe 1.1, "Run Programs, Scripts, and Existing Tools".

## See Also

Recipe 1.1, "Run Programs, Scripts, and Existing Tools"

Recipe 17.5, "Program: Invoke Simple Windows API Calls"

Recipe 17.6, "Define or Extend a .NET Class"

Recipe 17.8, "Access a .NET SDK Library"

# 17.5. Program: Invoke Simple Windows API Calls

There are times when neither PowerShell's cmdlets nor its scripting language directly support a feature you need. In most of those situations, PowerShell's direct support for the .NET Framework provides another avenue to let you accomplish your task. In some cases, though, even the .NET Framework does not support a feature you need to resolve a problem, and the only solution is to access the core Windows APIs.

For complex API calls (ones that take highly structured data), the solution is to use the Add-Type cmdlet (or write a PowerShell cmdlet) that builds on the Platform Invoke (P/Invoke) support in the .NET Framework. The P/Invoke support in the .NET Framework is designed to let you access core Windows APIs directly.

Although it is possible to determine these P/Invoke definitions yourself, it is usually easiest to build on the work of others. If you want to know how to call a specific Windows API from a .NET language, the P/Invoke .NET website (*http://www.pinvoke.net*) is the best place to start.

If the API you need to access is straightforward (one that takes and returns only simple data types), however, Example 17-4 can do most of the work for you.

For an example of this script in action, see Recipe 20.24, "Program: Create a Filesystem Hard Link".

*Example 17-4. Invoke-WindowsApi.ps1*

```
##############################################################################
##
## Invoke-WindowsApi
##
## From Windows PowerShell Cookbook (O'Reilly)
## by Lee Holmes (http://www.leeholmes.com/guide)
##
##############################################################################

<#
```

```
.SYNOPSIS

Invoke a native Windows API call that takes and returns simple data types.

.EXAMPLE

## Prepare the parameter types and parameters for the CreateHardLink function
PS > $filename = "c:\temp\hardlinked.txt"
PS > $existingFilename = "c:\temp\link_target.txt"
PS > Set-Content $existingFilename "Hard Link target"
PS > $parameterTypes = [string], [string], [IntPtr]
PS > $parameters = [string] $filename, [string] $existingFilename,
    [IntPtr]::Zero

## Call the CreateHardLink method in the Kernel32 DLL
PS > $result = Invoke-WindowsApi "kernel32" ([bool]) "CreateHardLink" `
    $parameterTypes $parameters
PS > Get-Content C:\temp\hardlinked.txt
Hard Link target

#>

param(
    ## The name of the DLL that contains the Windows API, such as "kernel32"
    [string] $DllName,

    ## The return type expected from Windows API
    [Type] $ReturnType,

    ## The name of the Windows API
    [string] $MethodName,

    ## The types of parameters expected by the Windows API
    [Type[]] $ParameterTypes,

    ## Parameter values to pass to the Windows API
    [Object[]] $Parameters
)

Set-StrictMode -Version 3

## Begin to build the dynamic assembly
$domain = [AppDomain]::CurrentDomain
$name = New-Object Reflection.AssemblyName 'PInvokeAssembly'
$assembly = $domain.DefineDynamicAssembly($name, 'Run')
$module = $assembly.DefineDynamicModule('PInvokeModule')
$type = $module.DefineType('PInvokeType', "Public,BeforeFieldInit")

## Go through all of the parameters passed to us.  As we do this,
## we clone the user's inputs into another array that we will use for
## the P/Invoke call.
```

```
$inputParameters = @()
$refParameters = @()

for($counter = 1; $counter -le $parameterTypes.Length; $counter++)
{
    ## If an item is a PSReference, then the user
    ## wants an [out] parameter.
    if($parameterTypes[$counter - 1] -eq [Ref])
    {
        ## Remember which parameters are used for [Out] parameters
        $refParameters += $counter

        ## On the cloned array, we replace the PSReference type with the
        ## .Net reference type that represents the value of the PSReference,
        ## and the value with the value held by the PSReference.
        $parameterTypes[$counter - 1] =
            $parameters[$counter - 1].Value.GetType().MakeByRefType()
        $inputParameters += $parameters[$counter - 1].Value
    }
    else
    {
        ## Otherwise, just add their actual parameter to the
        ## input array.
        $inputParameters += $parameters[$counter - 1]
    }
}

## Define the actual P/Invoke method, adding the [Out]
## attribute for any parameters that were originally [Ref]
## parameters.
$method = $type.DefineMethod(
    $methodName, 'Public,HideBySig,Static,PinvokeImpl',
    $returnType, $parameterTypes)
foreach($refParameter in $refParameters)
{
    [void] $method.DefineParameter($refParameter, "Out", $null)
}

## Apply the P/Invoke constructor
$ctor = [Runtime.InteropServices.DllImportAttribute].GetConstructor([string])
$attr = New-Object Reflection.Emit.CustomAttributeBuilder $ctor, $dllName
$method.SetCustomAttribute($attr)

## Create the temporary type, and invoke the method.
$realType = $type.CreateType()

$realType.InvokeMember(
    $methodName, 'Public,Static,InvokeMethod', $null, $null,$inputParameters)

## Finally, go through all of the reference parameters, and update the
## values of the PSReference objects that the user passed in.
```

```
foreach($refParameter in $refParameters)
{
    $parameters[$refParameter - 1].Value = $inputParameters[$refParameter - 1]
}
```

For more information about running scripts, see Recipe 1.1, "Run Programs, Scripts, and Existing Tools".

## See Also

Recipe 1.1, "Run Programs, Scripts, and Existing Tools"

Recipe 20.24, "Program: Create a Filesystem Hard Link"

# 17.6. Define or Extend a .NET Class

## Problem

You want to define a new .NET class or extend an existing one.

## Solution

Use the -TypeDefinition parameter of the Add-Type class, as in Example 17-5.

*Example 17-5. Invoke-AddTypeTypeDefinition.ps1*

```
##############################################################################
##
## Invoke-AddTypeTypeDefinition
##
## From Windows PowerShell Cookbook (O'Reilly)
## by Lee Holmes (http://www.leeholmes.com/guide)
##
##############################################################################

<#

.SYNOPSIS

Demonstrates the use of the -TypeDefinition parameter of the Add-Type
cmdlet.

#>

Set-StrictMode -Version 3

## Define the new C# class
$newType = @'
using System;
```

```
namespace PowerShellCookbook
{
    public class AddTypeTypeDefinitionDemo
    {
        public string SayHello(string name)
        {
            string result = String.Format("Hello {0}", name);
            return result;
        }
    }
}

'@

## Add it to the Powershell session
Add-Type -TypeDefinition $newType

## Show that we can access it like any other .NET type
$greeter = New-Object PowerShellCookbook.AddTypeTypeDefinitionDemo
$greeter.SayHello("World")
```

## Discussion

The Add-Type cmdlet is one of the major aspects of the *glue-like* nature of PowerShell, and it offers several unique ways to interact deeply with the .NET Framework. One of its major modes of operation comes from the -TypeDefinition parameter, which lets you define entirely new .NET classes. In addition to the example given in the Solution, Recipe 3.7, "Program: Create a Dynamic Variable" demonstrates an effective use of this technique.

Once you call the Add-Type cmdlet, PowerShell compiles the source code you provide into a real .NET class. This action is equivalent to defining the class in a traditional development environment, such as Visual Studio, and is just as powerful.

The thought of compiling source code as part of the execution of your script may concern you because of its performance impact. Fortunately, PowerShell saves your objects when it compiles them. If you call the Add-Type cmdlet a second time with the same source code and in the same session, PowerShell reuses the result of the first call. If you want to change the behavior of a type you've already loaded, exit your session and create it again.

PowerShell assumes C# as the default language for source code supplied to the -Type Definition parameter. In addition to C#, the Add-Type cmdlet also supports C# version 3 (LINQ, the var keyword, etc.), Visual Basic, and JScript. It also supports languages that implement the .NET-standard CodeProvider requirements (such as F#).

If the code you want to compile already exists in a file, you don't have to specify it in-line. Instead, you can provide its path to the -Path parameter. This parameter automatically detects the extension of the file and compiles using the appropriate language as needed.

In addition to supporting input from a file, you might also want to store the output into a file—such as a cmdlet DLL or console application. The Add-Type cmdlet makes this possible through the -OutputAssembly parameter. For example, the following adds a cmdlet on the fly:

```
PS > $cmdlet = @'
using System.Management.Automation;

namespace PowerShellCookbook
{
    [Cmdlet("Invoke", "NewCmdlet")]
    public class InvokeNewCmdletCommand : Cmdlet
    {
        [Parameter(Mandatory = true)]
        public string Name
        {
            get { return _name; }
            set { _name = value; }
        }
        private string _name;


        protected override void BeginProcessing()
        {
            WriteObject("Hello " + _name);
        }
    }
}

'@

PS > Add-Type -TypeDefinition $cmdlet -OutputAssembly MyNewModule.dll
PS > Import-Module .\MyNewModule.dll
PS > Invoke-NewCmdlet

cmdlet Invoke-NewCmdlet at command pipeline position 1
Supply values for the following parameters:
Name: World
Hello World
```

For advanced scenarios, you might want to customize how PowerShell compiles your source code: embedding resources, changing the warning options, and more. For this, use the -CompilerParameters parameter.

For an example of using the Add-Type cmdlet to generate inline C#, see Recipe 17.7, "Add Inline C# to Your PowerShell Script".

---

## See Also

Recipe 1.1, "Run Programs, Scripts, and Existing Tools"

Recipe 17.5, "Program: Invoke Simple Windows API Calls"

Recipe 17.7, "Add Inline C# to Your PowerShell Script"

Recipe 17.9, "Create Your Own PowerShell Cmdlet"

# 17.7. Add Inline C# to Your PowerShell Script

## Problem

You want to write a portion of your script in C# (or another .NET language).

## Solution

Use the `-MemberDefinition` parameter of the `Add-Type` class, as in Example 17-6.

*Example 17-6. Invoke-Inline.ps1*

```
##############################################################################
##
## Invoke-Inline
##
## From Windows PowerShell Cookbook (O'Reilly)
## by Lee Holmes (http://www.leeholmes.com/guide)
##
##############################################################################

<#

.SYNOPSIS

Demonstrates the Add-Type cmdlet to invoke inline C#

#>

Set-StrictMode -Version 3

$inlineType = Add-Type -Name InvokeInline_Inline -PassThru `
    -MemberDefinition @'
    public static int RightShift(int original, int places)
    {
        return original >> places;
    }
'@

$inlineType::RightShift(1024, 3)
```

# Discussion

One of the natural languages to explore after learning PowerShell is C#. It uses many of the same programming techniques as PowerShell, and it also uses the same classes and methods in the .NET Framework. In addition, C# sometimes offers language features or performance benefits that are not available through PowerShell.

Rather than having to move to C# completely for these situations, Example 17-6 demonstrates how you can use the Add-Type cmdlet to write and invoke C# directly in your script.

Once you call the Add-Type cmdlet, PowerShell compiles the source code you provide into a real .NET class. This action is equivalent to defining the class in a traditional development environment, such as Visual Studio, and gives you equivalent functionality. When you use the -MemberDefinition parameter, PowerShell adds the surrounding source code required to create a complete .NET class.

By default, PowerShell will place your resulting type in the Microsoft.Power Shell.Commands.AddType.AutoGeneratedTypes namespace. If you use the -Pass Thru parameter (and define your method as static), you don't need to pay much attention to the name or namespace of the generated type. However, if you do not define your method as static, you will need to use the New-Object cmdlet to create a new instance of the object before using it. In this case, you will need to use the full name of the resulting type when creating it. For example:

```
New-Object Microsoft.PowerShell.Commands.AddType.
   AutoGeneratedTypes.InvokeInline_Inline
```

 The thought of compiling source code as part of the execution of your script may concern you because of its performance impact. Fortunately, PowerShell saves your objects when it compiles them. If you call the Add-Type cmdlet a second time with the same source code and in the same session, PowerShell reuses the result of the first call. If you want to change the behavior of a type you've already loaded, exit your session and create it again.

PowerShell assumes C# as the default language of code supplied to the -Member Definition parameter. It also supports C# version 3 (LINQ, the var keyword, etc.), Visual Basic, and JScript. In addition, it supports languages that implement the .NET-standard CodeProvider requirements (such as F#).

For an example of the -MemberDefinition parameter being used as part of a larger script, see Recipe 17.4, "Access Windows API Functions". For an example of using the Add-Type cmdlet to create entire types, see Recipe 17.6, "Define or Extend a .NET Class".

---

## See Also

Recipe 17.4, "Access Windows API Functions"

Recipe 17.6, "Define or Extend a .NET Class"

# 17.8. Access a .NET SDK Library

## Problem

You want to access the functionality exposed by a .NET DLL, but that DLL is packaged as part of a developer-oriented software development kit (SDK).

## Solution

To create objects contained in a DLL, use the `-Path` parameter of the `Add-Type` cmdlet to load the DLL and the `New-Object` cmdlet to create objects contained in it. Example 17-7 illustrates this technique.

*Example 17-7. Interacting with classes from the SharpZipLib SDK DLL*

```
Add-Type -Path d:\bin\ICSharpCode.SharpZipLib.dll
$namespace = "ICSharpCode.SharpZipLib.Zip.{0}"

$zipName = Join-Path (Get-Location) "PowerShell_Scripts.zip"
$zipFile = New-Object ($namespace -f "ZipOutputStream") ([IO.File]::Create($zipName))

foreach($file in dir *.ps1)
{
   ## Add the file to the ZIP archive.
   $zipEntry = New-Object ($namespace -f "ZipEntry") $file.Name
   $zipFile.PutNextEntry($zipEntry)
}

$zipFile.Close()
```

## Discussion

While C# and VB.NET developers are usually the consumers of SDKs created for the .NET Framework, PowerShell lets you access the SDK features just as easily. To do this, use the `-Path` parameter of the `Add-Type` cmdlet to load the SDK assembly, and then work with the classes from that assembly as you would work with other classes in the .NET Framework.

Although PowerShell lets you access developer-oriented SDKs easily, it can't change the fact that these SDKs are developer-oriented. SDKs and programming interfaces are rarely designed with the administrator in mind, so be prepared to work with programming models that require multiple steps to accomplish your task.

To load any of the typical assemblies included in the .NET Framework, use the -Assembly parameter of the Add-Type cmdlet:

```
PS > Add-Type -Assembly System.Web
```

Like most PowerShell cmdlets, the Add-Type cmdlet supports wildcards to make long assembly names easier to type:

```
PS > Add-Type -Assembly system.win*.forms
```

If the wildcard matches more than one assembly, Add-Type generates an error.

The .NET Framework offers a similar feature through the LoadWithPartialName method of the System.Reflection.Assembly class, shown in Example 17-8.

*Example 17-8. Loading an assembly by its partial name*

```
PS > [Reflection.Assembly]::LoadWithPartialName("System.Web")

GAC    Version       Location
---    -------       --------
True   v2.0.50727    C:\WINDOWS\assembly\GAC_32\(...)\System.Web.dll

PS > [Web.HttpUtility]::UrlEncode("http://www.bing.com")
http%3a%2f%2fwww.bing.com
```

The difference between the two is that the LoadWithPartialName method is unsuitable for scripts that you want to share with others or use in a production environment. It loads the most current version of the assembly, which may not be the same as the version you used to develop your script. If that assembly changes between versions, your script will no longer work. The Add-Type command, on the other hand, internally maps the short assembly names to the fully qualified assembly names contained in a typical installation of the .NET Framework versions 2.0 and 3.5.

One thing you will notice when working with classes from an SDK is that it quickly becomes tiresome to specify their fully qualified type names. For example, zip-related classes from the SharpZipLib all start with ICSharpCode.SharpZipLib.Zip. This is called the *namespace* of that class. Most programming languages solve this problem with a using statement that lets you specify a list of namespaces for that language to search when you type a plain class name such as ZipEntry. PowerShell lacks a using statement, but the Solution demonstrates one of several ways to get the benefits of one.

For more information on how to manage these long class names, see Recipe 3.11, "Reduce Typing for Long Class Names".

Note that prepackaged SDKs aren't the only DLLs you can load this way. An SDK library is simply a DLL that somebody wrote, compiled, packaged, and released. If you are comfortable with any of the .NET languages, you can also create your own DLL, compile it, and use it exactly the same way. To see an example of this approach, see Recipe 17.6, "Define or Extend a .NET Class".

For more information about working with classes from the .NET Framework, see Recipe 3.9, "Create an Instance of a .NET Object".

## See Also

Recipe 3.9, "Create an Instance of a .NET Object"

Recipe 3.11, "Reduce Typing for Long Class Names"

Recipe 17.6, "Define or Extend a .NET Class"

# 17.9. Create Your Own PowerShell Cmdlet

## Problem

You want to write your own PowerShell cmdlet.

## Solution

To create a compiled cmdlet, use the PowerShell SDK (software development kit) as described on MSDN (the Microsoft Developer Network). To create a script-based cmdlet, see Recipe 11.15, "Provide -WhatIf, -Confirm, and Other Cmdlet Features".

## Discussion

As mentioned in "Structured Commands (Cmdlets)" (page vii), PowerShell cmdlets offer several significant advantages over traditional executable programs. From the user's perspective, cmdlets are incredibly consistent. Their support for strongly typed objects as input makes them incredibly powerful, too. From the cmdlet author's perspective, cmdlets are incredibly easy to write when compared to the amount of power they provide.

In most cases, writing a script-based cmdlet (also known as an advanced function) should be all you need. However, you can also use the C# programming language to create a cmdlet.

As with the ease of creating advanced functions, creating and exposing a new command-line parameter is as easy as creating a new public property on a class. Supporting a rich pipeline model is as easy as placing your implementation logic into one of three standard method overrides.

Although a full discussion on how to implement a cmdlet is outside the scope of this book, the following steps illustrate the process behind implementing a simple cmdlet. While implementation typically happens in a fully featured development environment (such as Visual Studio), Example 17-9 demonstrates how to compile a cmdlet simply through the *csc.exe* command-line compiler.

For more information on how to write a PowerShell cmdlet, see the MSDN topic "How to Create a Windows PowerShell Cmdlet," available here (*http://msdn.microsoft.com/en-us/library/ms714598.aspx*).

### Step 1: Download the PowerShell SDK

The PowerShell SDK contains samples, reference assemblies, documentation, and other information used in developing PowerShell cmdlets. Search for "PowerShell 2.0 SDK" here (*http://download.microsoft.com*) and download the latest PowerShell SDK.

### Step 2: Create a file to hold the cmdlet source code

Create a file called *InvokeTemplateCmdletCommand.cs* with the content from Example 17-9 and save it on your hard drive.

*Example 17-9. InvokeTemplateCmdletCommand.cs*

```
using System;
using System.ComponentModel;
using System.Management.Automation;

/*
To build and install:

1) Set-Alias csc $env:WINDIR\Microsoft.NET\Framework\v2.0.50727\csc.exe
2) $ref = [PsObject].Assembly.Location
3) csc /out:TemplateBinaryModule.dll
        /t:library InvokeTemplateCmdletCommand.cs /r:$ref
4) Import-Module .\TemplateBinaryModule.dll

To run:

PS >Invoke-TemplateCmdlet
*/

namespace Template.Commands
{
    [Cmdlet("Invoke", "TemplateCmdlet")]
    public class InvokeTemplateCmdletCommand : Cmdlet
```

```
    {
        [Parameter(Mandatory=true, Position=0, ValueFromPipeline=true)]
        public string Text
        {
            get
            {
                return text;
            }
            set
            {
                text = value;
            }
        }
        private string text;

        protected override void BeginProcessing()
        {
            WriteObject("Processing Started");
        }

        protected override void ProcessRecord()
        {
            WriteObject("Processing " + text);
        }

        protected override void EndProcessing()
        {
            WriteObject("Processing Complete.");
        }
    }
}
```

### Step 3: Compile the DLL

A PowerShell cmdlet is a simple .NET class. The DLL that contains one or more compiled cmdlets is called a *binary module*.

```
Set-Alias csc $env:WINDIR\Microsoft.NET\Framework\v2.0.50727\csc.exe
$ref = [PsObject].Assembly.Location
csc /out:TemplateBinaryModule.dll
    /t:library InvokeTemplateCmdletCommand.cs /r:$ref
```

For more information about binary modules, see Recipe 1.29, "Extend Your Shell with Additional Commands".

If you don't want to use *csc.exe* to compile the DLL, you can also use PowerShell's built-in Add-Type cmdlet. For more information about this approach, see Recipe 17.6, "Define or Extend a .NET Class".

### Step 4: Load the module

Once you have compiled the module, the final step is to load it:

```
Import-Module .\TemplateBinaryModule.dll
```

### Step 5: Use the module

Once you've added the module to your session, you can call commands from that module as you would call any other cmdlet.

```
PS > "Hello World" | Invoke-TemplateCmdlet
Processing Started
Processing Hello World
Processing Complete.
```

In addition to binary modules, PowerShell supports almost all of the functionality of cmdlets through advanced functions. If you want to create functions with the power of cmdlets and the ease of scripting, see Recipe 11.15, "Provide -WhatIf, -Confirm, and Other Cmdlet Features".

## See Also

"Structured Commands (Cmdlets)" (page vii)

Recipe 1.29, "Extend Your Shell with Additional Commands"

Recipe 11.15, "Provide -WhatIf, -Confirm, and Other Cmdlet Features"

Recipe 17.6, "Define or Extend a .NET Class"

# 17.10. Add PowerShell Scripting to Your Own Program

## Problem

You want to provide your users with an easy way to automate your program, but don't want to write a scripting language on your own.

## Solution

To build PowerShell scripting into your own program, use the PowerShell Hosting features as described on MSDN (the Microsoft Developer Network).

# Discussion

One of the fascinating aspects of PowerShell is how easily it lets you add many of its capabilities to your own program. This is because PowerShell is, at its core, a powerful engine that any application can use. The PowerShell console application is in fact just a text-based interface to this engine.

Although a full discussion of the PowerShell hosting model is outside the scope of this book, the following example illustrates the techniques behind exposing features of your application for your users to script.

To frame the premise of Example 17-10 (shown later), imagine an email application that lets you run rules when it receives an email. While you will want to design a standard interface that allows users to create simple rules, you also will want to provide a way for users to write incredibly complex rules. Rather than design a scripting language yourself, you can simply use PowerShell's scripting language. In the following example, we provide user-written scripts with a variable called $message that represents the current message and then runs the commands.

```
PS > Get-Content VerifyCategoryRule.ps1
if($message.Body -match "book")
{
    [Console]::WriteLine("This is a message about the book.")
}
else
{
    [Console]::WriteLine("This is an unknown message.")
}
PS > .\RulesWizardExample.exe (Resolve-Path VerifyCategoryRule.ps1)
This is a message about the book.
```

For more information on how to host PowerShell in your own application, see the MSDN topic "How to Create a Windows PowerShell Hosting Application," available here (*http://msdn.microsoft.com/en-us/library/ee706563.aspx*).

## Step 1: Download the PowerShell SDK

The PowerShell SDK contains samples, reference assemblies, documentation, and other information used in developing PowerShell cmdlets. Search for "PowerShell 2.0 SDK" here (*http://download.microsoft.com*) and download the latest PowerShell SDK.

## Step 2: Create a file to hold the hosting source code

Create a file called *RulesWizardExample.cs* with the content from Example 17-10, and save it on your hard drive.

*Example 17-10. RulesWizardExample.cs*

```
using System;
using System.Management.Automation;
```

```
using System.Management.Automation.Runspaces;

namespace Template
{

    // Define a simple class that represents a mail message
    public class MailMessage
    {
        public MailMessage(string to, string from, string body)
        {
            this.To = to;
            this.From = from;
            this.Body = body;
        }

        public String To;
        public String From;
        public String Body;
    }

    public class RulesWizardExample
    {
        public static void Main(string[] args)
        {
            // Ensure that they've provided some script text
            if(args.Length == 0)
            {
                Console.WriteLine("Usage:");
                Console.WriteLine(" RulesWizardExample <script text>");
                return;
            }

            // Create an example message to pass to our rules wizard
            MailMessage mailMessage =
                        new MailMessage(
                            "guide_feedback@LeeHolmes.com",
                            "guide_reader@example.com",
                            "This is a message about your book.");

            // Create a runspace, which is the environment for
            // running commands
            Runspace runspace = RunspaceFactory.CreateRunspace();
            runspace.Open();

            // Create a variable called "$message" in the runspace, and populate
            // it with a reference to the current message in our application.
            // Pipeline commands can interact with this object like any other
            // .Net object.
            runspace.SessionStateProxy.SetVariable("message", mailMessage);
```

```
        // Create a pipeline, and populate it with the script given in the
        // first command-line argument.
        Pipeline pipeline = runspace.CreatePipeline(args[0]);

        // Invoke (execute) the pipeline, and close the runspace.
        pipeline.Invoke();
        runspace.Close();
    }
  }
}
```

### Step 3: Compile and run the example

Although the example itself provides very little functionality, it demonstrates the core
concepts behind adding PowerShell scripting to your own program.

```
Set-Alias csc $env:WINDIR\Microsoft.NET\Framework\v2.0.50727\csc.exe
$dll = [PsObject].Assembly.Location
Csc RulesWizardExample.cs /reference:$dll
RulesWizardExample.exe <script commands to run>
```

Now we can run Example 17-10. Here we give it a simple rule to just output the sender
of the sample mail message:

```
PS > .\RulesWizardExample.exe '[Console]::WriteLine($message.From)'
guide_reader@example.com
```

## See Also

"Structured Commands (Cmdlets)" (page vii)

# Security and Script Signing

## 18.0. Introduction

Security plays two important roles in PowerShell. The first role is the security of PowerShell itself. Scripting languages have long been a vehicle of email-based malware on Windows, so PowerShell's security features have been carefully designed to thwart this danger. The second role is the set of security-related tasks you are likely to encounter when working with your computer: script signing, certificates, and credentials, just to name a few.

When it comes to talking about security in the scripting and command-line world, a great deal of folklore and superstition clouds the picture. One of the most common misconceptions is that scripting languages and command-line shells somehow let users bypass the security protections of the Windows graphical user interface.

The Windows security model protects resources—not the way you get to them. That is because, in effect, the programs that you run *are* you. If you can do it, so can a program. If a program can do it, then you can do it without having to use that program. For example, consider the act of changing critical data in the Windows Registry. If you use the Windows Registry Editor graphical user interface, it provides an error message when you attempt to perform an operation that you do not have permission for, as shown in Figure 18-1.

The Registry Editor provides this error message because it is *unable* to delete that key, not because it wanted to prevent you from doing it. Windows itself protects the registry keys, not the programs you use to access them.

Likewise, PowerShell provides an error message when you attempt to perform an operation that you do not have permission for—not because PowerShell contains extra security checks for that operation, but simply because Windows itself prevents the operation:

```
PS > New-Item "HKLM:\Software\Microsoft\Windows\CurrentVersion\Run\New"
New-Item : Requested registry access is not allowed.
At line:1 char:9
+ New-Item <<<< "HKLM:\Software\Microsoft\Windows\CurrentVersion\Run\New"
```

While perhaps clear after explanation, this misunderstanding often gets used as a reason
to prevent users from running command shells or scripting languages altogether.

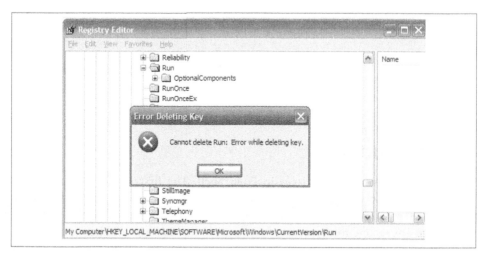

*Figure 18-1. Error message from the Windows Registry Editor*

# 18.1. Enable Scripting Through an Execution Policy

## Problem

PowerShell provides an error message, such as the following, when you try to run a
script:

```
PS > .\Test.ps1
File C:\temp\test.ps1 cannot be loaded because the execution of scripts is
disabled on this system. Please see "get-help about_signing" for more details.
At line:1 char:10
+ .\Test.ps1 <<<<
```

## Solution

To prevent this error message, use the `Set-ExecutionPolicy` cmdlet to change the
PowerShell execution policy to one of the policies that allow scripts to run:

```
Set-ExecutionPolicy RemoteSigned
```

# Discussion

As normally configured, PowerShell operates strictly as an interactive shell. By disabling the execution of scripts by default, PowerShell prevents malicious PowerShell scripts from affecting users who have PowerShell installed but who may never have used (or even heard of!) PowerShell.

You (as a reader of this book and PowerShell user) are not part of that target audience. You will want to configure PowerShell to run under one of the following five execution policies:

Restricted
> PowerShell operates as an interactive shell only. Attempting to run a script generates an error message. This is PowerShell's default execution policy.

AllSigned
> PowerShell runs only those scripts that contain a digital signature. When you attempt to run a script signed by a publisher that PowerShell hasn't seen before, PowerShell asks whether you trust that publisher to run scripts on your system.

RemoteSigned *(recommended)*
> PowerShell runs most scripts without prompting, but requires that scripts from the Internet contain a digital signature. As in AllSigned mode, PowerShell asks whether you trust that publisher to run scripts on your system when you run a script signed by a publisher it hasn't seen before. PowerShell considers a script to have come from the Internet when it has been downloaded to your computer by a popular communications program such as Internet Explorer, Outlook, or Messenger.

Unrestricted
> PowerShell does not require a digital signature on any script, but (like Windows Explorer) warns you when a script has been downloaded from the Internet.

Bypass
> PowerShell places the responsibility of security validation entirely upon the user.

When it comes to evaluating script signatures, always remember that a signed script does not mean a safe script! The signature on a script gives you a way to verify who the script came from, but not that you can trust its author to run commands on your system. You need to make that decision for yourself, which is why PowerShell asks you.

Run the Set-ExecutionPolicy cmdlet to configure the system's execution policy. It supports three scopes:

Process
> Impacts the current session and any that it launches. This scope modifies the PS ExecutionPolicyPreference environment variable and is also supported through the -ExecutionPolicy parameter to *PowerShell.exe*.

`CurrentUser`

> Modifies the execution policy for the current user, and stores its value in the `HKEY_CURRENT_USER` hive of the Windows Registry.

`LocalMachine`

> Modifies the execution policy for the entire machine, and stores its value in the `HKEY_LOCAL_MACHINE` hive of the Windows Registry. Modifying the execution policy at this scope requires that you launch PowerShell with Administrator privileges. If you want to configure your execution policy on Windows Vista or later, right-click the Windows PowerShell link for the option to launch PowerShell as the Administrator.

If you specify the value `Undefined` for the execution policy at a specific scope, PowerShell removes any execution policy you previously defined for that scope.

Alternatively, you can directly modify the registry key that PowerShell uses to store its execution policy. For the `CurrentUser` and `LocalMachine` scopes, this is the `Execution Policy` property under the registry path *SOFTWARE\Microsoft\PowerShell\1\ShellIds \Microsoft.PowerShell.*

In an enterprise setting, PowerShell also lets you override this local preference through Group Policy. For more information about PowerShell's Group Policy support, see Recipe 18.5, "Manage PowerShell Security in an Enterprise".

### Execution policies are not user restrictions

It is easy to understand the power of an execution policy to prevent scripts from running, but administrators often forget to consider *from whom*. They might think that enforcing an `AllSigned` policy is a way to prevent the *user* from running unapproved applications, when really it is designed as a way to prevent the *attacker* from running scripts that the user doesn't approve. This misconception is often wrongly reinforced by the location of the `ExecutionPolicy` configuration key in PowerShell version 1—in a registry location that only machine administrators have access to.

Systemwide PowerShell execution policies cannot prevent the user from doing something the user wants to do. That job is left to the Windows Account Model, which is designed as a security boundary. It controls what users can do: what files can be accessed, what registry keys can be accessed, and more. PowerShell is a user-mode application, and is therefore (as defined by the Windows security model) completely under the user's control.

Instead, execution policies are a user-focused feature, similar to seatbelts or helmets. It's best to keep them on, but you always have the option to take them off. PowerShell's installer sets the execution policy to `Restricted` as a safe default for the vast majority of Windows users who will never run a PowerShell script in their life. A system administrator might set the execution policy to `AllSigned` to define it as a best practice or to let nontechnical users run a subset of safe scripts.

At any time, users can decide otherwise. They can type the commands by hand, paste the script into their PowerShell prompt, or use any of a countless number of other workarounds. These are all direct results of a Windows core security principle: you have complete control over any application you are running. PowerShell makes this reality transparent through its fine-grained execution policy scopes.

At its core, execution policy scopes let administrators and users tailor their safety harnesses. Jane might be fluent and technical (and opt for a `RemoteSigned` execution policy), whereas Bob (another user of the same machine with different security preferences) can still get the benefits of an `AllSigned` default execution policy. In addition, agents or automation tools can invoke PowerShell commands without having to modify the permanent state of the system.

### See Also

Recipe 18.5, "Manage PowerShell Security in an Enterprise"

# 18.2. Disable Warnings for UNC Paths

## Problem

PowerShell warns you when it tries to load a script from an Intranet (UNC) path.

## Solution

If it makes sense, copy the file locally and run it from your local location. If you want to keep the script on the UNC path, enable Internet Explorer's `UncAsIntranet` setting, or add the UNC path to the list of trusted sites. Example 18-1 adds *server* to the list of trusted sites.

*Example 18-1. Adding a server to the list of trusted hosts*

```
$path = "HKLM:\SOFTWARE\Microsoft\Windows\CurrentVersion\Internet Settings\" +
    "ZoneMap\Domains\server"
New-Item -Path $path | New-ItemProperty -Name File -PropertyType DWORD -Value 2
```

## Discussion

When using an execution policy that detects Internet-based scripts, you may want to stop PowerShell from treating those scripts as remote.

In an enterprise setting, PowerShell sometimes warns of the dangers of Internet-based scripts even if they are located only on a network share. This is a security precaution, as it is possible for network paths (such as UNC shares) to be spoofed, or for the content of those scripts to be changed without your knowledge. If you have a high trust in your network and the security of the remote system, you might want to avoid these precautions.

To remove this warning, first ensure the scripts have not actually been downloaded from the Internet. The easiest way is to use the `Unblock-File` cmdlet to unblock the file and then restart PowerShell. Alternatively, you can right-click on the file from Windows Explorer, select Properties, and then click Unblock. This also requires that you restart PowerShell.

If unblocking the file does not resolve the issue (or is not an option), your machine has likely been configured to restrict access to network shares. This is common with Internet Explorer's Enhanced Security Configuration mode. To prevent this message, add the path of the network share to Internet Explorer's Intranet or Trusted Sites zone. For more information on managing Internet Explorer's zone mappings, see Recipe 21.7, "Add a Site to an Internet Explorer Security Zone".

If you are using an `Unrestricted` execution policy and want to get rid of this warning for remote files without altering the Trusted Sites zone, you can use the `Bypass` execution policy to bypass PowerShell's security features entirely. For more information about execution policies, see Recipe 18.1, "Enable Scripting Through an Execution Policy".

### See Also

Recipe 18.1, "Enable Scripting Through an Execution Policy"

Recipe 21.7, "Add a Site to an Internet Explorer Security Zone"

# 18.3. Sign a PowerShell Script, Module, or Formatting File

## Problem

You want to sign a PowerShell script, module, or formatting file so that it can be run on systems that have their execution policy set to require signed scripts.

## Solution

To sign the script with your standard code-signing certificate, use the `Set-AuthenticodeSignature` cmdlet:

```
$cert = @(Get-ChildItem cert:\CurrentUser\My -CodeSigning)[0]
Set-AuthenticodeSignature file.ps1 $cert
```

Alternatively, you can also use other traditional applications (such as *signtool.exe*) to sign PowerShell *.ps1*, *.psm1*, *.psd1*, and *.ps1xml* files.

## Discussion

Signing a script or formatting file provides you and your customers with two primary benefits: publisher identification and file integrity. When you sign a script, module, or formatting file, PowerShell appends your digital signature to the end of that file. This signature verifies that the file came from you and also ensures that nobody can tamper with the content in the file without detection. If you try to load a file that has been tampered with, PowerShell provides the following error message:

```
File C:\temp\test.ps1 cannot be loaded. The contents of file C:\temp\test.ps1
may have been tampered because the hash of the file does not match the hash
stored in the digital signature. The script will not execute on the system.
Please see "get-help about_signing" for more details.
At line:1 char:10
+ .\test.ps1 <<<<
```

When it comes to the signing of scripts, modules, and formatting files, PowerShell participates in the standard Windows Authenticode infrastructure. Because of that, techniques you may already know for signing files and working with their signatures continue to work with PowerShell scripts and formatting files. Although the Set-AuthenticodeSignature cmdlet is primarily designed to support scripts and formatting files, it also supports DLLs and other standard Windows executable file types.

To sign a file, the Set-AuthenticodeSignature cmdlet requires that you provide it with a valid code-signing certificate. Most certification authorities provide Authenticode code-signing certificates for a fee. By using an Authenticode code-signing certificate from a reputable certification authority (such as VeriSign or Thawte), you can be sure that all users will be able to verify the signature on your script. Some online services offer extremely cheap code-signing certificates, but be aware that many machines may be unable to verify the digital signatures created by those certificates.

 You can still gain many of the benefits of code signing on your own computers by generating your own code-signing certificate. While other computers will not be able to recognize the signature, it still provides tamper protection on your own computer. For more information about this approach, see Recipe 18.4, "Program: Create a Self-Signed Certificate".

The -TimeStampServer parameter lets you sign your script or formatting file in a way that makes the signature on your script or formatting file valid even after your code-signing certificate expires.

For more information about the Set-AuthenticodeSignature cmdlet, type **Get-Help Set-AuthenticodeSignature**.

## See Also

Recipe 18.4, "Program: Create a Self-Signed Certificate"

# 18.4. Program: Create a Self-Signed Certificate

## Discussion

It is possible to benefit from the tamper-protection features of signed scripts without having to pay for an official code-signing certificate. You do this by creating a *self-signed* certificate. Scripts signed with a self-signed certificate will not be recognized as valid on other computers, but you can still sign and use them on your own computer.

When Example 18-2 runs, it prompts you for a password. Windows uses this password to prevent malicious programs from automatically signing files on your behalf.

*Example 18-2. New-SelfSignedCertificate.ps1*

```
##############################################################################
##
## New-SelfSignedCertificate
##
## From Windows PowerShell Cookbook (O'Reilly)
## by Lee Holmes (http://www.leeholmes.com/guide)
##
##############################################################################

<#

.SYNOPSIS

Generate a new self-signed certificate. The certificate generated by these
commands allow you to sign scripts on your own computer for protection
from tampering. Files signed with this signature are not valid on other
computers.

.EXAMPLE

PS > New-SelfSignedCertificate.ps1
Creates a new self-signed certificate

#>

Set-StrictMode -Version 3

## Ensure we can find makecert.exe
if(-not (Get-Command makecert.exe -ErrorAction SilentlyContinue))
```

```
{
    $errorMessage = "Could not find makecert.exe. " +
        "This tool is available as part of Visual Studio, or the Windows SDK."

    Write-Error $errorMessage
    return
}

$keyPath = Join-Path ([IO.Path]::GetTempPath()) "root.pvk"

## Generate the local certification authority
makecert -n "CN=PowerShell Local Certificate Root" -a sha1 `
    -eku 1.3.6.1.5.5.7.3.3 -r -sv $keyPath root.cer `
    -ss Root -sr localMachine

## Use the local certification authority to generate a self-signed
## certificate
makecert -pe -n "CN=PowerShell User" -ss MY -a sha1 `
    -eku 1.3.6.1.5.5.7.3.3 -iv $keyPath -ic root.cer

## Remove the private key from the filesystem.
Remove-Item $keyPath

## Retrieve the certificate
Get-ChildItem cert:\currentuser\my -codesign |
    Where-Object { $_.Subject -match "PowerShell User" }
```

For more information about running scripts, see Recipe 1.1, "Run Programs, Scripts, and Existing Tools".

## See Also

Recipe 1.1, "Run Programs, Scripts, and Existing Tools"

# 18.5. Manage PowerShell Security in an Enterprise

## Problem

You want to control PowerShell's security features in an enterprise setting.

## Solution

You have two ways to manage PowerShell's security features enterprise-wide:

- Apply PowerShell's Group Policy templates to control PowerShell's execution policy through Group Policy.

- Deploy Microsoft Certificate Services to automatically generate Authenticode code-signing certificates for domain accounts.

## Discussion

Either separately or together, these features let you customize your PowerShell environment across your entire domain.

### Apply PowerShell's Group Policy templates

The administrative templates for Windows PowerShell let you override the machine's local execution policy preference at both the machine and per-user level. To obtain the PowerShell administrative templates, visit this site (*http://www.microsoft.com/down loads*) and search for "Administrative templates for Windows PowerShell."

 Although Group Policy settings override local preferences, PowerShell's execution policy should not be considered a security measure that protects the system from the user. It is a security measure that helps prevent untrusted scripts from running on the system. As mentioned in Recipe 18.1, "Enable Scripting Through an Execution Policy", PowerShell is only a vehicle that allows users to do what they already have the Windows permissions to do.

Once you install the administrative templates for Windows PowerShell, launch the Group Policy Object Editor MMC snap-in. Right-click Administrative Templates, and then select Add/Remove Administrative Templates. You will find the administrative template in the installation location you chose when you installed the administrative templates for Windows PowerShell. Once added, the Group Policy Editor MMC snap-in provides PowerShell as an option under its Administrative Templates node, as shown in Figure 18-2.

*Figure 18-2. PowerShell Group Policy configuration*

The default state is Not Configured. In this state, PowerShell takes its execution policy from the machine's local preference (as described in Recipe 18.1, "Enable Scripting Through an Execution Policy"). If you change the state to one of the Enabled options (or Disabled), PowerShell uses this configuration instead of the machine's local preference.

> PowerShell respects these Group Policy settings no matter what. This includes settings that the machine's administrator may consider to reduce security—such as an Unrestricted group policy overriding an AllSigned local preference.

Per-user Group Policy settings override the machine's local preference, whereas per-machine Group Policy settings override per-user settings.

### Deploy Microsoft Certificate Services

Although outside the scope of this book, Microsoft Certificate Services lets you automatically deploy code-signing certificates to any or all domain users. This provides a significant benefit, as it helps protect users from accidental or malicious script tampering.

For an introduction to this topic, visit this site (*http://technet.microsoft.com*) and search for "Enterprise Design for Certificate Services." For more information about script signing, see Recipe 18.3, "Sign a PowerShell Script, Module, or Formatting File".

## See Also

Recipe 18.1, "Enable Scripting Through an Execution Policy"

Recipe 18.3, "Sign a PowerShell Script, Module, or Formatting File"

---

# 18.6. Block Scripts by Publisher, Path, or Hash

## Problem

In addition to PowerShell's execution policy, you want to block scripts by their publisher, location, or similarity to a specific script.

## Solution

Create new Software Restriction Policy rules to enforce these requirements.

## Discussion

While this is not common, you may sometimes want to prevent PowerShell from running scripts signed by specific publishers, from a certain path, or with specific content. For all execution policies except `Bypass`, PowerShell lets you configure this through the computer's software restriction policies.

To configure these software restriction policies, launch the Local Security Policy MMC snap-in listed in the Administrative Tools group of the Start menu. Expand the Software Restriction Policies node, right-click Additional Rules, and then create the desired rules: certificate rules, path rule, or hash rules.

> In Windows 7, the PowerShell module for the AppLocker feature makes managing software restriction policies immensely easier. For more information, search the Internet for "AppLocker PowerShell."

Certificate rules let you configure certain certificates that PowerShell will never trust. Path rules let you define system paths that allow or disallow execution of PowerShell scripts from certain paths. Hash rules let you block specific scripts from execution if they are the same as the script you used to generate the rule.

Figure 18-3 shows how to add a new certificate rule.

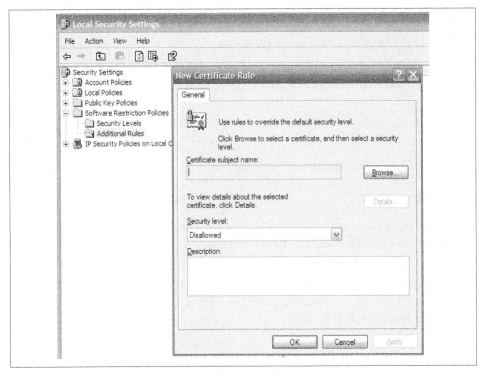

*Figure 18-3. Adding a new certificate rule*

Browse to the certificate that represents the publisher you want to block, and then click OK to block that publisher.

Rather than block specific certificates, you can also create a certificate policy that allows only certificates from a centrally administered whitelist. To do this, select either "Allow only all administrators to manage Trusted Publishers" or "Allow only enterprise administrators to manage Trusted Publishers" from the Trusted Publishers Management dialog.

## See Also

Recipe 18.1, "Enable Scripting Through an Execution Policy"

Recipe 18.3, "Sign a PowerShell Script, Module, or Formatting File"

# 18.7. Verify the Digital Signature of a PowerShell Script

## Problem

You want to verify the digital signature of a PowerShell script or formatting file.

## Solution

To validate the signature of a script or formatting file, use the `Get-Authenticode Signature` cmdlet:

```
PS > Get-AuthenticodeSignature .\test.ps1

    Directory: C:\temp

SignerCertificate                               Status    Path
-----------------                               ------    ----
FD48FAA9281A657DBD089B5A008FAFE61D3B32FD       Valid     test.ps1
```

## Discussion

The `Get-AuthenticodeSignature` cmdlet gets the Authenticode signature from a file. This can be a PowerShell script or formatting file, but the cmdlet also supports DLLs and other Windows standard executable file types.

By default, PowerShell displays the signature in a format that summarizes the certificate and its status. For more information about the signature, use the `Format-List` cmdlet, as shown in Example 18-3.

*Example 18-3. PowerShell displaying detailed information about an Authenticode signature*

```
PS > Get-AuthenticodeSignature .\test.ps1 | Format-List

SignerCertificate       : [Subject]
                            CN=PowerShell User

                          [Issuer]
                            CN=PowerShell Local Certificate Root

                          [Serial Number]
                            454D75B8A18FBDB445D8FCEC4942085C

                          [Not Before]
                            4/22/2007 12:32:37 AM

                          [Not After]
                            12/31/2039 3:59:59 PM

                          [Thumbprint]
                            FD48FAA9281A657DBD089B5A008FAFE61D3B32FD

TimeStamperCertificate :
Status                 : Valid
StatusMessage          : Signature verified.
Path                   : C:\temp\test.ps1
```

For more information about the `Get-AuthenticodeSignature` cmdlet, type **Get-Help Get-AuthenticodeSignature**.

# 18.8. Securely Handle Sensitive Information

## Problem

You want to request sensitive information from the user, but want to do this as securely as possible.

## Solution

To securely handle sensitive information, store it in a `SecureString` whenever possible. The `Read-Host` cmdlet (with the `-AsSecureString` parameter) lets you prompt the user for (and handle) sensitive information by returning the user's response as a `Secure String`:

```
PS > $secureInput = Read-Host -AsSecureString "Enter your private key"
Enter your private key:
PS > $secureInput
System.Security.SecureString
```

## Discussion

When you use any string in the .NET Framework (and therefore PowerShell), it retains that string so that it can efficiently reuse it later. Unlike most .NET data, unused strings persist even after you finish using them. When this data is in memory, there is always the chance that it could get captured in a crash dump or swapped to disk in a paging operation. Because some data (such as passwords and other confidential information) may be sensitive, the .NET Framework includes the `SecureString` class: a container for text data that the framework encrypts when it stores it in memory. Code that needs to interact with the plain-text data inside a `SecureString` does so as securely as possible.

When a cmdlet author asks you for sensitive data (for example, an encryption key), the best practice is to designate that parameter as a `SecureString` to help keep your information confidential. You can provide the parameter with a `SecureString` variable as input, or the host prompts you for the `SecureString` if you do not provide one. PowerShell also supports two cmdlets (`ConvertTo-SecureString` and `ConvertFrom-SecureString`) that let you securely persist this data to disk. For more information about securely storing information on disk, see Recipe 18.12, "Securely Store Credentials on Disk".

Credentials are a common source of sensitive information. See Recipe 18.9, "Securely Request Usernames and Passwords" for information on how to securely manage credentials in PowerShell.

By default, the `SecureString` cmdlets use the Windows Data Protection API (DPAPI) when they convert your `SecureString` to and from its text representation. The key it uses to encrypt your data is based on your Windows logon credentials, so only you can decrypt the data that you've encrypted. If you want the exported data to work on another system or separate user account, you can use the cmdlet options that let you provide an explicit key. PowerShell treats this sensitive data as an opaque blob—and so should you.

However, there are many instances when you may want to automatically provide the `SecureString` input to a cmdlet rather than have the host prompt you for it. In these situations, the ideal solution is to use the `ConvertTo-SecureString` cmdlet to import a previously exported `SecureString` from disk. This retains the confidentiality of your data and still lets you automate the input.

If the data is highly dynamic (for example, coming from a CSV), then the `ConvertTo-SecureString` cmdlet supports an `-AsPlainText` parameter:

```
$secureString = ConvertTo-SecureString "Kinda Secret" -AsPlainText -Force
```

Since you've already provided plain-text input in this case, placing this data in a `Secure String` no longer provides a security benefit. To prevent a false sense of security, the cmdlet requires the `-Force` parameter to convert plain-text data into a `SecureString`.

Once you have data in a `SecureString`, you may want to access its plain-text representation. PowerShell doesn't provide a direct way to do this, as that defeats the purpose of a `SecureString`. If you still want to convert a `SecureString` to plain text, you have two options:

- Use the `GetNetworkCredential()` method of the `PsCredential` class:

  ```
  $secureString = Read-Host -AsSecureString
  $temporaryCredential = New-Object `
      System.Management.Automation.PsCredential "TempUser",$secureString
  $unsecureString = $temporaryCredential.GetNetworkCredential().Password
  ```

- Use the .NET Framework's `Marshal` class:

  ```
  $secureString = Read-Host -AsSecureString
  $unsecureString = [Runtime.InteropServices.Marshal]::PtrToStringAuto(
      [Runtime.InteropServices.Marshal]::SecureStringToBSTR($secureString))
  ```

## See Also

Recipe 18.9, "Securely Request Usernames and Passwords"

Recipe 18.12, "Securely Store Credentials on Disk"

# 18.9. Securely Request Usernames and Passwords

## Problem

Your script requires that users provide it with a username and password, but you want to do this as securely as possible.

## Solution

To request a credential from the user, use the `Get-Credential` cmdlet:

```
$credential = Get-Credential
```

## Discussion

The `Get-Credential` cmdlet reads credentials from the user as securely as possible and ensures that the user's password remains highly protected the entire time. For an example of using the `Get-Credential` cmdlet effectively in a script, see Recipe 18.10, "Program: Start a Process as Another User".

Once you have the username and password, you can pass that information around to any other command that accepts a PowerShell credential object without worrying about disclosing sensitive information. If a command doesn't accept a PowerShell credential object (but does support a `SecureString` for its sensitive information), the resulting `PsCredential` object provides a `Username` property that returns the username in the credential and a `Password` property that returns a `SecureString` containing the user's password.

Unfortunately, not everything that requires credentials can accept either a PowerShell credential or `SecureString`. If you need to provide a credential to one of these commands or API calls, the `PsCredential` object provides a `GetNetworkCredential()` method to convert the PowerShell credential to a less secure `NetworkCredential` object. Once you've converted the credential to a `NetworkCredential`, the `UserName` and `Password` properties provide unencrypted access to the username and password from the original credential. Many network-related classes in the .NET Framework support the `NetworkCredential` class directly.

The NetworkCredential class is less secure than the PsCredential class because it stores the user's password in plain text. For more information about the security implications of storing sensitive information in plain text, see Recipe 18.8, "Securely Handle Sensitive Information".

If a frequently run script requires credentials, you might consider caching those credentials in memory to improve the usability of that script. For example, in the region of the script that calls the Get-Credential cmdlet, you can instead use the techniques shown by Example 18-4.

*Example 18-4. Caching credentials in memory to improve usability*

```
$credential = $null
if(Test-Path Variable:\Lee.Holmes.CommonScript.CachedCredential)
{
    $credential = ${GLOBAL:Lee.Holmes.CommonScript.CachedCredential}
}

${GLOBAL:Lee.Holmes.CommonScript.CachedCredential} =
    Get-Credential $credential

$credential = ${GLOBAL:Lee.Holmes.CommonScript.CachedCredential}
```

The script prompts the user for credentials the first time it is called but uses the cached credentials for subsequent calls. If your command is part of a PowerShell module, you can avoid storing the information in a global variable. For more information about this technique, see Recipe 11.7, "Write Commands That Maintain State".

To cache these credentials on disk (to support unattended operations), see Recipe 18.12, "Securely Store Credentials on Disk".

For more information about the Get-Credential cmdlet, type **Get-Help Get-Credential**.

## See Also

Recipe 11.7, "Write Commands That Maintain State"

Recipe 18.8, "Securely Handle Sensitive Information"

Recipe 18.10, "Program: Start a Process as Another User"

Recipe 18.12, "Securely Store Credentials on Disk"

# 18.10. Program: Start a Process as Another User

If your script requires user credentials, PowerShell offers the PsCredential object. This lets you securely store those credentials or pass them to other commands that accept

PowerShell credentials. When you write a script that accepts credentials, consider letting the user supply either a username or a preexisting credential. This is the model followed by the Get-Credential cmdlet, and it provides an intuitive user experience. Example 18-5 demonstrates a useful approach to support this model. As the framework for this demonstration, the script lets you start a process as another user. While the scenario addressed by this specific script is fully handled by the Start-Process cmdlet, it provides a useful framework for discussion.

*Example 18-5. Start-ProcessAsUser.ps1*

```
##############################################################################
##
## Start-ProcessAsUser
##
## From Windows PowerShell Cookbook (O'Reilly)
## by Lee Holmes (http://www.leeholmes.com/guide)
##
##############################################################################

<#

.SYNOPSIS

Launch a process under alternate credentials, providing functionality
similar to runas.exe.

.EXAMPLE

PS > $file = Join-Path ([Environment]::GetFolderPath("System")) certmgr.msc
PS > Start-ProcessAsUser Administrator mmc $file

#>

param(
    ## The credential to launch the process under
    $Credential = (Get-Credential),

    ## The process to start
    [Parameter(Mandatory = $true)]
    [string] $Process,

    ## Any arguments to pass to the process
    [string] $ArgumentList = ""
)

Set-StrictMode -Version 3

## Create a real credential if they supplied a username
$credential = Get-Credential $credential

## Exit if they canceled out of the credential dialog
```

```
if(-not ($credential -is "System.Management.Automation.PsCredential"))
{
    return
}

## Prepare the startup information (including username and password)
$startInfo = New-Object Diagnostics.ProcessStartInfo
$startInfo.Filename = $process
$startInfo.Arguments = $argumentList

## If we're launching as ourselves, set the "runas" verb
if(($credential.Username -eq "$ENV:Username") -or
    ($credential.Username -eq "\$ENV:Username"))
{
    $startInfo.Verb = "runas"
}
else
{
    $startInfo.UserName = $credential.Username
    $startInfo.Password = $credential.Password
    $startInfo.UseShellExecute = $false
}

## Start the process
[Diagnostics.Process]::Start($startInfo)
```

For a version of this script that lets you invoke PowerShell commands in an elevated session and easily interact with the results, see Recipe 18.11, "Program: Run a Temporarily Elevated Command".

For more information about running scripts, see Recipe 1.1, "Run Programs, Scripts, and Existing Tools".

### See Also

Recipe 1.1, "Run Programs, Scripts, and Existing Tools"

Recipe 18.11, "Program: Run a Temporarily Elevated Command"

# 18.11. Program: Run a Temporarily Elevated Command

One popular feature of many Unix-like operating systems is the sudo command: a feature that lets you invoke commands as another user without switching context.

This is a common desire in Windows Vista and above, where User Access Control (UAC) means that most interactive sessions do not have their Administrator privileges enabled. Enabling these privileges is often a clumsy task, requiring that you launch a new instance of PowerShell with the "Run as Administrator" option enabled.

Example 18-6 resolves many of these issues by launching an administrative shell for you and letting it participate in a regular (nonelevated) PowerShell pipeline.

To do this, it first streams all of your input into a richly structured CliXml file on disk. It invokes the elevated command and stores its results into another richly structured CliXml file on disk. Finally, it imports the structured data from disk and removes the temporary files.

*Example 18-6. Invoke-ElevatedCommand.ps1*

```
##############################################################################
##
## Invoke-ElevatedCommand
##
## From Windows PowerShell Cookbook (O'Reilly)
## by Lee Holmes (http://www.leeholmes.com/guide)
##
##############################################################################

<#

.SYNOPSIS

Runs the provided script block under an elevated instance of PowerShell as
through it were a member of a regular pipeline.

.EXAMPLE

PS > Get-Process | Invoke-ElevatedCommand.ps1 {
    $input | Where-Object { $_.Handles -gt 500 } } | Sort Handles

#>

param(
    ## The script block to invoke elevated
    [Parameter(Mandatory = $true)]
    [ScriptBlock] $Scriptblock,

    ## Any input to give the elevated process
    [Parameter(ValueFromPipeline = $true)]
    $InputObject,

    ## Switch to enable the user profile
    [switch] $EnableProfile
)

begin
{
    Set-StrictMode -Version 3
    $inputItems = New-Object System.Collections.ArrayList
}
```

```
process
{
    $null = $inputItems.Add($inputObject)
}

end
{
    ## Create some temporary files for streaming input and output
    $outputFile = [IO.Path]::GetTempFileName()
    $inputFile = [IO.Path]::GetTempFileName()

    ## Stream the input into the input file
    $inputItems.ToArray() | Export-CliXml -Depth 1 $inputFile

    ## Start creating the command line for the elevated PowerShell session
    $commandLine = ""
    if(-not $EnableProfile) { $commandLine += "-NoProfile " }

    ## Convert the command into an encoded command for PowerShell
    $commandString = "Set-Location '$($pwd.Path)'; " +
        "`$output = Import-CliXml '$inputFile' | " +
        "& {" + $scriptblock.ToString() + "} 2>&1; " +
        "`$output | Export-CliXml -Depth 1 '$outputFile'"

    $commandBytes = [System.Text.Encoding]::Unicode.GetBytes($commandString)
    $encodedCommand = [Convert]::ToBase64String($commandBytes)
    $commandLine += "-EncodedCommand $encodedCommand"

    ## Start the new PowerShell process
    $process = Start-Process -FilePath (Get-Command powershell).Definition `
        -ArgumentList $commandLine -Verb RunAs `
        -WindowStyle Hidden `
        -Passthru
    $process.WaitForExit()

    ## Return the output to the user
    if((Get-Item $outputFile).Length -gt 0)
    {
        Import-CliXml $outputFile
    }

    ## Clean up
    [Console]::WriteLine($outputFile)
    # Remove-Item $outputFile
    Remove-Item $inputFile
}
```

For more information about the CliXml commands, see Recipe 10.5, "Easily Import and Export Your Structured Data". For more information about running scripts, see Recipe 1.1, "Run Programs, Scripts, and Existing Tools".

## See Also

Recipe 1.1, "Run Programs, Scripts, and Existing Tools"

Recipe 10.5, "Easily Import and Export Your Structured Data"

# 18.12. Securely Store Credentials on Disk

## Problem

Your script performs an operation that requires credentials, but you don't want it to require user interaction when it runs.

## Solution

In PowerShell version 3, use the `Export-CliXml` and `Import-CliXml` cmdlets to import and export credentials. In PowerShell version 2, use the `ConvertFrom-SecureString` and `ConvertTo-SecureString` cmdlets.

### Save the credential's password to disk

The first step for storing a password on disk is usually a manual one. There is nothing mandatory about the filename, but we'll use a convention to name the file *Current Script.ps1.credential*. Given a credential that you've stored in the `$credential` variable, you can safely use the `Export-CliXml` cmdlet to save the credential to disk. Replace *CurrentScript* with the name of the script that will be loading it:

```
PS > $credPath = Join-Path (Split-Path $profile) CurrentScript.ps1.credential
PS > $credential | Export-CliXml $credPath
```

In PowerShell version 2, you must use the `ConvertFrom-SecureString` cmdlet:

```
PS > $credPath = Join-Path (Split-Path $profile) CurrentScript.ps1.credential
PS > $credential.Password | ConvertFrom-SecureString | Set-Content $credPath
```

### Recreate the credential from the password stored on disk

In the script that you want to run automatically, add the following commands for PowerShell version 3:

```
$credPath = Join-Path (Split-Path $profile) CurrentScript.ps1.credential
$credential = Import-CliXml $credPath
```

In PowerShell version 2, you must manually create a `PSCredential` object, using the password imported by the `ConvertTo-SecureString` cmdlet. Whereas the `Export-CliXml` cmdlet keeps track of the credential username automatically, this alternate approach needs to keep track of it by hand:

```
$credPath = Join-Path (Split-Path $profile) CurrentScript.ps1.credential
$password = Get-Content $credPath | ConvertTo-SecureString
$credential = New-Object System.Management.Automation.PsCredential `
    "CachedUser",$password
```

These commands create a new credential object (for the *CachedUser* user) and store that object in the $credential variable.

## Discussion

When reading the Solution, you might at first be wary of storing a password on disk. While it is natural (and prudent) to be cautious of littering your hard drive with sensitive information, the Export-CliXml cmdlet encrypts credential objects using the Windows standard Data Protection API. This ensures that only your user account can properly decrypt its contents. Similarly, the ConvertFrom-SecureString cmdlet also encrypts the password you provide.

While keeping a password secure is an important security feature, you may sometimes want to store a password (or other sensitive information) on disk so that other accounts have access to it. This is often the case with scripts run by service accounts or scripts designed to be transferred between computers. The ConvertFrom-SecureString and ConvertTo-SecureString cmdlets support this by letting you specify an encryption key.

 When used with a hardcoded encryption key, this technique no longer acts as a security measure. If a user can access the content of your automated script, that user has access to the encryption key. If the user has access to the encryption key, the user has access to the data you were trying to protect.

Although the Solution stores the password in the directory that contains your profile, you could also load it from the same location as your script. To learn how to load it from the same location as your script, see Recipe 16.6, "Find Your Script's Location".

For more information about the ConvertTo-SecureString and ConvertFrom-Secure String cmdlets, type **Get-Help ConvertTo-SecureString** or **Get-Help ConvertFrom-SecureString**.

## See Also

Recipe 16.6, "Find Your Script's Location"

# 18.13. Access User and Machine Certificates

## Problem

You want to retrieve information about certificates for the current user or local machine.

## Solution

To browse and retrieve certificates on the local machine, use PowerShell's certificate drive. This drive is created by the certificate provider, as shown in Example 18-7.

*Example 18-7. Exploring certificates in the certificate provider*

```
PS > Set-Location cert:\CurrentUser\
PS > $cert = Get-ChildItem -Rec -CodeSign
PS > $cert | Format-List

Subject      : CN=PowerShell User
Issuer       : CN=PowerShell Local Certificate Root
Thumbprint   : FD48FAA9281A657DBD089B5A008FAFE61D3B32FD
FriendlyName :
NotBefore    : 4/22/2007 12:32:37 AM
NotAfter     : 12/31/2039 3:59:59 PM
Extensions   : {System.Security.Cryptography.Oid, System.Security.
               Cryptography.Oid}
```

## Discussion

The certificate drive provides a useful way to navigate and view certificates for the current user or local machine. For example, if your execution policy requires the use of digital signatures, the following command tells you which publishers are trusted to run scripts on your system:

```
Get-ChildItem cert:\CurrentUser\TrustedPublisher
```

The certificate provider is probably most commonly used to select a code-signing certificate for the `Set-AuthenticodeSignature` cmdlet. The following command selects the "best" code-signing certificate (i.e., the one that expires last):

```
$certificates = Get-ChildItem Cert:\CurrentUser\My -CodeSign
$signingCert = @($certificates | Sort -Desc NotAfter)[0]
```

The `-CodeSign` parameter lets you search for certificates in the certificate store that support code signing. To search for certificates used for other purposes, see Recipe 18.14, "Program: Search the Certificate Store".

Although the certificate provider is useful for browsing and retrieving information from the computer's certificate stores, it does not let you add items to these locations. If you want to manage certificates in the certificate store, the `System.Security.`

`Cryptography.X509Certificates.X509Store` class (and other related classes from the `System.Security.Cryptography.X509Certificates` namespace) from the .NET Framework supports that functionality. For an example of this approach, see Recipe 18.15, "Add and Remove Certificates".

For more information about the certificate provider, type **Get-Help Certificate**.

## See Also

Recipe 18.14, "Program: Search the Certificate Store"

Recipe 18.15, "Add and Remove Certificates"

# 18.14. Program: Search the Certificate Store

One useful feature of the certificate provider is its support for a `-CodeSign` parameter that lets you search for certificates in the certificate store that support code signing.

This parameter is called a *dynamic parameter*: one that has been added by a provider to a core PowerShell cmdlet. You can discover the dynamic parameters for a provider by navigating to that provider and then reviewing the output of `Get-Command -Syntax`. For example:

```
PS > Set-Location cert:\
PS > Get-Command Get-ChildItem -Syntax
Get-ChildItem [[-Path] <String[]>] [[-Filter] <String>] (...) [-CodeSigningCert]
```

In addition to the output of `Get-Command`, the help topic for the provider often describes the dynamic parameters it supports. For a list of the provider help topics, type **Get-Help -Category Provider**.

Code-signing certificates are not the only kind of certificates, however; other frequently used certificate types are Encrypting File System, Client Authentication, and more.

Example 18-8 lets you search the certificate provider for certificates that support a given Enhanced Key Usage (EKU).

*Example 18-8. Search-CertificateStore.ps1*

```
##############################################################################
##
## Search-CertificateStore
##
## From Windows PowerShell Cookbook (O'Reilly)
## by Lee Holmes (http://www.leeholmes.com/guide)
##
##############################################################################

<#
```

```
.SYNOPSIS

Search the certificate provider for certificates that match the specified
Enhanced Key Usage (EKU.)

.EXAMPLE

PS > Search-CertificateStore "Encrypting File System"
Searches the certificate store for Encrypting File System certificates

#>

param(
    ## The friendly name of an Enhanced Key Usage
    ## (such as 'Code Signing')
    [Parameter(Mandatory = $true)]
    $EkuName
)

Set-StrictMode -Off

## Go through every certificate in the current user's "My" store
foreach($cert in Get-ChildItem cert:\CurrentUser\My)
{
    ## For each of those, go through its extensions
    foreach($extension in $cert.Extensions)
    {
        ## For each extension, go through its Enhanced Key Usages
        foreach($certEku in $extension.EnhancedKeyUsages)
        {
            ## If the friendly name matches, output that certificate
            if($certEku.FriendlyName -eq $ekuName)
            {
                $cert
            }
        }
    }
}
```

For more information about running scripts, see Recipe 1.1, "Run Programs, Scripts, and Existing Tools".

## See Also

Recipe 1.1, "Run Programs, Scripts, and Existing Tools"

# 18.15. Add and Remove Certificates

## Problem

You want to add and remove certificates in the certificate store.

## Solution

To remove a certificate, use the Remove-Item cmdlet. For example, to remove temporary certificates that you create when debugging SSL websites with the Fiddler HTTP debugging proxy:

```
PS Cert:\CurrentUser\My > dir |
    Where Subject -like "*OU=Created by http://www.fiddler2.com" | Remove-Item
```

To add a certificate, use the certificate store APIs from the .NET Framework, as shown in Example 18-9.

*Example 18-9. Adding certificates*

```
## Adding a certificate from disk
$cert = Get-PfxCertificate <path_to_certificate>
$store = New-Object System.Security.Cryptography.X509Certificates.X509Store `
    "TrustedPublisher","CurrentUser"
$store.Open("ReadWrite")
$store.Add($cert)
$store.Close()
```

## Discussion

The certificate drive provides a useful way to navigate and view certificates for the current user or local machine. For example, if your execution policy requires the use of digital signatures, the following command tells you which publishers are trusted to run scripts on your system:

```
Get-ChildItem cert:\CurrentUser\TrustedPublisher
```

If you want to remove a trusted publisher from this store, simply use the Remove-Item cmdlet to do so.

While it is easy to remove a certificate, adding a certificate is not as easy. For example, the Get-PfxCertificate cmdlet lets you review a certificate from a file that contains it, but it does not let you install it into the certificate store permanently. The .NET APIs provide the way to import the certificate for good.

For more information about retrieving certificates from the certificate provider, please see Recipe 18.13, "Access User and Machine Certificates". For more information about working with classes from the .NET Framework, please see Recipe 3.8, "Work with .NET Objects".

---

## See Also

Recipe 3.8, "Work with .NET Objects"

Recipe 18.13, "Access User and Machine Certificates"

# 18.16. Manage Security Descriptors in SDDL Form

## Problem

You want to work with a security identifier in Security Descriptor Definition Language (SDDL) form.

## Solution

Use the `System.Security.AccessControl.CommonSecurityDescriptor` class from the .NET Framework, as shown by Example 18-10.

*Example 18-10. Automating security configuration of the PowerShell Remoting Users group*

```
## Get the SID for the "PowerShell Remoting Users" group
$account = New-Object Security.Principal.NTAccount "PowerShell Remoting Users"
$sid = $account.Translate([Security.Principal.SecurityIdentifier]).Value

## Get the security descriptor for the existing configuration
$config = Get-PSSessionConfiguration Microsoft.PowerShell
$existingSddl = $config.SecurityDescriptorSddl

## Create a CommonSecurityDescriptor object out of the existing SDDL
## so that we don't need to manage the string by hand
$arguments = $false,$false,$existingSddl
$mapper = New-Object Security.AccessControl.CommonSecurityDescriptor $arguments

## Create a new access rule that adds the "PowerShell Remoting Users" group
$mapper.DiscretionaryAcl.AddAccess("Allow",$sid,268435456,"None","None")

## Get the new SDDL for that configuration
$newSddl = $mapper.GetSddlForm("All")

## Update the endpoint configuration
Set-PSSessionConfiguration Microsoft.PowerShell -SecurityDescriptorSddl $newSddl
```

## Discussion

Security descriptors are often shown (or requested) in SDDL form. The SDDL form of a security descriptor is cryptic, highly specific, and plain text. All of these aspects make this format difficult to work with reliably, so you can use the `System.Security.Access Control.CommonSecurityDescriptor` class from the .NET Framework to do most of the gritty work for you.

For more information about the SDDL format, see here (*http://msdn.microsoft.com/en-us/library/aa379570%28VS.85%29.aspx*). For an example of this in action, see Recipe 29.11, "Configure User Permissions for Remoting".

## See Also

Recipe 3.8, "Work with .NET Objects"

Recipe 29.11, "Configure User Permissions for Remoting"

# Integrated Scripting Environment

## 19.0. Introduction

While text-mode PowerShell is great for its efficiency and automation, there's not much to be said for its user interface. Most Windows key combinations don't work. Text selection and editing don't work. Rectangular text selection is strange, as is the lack of support for freely resizing the console window.

All of these are simple side effects of *PowerShell.exe* being a console application. These problems impact every console application in Windows and likely always will.

Aside from the user interface oddities, the fatal flaw with console applications comes from their lack of support for the Unicode standard: the way that most international languages represent their alphabets. While the Windows console supports a few basic non-English characters (such as accented letters), it provides full support for very little else.

This proves to be quite a problem for worldwide administrators! Since typing international characters directly at the command line was so difficult, administrators in many countries were forced to write scripts in Notepad in order to get full Unicode support, and then use PowerShell to run the scripts, even if the command was ultimately only a single line.

PowerShell resolves these issues by introducing the Integrated Scripting Environment (ISE).

The ISE gives PowerShell the user interface you expect from a modern application, supports full Unicode input and multiple tabbed sessions, and provides a great experience for interactive debugging.

Conceptually, the ISE consists of two main components (shown in Figure 19-1).

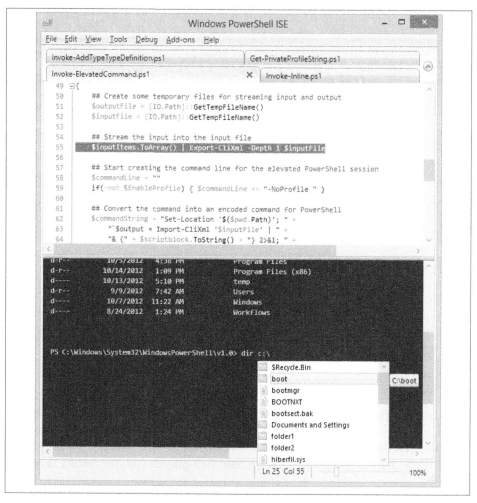

*Figure 19-1. Windows PowerShell Integrated Scripting Environment*

*Scripting pane*

The scripting pane is the top pane of the ISE, and it is geared toward multiline script editing and creation. It offers line numbering and syntax highlighting, and it supports a great debugging experience.

One unique aspect of the scripting pane is that it supports *selective execution*: the ability to run just what you've highlighted rather than the entire script you're working on. This makes script authoring a breeze. As you start to write your script, you can interactively experiment with commands until you get them right. Once they work as expected, you can keep them, move on, and then continue to build your script one piece at a time. As you've come to expect from PowerShell's console shell, script editing in the scripting pane supports tab completion of commands, parameters, paths, and more.

*Console pane*

The console pane, which sits in the bottom of the application, is where you'll spend most of your interactive sessions in the ISE. Like the command prompt in the PowerShell console, the console pane supports tab completion. Unlike the command pane in the console window, it supports standard Windows hotkeys, text selection, syntax highlighting, powerful IntelliSense, and more.

If you find your command growing too long, you can press Shift-Enter to enable multiline editing for the current command.

If you want the ISE to look like the regular PowerShell console (yet support easy resizing and intuitive hotkeys), simply select Show Script Pane Maximized from the Tools menu. You can then select Go to Console and Go to Script Pane to toggle between the fully immersive console and script editing modes.

In addition to these features, the PowerShell ISE offers extensive customization, scripting, and remoting support.

# 19.1. Debug a Script

## Problem

You want to use PowerShell's debugging commands through an interface more friendly than its `*-PsBreakpoint` cmdlets.

## Solution

Use the Debug menu in the ISE to add and remove breakpoints and manage debugging behavior when PowerShell reaches a breakpoint.

## Discussion

The PowerShell ISE gives you a rich set of interactive graphical debugging commands to help you diagnose errors in your scripts. It exposes these through the *Debug* menu, and it behaves like many other graphical debugging environments you may have experience with. Figure 19-2 shows the debugging option available in the ISE.

*Figure 19-2. Debugging options in the Integrated Scripting Environment*

To set a breakpoint, first save your script. Then, select the Toggle Breakpoint menu item, select the Toggle Breakpoint option that appears when you right-click in the lefthand margin of the ISE, or press F9. Once PowerShell hits the breakpoint in your script, it pauses to let you examine variables, script state, and whatever else interests you. To control the flow of execution, you can use the stepping commands: Step Over, Step Into, and Step Out.

Step Over continues to the next line of the script, executing (but not debugging into) any function calls that you come across. Step Into continues to the next line of the script, debugging into any function calls that you come across. If you are in a function, the Step Out command lets PowerShell complete execution of the function and resumes debugging once the function completes.

One unique aspect of debugging in the ISE is that it builds its support entirely on the core debugging cmdlets discussed in Chapter 14. Changes that you make from the debugging menu (such as adding a breakpoint) are immediately reflected in the cmdlets (such as listing breakpoints). Likewise, breakpoints that you add or modify from the integrated command line show up in the user interface as though you had created them from the Debug menu itself.

 In fact, the features exposed by PowerShell's breakpoint cmdlets in many cases surpass the functionality exposed by the ISE's debug menu. For example, the Set-PsDebug cmdlet supports command breakpoints, conditional breakpoints, variable breakpoints, and much more. For more information about the Set-PsDebug cmdlet, see Recipe 14.3, "Set a Script Breakpoint".

Unlike most graphical debugging environments, the PowerShell ISE makes it incredibly easy to investigate the dynamic state of your script while you are debugging it. For more information about how to investigate the state of your script while debugging, see Recipe 14.6, "Investigate System State While Debugging".

## See Also

Recipe 14.6, "Investigate System State While Debugging"

Chapter 14, *Debugging*

# 19.2. Customize Text and User Interface Colors

## Problem

You want to change the color scheme of the ISE or change the colors used for syntax highlighting.

## Solution

Review the properties of the $psISE.Options automatic variable, and customize the ones you want. For example, to give the console pane the same appearance as the PowerShell console (its default):

```
$psISE.Options.ConsolePaneBackgroundColor = "#012456"
$psISE.Options.ConsolePaneForegroundColor = "#EEEDF0"
$psISE.Options.ConsolePaneTextBackgroundColor = "#012456"
```

## Discussion

While working in the ISE, you might sometimes wonder, "Where is the Options dialog?"

Like many other applications, it is available through the Tools menu. That's not where configuration in the ISE ends, though. In addition, the ISE offers a wealth of configuration options through its $psISE automatic variable:

```
PS > $psISE.Options | Format-List

SelectedScriptPaneState        : Maximized
ShowDefaultSnippets            : True
ShowToolBar                    : False
ShowOutlining                  : True
ShowLineNumbers                : True
TokenColors                    : {[Attribute, #FF008080], [Command,
                                 #FF0000FF], [CommandArgument, #FF8A2BE2],
                                 [CommandParameter, #FF000080]...}

ConsoleTokenColors             : {[Attribute, #FFB0C4DE], [Command,
                                 #FFE0FFFF], [CommandArgument, #FFEE82EE],
                                 [CommandParameter, #FFFFE4B5]...}

XmlTokenColors                 : {[Comment, #FF006400], [CommentDelimiter,
                                 #FF008000], [ElementName, #FF8B0000],
                                 [MarkupExtension, #FFFF8C00]...}

DefaultOptions                 : Microsoft.PowerShell.Host.ISE.ISEOptions
FontSize                       : 9
Zoom                           : 100
FontName                       : Consolas
ErrorForegroundColor           : #FFFF0000
ErrorBackgroundColor           : #00FFFFFF
WarningForegroundColor         : #FFFF8C00
WarningBackgroundColor         : #00FFFFFF
VerboseForegroundColor         : #FF00FFFF
VerboseBackgroundColor         : #00FFFFFF
DebugForegroundColor           : #FF00FFFF
DebugBackgroundColor           : #00FFFFFF
ConsolePaneBackgroundColor     : #FF012456
ConsolePaneTextBackgroundColor : #FF012456
ConsolePaneForegroundColor     : #FFEEEDF0
ScriptPaneBackgroundColor      : #FFFFFFFF
ScriptPaneForegroundColor      : #FF000000
ShowWarningForDuplicateFiles   : True
ShowWarningBeforeSavingOnRun   : True
UseLocalHelp                   : True
AutoSaveMinuteInterval         : 2
MruCount                       : 10
ShowIntellisenseInConsolePane  : True
```

```
ShowIntellisenseInScriptPane          : True
UseEnterToSelectInConsolePaneIntellisense : True
UseEnterToSelectInScriptPaneIntellisense  : True
IntellisenseTimeoutInSeconds          : 3
```

You can change these options as easily as you change any other automatic variable—by assigning new values to its properties (as shown in the Solution). To apply these changes across all of your ISE sessions, simply store them in the host-specific profile file for the ISE. To edit this file, simply type: **ise $profile.CurrentUserCurrentHost**.

In addition to user interface customization, the ISE also lets you customize the colors it uses for syntax highlighting. It exposes these settings through the $psISE.Options.To kenColors automatic variable. For example, to change the coloring of variables to be bubble-gum pink, type:

```
$psIse.Options.TokenColors["Variable"] = "#FF11FF"
```

For more information about modifying your PowerShell profile, see Recipe 1.8, "Customize Your Shell, Profile, and Prompt".

## See Also

Recipe 1.8, "Customize Your Shell, Profile, and Prompt"

# 19.3. Connect to a Remote Computer

## Problem

You want to create a new tab in the ISE that represents a connection to a remote computer.

## Solution

Click the New Remote PowerShell Tab icon in the toolbar or File menu.

## Discussion

One of the features most requested for the PowerShell console application is support for multiple tabs and multiple sessions. As such, multitab support in the ISE is prominent—and gets a unique treatment.

To create a new tab that represents a local PowerShell session, simply click the New PowerShell Tab icon in the toolbar or File menu. If you want to connect to a remote computer instead, just click the New *Remote* PowerShell Tab menu or toolbar icon.

Once you've connected a remote PowerShell tab, interacting with a remote system is just like interacting with a local one. Prompts from the remote system show up like prompts from the local system, as do progress bars, credential requests, and PowerShell's other feedback mechanisms.

For more information about PowerShell Remoting, see Chapter 29.

### See Also

Chapter 29, *Remoting*

# 19.4. Extend ISE Functionality Through Its Object Model

## Problem

You want to customize the PowerShell ISE to add your own functionality and features.

## Solution

Explore and modify properties of the $psISE automatic variable to interact with the ISE's object model. For example, to clean up trailing spaces from the script you are currently editing, use the following:

```
$psISE.CurrentFile.Editor.Text =
    $psise.CurrentFile.Editor.Text -replace '(?m)\s+$',''
```

## Discussion

In addition to the features already available, the PowerShell ISE offers many additional customization opportunities through its *object model*. The object model exposes the nuts and bolts you need to create your own functionality—and makes it available through the $psISE automatic variable. Recipe 19.6, "Add an Item to the Tools Menu" demonstrates one aspect of the object model by showing how to add items to the Add-ons menu.

As with other .NET object models, the Get-Member and Format-List cmdlets are the keys to exploring the ISE's object model. At its first level, the object model gives you access to the current file, PowerShell tab, and ISE options:

```
PS > $psISE | Format-List


CurrentPowerShellTab : Microsoft.PowerShell.Host.ISE.PowerShellTab
CurrentFile          : Microsoft.PowerShell.Host.ISE.ISEFile
Options              : Microsoft.PowerShell.Host.ISE.ISEOptions
PowerShellTabs       : {PowerShell 1}
```

For example, the `$psISE.CurrentFile.Editor` variable provides programmatic access to the text and behavior of the current scripting pane:

```
PS > $psISE.CurrentFile.Editor | Get-Member

   TypeName: Microsoft.Windows.PowerShell.Gui.Internal.ScriptEditor

Name              MemberType Definition
----              ---------- ----------
PropertyChanged   Event      System.ComponentModel.PropertyChangedEventHandler...
Clear             Method     System.Void Clear()
EnsureVisible     Method     System.Void EnsureVisible(int lineNumber)
Equals            Method     bool Equals(System.Object obj)
Focus             Method     System.Void Focus()
GetHashCode       Method     int GetHashCode()
GetLineLength     Method     int GetLineLength(int lineNumber)
GetType           Method     type GetType()
InsertText        Method     System.Void InsertText(string text)
Select            Method     System.Void Select(int startLine, int startColumn,...
SetCaretPosition  Method     System.Void SetCaretPosition(int lineNumber, int c...
ToString          Method     string ToString()
CaretColumn       Property   System.Int32 CaretColumn {get;}
CaretLine         Property   System.Int32 CaretLine {get;}
LineCount         Property   System.Int32 LineCount {get;}
SelectedText      Property   System.String SelectedText {get;}
Text              Property   System.String Text {get;set;}
```

By building on the object model, you can write tools to automatically process your scripts (for example, commenting and uncommenting regions of your script, processing script output, and more).

For more information about working with .NET objects, see Recipe 3.8, "Work with .NET Objects".

## See Also

Recipe 3.8, "Work with .NET Objects"

Recipe 19.6, "Add an Item to the Tools Menu"

# 19.5. Quickly Insert Script Snippets

## Problem

You want to quickly insert common snippets of PowerShell script.

## Solution

Click Start Snippets from the ISE's Edit menu, or press Ctrl-J (see Figure 19-3).

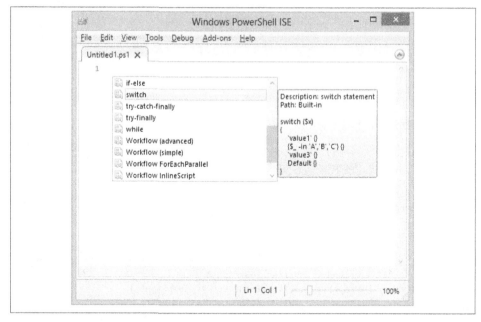

*Figure 19-3. Inserting a snippet*

## Discussion

Even with all of the great resources available, remembering the syntax for scripting constructs such as switch statements and comment-based help escapes all of us at some point in time. To help solve this problem, the Integrated Scripting Environment includes support for *snippets*—small sections of PowerShell script that you can insert simply by pressing Ctrl-J or by selecting the Start Snippets item in the Edit menu. Typing automatically searches for snippets that match the text you type.

By default, the ISE includes snippets for most sections of the PowerShell language. You can also extend this menu with snippets of your own.

If you'd like to create a simple snippet, simply run:

```
Show-Command New-ISESnippet
```

In the window that opens, Title represents the main title that will be shown in the drop-down box. Description represents the summary text that will be shown to the right of the menu. Text represents the text that will be used as the replacement text.

If you've got a multiline snippet that you'd like to add, PowerShell's splatting feature comes in handy:

```
$snippet = @{
    Title = "Header";
```

```
        Description = "Standard script header";
        Text = @"
##############################################
##
## My Standard Script Header
##
##############################################
"@
    }

    New-IseSnippet @snippet
```

For more information about splatting, see Recipe 11.14, "Dynamically Compose Command Parameters".

When you create a snippet, the ISE creates a file in a *Snippets* subdirectory of the directory that holds your profile. To remove a snippet, simply remove the corresponding file from your *Snippets* directory.

## See Also

Recipe 11.14, "Dynamically Compose Command Parameters"

# 19.6. Add an Item to the Tools Menu

## Problem

You want to add your own menu items and shortcuts to the ISE.

## Solution

Pick a display name, action, and (optional) shortcut, and then add those to the `$psISE.CurrentPowerShellTab.AddOnsMenu.Submenus` collection:

```
$psISE.CurrentPowerShellTab.AddOnsMenu.Submenus.Add(
    "PowerShell Blog",
    { Start-Process http://blogs.msdn.com/PowerShell },
    "Control+Alt+B")
```

## Discussion

As part of its extensibility features, the PowerShell ISE gives you complete access to a submenu of your very own: the Add-ons menu.

To work with the Add-ons menu, access the `$psISE.CurrentPowerShellTab.AddOnsMenu` variable.

By default, menu items that get added have no shortcuts, so you must click them to activate them. To add a typical menu shortcut that becomes active once the Add-ons menu is active, put an underscore (_) character before the letter that you want to activate your menu item.

To define a global hotkey (one that is available through the entire application), supply the keys as the third argument for the Add( ) method. If you don't want to assign a global hotkey, use $null as the third argument.

For more information about extending the ISE, see Recipe 19.4, "Extend ISE Functionality Through Its Object Model".

## See Also

Recipe 19.4, "Extend ISE Functionality Through Its Object Model"

# Administrator Tasks

Chapter 20, *Files and Directories*

Chapter 21, *The Windows Registry*

Chapter 22, *Comparing Data*

Chapter 23, *Event Logs*

Chapter 24, *Processes*

Chapter 25, *System Services*

Chapter 26, *Active Directory*

Chapter 27, *Enterprise Computer Management*

Chapter 28, *Windows Management Instrumentation*

Chapter 29, *Remoting*

Chapter 30, *Workflows*

Chapter 31, *Transactions*

Chapter 32, *Event Handling*

# Files and Directories

## 20.0. Introduction

One of the most common tasks when administering a system is working with its files and directories. This is true when you administer the computer at the command line, and it is true when you write scripts to administer it automatically.

Fortunately, PowerShell makes scripting files and directories as easy as working at the command line—a point that many seasoned programmers and scripters often miss. A perfect example of this comes when you wrestle with limited disk space and need to find the files taking up the most space.

A typical programmer might approach this task by writing functions to scan a specific directory of a system. For each file, they check whether the file is big enough to care about. If so, they add it to a list. For each directory in the original directory, the programmer repeats this process (until there are no more directories to process).

As the saying goes, though, "You can write C in any programming language." The habits and preconceptions you bring to a language often directly influence how open you are to advances in that language.

Being an administrative shell, PowerShell directly supports tasks such as visiting all the files in a subdirectory or moving a file from one directory to another. That complicated programmer-oriented script turns into a one-liner:

```
Get-ChildItem -Recurse | Sort-Object -Descending Length | Select -First 10
```

Before diving into your favorite programmer's toolkit, check to see what PowerShell supports in that area. In many cases, it can handle the task without requiring your programmer's bag of tricks.

# 20.1. Determine the Current Location

## Problem

You want to determine the current location from a script or command.

## Solution

To retrieve the current location, use the `Get-Location` cmdlet. The `Get-Location` cmdlet provides the drive and path as two common properties:

```
$currentLocation = (Get-Location).Path
```

As a short form for `(Get-Location).Path`, use the `$pwd` automatic variable.

## Discussion

The `Get-Location` cmdlet returns information about the current location. From the information it returns, you can access the current drive, provider, and path.

This current location affects PowerShell commands and programs that you launch from PowerShell. This does not apply when you interact with the .NET Framework, however. If you need to call a .NET method that interacts with the filesystem, always be sure to provide fully qualified paths:

```
[System.IO.File]::ReadAllText("c:\temp\file.txt")
```

If you are sure that the file exists, the `Resolve-Path` cmdlet lets you translate a relative path to an absolute path:

```
$filePath = (Resolve-Path file.txt).Path
```

If the file does not exist, use the `Join-Path` cmdlet in combination with the `Get-Location` cmdlet to specify the file:

```
$filePath = Join-Path (Get-Location) file.txt
```

Another alternative that combines the functionality of both approaches is a bit more advanced but also lets you specify relative locations. It comes from methods in the PowerShell `$executionContext` variable, which provides functionality normally used by cmdlet and provider authors:

```
$executionContext.SessionState.Path. `
    GetUnresolvedProviderPathFromPSPath("..\file.txt")
```

For more information about the `Get-Location` cmdlet, type **Get-Help Get-Location**.

# 20.2. Get the Files in a Directory

## Problem

You want to get or list the files in a directory.

## Solution

To retrieve the list of files in a directory, use the Get-ChildItem cmdlet. To get a specific item, use the Get-Item cmdlet.

- To list all items in the current directory, use the Get-ChildItem cmdlet:

  ```
  Get-ChildItem
  ```

- To list all items that match a wildcard, supply a wildcard to the Get-ChildItem cmdlet:

  ```
  Get-ChildItem *.txt
  ```

- To list all files that match a wildcard in the current directory (and all its children), use the -Recurse parameter of the Get-ChildItem cmdlet:

  ```
  Get-ChildItem *.txt -Recurse
  ```

- To list all directories in the current directory, use the -Attributes parameter:

  ```
  Get-ChildItem -Attributes Directory
  dir -ad
  ```

- To get information about a specific item, use the Get-Item cmdlet:

  ```
  Get-Item test.txt
  ```

## Discussion

Although most commonly used on the filesystem, the Get-ChildItem and Get-Item cmdlets in fact work against any items on any of the PowerShell drives. In addition to A: through Z: (the standard filesystem drives), they also work on Alias:, Cert:, Env:, Function:, HKLM:, HKCU:, and Variable:.

While the Solution demonstrates some simple wildcard scenarios that the Get-ChildItem cmdlet supports, PowerShell in fact enables several more advanced scenarios. For more information about these scenarios, see Recipe 20.6, "Find Files That Match a Pattern". One specific point of interest is that the third example in the Solution lists files that match a wildcard in a directory and all its children. That example works on any PowerShell provider. However, PowerShell can retrieve your results more quickly if you use a provider-specific filter, as described in Recipe 20.6, "Find Files That Match a Pattern".

Versions 1 and 2 of PowerShell had issues when you used the syntax in the Solution to recursively search for files. If you need to support PowerShell version 1 or 2, use the Include parameter: `Get-ChildItem -Include *.txt -Recurse`.

When you're working in the filesystem, the `Get-ChildItem` cmdlet exposes several parameters (`-Directory`, `-File`, `-ReadOnly`, `-Hidden`, and `-System`) to make filtering as simple as possible. These parameters have aliases as well (for example, `-ad`), making short work of most common tasks:

```
Get-ChildItem -Directory
dir -ad
```

For less common attributes, the `-Attributes` parameter supports powerful filtering against all other file and directory properties. At its most basic level, you can supply any standard file attribute. PowerShell only returns files with that attribute set:

```
Get-ChildItem -Attributes Compressed
```

To return items that do not have an attribute set (a "not" scenario), use an exclamation point:

```
Get-ChildItem -Attributes !Archive
```

To return items that have *any* of several attributes set (an "or" scenario), use a comma:

```
Get-ChildItem -Attributes "Hidden, ReadOnly"
```

To return items that have *all* of several attributes set (an "and" scenario), use a plus:

```
Get-ChildItem -Attributes "ReadOnly + Hidden"
```

You can combine these filters at will. For example, to find all items that are `ReadOnly` or `Hidden` and not `System`:

```
Get-ChildItem c:\ -Attributes "ReadOnly, Hidden + !System"
```

The `-Attributes` parameter was introduced in PowerShell version 3. If you require a solution that works on PowerShell version 2, you can script against file properties (such as `PSIsContainer`) and attributes directly.

In the filesystem, these cmdlets return objects from the .NET Framework that represent files and directories—instances of `System.IO.FileInfo` and `System.IO.Direct oryInfo` classes, respectively. Each provides a great deal of useful information: attributes, modification times, full name, and more. Although the default directory listing exposes a lot of information, PowerShell provides even more. For more information about working with classes from the .NET Framework, please see Recipe 3.8, "Work with .NET Objects".

## See Also

Recipe 3.8, "Work with .NET Objects"

Recipe 20.6, "Find Files That Match a Pattern"

# 20.3. Find All Files Modified Before a Certain Date

## Problem

You want to find all files last modified before a certain date.

## Solution

To find all files modified before a certain date, use the Get-ChildItem cmdlet to list the files in a directory, and then use the Where-Object cmdlet to compare the LastWrite Time property to the date you are interested in. For example, to find all files created before the year 2007:

```
Get-ChildItem -Recurse | Where-Object { $_.LastWriteTime -lt "01/01/2007" }
```

## Discussion

A common reason to compare files against a certain date is to find recently modified (or not recently modified) files. The code for this looks almost the same as the example given by the Solution, except your script can't know the exact date to compare against.

In this case, the AddDays() method in the .NET Framework's DateTime class gives you a way to perform some simple calendar arithmetic. If you have a DateTime object, you can add or subtract time from it to represent a different date altogether. For example, to find all files modified in the last 30 days:

```
$compareDate = (Get-Date).AddDays(-30)
Get-ChildItem -Recurse | Where-Object { $_.LastWriteTime -ge $compareDate }
```

Similarly, to find all files more than 30 days old:

```
$compareDate = (Get-Date).AddDays(-30)
Get-ChildItem -Recurse | Where-Object { $_.LastWriteTime -lt $compareDate }
```

In this example, the Get-Date cmdlet returns an object that represents the current date and time. You call the AddDays() method to subtract 30 days from that time, which stores the date representing "30 days ago" in the $compareDate variable. Next, you compare that date against the LastWriteTime property of each file that the Get-ChildItem cmdlet returns.

The DateTime class is the administrator's favorite calendar!

```
PS > [DateTime]::IsLeapYear(2008)
True
PS > $daysTillChristmas = [DateTime] "December 25" - (Get-Date)
PS > $daysTillChristmas.Days
327
```

For more information about the Get-ChildItem cmdlet, type **Get-Help Get-ChildItem**. For more information about the Where-Object cmdlet, see Recipe 2.1, "Filter Items in a List or Command Output".

## See Also

Recipe 2.1, "Filter Items in a List or Command Output"

# 20.4. Clear the Content of a File

## Problem

You want to clear the content of a file.

## Solution

To clear the content of a file, use the Clear-Content cmdlet, as shown by Example 20-1.

*Example 20-1. Clearing content from a file*

```
PS > Get-Content test.txt
Hello World
PS > Clear-Content test.txt
PS > Get-Content test.txt
PS > Get-Item test.txt


    Directory: C:\temp


Mode                LastWriteTime     Length Name
----                -------------     ------ ----
-a---          4/23/2007   8:05 PM         0 test.txt
```

## Discussion

The (aptly named) Clear-Content cmdlet clears the content from an item. Although the Solution demonstrates this only for files in the filesystem, it in fact applies to any PowerShell providers that support the concept of "content." Examples of other drives that support these content concepts are *Function:, Alias:,* and *Variable:.*

---

For information on how to remove an item entirely, see Recipe 20.13, "Remove a File or Directory".

For more information about the `Remove-Item` or `Clear-Content` cmdlets, type **Get-Help Remove-Item** or **Get-Help Clear-Content**.

## See Also

Recipe 20.13, "Remove a File or Directory"

# 20.5. Manage and Change the Attributes of a File

## Problem

You want to update the `ReadOnly`, `Hidden`, or `System` attributes of a file.

## Solution

Most of the time, you will want to use the familiar *attrib.exe* program to change the attributes of a file:

```
attrib +r test.txt
attrib -s test.txt
```

To set only the `ReadOnly` attribute, you can optionally set the `IsReadOnly` property on the file:

```
$file = Get-Item test.txt
$file.IsReadOnly = $true
```

To apply a specific set of attributes, use the `Attributes` property on the file:

```
$file = Get-Item test.txt
$file.Attributes = "ReadOnly,NotContentIndexed"
```

Directory listings show the attributes on a file, but you can also access the `Mode` or `Attributes` property directly:

```
PS > $file.Attributes = "ReadOnly","System","NotContentIndexed"
PS > $file.Mode
--r-s
PS > $file.Attributes
ReadOnly, System, NotContentIndexed
```

## Discussion

When the `Get-Item` or `Get-ChildItem` cmdlets retrieve a file, the resulting output has an `Attributes` property. This property doesn't offer much in addition to the regular *attrib.exe* program, although it does make it easier to set the attributes to a specific state.

Be aware that setting the Hidden attribute on a file removes it from most default views. If you want to retrieve it after hiding it, most commands require a -Force parameter. Similarly, setting the ReadOnly attribute on a file causes most write operations on that file to fail unless you call that command with the -Force parameter.

If you want to add an attribute to a file using the Attributes property (rather than *attrib.exe* for some reason), this is how you would do that:

```
$file = Get-Item test.txt
$readOnly = [IO.FileAttributes] "ReadOnly"
$file.Attributes = $file.Attributes -bor $readOnly
```

For more information about working with classes from the .NET Framework, see Recipe 3.8, "Work with .NET Objects".

### See Also

Recipe 3.8, "Work with .NET Objects"

# 20.6. Find Files That Match a Pattern

## Problem

You want to get a list of files that match a specific pattern.

## Solution

Use the Get-ChildItem cmdlet for both simple and advanced wildcard support:

- To find all items in the current directory that match a PowerShell wildcard, supply that wildcard to the Get-ChildItem cmdlet:

    ```
    Get-ChildItem *.txt
    ```

- To find all items in the current directory that match a *provider-specific* filter, supply that filter to the -Filter parameter:

    ```
    Get-ChildItem -Filter *~2*
    ```

- To find all items in the current directory that do not match a PowerShell wildcard, supply that wildcard to the -Exclude parameter:

    ```
    Get-ChildItem -Exclude *.txt
    ```

- To find all items in subdirectories that match a PowerShell wildcard, use the -Include and -Recurse parameters, or use the wildcard as part of the -Path parameter:

```
Get-ChildItem -Include *.txt -Recurse
Get-ChildItem *.txt -Recurse
Get-ChildItem -Path c:\temp\*.txt -Recurse
```

- To find all items in subdirectories that match a *provider-specific* filter, use the -Filter and -Recurse parameters:

```
Get-ChildItem -Filter *.txt -Recurse
```

- To find all items in subdirectories that do not match a PowerShell wildcard, use the -Exclude and -Recurse parameters:

```
Get-ChildItem -Exclude *.txt -Recurse
```

Use the Where-Object cmdlet for advanced regular expression support:

- To find all items with a filename that matches a regular expression, use the Where-Object cmdlet to compare the Name property to the regular expression:

```
Get-ChildItem | Where-Object { $_.Name -match '^KB[0-9]+\.log$' }
```

- To find all items with a directory name that matches a regular expression, use the Where-Object cmdlet to compare the DirectoryName property to the regular expression:

```
Get-ChildItem -Recurse | Where-Object { $_.DirectoryName -match 'Release' }
```

- To find all items with a directory name or filename that matches a regular expression, use the Where-Object cmdlet to compare the FullName property to the regular expression:

```
Get-ChildItem -Recurse | Where-Object { $_.FullName -match 'temp' }
```

## Discussion

The Get-ChildItem cmdlet supports wildcarding through three parameters:

Path

The -Path parameter is the first (and default) parameter. While you can enter simple paths such as ., C:\, or D:\Documents, you can also supply paths that include wildcards—such as *, *.txt, [a-z]???.log, or even C:\win*\*.N[a-f]?\ F*\v2* \csc.exe.

Include/Exclude

The -Include and -Exclude parameters act as a filter on wildcarding that happens on the -Path parameter. If you specify the -Recurse parameter, the -Include and -Exclude wildcards apply to all items returned.

The most common mistake with the -Include parameter comes when you use it against a path with no wildcards. For example, this doesn't seem to produce the expected results:

```
Get-ChildItem $env:WINDIR -Include *.log
```

That command produces no results because you have not supplied an item wildcard to the path. Instead, the correct command is:

```
Get-ChildItem $env:WINDIR\* -Include *.log
```

Or simply:

```
Get-ChildItem $env:WINDIR\*.log
```

### Filter

The -Filter parameter lets you filter results based on the *provider-specific* filtering language of the provider from which you retrieve items. Since PowerShell's wildcarding support closely mimics filesystem wildcards, and most people use the -Filter parameter only on the filesystem, this seems like a redundant (and equivalent) parameter. A SQL provider, however, would use SQL syntax in its -Filter parameter. Likewise, an Active Directory provider would use LDAP paths in its -Filter parameter.

It may not be obvious, but the filesystem provider's filtering language is not exactly the same as the PowerShell wildcard syntax. For example, the -Filter parameter matches against the short filenames, too:

```
PS > Get-ChildItem | Select-Object Name

Name
----
A Long File Name With Spaces Also.txt
A Long File Name With Spaces.txt

PS > Get-ChildItem *1* | Select-Object Name
PS > Get-ChildItem -Filter *1* | Select-Object Name

Name
----
A Long File Name With Spaces.txt
```

On the other hand, PowerShell's wildcard syntax supports far more than the filesystem's native filtering language. For more information about PowerShell's wildcard syntax, type **Get-Help About_WildCard**.

When you want to perform even more advanced filtering than what PowerShell's wildcarding syntax offers, the Where-Object cmdlet provides infinite possibilities. For example, to exclude certain directories from a search, use the following:

```
Get-ChildItem -Rec | Where-Object { $_.DirectoryName -notmatch "Debug" }
```

Since the syntax of the Where-Object cmdlet can sometimes be burdensome for simple queries, the simplified Where-Object syntax in Recipe 2.3, "Program: Simplify Most Where-Object Filters" provides an attractive alternative:

```
Get-ChildItem -Rec | ? DirectoryName -notmatch Debug
```

For a filter that is difficult (or impossible) to specify programmatically, use the Out-GridView cmdlet as demonstrated in Recipe 2.4, "Program: Interactively Filter Lists of Objects" to interactively filter the output.

Because of PowerShell's pipeline model, an advanced file set generated by Get-ChildItem automatically turns into an advanced file set for other cmdlets to operate on:

```
PS > Get-ChildItem -Rec | Where-Object { $_.Length -gt 20mb } |
    Sort-Object -Descending Length | Select-FilteredObject |
    Remove-Item -WhatIf

What if: Performing operation "Remove File" on Target "C:\temp\backup092.zip".
What if: Performing operation "Remove File" on Target "C:\temp\slime.mov".
What if: Performing operation "Remove File" on Target "C:\temp\hello.mov".
```

For more information about the Get-ChildItem cmdlet, type **Get-Help Get-ChildItem**.

For more information about the Where-Object cmdlet, type **Get-Help Where-Object**.

## See Also

Recipe 2.3, "Program: Simplify Most Where-Object Filters"

Recipe 2.4, "Program: Interactively Filter Lists of Objects"

# 20.7. Manage Files That Include Special Characters

## Problem

You want to use a cmdlet that supports wildcarding but provide a filename that includes wildcard characters.

## Solution

To prevent PowerShell from treating those characters as wildcard characters, use the cmdlet's -LiteralPath (or similarly named) parameter if it defines one:

```
Get-ChildItem -LiteralPath '[My File].txt'
```

## Discussion

One consequence of PowerShell's advanced wildcard support is that the square brackets used to specify character ranges sometimes conflict with actual filenames. Consider the following example:

```
PS > Get-ChildItem | Select-Object Name

Name
----
[My File].txt

PS > Get-ChildItem '[My File].txt' | Select-Object Name
PS > Get-ChildItem -LiteralPath '[My File].txt' | Select-Object Name

Name
----
[My File].txt
```

The first command clearly demonstrates that we have a file called *[My File].txt*. When we try to retrieve it (passing its name to the `Get-ChildItem` cmdlet), we see no results. Since square brackets are wildcard characters in PowerShell (as are * and ?), the text we provided turns into a search expression rather than a filename.

The `-LiteralPath` parameter (or a similarly named parameter in other cmdlets) tells PowerShell that the filename is named exactly—not a wildcard search term.

In addition to wildcard matching, filenames may sometimes run afoul of PowerShell escape sequences. For example, the backtick character ( ` ) in PowerShell means the start of an escape sequence, such as `` `t `` (tab), `` `n `` (newline), or `` `a `` (alarm). To prevent PowerShell from interpreting a backtick as an escape sequence, surround that string in single quotes instead of double quotes.

For more information about the `Get-ChildItem` cmdlet, type **Get-Help Get-ChildItem**. For more information about PowerShell's special characters, type **Get-Help About_ Special_Characters**.

# 20.8. Program: Get Disk Usage Information

When disk space starts running low, you'll naturally want to find out where to focus your cleanup efforts. Sometimes you may tackle this by looking for large directories (including the directories in them), but other times, you may solve this by looking for directories that are large simply from the files they contain.

To review the disk usage statistics for an entire drive, use the Get-PSDrive cmdlet.

---

Example 20-2 collects both types of data. It also demonstrates an effective use of *calculated properties*. Like the Add-Member cmdlet, calculated properties let you add properties to output objects by specifying the expression that generates their data.

For more information about calculated properties and the Add-Member cmdlet, see Recipe 3.15, "Add Custom Methods and Properties to Objects".

*Example 20-2. Get-DiskUsage.ps1*

```
##############################################################################
##
## Get-DiskUsage
##
## From Windows PowerShell Cookbook (O'Reilly)
## by Lee Holmes (http://www.leeholmes.com/guide)
##
##############################################################################

<#

.SYNOPSIS

Retrieve information about disk usage in the current directory and all
subdirectories. If you specify the -IncludeSubdirectories flag, this
script accounts for the size of subdirectories in the size of a directory.

.EXAMPLE

PS > Get-DiskUsage
Gets the disk usage for the current directory.

.EXAMPLE

PS > Get-DiskUsage -IncludeSubdirectories
Gets the disk usage for the current directory and those below it,
adding the size of child directories to the directory that contains them.

#>

param(
    ## Switch to include subdirectories in the size of each directory
    [switch] $IncludeSubdirectories
)

Set-StrictMode -Version 3

## If they specify the -IncludeSubdirectories flag, then we want to account
## for all subdirectories in the size of each directory
if($includeSubdirectories)
{
    Get-ChildItem -Directory |
        Select-Object Name,
```

```
                @{ Name="Size";
                Expression={ ($_ | Get-ChildItem -Recurse |
                    Measure-Object -Sum Length).Sum + 0 } }
}
## Otherwise, we just find all directories below the current directory,
## and determine their size
else
{
    Get-ChildItem -Recurse -Directory |
        Select-Object FullName,
            @{ Name="Size";
            Expression={ ($_ | Get-ChildItem |
                Measure-Object -Sum Length).Sum + 0 } }
}
```

For more information about running scripts, see Recipe 1.1, "Run Programs, Scripts, and Existing Tools".

## See Also

Recipe 1.1, "Run Programs, Scripts, and Existing Tools"

Recipe 3.15, "Add Custom Methods and Properties to Objects"

# 20.9. Monitor a File for Changes

## Problem

You want to monitor the end of a file for new content.

## Solution

To monitor the end of a file for new content, use the -Wait parameter of the Get-Content cmdlet:

```
Get-Content log.txt -Wait
```

## Discussion

The -Wait parameter of the Get-Content cmdlet acts much like the traditional Unix tail command with the --follow parameter. If you provide the -Wait parameter, the Get-Content cmdlet reads the content of the file but doesn't exit. When a program appends new content to the end of the file, the Get-Content cmdlet returns that content and continues to wait.

If you want to monitor a large file, the initial output displayed by the -Wait parameter Get-Content might flood your screen or take a long time to complete. To read from the end of the file, use the -Tail parameter. For example, to start with the final 10 lines:

```
Get-Content log.txt -Tail 10 -Wait
```

For more information about the Get-Content cmdlet, type **Get-Help Get-Content**. For more information about the -Wait parameter, type **Get-Help FileSystem**.

# 20.10. Get the Version of a DLL or Executable

## Problem

You want to examine the version information of a file.

## Solution

Use the Get-Item cmdlet to retrieve the file, and then access the VersionInfo property to retrieve its version information:

```
PS > $file = Get-Item $pshome\powershell.exe
PS > $file.VersionInfo

ProductVersion   FileVersion     FileName
--------------   -----------     --------
6.2.9200.16384   6.2.9200.16384  C:\Win...\WindowsPowerShell\v1.0\powershell.exe
```

## Discussion

One common task in system administration is identifying file and version information of installed software. PowerShell makes this simple through the VersionInfo property that it automatically attaches to files that you retrieve through the Get-Item cmdlet. To generate a report for a directory, simply pass the output of Get-ChildItem to the Select-Object cmdlet, and use the -ExpandProperty parameter to expand the VersionInfo property.

```
PS > Get-ChildItem $env:WINDIR |
    Select -Expand VersionInfo -ErrorAction SilentlyContinue

ProductVersion   FileVersion     FileName
--------------   -----------     --------
                                 C:\Windows\autologon.log
6.0.6000.16386   6.0.6000.1638... C:\Windows\bfsvc.exe
                                 C:\Windows\bootstat.dat
                                 C:\Windows\DtcInstall.log
6.0.6000.16386   6.0.6000.1638... C:\Windows\explorer.exe
```

```
6.0.6000.16386   6.0.6000.1638... C:\Windows\fveupdate.exe
6.0.6000.16386   6.0.6000.1638... C:\Windows\HelpPane.exe
6.0.6000.16386   6.0.6000.1638... C:\Windows\hh.exe
(...)
```

For more information about the Get-ChildItem cmdlet, see Recipe 20.2, "Get the Files in a Directory".

## See Also

Recipe 20.2, "Get the Files in a Directory"

# 20.11. Program: Get the MD5 or SHA1 Hash of a File

File hashes provide a useful way to check for damage or modification to a file. A digital hash acts like the fingerprint of a file and detects even minor modifications. If the content of a file changes, then so does its hash. Many online download services provide the hash of a file on that file's download page so you can determine whether the transfer somehow corrupted the file (see Figure 20-1).

↑ Top of page

**Additional Information**
To verify that your download of the ISO file for the Windows SDK is not corrupt, here is some verification information:
AutoCRC: 0x3DFD5327
Size: 1.15 GB (1,245,220,864 bytes)
MD5 hash: c2ee660c326940d4ea78e7b6e48afb98
SHA-1 hash: 573f966ed120aeda74755283fb6112f1094327dc

*Figure 20-1. File hashes as a verification mechanism*

There are three common ways to generate the hash of a file: MD5, SHA1, and SHA256. The most common is MD5, and the next most common is SHA1. While popular, these hash types can be trusted to detect only accidental file modification. They can be fooled if somebody wants to tamper with the file without changing its hash. The SHA256 algorithm can be used to protect against even intentional file tampering.

Example 20-3 lets you determine the hash of a file (or of multiple files if provided by the pipeline).

*Example 20-3. Get-FileHash.ps1*

```
##############################################################################
##
## Get-FileHash
##
## From Windows PowerShell Cookbook (O'Reilly)
## by Lee Holmes (http://www.leeholmes.com/guide)
##
```

```
##############################################################################

<#

.SYNOPSIS

Get the hash of an input file.

.EXAMPLE

PS > Get-FileHash myFile.txt
Gets the hash of a specific file

.EXAMPLE

dir | Get-FileHash
Gets the hash of files from the pipeline

.EXAMPLE

Get-FileHash myFile.txt -Hash SHA1
Gets the hash of myFile.txt, using the SHA1 hashing algorithm

#>

param(
    ## The path of the file to check
    $Path,

    ## The algorithm to use for hash computation
    [ValidateSet("MD5", "SHA1", "SHA256", "SHA384", "SHA512")]
    $HashAlgorithm = "MD5"
)

Set-StrictMode -Version 3

## Create the hash object that calculates the hash of our file.
$hashType = [Type] "System.Security.Cryptography.$HashAlgorithm"
$hasher = $hashType::Create()

## Create an array to hold the list of files
$files = @()

## If they specified the filename as a parameter, add that to the list
## of files to process
if($path)
{
    $files += $path
}
## Otherwise, take the files that they piped in to the script.
## For each input file, put its full name into the file list
else
```

```
{
    $files += @($input | Foreach-Object { $_.FullName })
}

## Go through each of the items in the list of input files
foreach($file in $files)
{
    ## Skip the item if it is not a file
    if(-not (Test-Path $file -Type Leaf)) { continue }

    ## Convert it to a fully-qualified path
    $filename = (Resolve-Path $file).Path

    ## Use the ComputeHash method from the hash object to calculate
    ## the hash
    $inputStream = New-Object IO.StreamReader $filename
    $hashBytes = $hasher.ComputeHash($inputStream.BaseStream)
    $inputStream.Close()

    ## Convert the result to hexadecimal
    $builder = New-Object System.Text.StringBuilder
    $hashBytes | Foreach-Object { [void] $builder.Append($_.ToString("X2")) }

    ## Return a custom object with the important details from the
    ## hashing
    $output = New-Object PsObject -Property @{
        Path = ([IO.Path]::GetFileName($file));
        HashAlgorithm = $hashAlgorithm;
        HashValue = $builder.ToString()
    }

    $output
}
```

For more information about running scripts, see Recipe 1.1, "Run Programs, Scripts, and Existing Tools".

## See Also

Recipe 1.1, "Run Programs, Scripts, and Existing Tools"

# 20.12. Create a Directory

## Problem

You want to create a directory or file folder.

---

## Solution

To create a directory, use the md or mkdir function:

```
PS > md NewDirectory


    Directory: C:\temp


Mode              LastWriteTime     Length Name
----              -------------     ------ ----
d----         4/29/2007   7:31  PM         NewDirectory
```

## Discussion

The md and mkdir functions are simple wrappers around the more sophisticated New-Item cmdlet. As you might guess, the New-Item cmdlet creates an item at the location you provide. To create a directory using the New-Item cmdlet directly, supply Directory to the -Type parameter.

```
New-Item -Path C:\Temp\NewDirectory -Type Directory
```

The New-Item cmdlet doesn't work against only the filesystem, however. Any providers that support the concept of items automatically support this cmdlet as well.

For more information about the New-Item cmdlet, type **Get-Help New-Item**.

# 20.13. Remove a File or Directory

## Problem

You want to remove a file or directory.

## Solution

To remove a file or directory, use the Remove-Item cmdlet:

```
PS > Test-Path NewDirectory
True
PS > Remove-Item NewDirectory
PS > Test-Path NewDirectory
False
```

## Discussion

The Remove-Item cmdlet removes an item from the location you provide. The RemoveItem cmdlet doesn't work against only the filesystem, however. Any providers that support the concept of items automatically support this cmdlet as well.

The Remove-Item cmdlet lets you specify multiple files through its Path, Include, Exclude, and Filter parameters. For information on how to use these parameters effectively, see Recipe 20.6, "Find Files That Match a Pattern".

If the item is a container (for example, a directory), PowerShell warns you that your action will also remove anything inside that container. You can provide the -Recurse flag if you want to prevent this message.

For more information about the Remove-Item cmdlet, type **Get-Help Remove-Item**.

## See Also

Recipe 20.6, "Find Files That Match a Pattern"

# 20.14. Rename a File or Directory

## Problem

You want to rename a file or directory.

## Solution

To rename an item in a provider, use the Rename-Item cmdlet:

```
PS > Rename-Item example.txt example2.txt
```

## Discussion

The Rename-Item cmdlet changes the name of an item.

Some shells let you rename multiple files at the same time. In those shells, the command looks like this:

```
ren *.gif *.jpg
```

PowerShell does not support this syntax, but provides even more power through its -replace operator. As a simple example, we can emulate the preceding command:

```
Get-ChildItem *.gif | Rename-Item -NewName { $_.Name -replace '.gif$','.jpg' }
```

This syntax provides an immense amount of power. Consider removing underscores from filenames and replacing them with spaces:

```
Get-ChildItem *_* | Rename-Item -NewName { $_.Name -replace '_',' ' }
```

or restructuring files in a directory with the naming convention of <*Report_Project_ Quarter*>.*txt*:

```
PS > Get-ChildItem | Select Name

Name
----
Report_Project1_Q3.txt
Report_Project1_Q4.txt
Report_Project2_Q1.txt
```

You might want to change that to *<Quarter_Project>.txt* with an advanced replacement pattern:

```
PS > Get-ChildItem |
    Rename-Item -NewName { $_.Name -replace '.*_(.*)_(.*)\.txt','$2_$1.txt' }

PS > Get-ChildItem | Select Name

Name
----
Q1_Project2.txt
Q3_Project1.txt
Q4_Project1.txt
```

For more information about the `-replace` operator, see Recipe 5.8, "Replace Text in a String".

Like the other `*-Item` cmdlets, the `Rename-Item` doesn't work against only the filesystem. Any providers that support the concept of items automatically support this cmdlet as well. For more information about the `Rename-Item` cmdlet, type **Get-Help Rename-Item**.

## See Also

Recipe 5.8, "Replace Text in a String"

# 20.15. Move a File or Directory

## Problem

You want to move a file or directory.

## Solution

To move a file or directory, use the `Move-Item` cmdlet:

```
PS > Move-Item example.txt c:\temp\example2.txt
```

## Discussion

The Move-Item cmdlet moves an item from one location to another. Like the other *-Item cmdlets, Move-Item doesn't work against only the filesystem. Any providers that support the concept of items automatically support this cmdlet as well.

 The Move-Item cmdlet lets you specify multiple files through its Path, Include, Exclude, and Filter parameters. For information on how to use these parameters effectively, see Recipe 20.6, "Find Files That Match a Pattern".

Although the Move-Item cmdlet works in every provider, you cannot move items between providers. For more information about the Move-Item cmdlet, type **Get-Help Move-Item**.

## See Also

Recipe 20.6, "Find Files That Match a Pattern"

# 20.16. Create and Map PowerShell Drives

## Problem

You want to create a custom drive letter for use within PowerShell.

## Solution

To create a custom drive, use the New-PSDrive cmdlet:

```
PS > $myDocs = [Environment]::GetFolderPath("MyDocuments")
PS > New-PSDrive -Name MyDocs -Root $myDocs -PSProvider FileSystem

Name          Used (GB)      Free (GB) Provider      Root
----          ---------      --------- --------      ----
MyDocs                        1718.98 FileSystem     G:\Lee

PS > dir MyDocs:\Cookbook

    Directory: G:\Lee\Cookbook

Mode                LastWriteTime     Length Name
----                -------------     ------ ----
d----         7/10/2012   1:12 PM            Admin
d----         2/15/2010  10:39 AM            chapters
(...)
```

To create a custom drive available throughout all of Windows, use the `-Persist` flag:

```
PS > $serverDocs = "\\server\shared\documents"
PS > New-PSDrive -Name Z -Root $serverDocs -PSProvider FileSystem -Persist
```

## Discussion

In addition to the standard drive letters you are used to (*A:* through *Z:*), PowerShell also lets you define drives with completely custom names. Using the `New-PSDrive` cmdlet, you can create friendly drive names for all of your most commonly used paths.

When you use the `New-PSDrive` cmdlet to create a custom drive mapping, PowerShell automatically creates a new virtual drive with the name and root location that you specify. This mapping exists only for the current PowerShell session, so be sure to put it in your PowerShell profile if you want it to be available in every session.

To see the available drives in your session, type `Get-PSDrive`.

While extremely flexible and powerful, custom drives created this way come with some limitations. PowerShell's core commands (`Get-Item`, `Get-Content`, etc.) all understand how to handle these virtual drives, but most of the rest of the system does not:

```
PS > more.com MyDocs:\blogMonitor.csv
Cannot access file G:\lee\MyDocs:\blogMonitor.csv
```

To resolve this issue, use the `Get-Item` cmdlet to convert these virtual filenames to their real filenames:

```
more.com (Get-Item MyDocs:\blogMonitor.csv)
```

While creating custom drives can provide easier access to local files, a common scenario with the `New-PSDrive` cmdlet is to map a drive to provide access to network resources. To do this, simply supply a UNC path to the `-Root` parameter of `New-PSDrive`.

When you supply a UNC path to the `-Root` parameter, PowerShell also supports a `-Persist` flag. When you specify `-Persist`, your drive becomes a persistent PowerShell drive and survives across PowerShell sessions. Unlike locally mapped drives, the items in this drive become available to all of Windows in a way that all applications can understand. For most purposes, this `-Persist` parameter can replace the `net use` command you are most likely familiar with.

 The primary limitation to the `-Persist` flag is that you can only use the traditional single-letter drive names (*A:* through *Z:*) as the names of drives you create.

To remove a persistent mapped drive, use the `Remove-PSDrive` cmdlet:

```
Remove-PSDrive -Name Z
```

One additional benefit of drives created with the -Persist flag is that they support the use of alternate credentials. If you supply a -Credential parameter when mapping a network drive, PowerShell will use that credential any time it uses that drive to access files on the network location.

# 20.17. Access Long File and Directory Names

## Problem

You want to access a file in a deeply nested directory.

## Solution

Use the -Persist parameter of the New-PSDrive cmdlet to create a new drive, using the long portion of the path as the root:

```
PS > $root = "\\server\share\some_long_directory_name"
PS > New-PSDrive -Name L -Root $root -PSProvider FileSystem -Persist
PS > Get-Item L:\some_long_file_name.txt
```

## Discussion

When working on some complicated directory structures, you may get the following error message:

```
Get-ChildItem : The specified path, file name, or both are too long. The fully
qualified file name must be less than 260 characters, and the directory name
must be less than 248 characters.
```

This is caused by the MAX_PATH limitation built into most of Windows. This limitation enforces—not surprisingly—the maximum length of a path. If you try to create a file or directory structure in Windows Explorer longer than 260 characters, you will get an error. If you try to interact with a file or directory structure in Windows longer than 260 characters, you will get an error.

Then how did something manage to create this problematic file? It's because Windows actually has a limitation of *32,000* characters. If you tread carefully, there are funcitons in Windows that let you create and work with files longer than 260 characters.

Unfortunately, support for huge filenames only became mainstream with the release of Windows XP. Before that, the vast majority of Windows was written to understand only paths of fewer than 260 characters. Since most of Windows can't work with long file-names, the system prevents ad hoc interaction with them—through Windows Explorer, the .NET Framework, and more.

If you find yourself in the situation of having to work with long filenames, the solution is to map a new drive (using the -Persist parameter), putting as much of the long path into the drive's `-Root` parameter as possible. This mapping happens very deeply within Windows, so applications that can't understand long filenames aren't even aware. Rather than *\\server\share\some_long_directory_name\some_long_file_name.txt*, they simply see *L:\some_long_file_name.txt*.

For more information about the `New-PSDrive` cmdlet, see Recipe 20.16, "Create and Map PowerShell Drives".

## See Also

Recipe 20.16, "Create and Map PowerShell Drives"

# 20.18. Unblock a File

## Problem

You want to prevent Windows Explorer or PowerShell from warning that a file has been downloaded from the Internet.

## Solution

Use the `Unblock-File` cmdlet to clear the "Downloaded from the Internet" flag on a file:

```
PS > Unblock-File c:\downloads\file.zip
```

To unblock many files (for example, an expanded ZIP archive), pipe the results of the `Get-ChildItem` cmdlet into the `Unblock-File` cmdlet:

```
PS > Get-ChildItem -Recurse | Unblock-File
```

## Discussion

When you download a file from the Internet, many web browsers, email clients, and chat programs add a marker to the file that identifies it as having come from the Internet. This marker is contained in the `Zone.Identifier` alternate data stream:

```
PS > Get-Item .\Download.zip -Stream *

   FileName: C:\Users\Lee\Downloads\Download.zip

Stream                 Length
------                 ------
:$DATA                 1010884
Zone.Identifier            26
```

```
PS > Get-Content .\Download.zip -Stream Zone.Identifier
[ZoneTransfer]
ZoneId=3
```

When you try to use Windows Explorer to launch an application with this zone identifier, Windows cautions you that the program has been downloaded from the Internet. Similarly, PowerShell cautions you when you try to run a script that has been downloaded from the Internet.

To prevent this warning, simply run the Unblock-File cmdlet. This cmdlet removes the Zone.Identifier alternate data stream.

If you unblock a script after getting the warning that it has been downloaded from the Internet, you will have to restart PowerShell to see the effect.

For more information about alternate data streams, see Recipe 20.19, "Interact with Alternate Data Streams".

## See Also

Recipe 20.19, "Interact with Alternate Data Streams"

# 20.19. Interact with Alternate Data Streams

## Problem

You want to access and manage the alternate data streams associated with a file.

## Solution

Use the -Stream parameter of the Get-Item, Get-Content, Remove-Item, Set-Content, Clear-Content, and Add-Content cmdlets:

```
PS C:\Downloads > Get-Item * -Stream Zone.Identifier -ErrorAction Ignore |
    Select Filename, Length | Format-Table -Auto

FileName                        Length
--------                        ------
C:\Downloads\a.zip              26
C:\Downloads\b.exe              26
C:\Downloads\c.txt              26

PS > Get-Content .\a.zip -Stream Zone.Identifier
[ZoneTransfer]
ZoneId=3
```

Additionally, use the colon syntax to name a specific stream in a filename:

---

```
PS C:\Downloads > Get-Content .\a.zip:Zone.Identifier
[ZoneTransfer]
ZoneId=3
```

## Discussion

In addition to storing the basic content of files, Windows supports a mechanism called *alternate data streams* to store additional metadata about these files.

```
PS > Get-Item .\a.zip -Stream *


    FileName: C:\Downloads\a.zip

Stream                        Length
------                        ------
:$DATA                       6878348
Zone.Identifier                   26
```

The :$DATA stream represents the content you normally see when you open a file.

In this example, the file has an additional alternate data stream, called Zone.Identifi er. When you download a file from the Internet, many web browsers, email clients, and chat programs add a marker to the file that identifies it as having come from the Internet. They place this marker in the Zone.Identifier alternate data stream.

To place your own content in a stream, you can use the Set-Content cmdlet:

```
PS > Set-Content .\a.zip:MyCustomStream -Value "Hello World"
PS > Get-Item .\a.zip -Stream *


    FileName: C:\Downloads\a.zip

Stream                        Length
------                        ------
:$DATA                       6878348
MyCustomStream                    13
Zone.Identifier                   26


PS > Get-Content .\a.zip:MyCustomStream
Hello World
```

While it is an attractive idea to store additional data in alternate data streams, you should use them with caution. Many programs are unaware of alternate data streams, and unintentionally remove them when copying or modifying the file. For example, transferring a file over Remote Desktop or FTP does not retain the alternate data streams. Additionally, they are not retained when you copy files to filesystems based on the FAT32 format—USB keys being the most common example.

By far, our most frequent brush with alternate data streams comes from the warning generated by Windows and PowerShell when a file has been downloaded from the Internet. To learn how to remove this warning, see Recipe 20.18, "Unblock a File".

## See Also

Recipe 20.18, "Unblock a File"

# 20.20. Program: Move or Remove a Locked File

Once in a while, you'll run into a file that's been locked by the operating system, and you'll want to move it or delete it.

This is a common problem encountered by patches, installers, and hotfixes, so Windows has a special mechanism that lets it move files before any process has the chance to lock it. If a file that an installer needs to change is locked, it uses this special mechanism to complete its setup tasks. Windows can do this only during a reboot, which is why you sometimes receive warnings from installers about locked files requiring a restart.

The underlying mechanism that enables this is the MoveFileEx Windows API. Calling this API with the MOVEFILE_DELAY_UNTIL_REBOOT flag tells Windows to move (or delete) your file at the next boot. If you specify a source and destination path, Windows moves the file. If you specify $null as a destination path, Windows deletes the file.

Example 20-4 uses the Add-Type cmdlet to expose this functionality through PowerShell. While it exposes only the functionality to move locked files, you can easily rename it and modify it to delete locked files.

*Example 20-4. Move-LockedFile.ps1*

```
##############################################################################
##
## Move-LockedFile
##
## From Windows PowerShell Cookbook (O'Reilly)
## by Lee Holmes (http://www.leeholmes.com/guide)
##
##############################################################################

<#

.SYNOPSIS

Registers a locked file to be moved at the next system restart.

.EXAMPLE

PS > Move-LockedFile c:\temp\locked.txt c:\temp\locked.txt.bak
```

```
#>

param(
    ## The current location of the file to move
    $Path,

    ## The target location of the file
    $Destination
)

Set-StrictMode -Version 3

## Convert the path and destination to fully qualified paths
$path = (Resolve-Path $path).Path
$destination = $executionContext.SessionState.`
    Path.GetUnresolvedProviderPathFromPSPath($destination)

## Define a new .NET type that calls into the Windows API to
## move a locked file.
$MOVEFILE_DELAY_UNTIL_REBOOT = 0x00000004
$memberDefinition = @'
[DllImport("kernel32.dll", SetLastError=true, CharSet=CharSet.Auto)]
public static extern bool MoveFileEx(
    string lpExistingFileName, string lpNewFileName, int dwFlags);
'@
$type = Add-Type -Name MoveFileUtils `
    -MemberDefinition $memberDefinition -PassThru

## Move the file
$type::MoveFileEx($path, $destination, $MOVEFILE_DELAY_UNTIL_REBOOT)
```

For more information about interacting with the Windows API, see Recipe 17.4, "Access Windows API Functions". For more information about running scripts, see Recipe 1.1, "Run Programs, Scripts, and Existing Tools".

## See Also

Recipe 1.1, "Run Programs, Scripts, and Existing Tools"

Recipe 17.4, "Access Windows API Functions"

# 20.21. Get the ACL of a File or Directory

## Problem

You want to retrieve the ACL of a file or directory.

## Solution

To retrieve the ACL of a file, use the `Get-Acl` cmdlet:

```
PS > Get-Acl example.txt

    Directory: C:\temp

Path                    Owner                   Access
----                    -----                   ------
example.txt             LEE-DESK\Lee            BUILTIN\Administrator...
```

## Discussion

The `Get-Acl` cmdlet retrieves the security descriptor of an item. This cmdlet doesn't work against only the filesystem, however. Any provider (for example, the registry provider) that supports the concept of security descriptors also supports the `Get-Acl` cmdlet.

The `Get-Acl` cmdlet returns an object that represents the security descriptor of the item and is specific to the provider that contains the item. In the filesystem, this returns a .NET `System.Security.AccessControl.FileSecurity` object that you can explore for further information. For example, Example 20-5 searches a directory for possible ACL misconfigurations by ensuring that each file contains an Administrator, Full Control ACL.

*Example 20-5. Get-AclMisconfiguration.ps1*

```
##############################################################################
##
## Get-AclMisconfiguration
##
## From Windows PowerShell Cookbook (O'Reilly)
## by Lee Holmes (http://www.leeholmes.com/guide)
##
##############################################################################

<#

.SYNOPSIS

Demonstration of functionality exposed by the Get-Acl cmdlet. This script
goes through all access rules in all files in the current directory, and
ensures that the Administrator group has full control of that file.

#>

Set-StrictMode -Version 3

## Get all files in the current directory
foreach($file in Get-ChildItem)
```

```
{
    ## Retrieve the ACL from the current file
    $acl = Get-Acl $file
    if(-not $acl)
    {
        continue
    }

    $foundAdministratorAcl = $false

    ## Go through each access rule in that ACL
    foreach($accessRule in $acl.Access)
    {
        ## If we find the Administrator, Full Control access rule,
        ## then set the $foundAdministratorAcl variable
        if(($accessRule.IdentityReference -like "*Administrator*") -and
            ($accessRule.FileSystemRights -eq "FullControl"))
        {
            $foundAdministratorAcl = $true
        }
    }

    ## If we didn't find the Administrator ACL, output a message
    if(-not $foundAdministratorAcl)
    {
        "Found possible ACL Misconfiguration: $file"
    }
}
```

For more information about the Get-Acl command, type **Get-Help Get-Acl**. For more information about working with classes from the .NET Framework, see Recipe 3.8, "Work with .NET Objects". For more information about running scripts, see Recipe 1.1, "Run Programs, Scripts, and Existing Tools".

## See Also

Recipe 1.1, "Run Programs, Scripts, and Existing Tools"

Recipe 3.8, "Work with .NET Objects"

# 20.22. Set the ACL of a File or Directory

## Problem

You want to change the ACL of a file or directory.

## Solution

To change the ACL of a file, use the `Set-Acl` cmdlet. This example prevents the `Guest` account from accessing a file:

```
$acl = Get-Acl example.txt
$arguments = "LEE-DESK\Guest","FullControl","Deny"
$accessRule =
    New-Object System.Security.AccessControl.FileSystemAccessRule $arguments
$acl.SetAccessRule($accessRule)
$acl | Set-Acl example.txt
```

## Discussion

The `Set-Acl` cmdlet sets the security descriptor of an item. This cmdlet doesn't work against only the filesystem, however. Any provider (for example, the registry provider) that supports the concept of security descriptors also supports the `Set-Acl` cmdlet.

The `Set-Acl` cmdlet requires that you provide it with an ACL to apply to the item. While it is possible to construct the ACL from scratch, it is usually easiest to retrieve it from the item beforehand (as demonstrated in the Solution). To retrieve the ACL, use the `Get-Acl` cmdlet. Once you've modified the access control rules on the ACL, simply pipe them to the `Set-Acl` cmdlet to make them permanent.

In the Solution, the `$arguments` list that we provide to the `FileSystemAccessRule` constructor explicitly sets a `Deny` rule on the `Guest` account of the `LEE-DESK` computer for `FullControl` permission. For more information about working with classes from the .NET Framework (such as the `FileSystemAccessRule` class), see Recipe 3.8, "Work with .NET Objects".

Although the `Set-Acl` command is powerful, you may already be familiar with command-line tools that offer similar functionality (such as *cacls.exe*). Although these tools generally do not work on the registry (or other providers that support PowerShell security descriptors), you can, of course, continue to use these tools from PowerShell.

For more information about the `Set-Acl` cmdlet, type **Get-Help Set-Acl**. For more information about the `Get-Acl` cmdlet, see Recipe 20.21, "Get the ACL of a File or Directory".

## See Also

Recipe 3.8, "Work with .NET Objects"

Recipe 20.21, "Get the ACL of a File or Directory"

# 20.23. Program: Add Extended File Properties to Files

The Explorer shell provides useful information about a file when you click on its Properties dialog. It includes the authoring information, image information, music information, and more (see Figure 20-2).

*Figure 20-2. Extended file properties in Windows Explorer*

PowerShell doesn't expose this information by default, but it is possible to obtain these properties from the `Shell.Application` COM object. Example 20-6 does just that—and adds this extended information as properties to the files returned by the `Get-ChildItem` cmdlet.

*Example 20-6. Add-ExtendedFileProperties.ps1*

```
##############################################################################
##
## Add-ExtendedFileProperties
##
## From Windows PowerShell Cookbook (O'Reilly)
## by Lee Holmes (http://www.leeholmes.com/guide)
##
##############################################################################

<#

.SYNOPSIS

Add the extended file properties normally shown in Explorer's
"File Properties" tab.

.EXAMPLE

PS > Get-ChildItem | Add-ExtendedFileProperties.ps1 | Format-Table Name,"Bit Rate"

#>
```

```
begin
{
    Set-StrictMode -Version 3

    ## Create the Shell.Application COM object that provides this
    ## functionality
    $shellObject = New-Object -Com Shell.Application

    ## Store the property names and identifiers for all of the shell
    ## properties
    $itemProperties = $null
}

process
{
    ## Get the file from the input pipeline. If it is just a filename
    ## (rather than a real file,) piping it to the Get-Item cmdlet will
    ## get the file it represents.
    $fileItem = $_ | Get-Item

    ## Don't process directories
    if($fileItem.PsIsContainer)
    {
        $fileItem
        return
    }

    ## Extract the filename and directory name
    $directoryName = $fileItem.DirectoryName
    $filename = $fileItem.Name

    ## Create the folder object and shell item from the COM object
    $folderObject = $shellObject.NameSpace($directoryName)
    $item = $folderObject.ParseName($filename)

    ## Populate the item properties
    if(-not $itemProperties)
    {
        $itemProperties = @{}

        $counter = 0
        $columnName = ""
        do
        {
            $columnName = $folderObject.GetDetailsOf(
                $folderObject.Items, $counter)
            if($columnName) { $itemProperties[$counter] = $columnName }

            $counter++
        } while($columnName)
    }
```

```
## Now, go through each property and add its information as a
## property to the file we are about to return
foreach($itemProperty in $itemProperties.Keys)
{
    $fileItem | Add-Member NoteProperty $itemProperties[$itemProperty] `
        $folderObject.GetDetailsOf($item, $itemProperty) -ErrorAction `
        SilentlyContinue
}

## Finally, return the file with the extra shell information
$fileItem
}
```

For more information about running scripts, see Recipe 1.1, "Run Programs, Scripts, and Existing Tools".

## See Also

Recipe 1.1, "Run Programs, Scripts, and Existing Tools"

# 20.24. Program: Create a Filesystem Hard Link

It is sometimes useful to refer to the same file by two different names or locations. You can't solve this problem by copying the item, because modifications to one file do not automatically affect the other.

The solution to this is called a *hard link*, an item of a new name that points to the data of another file. The Windows operating system supports hard links, but only Windows Vista includes a utility that lets you create them.

Example 20-7 lets you create hard links without needing to install additional tools. It uses (and requires) the *Invoke-WindowsApi.ps1* script provided in Recipe 17.5, "Program: Invoke Simple Windows API Calls".

*Example 20-7. New-FilesystemHardLink.ps1*

```
##############################################################################
##
## New-FileSystemHardLink
##
## From Windows PowerShell Cookbook (O'Reilly)
## by Lee Holmes (http://www.leeholmes.com/guide)
##
##############################################################################

<#
```

```
.SYNOPSIS

Create a new hard link, which allows you to create a new name by which you
can access an existing file. Windows only deletes the actual file once
you delete all hard links that point to it.

.EXAMPLE

PS > "Hello" > test.txt
PS > dir test* | select name

Name
----
test.txt

PS > .\New-FilesystemHardLink.ps1 test.txt test2.txt
PS > type test2.txt
Hello
PS > dir test* | select name

Name
----
test.txt
test2.txt

#>

param(
    ## The existing file that you want the new name to point to
    [string] $Path,

    ## The new filename you want to create
    [string] $Destination
)

Set-StrictMode -Version 3

## Ensure that the provided names are absolute paths
$filename = $executionContext.SessionState.`
    Path.GetUnresolvedProviderPathFromPSPath($destination)
$existingFilename = Resolve-Path $path

## Prepare the parameter types and parameters for the CreateHardLink function
$parameterTypes = [string], [string], [IntPtr]
$parameters = [string] $filename, [string] $existingFilename, [IntPtr]::Zero

## Call the CreateHardLink method in the Kernel32 DLL
$currentDirectory = Split-Path $myInvocation.MyCommand.Path
$invokeWindowsApiCommand = Join-Path $currentDirectory Invoke-WindowsApi.ps1
$result = & $invokeWindowsApiCommand "kernel32" `
    ([bool]) "CreateHardLink" $parameterTypes $parameters
```

```
## Provide an error message if the call fails
if(-not $result)
{
    $message = "Could not create hard link of $filename to " +
        "existing file $existingFilename"
    Write-Error $message
}
```

For more information about running scripts, see Recipe 1.1, "Run Programs, Scripts, and Existing Tools".

## See Also

Recipe 1.1, "Run Programs, Scripts, and Existing Tools"

Recipe 17.5, "Program: Invoke Simple Windows API Calls"

# 20.25. Program: Create a ZIP Archive

When transporting or archiving files, it is useful to store those files in an archive. ZIP archives are the most common type of archive, so it would be useful to have a script to help manage them.

For many purposes, traditional command-line ZIP archive utilities may fulfill your needs. If they do not support the level of detail or interaction that you need for administrative tasks, a more programmatic alternative is attractive.

Example 20-8 lets you create ZIP archives simply by piping files into them.

*Example 20-8. New-ZipFile.ps1*

```
##############################################################################
##
## New-ZipFile
##
## From Windows PowerShell Cookbook (O'Reilly)
## by Lee Holmes (http://www.leeholmes.com/guide)
##
##############################################################################

<#

.SYNOPSIS

Create a zip file from any files piped in.

.EXAMPLE

PS > dir *.ps1 | New-ZipFile scripts.zip
Copies all PS1 files in the current directory to scripts.zip
```

```
.EXAMPLE

PS > "readme.txt" | New-ZipFile docs.zip
Copies readme.txt to docs.zip

#>

param(
    ## The name of the zip archive to create
    $Path = $(throw "Specify a zip file name"),

    ## Switch to delete the zip archive if it already exists.
    [Switch] $Force
)

Set-StrictMode -Version 3

## Create the Zip File
$zipName = $executionContext.SessionState.`
    Path.GetUnresolvedProviderPathFromPSPath($Path)

## Check if the file exists already. If it does, check
## for -Force - generate an error if not specified.
if(Test-Path $zipName)
{
    if($Force)
    {
        Remove-Item $zipName -Force
    }
    else
    {
        throw "Item with specified name $zipName already exists."
    }
}

## Add the DLL that helps with file compression
Add-Type -Assembly System.IO.Compression.FileSystem

try
{
    ## Open the Zip archive
    $archive = [System.IO.Compression.ZipFile]::Open($zipName, "Create")

    ## Go through each file in the input, adding it to the Zip file
    ## specified
    foreach($file in $input)
    {
        ## Skip the current file if it is the zip file itself
        if($file.FullName -eq $zipName)
        {
            continue
```

```
    }

    ## Skip directories
    if($file.PSIsContainer)
    {
        continue
    }

    $item = $file | Get-Item
    $null = [System.IO.Compression.ZipFileExtensions]::CreateEntryFromFile(
        $archive, $item.FullName, $item.Name)
    }
}
finally
{
    ## Close the file
    $archive.Dispose()
    $archive = $null
}
```

For more information about running scripts, see Recipe 1.1, "Run Programs, Scripts, and Existing Tools".

## See Also

Recipe 1.1, "Run Programs, Scripts, and Existing Tools"

# The Windows Registry

## 21.0. Introduction

As the configuration store for the vast majority of applications, the registry plays a central role in system administration. It is also generally hard to manage.

Although command-line tools (such as *reg.exe*) exist to help you work with the registry, their interfaces are usually inconsistent and confusing. The Registry Editor graphical user interface is easy to use, but it does not support scripted administration.

PowerShell tackles this problem by exposing the Windows Registry as a navigation provider: a data source that you navigate and manage in exactly the same way that you work with the filesystem.

## 21.1. Navigate the Registry

### Problem

You want to navigate and explore the Windows Registry.

### Solution

Use the Set-Location cmdlet to navigate the registry, just as you would navigate the filesystem:

```
PS > Set-Location HKCU:
PS > Set-Location \Software\Microsoft\Windows\CurrentVersion\Run
PS > Get-Location

Path
----
HKCU:\Software\Microsoft\Windows\CurrentVersion\Run
```

## Discussion

PowerShell lets you navigate the Windows Registry in exactly the same way that you navigate the filesystem, certificate drives, and other navigation-based providers. Like these other providers, the registry provider supports the Set-Location cmdlet (with the standard aliases of sl, cd, and chdir), Push-Location (with the standard alias pushd), Pop-Location (with the standard alias popd), and more.

For information about how to change registry keys once you get to a registry location, see Recipe 21.3, "Modify or Remove a Registry Key Value". For more information about the registry provider, type **Get-Help Registry**.

## See Also

Recipe 21.3, "Modify or Remove a Registry Key Value"

# 21.2. View a Registry Key

## Problem

You want to view the value of a specific registry key.

## Solution

To retrieve the value(s) of a registry key, use the Get-ItemProperty cmdlet, as shown in Example 21-1.

*Example 21-1. Retrieving properties of a registry key*

```
PS > Set-Location HKCU:
PS > Set-Location \Software\Microsoft\Windows\CurrentVersion\Run
PS > Get-ItemProperty .


PSPath                : Microsoft.PowerShell.Core\Registry::HKEY_CURRENT_U
                        SER\Software\Microsoft\Windows\CurrentVersion\Run
PSParentPath          : Microsoft.PowerShell.Core\Registry::HKEY_CURRENT_U
                        SER\Software\Microsoft\Windows\CurrentVersion
PSChildName           : Run
PSDrive               : HKCU
PSProvider            : Microsoft.PowerShell.Core\Registry
FolderShare           : "C:\Program Files\FolderShare\FolderShare.exe" /
                        background
TaskSwitchXP          : d:\lee\tools\TaskSwitchXP.exe
ctfmon.exe            : C:\WINDOWS\system32\ctfmon.exe
Ditto                 : C:\Program Files\Ditto\Ditto.exe
QuickTime Task        : "C:\Program Files\QuickTime Alternative\qttask.exe
                        " -atboottime
H/PC Connection Agent : "C:\Program Files\Microsoft ActiveSync\wcescomm.exe"
```

## Discussion

In the registry provider, PowerShell treats registry keys as items and key values as properties of those items. To get the properties of an item, use the `Get-ItemProperty` cmdlet. The `Get-ItemProperty` cmdlet has the standard alias `gp`.

Example 21-1 lists all property values associated with that specific key. To retrieve the value of a specific item, access it as you would access a property on a .NET object, or anywhere else in PowerShell:

```
PS > $item = Get-ItemProperty .
PS > $item.TaskSwitchXp
d:\lee\tools\TaskSwitchXP.exe
```

If you want to do this all at once, the command looks like:

```
PS > $runKey = "HKCU:\Software\Microsoft\Windows\CurrentVersion\Run"
PS > (Get-ItemProperty $runKey).TaskSwitchXp
d:\lee\tools\TaskSwitchXP.exe
```

For more information about the `Get-ItemProperty` cmdlet, type **Get-Help Get-ItemProperty**. For more information about the registry provider, type **Get-Help Registry**.

# 21.3. Modify or Remove a Registry Key Value

## Problem

You want to modify or remove a property of a specific registry key.

## Solution

To set the value of a registry key, use the `Set-ItemProperty` cmdlet:

```
PS > (Get-ItemProperty .).MyProgram
c:\temp\MyProgram.exe
PS > Set-ItemProperty . MyProgram d:\Lee\tools\MyProgram.exe
PS > (Get-ItemProperty .).MyProgram
d:\Lee\tools\MyProgram.exe
```

To remove the value of a registry key, use the `Remove-ItemProperty` cmdlet:

```
PS > Remove-ItemProperty . MyProgram
PS > (Get-ItemProperty .).MyProgram
```

## Discussion

In the registry provider, PowerShell treats registry keys as items and key values as properties of those items. To change the value of a key property, use the Set-ItemProperty cmdlet. The Set-ItemProperty cmdlet has the standard alias sp. To remove a key property altogether, use the Remove-ItemProperty cmdlet.

 As always, use caution when changing information in the registry. Deleting or changing the wrong item can easily render your system unbootable.

For more information about the Get-ItemProperty cmdlet, type **Get-Help Get-ItemProperty**. For information about the Set-ItemProperty and Remove-Item Property cmdlets, type **Get-Help Set-ItemProperty** or **Get-Help Remove-Item Property**, respectively. For more information about the registry provider, type **Get-Help Registry**.

# 21.4. Create a Registry Key Value

## Problem

You want to add a new key value to an existing registry key.

## Solution

To add a value to a registry key, use the New-ItemProperty cmdlet. Example 21-2 adds *MyProgram.exe* to the list of programs that start when the current user logs in.

*Example 21-2. Creating new properties on a registry key*

```
PS > Set-Location HKCU:\Software\Microsoft\Windows\CurrentVersion\Run
PS > New-ItemProperty . -Name MyProgram -Value c:\temp\MyProgram.exe

PSPath        : Microsoft.PowerShell.Core\Registry::HKEY_CURRENT_USER
                \Software\Microsoft\Windows\CurrentVersion\Run
PSParentPath  : Microsoft.PowerShell.Core\Registry::HKEY_CURRENT_USER
                \Software\Microsoft\Windows\CurrentVersion
PSChildName   : Run
PSDrive       : HKCU
PSProvider    : Microsoft.PowerShell.Core\Registry
MyProgram     : c:\temp\MyProgram.exe

PS > Get-ItemProperty .

PSPath                 : Microsoft.PowerShell.Core\Registry::HKEY_CURRENT_
                         USER\Software\Microsoft\Windows\CurrentVersion\Run
```

```
PSParentPath            : Microsoft.PowerShell.Core\Registry::HKEY_CURRENT_
                          USER\Software\Microsoft\Windows\CurrentVersion
PSChildName             : Run
PSDrive                 : HKCU
PSProvider              : Microsoft.PowerShell.Core\Registry
FolderShare             : "C:\Program Files\FolderShare\FolderShare.exe"
                          /background
TaskSwitchXP            : d:\lee\tools\TaskSwitchXP.exe
ctfmon.exe              : C:\WINDOWS\system32\ctfmon.exe
Ditto                   : C:\Program Files\Ditto\Ditto.exe
QuickTime Task          : "C:\Program Files\QuickTime Alternative\qttask.exe"
                          -atboottime
H/PC Connection Agent   : "C:\Program Files\Microsoft ActiveSync\wcescomm.exe"
MyProgram               : c:\temp\MyProgram.exe
```

## Discussion

In the registry provider, PowerShell treats registry keys as items and key values as properties of those items. To create a key property, use the New-ItemProperty cmdlet.

For more information about the New-ItemProperty cmdlet, type **Get-Help New-ItemProperty**. For more information about the registry provider, type **Get-Help Registry**.

# 21.5. Remove a Registry Key

## Problem

You want to remove a registry key and all its properties.

## Solution

To remove a registry key, use the Remove-Item cmdlet:

```
PS > dir

    Hive: HKEY_CURRENT_USER\Software\Microsoft\Windows\CurrentVersion\Run

SKC  VC Name                           Property
---  -- ----                           --------
  0   0 Spyware                        {}

PS > Remove-Item Spyware
```

## Discussion

As mentioned in Recipe 21.4, "Create a Registry Key Value", the registry provider lets you remove items and containers with the Remove-Item cmdlet. The Remove-Item cmdlet has the standard aliases rm, rmdir, del, erase, and rd.

As always, use caution when changing information in the registry. Deleting or changing the wrong item can easily render your system unbootable.

As in the filesystem, the Remove-Item cmdlet lets you specify multiple files through its Path, Include, Exclude, and Filter parameters. For information on how to use these parameters effectively, see Recipe 20.6, "Find Files That Match a Pattern".

For more information about the Remove-Item cmdlet, type **Get-Help Remove-Item**. For more information about the registry provider, type **Get-Help Registry**.

### See Also

Recipe 20.6, "Find Files That Match a Pattern"

Recipe 21.4, "Create a Registry Key Value"

# 21.6. Safely Combine Related Registry Modifications

## Problem

You have several related registry modifications, and you want to group them so that either they all apply or none apply.

## Solution

Use the Start-Transaction cmdlet to start a transaction, and make your registry modifications within it. Use the Complete-Transaction cmdlet to make the registry modifications permanent:

```
PS > Set-Location HKCU:
PS > Start-Transaction

Suggestion [1,Transactions]: Once a transaction is started, only commands
that get called with the -UseTransaction flag become part of that transaction.
PS > mkdir TempKey -UseTransaction

    Hive: HKEY_CURRENT_USER

SKC  VC Name                           Property
---  -- ----                           --------
  0   0 TempKey                        {}


PS > Set-Location TempKey -UseTransaction
PS > New-Item TempKey2 -UseTransaction

    Hive: HKEY_CURRENT_USER\TempKey
```

```
SKC  VC Name                          Property
---  -- ----                          --------
  0   0 TempKey2                      {}

PS > Set-Location \
PS > Get-ChildItem TempKey
Get-ChildItem : Cannot find path 'HKEY_CURRENT_USER\TempKey' because it
does not exist.
At line:1 char:14
+ Get-ChildItem <<<<  TempKey
    + CategoryInfo          : ObjectNotFound: (HKEY_CURRENT_USER\TempKey:
    String) [Get-ChildItem], ItemNotFoundException
    + FullyQualifiedErrorId : PathNotFound,Microsoft.PowerShell.Commands.
    GetChildItemCommand

PS > Complete-Transaction
PS > Get-ChildItem TempKey


    Hive: HKEY_CURRENT_USER\TempKey

SKC  VC Name                          Property
---  -- ----                          --------
  0   0 TempKey2                      {}
```

## Discussion

When working in the registry, you might sometimes want to chain a set of related changes and be sure that they all get applied as a single unit. These are goals known as *atomicity* and *consistency*: the desire to avoid situations where an error during any step of the operation could cause an inconsistent system state if the other operations are not also successful.

To support this type of management task, PowerShell supports a change management strategy known as *transactions*. On Windows Vista and later, PowerShell's registry provider fully supports transactions.

When you start a transaction, any commands in that transaction are virtual and don't actually apply to the system until you complete the transaction. Within the context of the transaction, through, each participating command sees the system as though the state really had changed. Once you complete a transaction, changes are applied as a single unit.

Some systems that support transactions (such as databases) put locks on any resources that are being changed by a transaction. If another user tries to modify the locked resources, the user gets an error message. This is not supported in the Windows Registry.

If something alters a resource that your transaction depends on, the changes contained in your transaction will be abandoned and you will receive an error message when you try to complete that transaction. For more information about transactions, see Chapter 31.

## See Also

Chapter 31, *Transactions*

# 21.7. Add a Site to an Internet Explorer Security Zone

## Problem

You want to add a site to a specific Internet Explorer security zone.

## Solution

To create the registry keys and properties required to add a site to a specific security zone, use the `New-Item` and `New-ItemProperty` cmdlets. Example 21-3 adds *www.example.com* to the list of sites trusted by Internet Explorer.

*Example 21-3. Adding www.example.com to the list of trusted sites in Internet Explorer*

```
Set-Location "HKCU:\Software\Microsoft\Windows\CurrentVersion\Internet Settings"
Set-Location ZoneMap\Domains
New-Item example.com
Set-Location example.com
New-Item www
Set-Location www
New-ItemProperty . -Name http -Value 2 -Type DWORD
```

## Discussion

One task that requires modifying data in the registry is working with Internet Explorer to add and remove sites from its different security zones.

Internet Explorer stores its zone mapping information in the registry at *HKCU:\Software\Microsoft\Windows\CurrentVersion\Internet Settings\ZoneMap\Domains*. Below that key, Explorer stores the domain name (such as `leeholmes.com`) with the hostname (such as `www`) as a subkey of that one (see Figure 21-1). In the host key, Explorer stores a property (such as `http`) with a `DWORD` value that corresponds to the zone identifier.

*Figure 21-1. Internet Explorer zone configuration*

The Internet Explorer zone identifiers are:

- My Computer
- Local intranet
- Trusted sites
- Internet
- Restricted sites

When Internet Explorer is configured in its Enhanced Security Configuration mode, you must also update entries under the EscDomains key.

 Once a machine has enabled Internet Explorer's Enhanced Security Configuration, those settings persist even after you remove Enhanced Security Configuration. The following commands let your machine trust UNC paths again:

```
Set-Location "HKCU:\Software\Microsoft\Windows\"
Set-Location "CurrentVersion"
Set-Location "Internet Settings"
Set-ItemProperty ZoneMap UNCAsIntranet -Type DWORD 1
Set-ItemProperty ZoneMap IntranetName -Type DWORD 1
```

To remove the zone mapping for a specific domain, use the Remove-Item cmdlet:

```
PS > Get-ChildItem

    Hive: HKEY_CURRENT_USER\Software\…\Internet Settings\ZoneMap\Domains

SKC VC Name                               Property
--- -- ----                               --------
  1  0 example.com                        {}

PS > Remove-Item -Recurse example.com
PS > Get-ChildItem
PS >
```

For more information about using the Internet Explorer registry entries to configure security zones, see the Microsoft KB article "Description of Internet Explorer Security Zones Registry Entries" here (*http://support.microsoft.com/kb/182569*). For more information about managing Internet Explorer's Enhanced Security Configuration, search for it here (*http://technet.microsoft.com*).

For more information about modifying data in the registry, see Recipe 21.3, "Modify or Remove a Registry Key Value".

### See Also

Recipe 21.3, "Modify or Remove a Registry Key Value"

# 21.8. Modify Internet Explorer Settings

## Problem

You want to modify Internet Explorer's configuration options.

## Solution

To modify the Internet Explorer configuration registry keys, use the `Set-ItemProperty` cmdlet. For example, to update the proxy:

```
Set-Location "HKCU:\Software\Microsoft\Windows\CurrentVersion\Internet Settings"
Set-ItemProperty . -Name ProxyServer -Value http://proxy.example.com
Set-ItemProperty . -Name ProxyEnable -Value 1
```

## Discussion

Internet Explorer stores its main configuration information as properties on the registry key *HKCU:\Software\Microsoft\Windows\CurrentVersion\Internet Settings*. To change these properties, use the `Set-ItemProperty` cmdlet as demonstrated in the Solution.

Another common set of properties to tweak are the configuration parameters that define a security zone. An example of this is to prevent scripts from running in the Restricted Sites zone. For each zone, Internet Explorer stores this information as properties of the registry key *HKCU:\Software\Microsoft\Windows\CurrentVersion\Internet Settings \Zones\<Zone>*, where *<Zone>* represents the zone identifier (0, 1, 2, 3, or 4) to manage.

The Internet Explorer zone identifiers are:

- My Computer
- Local intranet
- Trusted sites
- Internet
- Restricted sites

The names of the properties in this key are not designed for human consumption, as they carry illuminating titles such as 1A04 and 1809. While they are not well named, you can still script them.

For more information about using the Internet Explorer registry settings to configure security zones, see the Microsoft KB article "Description of Internet Explorer Security Zones Registry Entries" here (*http://support.microsoft.com/kb/182569*).

For more information about modifying data in the registry, see Recipe 21.3, "Modify or Remove a Registry Key Value".

## See Also

Recipe 21.3, "Modify or Remove a Registry Key Value"

# 21.9. Program: Search the Windows Registry

Although the Windows Registry Editor is useful for searching the registry, sometimes it might not provide the power you need. For example, the Registry Editor does not support searches with wildcards or regular expressions.

In the filesystem, we have the `Select-String` cmdlet to search files for content. PowerShell does not offer that ability for other stores, but we can write a script to do it. The key here is to think of registry key values like you think of content in a file:

- Directories have items; items have content.
- Registry keys have properties; properties have values.

Example 21-4 goes through all registry keys (and their values) for a search term and returns information about the match.

*Example 21-4. Search-Registry.ps1*

```
##############################################################################
##
## Search-Registry
##
## From Windows PowerShell Cookbook (O'Reilly)
## by Lee Holmes (http://www.leeholmes.com/guide)
##
##############################################################################

<#

.SYNOPSIS

Search the registry for keys or properties that match a specific value.

.EXAMPLE

PS > Set-Location HKCU:\Software\Microsoft\
PS > Search-Registry Run

#>

param(
    ## The text to search for
    [Parameter(Mandatory = $true)]
    [string] $Pattern
)

Set-StrictMode -Off

## Helper function to create a new object that represents
## a registry match from this script
function New-RegistryMatch
{
    param( $matchType, $keyName, $propertyName, $line )

    $registryMatch = New-Object PsObject -Property @{
        MatchType = $matchType;
        KeyName = $keyName;
        PropertyName = $propertyName;
        Line = $line
    }

    $registryMatch
}

## Go through each item in the registry
foreach($item in Get-ChildItem -Recurse -ErrorAction SilentlyContinue)
{
    ## Check if the key name matches
```

```
if($item.Name -match $pattern)
{
    New-RegistryMatch "Key" $item.Name $null $item.Name
}

## Check if a key property matches
foreach($property in (Get-ItemProperty $item.PsPath).PsObject.Properties)
{
    ## Skip the property if it was one PowerShell added
    if(($property.Name -eq "PSPath") -or
       ($property.Name -eq "PSChildName"))
    {
        continue
    }

    ## Search the text of the property
    $propertyText = "$($property.Name)=$($property.Value)"
    if($propertyText -match $pattern)
    {
        New-RegistryMatch "Property" $item.Name `
            property.Name $propertyText
    }
}
}
}
```

For more information about running scripts, see Recipe 1.1, "Run Programs, Scripts, and Existing Tools".

## See Also

Recipe 1.1, "Run Programs, Scripts, and Existing Tools"

# 21.10. Get the ACL of a Registry Key

## Problem

You want to retrieve the ACL of a registry key.

## Solution

To retrieve the ACL of a registry key, use the Get-Acl cmdlet:

```
PS > Get-Acl HKLM:\Software

Path                    Owner                   Access
----                    -----                   ------
Microsoft.PowerShell.... BUILTIN\Administrators  CREATOR OWNER Allow ....
```

## Discussion

As mentioned in Recipe 20.21, "Get the ACL of a File or Directory", the `Get-Acl` cmdlet retrieves the security descriptor of an item. This cmdlet doesn't work against only the registry, however. Any provider (for example, the filesystem provider) that supports the concept of security descriptors also supports the `Get-Acl` cmdlet.

The `Get-Acl` cmdlet returns an object that represents the security descriptor of the item and is specific to the provider that contains the item. In the registry provider, this returns a .NET `System.Security.AccessControl.RegistrySecurity` object that you can explore for further information. For an example of changing the ACL of a registry key with this result, see Recipe 21.11, "Set the ACL of a Registry Key". For an example of a script that works with ACLs, see Recipe 20.21, "Get the ACL of a File or Directory".

For more information about the `Get-Acl` command, type **Get-Help Get-Acl**. For more information about working with classes from the .NET Framework, see Recipe 3.8, "Work with .NET Objects".

## See Also

Recipe 3.8, "Work with .NET Objects"

Recipe 20.21, "Get the ACL of a File or Directory"

Recipe 21.11, "Set the ACL of a Registry Key"

# 21.11. Set the ACL of a Registry Key

## Problem

You want to change the ACL of a registry key.

## Solution

To set the ACL on a registry key, use the `Set-Acl` cmdlet. This example grants an account write access to a registry key under *HKLM:\Software*. This is especially useful for programs that write to administrator-only regions of the registry, which prevents them from running under a nonadministrator account.

```
##############################################################################
##
## Grant-RegistryAccessFullControl
##
## From Windows PowerShell Cookbook (O'Reilly)
## by Lee Holmes (http://www.leeholmes.com/guide)
##
##############################################################################
```

```
<#

.SYNOPSIS

Grants full control access to a user for the specified registry key.

.EXAMPLE

PS > $registryPath = "HKLM:\Software\MyProgram"
PS > Grant-RegistryAccessFullControl "LEE-DESK\LEE" $registryPath

#>

param(
    ## The user to grant full control
    [Parameter(Mandatory = $true)]
    $User,

    ## The registry path that should have its permissions modified
    [Parameter(Mandatory = $true)]
    $RegistryPath
)

Set-StrictMode -Version 3

Push-Location
Set-Location -LiteralPath $registryPath

## Retrieve the ACL from the registry key
$acl = Get-Acl .

## Prepare the access rule, and set the access rule
$arguments = $user,"FullControl","Allow"
$accessRule = New-Object Security.AccessControl.RegistryAccessRule $arguments
$acl.SetAccessRule($accessRule)

## Apply the modified ACL to the regsitry key
$acl | Set-Acl  .

Pop-Location
```

## Discussion

As mentioned in Recipe 20.22, "Set the ACL of a File or Directory", the Set-Acl cmdlet sets the security descriptor of an item. This cmdlet doesn't work against only the registry, however. Any provider (for example, the filesystem provider) that supports the concept of security descriptors also supports the Set-Acl cmdlet.

The Set-Acl cmdlet requires that you provide it with an ACL to apply to the item. Although it is possible to construct the ACL from scratch, it is usually easiest to retrieve it from the item beforehand (as demonstrated in the Solution). To retrieve the ACL, use the Get-Acl cmdlet. Once you've modified the access control rules on the ACL, simply pipe them to the Set-Acl cmdlet to make them permanent.

In the Solution, the $arguments list that we provide to the RegistryAccessRule constructor explicitly sets an Allow rule on the Lee account of the LEE-DESK computer for FullControl permission. For more information about working with classes from the .NET Framework (such as the RegistryAccessRule class), see Recipe 3.8, "Work with .NET Objects".

Although the Set-Acl command is powerful, you may already be familiar with command-line tools that offer similar functionality (such as *SubInAcl.exe*). You can, of course, continue to use these tools from PowerShell.

For more information about the Set-Acl cmdlet, type **Get-Help Set-Acl**. For more information about the Get-Acl cmdlet, see Recipe 21.10, "Get the ACL of a Registry Key".

## See Also

Recipe 3.8, "Work with .NET Objects"

Recipe 20.22, "Set the ACL of a File or Directory"

Recipe 21.10, "Get the ACL of a Registry Key"

# 21.12. Work with the Registry of a Remote Computer

## Problem

You want to work with the registry keys and values of a remote computer.

## Solution

To work with the registry of a remote computer, use the scripts provided in this chapter: Get-RemoteRegistryChildItem (Recipe 21.13, "Program: Get Registry Items from Remote Machines"), Get-RemoteRegistryKeyProperty (Recipe 21.14, "Program: Get Properties of Remote Registry Keys"), and Set-RemoteRegistryKeyProperty (Recipe 21.15, "Program: Set Properties of Remote Registry Keys"). These scripts require that the remote computer has the remote registry service enabled and running. Example 21-5 updates the PowerShell execution policy of a remote machine.

*Example 21-5. Setting the PowerShell execution policy of a remote machine*

```
PS > $registryPath = "HKLM:\Software\Microsoft\PowerShell\1"
PS > Get-RemoteRegistryChildItem LEE-DESK $registryPath

SKC  VC Name                       Property
---  -- ----                       --------
  0   1 1033                       {Install}
  0   5 PowerShellEngine           {ApplicationBase, ConsoleHost...
  2   0 PowerShellSnapIns          {}
  1   0 ShellIds                   {}

PS > Get-RemoteRegistryChildItem LEE-DESK $registryPath\ShellIds

SKC  VC Name                       Property
---  -- ----                       --------
  0   2 Microsoft.PowerShell       {Path, ExecutionPolicy}

PS > $registryPath = "HKLM:\Software\Microsoft\PowerShell\1\" +
    "ShellIds\Microsoft.PowerShell"

PS > Get-RemoteRegistryKeyProperty LEE-DESK $registryPath ExecutionPolicy

ExecutionPolicy
---------------
Unrestricted

PS > Set-RemoteRegistryKeyProperty LEE-DESK $registryPath `
    "ExecutionPolicy" "RemoteSigned"

PS > Get-RemoteRegistryKeyProperty LEE-DESK $registryPath ExecutionPolicy

ExecutionPolicy
---------------
RemoteSigned
```

## Discussion

Although this specific task is perhaps better solved through PowerShell's Group Policy support, it demonstrates a useful scenario that includes both remote registry exploration and modification.

If the remote computer does not have the remote registry service running (but does have WMI enabled), you can use WMI's StdRegProv class to work with the registry as well. The following example demonstrates how to get and set the registry key that controls Remote Desktop:

```
$HKEY_CLASSES_ROOT = [Convert]::ToUInt32(80000000, 16)
$HKEY_CURRENT_USER = [Convert]::ToUInt32(80000001, 16)
$HKEY_LOCAL_MACHINE = [Convert]::ToUInt32(80000002, 16)
$HKEY_USERS = [Convert]::ToUInt32(80000003, 16)
$HKEY_CURRENT_CONFIG = [Convert]::ToUInt32(80000005, 16)
```

```
## Connect to the registry via WMI
$reg = Get-CimClass -ComputerName LEE-DESK `
    -Namespace root\default StdRegProv

## Get and set DWORD values on the remote machine
$reg | Invoke-CimMethod -Name GetDWORDValue -Arguments @{
    hDefKey = $HKEY_LOCAL_MACHINE;
    sSubKeyName = "SYSTEM\CurrentControlSet\Control\Terminal Server";
    sValueName = "fDenyTSConnections"
}

$reg | Invoke-CimMethod -Name SetDWORDValue -Arguments @{
    hDefKey = $HKEY_LOCAL_MACHINE;
    sSubKeyName = "SYSTEM\CurrentControlSet\Control\Terminal Server";
    sValueName = "fDenyTSConnections";
    uValue = 0
}
```

For more information about the `Get-RemoteRegistryChildItem`, `Get-RemoteRegistryKeyProperty`, and `Set-RemoteRegistryKeyProperty` scripts, see Recipes 21.13, 21.14, and 21.15.

### See Also

Recipe 21.13, "Program: Get Registry Items from Remote Machines"

Recipe 21.14, "Program: Get Properties of Remote Registry Keys"

Recipe 21.15, "Program: Set Properties of Remote Registry Keys"

# 21.13. Program: Get Registry Items from Remote Machines

Although PowerShell does not directly let you access and manipulate the registry of a remote computer, it still supports this by working with the .NET Framework. The functionality exposed by the .NET Framework is a bit more developer-oriented than we want, so we can instead use a script to make it easier to work with.

Example 21-6 lets you list child items in a remote registry key, much like you do on the local computer. In order for this script to succeed, the target computer must have the remote registry service enabled and running.

*Example 21-6. Get-RemoteRegistryChildItem.ps1*

```
##############################################################################
##
## Get-RemoteRegistryChildItem
##
## From Windows PowerShell Cookbook (O'Reilly)
```

```
## by Lee Holmes (http://www.leeholmes.com/guide)
##
#############################################################################

<#

.SYNOPSIS

Get the list of subkeys below a given key on a remote computer.

.EXAMPLE

Get-RemoteRegistryChildItem LEE-DESK HKLM:\Software

#>

param(
    ## The computer that you wish to connect to
    [Parameter(Mandatory = $true)]
    $ComputerName,

    ## The path to the registry items to retrieve
    [Parameter(Mandatory = $true)]
    $Path
)

Set-StrictMode -Version 3

## Validate and extract out the registry key
if($path -match "^HKLM:\\(.*)")
{
    $baseKey = [Microsoft.Win32.RegistryKey]::OpenRemoteBaseKey(
        "LocalMachine", $computername)
}
elseif($path -match "^HKCU:\\(.*)")
{
    $baseKey = [Microsoft.Win32.RegistryKey]::OpenRemoteBaseKey(
        "CurrentUser", $computername)
}
else
{
    Write-Error ("Please specify a fully qualified registry path " +
        "(i.e.: HKLM:\Software) of the registry key to open.")
    return
}

## Open the key
$key = $baseKey.OpenSubKey($matches[1])

## Retrieve all of its children
foreach($subkeyName in $key.GetSubKeyNames())
{
```

```
## Open the subkey
$subkey = $key.OpenSubKey($subkeyName)

## Add information so that PowerShell displays this key like regular
## registry key
$returnObject = [PsObject] $subKey
$returnObject | Add-Member NoteProperty PsChildName $subkeyName
$returnObject | Add-Member NoteProperty Property $subkey.GetValueNames()

## Output the key
$returnObject

## Close the child key
$subkey.Close()
}

## Close the key and base keys
$key.Close()
$baseKey.Close()
```

For more information about running scripts, see Recipe 1.1, "Run Programs, Scripts, and Existing Tools".

## See Also

Recipe 1.1, "Run Programs, Scripts, and Existing Tools"

# 21.14. Program: Get Properties of Remote Registry Keys

Although PowerShell does not directly let you access and manipulate the registry of a remote computer, it still supports this by working with the .NET Framework. The functionality exposed by the .NET Framework is a bit more developer-oriented than we want, so we can instead use a script to make it easier to work with.

Example 21-7 lets you get the properties (or a specific property) from a given remote registry key. In order for this script to succeed, the target computer must have the remote registry service enabled and running.

*Example 21-7. Get-RemoteRegistryKeyProperty.ps1*

```
##############################################################################
##
## Get-RemoteRegistryKeyProperty
##
## From Windows PowerShell Cookbook (O'Reilly)
## by Lee Holmes (http://www.leeholmes.com/guide)
##
##############################################################################

<#
```

```
    .SYNOPSIS

    Get the value of a remote registry key property

    .EXAMPLE

    PS > $registryPath =
        "HKLM:\software\Microsoft\PowerShell\1\ShellIds\Microsoft.PowerShell"
    PS > Get-RemoteRegistryKeyProperty LEE-DESK $registryPath ExecutionPolicy

    #>

    param(
        ## The computer that you wish to connect to
        [Parameter(Mandatory = $true)]
        $ComputerName,

        ## The path to the registry item to retrieve
        [Parameter(Mandatory = $true)]
        $Path,

        ## The specific property to retrieve
        $Property = "*"
    )

    Set-StrictMode -Version 3

    ## Validate and extract out the registry key
    if($path -match "^HKLM:\\(.*)")
    {
        $baseKey = [Microsoft.Win32.RegistryKey]::OpenRemoteBaseKey(
            "LocalMachine", $computername)
    }
    elseif($path -match "^HKCU:\\(.*)")
    {
        $baseKey = [Microsoft.Win32.RegistryKey]::OpenRemoteBaseKey(
            "CurrentUser", $computername)
    }
    else
    {
        Write-Error ("Please specify a fully qualified registry path " +
            "(i.e.: HKLM:\Software) of the registry key to open.")
        return
    }

    ## Open the key
    $key = $baseKey.OpenSubKey($matches[1])
    $returnObject = New-Object PsObject

    ## Go through each of the properties in the key
    foreach($keyProperty in $key.GetValueNames())
```

```
{
    ## If the property matches the search term, add it as a
    ## property to the output
    if($keyProperty -like $property)
    {
        $returnObject |
            Add-Member NoteProperty $keyProperty $key.GetValue($keyProperty)
    }
}

## Return the resulting object
$returnObject

## Close the key and base keys
$key.Close()
$baseKey.Close()
```

For more information about running scripts, see Recipe 1.1, "Run Programs, Scripts, and Existing Tools".

## See Also

Recipe 1.1, "Run Programs, Scripts, and Existing Tools"

# 21.15. Program: Set Properties of Remote Registry Keys

Although PowerShell does not directly let you access and manipulate the registry of a remote computer, it still supports this by working with the .NET Framework. The functionality exposed by the .NET Framework is a bit more developer-oriented than we want, so we can instead use a script to make it easier to work with.

Example 21-8 lets you set the value of a property on a given remote registry key. In order for this script to succeed, the target computer must have the remote registry service enabled and running.

*Example 21-8. Set-RemoteRegistryKeyProperty.ps1*

```
##############################################################################
##
## Set-RemoteRegistryKeyProperty
##
## From Windows PowerShell Cookbook (O'Reilly)
## by Lee Holmes (http://www.leeholmes.com/guide)
##
##############################################################################

<#

.SYNOPSIS
```

```
Set the value of a remote registry key property

.EXAMPLE

PS >$registryPath =
    "HKLM:\software\Microsoft\PowerShell\1\ShellIds\Microsoft.PowerShell"
PS >Set-RemoteRegistryKeyProperty LEE-DESK $registryPath `
    "ExecutionPolicy" "RemoteSigned"

#>

param(
    ## The computer to connect to
    [Parameter(Mandatory = $true)]
    $ComputerName,

    ## The registry path to modify
    [Parameter(Mandatory = $true)]
    $Path,

    ## The property to modify
    [Parameter(Mandatory = $true)]
    $PropertyName,

    ## The value to set on the property
    [Parameter(Mandatory = $true)]
    $PropertyValue
)

Set-StrictMode -Version 3

## Validate and extract out the registry key
if($path -match "^HKLM:\\(.*)")
{
    $baseKey = [Microsoft.Win32.RegistryKey]::OpenRemoteBaseKey(
        "LocalMachine", $computername)
}
elseif($path -match "^HKCU:\\(.*)")
{
    $baseKey = [Microsoft.Win32.RegistryKey]::OpenRemoteBaseKey(
        "CurrentUser", $computername)
}
else
{
    Write-Error ("Please specify a fully qualified registry path " +
        "(i.e.: HKLM:\Software) of the registry key to open.")
    return
}

## Open the key and set its value
$key = $baseKey.OpenSubKey($matches[1], $true)
$key.SetValue($propertyName, $propertyValue)
```

```
## Close the key and base keys
$key.Close()
$baseKey.Close()
```

For more information about running scripts, see Recipe 1.1, "Run Programs, Scripts, and Existing Tools".

## See Also

Recipe 1.1, "Run Programs, Scripts, and Existing Tools"

# 21.16. Discover Registry Settings for Programs

## Problem

You want to automate the configuration of a program, but that program does not document its registry configuration settings.

## Solution

To discover a registry setting for a program, use the Sysinternals Process Monitor to observe registry access by that program. Process Monitor is available here (*http://www.microsoft.com/technet/sysinternals/FileAndDisk/processmonitor.mspx*).

## Discussion

In an ideal world, all programs would fully support command-line administration and configuration through PowerShell cmdlets. Many programs do not, however, so the solution is to look through their documentation in the hope that they list the registry keys and properties that control their settings. While many programs document their registry configuration settings, many still do not.

Although these programs may not document their registry settings, you can usually observe their registry access activity to determine the registry paths they use. To illustrate this, we will use the Sysinternals Process Monitor to discover PowerShell's execution policy configuration keys. Although PowerShell documents these keys *and* makes its automated configuration a breeze, this example illustrates the general technique.

### Launch and configure Process Monitor

Once you've downloaded Process Monitor, the first step is to filter its output to include only the program you are interested in. By default, Process Monitor logs almost all registry and file activity on the system.

First, launch Process Monitor, and then press Ctrl-E (or click the magnifying glass icon) to temporarily prevent it from capturing any data (see Figure 21-2). Next, press Ctrl-X (or click the white sheet with an eraser icon) to clear the extra information that it captured automatically. Finally, drag the target icon and drop it on top of the application in question. You can press Ctrl-L (or click the funnel icon) to see the filter that Process Monitor now applies to its output.

*Figure 21-2. Process Monitor ready to capture*

### Prepare to manually set the configuration option

Next, prepare to manually set the program's configuration option. Usually, this means typing and clicking all the property settings, but just not clicking OK or Apply. For this PowerShell example, type the Set-ExecutionPolicy command line, but do not press Enter (see Figure 21-3).

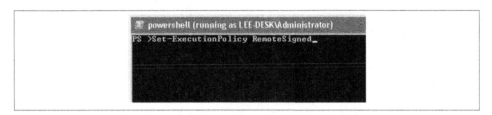

*Figure 21-3. Preparing to apply the configuration option*

### Tell Process Monitor to begin capturing information

Switch to the Process Monitor window, and then press Ctrl-E (or click the magnifying glass icon). Process Monitor now captures all registry access for the program in question.

### Manually set the configuration option

Click OK, Apply, or whatever action it takes to actually complete the program's configuration. For the PowerShell example, this means pressing Enter.

### Tell Process Monitor to stop capturing information

Switch again to the Process Monitor window, and then press Ctrl-E (or click the magnifying glass icon). Process Monitor now no longer captures the application's activity.

### Review the capture logs for registry modification

The Process Monitor window now shows all registry keys that the application interacted with when it applied its configuration setting.

Press Ctrl-F (or click the binoculars icon), and then search for `RegSetValue`. Process Monitor highlights the first modification to a registry key, as shown in Figure 21-4.

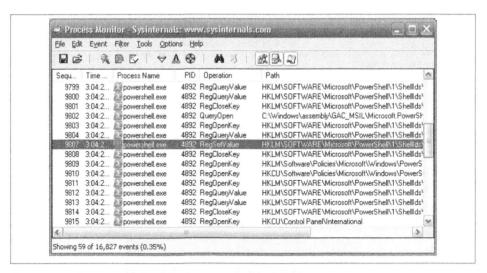

*Figure 21-4. Process Monitor's registry access detail*

Press Enter (or double-click the highlighted row) to see the details about this specific registry modification. In this example, we can see that PowerShell changed the value of the `ExecutionPolicy` property (under *HKLM:\Software\Microsoft\PowerShell\1\Shell Ids\Microsoft.PowerShell*) to `RemoteSigned`. Press F3 to see the next entry that corresponds to a registry modification.

### Automate these registry writes

Now that you know all registry writes that the application performed when it updated its settings, judgment and experimentation will help you determine which modifications actually represent this setting. Since PowerShell performed only one registry write (to a key that very obviously represents the execution policy), the choice is pretty clear in this example.

Once you've discovered the registry keys, properties, and values that the application uses to store its configuration data, you can use the techniques discussed in Recipe 21.3, "Modify or Remove a Registry Key Value" to automate these configuration settings, as in the following example:

```
PS > $key = "HKLM:\Software\Microsoft\PowerShell\1\" +
    "ShellIds\Microsoft.PowerShell"

PS > Set-ItemProperty $key ExecutionPolicy AllSigned
PS > Get-ExecutionPolicy
AllSigned
PS > Set-ItemProperty $key ExecutionPolicy RemoteSigned
PS > Get-ExecutionPolicy
RemoteSigned
```

## See Also

Recipe 21.3, "Modify or Remove a Registry Key Value"

# Comparing Data

## 22.0. Introduction

When you're working in PowerShell, it is common to work with collections of objects. Most PowerShell commands generate objects, as do many of the methods that you work with in the .NET Framework. To help you work with these object collections, PowerShell introduces the `Compare-Object` cmdlet. The `Compare-Object` cmdlet provides functionality similar to the well-known `diff` commands, but with an object-oriented flavor.

## 22.1. Compare the Output of Two Commands

### Problem

You want to compare the output of two commands.

### Solution

To compare the output of two commands, store the output of each command in variables, and then use the `Compare-Object` cmdlet to compare those variables:

```
PS > notepad
PS > $processes = Get-Process
PS > Stop-Process -ProcessName Notepad
PS > $newProcesses = Get-Process
PS > Compare-Object $processes $newProcesses

InputObject                          SideIndicator
-----------                          -------------
System.Diagnostics.Process (notepad) <=
```

## Discussion

The Solution shows how to determine which processes have exited between the two calls to Get-Process. The SideIndicator of <= tells us that the process was present in the left collection ($processes) but not in the right ($newProcesses). To work with the actual object that was different, access the InputObject property:

```
PS > $diff = @(Compare-Object $processes $newProcesses)[0]
PS > $process = $diff.InputObject
PS > $process.Handles
55
```

By default, the Compare-Object cmdlet uses the comparison functionality built into most .NET objects. This works as expected most of the time, but sometimes you might want to override that comparison behavior. For example, you might want two processes to be considered different if their memory usage changes. In that case, use the -Property parameter.

```
PS > Compare-Object $processes $newProcesses -Property Name,WS | Sort Name
```

| Name | WS | SideIndicator |
| ---- | -- | ------------- |
| dwm | 31358976 | <= |
| dwm | 29540352 | => |
| explorer | 37969920 | <= |
| explorer | 38023168 | => |
| lsass | 1548288 | => |
| lsass | 1372160 | <= |
| notepad | 5701632 | <= |
| notepad | 2891776 | => |
| powershell | 44281856 | => |
| powershell | 44290048 | <= |
| SearchIndexer | 13606912 | => |
| SearchIndexer | 13619200 | <= |
| svchost | 56061952 | <= |
| svchost | 43982848 | <= |
| svchost | 56037376 | => |
| svchost | 44048384 | => |
| svchost | 12193792 | <= |
| svchost | 12201984 | => |
| taskeng | 9220096 | <= |
| taskeng | 9228288 | => |

When you use the -Property parameter, the Compare-Object cmdlet outputs custom objects that have only the properties you used in the comparison. If you still want access to the original objects used in the comparison, also use the -PassThru parameter. In that case, PowerShell instead adds the SideIndicator property to the original objects.

If the objects you are comparing are already in proper order (for example, the lines in a file), you can improve the performance of the comparison process by using the -SyncWindow parameter. A sync window of five, for example, looks for differences only within the surrounding five objects.

For more information about the Compare-Object cmdlet, type **Get-Help Compare-Object**.

# 22.2. Determine the Differences Between Two Files

## Problem

You want to determine the differences between two files.

## Solution

To determine simple differences in the content of each file, store their content in variables, and then use the Compare-Object cmdlet to compare those variables:

```
PS > "Hello World" > c:\temp\file1.txt
PS > "Hello World" > c:\temp\file2.txt
PS > "More Information" >> c:\temp\file2.txt
PS > $content1 = Get-Content c:\temp\file1.txt
PS > $content2 = Get-Content c:\temp\file2.txt
PS > Compare-Object $content1 $content2

InputObject                     SideIndicator
-----------                     -------------
More Information                =>
```

## Discussion

The primary focus of the Compare-Object cmdlet is to compare two unordered sets of objects. Although those sets of objects can be strings (as in the content of two files), the output of Compare-Object when run against files is usually counterintuitive because of the content losing its order.

When comparing large files (or files where the order of comparison matters), you can still use traditional file comparison tools such as *diff.exe* or the WinDiff application that comes with both the Windows Support Tools and Visual Studio.

For more information about the Compare-Object cmdlet, type **Get-Help Compare-Object**.

## 22.3. Verify Integrity of File Sets

### Problem

You want to determine whether any files in a set of files have been modified or damaged.

### Solution

To verify the integrity of file sets, use the Get-FileHash script provided in Recipe 20.11, "Program: Get the MD5 or SHA1 Hash of a File" to generate the signatures of the files in question. Do the same for the files on a known good system. Finally, use the Compare-Object cmdlet to compare those two sets.

### Discussion

To generate the information from the files in question, use a command like:

```
dir C:\Windows\System32\WindowsPowerShell\v1.0 | Get-FileHash |
    Export-CliXml c:\temp\PowerShellHashes.clixml
```

This command gets the hash values of the files from *C:\Windows\System32\WindowsPowerShell\v1.0*, and uses the Export-CliXml cmdlet to store that data in a file.

Transport this file to a system with files in a known good state, and then import the data from that file.

```
$otherHashes = Import-CliXml c:\temp\PowerShellHashes.clixml
```

 You can also map a network drive to the files in question and skip the export, transport, and import steps altogether:

```
$path = "\\lee-desk\c$\Windows\System32\WindowsPowerShell\v1.0"
New-PSDrive -Name x -Root $path -PSProvider FileSystem
$otherHashes = dir x: | Get-FileHash
```

Generate the information from the files you know are in a good state:

```
$knownHashes = dir C:\Windows\System32\WindowsPowerShell\v1.0 |
    Get-FileHash
```

Finally, use the Compare-Object cmdlet to detect any differences:

```
Compare-Object $otherHashes $knownHashes -Property Path,HashValue
```

If there are any differences, the Compare-Object cmdlet displays them in a list, as shown in Example 22-1.

*Example 22-1. The Compare-Object cmdlet showing differences between two files*

```
PS > Compare-Object $otherHashes $knownHashes -Property Path,HashValue
Path                    HashValue               SideIndicator
----                    ---------               -------------
system.management.aut... 247F291CCDA8E669FF9FA... =>
system.management.aut... 5A68BC5819E29B8E3648F... <=

PS > Compare-Object $otherHashes $knownHashes -Property Path,HashValue |
Select-Object Path

Path
----
system.management.automation.dll-help.xml
system.management.automation.dll-help.xml
```

For more information about the Compare-Object cmdlet, type **Get-Help Compare-Object**. For more information about the Export-CliXml and Import-CliXml cmdlets, type **Get-Help Export-CliXml and Get-Help Import-CliXml**, respectively.

## See Also

Recipe 20.11, "Program: Get the MD5 or SHA1 Hash of a File"

# Event Logs

## 23.0. Introduction

Event logs form the core of most monitoring and diagnosis on Windows. To support this activity, PowerShell offers both the `Get-EventLog` and `Get-WinEvent` cmdlets to let you query and work with event log data on a system. In addition to simple event log retrieval, PowerShell also includes many other cmdlets to create, delete, customize, and interact with event logs.

In addition to the (now "classic") event logs exposed by the `*-EventLog` cmdlets, Windows Vista and beyond have a significantly expanded and revamped event logging system compared to Windows XP. The features of the new system are different enough that we expose them through an entirely new `Get-WinEvent` cmdlet. If you need to read events from Vista-style event logs, you'll need the `Get-WinEvent` cmdlet. If you need to read events from classic event logs, the choice is up to you.

## 23.1. List All Event Logs

### Problem

You want to determine which event logs exist on a system.

### Solution

To list all classic event logs on a system, use the `-List` parameter of the `Get-EventLog` cmdlet:

```
PS > Get-EventLog -List

  Max(K) Retain OverflowAction          Entries Log
  ------ ------ --------------          ------- ---
  20,480      0 OverwriteAsNeeded         1,933 Application
  15,168      0 OverwriteAsNeeded             0 DFS Replication
  20,480      0 OverwriteAsNeeded             0 HardwareEvents
     512      7 OverwriteOlder                0 Internet Explorer
  20,480      0 OverwriteAsNeeded             0 Key Management Service
   8,192      0 OverwriteAsNeeded             0 Media Center
     128      0 OverwriteAsNeeded             2 OAlerts
   1,024      7 OverwriteOlder              424 ScriptEvents
  20,480      0 OverwriteAsNeeded        39,006 Security
  20,480      0 OverwriteAsNeeded        55,958 System
  15,360      0 OverwriteAsNeeded         2,865 Windows PowerShell
```

On Windows Vista or later, you can also use the Get-WinEvent cmdlet. In addition to classic event logs, the Get-WinEvent cmdlet supports Application and Services event logs:

```
PS > Get-WinEvent -ListLog * | Select LogName,RecordCount

LogName                                       RecordCount
-------                                       -----------
Application                                          1933
DFS Replication                                         0
HardwareEvents                                          0
Internet Explorer                                       0
Key Management Service                                  0
Media Center                                            0
OAlerts                                                 2
ScriptEvents                                          424
Security                                            39005
System                                              55957
Windows PowerShell                                   2865
ForwardedEvents
Microsoft-Windows-Backup                                0
Microsoft-Windows-Bits-Client/Ana ...
Microsoft-Windows-Bits-Client/Oper...                2232
Microsoft-Windows-Bluetooth-MTPEnu...                   0
Microsoft-Windows-CAPI2/Operational
(...)
```

To browse event logs using the Windows Event Viewer graphical user interface, use the Show-EventLog cmdlet.

## Discussion

The -List parameter of the Get-EventLog cmdlet generates a list of the event logs registered on the system. In addition to supporting event logs on the current system, all of PowerShell's event log cmdlets let you supply the -ComputerName parameter to interact with event logs on a remote system.

Once you've determined which event log you are interested in, you can use the Get-EventLog and Get-WinEvent cmdlets to search, filter, and retrieve specific entries from those logs. For information on how to retrieve event log entries, see Recipes 23.2, 23.3, and 23.4.

For more information about the Get-EventLog cmdlet, type **Get-Help Get-EventLog**. For more information about the Get-WinEvent cmdlet, type **Get-Help Get-WinEvent**.

## See Also

Recipe 23.2, "Get the Newest Entries from an Event Log"

Recipe 23.3, "Find Event Log Entries with Specific Text"

Recipe 23.4, "Retrieve and Filter Event Log Entries"

# 23.2. Get the Newest Entries from an Event Log

## Problem

You want to retrieve the most recent entries from an event log.

## Solution

To retrieve the most recent entries from an event log, use the -Newest parameter of the Get-EventLog cmdlet, as shown in Example 23-1.

*Example 23-1. Retrieving the 10 newest entries from the System event log*

```
PS > Get-EventLog System -Newest 10 | Format-Table Index,Source,Message -Auto

Index Source                  Message
----- ------                  -------
 2922 Service Control Manager The Background Intelligent Transfer Servi...
 2921 Service Control Manager The Background Intelligent Transfer Servi...
 2920 Service Control Manager The Logical Disk Manager Administrative S...
 2919 Service Control Manager The Logical Disk Manager Administrative S...
 2918 Service Control Manager The Logical Disk Manager Administrative S...
 2917 TermServDevices         Driver Microsoft XPS Document Writer requ...
```

```
2916 Print            Printer Microsoft Office Document Image W...
2915 Print            Printer Microsoft Office Document Image W...
2914 Print            Printer Microsoft Office Document Image W...
2913 TermServDevices  Driver Microsoft Shared Fax Driver requir...
```

Alternatively, use the -MaxEvents parameter of the Get-WinEvent cmdlet:

```
PS > Get-WinEvent Application -MaxEvents 10 |
    Format-Table ProviderName,Id,Message -Auto

ProviderName            Id Message
------------            -- -------
VSS                   8224 The VSS service is shutting down due to ...
System Restore        8194 Successfully created restore point (Proc...
System Restore        8194 Successfully created restore point (Proc...
VSS                   8224 The VSS service is shutting down due to ...
System Restore        8211 Successfully created scheduled restore p...
System Restore        8194 Successfully created restore point (Proc...
Microsoft-Windows-MSDTC 2 4202 MSDTC started with the following setting...
VSS                   8224 The VSS service is shutting down due to ...
System Restore        8211 Successfully created scheduled restore p...
System Restore        8194 Successfully created restore point (Proc...
```

## Discussion

The -Newest parameter of the Get-EventLog cmdlet retrieves the most recent entries from an event log that you specify. To list the event logs available on the system, see Recipe 23.1, "List All Event Logs". The Get-WinEvent cmdlet returns the most recent entries by default, so no specific parameter is required.

For more information about the Get-EventLog cmdlet, type **Get-Help Get-EventLog**.

## See Also

Recipe 23.1, "List All Event Logs"

# 23.3. Find Event Log Entries with Specific Text

## Problem

You want to retrieve all event log entries that contain a given term.

## Solution

To find specific event log entries, use the Get-EventLog or Get-WinEvent cmdlet to retrieve the items, and then pipe them to the Where-Object cmdlet to filter them, as shown in Example 23-2.

---

*Example 23-2. Searching the event log for entries that mention the term "disk"*

```
PS > Get-EventLog System | Where-Object { $_.Message -match "disk" }

Index Time            Type Source            EventID Message
----- ----            ---- ------            ------- -------
 2920 May 06 09:18    Info Service Control M...   7036 The Logical Disk...
 2919 May 06 09:17    Info Service Control M...   7036 The Logical Disk...
 2918 May 06 09:17    Info Service Control M...   7035 The Logical Disk...
 2884 May 06 00:28    Erro sr                        1 The System Resto...
 2333 Apr 03 00:16    Erro Disk                     11 The driver detec...
 2332 Apr 03 00:16    Erro Disk                     11 The driver detec...
 2131 Mar 27 13:59    Info Service Control M...   7036 The Logical Disk...
 2127 Mar 27 12:48    Info Service Control M...   7036 The Logical Disk...
 2126 Mar 27 12:48    Info Service Control M...   7035 The Logical Disk...
 2123 Mar 27 12:31    Info Service Control M...   7036 The Logical Disk...
 2122 Mar 27 12:29    Info Service Control M...   7036 The Logical Disk...
 2121 Mar 27 12:29    Info Service Control M...   7035 The Logical Disk...
```

## Discussion

Since the Get-EventLog cmdlet retrieves rich objects that represent event log entries, you can pipe them to the Where-Object cmdlet for equally rich filtering.

By default, PowerShell's default table formatting displays a summary of event log entries. If you are searching the event log message, however, you are probably interested in seeing more details about the message itself. In this case, use the Format-List cmdlet to format these entries in a more detailed list view. Example 23-3 shows this view.

*Example 23-3. A detailed list view of an event log entry*

```
PS > Get-EventLog System | Where-Object { $_.Message -match "disk" } |
    Format-List

Index              : 2920
EntryType          : Information
EventID            : 7036
Message            : The Logical Disk Manager Administrative Service
                     service entered the stopped state.
Category           : (0)
CategoryNumber     : 0
ReplacementStrings : {Logical Disk Manager Administrative Service, stopped
                     }
Source             : Service Control Manager
TimeGenerated      : 5/6/2007 9:18:25 AM
TimeWritten        : 5/6/2007 9:18:25 AM
UserName           :

Index              : 2919
(...)
```

For more information about the Get-EventLog cmdlet, type **Get-Help Get-EventLog**. For more information about filtering command output, see Recipe 2.1, "Filter Items in a List or Command Output".

## See Also

Recipe 2.1, "Filter Items in a List or Command Output"

# 23.4. Retrieve and Filter Event Log Entries

## Problem

You want to retrieve a specific event log entry or filter a log based on advanced search criteria.

## Solution

To retrieve a specific event log entry, use the Get-EventLog cmdlet to retrieve the entries in the event log, and then pipe them to the Where-Object cmdlet to filter them to the one you are looking for.

```
PS > Get-EventLog System | Where-Object { $_.Index -eq 2920 }

Index Time          Type Source              EventID Message
----- ----          ---- ------              ------- -------
 2920 May 06 09:18  Info Service Control M...    7036 The Logical Disk...
```

For more advanced (or performance-sensitive) queries, use the -FilterXml, the -FilterHashtable, or the -FilterXPath parameters of the Get-WinEvent cmdlet:

```
Get-WinEvent -LogName "System" -FilterXPath "*[System[EventRecordID = 2920]]"
```

## Discussion

If you've listed the items in an event log or searched it for entries that have a message with specific text, you often want to get more details about a specific event log entry.

Since the Get-EventLog cmdlet retrieves rich objects that represent event log entries, you can pipe them to the Where-Object cmdlet for equally rich filtering.

By default, PowerShell's default table formatting displays a summary of event log entries. If you are retrieving a specific entry, however, you are probably interested in seeing more details about the entry. In this case, use the Format-List cmdlet to format these entries in a more detailed list view, as shown in Example 23-4.

*Example 23-4. A detailed list view of an event log entry*

```
PS > Get-EventLog System | Where-Object { $_.Index -eq 2920 } |
    Format-List

Index             : 2920
EntryType         : Information
EventID           : 7036
Message           : The Logical Disk Manager Administrative Service
                    service entered the stopped state.
Category          : (0)
CategoryNumber    : 0
ReplacementStrings : {Logical Disk Manager Administrative Service, stopped
                    }
Source            : Service Control Manager
TimeGenerated     : 5/6/2007 9:18:25 AM
TimeWritten       : 5/6/2007 9:18:25 AM
UserName          :

Index             : 2919
(...)
```

While the `Where-Object` cmdlet works well for simple (or one-off) tasks, the `Get-WinEvent` cmdlet offers three parameters that can make your event log searches both more powerful and more efficient.

### Efficiently processing simple queries

If you have a simple event log query, you can use the `-FilterHashtable` parameter of the `Get-WinEvent` cmdlet to filter the event log very efficiently.

> The `-FilterHashtable` parameter works only on Windows 7. On Windows Vista, it generates an error: "The parameter is incorrect."

The hashtable that you supply to this parameter lets you filter on `LogName`, `Provider Name`, `Path`, `Keywords`, `ID`, `Level`, `StartTime`, `EndTime`, and `UserID`. This can replace many `Where-Object` style filtering operations. This example retrieves all critical and error events in the System event log:

```
Get-WinEvent -FilterHashtable @{ LogName = "System"; Level = 1,2 }
```

### Automating GUI-generated searches

When you are reviewing an event log, the Windows Event Viewer offers a Filter Current Log action on the righthand side. This interface lets you select data ranges, event severity, keywords, task categories, and more. After customizing a filter, you can click the XML tab to see an XML representation of your query. You can copy and paste that XML directly into a here string in a script, and then pass it to the -FilterXml parameter of the Get-WinEvent cmdlet:

```
## Gets all Critical and Error events from the last 24 hours
$xml = @'
<QueryList>
  <Query Id="0" Path="System">
    <Select Path="System">
        *[System[(Level=1  or Level=2) and
            TimeCreated[timediff(@SystemTime) &lt;= 86400000]]]
    </Select>
  </Query>
</QueryList>
'@

Get-WinEvent -FilterXml $xml
```

## Performing complex event analysis and correlation

Under the covers, event logs store their event information in an XML format. In addition to the -FilterHashtable and -FilterXml parameters, the Get-WinEvent cmdlet lets you filter event logs with a subset of the standard XPath XML querying language. XPath lets your filters describe complex hierarchical queries, value ranges, and more.

 Like regular expressions, the XPath query language is by no means simple or easy to understand. This parameter can help if you already have some degree of knowledge or comfort in XPath, but don't let it intimidate or frustrate you. There is always more than one way to do it.

While the XPath querying language is powerful, the type of rules you can express ultimately depend on what is contained in the XML of the actual events. To see what can be contained in the XML of an event, search MSDN for "Windows 'event schema.'" The online reference is useful, but actual events tend to contain an extremely small subset of the supported XML nodes. Because of that, you might have more success reviewing the XML of events that interest you and forming XPath queries based on those. Here are some example queries that build on the -FilterXPath parameter:

```
## Search by Event ID
Get-WinEvent -LogName "System" -FilterXPath "*[System[(EventID=1)]]"

## Search for events associated with a given Process ID
Get-WinEvent -LogName "System" -FilterXPath "*[System/Execution[@ProcessID=428]]"

## Search for events that have 'Volume Shadow Copy' as one of the
## replacement strings
```

```
Get-WinEvent -LogName "System" -FilterXPath `
    "*[EventData[Data = 'Volume Shadow Copy']]"

## Search for Windows Installer Events associated with Vista SP1
$query = "*[UserData/CbsPackageInitiateChanges[PackageIdentifier = 'KB936330']]"
Get-WinEvent -LogName "System" -FilterXPath $query
```

## See Also

Recipe 2.1, "Filter Items in a List or Command Output"

Appendix C, *XPath Quick Reference*

# 23.5. Find Event Log Entries by Their Frequency

## Problem

You want to find the event log entries that occur most frequently.

## Solution

To find event log entries by frequency, use the Get-EventLog cmdlet to retrieve the entries in the event log, and then pipe them to the Group-Object cmdlet to group them by their message.

```
PS > Get-EventLog System | Group-Object Message | Sort-Object -Desc Count

Count Name                      Group
----- ----                      -----
  161 Driver Microsoft XPS D... {LEE-DESK, LEE-DESK, LEE-DESK, LEE-DESK...
   23 The Background Intelli... {LEE-DESK, LEE-DESK, LEE-DESK, LEE-DESK...
   23 The Background Intelli... {LEE-DESK, LEE-DESK, LEE-DESK, LEE-DESK...
    3 The Logical Disk Manag... {LEE-DESK, LEE-DESK, LEE-DESK}
    3 The Logical Disk Manag... {LEE-DESK, LEE-DESK, LEE-DESK}
    3 The Logical Disk Manag... {LEE-DESK, LEE-DESK, LEE-DESK}
(...)
```

## Discussion

The Group-Object cmdlet is a useful way to determine which events occur most frequently on your system. It also provides a useful way to summarize the information in the event log.

If you want more information about the items in a specific group, use the Where-Object cmdlet. Since we used the Message property in the Group-Object cmdlet, we need to filter on Message in the Where-Object cmdlet. For example, to learn more about the entries relating to the Microsoft XPS Driver (from the scenario in the Solution):

```
PS > Get-EventLog System |
    Where-Object { $_.Message -like "Driver Microsoft XPS*" }

Index Time           Type Source            EventID Message
----- ----           ---- ------            ------- -------
 2917 May 06 09:13   Erro TermServDevices      1111 Driver Microsoft...
 2883 May 05 10:40   Erro TermServDevices      1111 Driver Microsoft...
 2877 May 05 08:10   Erro TermServDevices      1111 Driver Microsoft...
(...)
```

If grouping by message doesn't provide useful information, you can group by any other property—such as source:

```
PS > Get-EventLog Application | Group-Object Source

Count Name                      Group
----- ----                      -----
    4 Application                {LEE-DESK, LEE-DESK, LEE-DESK, LEE-DESK}
  191 Media Center Scheduler     {LEE-DESK, LEE-DESK, LEE-DESK, LEE-DESK...
 1082 MSSQL$SQLEXPRESS           {LEE-DESK, LEE-DESK, LEE-DESK, LEE-DESK...
(...)
```

If you've listed the items in an event log or searched it for entries that have a message with specific text, you often want to get more details about a specific event log entry.

By default, PowerShell's default table formatting displays a summary of event log entries. If you are retrieving a specific entry, however, you are probably interested in seeing more details about the entry. In this case, use the Format-List cmdlet to format these entries in a more detailed list view, as shown in Example 23-5.

*Example 23-5. A detailed list view of an event log entry*

```
PS > Get-EventLog System | Where-Object { $_.Index -eq 2917 } |
    Format-List

Index             : 2917
EntryType         : Error
EventID           : 1111
Message           : Driver Microsoft XPS Document Writer required for printer
                    Microsoft XPS Document Writer is unknown. Contact
                    the administrator to install the driver before you
                    log in again.
Category          : (0)
CategoryNumber    : 0
ReplacementStrings : {Microsoft XPS Document Writer, Microsoft XPS Document
                    Writer}
Source            : TermServDevices
TimeGenerated     : 5/6/2007 9:13:31 AM
TimeWritten       : 5/6/2007 9:13:31 AM
UserName          :
```

For more information about the Get-EventLog cmdlet, type **Get-Help Get-EventLog**. For more information about filtering command output, see Recipe 2.1, "Filter Items in a List or Command Output". For more information about the Group-Object cmdlet, type **Get-Help Group-Object**.

## See Also

Recipe 2.1, "Filter Items in a List or Command Output"

# 23.6. Back Up an Event Log

## Problem

You want to store the information in an event log in a file for storage or later review.

## Solution

To store event log entries in a file, use the *wevtutil.exe* application:

```
PS > wevtutil epl System c:\temp\system.bak.evtx
```

After exporting the event log, use the Get-WinEvent cmdlet to query the exported log as though it were live:

```
PS > Get-WinEvent -FilterHashtable @{
    LogName="System"; Level=1,2 } -MaxEvents 2 | Format-Table -Auto

TimeCreated             ProviderName Id Message
-----------             ------------ -- -------
2/15/2010 11:49:31 AM Ntfs           55 The file system structure on the disk is...
2/15/2010 11:49:31 AM Ntfs           55 The file system structure on the disk is...

PS > Get-WinEvent -FilterHashtable @{
    Path="c:\temp\system.bak.evtx"; Level=1,2 } -MaxEvents 2 |
    Format-Table -Auto

TimeCreated             ProviderName Id Message
-----------             ------------ -- -------
2/15/2010 11:49:31 AM Ntfs           55 The file system structure on the disk is...
2/15/2010 11:49:31 AM Ntfs           55 The file system structure on the disk is...
```

If you need to process the event logs on a system where the Get-WinEvent cmdlet is not available, use the Get-EventLog cmdlet to retrieve the entries in the event log, and then pipe them to the Export-CliXml cmdlet to store them in a file.

```
Get-EventLog System | Export-CliXml c:\temp\SystemLogBackup.clixml
```

## Discussion

While there is no PowerShell cmdlet to export event logs, the *wevtutil.exe* application provides an easy way to save an event log to disk in its full fidelity. After exporting the event log, you can import it again, or even use the Get-WinEvent cmdlet to query against it directly.

If you want to analyze the event logs on a machine where the Get-WinEvent cmdlet is not available, you can use the Export-CliXml cmdlet to save event logs to disk—just as PowerShell lets you save any other structured data to disk. Once you've exported the events from an event log, you can archive them, or use the Import-CliXml cmdlet to review them on any machine that has PowerShell installed:

```
PS > $archivedLogs = Import-CliXml c:\temp\SystemLogBackup.clixml
PS > $archivedLogs | Group Source

Count Name                      Group
----- ----                      -----
  856 Service Control Manager   {LEE-DESK, LEE-DESK, LEE-DESK, LEE-DESK...
  640 TermServDevices           {LEE-DESK, LEE-DESK, LEE-DESK, LEE-DESK...
   91 Print                     {LEE-DESK, LEE-DESK, LEE-DESK, LEE-DESK...
  100 WMPNetworkSvc             {LEE-DESK, LEE-DESK, LEE-DESK, LEE-DESK...
  123 Tcpip                     {LEE-DESK, LEE-DESK, LEE-DESK, LEE-DESK...
(...)
```

In addition to the Export-CliXml cmdlet, you can also use WMI's Win32_NTEventLog File class to back up classic event logs:

```
$log = Get-CimInstance Win32_NTEventLogFile -Filter "LogFileName = 'Application'"
$log | Invoke-CimMethod -Name BackupEventLog -Arguments @{
    ArchiveFileName = "c:\temp\application_backup.log" }
```

After saving a log, you can use the Open Saved Log feature in the Windows Event Viewer to review it.

For more information about the Get-EventLog cmdlet, type **Get-Help Get-EventLog**. For more information about the Export-CliXml and Import-CliXml cmdlets, type **Get-Help Export-CliXml** and **Get-Help Import-CliXml**, respectively.

# 23.7. Create or Remove an Event Log

## Problem

You want to create or remove an event log.

## Solution

Use the New-EventLog and Remove-EventLog cmdlets to create and remove event logs:

```
PS > New-EventLog -Logname ScriptEvents -Source PowerShellCookbook
PS > Get-EventLog -List

  Max(K) Retain OverflowAction          Entries Log
  ------ ------ --------------          ------- ---
  20,480      0 OverwriteAsNeeded         1,930 Application
(...)
     512      7 OverwriteOlder                0 ScriptEvents
(...)
  15,360      0 OverwriteAsNeeded         2,847 Windows PowerShell

PS > Remove-EventLog ScriptEvents
```

Both cmdlets support remote administration via the `-ComputerName` parameter.

## Discussion

Although Windows offers the standard Application event log, you might sometimes want to make separate event logs to hold events of special interest. For this, PowerShell includes the New-EventLog cmdlet. It takes two parameters: the event log name and the source identifier for events. If the event log does not already exist, PowerShell creates it. If both the event log and event log source already exist, the New-EventLog cmdlet generates an error.

After you create the event log, the Limit-EventLog cmdlet lets you manage its retention policy. For more information about the Limit-EventLog cmdlet, see Recipe 23.10, "Clear or Maintain an Event Log".

The Remove-EventLog cmdlet lets you remove both event logs and event log sources.

 Be careful when deleting event logs, as it is difficult to recreate all the event sources if you delete the wrong log by accident. If you delete a standard event log, you have little hope for recovery.

To remove just an event log source, use the `-Source` parameter:

```
Remove-EventLog -Source PowerShellCookbook
```

To remove an event log altogether, specify the log name in the `-Logname` parameter:

```
Remove-EventLog -LogName ScriptEvents
```

Once you have created an event log, you can use the Write-EventLog cmdlet to work with it. For more information about writing to event logs, see Recipe 23.8, "Write to an Event Log".

## See Also

Recipe 23.8, "Write to an Event Log"

# 23.8. Write to an Event Log

## Problem

You want to add an entry to an event log.

## Solution

Use the `Write-EventLog` cmdlet to write events to an event log:

```
PS > Write-EventLog -LogName ScriptEvents -Source PowerShellCookbook `
    -EventId 1234 -Message "Hello World"

PS > Get-EventLog ScriptEvents | Select EntryType,Source,InstanceId,Message

        EntryType Source                    InstanceId Message
        --------- ------                    ---------- -------
        Information PowerShellCookbook            1234 Hello World
```

## Discussion

The `Write-EventLog` cmdlet lets you write event log messages to a specified event log. To write an event log message, you must supply a valid log name and a registered event log source. If you need to create a new event log or register a new event source, see Recipe 23.7, "Create or Remove an Event Log".

In addition to the log name and source, the `Write-EventLog` cmdlet also requires an event ID and message. Within an event log and event source, each event ID should uniquely identify the situation being logged: for example, *logon failure* or *disk full*. This makes it easy for scripts and other management tasks to automatically respond to system events. The event message should elaborate on the situation being logged (for example, the username or drive letter), but should not be required to identify its reason.

## See Also

Recipe 23.7, "Create or Remove an Event Log"

# 23.9. Run a PowerShell Script for Windows Event Log Entries

## Problem

You want to run a PowerShell script when the system generates a specific event log entry.

## Solution

Use the *schtasks.exe* tool to define a new task that reacts to event log entries. As its action, call *powershell.exe* with the arguments to disable the profile, customize the execution policy, hide its window, and launch a script:

```
$cred = Get-Credential
$password = $cred.GetNetworkCredential().Password

## Define the command that task scheduler should run when the event
## occurs
$command = "PowerShell -NoProfile -ExecutionPolicy RemoteSigned " +
    "-WindowStyle Hidden -File 'C:\Program Files\TaskScripts\ScriptEvents.ps1'"

## Create a new scheduled task
SCHTASKS /Create /TN "ScriptEvents Monitor" /TR $command /SC ONEVENT `
         /RL Highest /RU $cred.Username /RP $password `
         /EC ScriptEvents /MO *[System/EventID=1010]
```

## Discussion

In Vista and beyond, the Windows event log lets you define custom actions that launch when an event is generated. Although you can use the user interface to create these tasks and filters, the *schtasks.exe* tool lets you create them all from the automation-friendly command line.

As an example of this in action, imagine trying to capture the processes running on a system when a problematic event occurs. That script might look like:

```
$logTag = "{0:yyyyMMdd_HHmm}" -f (Get-Date)
$logPath = 'C:\Program Files\TaskScripts\ScriptEvents-{0}.txt' -f $logTag

Start-Transcript -Path $logPath

Get-CimInstance Win32_OperatingSystem | Format-List | Out-String
Get-Process | Format-Table | Out-String

Stop-Transcript
```

After generating an event, we can see the log being created just moments after:

```
PS > dir

    Directory: C:\Program Files\TaskScripts

Mode                LastWriteTime     Length Name
----                -------------     ------ ----
-a---         2/21/2010   8:38 PM        278 ScriptEvents.ps1

PS > Write-EventLog -LogName ScriptEvents -Source PowerShellCookbook `
    -EventId 1010 -Message "Hello World"
```

```
PS > dir

    Directory: C:\Program Files\TaskScripts

Mode                LastWriteTime     Length Name
----                -------------     ------ ----
-a---        2/21/2010   9:50 PM      12766 ScriptEvents-20100221_2150.txt
-a---        2/21/2010   8:38 PM        278 ScriptEvents.ps1
```

When we define the task, we use the /TN parameter to define a name for our task. As the command (specified by the /TR parameter), we tell Windows to launch *Power Shell.exe* with several parameters to customize its environment. We use the /RL parameter to ensure that the task is run with elevated permissions (as it writes to the *Program Files* directory). To define the actual event log filter, we use the /EC parameter to define the event channel—in this case, the ScriptEvents log. In the /MO ("modifier") parameter, we specify the XPath filter required to match events that we care about. In this case, we search for EventId 1010. The System/ prefix doesn't tell Windows to search the System event log; it tells it to look in the standard system properties: EventID, Level, Task, Keywords, Computer, and more.

For more information about the event viewer's XPath syntax, see Recipe 23.4, "Retrieve and Filter Event Log Entries".

## See Also

Recipe 1.16, "Invoke a PowerShell Command or Script from Outside PowerShell"

Recipe 23.4, "Retrieve and Filter Event Log Entries"

# 23.10. Clear or Maintain an Event Log

## Problem

You want to clear an event log or manage its retention policy.

## Solution

Use the Limit-EventLog cmdlet to manage the retention policy (days, size, and overflow behavior) of an event log. Use the Clear-EventLog cmdlet to clear it completely:

```
PS > Get-EventLog -List | Where-Object { $_.Log -eq "ScriptEvents" }

  Max(K) Retain OverflowAction        Entries Log
  ------ ------ --------------        ------- ---
   2,048      7 OverwriteOlder            872 ScriptEvents

PS > Clear-EventLog ScriptEvents
PS > Get-EventLog -List | Where-Object { $_.Log -eq "ScriptEvents" }
```

```
  Max(K) Retain OverflowAction        Entries Log
  ------ ------ --------------        ------- ---
   2,048      7 OverwriteOlder              0 ScriptEvents

PS > Limit-EventLog -LogName ScriptEvents -MaximumSize 1024kb
PS > 1..10000 | Foreach-Object {
    Write-EventLog -LogName ScriptEvents -Source PowerShellCookbook `
        -EventId 1234 -Message ('A' * 1000)
}

PS > Get-EventLog -List | Where-Object { $_.Log -eq "ScriptEvents" }

  Max(K) Retain OverflowAction        Entries Log
  ------ ------ --------------        ------- ---
   1,024      7 OverwriteOlder            424 ScriptEvents
```

Both cmdlets support remote administration via the -ComputerName parameter.

## Discussion

While the default policies of most event logs are sensible, PowerShell still provides commands to help you manage how much information each event log retains.

For permanent policy changes, use the Limit-EventLog cmdlet. This cmdlet lets you limit the log size, maximum event age, and overwrite behavior for the event log that you apply it to. While the size and age limits are fairly self-describing parameters, configuring the overflow behavior is more subtle.

The -OverflowAction parameter supports one of three options. Each describes a different strategy for Windows to take when writing to a full event log:

DoNotOverwrite
: Discards new entries.

OverwriteAsNeeded
: Overwrites the oldest entry.

OverwriteOlder
: Overwrites entries older than the age limit specified for the event log (via the RetentionDays parameter). If there are no old entries to overwrite, Windows discards the new entry.

To clear an event log entirely, use the Clear-EventLog cmdlet. If you want to save the contents of the event log before clearing it, see Recipe 23.6, "Back Up an Event Log". PowerShell does not include a cmdlet to clear the new event logs supported by Vista and later (as exposed by the `Get-WinEvent` cmdlet), but you can use the `[System.Diagnostics.Eventing.Reader.EventLogSession]::GlobalSession.ClearLog()` method from the .NET Framework to clear these event logs. For more information about working with .NET objects, see Recipe 3.8, "Work with .NET Objects".

If you want to remove an event log entirely, see Recipe 23.7, "Create or Remove an Event Log".

## See Also

Recipe 3.8, "Work with .NET Objects"

Recipe 23.6, "Back Up an Event Log"

Recipe 23.7, "Create or Remove an Event Log"

# 23.11. Access Event Logs of a Remote Machine

## Problem

You want to access event log entries from a remote machine.

## Solution

To access event logs on a remote machine, use the `-ComputerName` parameter of any of the `EventLog` cmdlets:

```
PS > Get-EventLog System -ComputerName LEE-DESK | Group-Object Source

Count Name                    Group
----- ----                    -----
   91 Print                   {LEE-DESK, LEE-DESK, LEE-DESK, LEE-DESK...
  640 TermServDevices         {LEE-DESK, LEE-DESK, LEE-DESK, LEE-DESK...
  148 W32Time                 {LEE-DESK, LEE-DESK, LEE-DESK, LEE-DESK...
  100 WMPNetworkSvc           {LEE-DESK, LEE-DESK, LEE-DESK, LEE-DESK...
  856 Service Control Manager {LEE-DESK, LEE-DESK, LEE-DESK, LEE-DESK...
  123 Tcpip                   {LEE-DESK, LEE-DESK, LEE-DESK, LEE-DESK...
(...)
```

To use the graphical event log viewer to browse event logs on a remote machine, use the `Show-EventLog` cmdlet:

```
Show-EventLog Computername
```

## Discussion

The `-ComputerName` parameter of the `*-EventLog` cmdlets makes it easy to manage event logs of remote computers. Using these cmdlets, you can create event logs, remove event logs, write event log entries, and more.

If you want to use a graphical user interface to work with event logs on a remote machine in a more ad hoc way, use the Show-EventLog cmdlet. If the Remote Eventlog Management firewall rule is enabled on the remote computer (and you have the appropriate permissions), PowerShell launches the Windows Event Viewer targeted to that machine (see Figure 23-1).

*Figure 23-1. Event Viewer targeting a remote machine*

By default, the Windows Event Viewer tries to use the credentials of your current account to connect to the remote computer. If you need to connect as another account, click the "Connect to Another Computer" action on the righthand side of the Event Viewer window that opens. In that window, specify both the remote computer name and new user information.

For information about how to get event logs, see Recipe 23.1, "List All Event Logs". For more information about how to create or delete event logs, see Recipe 23.7, "Create or Remove an Event Log". For more information about how to write event log entries, see Recipe 23.8, "Write to an Event Log".

## See Also

Recipe 23.1, "List All Event Logs"

Recipe 23.7, "Create or Remove an Event Log"

Recipe 23.8, "Write to an Event Log"

# Processes

## 24.0. Introduction

Working with system processes is a natural aspect of system administration. It is also the source of most of the regular expression magic and kung fu that make system administrators proud. After all, who wouldn't boast about this Unix one-liner to stop all processes using more than 100 MB of memory:

```
ps -el | awk '{ if ( $6 > (1024*100)) { print $3 } }' | grep -v PID | xargs kill
```

While helpful, it also demonstrates the inherently fragile nature of pure text processing. For this command to succeed, it must:

- Depend on the ps command to display memory usage in column 6
- Depend on column 6 of the ps command's output to represent the memory usage in kilobytes
- Depend on column 3 of the ps command's output to represent the process ID
- Remove the header column from the ps command's output

While the ps command has parameters that simplify some of this work, this form of "prayer-based parsing" is common when manipulating the output of tools that produce only text.

Since PowerShell's Get-Process cmdlet returns information as highly structured .NET objects, fragile text parsing becomes a thing of the past:

```
Get-Process | Where-Object { $_.WorkingSet -gt 100mb } | Stop-Process -WhatIf
```

If brevity is important, PowerShell defines aliases to make most commands easier to type:

```
gps | ? { $_.WS -gt 100mb } | kill -WhatIf
```

In addition to simple process control, PowerShell also offers commands for starting processes, customizing their execution environment, waiting for processes to exit, and more.

# 24.1. List Currently Running Processes

## Problem

You want to see which processes are running on the system.

## Solution

To retrieve the list of currently running processes, use the Get-Process cmdlet:

```
PS > Get-Process

Handles  NPM(K)  PM(K)  WS(K)  VM(M)  CPU(s)     Id ProcessName
-------  ------  -----  -----  -----  ------     -- -----------
    274       6   1328   3940     33           1084 alg
     85       4   3816   6656     57    5.67   3460 AutoHotkey
     50       2   2292   1980     14  384.25   1560 BrmfRsmg
     71       3   2520   4680     35    0.42   2592 cmd
    946       7   3676   6204     32            848 csrss
     84       4    732   2248     22           3144 csrss
     68       4    936   3364     30    0.38   3904 ctfmon
    243       7   3648   9324     48    2.02   2892 Ditto
(...)
```

## Discussion

The Get-Process cmdlet retrieves information about all processes running on the system. Because these are rich .NET objects (of the type System.Diagnostics.Process), advanced filters and operations are easier than ever before.

For example, to find all processes using more than 100 MB of memory:

```
PS > Get-Process | Where-Object { $_.WorkingSet -gt 100mb }

Handles  NPM(K)  PM(K)  WS(K)   VM(M)  CPU(s)     Id ProcessName
-------  ------  -----  -----   -----  ------     -- -----------
   1458      29  83468 105824    273  323.80   3992 BigBloatedApp
```

To group processes by company:

```
PS > Get-Process | Group-Object Company

Count Name                      Group
----- ----                      -----
   39                           {alg, csrss, csrss, dllhost...}
    4                           {AutoHotkey, Ditto, gnuserv, mafwTray}
```

```
      1 Brother Industries, Ltd.  {BrmfRsmg}
     19 Microsoft Corporation      {cmd, ctfmon, EXCEL, explorer...}
      1 Free Software Foundation   {emacs}
      1 Microsoft (R) Corporation {FwcMgmt}
(...)
```

Or perhaps to sort by start time (with the most recent first):

```
PS > Get-Process | Sort -Descending StartTime | Select-Object -First 10

Handles  NPM(K)    PM(K)     WS(K) VM(M)   CPU(s)     Id ProcessName
-------  ------    -----     ----- -----   ------     -- -----------
   1810      39    53616     33964   193   318.02   1452 iTunes
    675       6    41472     50180   146    49.36    296 powershell
   1240      35    48220     58860   316   167.58   4012 OUTLOOK
    305       8     5736      2460   105    21.22   3384 WindowsSearch...
    464       7    29704     30920   153     6.00   3680 powershell
   1458      29    83468    105824   273   324.22   3992 iexplore
    478       6    24620     23688   143    17.83   3548 powershell
    222       8     8532     19084   144    20.69   3924 EXCEL
     14       2      396      1600    15     0.06   2900 logon.scr
    544      18    21336     50216   294   180.72   2660 WINWORD
```

These advanced tasks become incredibly simple due to the rich amount of information that PowerShell returns for each process. For more information about the Get-Process cmdlet, type **Get-Help Get-Process**. For more information about filtering, grouping, and sorting in PowerShell commands, see Recipe 2.1, "Filter Items in a List or Command Output".

For more information about working with classes from the .NET Framework, see Recipe 3.8, "Work with .NET Objects".

## See Also

Recipe 2.1, "Filter Items in a List or Command Output"

Recipe 3.8, "Work with .NET Objects"

# 24.2. Launch the Application Associated with a Document

## Problem

You want to launch the application associated with a document or with another shell association.

## Solution

Use the Start-Process cmdlet (or its start alias) to launch the document or location:

```
PS > Start-Process http://blogs.msdn.com/powershell
PS > start http://www.bing.com
PS > start c:\temp\output.csv
```

To launch one of the predefined actions for a document (usually exposed through its right-click menu), use the -Verb parameter:

```
start c:\documents\MyDoc.docx -Verb Print
```

## Discussion

The Start-Process cmdlet gives you a great deal of flexibility over how you launch an application. In addition to launching applications, it also gives you access to Windows *shell associations*: functionality associated with URLs and documents.

Windows defines many shell associations: for HTTP websites, FTP locations, and even Explorer-specific behavior. For example, to launch the All Tasks view of the Windows control panel:

```
start 'shell:::{ED7BA470-8E54-465E-825C-99712043E01C}'
```

If the document you are launching defines an action (such as Edit or Print), you can use the -Verb parameter to invoke that action.

For more information about the Start-Process cmdlet and launching system processes, see Recipe 24.3, "Launch a Process".

## See Also

Recipe 24.3, "Launch a Process"

# 24.3. Launch a Process

## Problem

You want to launch a new process on the system, but you also want to configure its startup environment.

## Solution

To launch a new process, use the Start-Process cmdlet.

```
PS > Start-Process mmc -Verb RunAs -WindowStyle Maximized
```

For advanced tasks that are not covered by the Start-Process cmdlet, call the [System.Diagnostics.Process]::Start() method. To control the process's startup environment, supply it with a System.Diagnostics.ProcessStartInfo object that you prepare, as shown in Example 24-1.

---

*Example 24-1. Configuring the startup environment of a new process*

```
$processname = "powershell.exe"

## Prepare to invoke the process
$processStartInfo = New-Object System.Diagnostics.ProcessStartInfo
$processStartInfo.FileName = (Get-Command $processname).Definition
$processStartInfo.WorkingDirectory = (Get-Location).Path
if($argumentList) { $processStartInfo.Arguments = $argumentList }
$processStartInfo.UseShellExecute = $false

## Always redirect the input and output of the process.
## Sometimes we will capture it as binary, other times we will
## just treat it as strings.
$processStartInfo.RedirectStandardOutput = $true
$processStartInfo.RedirectStandardInput = $true

$process = [System.Diagnostics.Process]::Start($processStartInfo)
```

## Discussion

Normally, launching a process in PowerShell is as simple as typing the program name:

```
PS > notepad c:\temp\test.txt
```

However, you may sometimes need detailed control over the process details, such as its credentials, working directory, window style, and more. In those situations, use the Start-Process cmdlet. It exposes most of these common configuration options through simple parameters.

> For an example of how to start a process as another user (or as an elevated PowerShell command), see Recipe 18.10, "Program: Start a Process as Another User".

If your needs are more complex than the features offered by the Start-Process cmdlet, you can use the [System.Diagnostics.Process]::Start() method from the .NET Framework to provide that additional functionality. Example 24-1 is taken from Recipe 2.10, "Capture and Redirect Binary Process Output", and gives an example of this type of advanced requirement.

For more information about launching programs from PowerShell, see Recipe 1.1, "Run Programs, Scripts, and Existing Tools". For more information about working with classes from the .NET Framework, see Recipe 3.8, "Work with .NET Objects".

## See Also

Recipe 1.1, "Run Programs, Scripts, and Existing Tools"

Recipe 3.8, "Work with .NET Objects"

# 24.4. Stop a Process

## Problem

You want to stop (or kill) a process on the system.

## Solution

To stop a process, use the Stop-Process cmdlet, as shown in Example 24-2.

*Example 24-2. Stopping a process using the Stop-Process cmdlet*

```
PS > notepad
PS > Get-Process Notepad

Handles  NPM(K)  PM(K)  WS(K)  VM(M)  CPU(s)    Id ProcessName
-------  ------  -----  -----  -----  ------    -- -----------
     42       3   1276   3916     32    0.09  3520 notepad

PS > Stop-Process -ProcessName notepad
PS > Get-Process Notepad
Get-Process : Cannot find a process with the name 'Notepad'. Verify the
process name and call the cmdlet again.
At line:1 char:12
+ Get-Process <<<< Notepad
```

## Discussion

Although the parameters of the Stop-Process cmdlet are useful in their own right, PowerShell's pipeline model lets you be even more precise. The Stop-Process cmdlet stops any processes that you pipeline into it, so an advanced process set generated by Get-Process automatically turns into an advanced process set for the Stop-Process cmdlet to operate on:

```
PS > Get-Process | Where-Object { $_.WorkingSet -lt 10mb } |
    Sort-Object -Descending Name | Stop-Process -WhatIf

What if: Performing operation "Stop-Process" on Target "svchost (1368)".
What if: Performing operation "Stop-Process" on Target "sqlwriter (1772)".
What if: Performing operation "Stop-Process" on Target "qttask (3672)".
What if: Performing operation "Stop-Process" on Target "Ditto (2892)".
What if: Performing operation "Stop-Process" on Target "ctfmon (3904)".
```

```
What if: Performing operation "Stop-Process" on Target "csrss (848)".
What if: Performing operation "Stop-Process" on Target "BrmfRsmg (1560)".
What if: Performing operation "Stop-Process" on Target "AutoHotkey (3460)".
What if: Performing operation "Stop-Process" on Target "alg (1084)".
```

 Notice that this example uses the -WhatIf flag on the Stop-Process cmdlet. This flag lets you see what would happen if you were to run the command, but doesn't actually perform the action.

Another common need when it comes to stopping a process is simply waiting for one to exit. Most scripts handle this by creating a loop that exits only when the Get-Process cmdlet returns no results for the process in question. PowerShell greatly simplifies this need by offering the Wait-Process cmdlet, which lets you pause your script until the specified process has exited. If you still want some degree of control while waiting for the process to stop, the -Timeout parameter lets you control how long PowerShell should wait for the process to exit. When the timeout elapses, PowerShell returns control to your script—giving you the opportunity to continue waiting, forcibly terminate the process, or do whatever else you wish.

For more information about the Stop-Process cmdlet, type **Get-Help Stop-Process**. For more information about the Wait-Process cmdlet, type **Get-Help Wait-Process**.

# 24.5. Get the Owner of a Process

## Problem

You want to know the user account that launched a given process.

## Solution

Use the GetOwner method of the Win32_Process class.

```
PS > $id = Get-Process -Name Notepad | Foreach-Object Id
PS > Get-CimInstance Win32_Process -Filter "ProcessId = '$id'" |
    Invoke-CimMethod -Name GetOwner

Domain       ReturnValue User PSComputerName
------       ----------- ---- --------------
LEE-DESK               0 Lee
```

## Discussion

While the output returned by the Get-Process command contains a lot of information, it doesn't return the owner of a process. For this, we can rely on the Win32_Process class from WMI.

The Get-CimInstance command doesn't let you filter on process names, so this becomes a two-step solution: use the Get-Process cmdlet to retrieve the process you care about by name, and then use the Get-CimInstance cmdlet to return additional information about the process with that ID.

Once we have a CIM instance, we can pipe it to the Invoke-CimMethod cmdlet. For more information about invoking WMI methods, see Recipe 28.3, "Invoke a Method on a WMI Instance or Class".

## See Also

Recipe 28.3, "Invoke a Method on a WMI Instance or Class"

# 24.6. Get the Parent Process of a Process

## Problem

You want to know the process that launched a given process.

## Solution

Use the ParentProcessId property of the Win32_Process class.

```
PS > $process = Get-Process -Name Notepad
PS > $id = $process.Id
PS > $instance = Get-CimInstance Win32_Process -Filter "ProcessId = '$id'"
PS > $instance.ParentProcessId
3376
PS > $parentProcess = Get-Process -Id $instance.ParentProcessId
PS > $parentProcess


Handles  NPM(K)    PM(K)     WS(K) VM(M)   CPU(s)     Id ProcessName
-------  ------    -----     ----- -----   ------     -- -----------
    529      31    72196     87928   659     9.86   3376 powershell
```

## Discussion

While the output returned by the Get-Process command contains a lot of information, it doesn't return the parent of a process. For this, we can rely on the Win32_Process class from WMI.

The Get-CimInstance command doesn't let you filter on process names, so this becomes a two-step solution: use the Get-Process cmdlet to retrieve the process you care about by name, and then use the Get-CimInstance cmdlet to return additional information about the process with that ID.

Once we have a CIM instance, we can access the ParentProcessId property.

Beware of how you use this information. Windows records the parent process ID when a process is launched, but there's no guarantee that the parent process didn't exit after launching the process in question. Since Windows recycles process IDs, this property can sometimes appear to return incorrect results. To validate this in important situations, you can compare the StartTime properties of the processes:

```
PS > $parentProcess.StartTime -lt $process.StartTime
True
```

For more information about working with WMI properties, see Recipe 28.1, "Access Windows Management Instrumentation and CIM Data".

## See Also

Recipe 28.1, "Access Windows Management Instrumentation and CIM Data"

# 24.7. Debug a Process

## Problem

You want to attach a debugger to a running process on the system.

## Solution

To debug a process, use the Debug-Process cmdlet.

## Discussion

If you have a software debugger installed on your computer (such as Visual Studio or the Debugging Tools for Windows), the Debug-Process cmdlet lets you start a debugging session from the PowerShell command line. It is not designed to automate the debugging tools after launching them, but it does provide a useful shortcut.

 To debug a PowerShell script, see Chapter 14.

The Debug-Process cmdlet launches the systemwide debugger, as configured in the *HKLM:\Software\Microsoft\Windows NT\CurrentVersion\AeDebug* registry key. To change the debugger launched by this cmdlet (and other tools that launch the default debugger), change the Debugger property:

```
PS > Get-Location

Path
```

```
----
HKLM:\Software\Microsoft\Windows NT\CurrentVersion\AeDebug


PS > Get-ItemProperty .


PSPath              : Microsoft.PowerShell.Core\Registry::HKEY_LOCAL_MACHINE
                      \Software\Microsoft\Windows NT\CurrentVersion\AeDebug
PSParentPath        : Microsoft.PowerShell.Core\Registry::HKEY_LOCAL_MACHINE
                      \Software\Microsoft\Windows NT\CurrentVersion
PSChildName         : AeDebug
PSDrive             : HKLM
PSProvider          : Microsoft.PowerShell.Core\Registry
UserDebuggerHotKey  : 0
Debugger            : "c:\Windows\system32\vsjitdebugger.exe" -p %ld -e %ld
```

For more information about the Debug-Process cmdlet, type **Get-Help Debug-Process**.

## See Also

Chapter 14, *Debugging*

# System Services

## 25.0. Introduction

As the support mechanism for many administrative tasks on Windows, managing and working with system services naturally fits into the administrator's toolbox.

PowerShell offers a handful of cmdlets to help make working with system services easier: from listing services to lifecycle management and even to service installation.

## 25.1. List All Running Services

### Problem

You want to see which services are running on the system.

### Solution

To list all running services, use the Get-Service cmdlet:

```
PS > Get-Service

Status    Name          DisplayName
------    ----          -----------
Running   ADAM_Test     Test
Stopped   Alerter       Alerter
Running   ALG           Application Layer Gateway Service
Stopped   AppMgmt       Application Management
Stopped   aspnet_state  ASP.NET State Service
Running   AudioSrv      Windows Audio
Running   BITS          Background Intelligent Transfer Ser...
Running   Browser       Computer Browser
(...)
```

## Discussion

The Get-Service cmdlet retrieves information about all services running on the system. Because these are rich .NET objects (of the type System.ServiceProcess.ServiceController), you can apply advanced filters and operations to make managing services straightforward.

For example, to find all running services:

```
PS > Get-Service | Where-Object { $_.Status -eq "Running" }

Status   Name                DisplayName
------   ----                -----------
Running  ADAM_Test           Test
Running  ALG                 Application Layer Gateway Service
Running  AudioSrv            Windows Audio
Running  BITS                Background Intelligent Transfer Ser...
Running  Browser             Computer Browser
Running  COMSysApp           COM+ System Application
Running  CryptSvc            Cryptographic Services
```

Or, to sort services by the number of services that depend on them:

```
PS > Get-Service | Sort-Object -Descending { $_.DependentServices.Count }

Status   Name                DisplayName
------   ----                -----------
Running  RpcSs               Remote Procedure Call (RPC)
Running  PlugPlay            Plug and Play
Running  lanmanworkstation   Workstation
Running  SSDPSRV             SSDP Discovery Service
Running  TapiSrv             Telephony
(...)
```

Since PowerShell returns full-fidelity .NET objects that represent system services, these tasks and more become incredibly simple due to the rich amount of information that PowerShell returns for each service. For more information about the Get-Service cmdlet, type **Get-Help Get-Service**. For more information about filtering, grouping, and sorting in PowerShell commands, see Recipe 2.1, "Filter Items in a List or Command Output".

> The Get-Service cmdlet displays most (but not all) information about running services. For additional information (such as the service's startup mode), use the Get-CimInstance cmdlet:
>
> ```
> $service = Get-CimInstance Win32_Service |
>     Where-Object { $_.Name -eq "AudioSrv" }
> $service.StartMode
> ```

In addition to supporting services on the local machine, the Get-Service cmdlet lets you retrieve and manage services on a remote machine as well:

```
PS > Get-Service -Computer <Computer> |
    Sort-Object -Descending { $_.DependentServices.Count }

Status   Name          DisplayName
------   ----          -----------
Running  RpcEptMapper  RPC Endpoint Mapper
Running  DcomLaunch    DCOM Server Process Launcher
Running  RpcSs         Remote Procedure Call (RPC)
Running  PlugPlay      Plug and Play
Running  nsi           Network Store Interface Service
Running  SamSs         Security Accounts Manager
(...)
```

For more information about working with classes from the .NET Framework, see Recipe 3.8, "Work with .NET Objects". For more information about working with the Get-CimInstance cmdlet, see Chapter 28.

## See Also

Recipe 2.1, "Filter Items in a List or Command Output"

Recipe 3.8, "Work with .NET Objects"

Chapter 28, *Windows Management Instrumentation*

# 25.2. Manage a Running Service

## Problem

You want to manage a running service.

## Solution

To stop a service, use the Stop-Service cmdlet:

```
PS > Stop-Service AudioSrv -WhatIf
What if: Performing operation "Stop-Service" on Target "Windows Audio
(AudioSrv)".
```

Likewise, use the Suspend-Service, Restart-Service, and Resume-Service cmdlets to suspend, restart, and resume services, respectively.

## Discussion

The Stop-Service cmdlet lets you stop a service either by name or display name.

Notice that the Solution uses the -WhatIf flag on the Stop-Service cmdlet. This parameter lets you see what would happen if you were to run the command but doesn't actually perform the action.

For more information about the Stop-Service cmdlet, type **Get-Help Stop-Service**. If you want to suspend, restart, or resume a service, see the help for the Suspend-Service, Restart-Service, and Resume-Service cmdlets, respectively.

To configure a service (for example, its description or startup type), see Recipe 25.3, "Configure a Service". In addition to letting you configure a service, the Set-Service cmdlet described in that recipe also lets you stop a service on a remote computer.

### See Also

Recipe 25.3, "Configure a Service"

Chapter 28, *Windows Management Instrumentation*

# 25.3. Configure a Service

## Problem

You want to configure properties or startup behavior of a service.

## Solution

To configure a service, use the Set-Service cmdlet:

```
PS > Set-Service WinRM -DisplayName 'Windows Remote Management (WS-Management)' `
    -StartupType Manual
```

## Discussion

The Set-Service cmdlet lets you manage the configuration of a service: its name, display name, description, and startup type.

If you change the startup type of a service, your natural next step is to verify that the changes were applied correctly. Recipe 25.1, "List All Running Services" shows how to view the properties of a service, including the WMI-based workaround to examine the startup type.

In addition to letting you configure services on the local computer, the `Set-Service` cmdlet also offers the `-ComputerName` parameter to configure services on remote computers.

## See Also

Recipe 25.1, "List All Running Services"

# Active Directory

## 26.0. Introduction

By far, the one thing that makes system administration on the Windows platform unique is its interaction with Active Directory. As the centralized authorization, authentication, and information store for Windows networks, Active Directory automation forms the core of many enterprise administration tasks.

In the core PowerShell language, the primary way to interact with Active Directory comes through its support for Active Directory Service Interface (ADSI) type shortcuts.

In addition, the Active Directory team has created an immensely feature-filled Power-Shell module to manage Active Directory domains. The Active Directory module includes a PowerShell provider (Set-Location AD:\) and almost 100 task-specific PowerShell cmdlets.

Working with the Active Directory module has two requirements:

*Support from the server*
> This module works with any domain that has enabled the Active Directory Web Services feature. Windows Server 2008 R2 enables this feature by default on Active Directory instances, and you can install it on any recent server operating system from Windows Server 2003 on.

*Support from the client*
> The module itself is included in the Windows 7 Remote Server Administration Tools (RSAT) package. After downloading and installing the package, you can enable it through the "Turn Windows Features On or Off" dialog in the Control Panel.

If working with the Active Directory module is an option at all, import it and use its commands. The Get-Command and Get-Help commands should be the two key steps you need to get started. In addition to the help built into the commands, MSDN provides a great task-based introduction to the Active Directory module here (*http://bit.ly/ UHHaIO*).

If the Active Directory module is not an option, PowerShell provides fluid integration with Active Directory through its [adsi] and [adsisearcher] built-in type shortcuts. This chapter covers their use for most common Active Directory tasks.

# 26.1. Test Active Directory Scripts on a Local Installation

## Problem

You want to test your Active Directory scripts against a local installation.

## Solution

To test your scripts against a local system, install Active Directory Lightweight Directory Services (AD LDS) and its sample configuration.

## Discussion

For most purposes, Active Directory Lightweight Services works as a lightweight version of Active Directory. Although it doesn't support any of Active Directory's infrastructure features, its programming model is close enough that you can easily use it to experiment with Active Directory scripting. Until recently, Active Directory Lightweight Directory Services was known as Active Directory Application Mode (ADAM). AD LDS is not supported on Windows XP, and so the Microsoft Download Center continues to provide a download of ADAM that supports Windows XP. To test your scripts against a local installation, you'll need to install either AD LDS or ADAM, and then create a test instance.

### Verify prerequisites

If you want to test AD LDS on a recent *server* operating system, simply enable it through the Optional Component Manager.

If you want to install it on a client operating system, you have two options. If you have Windows 7 or Windows Vista, download AD LDS. If you have Windows XP (or want to install in Windows XP mode), download ADAM.

## Install ADAM

The first step to installing AD LDS or ADAM is to download it. Microsoft provides both free of charge from the Download Center. You can obtain either by searching for "Active Directory Application Mode" or "AD LDS" here (*http://download.microsoft.com*).

Once you've downloaded it, run the setup program. Figure 26-1 shows the ADAM setup wizard on Windows XP.

*Figure 26-1. ADAM's post-installation screen*

## Create a test instance

From the ADAM menu in the Windows Start menu, select "Create an ADAM instance." On the Setup Options page that appears next, select "A unique instance." On the Instance Name page, type **Test** as an instance name. On the Ports page, accept the default ports, and then on the Application Directory Partition page, select "Yes, create an application directory partition." As the partition name, type **DC=Fabrikam,DC=COM**, as shown in Figure 26-2.

In the next pages, accept the default file locations, service accounts, and administrators.

When the setup wizard gives you the option to import LDIF files, import all available files except for *MS-AZMan.LDF*. Click Next on this page and the confirmation page to complete the instance setup.

*Figure 26-2. Creating a partition of a test ADAM instance*

Open a PowerShell window, and test your new instance:

```
PS > [adsi] "LDAP://localhost:389/dc=Fabrikam,dc=COM"

distinguishedName
-----------------
{DC=Fabrikam,DC=COM}
```

The [adsi] tag is a *type shortcut*, like several other type shortcuts in PowerShell. The [adsi] type shortcut provides a quick way to create and work with directory entries through Active Directory Service Interfaces.

 When you first try this shortcut, you may receive this unhelpful error message:

```
format-default : The following exception occurred while retrieving
member "PSComputerName": "Unknown error (0x80005000)"
```

If you receive this error, ensure that you've capitalized the LDAP in LDAP://localhost:389/.

Although scripts that act against an ADAM test environment are almost identical to those that operate directly against Active Directory, there are a few minor differences. ADAM scripts specify the host and port in their binding string (that is, localhost:389/), whereas Active Directory scripts do not.

For more information about type shortcuts in PowerShell, see "Working with the .NET Framework" (page 891).

## See Also

"Working with the .NET Framework" (page 891)

# 26.2. Create an Organizational Unit

## Problem

You want to create an organizational unit (OU) in Active Directory.

## Solution

To create an organizational unit in a container, use the [adsi] type shortcut to bind to a part of the Active Directory, and then call the Create() method.

```
$domain = [adsi] "LDAP://localhost:389/dc=Fabrikam,dc=COM"
$salesOrg = $domain.Create("OrganizationalUnit", "OU=Sales")
$salesOrg.Put("Description", "Sales Headquarters, SF")
$salesOrg.Put("wwwHomePage", "http://fabrikam.com/sales")
$salesOrg.SetInfo()
```

## Discussion

The Solution shows an example of creating a Sales organizational unit (OU) at the root of the organization. You can use the same syntax to create OUs under other OUs as well. Example 26-1 demonstrates how to create more sales divisions.

*Example 26-1. Creating North, East, and West sales divisions*

```
$sales = [adsi] "LDAP://localhost:389/ou=Sales,dc=Fabrikam,dc=COM"

$east = $sales.Create("OrganizationalUnit", "OU=East")
$east.Put("wwwHomePage", "http://fabrikam.com/sales/east")
$east.SetInfo()

$west = $sales.Create("OrganizationalUnit", "OU=West")
$west.Put("wwwHomePage", "http://fabrikam.com/sales/west")
$west.SetInfo()

$north = $sales.Create("OrganizationalUnit", "OU=North")
$north.Put("wwwHomePage", "http://fabrikam.com/sales/north")
$north.SetInfo()
```

When you initially create an item, notice that you need to use the Put() method to set properties on the new item. Once you've created the item, you can instead use simple property access to change those properties. For more information about changing properties of an organizational unit, see Recipe 26.4, "Modify Properties of an Organizational Unit".

To check that these OUs have been created, see Recipe 26.6, "Get the Children of an Active Directory Container".

Using the Active Directory module, the cmdlet to create an organizational unit is New-ADOrganizationalUnit. For more information on how to accomplish these tasks through the Active Directory module, see here (*http://bit.ly/UHHaIO*).

### See Also

Recipe 26.4, "Modify Properties of an Organizational Unit"

Recipe 26.6, "Get the Children of an Active Directory Container"

# 26.3. Get the Properties of an Organizational Unit

## Problem

You want to get and list the properties of a specific OU.

## Solution

To list the properties of an OU, use the [adsi] type shortcut to bind to the OU in Active Directory, and then pass the OU to the Format-List cmdlet:

```
$organizationalUnit =
  [adsi] "LDAP://localhost:389/ou=West,ou=Sales,dc=Fabrikam,dc=COM"

$organizationalUnit | Format-List *
```

## Discussion

The Solution retrieves the Sales West OU. By default, the Format-List cmdlet shows only the distinguished name of the group, so we type **Format-List** * to display all properties.

If you know the property for which you want the value, you can specify it by name:

```
PS > $organizationalUnit.wWWHomePage
http://fabrikam.com/sales/west
```

If you are having trouble getting a property that you know exists, you can also retrieve the property using the Get() method on the container. While the name property can be accessed using the usual property syntax, the following example demonstrates the alternative approach:

```
PS > $organizationalUnit.Get("name")
West
```

Using the Active Directory module, the cmdlet to get the properties of an organizational unit is Get-ADOrganizationalUnit. For more information on how to accomplish these tasks through the Active Directory module, see here (*http://bit.ly/UHHaIO*).

# 26.4. Modify Properties of an Organizational Unit

## Problem

You want to modify properties of a specific OU.

## Solution

To modify the properties of an OU, use the [adsi] type shortcut to bind to the OU in Active Directory. If the property has already been set, you can change the value of a property as you would with any other PowerShell object. If you are setting a property for the first time, use the Put() method. Finally, call the SetInfo() method to apply the changes.

```
$organizationalUnit =
  [adsi] "LDAP://localhost:389/ou=West,ou=Sales,dc=Fabrikam,dc=COM"

$organizationalUnit.Put("Description", "Sales West Organization")
$organizationalUnit.wwwHomePage = "http://fabrikam.com/sales/west/fy2012"
$organizationalUnit.SetInfo()
```

## Discussion

The Solution retrieves the Sales West OU. It then sets the description to Sales West Organization, updates the home page, and then applies those changes to Active Directory.

Using the Active Directory module, the cmdlet to modify the properties of an organizational unit is Set-ADOrganizationalUnit. For more information on how to accomplish these tasks through the Active Directory module, see this site (*http://bit.ly/UHHaIO*).

# 26.5. Delete an Organizational Unit

## Problem

You want to delete a specific OU.

## Solution

To delete an OU, use the [adsi] type shortcut to bind to the OU in Active Directory. Finally, call its DeleteTree() method to apply the changes.

```
$organizationalUnit =
   [adsi] "LDAP://localhost:389/ou=North,ou=Sales,dc=Fabrikam,dc=COM"
$organizationalUnit.DeleteTree()
```

## Discussion

The Solution retrieves the Sales North OU. It then calls the DeleteTree() method to permanently delete the organizational unit and all of its children.

Using the Active Directory module, the cmdlet to remove an organizational unit is Remove-ADOrganizationalUnit. For more information on how to accomplish these tasks through the Active Directory module, see here (*http://bit.ly/UHHaIO*).

# 26.6. Get the Children of an Active Directory Container

## Problem

You want to list all the children of an Active Directory container.

## Solution

To list the items in a container, use the [adsi] type shortcut to bind to the OU in Active Directory, and then access the Children property of that container:

```
$sales =
   [adsi] "LDAP://localhost:389/ou=Sales,dc=Fabrikam,dc=COM"
$sales.Children
```

## Discussion

The Solution lists all the children of the Sales OU. This is the level of information you typically get from selecting a node in the ADSIEdit MMC snap-in. If you want to filter this information to include only users, other organizational units, or more complex queries, see Recipe 26.9, "Search for a User Account".

Using the Active Directory module, the Active Directory provider lets you get the children of an organizational unit. For example:

```
PS > Set-Location 'AD:\ou=Sales,dc=Fabrikam,dc=COM'
PS > dir
```

For more information on how to accomplish these tasks through the Active Directory module, see this site (*http://bit.ly/UHHaIO*).

---

## See Also

Recipe 26.9, "Search for a User Account"

# 26.7. Create a User Account

## Problem

You want to create a user account in a specific OU.

## Solution

To create a user in a container, use the [adsi] type shortcut to bind to the OU in Active Directory, and then call the Create() method:

```
$salesWest =
  [adsi] "LDAP://localhost:389/ou=West,ou=Sales,dc=Fabrikam,dc=COM"

$user = $salesWest.Create("User", "CN=MyerKen")
$user.Put("userPrincipalName", "Ken.Myer@fabrikam.com")
$user.Put("displayName", "Ken Myer")
$user.SetInfo()
```

## Discussion

The Solution creates a user under the Sales West organizational unit. It sets the user PrincipalName (a unique identifier for the user), as well as the user's display name.

 If this step generates an error saying, "The specified directory service attribute or value does not exist," verify that you properly imported the LDIF files at the beginning of the ADAM installation steps. Importing those LDIF files creates the Active Directory schema required for many of these steps.

When you run this script against a real Active Directory deployment (as opposed to an ADAM instance), be sure to update the sAMAccountName property, or you'll get an autogenerated default.

To check that these users have been created, see Recipe 26.6, "Get the Children of an Active Directory Container". If you need to create users in bulk, see Recipe 26.8, "Program: Import Users in Bulk to Active Directory".

Using the Active Directory module, the cmdlet to create a user account is New-ADUser. For more information on how to accomplish these tasks through the Active Directory module, see this site (*http://bit.ly/UHHaIO*).

## See Also

Recipe 26.6, "Get the Children of an Active Directory Container"

Recipe 26.8, "Program: Import Users in Bulk to Active Directory"

# 26.8. Program: Import Users in Bulk to Active Directory

When importing several users into Active Directory, it quickly becomes tiresome to do it by hand (or even to script the addition of each user one by one). To solve this problem, we can put all our data into a CSV, and then do a bulk import from the information in the CSV.

Example 26-2 supports this in a flexible way. You provide a container to hold the user accounts and a CSV that holds the account information. For each row in the CSV, the script creates a user from the data in that row. The only mandatory column is a CN column to define the common name of the user. Any other columns, if present, represent other Active Directory attributes you want to define for that user.

*Example 26-2. Import-ADUser.ps1*

```
###########################################################################
##
## Import-AdUser
##
## From Windows PowerShell Cookbook (O'Reilly)
## by Lee Holmes (http://www.leeholmes.com/guide)
##
###########################################################################

<#

.SYNOPSIS

Create users in Active Directory from the content of a CSV.

.DESCRIPTION

In the user CSV, one column must be named "CN" for the username.
All other columns represent properties in Active Directory for that user.

For example:
CN,userPrincipalName,displayName,manager
MyerKen,Ken.Myer@fabrikam.com,Ken Myer,
DoeJane,Jane.Doe@fabrikam.com,Jane Doe,"CN=MyerKen,OU=West,OU=Sales,DC=..."
SmithRobin,Robin.Smith@fabrikam.com,Robin Smith,"CN=MyerKen,OU=West,OU=..."

.EXAMPLE
```

```
PS > $container = "LDAP://localhost:389/ou=West,ou=Sales,dc=Fabrikam,dc=COM"
PS > Import-ADUser.ps1 $container .\users.csv

#>

param(
    ## The container in which to import users
    ## For example:
    ## "LDAP://localhost:389/ou=West,ou=Sales,dc=Fabrikam,dc=COM)")
    [Parameter(Mandatory = $true)]
    $Container,

    ## The path to the CSV that contains the user records
    [Parameter(Mandatory = $true)]
    $Path
)

Set-StrictMode -Off

## Bind to the container
$userContainer = [adsi] $container

## Ensure that the container was valid
if(-not $userContainer.Name)
{
    Write-Error "Could not connect to $container"
    return
}

## Load the CSV
$users = @(Import-Csv $Path)
if($users.Count -eq 0)
{
    return
}

## Go through each user from the CSV
foreach($user in $users)
{
    ## Pull out the name, and create that user
    $username = $user.CN
    $newUser = $userContainer.Create("User", "CN=$username")

    ## Go through each of the properties from the CSV, and set its value
    ## on the user
    foreach($property in $user.PsObject.Properties)
    {
        ## Skip the property if it was the CN property that sets the
        ## username
        if($property.Name -eq "CN")
        {
            continue
```

```
    }

    ## Ensure they specified a value for the property
    if(-not $property.Value)
    {
        continue
    }

    ## Set the value of the property
    $newUser.Put($property.Name, $property.Value)
    }

    ## Finalize the information in Active Directory
    $newUser.SetInfo()
}
```

For more information about running scripts, see Recipe 1.1, "Run Programs, Scripts, and Existing Tools".

## See Also

Recipe 1.1, "Run Programs, Scripts, and Existing Tools"

# 26.9. Search for a User Account

## Problem

You want to search for a specific user account, but you don't know the user's distinguished name (DN).

## Solution

To search for a user in Active Directory, use the [adsi] type shortcut to bind to a container that holds the user account, and then use the [adsisearcher] type shortcut to search for the user:

```
$domain = [adsi] "LDAP://localhost:389/dc=Fabrikam,dc=COM"
$searcher = [adsisearcher] $domain
$searcher.Filter = '(&(objectClass=User)(displayName=Ken Myer))'
$userResult = $searcher.FindOne()
$user = $userResult.GetDirectoryEntry()
$user
```

## Discussion

When you don't know the full distinguished name (DN) of a user account, the [adsi searcher] type shortcut lets you search for it.

You provide an LDAP filter (in this case, searching for users with the display name of Ken Myer), and then call the FindOne() method. The FindOne() method returns the first search result that matches the filter, so we retrieve its actual Active Directory entry. If you expect your query to return multiple results, use the FindAll() method instead. Although the Solution searches on the user's display name, you can search on any field in Active Directory—the userPrincipalName and sAMAccountName are two other good choices.

When you do this search, always try to restrict it to the lowest level of the domain possible. If we know that Ken Myer is in the Sales OU, it would be better to bind to that OU instead:

```
$domain = [adsi] "LDAP://localhost:389/ou=Sales,dc=Fabrikam,dc=COM"
```

For more information about the LDAP search filter syntax, search here (*http:// msdn.microsoft.com*) for "Search Filter Syntax."

Using the Active Directory module, the cmdlet to search for a user account is Get-ADUser. While you can use a LDAP filter to search for users, the Get-ADUser cmdlet also lets you supply PowerShell expressions:

```
Get-ADUser -Filter { Name -like "*Ken*" }
```

For more information on how to accomplish these tasks through the Active Directory module, see this site (*http://bit.ly/UHHaIO*).

# 26.10. Get and List the Properties of a User Account

## Problem

You want to get and list the properties of a specific user account.

## Solution

To list the properties of a user account, use the [adsi] type shortcut to bind to the user in Active Directory, and then pass the user to the Format-List cmdlet:

```
$user =
  [adsi] "LDAP://localhost:389/cn=MyerKen,ou=West,ou=Sales,dc=Fabrikam,dc=COM"

$user | Format-List *
```

## Discussion

The Solution retrieves the MyerKen user from the Sales West OU. By default, the Format-List cmdlet shows only the distinguished name of the user, so we type **Format-List** * to display all properties.

If you know the property for which you want the value, specify it by name:

```
PS > $user.DirectReports
CN=SmithRobin,OU=West,OU=Sales,DC=Fabrikam,DC=COM
CN=DoeJane,OU=West,OU=Sales,DC=Fabrikam,DC=COM
```

If you are having trouble getting a property that you know exists, you can also retrieve the property using the Get() method on the container. While the userPrincipalName property can be accessed using the usual property syntax, the following example demonstrates the alternate approach:

```
PS > $user.Get("userPrincipalName")
Ken.Myer@fabrikam.com
```

Using the Active Directory module, the cmdlet to retrieve a user account is Get-ADUser. For more information on how to accomplish these tasks through the Active Directory module, see this site (*http://bit.ly/UHHaIO*).

# 26.11. Modify Properties of a User Account

## Problem

You want to modify properties of a specific user account.

## Solution

To modify a user account, use the [adsi] type shortcut to bind to the user in Active Directory. If the property has already been set, you can change the value of a property as you would with any other PowerShell object. If you are setting a property for the first time, use the Put() method. Finally, call the SetInfo() method to apply the changes.

```
$user =
  [adsi] "LDAP://localhost:389/cn=MyerKen,ou=West,ou=Sales,dc=Fabrikam,dc=COM"

$user.Put("Title", "Sr. Exec. Overlord")
$user.SetInfo()
```

## Discussion

The Solution retrieves the MyerKen user from the Sales West OU. It then sets the user's title to Sr. Exec. Overlord and applies those changes to Active Directory.

The cmdlet to modify a user account using the Active Directory module is Set-ADUser. For more information on how to accomplish these tasks through the Active Directory module, see this site (*http://bit.ly/UHHaIO*).

# 26.12. Change a User Password

## Problem

You want to change a user's password.

## Solution

To change a user's password, use the [adsi] type shortcut to bind to the user in Active Directory, and then call the SetPassword() method:

```
$user =
  [adsi] "LDAP://localhost:389/cn=MyerKen,ou=West,ou=Sales,dc=Fabrikam,dc=COM"
$user.SetPassword("newpassword")
```

## Discussion

Changing a user password in Active Directory is a relatively straightforward operation, requiring simply calling the SetPassword() method.

 Unfortunately, configuring your local experimental ADAM instance to support password changes is complicated and beyond the scope of this book.

One thing to notice is that the SetPassword() method takes a plain-text password as its input. Active Directory protects this password as it sends it across the network, but storing passwords securely until needed is a security best practice. Recipe 18.8, "Securely Handle Sensitive Information" discusses how to handle sensitive strings and also shows you how to convert one back to plain text when needed.

The cmdlet to change a user password using the Active Directory module is Set-ADAccountPassword. For more information on how to accomplish these tasks through the Active Directory module, see this site (*http://bit.ly/UHHaIO*).

## See Also

Recipe 18.8, "Securely Handle Sensitive Information"

# 26.13. Create a Security or Distribution Group

## Problem

You want to create a security or distribution group.

## Solution

To create a security or distribution group, use the `[adsi]` type shortcut to bind to a container in Active Directory, and then call the `Create()` method:

```
$salesWest =
  [adsi] "LDAP://localhost:389/ou=West,ou=Sales,dc=Fabrikam,dc=COM"
$management = $salesWest.Create("Group", "CN=Management")
$management.SetInfo()
```

## Discussion

The Solution creates a group named `Management` in the `Sales West` OU.

 When you run this script against a real Active Directory deployment (as opposed to an ADAM instance), be sure to update the `sAMAccount Name` property, or you'll get an autogenerated default.

When you create a group in Active Directory, it is customary to also set the type of group by defining the `groupType` attribute on that group. To specify a group type, use the `-bor` operator to combine group flags, and use the resulting value as the `groupType` property. Example 26-3 defines the group as a global, security-enabled group.

*Example 26-3. Creating an Active Directory security group with a custom groupType*

```
$ADS_GROUP_TYPE_GLOBAL_GROUP = 0x00000002
$ADS_GROUP_TYPE_DOMAIN_LOCAL_GROUP = 0x00000004
$ADS_GROUP_TYPE_LOCAL_GROUP = 0x00000004
$ADS_GROUP_TYPE_UNIVERSAL_GROUP = 0x00000008
$ADS_GROUP_TYPE_SECURITY_ENABLED = 0x80000000

$salesWest =
  [adsi] "LDAP://localhost:389/ou=West,ou=Sales,dc=Fabrikam,dc=COM"

$groupType = $ADS_GROUP_TYPE_SECURITY_ENABLED -bor
    $ADS_GROUP_TYPE_GLOBAL_GROUP

$management = $salesWest.Create("Group", "CN=Management")
$management.Put("groupType", $groupType)
$management.SetInfo()
```

If you need to create groups in bulk from the data in a CSV, the `Import-ADUser` script given in Recipe 26.8, "Program: Import Users in Bulk to Active Directory" provides an excellent starting point. To make the script create groups instead of users, change this line:

```
$newUser = $userContainer.Create("User", "CN=$username")
```

to this:

```
$newUser = $userContainer.Create("Group", "CN=$username")
```

If you change the script to create groups in bulk, it is helpful to also change the variable names ($user, $users, $username, and $newUser) to correspond to group-related names: $group, $groups, $groupname, and $newgroup.

The cmdlet to create a group using the Active Directory module is New-ADGroup. For more information on how to accomplish these tasks through the Active Directory module, see this site (*http://bit.ly/UHHaIO*).

## See Also

Recipe 26.8, "Program: Import Users in Bulk to Active Directory"

# 26.14. Search for a Security or Distribution Group

## Problem

You want to search for a specific group, but you don't know its distinguished name (DN).

## Solution

To search for a security or distribution group, use the [adsi] type shortcut to bind to a container that holds the group, and then use the [adsisearcher] type shortcut to search for the group:

```
$domain = [adsi] "LDAP://localhost:389/dc=Fabrikam,dc=COM"
$searcher = [adsisearcher] $domain
$searcher.Filter = '(&(objectClass=Group)(name=Management))'
$groupResult = $searcher.FindOne()
$group = $groupResult.GetDirectoryEntry()
$group
```

## Discussion

When you don't know the full distinguished name (DN) of a group, the [adsisearch er] type shortcut lets you search for it.

You provide an LDAP filter (in this case, searching for groups with the name of Management), and then call the FindOne() method. The FindOne() method returns the first search result that matches the filter, so we retrieve its actual Active Directory entry. If you expect your query to return multiple results, use the FindAll() method instead. Although the Solution searches on the group's name, you can search on any field in Active Directory—the mailNickname and sAMAccountName are two other good choices.

When you do this search, always try to restrict it to the lowest level of the domain possible. If we know that the Management group is in the Sales OU, it would be better to bind to that OU instead:

```
$domain = [adsi] "LDAP://localhost:389/ou=Sales,dc=Fabrikam,dc=COM"
```

For more information about the LDAP search filter syntax, search here (*http://msdn.microsoft.com*) for "Search Filter Syntax."

The cmdlet to search for a security or distribution group using the Active Directory module is Get-ADGroup. While you can use a LDAP filter to search for a group, the Get-ADGroup cmdlet also lets you supply PowerShell expressions:

```
Get-ADGroup -Filter { Name -like "*Management*" }
```

For more information on how to accomplish these tasks through the Active Directory module, see this site (*http://bit.ly/UHHaIO*).

# 26.15. Get the Properties of a Group

## Problem

You want to get and list the properties of a specific security or distribution group.

## Solution

To list the properties of a group, use the [adsi] type shortcut to bind to the group in Active Directory, and then pass the group to the Format-List cmdlet:

```
$group =
  [adsi] "LDAP://localhost:389/cn=Management,ou=West,ou=Sales,dc=Fabrikam,dc=COM"

$group | Format-List *
```

## Discussion

The Solution retrieves the Management group from the Sales West OU. By default, the Format-List cmdlet shows only the DN of the group, so we type **Format-List \*** to display all properties.

If you know the property for which you want the value, specify it by name:

```
PS > $group.Member
CN=SmithRobin,OU=West,OU=Sales,DC=Fabrikam,DC=COM
CN=MyerKen,OU=West,OU=Sales,DC=Fabrikam,DC=COM
```

If you are having trouble getting a property that you know exists, you can also retrieve the property using the Get() method on the container. While the name property can be accessed using the usual property syntax, the following example demonstrates the alternative approach:

```
PS > $group.Get("name")
Management
```

The cmdlet to get the properties of a group using the Active Directory module is Get-ADGroup. For more information on how to accomplish these tasks through the Active Directory module, see this site (*http://bit.ly/UHHaIO*).

# 26.16. Find the Owner of a Group

## Problem

You want to get the owner of a security or distribution group.

## Solution

To determine the owner of a group, use the [adsi] type shortcut to bind to the group in Active Directory, and then retrieve the ManagedBy property:

```
$group =
    [adsi] "LDAP://localhost:389/cn=Management,ou=West,ou=Sales,dc=Fabrikam,dc=COM"

$group.ManagedBy
```

## Discussion

The Solution retrieves the owner of the Management group from the Sales West OU. To do this, it accesses the ManagedBy property of that group. This property exists only when populated by the administrator of the group but is fairly reliable: Active Directory administrators consider it a best practice to create and populate this property.

The cmdlet to find the owner of a group using the Active Directory module is Get-ADGroup. This cmdlet does not retrieve the ManagedBy property by default, so you also need to specify ManagedBy as the value of the -Property parameter. For more information on how to accomplish these tasks through the Active Directory module, see this site (*http://bit.ly/UHHaIO*).

# 26.17. Modify Properties of a Security or Distribution Group

## Problem

You want to modify properties of a specific security or distribution group.

## Solution

To modify a security or distribution group, use the [adsi] type shortcut to bind to the group in Active Directory. If the property has already been set, you can change the value of a property as you would with any other PowerShell object. If you are setting a property for the first time, use the Put() method. Finally, call the SetInfo() method to apply the changes.

```
$group =
  [adsi] "LDAP://localhost:389/cn=Management,ou=West,ou=Sales,dc=Fabrikam,dc=COM"

PS > $group.Put("Description", "Managers in the Sales West Organization")
PS > $group.SetInfo()
PS > $group.Description
```

## Discussion

The Solution retrieves the Management group from the Sales West OU. It then sets the description to "Managers in the Sales West Organization," and applies those changes to Active Directory.

The cmdlet to modify the properties of a security or distribution group using the Active Directory module is Set-ADGroup. For more information on how to accomplish these tasks through the Active Directory module, see here (*http://bit.ly/UHHaIO*).

# 26.18. Add a User to a Security or Distribution Group

## Problem

You want to add a user to a security or distribution group.

## Solution

To add a user to a security or distribution group, use the [adsi] type shortcut to bind to the group in Active Directory, and then call the Add() method:

```
$management =
  [adsi] "LDAP://localhost:389/cn=Management,ou=West,ou=Sales,dc=Fabrikam,dc=COM"

$user = "LDAP://localhost:389/cn=MyerKen,ou=West,ou=Sales,dc=Fabrikam,dc=COM"
$management.Add($user)
```

## Discussion

The Solution adds the MyerKen user to a group named Management in the Sales West OU. To check whether you have added the user successfully, see Recipe 26.20, "List a User's Group Membership".

The cmdlet to add a user to a security or distribution group using the Active Directory module is Add-ADGroupMember. For more information on how to accomplish these tasks through the Active Directory module, see here (*http://bit.ly/UHHaIO*).

## See Also

Recipe 26.20, "List a User's Group Membership"

# 26.19. Remove a User from a Security or Distribution Group

## Problem

You want to remove a user from a security or distribution group.

## Solution

To remove a user from a security or distribution group, use the [adsi] type shortcut to bind to the group in Active Directory, and then call the Remove() method:

```
$management =
  [adsi] "LDAP://localhost:389/cn=Management,ou=West,ou=Sales,dc=Fabrikam,dc=COM"

$user = "LDAP://localhost:389/cn=MyerKen,ou=West,ou=Sales,dc=Fabrikam,dc=COM"
$management.Remove($user)
```

## Discussion

The Solution removes the MyerKen user from a group named Management in the Sales West OU. To check whether you have removed the user successfully, see Recipe 26.20, "List a User's Group Membership".

The cmdlet to remove a user from a security or distribution group using the Active Directory module is `Remove-ADGroupMember`. For more information on how to accomplish these tasks through the Active Directory module, see this site (*http://bit.ly/UHHaIO*).

## See Also

Recipe 26.20, "List a User's Group Membership"

# 26.20. List a User's Group Membership

## Problem

You want to list the groups to which a user belongs.

## Solution

To list a user's group membership, use the `[adsi]` type shortcut to bind to the user in Active Directory, and then access the `MemberOf` property:

```
$user =
  [adsi] "LDAP://localhost:389/cn=MyerKen,ou=West,ou=Sales,dc=Fabrikam,dc=COM"
$user.MemberOf
```

## Discussion

The Solution lists all groups in which the `MyerKen` user is a member. Since Active Directory stores this information as a user property, this is simply a specific case of retrieving information about the user. For more information about retrieving information about a user, see Recipe 26.10, "Get and List the Properties of a User Account".

The cmdlet to retrieve a user's group membership using the Active Directory module is `Get-ADUser`. This cmdlet does not retrieve the `MemberOf` property by default, so you also need to specify `MemberOf` as the value of the `-Property` parameter. For more information on how to accomplish these tasks through the Active Directory module, see this site (*http://bit.ly/UHHaIO*).

## See Also

Recipe 26.10, "Get and List the Properties of a User Account"

# 26.21. List the Members of a Group

## Problem

You want to list all the members in a group.

## Solution

To list the members of a group, use the [adsi] type shortcut to bind to the group in Active Directory, and then access the Member property:

```
$group =
   [adsi] "LDAP://localhost:389/cn=Management,ou=West,ou=Sales,dc=Fabrikam,dc=COM"
$group.Member
```

## Discussion

The Solution lists all members of the Management group in the Sales West OU. Since Active Directory stores this information as a property of the group, this is simply a specific case of retrieving information about the group. For more information about retrieving information about a group, see Recipe 26.15, "Get the Properties of a Group".

The cmdlet to list the members of a security or distribution group using the Active Directory module is Get-ADGroupMember. For more information on how to accomplish these tasks through the Active Directory module, see this site (*http://bit.ly/UHHaIO*).

## See Also

Recipe 26.15, "Get the Properties of a Group"

# 26.22. List the Users in an Organizational Unit

## Problem

You want to list all the users in an OU.

## Solution

To list the users in an OU, use the [adsi] type shortcut to bind to the OU in Active Directory. Use the [adsisearcher] type shortcut to create a searcher for that OU, and then set its Filter property to (objectClass=User). Finally, call the searcher's FindAll() method to perform the search.

```
$sales =
   [adsi] "LDAP://localhost:389/ou=Sales,dc=Fabrikam,dc=COM"
```

```
$searcher = [adsisearcher] $sales
$searcher.Filter = '(objectClass=User)'
$searcher.FindAll()
```

## Discussion

The Solution lists all users in the Sales OU. It does this through the [adsisearcher] type shortcut, which lets you search and query Active Directory. The Filter property specifies an LDAP filter string.

 By default, an [adsisearcher] searches the given container and all containers below it. Set the SearchScope property to change this behavior. A value of Base searches only the current container, whereas a value of OneLevel searches only the immediate children.

For more information about working with classes from the .NET Framework, see Recipe 3.8, "Work with .NET Objects".

The cmdlet to list the users in an organizational unit using the Active Directory module is Get-ADUser. To restrict the results to a specific organizational unit, specify that OU as the -SearchBase parameter. Alternatively, navigate to that path in the Active Directory provider, and then call the Get-ADUser cmdlet. For more information on how to accomplish these tasks through the Active Directory module, see this site (*http://bit.ly/UHHaIO*).

## See Also

Recipe 3.8, "Work with .NET Objects"

# 26.23. Search for a Computer Account

## Problem

You want to search for a specific computer account, but you don't know its distinguished name (DN).

## Solution

To search for a computer account, use the [adsi] type shortcut to bind to a container that holds the account, and then use the [adsisearcher] type shortcut to search for the account:

```
$domain = [adsi] "LDAP://localhost:389/dc=Fabrikam,dc=COM"
$searcher = [adsisearcher] $domain
$searcher.Filter = '(&(objectClass=Computer)(name=kenmyer_laptop))'
$computerResult = $searcher.FindOne()
$computer = $computerResult.GetDirectoryEntry()
```

## Discussion

When you don't know the full distinguished name (DN) of a computer account, the [adsisearcher] type shortcut lets you search for it.

 This recipe requires a full Active Directory instance, as neither ADAM nor AD LDS supports computer objects.

You provide an LDAP filter (in this case, searching for computers with the name of kenmyer_laptop), and then call the FindOne() method. The FindOne() method returns the first search result that matches the filter, so we retrieve its actual Active Directory entry. If you expect your query to return multiple results, use the FindAll() method instead. Although the solution searches on the computer's name, you can search on any field in Active Directory. The sAMAccountName and operating system characteristics (operatingSystem, operatingSystemVersion, operatingSystemServicePack) are other good choices.

When you do this search, always try to restrict it to the lowest level of the domain possible. If you know that the computer is in the Sales OU, it would be better to bind to that OU instead:

```
$domain = [adsi] "LDAP://localhost:389/ou=Sales,dc=Fabrikam,dc=COM"
```

For more information about the LDAP search filter syntax, search here (*http://msdn.microsoft.com*) for "Search Filter Syntax."

The cmdlet to search for a computer account using the Active Directory module is Get-ADComputer. While you can use a LDAP filter to search for a computer, the Get-ADComputer cmdlet also lets you supply PowerShell expressions:

```
Get-ADComputer -Filter { Name -like "*kenmyer*" }
```

For more information on how to accomplish these tasks through the Active Directory module, see this site (*http://bit.ly/UHHaIO*).

# 26.24. Get and List the Properties of a Computer Account

## Problem

You want to get and list the properties of a specific computer account.

## Solution

To list the properties of a computer account, use the [adsi] type shortcut to bind to the computer in Active Directory and then pass the computer to the Format-List cmdlet:

```
$computer =
  [adsi] "LDAP://localhost:389/cn=laptop_212,ou=West,ou=Sales,dc=Fabrikam,dc=COM"

$computer | Format-List *
```

## Discussion

The Solution retrieves the kenmyer_laptop computer from the Sales West OU. By default, the Format-List cmdlet shows only the distinguished name of the computer, so we type **Format-List *** to display all properties.

> This recipe requires a full Active Directory instance, as neither ADAM nor AD LDS supports computer objects.

If you know the property for which you want the value, specify it by name:

```
PS > $computer.OperatingSystem
Windows Server 2003
```

If you are having trouble getting a property that you know exists, you can also retrieve the property using the Get() method on the container. While the operatingSystem property can be accessed using the usual property syntax, the following example demonstrates the alternative approach:

```
PS > $computer.Get("operatingSystem")
Windows Server 2003
```

Using the Active Directory module, the cmdlet to list the properties of a computer account is Get-ADComputer. For more information on how to accomplish these tasks through the Active Directory module, see here (*http://bit.ly/UHHaIO*).

# Enterprise Computer Management

## 27.0. Introduction

When working with Windows systems across an enterprise, this question often arises: "How do I do <some task> in PowerShell?" In an administrator's perfect world, anybody who designs a feature with management implications also supports (via PowerShell cmdlets) the tasks that manage that feature. Many management tasks have been around longer than PowerShell, though, so the answer can sometimes be, "The same way you did it before PowerShell."

That's not to say that your life as an administrator doesn't improve with the introduction of PowerShell, however. Pre-PowerShell administration tasks generally fall into one of several models: command-line utilities, Windows Management Instrumentation (WMI) interaction, registry manipulation, file manipulation, interaction with COM objects, or interaction with .NET objects.

PowerShell makes it easier to interact with all these task models, and therefore makes it easier to manage functionality that depends on them.

## 27.1. Join a Computer to a Domain or Workgroup

### Problem

You want to join a computer to a domain or workgroup.

### Solution

Use the -DomainName parameter of the Add-Computer cmdlet to add a computer to a domain. Use the -WorkGroupName parameter to add it to a workgroup.

```
PS > Add-Computer -DomainName MyDomain -Credential MyDomain\MyUser
PS > Restart-Computer
```

## Discussion

The Add-Computer cmdlet's name is fairly self-descriptive: it lets you add a computer to a domain or workgroup. Since a domain join only takes effect once you restart the computer, always call the Restart-Computer cmdlet after joining a domain.

In addition to supporting the local computer, the Add-Computer cmdlet lets you add remote computers to a domain, as well. Adding a remote computer to a domain requires that it have WMI enabled, and that you have the administrative privileges on the remote computer.

Perhaps the most complex parameter of the Add-Computer cmdlet is the -Unsecure parameter. When you add a computer to a domain, a machine account is normally created with a unique password. An unsecure join (as enabled by the -Unsecure parameter) instead uses a default password: the first 14 characters of the computer name, all in lowercase. Once the domain join is complete, the system automatically changes the password. This parameter is primarily intended for unattended installations.

To remove a computer from a domain, see Recipe 27.2, "Remove a Computer from a Domain".

## See Also

Recipe 27.2, "Remove a Computer from a Domain"

# 27.2. Remove a Computer from a Domain

## Problem

You want to remove a computer from a domain.

## Solution

Use the Remove-Computer cmdlet to depart a domain.

```
PS > Remove-Computer
PS > Restart-Computer
```

## Discussion

The Remove-Computer cmdlet lets you remove a computer from a domain. In addition to supporting the local computer, the Remove-Computer cmdlet lets you remove a remote computer. Removing a remote computer from a domain requires that it have WMI enabled, and that you have the administrative privileges on the remote computer.

Once you remove a computer from a domain, it reverts to its default workgroup. Since domain changes only take effect once you restart the computer, always call the Restart-Computer cmdlet after departing a domain.

Once you remove a computer from a domain, you can no longer use domain credentials to manage that computer. Before departing a domain, make sure that you know (or create) a local administrator's account for that machine.

To rejoin a domain, see Recipe 27.1, "Join a Computer to a Domain or Workgroup".

## See Also

Recipe 27.1, "Join a Computer to a Domain or Workgroup"

# 27.3. Rename a Computer

## Problem

You want to rename a computer in a workgroup or domain.

## Solution

Use the Rename-Computer cmdlet to rename a computer.

```
PS > Rename-Computer -NewName <NewName>
PS > Restart-Computer
```

## Discussion

The Rename-Computer lets you rename a computer. In addition to supporting the local computer, the Rename-Computer cmdlet lets you rename a remote computer. Renaming a remote computer from a domain requires that it have WMI enabled, and that you have the administrative privileges on the remote computer.

Since a name change only takes effect once you restart the computer, always call the Restart-Computer cmdlet after renaming a computer.

# 27.4. Program: List Logon or Logoff Scripts for a User

The Group Policy system in Windows stores logon and logoff scripts under the two registry keys *HKLM:\SOFTWARE\Microsoft\Windows\CurrentVersion\Group Policy \State\<UserSID>\Scripts\Logon* and *HKLM:\SOFTWARE\Microsoft\Windows\Cur rentVersion\Group Policy\State\<UserSID>\Scripts\Logoff*. Each key has a subkey for each Group Policy object that applies. Each of those child keys has another level of keys that correspond to individual scripts that apply to the user.

This can be difficult to investigate when you don't know the SID of the user in question, so Example 27-1 automates the mapping of username to SID, as well as all the registry manipulation tasks required to access this information.

*Example 27-1. Get-UserLogonLogoffScript.ps1*

```
##############################################################################
##
## Get-UserLogonLogoffScript
##
## From Windows PowerShell Cookbook (O'Reilly)
## by Lee Holmes (http://www.leeholmes.com/guide)
##
##############################################################################

<#

.SYNOPSIS

Get the logon or logoff scripts assigned to a specific user

.EXAMPLE

Get-UserLogonLogoffScript LEE-DESK\LEE Logon
Gets all logon scripts for the user 'LEE-DESK\Lee'

#>

param(
    ## The username to examine
    [Parameter(Mandatory = $true)]
    $Username,

    [Parameter(Mandatory = $true)]
    [ValidateSet("Logon","Logoff")]
    $ScriptType
)

Set-StrictMode -Version 3

## Find the SID for the username
$account = New-Object System.Security.Principal.NTAccount $username
```

```
$sid =
    $account.Translate([System.Security.Principal.SecurityIdentifier]).Value

## Map that to their Group Policy scripts
$registryKey = "HKLM:\SOFTWARE\Microsoft\Windows\CurrentVersion\" +
    "Group Policy\State\$sid\Scripts"

if(-not (Test-Path $registryKey))
{
    return
}

## Go through each of the policies in the specified key
foreach($policy in Get-ChildItem $registryKey\$scriptType)
{
    ## For each of the scripts in that policy, get its script name
    ## and parameters
    foreach($script in Get-ChildItem $policy.PsPath)
    {
        Get-ItemProperty $script.PsPath | Select Script,Parameters
    }
}
```

For more information about working with the Windows Registry in PowerShell, see Chapter 21. For more information about running scripts, see Recipe 1.1, "Run Programs, Scripts, and Existing Tools".

## See Also

Recipe 1.1, "Run Programs, Scripts, and Existing Tools"

Chapter 21, *The Windows Registry*

# 27.5. Program: List Startup or Shutdown Scripts for a Machine

The Group Policy system in Windows stores startup and shutdown scripts under the registry keys *HKLM:\SOFTWARE\Policies\Microsoft\Windows\System\Scripts\Startup* and *HKLM:\SOFTWARE\Policies\Microsoft\Windows\System\Scripts\Shutdown*. Each key has a subkey for each Group Policy object that applies. Each of those child keys has another level of keys that correspond to individual scripts that apply to the machine.

Example 27-2 allows you to easily retrieve and access the startup and shutdown scripts for a machine.

*Example 27-2. Get-MachineStartupShutdownScript.ps1*

```
##############################################################################
##
## Get-MachineStartupShutdownScript
##
## From Windows PowerShell Cookbook (O'Reilly)
## by Lee Holmes (http://www.leeholmes.com/guide)
##
##############################################################################

<#

.SYNOPSIS

Get the startup or shutdown scripts assigned to a machine

.EXAMPLE

PS > Get-MachineStartupShutdownScript -ScriptType Startup
Gets startup scripts for the machine

#>

param(
    ## The type of script to search for: Startup, or Shutdown.
    [Parameter(Mandatory = $true)]
    [ValidateSet("Startup","Shutdown")]
    $ScriptType
)

Set-StrictMode -Version 3

## Store the location of the Group Policy scripts for the machine
$registryKey = "HKLM:\SOFTWARE\Policies\Microsoft\Windows\System\Scripts"

## There may be no scripts defined
if(-not (Test-Path $registryKey))
{
    return
}

## Go through each of the policies in the specified key
foreach($policy in Get-ChildItem $registryKey\$scriptType)
{
    ## For each of the scripts in that policy, get its script name
    ## and parameters
    foreach($script in Get-ChildItem $policy.PsPath)
    {
        Get-ItemProperty $script.PsPath | Select Script,Parameters
    }
}
```

For more information about working with the Windows Registry in PowerShell, see Chapter 21. For more information about running scripts, see Recipe 1.1, "Run Programs, Scripts, and Existing Tools".

## See Also

Recipe 1.1, "Run Programs, Scripts, and Existing Tools"

Chapter 21, *The Windows Registry*

# 27.6. Deploy PowerShell-Based Logon Scripts

## Problem

You want to use a PowerShell script in a logon, logoff, startup, or shutdown script.

## Solution

In Windows 7 (and Windows Server 2008 R2), simply add a new script in the PowerShell Scripts tab.

For other operating systems, open the Scripts tab, and click "Add a Script." Use *power-shell.exe* as the script name, and the following as its parameters:

```
-NoProfile -NonInteractive -ExecutionPolicy ByPass -File "script" arguments
```

## Discussion

In the first version of PowerShell, launching a PowerShell script as a Group Policy script was a difficult task. Although you could use the `-Command` parameter of *powershell.exe* to invoke a command, the quoting rules made it difficult to specify the script correctly. After getting the quoting rules correct, you still had to contend with the Execution Policy of the client computer.

Fortunately, the situation improved significantly. First of all, Group Policy now supports PowerShell scripts as first-class citizens for the four different user and computer scripts.

When Group Policy's native support is not an option, *PowerShell.exe* includes two parameters that make it easier to control the execution environment: `-ExecutionPolicy` and `-File`. For more information about these (and PowerShell's other) parameters, see Recipe 1.16, "Invoke a PowerShell Command or Script from Outside PowerShell".

## See Also

Recipe 1.16, "Invoke a PowerShell Command or Script from Outside PowerShell"

# 27.7. Enable or Disable the Windows Firewall

## Problem

You want to enable or disable the Windows Firewall.

## Solution

To manage the Windows Firewall, use the `LocalPolicy.CurrentProfile.FirewallEn`
`abled` property of the `HNetCfg.FwMgr` COM object:

```
PS > $firewall = New-Object -com HNetCfg.FwMgr
PS > $firewall.LocalPolicy.CurrentProfile.FirewallEnabled = $true
PS > $firewall.LocalPolicy.CurrentProfile.FirewallEnabled
True
```

## Discussion

The `HNetCfg.FwMgr` COM object provides programmatic access to the Windows Firewall in Windows XP SP2 and later. The `LocalPolicy.CurrentProfile` property provides the majority of its functionality.

For more information about managing the Windows Firewall through its COM API,
visit here (*http://msdn.microsoft.com*) and search for "Using Windows Firewall API."
The documentation provides examples in VBScript but gives a useful overview of the
functionality available.

If you are unfamiliar with the VBScript-specific portions of the documentation, the
Microsoft Script Center provides a useful guide (*http://www.microsoft.com/technet/
scriptcenter/topics/winpsh/convert/default.mspx*) to help you convert from VBScript to
PowerShell.

For more information about working with COM objects in PowerShell, see Recipe 17.1,
"Automate Programs Using COM Scripting Interfaces".

## See Also

Recipe 17.1, "Automate Programs Using COM Scripting Interfaces"

# 27.8. Open or Close Ports in the Windows Firewall

## Problem

You want to open or close ports in the Windows Firewall.

## Solution

To open or close ports in the Windows Firewall, use the `LocalPolicy.CurrentProfile.GloballyOpenPorts` collection of the `HNetCfg.FwMgr` COM object.

To open a port, create a `HNetCfg.FWOpenPort` COM object to represent the port, and then add it to the `GloballyOpenPorts` collection:

```
$PROTOCOL_TCP = 6
$firewall = New-Object -com HNetCfg.FwMgr
$port = New-Object -com HNetCfg.FWOpenPort

$port.Name = "Webserver at 8080"
$port.Port = 8080
$port.Protocol = $PROTOCOL_TCP

$firewall.LocalPolicy.CurrentProfile.GloballyOpenPorts.Add($port)
```

To close a port, remove it from the `GloballyOpenPorts` collection:

```
$PROTOCOL_TCP = 6
$firewall.LocalPolicy.CurrentProfile.
    GloballyOpenPorts.Remove(8080, $PROTOCOL_TCP)
```

## Discussion

The `HNetCfg.FwMgr` COM object provides programmatic access to the Windows Firewall in Windows XP SP2 and later. The `LocalPolicy.CurrentProfile` property provides the majority of its functionality.

For more information about managing the Windows Firewall through its COM API, visit here (*http://msdn.microsoft.com*) and search for "Using Windows Firewall API." The documentation provides examples in VBScript but gives a useful overview of the functionality available.

If you are unfamiliar with the VBScript-specific portions of the documentation, the Microsoft Script Center provides a useful guide (*http://www.microsoft.com/technet/scriptcenter/topics/winpsh/convert/default.mspx*) to help you convert from VBScript to PowerShell.

For more information about working with COM objects in PowerShell, see Recipe 17.1, "Automate Programs Using COM Scripting Interfaces".

## See Also

Recipe 17.1, "Automate Programs Using COM Scripting Interfaces"

# 27.9. Program: List All Installed Software

The best place to find information about currently installed software is actually from the place that stores information about how to uninstall it: the *HKLM:\SOFTWARE \Microsoft\Windows\CurrentVersion\Uninstall* registry key.

Each child of that registry key represents a piece of software you can uninstall—traditionally through the Add/Remove Programs entry in the Control Panel. In addition to the DisplayName of the application, other useful properties usually exist (depending on the application). Examples include Publisher, UninstallString, and HelpLink.

To see all the properties available from software installed on your system, type the following:

```
$properties = Get-InstalledSoftware |
    Foreach-Object { $_.PsObject.Properties }

$properties | Select-Object Name | Sort-Object -Unique Name
```

This lists all properties mentioned by at least one installed application (although very few are shared by all installed applications).

To work with this data, though, you first need to retrieve it. Example 27-3 provides a script to list all installed software on the current system, returning all information as properties of PowerShell objects.

*Example 27-3. Get-InstalledSoftware.ps1*

```
##############################################################################
##
## Get-InstalledSoftware
##
## From Windows PowerShell Cookbook (O'Reilly)
## by Lee Holmes (http://www.leeholmes.com/guide)
##
##############################################################################

<#

.SYNOPSIS

Lists installed software on the current computer.

.EXAMPLE

PS > Get-InstalledSoftware *Frame* | Select DisplayName

DisplayName
-----------
Microsoft .NET Framework 3.5 SP1
Microsoft .NET Framework 3.5 SP1
```

```
Hotfix for Microsoft .NET Framework 3.5 SP1 (KB953595)
Hotfix for Microsoft .NET Framework 3.5 SP1 (KB958484)
Update for Microsoft .NET Framework 3.5 SP1 (KB963707)

#>

param(
    ## The name of the software to search for
    $DisplayName = "*"
)

Set-StrictMode -Off

## Get all the listed software in the Uninstall key
$keys =
    Get-ChildItem HKLM:\SOFTWARE\Microsoft\Windows\CurrentVersion\Uninstall

## Get all of the properties from those items
$items = $keys | Foreach-Object { Get-ItemProperty $_.PsPath }

## For each of those items, display the DisplayName and Publisher
foreach($item in $items)
{
    if(($item.DisplayName) -and ($item.DisplayName -like $displayName))
    {
        $item
    }
}
```

For more information about working with the Windows Registry in PowerShell, see Chapter 21. For more information about running scripts, see Recipe 1.1, "Run Programs, Scripts, and Existing Tools".

## See Also

Recipe 1.1, "Run Programs, Scripts, and Existing Tools"

Chapter 21, *The Windows Registry*

# 27.10. Uninstall an Application

## Problem

You want to uninstall a specific software application.

## Solution

To uninstall an application, use the `Get-InstalledSoftware` script provided in Recipe 27.9, "Program: List All Installed Software" to retrieve the command that uninstalls the software. Since the `UninstallString` uses batch file syntax, use *cmd.exe* to launch the uninstaller:

```
PS > $software = Get-InstalledSoftware UnwantedProgram
PS > cmd /c $software.UninstallString
```

Alternatively, use the `Win32_Product` WMI class for an unattended installation:

```
$application = Get-CimInstance Win32_Product -filter "Name='UnwantedProgram'"
$application | Invoke-CimMethod -Name Uninstall
```

## Discussion

The `UninstallString` provided by applications starts the interactive experience you would see if you were to uninstall the application through the Add/Remove Programs entry in the Control Panel. If you need to remove the software in an unattended manner, you have two options: use the "quiet mode" of the application's uninstaller (for example, the `/quiet` switch to *msiexec.exe*) or use the software removal functionality of the `Win32_Product` WMI class as demonstrated in the solution.

For more information about working with WMI in PowerShell, see Recipe 28.1, "Access Windows Management Instrumentation and CIM Data".

## See Also

Recipe 27.9, "Program: List All Installed Software"

Recipe 28.1, "Access Windows Management Instrumentation and CIM Data"

# 27.11. Manage Computer Restore Points

## Problem

You want to create a computer restore point, restore a computer to a previous restore point, or manage the schedule for automatic restore points.

## Solution

Use the `Enable-ComputerRestore` and `Disable-ComputerRestore` cmdlets to enable and disable automatic computer checkpoints. Use the `Get-ComputerRestorePoint` and `Restore-Computer` cmdlets to list all restore points and to restore a computer to one of them, respectively. Use the `Checkpoint-Computer` cmdlet to create a new system restore point.

```
PS > Get-ComputerRestorePoint |
    Select Description,SequenceNumber,RestorePointType |
    Format-Table -Auto


Description            SequenceNumber RestorePointType
-----------           -------------- ----------------
Windows Update                   122                0
Windows Update                   123                0
Scheduled Checkpoint             124                7
Scheduled Checkpoint             125                7
Windows Update                   126                0
Scheduled Checkpoint             127                7
Scheduled Checkpoint             128                7
Windows Update                   129                0
Scheduled Checkpoint             130                7
Windows Update                   131                0
Scheduled Checkpoint             132                7
Windows Update                   133                0
Manual Checkpoint                134                0
Before driver updates            135                0


PS > Checkpoint-Computer "Before driver updates"
```

## Discussion

The computer restore point cmdlets give you an easy way to manage Windows system restore points. You can use the Checkpoint-Computer to create a new restore point before a potentially disruptive installation or system change. Figure 27-1 shows the Checkpoint-Computer cmdlet in progress. If you need to restore the computer to a previous state, you can use the Get-ComputerRestorePoint cmdlet to list existing restore points, and then use the Restore-Computer cmdlet to restore the computer to its previously saved state.

System restore points are finely tuned toward managing the state of the operating system, and are not designed to protect user data. System restore points primarily protect the Windows Registry, core operating system files, local user profiles, and COM and WMI registration databases.

To conserve disk space, Windows limits the amount of space consumed by restore points, and removes the oldest restore points as needed. If you plan to create manual checkpoints more frequently than the ones automatically scheduled by Windows, consider increasing the amount of space dedicated to system restore points. If you don't, you run the risk of being unable to recover from system errors that took you a long time to detect.

By default, Windows schedules automatic restore points for your main system volume. To enable or disable these automatic checkpoints for this (or any) volume, use the Enable-ComputerRestore and Disable-ComputerRestore cmdlets.

On Windows 7, the Control Panel lets you configure how much space Windows reserves for restore points. To do this, open the System group in the Control Panel, and then open System Protection. On Windows Vista, use the *vssadmin.exe* tool to manage this policy.

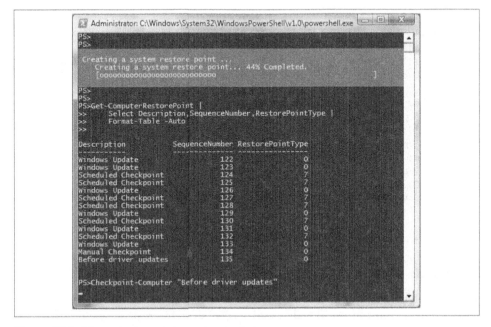

*Figure 27-1. Managing computer restore points*

# 27.12. Reboot or Shut Down a Computer

## Problem

You want to restart or shut down a local or remote computer.

## Solution

Use the `Restart-Computer` cmdlet to restart a computer:

```
PS > Restart-Computer -ComputerName Computer
```

Use the `Stop-Computer` cmdlet to shut it down entirely:

```
PS > Stop-Computer -ComputerName Computer
```

If you want to perform the same action on many computers, use the cmdlet's throttling support:

```
PS > $computers = Get-Content computers.txt
PS > Restart-Computer -ComputerName $computers -ThrottleLimit
```

## Discussion

Both the Restart-Computer and Stop-Computer cmdlets let you manage the reboot and shutdown process of a local or remote computer. Since they build on PowerShell's WMI support, they also offer the -ThrottleLimit parameter to let you control how many machines should be controlled at a time.

By default, these cmdlets reject a restart or a shutdown if a user is logged on to the computer. To restart the computer anyway, use the -Force parameter to override this behavior.

 While restarting a computer, you might sometimes want to have the computer take some action after it comes back online. To do this, create a new scheduled task with an -AtStartup trigger. For more information, see Recipe 27.14, "Manage Scheduled Tasks on a Computer".

If you want to wait for the computer to restart before continuing with a script, use the -Wait parameter. This waits until a PowerShell Remoting connection can be successfully made to the target computer. If you need only WSMan or WMI connectivity, use the -For parameter:

```
PS > Restart-Computer -ComputerName Computer -Wait -For Wmi
```

Rather than shut down or restart a computer, you might instead want to suspend or hibernate it. While neither the Restart-Computer nor Stop-Computer cmdlets support this, you can use the System.Windows.Forms.Application class from the .NET Framework to do so:

```
Add-Type -Assembly System.Windows.Forms
[System.Windows.Forms.Application]::SetSuspendState("Suspend", $false, $false)
```

```
Add-Type -Assembly System.Windows.Forms
[System.Windows.Forms.Application]::SetSuspendState("Hibernate", $false, $false)
```

This technique does not let you suspend or hibernate remote computers, but you can use PowerShell Remoting to invoke those commands on remote systems.

For more information about PowerShell Remoting, see Chapter 29.

## See Also

Recipe 27.14, "Manage Scheduled Tasks on a Computer"

Chapter 29, *Remoting*

---

# 27.13. Determine Whether a Hotfix Is Installed

## Problem

You want to determine whether a specific hotfix is installed on a system.

## Solution

To retrieve a list of hotfixes applied to the system, use the Get-Hotfix cmdlet:

```
PS > Get-HotFix KB968930 | Format-List

Description         : Windows Management Framework Core
FixComments         : Update
HotFixID            : KB968930
InstallDate         :
InstalledBy         : XPMUser
InstalledOn         :
Name                :
ServicePackInEffect : SP10
Status              :
```

To search by description, use the -Description parameter:

```
PS > Get-HotFix -Description *Framework* | Format-List

Description         : Windows Management Framework Core
FixComments         : Update
HotFixID            : KB968930
InstallDate         :
InstalledBy         : XPMUser
InstalledOn         :
Name                :
ServicePackInEffect : SP10
Status              :
```

## Discussion

The Get-Hotfix cmdlet lets you determine whether a hotfix is installed on a specific system. By default, it retrieves hotfixes from the local system, but you can use the -ComputerName parameter to retrieve hotfix information from a remote system.

# 27.14. Manage Scheduled Tasks on a Computer

## Problem

You want to schedule a task on a computer.

## Solution

To schedule a task, use the `Register-ScheduledJob` cmdlet.

```
$trigger = New-ScheduledTaskTrigger -Once -At (Get-Date) `
    -RepetitionInterval (New-TimeSpan -Hours 1) `
    -RepetitionDuration ([TimeSpan]::MaxValue)

Register-ScheduledJob -Name blogMonitor -Trigger $trigger -ScriptBlock {
    $myDocs = [Environment]::GetFolderPath("MyDocuments")
    $outputPath = Join-Path $myDocs blogMonitor.csv
    Test-Uri http://www.leeholmes.com/blog | Export-Csv -Append $outputPath
}
```

To view the list of scheduled jobs:

```
PS > Get-ScheduledJob

Id        Name          JobTriggers      Command
--        ----          -----------      -------
1         blogMonitor   1                ...
```

To remove a scheduled job, use the `Unregister-ScheduledJob` cmdlet:

```
PS > Register-ScheduledJob -Name UnwantedScheduledJob -ScriptBlock { "Oops" }

Id        Name          JobTriggers      Command
--        ----          -----------      -------
2         UnwantedSche... 0              "Oops"

PS > Unregister-ScheduledJob -Name UnwantedScheduledJob
```

## Discussion

PowerShell scheduled jobs offer an extremely easy way to automate system actions, PowerShell-based or otherwise.

Unlike scheduled *tasks* (as exposed by the Task Scheduler and `*-ScheduledTask` cmdlets), scheduled jobs give you the full experience you are used to with regular PowerShell jobs: background execution, state monitoring, rich object-based output, and a standard set of cmdlets. The primary difference is that `Register-ScheduledJob` cmdlet runs the script block you provide in the future.

For more information about PowerShell jobs, see Recipe 1.5, "Invoke a Long-Running or Background Command".

Scheduled jobs are based on two concepts: a job (the familiar PowerShell concept of a command-line or script block that runs in the background), and the thing that triggers it.

In its simplest form, a scheduled job can be registered with no trigger at all. In that case, the -DefinitionName parameter of the Start-Job cmdlet starts the actual job:

```
PS > Register-ScheduledJob -Name DateChecker -ScriptBlock { Get-Date }

Id Name          JobTriggers Command      Enabled
-- ----          ----------- -------      -------
4  DateChecker   0                        Get-Date     True


PS > Start-Job -DefinitionName DateChecker

Id Name          PSJobTypeName   State   HasMoreData Location  Command
-- ----          -------------   -----   ----------- --------  -------
2  DateChecker   PSScheduledJob  Running True                 localhost Get-Date


PS > Receive-Job  -Id 2

Saturday, September 1, 2012 9:27:30 PM
```

Running a job this way isn't much use, however. To make it useful, you'll want to attach a trigger. For example, to reset a development web server that is causing issues:

```
$trigger = New-ScheduledTaskTrigger -Daily -At "3:00 AM"
Register-ScheduledJob -Name WebsiteFix -ScriptBlock { iisreset }
```

For most scheduled tasks, the -Daily, -Weekly, -AtStartup, and -AtLogOn parameters will be all you need. Use the -At parameter to specify the start of this repetition. The -At parameter is a DateTime object, so most natural forms of dates and times (such as 3:00 AM) will work. If you want to be more specific, you can use the Get-Date cmdlet:

```
$date = Get-Date -Hour 15 -Minute 59
$trigger = New-ScheduledTaskTrigger -Daily -At $date
```

If the built-in daily or weekly patterns don't work, you can use the -Once parameter. By default, this schedules a task to run only once in the future:

```
$trigger = New-ScheduledTaskTrigger -Once -At "9/2/2012 10:00 AM"
```

However, you can also use the -Once parameter to schedule tasks that *start* at the time you supply, but then repeat at intervals more granular than simply daily or weekly. The -RepetitionInterval parameter defines how long the task scheduler should wait between invocations, while the -RepetitionDuration defines how far in the future the job will be allowed to run.

For example, to create a scheduled task that kills a specific runaway process every five minutes forever:

```
PS > $t = New-ScheduledTaskTrigger -Once -At (Get-Date) `
    -RepetitionInterval (New-TimeSpan -Minutes 5) `
    -RepetitionDuration ([TimeSpan]::MaxValue)
PS > Register-ScheduledJob -ScriptBlock { Stop-Process -Name RunawayProcess } `
    -Trigger $t -Name Zombie


Id        Name          JobTriggers      Command
--        ----          -----------      -------
31        Zombie        1                Stop-Process -Name RunawayProcess
```

When registering scheduled jobs, you can also provide options to the -Scheduled
JobOption parameter. To create the options used for this parameter, use the
New-ScheduledJobOption cmdlet. You'll rarely need most of them, but the
-RequireNetwork parameter deserves special attention.

As with PowerShell Remoting connections, scheduled tasks don't let you automatically
connect to network resources such as UNC paths and Active Directory. Doing this
requires that the scheduled task store your credentials, which becomes an annoyance
to keep up to date whenever your system requires you to change your password.

If your scheduled task fails when trying to access network locations, you can specify the
-RequireNetwork parameter to get around this issue. If you use this parameter, you'll
also have to provide your credentials when registering the scheduled job. If you change
your password, be sure to use the Set-ScheduledJob cmdlet to update your credential.

In addition to scheduling new commands on the system, you may want to interact with
tasks scheduled by other programs or applications. Tasks scheduled by other programs
don't have the rich job model that PowerShell does, but are used frequently for simple
task invocation. If you have access to a Windows 8 computer, use the ScheduledTask
cmdlet:

```
PS > Get-Command -Noun ScheduledTask
(...)

PS > Get-Help -Command Register-ScheduledTask
(...)

PS > Get-ScheduledTask -TaskName ProactiveScan | Format-List


Actions            : {MSFT_TaskComHandlerAction}
Author             : Microsoft Corporation
Date               :
Description        : NTFS Volume Health Scan
Documentation      :
Principal          : MSFT_TaskPrincipal2
SecurityDescriptor : D:AI(A;;FA;;;BA)(A;;FA;;;SY)(A;;FRFX;;;LS)(A;;FR;;;AU)
Settings           : MSFT_TaskSettings3
Source             : Microsoft Corporation
State              : Ready
TaskName           : ProactiveScan
```

```
TaskPath          : \Microsoft\Windows\Chkdsk\
Triggers          :
URI               : \Microsoft\Windows\Chkdsk\ProactiveScan
Version           :
PSComputerName    :
```

On Windows 7 or before, use the *schtasks.exe* application. As of Windows Vista, it has been enhanced to support event triggers, conditions, and additional settings.

For more information about the *schtasks.exe* application, type **schtasks /?**.

For more information about automating PowerShell from other applications, see Recipe 1.16, "Invoke a PowerShell Command or Script from Outside PowerShell".

## See Also

Recipe 1.5, "Invoke a Long-Running or Background Command"

Recipe 1.16, "Invoke a PowerShell Command or Script from Outside PowerShell"

# 27.15. Retrieve Printer Information

## Problem

You want to get information about printers on the current system.

## Solution

To retrieve information about printers attached to the system, use the Win32_Printer WMI class:

```
PS > Get-CimInstance Win32_Printer | Select-Object Name,PrinterStatus

Name                                                    PrinterStatus
----                                                    -------------
Microsoft Office Document Image Wr...                               3
Microsoft Office Document Image Wr...                               3
CutePDF Writer                                                     3
Brother DCP-1000                                                   3
```

To retrieve information about a specific printer, apply a filter based on its name:

```
PS > $device = Get-CimInstance Win32_Printer -Filter "Name='Brother DCP-1000'"
PS > $device | Format-List *
Status                 : Unknown
Name                   : Brother DCP-1000
Attributes             : 588
Availability           :
AvailableJobSheets     :
AveragePagesPerMinute  : 0
```

```
Capabilities            : {4, 2, 5}
CapabilityDescriptions  : {Copies, Color, Collate}
Caption                 : Brother DCP-1000
(...)
```

To retrieve specific properties, access them as you would access properties on other PowerShell objects:

```
PS > $device.VerticalResolution
600
PS > $device.HorizontalResolution
600
```

## Discussion

The example in the Solution uses the Win32_Printer WMI class to retrieve information about installed printers on the computer. While the Win32_Printer class gives access to the most commonly used information, WMI supports several additional printer-related classes: Win32_TCPIPPrinterPort, Win32_PrinterDriver, CIM_Printer, Win32_PrinterConfiguration, Win32_PrinterSetting, Win32_PrinterController, Win32_PrinterShare, and Win32_PrinterDriverDll. For more information about working with WMI in PowerShell, see Recipe 28.1, "Access Windows Management Instrumentation and CIM Data".

## See Also

Recipe 28.1, "Access Windows Management Instrumentation and CIM Data"

# 27.16. Retrieve Printer Queue Statistics

## Problem

You want to get information about print queues for printers on the current system.

## Solution

To retrieve information about printers attached to the system, use the Win32 _PerfFormattedData_Spooler_PrintQueue WMI class:

```
PS > Get-CimInstance Win32_PerfFormattedData_Spooler_PrintQueue |
    Select Name,TotalJobsPrinted

Name                                             TotalJobsPrinted
----                                             ----------------
Microsoft Office Document Image Wr...                           0
```

```
Microsoft Office Document Image Wr...                              0
CutePDF Writer                                                    0
Brother DCP-1000                                                  2
_Total                                                           2
```

To retrieve information about a specific printer, apply a filter based on its name, as shown in Example 27-4.

*Example 27-4. Retrieving information about a specific printer*

```
PS > $queueClass = "Win32_PerfFormattedData_Spooler_PrintQueue"
PS > $filter = "Name='Brother DCP-1000'"
PS > $stats = Get-CimInstance $queueClass -Filter $filter
PS > $stats | Format-List *

AddNetworkPrinterCalls      : 129
BytesPrintedPersec          : 0
Caption                     :
Description                 :
EnumerateNetworkPrinterCalls : 0
Frequency_Object            :
Frequency_PerfTime          :
Frequency_Sys100NS          :
JobErrors                   : 0
Jobs                        : 0
JobsSpooling                : 0
MaxJobsSpooling             : 1
MaxReferences               : 3
Name                        : Brother DCP-1000
NotReadyErrors              : 0
OutofPaperErrors            : 0
References                  : 2
Timestamp_Object            :
Timestamp_PerfTime          :
Timestamp_Sys100NS          :
TotalJobsPrinted            : 2
TotalPagesPrinted           : 0
```

To retrieve specific properties, access them as you would access properties on other PowerShell objects:

```
PS > $stats.TotalJobsPrinted
2
```

## Discussion

The `Win32_PerfFormattedData_Spooler_PrintQueue` WMI class provides access to the various Windows performance counters associated with print queues. Because of this, you can also access them through the .NET Framework, as mentioned in Recipe 17.3, "Access Windows Performance Counters":

```
PS > Get-Counter "\Print Queue($printer)\Jobs" | Select -Expand CounterSamples |
    Select InstanceName,CookedValue | Format-Table -Auto

InstanceName          CookedValue
------------          -----------
brother dcp-1000 usb            1
```

For more information about working with WMI in PowerShell, see Recipe 28.1, "Access Windows Management Instrumentation and CIM Data".

## See Also

Recipe 17.3, "Access Windows Performance Counters"

Recipe 28.1, "Access Windows Management Instrumentation and CIM Data"

# 27.17. Manage Printers and Print Queues

## Problem

You want to clear pending print jobs from a printer.

## Solution

To manage printers attached to the system, use the `Win32_Printer` WMI class. By default, the WMI class lists all printers:

```
PS > Get-CimInstance Win32_Printer | Select-Object Name,PrinterStatus

Name                                               PrinterStatus
----                                               -------------
Microsoft Office Document Image Wr...                          3
Microsoft Office Document Image Wr...                          3
CutePDF Writer                                                3
Brother DCP-1000                                              3
```

To clear the print queue of a specific printer, apply a filter based on its name and call the `CancelAllJobs()` method:

```
PS > $device = Get-CimInstance Win32_Printer -Filter "Name='Brother DCP-1000'"
PS > $device | Invoke-CimMethod -Name CancelAllJobs

__GENUS          : 2
__CLASS          : __PARAMETERS
__SUPERCLASS     :
__DYNASTY        : __PARAMETERS
__RELPATH        :
__PROPERTY_COUNT : 1
__DERIVATION     : {}
```

```
__SERVER       :
__NAMESPACE    :
__PATH         :
ReturnValue    : 5
```

## Discussion

The example in the Solution uses the `Win32_Printer` WMI class to cancel all jobs for a printer. In addition to cancelling all print jobs, the `Win32_Printer` class supports other tasks:

```
PS > Get-CimClass Win32_Printer | Foreach-Object CimClassMethods

Name                       ReturnType Parameters
----                       ---------- ----------
SetPowerState              UInt32 {PowerState, Time}
Reset                      UInt32 {}
Pause                      UInt32 {}
Resume                     UInt32 {}
CancelAllJobs              UInt32 {}
AddPrinterConnection       UInt32 {Name}
RenamePrinter              UInt32 {NewPrinterName}
PrintTestPage              UInt32 {}
SetDefaultPrinter          UInt32 {}
GetSecurityDescriptor      UInt32 {Descriptor}
SetSecurityDescriptor      UInt32 {Descriptor}
```

For more information about working with WMI in PowerShell, see Recipe 28.1, "Access Windows Management Instrumentation and CIM Data".

## See Also

Recipe 28.1, "Access Windows Management Instrumentation and CIM Data"

# 27.18. Program: Summarize System Information

WMI provides an immense amount of information about the current system or remote systems. In fact, the *msinfo32.exe* application traditionally used to gather system information is based largely on WMI.

The script shown in Example 27-5 summarizes the most common information, but WMI provides a great deal more than that. For a list of other commonly used WMI classes, see Appendix G. For more information about working with WMI in PowerShell, see Recipe 28.1, "Access Windows Management Instrumentation and CIM Data".

*Example 27-5. Get-DetailedSystemInformation.ps1*

```
##############################################################################
##
## Get-DetailedSystemInformation
```

```
##
## From Windows PowerShell Cookbook (O'Reilly)
## by Lee Holmes (http://www.leeholmes.com/guide)
##
###############################################################################

<#

.SYNOPSIS

Get detailed information about a system.

.EXAMPLE

PS > Get-DetailedSystemInformation LEE-DESK > output.txt
Gets detailed information about LEE-DESK and stores the output into output.txt

#>

param(
    ## The computer to analyze
    $Computer = "."
)

Set-StrictMode -Version 3

"#"*80
"System Information Summary"
"Generated $(Get-Date)"
"#"*80
""
""


"#"*80
"Computer System Information"
"#"*80
Get-CimInstance Win32_ComputerSystem -Computer $computer | Format-List *

"#"*80
"Operating System Information"
"#"*80
Get-CimInstance Win32_OperatingSystem -Computer $computer | Format-List *

"#"*80
"BIOS Information"
"#"*80
Get-CimInstance Win32_Bios -Computer $computer | Format-List *

"#"*80
"Memory Information"
"#"*80
Get-CimInstance Win32_PhysicalMemory -Computer $computer | Format-List *
```

```
"#"*80
"Physical Disk Information"
"#"*80
Get-CimInstance Win32_DiskDrive -Computer $computer | Format-List *

"#"*80
"Logical Disk Information"
"#"*80
Get-CimInstance Win32_LogicalDisk -Computer $computer | Format-List *
```

For more information about running scripts, see Recipe 1.1, "Run Programs, Scripts, and Existing Tools".

## See Also

Recipe 1.1, "Run Programs, Scripts, and Existing Tools"

Recipe 28.1, "Access Windows Management Instrumentation and CIM Data"

Appendix G, *WMI Reference*

# 27.19. Renew a DHCP Lease

## Problem

You want to renew the DHCP lease for a connection on a computer.

## Solution

To renew DHCP leases, use the `ipconfig` application. To renew the lease on all connections:

```
PS > ipconfig /renew
```

To renew the lease on a specific connection:

```
PS > ipconfig /renew "Wireless Network Connection 4"
```

## Discussion

The standard `ipconfig` application works well to manage network configuration options on a local machine. To renew the lease on a remote computer, you have two options.

---

### Use the Win32_NetworkAdapterConfiguration WMI class

To renew the lease on a remote computer, use the `Win32_NetworkAdapter Configuration` WMI class. The WMI class requires that you know the description of the network adapter, so first obtain that by reviewing the output of `Get-CimInstance Win32_NetworkAdapterConfiguration -Computer ComputerName`:

```
PS > Get-CimInstance Win32_NetworkAdapterConfiguration -Computer LEE-DESK

(...)
DHCPEnabled      : True
IPAddress        : {192.168.1.100}
DefaultIPGateway : {192.168.1.1}
DNSDomain        : hsd1.wa.comcast.net.
ServiceName      : USB_RNDIS
Description      : Linksys Wireless-G USB Network Adapter with (...)
Index            : 13
(...)
```

Knowing which adapter you want to renew, call its `RenewDHCPLease()` method:

```
$description = "Linksys Wireless-G USB"
$adapter = Get-CimInstance Win32_NetworkAdapterConfiguration -Computer LEE-DESK |
    Where-Object { $_.Description -match $description}
$adapter | Invoke-CimMethod -Name RenewDHCPLease
```

### Run ipconfig on the remote computer

Another way to renew the DHCP lease on a remote computer is to use either PowerShell Remoting or the solution offered by Recipe 29.7, "Program: Invoke a PowerShell Expression on a Remote Machine":

```
PS > Invoke-Command LEE-DESK { ipconfig /renew }
PS > Invoke-RemoteExpression \\LEE-DESK { ipconfig /renew }
```

For more information about working with WMI in PowerShell, see Recipe 28.1, "Access Windows Management Instrumentation and CIM Data".

## See Also

Recipe 28.1, "Access Windows Management Instrumentation and CIM Data"

Recipe 29.7, "Program: Invoke a PowerShell Expression on a Remote Machine"

# 27.20. Assign a Static IP Address

## Problem

You want to assign a static IP address to a computer.

## Solution

Use the `Win32_NetworkAdapterConfiguration` WMI class to manage network settings for a computer:

```
$description = "Linksys Wireless-G USB"
$staticIp = "192.168.1.100"
$subnetMask = "255.255.255.0"
$gateway = "192.168.1.1"

$adapter = Get-CimInstance Win32_NetworkAdapterConfiguration -Computer LEE-DESK |
    Where-Object { $_.Description -match $description}
$adapter | Invoke-CimMethod -Name EnableStatic -Arguments @{
    IPAddress = $staticIp; SubnetMask = $subnetMask }
$adapter | Invoke-CimMethod -Name SetGateways -Arguments @{
    DefaultIPGateway = $gateway; GatewayCostMetric = [UInt16] 1 }
```

## Discussion

When you are managing network settings for a computer, the `Win32_Network AdapterConfiguration` WMI class requires that you know the description of the network adapter. Obtain that by reviewing the output of `Get-CimInstance Win32_Network AdapterConfiguration -Computer ComputerName`:

```
PS > Get-CimInstance Win32_NetworkAdapterConfiguration -Computer LEE-DESK

(...)
DHCPEnabled      : True
IPAddress        : {192.168.1.100}
DefaultIPGateway : {192.168.1.1}
DNSDomain        : hsd1.wa.comcast.net.
ServiceName      : USB_RNDIS
Description      : Linksys Wireless-G USB Network Adapter with (...)
Index            : 13
(...)
```

Knowing which adapter you want to renew, you can now call methods on that object as illustrated in the solution. To enable DHCP on an adapter again, use the `EnableDHCP()` method:

```
PS > $adapter | Invoke-CimMethod -Name EnableDHCP
```

For more information about working with WMI in PowerShell, see Recipe 28.1, "Access Windows Management Instrumentation and CIM Data".

## See Also

Recipe 28.1, "Access Windows Management Instrumentation and CIM Data"

# 27.21. List All IP Addresses for a Computer

## Problem

You want to list all IP addresses for a computer.

## Solution

To list IP addresses assigned to a computer, use the `ipconfig` application:

```
PS > ipconfig
```

## Discussion

The standard `ipconfig` application works well to manage network configuration options on a local machine. To view IP addresses on a remote computer, you have two options.

### Use the Win32_NetworkAdapterConfiguration WMI class

To view the IP addresses of a remote computer, use the `Win32_NetworkAdapterConfi guration` WMI class. Since that lists all network adapters, use the `Where-Object` cmdlet to restrict the results to those with an IP address assigned to them:

```
PS > Get-CimInstance Win32_NetworkAdapterConfiguration -Computer LEE-DESK |
    Where-Object { $_.IpEnabled }


DHCPEnabled       : True
IPAddress         : {192.168.1.100}
DefaultIPGateway  : {192.168.1.1}
DNSDomain         : hsd1.wa.comcast.net.
ServiceName       : USB_RNDIS
Description       : Linksys Wireless-G USB Network Adapter with SpeedBooste
                    r v2 - Packet Scheduler Miniport
Index             : 13
```

### Run ipconfig on the remote computer

Another way to view the IP addresses of a remote computer is to use either PowerShell Remoting or the solution offered by Recipe 29.7, "Program: Invoke a PowerShell Expression on a Remote Machine":

```
PS > Invoke-Command LEE-DESK { ipconfig }
PS > Invoke-RemoteExpression \\LEE-DESK { ipconfig }
```

For more information about working with WMI in PowerShell, see Recipe 28.1, "Access Windows Management Instrumentation and CIM Data".

---

## See Also

Recipe 28.1, "Access Windows Management Instrumentation and CIM Data"

Recipe 29.7, "Program: Invoke a PowerShell Expression on a Remote Machine"

# 27.22. List Network Adapter Properties

## Problem

You want to retrieve information about network adapters on a computer.

## Solution

To retrieve information about network adapters on a computer, use the `Win32_NetworkAdapterConfiguration` WMI class:

```
Get-CimInstance Win32_NetworkAdapterConfiguration -Computer <ComputerName>
```

To list only those with IP addresses assigned to them, use the `Where-Object` cmdlet to filter on the `IpEnabled` property:

```
PS > Get-CimInstance Win32_NetworkAdapterConfiguration -Computer LEE-DESK |
    Where-Object { $_.IpEnabled }


DHCPEnabled       : True
IPAddress         : {192.168.1.100}
DefaultIPGateway  : {192.168.1.1}
DNSDomain         : hsd1.wa.comcast.net.
ServiceName       : USB_RNDIS
Description       : Linksys Wireless-G USB Network Adapter with SpeedBooster
                    v2 - Packet Scheduler Miniport
Index             : 13
```

## Discussion

The solution uses the `Win32_NetworkAdapterConfiguration` WMI class to retrieve information about network adapters on a given system. By default, PowerShell displays only the most important information about the network adapter, but it provides access to much more.

To see all information available, use the `Format-List` cmdlet, as shown in Example 27-6.

*Example 27-6. Using the Format-List cmdlet to see detailed information about a network adapter*

```
PS > $adapter = Get-CimInstance Win32_NetworkAdapterConfiguration |
    Where-Object { $_.IpEnabled }
```

```
PS > $adapter
DHCPEnabled      : True
IPAddress        : {192.168.1.100}
DefaultIPGateway : {192.168.1.1}
DNSDomain        : hsd1.wa.comcast.net.
ServiceName      : USB_RNDIS
Description      : Linksys Wireless-G USB Network Adapter with SpeedBooster
                   v2 - Packet Scheduler Miniport
Index            : 13

PS > $adapter | Format-List *

DHCPLeaseExpires            : 20070521221927.000000-420
Index                       : 13
Description                 : Linksys Wireless-G USB Network Adapter with
                                SpeedBooster v2 - Packet Scheduler Miniport
DHCPEnabled                 : True
DHCPLeaseObtained           : 20070520221927.000000-420
DHCPServer                  : 192.168.1.1
DNSDomain                   : hsd1.wa.comcast.net.
DNSDomainSuffixSearchOrder  :
DNSEnabledForWINSResolution : False
DNSHostName                 : Lee-Desk
DNSServerSearchOrder        : {68.87.69.146, 68.87.85.98}
DomainDNSRegistrationEnabled : False
FullDNSRegistrationEnabled  : True
IPAddress                   : {192.168.1.100}
IPConnectionMetric          : 25
IPEnabled                   : True
IPFilterSecurityEnabled     : False
WINSEnableLMHostsLookup     : True
(...)
```

To retrieve specific properties, access them as you would access properties on other PowerShell objects:

```
PS > $adapter.MacAddress
00:12:17:77:B4:EB
```

For more information about working with WMI in PowerShell, see Recipe 28.1, "Access Windows Management Instrumentation and CIM Data".

## See Also

Recipe 28.1, "Access Windows Management Instrumentation and CIM Data"

# Windows Management Instrumentation

## 28.0. Introduction

Windows Management Instrumentation (WMI) has long been a core management feature in Windows. It offers amazing breadth, wide reach, and ubiquitous remoting.

What WMI lacked in the past, though, was a good way to get to it. Graphically, the *wbemtest.exe* utility lets you experiment with WMI, its namespaces, and classes. It truly is a testing tool, though, as its complex user interface makes it impractical to use for most scenarios (see Figure 28-1).

A more user-friendly alternative is the *wmic.exe* command-line tool. The WMIC tool lets you interactively query WMI—but more importantly, automate its behavior. As with PowerShell, results within WMIC retain a great deal of their structured information and let you write fairly detailed queries:

```
PS > WMIC logicaldisk WHERE drivetype=3 `
    GET "name,freespace,SystemName,FileSystem,Size"

FileSystem  FreeSpace    Name  Size        SystemName
NTFS        10587656192  C:    34357637120 LEEHOLMES1C23
```

The language is limited, however, and all of the data's structure is lost once WMIC converts its output to text.

By far, the most popular user interface for WMI has been VBScript, the administrator's traditional scripting language. VBScript offers much richer language facilities than WMIC and retains WMI's structured data for the entire duration of your script.

*Figure 28-1. Using wbemtest.exe to retrieve a Win32_Process*

VBScript has its own class of usability difficulties, however. For example, generating a report of the processes running on a computer often ends up looking like this:

```
strComputer = "atl-dc-01"
Set objWMIService = GetObject("winmgmts:" _
    & "{impersonationLevel=impersonate}!\\" _
    & strComputer & "\root\cimv2")
Set colProcessList = objWMIService.ExecQuery _
    ("Select * from Win32_Process")
For Each objProcess in colProcessList
    Wscript.Echo "Process: " & objProcess.Name
    Wscript.Echo "Process ID: " & objProcess.ProcessID
    Wscript.Echo "Thread Count: " & objProcess.ThreadCount
    Wscript.Echo "Page File Size: " _
        & objProcess.PageFileUsage
    Wscript.Echo "Page Faults: " _
        & objProcess.PageFaults
    Wscript.Echo "Working Set Size: " _
        & objProcess.WorkingSetSize
Next
```

It also requires that you write an entire *script*, and it offers no lightweight interactive experience. The Microsoft Scripting Guys' Scriptomatic tool helps make it easier to create many of these mundane scripts, but it still doesn't address one-off queries.

Enter PowerShell.

PowerShell elevates WMI to a first-class citizen for both ad hoc and structured queries. Since most of the template VBScript for dealing with WMI instances ends up being used to display the results, PowerShell eliminates this step completely. The PowerShell equivalent of the preceding VBScript is simply:

```
Get-CimInstance Win32_Process -Computer atl-dc-01
```

Or, if you want a subset of properties:

```
Get-CimInstance Win32_Process | Select Name,ProcessId,ThreadCount
```

By providing a deep and user-friendly integration with WMI, PowerShell puts a great deal of functionality at the fingertips of every administrator.

## The Shift to CIM

While you may be most familiar with WMI on Windows, the concepts you've become familiar with are actually an implementation of the Distributed Management Task Force (DMTF) standard. However, the DMTF standard has advanced significantly since WMI was introduced, and improvements to WMI in the meantime have created a set of differences—both technical and philosophical—that are hard to reconcile.

To address these differences, PowerShell version 3 introduces the `CimCmdlets` module. The commands in this module are fully aligned to the CIM standard. They use standard CIM namespaces and schemas, use the standard WS-MAN communication protocol, and represent objects in a standard way.

The benefit of this transition is enormous. Expertise that you gained using the WMI cmdlets essentially applied only to interactions with Windows systems. With the CIM cmdlets, though, expertise that you gain applies to a broad spectrum of vendors and devices.

While PowerShell's WMI cmdlets will be supported for the foreseeable future, moving to the CIM-based cmdlets now is a wise investment in your future.

# 28.1. Access Windows Management Instrumentation and CIM Data

## Problem

You want to work with data and functionality provided by the WMI and CIM facilities in Windows.

## Solution

To retrieve all instances of a WMI or CIM class, use the Get-CimInstance cmdlet:

```
Get-CimInstance -ComputerName Computer -Class Win32_Bios
```

To retrieve specific instances of a WMI or CIM class using a filter, supply an argument to the -Filter parameter of the Get-CimInstance cmdlet. This is the WHERE clause of a WQL statement, but without the WHERE keyword:

```
Get-CimInstance Win32_Service -Filter "StartMode = 'Auto'"
```

For WMI instances specifically, you can use the [Wmi] type shortcut:

```
[Wmi] 'Win32_Service.Name="winmgmt"'
```

To retrieve instances of a class using WMI's WQL language, use the -Query parameter of Get-CimInstance:

```
Get-CimInstance -Query "SELECT * FROM Win32_Service WHERE StartMode = 'Auto'"
```

For WMI instance specifically, use the [WmiSearcher] type shortcut:

```
$query = [WmiSearcher] "SELECT * FROM Win32_Service WHERE StartMode = 'Auto'"
$query.Get()
```

To retrieve a property of a WMI or CIM instance, access that property as you would access a .NET property:

```
$service = [Wmi] 'Win32_Service.Name="winmgmt"'
$service.StartMode
```

To invoke a method on a CIM instance, use the Invoke-CimMethod cmdlet:

```
$service = Get-CimInstance Win32_Service -Filter "Name = 'winmgmt'"
$service | Invoke-CimMethod -Name ChangeStartMode -Arguments @{
    StartMode = "Manual" }
```

Alternatively, for WMI instances specifically, invoke that method as you would invoke a .NET method:

```
$service = [Wmi] 'Win32_Service.Name="winmgmt"'
$service.ChangeStartMode("Manual")
$service.ChangeStartMode("Automatic")
```

To invoke a method on a WMI class, use the `Invoke-CimMethod` cmdlet. You can also use the `[WmiClass]` type shortcut to access that WMI class. Then, invoke that method as you would invoke a .NET method:

```
Invoke-CimMethod -Class Win32_Process -Name Create -Arguments @{
    CommandLine = "notepad" }

$class = [WmiClass] "Win32_Process"
$class.Create("Notepad")
```

To retrieve a WMI class from a specific namespace, use its fully qualified name along with the `[WmiClass]` type shortcut:

```
[WmiClass] "\\COMPUTER\Root\Cimv2:Win32_Process"
```

## Discussion

Working with WMI has long been a staple of managing Windows systems—especially systems that are part of corporate domains or enterprises. WMI supports a huge number of Windows management tasks, albeit not in a very user-friendly way.

Traditionally, administrators required either VBScript or the WMIC command-line tool to access and manage these systems through WMI. While powerful and useful, these techniques still provided plenty of opportunities for improvement. VBScript lacks support for an ad hoc investigative approach, and WMIC fails to provide (or take advantage of) knowledge that applies to anything outside WMIC.

In comparison, PowerShell lets you work with WMI and CIM just like you work with the rest of the shell. WMI and CIM instances provide methods and properties, and you work with them the same way you work with methods and properties of other objects in PowerShell.

Not only does PowerShell make working with WMI instances and classes easy once you have them, but it also provides a clean way to access them in the first place. For most tasks, you need only to use the simple `[Wmi]`, `[WmiClass]`, or `[WmiSearcher]` syntax as shown in the Solution.

Along with WMI's huge scope, though, comes a related problem: finding the WMI class that accomplishes your task. To assist you in learning what WMI or CIM classes are available, Appendix G provides a helpful listing of the most common ones. For a script that helps you search for WMI classes by name, description, property name, or property description, see Recipe 28.5, "Program: Search for WMI Classes".

Some advanced WMI tasks require that you enable your security privileges or adjust the packet privacy settings used in your request. All of PowerShell's WMI cmdlets support these options through built-in parameters.

When you want to access a specific WMI instance with the [Wmi] accelerator, you might at first struggle to determine what properties WMI lets you search on. These properties are called key properties on the class. For a script that lists these key properties, see Recipe 28.4, "Program: Determine Properties Available to WMI and CIM Filters".

For more information about the Get-CimInstance cmdlet, type **Get-Help Get-CimInstance**.

### See Also

Recipe 28.4, "Program: Determine Properties Available to WMI and CIM Filters"

Recipe 28.5, "Program: Search for WMI Classes"

Appendix G, *WMI Reference*

# 28.2. Modify the Properties of a WMI or CIM Instance

## Problem

You want to modify the properties of a WMI or CIM instance.

## Solution

Use the Set-CimInstance cmdlet:

```
PS > $bootVolume = Get-CimInstance Win32_LogicalDisk |
    Where-Object { $_.DeviceID -eq 'C:' }

PS > $bootVolume

DeviceID     : C:
DriveType    : 3
ProviderName :
FreeSpace    : 10587656192
Size         : 34357637120
VolumeName   : Boot Volume

PS > $bootVolume | Set-CimInstance -Arguments @{
    VolumeName = 'Operating System' }

DeviceID     : C:
DriveType    : 3
ProviderName :
FreeSpace    : 10587656192
Size         : 34357637120
VolumeName   : Operating System
```

# Discussion

Although you can assign new property values to the objects output by Get-CimInstance, changes you make ultimately are not reflected in the permanent system state, as this example shows:

```
PS > $bootVolume = Get-CimInstance Win32_LogicalDisk |
    Where-Object { $_.DeviceID -eq 'C:' }

PS > $bootVolume

DeviceID     : C:
DriveType    : 3
ProviderName :
FreeSpace    : 10587656192
Size         : 34357637120
VolumeName   : Vista

PS > $bootVolume.VolumeName = "Boot Volume"

PS > Get-CimInstance Win32_LogicalDisk |
    Where-Object { $_.DeviceID -eq 'C:' }


DeviceID     : C:
DriveType    : 3
ProviderName :
FreeSpace    : 10587652096
Size         : 34357637120
VolumeName   : Vista
```

Instead, the Set-CimInstance cmdlet lets you permanently modify values of WMI and CIM instances. While the Set-CimInstance cmdlet supports WMI instances as pipeline input, you can also use the -Query parameter to select the instance you want to modify:

```
Set-CimInstance -Query "SELECT * FROM Win32_LogicalDisk WHERE DeviceID='C:'" `
    -Property @{ VolumeName="Vista" }
```

To determine which properties can be modified on an instance, you need to investigate the CIM class that defines it. Each CIM class has a CimClassProperties collection, and each property has a Qualifiers collection. If Write is one of the qualifiers, then that property is writeable:

```
PS > Get-CimClass Win32_LogicalDisk | Foreach-Object CimClassProperties

(...)
Name               : VolumeName
Value              :
CimType            : String
Flags              : Property, NullValue
Qualifiers         : {MappingStrings, read, write}
ReferenceClassName :
```

```
Name              : VolumeSerialNumber
Value             :
CimType           : String
Flags             : Property, ReadOnly, NullValue
Qualifiers        : {MappingStrings, read}
ReferenceClassName :
(...)
```

To automatically see all writeable classes in the ROOT\CIMV2 namespace, simply run this snippet of PowerShell script:

```
Get-CimClass Win32_LogicalDisk | Foreach-Object {
    $_.CimClassName; $_.CimClassProperties |
    Where-Object { $_.Qualifiers["Write"] } | Foreach-Object Name
}
```

When dealing with the WMI-related cmdlets, the Set-WmiInstance cmdlet lets you configure impersonation, authentication, and privilege restrictions. For more information about working with WMI classes, see Recipe 28.1, "Access Windows Management Instrumentation and CIM Data".

## See Also

Recipe 28.1, "Access Windows Management Instrumentation and CIM Data"

Appendix G, *WMI Reference*

# 28.3. Invoke a Method on a WMI Instance or Class

## Problem

You want to invoke a method supported by a WMI instance or class.

## Solution

Use the Invoke-CimMethod cmdlet:

```
PS > Invoke-CimMethod -Class Win32_Process -Name Create -Arguments @{
    CommandLine = "notepad" }
(notepad starts)

ProcessId                              ReturnValue PSComputerName
---------                              ----------- --------------
     5976                                        0</leeholmes1c23
```

# Discussion

As with .NET types, WMI classes describe the functionality and features of a related set of items. For example, the Win32_Process class describes the features and behavior of an entity called an operating system process. When WMI or CIM returns information about a specific *operating system process*, that is called an *instance*.

As with static methods on .NET types, many WMI and CIM classes offer methods that relate broadly to the entity they try to represent. For example, the Win32_Process class defines methods to start processes, stop them, and more. To invoke any of these methods, call the Invoke-CimMethod cmdlet.

While you may already know the method you want to call, PowerShell also offers a way to see the methods exposed by WMI and CIM classes on your system. Each WMI class has a CimClassMethods collection, and reviewing that collection lists all methods supported by that class. The following snippet lists all methods supported by the Win32_Process class:

```
Get-CimClass Win32_Process | Foreach-Object CimClassMethods
```

Once you find a method you want to invoke, you can access the Parameters property to see how to invoke the method:

```
PS > $methods = Get-CimClass Win32_Process | Foreach-Object CimClassMethods
PS > $methods | Where-Object Name -eq Create | Foreach-Object Parameters

Name                       CimType Qualifiers
----                       ------- ----------
CommandLine                 String {ID, In, MappingStrings}
CurrentDirectory            String {ID, In, MappingStrings}
ProcessStartupInformation Instance {EmbeddedInstance, ID, In, MappingStrings}
ProcessId                   UInt32 {ID, MappingStrings, Out}
```

When you're dealing with WMI-related cmdlets, the Invoke-WmiMethod cmdlet lets you configure impersonation, authentication, and privilege restrictions.

In addition to the Invoke-CimMethod cmdlet, the [WmiClass] type shortcut also lets you refer to a WMI class and invoke its methods:

```
$processClass = [WmiClass] "Win32_Process"
$processClass.Create("notepad.exe")
```

This method, however, does not easily support customization of impersonation, authentication, or privilege restrictions.

For more information about working with WMI classes, see Recipe 28.1, "Access Windows Management Instrumentation and CIM Data".

## See Also

Recipe 28.1, "Access Windows Management Instrumentation and CIM Data"

Appendix G, *WMI Reference*

# 28.4. Program: Determine Properties Available to WMI and CIM Filters

When you want to access a specific WMI or CIM instance with PowerShell, you might at first struggle to determine what properties WMI or CIM lets you search on. These properties are called *key properties* on the class. Example 28-1 gets all the properties you can use in a WMI filter for a given class.

*Example 28-1. Get-WmiClassKeyProperty.ps1*

```
##############################################################################
##
## Get-WmiClassKeyProperty
##
## From Windows PowerShell Cookbook (O'Reilly)
## by Lee Holmes (http://www.leeholmes.com/guide)
##
##############################################################################

<#

.SYNOPSIS

Get all of the properties that you may use in a WMI filter for a given class.

.EXAMPLE

PS > Get-WmiClassKeyProperty Win32_Process
Handle

#>

param(
    ## The WMI class to examine
    [WmiClass] $WmiClass
)

Set-StrictMode -Version 3

## WMI classes have properties
foreach($currentProperty in $wmiClass.Properties)
{
    ## WMI properties have qualifiers to explain more about them
    foreach($qualifier in $currentProperty.Qualifiers)
```

```
        {
            ## If it has a 'Key' qualifier, then you may use it in a filter
            if($qualifier.Name -eq "Key")
            {
                $currentProperty.Name
            }
        }
    }
}
```

For more information about running scripts, see Recipe 1.1, "Run Programs, Scripts, and Existing Tools".

## See Also

Recipe 1.1, "Run Programs, Scripts, and Existing Tools"

# 28.5. Program: Search for WMI Classes

Along with WMI's huge scope comes a related problem: finding the WMI class that accomplishes your task. To help you learn what WMI classes are available, Appendix G provides a helpful listing of the most common ones. If you want to dig a little deeper, though, Example 28-2 lets you search for WMI classes by name, description, property name, or property description.

*Example 28-2. Search-WmiNamespace.ps1*

```
##############################################################################
##
## Search-WmiNamespace
##
## From Windows PowerShell Cookbook (O'Reilly)
## by Lee Holmes (http://www.leeholmes.com/guide)
##
##############################################################################

<#

.SYNOPSIS

Search the WMI classes installed on the system for the provided match text.

.EXAMPLE

PS > Search-WmiNamespace Registry
Searches WMI for any classes or descriptions that mention "Registry"

.EXAMPLE

Search-WmiNamespace Process ClassName,PropertyName
Searchs WMI for any classes or properties that mention "Process"
```

```
.EXAMPLE

Search-WmiNamespace CPU -Detailed
Searches WMI for any class names, descriptions, or properties that mention
"CPU"

#>

param(
    ## The pattern to search for
    [Parameter(Mandatory = $true)]
    [string] $Pattern,

    ## Switch parameter to look for class names, descriptions, or properties
    [switch] $Detailed,

    ## Switch parameter to look for class names, descriptions, properties, and
    ## property description.
    [switch] $Full,

    ## Custom match options.
    ## Supports any or all of the following match options:
    ## ClassName, ClassDescription, PropertyName, PropertyDescription
    [string[]] $MatchOptions = ("ClassName","ClassDescription")
)

Set-StrictMode -Off

## Helper function to create a new object that represents
## a Wmi match from this script
function New-WmiMatch
{
    param( $matchType, $className, $propertyName, $line )

    $wmiMatch = New-Object PsObject -Property @{
        MatchType = $matchType;
        ClassName = $className;
        PropertyName = $propertyName;
        Line = $line
    }

    $wmiMatch
}

## If they've specified the -detailed or -full options, update
## the match options to provide them an appropriate amount of detail
if($detailed)
{
    $matchOptions = "ClassName","ClassDescription","PropertyName"
}
```

```
if($full)
{
    $matchOptions =
        "ClassName","ClassDescription","PropertyName","PropertyDescription"
}

## Verify that they specified only valid match options
foreach($matchOption in $matchOptions)
{
    $fullMatchOptions =
        "ClassName","ClassDescription","PropertyName","PropertyDescription"

    if($fullMatchOptions -notcontains $matchOption)
    {
        $error = "Cannot convert value {0} to a match option. " +
            "Specify one of the following values and try again. " +
            "The possible values are ""{1}""."
        $ofs = ", "
        throw ($error -f $matchOption, ([string] $fullMatchOptions))
    }
}

## Go through all of the available classes on the computer
foreach($class in Get-WmiObject -List -Rec)
{
    ## Provide explicit get options, so that we get back descriptios
    ## as well
    $managementOptions = New-Object System.Management.ObjectGetOptions
    $managementOptions.UseAmendedQualifiers = $true
    $managementClass =
        New-Object Management.ManagementClass $class.Name,$managementOptions

    ## If they want us to match on class names, check if their text
    ## matches the class name
    if($matchOptions -contains "ClassName")
    {
        if($managementClass.Name -match $pattern)
        {
            New-WmiMatch "ClassName" `
                $managementClass.Name $null $managementClass.__PATH
        }
    }

    ## If they want us to match on class descriptions, check if their text
    ## matches the class description
    if($matchOptions -contains "ClassDescription")
    {
        $description =
            $managementClass.Qualifiers |
                foreach { if($_.Name -eq "Description") { $_.Value } }
        if($description -match $pattern)
        {
```

```
        New-WmiMatch "ClassDescription" `
            $managementClass.Name $null $description
    }
}

## Go through the properties of the class
foreach($property in $managementClass.Properties)
{
    ## If they want us to match on property names, check if their text
    ## matches the property name
    if($matchOptions -contains "PropertyName")
    {
        if($property.Name -match $pattern)
        {
            New-WmiMatch "PropertyName" `
                $managementClass.Name $property.Name $property.Name
        }
    }

    ## If they want us to match on property descriptions, check if
    ## their text matches the property name
    if($matchOptions -contains "PropertyDescription")
    {
        $propertyDescription =
            $property.Qualifiers |
                foreach { if($_.Name -eq "Description") { $_.Value } }
        if($propertyDescription -match $pattern)
        {
            New-WmiMatch "PropertyDescription" `
                $managementClass.Name $property.Name $propertyDescription
        }
    }
}
}
```

For more information about running scripts, see Recipe 1.1, "Run Programs, Scripts, and Existing Tools".

## See Also

Recipe 1.1, "Run Programs, Scripts, and Existing Tools"

Appendix G, *WMI Reference*

# 28.6. Use .NET to Perform Advanced WMI Tasks

## Problem

You want to work with advanced features of WMI, but PowerShell's access (through the [Wmi], [WmiClass], and [WmiSearcher] accelerators) does not directly support them.

# Solution

To interact with advanced features of WMI objects, access their methods and properties.

### Advanced instance features

To get CIM instances related to a given instance (its *associators*), use the `Get-CimAssociatedInstance` cmdlet:

```
Get-CimInstance Win32_Service -Filter "Name='winmgmt'" |
    Get-CimAssociatedInstance
```

When dealing with the WMI cmdlets, use the `GetRelated()` method:

```
$instance = [Wmi] 'Win32_Service.Name="winmgmt"'
$instance.GetRelated()
```

When dealing with the WMI cmdlets (as opposed to CIM cmdlets), connectivity options play a major role in some scenarios. To change advanced scope options, access the `Scope.Options` property. While the `Invoke-WmiMethod` cmdlet lets you enable privileges directly through a parameter, this example provides another option:

```
$system = Get-WmiObject Win32_OperatingSystem
$system.Scope.Options.EnablePrivileges = $true
$system.SetDateTime($system.ConvertFromDateTime("01/01/2007"))
```

### Advanced class features

To retrieve the WMI properties and qualifiers of a class, access the `CimClassProperties` property:

```
$class = Get-CimClass Win32_Process
$class.CimClassProperties
```

### Advanced query feature

When dealing with the WMI cmdlets, advanced query options play a major role in some scenarios. To configure connection options on a query, such as Packet Privacy and Authentication, set the options on the `Scope` property:

```
$credential = Get-Credential
$query = [WmiSearcher] "SELECT * FROM IISWebServerSetting"
$query.Scope.Path = "\\REMOTE_COMPUTER\Root\MicrosoftIISV2"
$query.Scope.Options.Username = $credential.Username
$query.Scope.Options.Password = $credential.GetNetworkCredential().Password
$query.Scope.Options.Authentication = "PacketPrivacy"
$query.get() | Select-Object AnonymousUserName
```

## Discussion

The [Wmi], [WmiClass], and [WmiSearcher] type shortcuts return instances of .NET System.Management.ManagementObject, System.Management.ManagementClass, and System.Management.ManagementObjectSearcher classes, respectively.

As might be expected, the .NET Framework provides comprehensive support for WMI queries, with PowerShell providing an easier-to-use interface to that support. If you need to step outside the support offered directly by PowerShell, these classes in the .NET Framework provide an advanced outlet.

For more information about working with classes from the .NET Framework, see Recipe 3.8, "Work with .NET Objects".

## See Also

Recipe 3.8, "Work with .NET Objects"

# 28.7. Improve the Performance of Large-Scale WMI Operations

## Problem

You want to perform a large-scale WMI operation across many computers, and you want to control how many computers should be managed at a time.

## Solution

Use the -ThrottleLimit parameter on the Get-WmiObject cmdlet, and invoke that cmdlet as a job:

```
$computers = Get-Content computers.txt
Get-WmiObject Win32_OperatingSystem -Computer $computers -ThrottleLimit 10 -AsJob
```

## Discussion

One problem with large-scale WMI operations against many computers is that most scripts invoke them sequentially. If your script acts against 10,000 servers, it will usually process the first computer, and then retrieve the results. Next, it will process the second computer, and then retrieve its results. Since WMI operations are traditionally network-bound, your script spends the vast majority of its time simply waiting for results from remote computers.

A genesis for this feature was a sobering story we heard from one of our large customers. The customer's scripts had to deal with so many computers that the customer would have to start a second script before the first had finished!

The solution to this quandary comes from invoking the commands in parallel. Not entirely in parallel, however, as most machines would buckle under the load of 10,000 active WMI queries. While it is possible to recognize the solution and pitfalls, actually implementing it is something different altogether. Even with the proper skill set, a job manager that supports automatic throttling is usually not high on an administrator's list of priorities when compared to the collection of fires the administrator needs to put out.

Instead, PowerShell's WMI cmdlets handle all of this complexity for you. For more information about PowerShell's job support, see Recipe 1.5, "Invoke a Long-Running or Background Command".

The -AsJob parameter is not supported for CIM-based cmdlets.

## See Also

Recipe 1.5, "Invoke a Long-Running or Background Command"

# 28.8. Convert a VBScript WMI Script to PowerShell

## Problem

You want to perform a WMI or CIM task in PowerShell, but you can find only VBScript examples that demonstrate the solution to the problem.

## Solution

To accomplish the task of a script that retrieves data from a computer, use the Get-CimInstance cmdlet:

```
foreach($printer in Get-CimInstance -Computer COMPUTER Win32_Printer)
{
    ## Work with the properties
    $printer.Name
}
```

To accomplish the task of a script that calls methods on an instance, use the [Wmi] or [WmiSearcher] accelerators to retrieve the instances, and then call methods on the instances like you would call any other PowerShell method.

```
$service = [WMI] 'Win32_Service.Name="winmgmt"'
$service.ChangeStartMode("Manual")
$service.ChangeStartMode("Automatic")
```

Additionally, you can use the `Get-CimInstance` and `Invoke-CimMethod` cmdlets to do the same:

```
$service = Get-CimInstance Win32_Service -Filter "Name = 'winmgmt'"
$service | Invoke-CimMethod -Name ChangeStartMode -Arguments @{
    StartMode = "Manual" }
$service | Invoke-CimMethod -Name ChangeStartMode -Arguments @{
    StartMode = "Automatic" }
```

To accomplish the task of a script that calls methods on a class, use the `Invoke-CimMethod` cmdlet, or use the `[WmiClass]` accelerator to retrieve the class, and then call methods on the class like you would call any other PowerShell method:

```
Invoke-CimMethod -Class Win32_Process -Name Create -Arguments @{
    CommandLine = "notepad" }

$class = [WmiClass] "Win32_Process"
$class.Create("Notepad")
```

## Discussion

For many years, VBScript has been the preferred language that administrators use to access WMI data. Because of that, the vast majority of scripts available in books and on the Internet come written in VBScript.

These scripts usually take one of three forms: retrieving data and accessing properties, calling methods of an instance, and calling methods of a class.

 Although most WMI scripts on the Internet accomplish unique tasks, PowerShell supports many of the traditional WMI tasks natively. If you want to translate a WMI example to PowerShell, first check that there aren't any PowerShell cmdlets that might accomplish the task directly.

### Retrieving data

One of the most common uses of WMI is for data collection and system inventory tasks. A typical VBScript that retrieves data looks like Example 28-3.

*Example 28-3. Retrieving printer information from WMI using VBScript*

```
strComputer = "."
Set objWMIService = GetObject("winmgmts:" _
    & "{impersonationLevel=impersonate}!\\" & strComputer & "\root\cimv2")

Set colInstalledPrinters = objWMIService.ExecQuery _
    ("Select * from Win32_Printer")
```

```
For Each objPrinter in colInstalledPrinters
    Wscript.Echo "Name: " & objPrinter.Name
    Wscript.Echo "Location: " & objPrinter.Location
    Wscript.Echo "Default: " & objPrinter.Default
Next
```

The first three lines prepare a WMI connection to a given computer and namespace. The next two lines of code prepare a WMI query that requests all instances of a class. The For Each block loops over all the instances, and the objPrinter.*Property* statements interact with properties on those instances.

In PowerShell, the Get-CimInstance cmdlet takes care of most of that by retrieving all instances of a class from the computer and namespace that you specify. The first five lines of code then become:

```
$installedPrinters = Get-CimInstance Win32_Printer -ComputerName computer
```

If you need to specify a different computer, namespace, or query restriction, the Get-CimInstance cmdlets supports those through optional parameters.

In PowerShell, the For Each block becomes:

```
foreach($printer in $installedPrinters)
{
    $printer.Name
    $printer.Location
    $printer.Default
}
```

Notice that we spend the bulk of the PowerShell conversion of this script showing how to access properties. If you don't actually need to work with the properties (and only want to display them for reporting purposes), PowerShell's formatting commands simplify that even further:

```
Get-CimInstance Win32_Printer -ComputerName computer |
    Format-List Name,Location,Default
```

For more information about working with the Get-CimInstance cmdlet, see Recipe 28.1, "Access Windows Management Instrumentation and CIM Data".

### Calling methods on an instance

Although data retrieval scripts form the bulk of WMI management examples, another common task is to call methods of an instance that invoke actions.

For example, Example 28-4 changes the startup type of a service.

*Example 28-4. Changing the startup type of a service from WMI using VBScript*

```
strComputer = "."
Set objWMIService = GetObject("winmgmts:" _
```

```
    & "{impersonationLevel=impersonate}!\\" & strComputer & "\root\cimv2")

Set colServiceList = objWMIService.ExecQuery _
    ("Select * from Win32_Service where StartMode = 'Manual'")

For Each objService in colServiceList
    errReturnCode = objService.ChangeStartMode("Disabled")
Next
```

The first three lines prepare a WMI connection to a given computer and namespace. The next two lines of code prepare a WMI query that requests all instances of a class and adds an additional filter (`StartMode = 'Manual'`) to the query. The `For Each` block loops over all the instances, and the `objService.Change(…)` statement calls the `Change()` method on the service.

In PowerShell, the `Get-CimInstance` cmdlet takes care of most of the setup by retrieving all instances of a class from the computer and namespace that you specify. The first five lines of code then become:

```
$services = Get-CimInstance Win32_Service -Filter "StartMode = 'Manual'"
```

If you need to specify a different computer or namespace, the `Get-CimInstance` cmdlet supports those through optional parameters.

In PowerShell, the `For Each` block becomes:

```
foreach($service in $services)
{
    $service | Invoke-CimMethod -Name ChangeStartMode -Arguments @{
    StartMode = "Manual" }
}
```

For more information about working with the `Get-CimInstance` cmdlet, see Recipe 28.1, "Access Windows Management Instrumentation and CIM Data".

### Calling methods on a class

Although less common than calling methods on an instance, it is sometimes helpful to call methods on a WMI class. PowerShell makes this work almost exactly like calling methods on an instance.

For example, a script that creates a process on a remote computer looks like this:

```
strComputer = "COMPUTER"
Set objWMIService = GetObject _
    ("winmgmts:\\" & strComputer & "\root\cimv2:Win32_Process")

objWMIService.Create("notepad.exe")
```

The first three lines prepare a WMI connection to a given computer and namespace. The final line calls the `Create()` method on the class.

---

In PowerShell, the `Invoke-CimMethod` cmdlet lets you easily work with methods on a class. The entire segment of code then becomes:

```
Invoke-CimMethod -Computername COMPUTER -Class Win32_Process -Name Create `
    -Arguments @{ CommandLine = "notepad" }
```

For more information about invoking methods on WMI classes, see Recipe 28.3, "Invoke a Method on a WMI Instance or Class".

## See Also

Recipe 28.1, "Access Windows Management Instrumentation and CIM Data"

Recipe 28.3, "Invoke a Method on a WMI Instance or Class"

# Remoting

## 29.0. Introduction

PowerShell's support for local and interactive computer automation makes it an incredibly attractive platform for computer management and administration. Its rich, object-flavored perspective takes even the simplest of management tasks to the next level.

While PowerShell supports interaction with traditional remoting technologies (SSH, FTP, Telnet, PsExec, and more), that support is fairly equivalent to that offered by any other shell. Where PowerShell's remote management really takes off is, unsurprisingly, through its unique object-based approach.

Of course, any feature that provides remote access to your systems should be viewed with a cautious eye. Security is a natural concern with any technology that supports network connections, and is something that the PowerShell Remoting feature takes very seriously. In addition, ubiquitous support for remote headless management across your entire enterprise is a core value that any sane server platform offers. How does Windows Server ensure that both hold true? As of PowerShell version 3, PowerShell Remoting is enabled by default for most common remote management scenarios:

- On desktop machines (i.e., Windows 8 client), PowerShell does not listen to network connections by default and must be explicitly activated.

- On untrusted networks (i.e., a server that accepts connections from the Internet), PowerShell listens only to network connections that originate from that same subnet. Machines on the same subnet are generally connected to the same physical network.

- On trusted networks (i.e., a domain or network interface explicitly marked as trusted), PowerShell listens to network connections by default.

With these protections in place, PowerShell Remoting offers a robust, reliable, and secure way to remotely manage your machines.

To create PowerShell Remoting, the PowerShell and Windows Remote Management (WinRM) teams worked together closely to create a combined release known as the *Windows Management Framework*. Designing a rich remoting experience was one of the top focuses of their collaboration. Starting with standard *interactive remoting*, PowerShell lets you easily connect to a remote system and work with it one to one:

```
PS > Enter-PSSession Lee-Desk
[Lee-Desk]: PS > Get-Process -n PowerShell

Handles  NPM(K)    PM(K)      WS(K) VM(M)   CPU(s)     Id Process   PSComputer
                                                          Name       Name
-------  ------    -----      ----- -----   ------     -- --------- ---------
    628      17    39084      58908   214     4.26   7540 powers... lee-des...
```

If you want to import the commands from that remote system (but still have them run on the remote system), *implicit remoting* often lets you forget you are managing a remote system altogether. Expanding on interactive and implicit remoting, large-scale *fan-out* remoting is a natural next step. Fan-out remoting lets you manage many computers at a time in a bulk, command-based approach:

```
PS > Invoke-Command Lee-Desk { Get-Process -n PowerShell } -Cred Lee

Handles  NPM(K)    PM(K)      WS(K) VM(M)   CPU(s)     Id Process   PSComputer
                                                          Name       Name
-------  ------    -----      ----- -----   ------     -- --------- ---------
    628      17    39084      58908   214     4.26   7540 powers... lee-des...
```

As with the rest of PowerShell, fan-out remoting offers a unique, object-focused treatment that elevates its experience past plain-text-based approaches.

# 29.1. Find Commands That Support Their Own Remoting

## Problem

You want to find commands that let you access remote computers but that don't require PowerShell Remoting.

## Solution

Use the -ParameterName parameter of the Get-Command cmdlet to find all commands that expose a -ComputerName parameter. This parameter was introduced in PowerShell version 3:

```
PS > Get-Command -CommandType Cmdlet -ParameterName ComputerName

CommandType     Name                    Definition
-----------     ----                    ----------
Cmdlet          Clear-EventLog          Clear-EventLog [-LogName]...
Cmdlet          Connect-WSMan           Connect-WSMan [[-Computer...
Cmdlet          Disconnect-WSMan        Disconnect-WSMan [[-Compu...
Cmdlet          Enter-PSSession         Enter-PSSession [-Compute...
Cmdlet          Get-Counter             Get-Counter [[-Counter] <...
Cmdlet          Get-EventLog            Get-EventLog [-LogName] <...
Cmdlet          Get-HotFix              Get-HotFix [[-Id] <String...
Cmdlet          Get-Process             Get-Process [[-Name] <Str...
(...)
```

Alternatively, if only PowerShell version 2 is available, use the Get-Command cmdlet to retrieve all cmdlets. Then use the Where-Object cmdlet to access the Parameters collection to find all commands that expose a -ComputerName parameter:

```
Get-Command -CommandType Cmdlet | Where-Object { $_.Parameters["ComputerName"] }
```

## Discussion

While PowerShell Remoting offers great power and consistency, sometimes you might need to invoke a command against a system that does not have PowerShell installed. A simple Remote Desktop session is a common approach, but PowerShell still offers plenty of remote management options that work independently of its core remoting support.

Each command shown by the output of Get-Command that exposes a -ComputerName parameter does so using its own built-in remoting technology. The WMI cmdlets use a WMI-specific form of DCOM-based remoting. The WSMan cmdlets use SOAP-based remoting. Many of the other cmdlets offer RPC-based remoting.

By building on their own existing remoting protocols, these commands integrate easily with environments that have already enabled WMI or event log management, for example. Since these protocols are designed to handle only their specific technology, often they can offer performance benefits as well.

Despite their benefits, commands that offer a -ComputerName parameter can't replace a generalized remoting technology for most purposes. Since each command builds on its own protocol, using that command means managing firewall rules, services, and more. Command-based remoting generally offers limited functionality as well, and something as simple as alternate credentials is rarely supported.

For more information about enabling PowerShell Remoting, see Recipe 29.2, "Enable PowerShell Remoting on a Computer".

## See Also

Recipe 29.2, "Enable PowerShell Remoting on a Computer"

# 29.2. Enable PowerShell Remoting on a Computer

## Problem

You want to allow remote management of a computer via PowerShell Remoting.

## Solution

Use the `Enable-PSRemoting` cmdlet to enable PowerShell Remoting:

```
PS > Enable-PSRemoting

WinRM Quick Configuration
Running command "Set-WSManQuickConfig" to enable this machine for remote
management through WinRM service.
 This includes:
    1. Starting or restarting (if already started) the WinRM service
    2. Setting the WinRM service type to autostart
    3. Creating a listener to accept requests on any IP address
    4. Enabling firewall exception for WS-Management traffic (for http only).

Do you want to continue?
[Y] Yes  [A] Yes to All  [N] No  [L] No to All  [S] Suspend  [?] Help
(default is "Y"): Y

WinRM has been updated to receive requests.
WinRM service type changed successfully.
WinRM service started.
Configured LocalAccountTokenFilterPolicy to grant administrative rights
remotely to local users.

WinRM has been updated for remote management.
Created a WinRM listener on HTTP://* to accept WS-Man requests to any IP on
this machine.
WinRM firewall exception enabled.
```

## Discussion

As mentioned in this chapter's introduction, PowerShell version 3 enables remoting by default for typical management scenarios: servers within a trusted or domain network and within the local subnet. On client machines or untrusted networks, PowerShell does not listen to network connections by default and it must be explicitly enabled.

PowerShell Remoting does not require any specific configuration to let you connect to a remote computer, but it does require a configuration step to allow connections from remote computers.

### Enable remoting on a single local machine

Once you've decided to enable remoting, PowerShell makes this a snap (after informing you of the impact). Simply call `Enable-PSRemoting` from an elevated shell. The solution demonstrates this approach. To bypass any user prompts or confirmation, also specify the `-Force` flag.

By default, `Enable-PSRemoting` is blocked on networks identified as public networks. If you generally trust the network you are connected to, use the `Set-Net ConnectionProfile` cmdlet to change the network profile to private:

```
PS > Set-NetConnectionProfile -NetworkCategory Private
```

If you don't generally trust the network you are connected to but want to enable PowerShell Remoting, use the `-SkipNetworkProfileCheck` parameter.

As part of the `Enable-PSRemoting` process, PowerShell connects to the local WS-Management service to create and configure a new endpoint. This is done through a local network connection, so it is impacted by the Windows restrictions on network connections. For example, Windows does not allow network connections to any account that has a blank password. If your administrator account has a blank password, PowerShell will be unable to properly create and configure the WSMan endpoint.

### Enable remoting on a remote machine

Remotely enabling PowerShell Remoting offers many unique challenges. Although you can certainly use Remote Desktop to connect to the system (and then essentially enable it locally), Remote Desktop does not lend itself to automation.

Instead, you can leverage another remoting technology that does lend itself to automation: Windows Management Instrumentation (WMI). WMI is enabled on most domain machines, but it offers only a minor facility for remote command execution: the `Cre ate()` method of the `Win32_Process` WMI class. For more information about this approach, see Recipe 29.6, "Program: Remotely Enable PowerShell Remoting".

### Enable remoting in an enterprise

If you want to enable PowerShell Remoting in an enterprise, Group Policy is the most flexible and scalable option. Through Group Policy settings, you can enable automatic configuration of WinRM endpoints and firewall rules. For more information about this approach, type `Get-Help about_remote_troubleshooting`.

## See Also

Recipe 29.6, "Program: Remotely Enable PowerShell Remoting"

# 29.3. Interactively Manage a Remote Computer

## Problem

You want to interactively work with a remote computer as though it were a local PowerShell session.

## Solution

Use the `Enter-PSSession` cmdlet to connect to a remote session and manage it interactively:

```
PS > Enter-PSSession Lee-Desk
[lee-desk]: PS E:\Lee> Get-Process -Name PowerShell

Handles  NPM(K)    PM(K)      WS(K) VM(M)   CPU(s)     Id ProcessName
-------  ------    -----      ----- -----   ------     -- -----------
   2834      14    85500      86256   218 ...22.83   8396 powershell
    421      12    39220      54204   189    7.41    9708 powershell

[lee-desk]: PS E:\Lee> exit
PS >
```

If your current account does not have access to the remote computer, you can use the `-Credential` parameter to supply alternate credentials:

```
PS > $cred = Get-Credential LEE-DESK\Lee
PS > Enter-PSSession Lee-Desk -Cred $cred
```

## Discussion

Like many traditional shells, PowerShell Remoting offers a simple, direct, interactive management experience known simply as *interactive remoting*. Just as in your local PowerShell sessions, you type commands and see their output. This remote PowerShell is just as powerful as your local one; all of the filtering, pipelining, and integrated language features continue to work.

Two aspects make an interactive remote session different from a local one, however.

The first thing to note is that your remote PowerShell sessions have no associated desktop or graphical user interface. PowerShell will launch Notepad if you ask it to, but the user interface won't be displayed to anybody.

When you use your normal technique (i.e., `PS > notepad.exe`) to launch an application in interactive remoting, PowerShell waits for it to close before returning control to you. This ends up blocking your session, so press Ctrl-C to regain control of your session. If you want to launch a graphical application, use either the `Start-Process` cmdlet or command-based remoting.

Also, if you launch a program (such as *edit.com* or *ftp.exe*'s interactive mode) that directly interacts with the console window for its user interface, this program will not work as expected. Some applications (such as *ftp.exe*'s interactive mode) detect that they have no console window available and simply exit. Others (such as *edit.com*) hang and cause PowerShell's interactive remoting to become unresponsive as well. To break free from misbehaving applications like this, press Ctrl-C.

The second aspect to interactive remoting is shared by all Windows network technologies that work without explicit credentials: the double-hop problem. Once you've connected to a computer remotely, Windows gives you full access to all local resources as though you were logged into the computer directly. When it comes to *network* resources, however, Windows prevents your user information from being automatically used on another computer. This typically shows up when you're trying to access either restricted network shares from a remoting system or intranet websites that require implicit authentication. For information about how to launch a remoting session that supports this type of credential forwarding, see Recipe 29.14, "Create Sessions with Full Network Access".

In addition to supplying a computer name to the `Enter-PSSession` cmdlet, you can also use the `New-PSSession` cmdlet to connect to a computer. After connecting, you can enter and exit that session at will:

```
PS > $session = New-PSSession Lee-Desk -Cred $cred
PS > Get-PSSession

 Id Name          ComputerName   State    ConfigurationName    Availability
 -- ----          ------------   -----    -----------------    ------------
  1 Session1      lee-desk       Opened   Microsoft.PowerShell ...lable


PS > Enter-PSSession $session
[lee-desk]: PS E:\Lee> Start-Process calc
[lee-desk]: PS E:\Lee> Get-Process -n calc

Handles  NPM(K)    PM(K)      WS(K) VM(M)   CPU(s)     Id ProcessName
-------  ------    -----      ----- -----   ------     -- -----------
     64       5     4172       7272    44     0.06   7148 calc
```

```
[lee-desk]: PS E:\Lee> exit
PS > Get-Process -n calc
Get-Process : Cannot find a process with the name "calc". Verify the process
name and call the cmdlet again.

PS > Enter-PSSession $session
[lee-desk]: PS E:\Lee> Get-Process -n calc

Handles  NPM(K)    PM(K)     WS(K) VM(M)   CPU(s)     Id ProcessName
-------  ------    -----     ----- -----   ------     -- -----------
     64       5     4172      7272    44     0.06   7148 calc


[lee-desk]: PS E:\Lee>
```

After creating a session, you can even combine interactive remoting with bulk, command-based *fan-out* remoting. For more information about command-based remoting, see Recipe 29.4, "Invoke a Command on a Remote Computer".

When working with a PowerShell session, you may have commands that require access to network resources such as file shares. If this is a requirement for a session you're creating on the local machine, you can use the -EnableNetworkAccess parameter of the different PowerShell Remoting cmdlets. If this is a session you're creating on another machine, you'll need to use the CredSSP authentication mechanism. For more information on enabling and using CredSSP, see Recipe 29.14, "Create Sessions with Full Network Access".

### See Also

Recipe 29.4, "Invoke a Command on a Remote Computer"

Recipe 29.14, "Create Sessions with Full Network Access"

# 29.4. Invoke a Command on a Remote Computer

## Problem

You want to invoke a command on one or many remote computer(s).

## Solution

Use the Invoke-Command cmdlet:

```
PS > Invoke-Command -Computer Lee-Desk,LEEHOLMES1C23 -Command { Get-PsDrive } |
    Format-Table Name,Used,Free,PSComputerName -Auto
```

```
Name          Used          Free          PSComputerName
----          ----          ----          --------------
Alias                                     lee-desk
C             44830642176   105206947840  lee-desk
E             37626998784   61987717120   lee-desk
F             126526734336  37394722816   lee-desk
G             93445226496   6986330112    lee-desk
H             1703936       0             lee-desk
I             349184        18099200      lee-desk
J             40442880      0             lee-desk
C             24018575360   10339061760   leeholmes1c23
D             0                           leeholmes1c23
(...)
```

If your current account does not have access to the remote computer, you can use the -Credential parameter to supply alternate credentials:

```
PS > $cred = Get-Credential LEE-DESK\Lee
PS > Invoke-Command Lee-Desk { Get-Process } -Cred $cred
```

## Discussion

As shown in Recipe 29.3, "Interactively Manage a Remote Computer", PowerShell offers simple interactive remoting to handle situations when you want to quickly explore or manage a single remote system. For many scenarios, though, one-to-one interactive remoting is not realistic. Simple automation (which by definition is noninteractive) is the most basic example, but another key point is large-scale automation.

Running a command (or set of commands) against a large number of machines has always been a challenging task. To address both one-to-one automation as well as large-scale automation, PowerShell supports *fan-out* remoting: a command-based, batch-oriented approach to system management.

Fan-out remoting integrates all of the core features you've come to expect from your local PowerShell experience: richly structured output, consistency, and most of all, reach. While a good number of PowerShell cmdlets support their own native form of remoting, PowerShell's support provides it to every command—cmdlets as well as console applications.

When you call the Invoke-Command cmdlet simply with a computer name and script block, PowerShell automatically connects to that machine, invokes the command, and returns the results:

```
PS > $result = Invoke-Command leeholmes1c23 { Get-PSDrive }
PS > $result | Format-Table Name,Used,Free,Root,PSComputerName -Auto

Name          Used Free     Root         PSComputerName
----          ---- ----     ----         --------------
A             0             A:\          leeholmes1c23
```

```
Alias                                              leeholmes1c23
C          24018575360 10339061760 C:\              leeholmes1c23
cert                                  \            leeholmes1c23
D                    0              D:\             leeholmes1c23
Env                                                leeholmes1c23
Function                                           leeholmes1c23
HKCU                             HKEY_CURRENT_USER  leeholmes1c23
HKLM                             HKEY_LOCAL_MACHINE leeholmes1c23
Variable                                           leeholmes1c23
WSMan                                              leeholmes1c23
```

So far, this remoting experience looks similar to many other technologies. Notice the PSComputerName property, though. PowerShell automatically adds this property to all of your results, which lets you easily work with the output of multiple computers at once. We get to see PowerShell's unique remoting treatment once we start working with results. For example:

```
PS > $result | Sort Name | Where { $_.Root -like "*\*" }

Name            Used (GB)    Free (GB) Provider    Root
----            ---------    --------- --------    ----
A                                                  A:\
C                 22.37         9.63              C:\
cert                                               \
D                                                 D:\

PS > $result[2].Used
24018575360
PS > $result[2].Used * 4
96074301440
```

Rather than transport plain text like other remoting technologies, PowerShell transports data in a way that preserves a great deal of information about the original command output. Before sending objects to you, PowerShell *serializes* them into a format that can be moved across the network. This format retains the following "primitive" types, and converts all others to their string representation:

| | | | |
|---|---|---|---|
| Byte | UInt16 | TimeSpan | SecureString |
| SByte | UInt32 | DateTime | Boolean |
| Byte[] | UInt64 | ProgressRecord | Guid |
| Int16 | Decimal | Char | Uri |
| Int32 | Single | String | Version |
| Int64 | Double | XmlDocument | |

Perhaps most importantly, serialization removes all methods from non-primitive objects. By converting these objects to what are called *property bags*, your scripts can depend on an interface that won't change between PowerShell releases, .NET Framework releases, or operating system releases.

When the objects reach your computer, PowerShell *rehydrates* them. During this process, it creates objects that have their original structure and repopulates the properties. Any properties that were primitive types will again be fully functional: integer properties can be sorted and computed, XML documents can be navigated, and more.

When PowerShell reassembles an object, it prepends `Deserialized` to its type name. When PowerShell displays a deserialized object, it will use any formatting definitions that apply to the full-fidelity object:

```
PS > $result[2] | Get-Member


    TypeName: Deserialized.System.Management.Automation.PSDriveInfo

Name                MemberType   Definition
----                ----------   ----------
ToString            Method       string ToString(), string ToString(stri...
Free                NoteProperty System.UInt64 Free=10339061760
PSComputerName      NoteProperty System.String PSComputerName=leeholmes1c23
PSShowComputerName  NoteProperty System.Boolean PSShowComputerName=True
RunspaceId          NoteProperty System.Guid RunspaceId=33f45afd-2381-44...
Used                NoteProperty System.UInt64 Used=24018575360
Credential          Property     Deserialized.System.Management.Automati...
CurrentLocation     Property     System.String {get;set;}
Description         Property     System.String {get;set;}
Name                Property     System.String {get;set;}
Provider            Property     System.String {get;set;}
Root                Property     System.String {get;set;}
```

In addition to supplying a computer name to the `Invoke-Command` cmdlet, you can also use the `New-PSSession` cmdlet to connect to a computer. After connecting, you can invoke commands in that session at will:

```
PS > $session = New-PSSession leeholmes1c23 -Cred $cred
PS > Get-PSSession

Id Name      ComputerName   State   ConfigurationName     Availability
-- ----      ------------   -----   -----------------     ------------
 1 Session1  leeholmes1c23  Opened  Microsoft.PowerShell  ...lable

PS > Invoke-Command -Session $session { Get-Process -Name PowerShell }
```

| Handles | NPM(K) | PM(K) | WS(K) | VM(M) | CPU(s) | Id | Process Name | PSCompu terName |
|---|---|---|---|---|---|---|---|---|
| ------- | ------ | ----- | ----- | ----- | ------ | -- | -------- | ------- |
| 716 | 12 | 48176 | 65060 | 201 | 23.31 | 4684 | power... | leeh... |

After creating a session, you can even combine commands with interactive remoting, as shown in Recipe 29.3, "Interactively Manage a Remote Computer".

 If network interruptions cause an interruption in your session, Power-Shell tries to automatically disconnect your session so that you can reconnect to it when you again have network availability. For more information, see Recipe 29.5, "Disconnect and Reconnect PowerShell Sessions".

Using these techniques, you can easily scale your automation across many, many machines. For more information about this technique, see Recipe 29.17, "Invoke a Command on Many Computers".

One of the primary challenges you will run into with fan-out remoting is shared by all of the Windows network technologies that work without explicit credentials: the *double-hop problem*. Once you've connected to a computer remotely, Windows gives you full access to all local resources as though you were logged into the computer directly. When it comes to *network* resources, however, Windows prevents your user information from being automatically used on another computer. This typically shows up when you try to access restricted network shares from a remoting system or intranet websites that require implicit authentication. For information about how to launch a remoting session that supports this type of credential forwarding, see Recipe 29.14, "Create Sessions with Full Network Access".

## See Also

Recipe 29.3, "Interactively Manage a Remote Computer"

Recipe 29.14, "Create Sessions with Full Network Access"

Recipe 29.17, "Invoke a Command on Many Computers"

# 29.5. Disconnect and Reconnect PowerShell Sessions

## Problem

You have an active PowerShell session and want to disconnect from it, or reconnect to it.

# Solution

If you have an active PowerShell session, use the `Disconnect-PSSession` cmdlet to disconnect from it. Use the `Connect-PSSession` to reconnect at a later time:

```
PS > $s = New-PSSession RemoteComputer -Name ConnectTest
PS > Invoke-Command $s { $saved = "Hello World" }
PS > Disconnect-PSSession $s

 Id Name           ComputerName    State         ConfigurationName
 -- ----           ------------    -----         -----------------
  7 ConnectTest    RemoteComputer  Disconnected  Microsoft.PowerShell

## From potentially another shell or computer
PS > $s2 = Get-PSSession -ComputerName RemoteComputer -Name ConnectTest
PS > Connect-PSSession $s2

 Id Name           ComputerName    State         ConfigurationName
 -- ----           ------------    -----         -----------------
  7 ConnectTest    RemoteComputer  Disconnected  Microsoft.PowerShell

PS > Invoke-Command $s2 { $saved }
Hello World
```

# Discussion

In PowerShell version 2, one problem with PowerShell Remoting was that closing your local shell automatically closed any remote shells you had connected to. If your remote shell had valuable information in it or was running jobs, this information was lost.

To resolve this issue, PowerShell version 3 introduces the `Disconnect-PSSession` and `Connect-PSSession` cmdlets. These let you disconnect and connect to remote sessions, respectively.

> If you are experimenting with this on a Windows 8 machine and use your Microsoft ID to log in, you will have to use the *local* account name when reconnecting to your session. For example:
>
> ```
> ## Logged in as example@live.com, computer name is "MyComputer"
> $s = New-PSSession -Credential MyComputer\example
> Disconnect-PSSession $s
>
> ## Later
> Connect-PSSession -Computername MyComputer
>     -Credential MyComputer\example
> ```

When you want to discover disconnected sessions on a remote computer, use the `-ComputerName` parameter of the `Get-PSSession` cmdlet to retrieve them.

In addition to disconnecting specific sessions, you can invoke a long-running command on a computer and immediately disconnect from it. For this purpose, the Invoke-Command cmdlet offers the -InDisconnectedSession parameter:

```
PS > Invoke-Command RemoteComputer {
    1..10 | % { Start-Sleep -Seconds 10; $_ } } -InDisconnectedSession

 Id Name            ComputerName    State          ConfigurationName
 -- ----            ------------    -----          -----------------
  3 Session2        RemoteComputer  Disconnected   Microsoft.PowerShell

PS > $s = Get-PSSession -Computername RemoteComputer -Name Session2

PS > Connect-PSSession $s

 Id Name            ComputerName    State          ConfigurationName
 -- ----            ------------    -----          -----------------
  3 Session2        RemoteComputer  Opened         Microsoft.PowerShell

PS > Receive-PSSession $s
1
2
3
(...)
```

When you use the -InDisconnectedSession parameter, the command you run is likely to generate output. If it generates more than a megabyte of output while disconnected, PowerShell pauses your command until you connect and call the Receive-PSSession command to retrieve it. When calculating this megabyte of output, PowerShell considers only output that would normally have been sent directly to the connected client—output that you would typically see on your screen. Output stored in variables does not count toward this limit, nor does output that you redirect to files.

If you'd like PowerShell to keep running your command no matter how much output it generates, you can use the OutputBufferingMode property of the -SessionOption parameter:

```
Invoke-Command RemoteComputer {
    ... commands ...
} -InDisconnectedSession -SessionOption @{ OutputBufferingMode = "Drop" }
```

When you specify Drop as the OutputBufferingMode, PowerShell retains only the last megabyte of output.

## See Also

Recipe 29.3, "Interactively Manage a Remote Computer"

Recipe 29.4, "Invoke a Command on a Remote Computer"

# 29.6. Program: Remotely Enable PowerShell Remoting

Although not required for Windows Server 2012, you may sometimes need to remotely enable PowerShell Remoting. As mentioned in Recipe 29.2, "Enable PowerShell Remoting on a Computer", the Enable-PSRemoting cmdlet uses a local network connection to create and configure its WS-Management endpoint.

Windows places many restrictions on remote commands that attempt to invoke other remote commands—also known as the *double-hop problem*. If you attempt to call Enable-PSRemoting from a remote system on a system with PowerShell version 2, your account privileges are disabled during the WSMan configuration's second hop.

Scheduled tasks offer one way to solve this problem, as they let you create a task with the full credentials required to interact with network resources. Unfortunately, most machines are not configured to support remote task management. Most are, however, configured to support WMI connections. As a bootstrapping step, we can use the Create() method of the Win32_Process class to launch an instance of PowerShell, and then provide PowerShell with a script to create, launch, and delete a scheduled task that ultimately configures PowerShell Remoting.

The script shown in Example 29-1 automates this cumbersome process.

*Example 29-1. Enable-RemotePSRemoting.ps1*

```
#############################################################################
##
## Enable-RemotePsRemoting
##
## From Windows PowerShell Cookbook (O'Reilly)
## by Lee Holmes (http://www.leeholmes.com/guide)
##
#############################################################################

<#

.SYNOPSIS

Enables PowerShell Remoting on a remote computer. Requires that the machine
responds to WMI requests, and that its operating system is Windows Vista or
later.

.EXAMPLE

PS > Enable-RemotePsRemoting <Computer>

#>

param(
    ## The computer on which to enable remoting
    $Computername,
```

```
        ## The credential to use when connecting
        $Credential = (Get-Credential)
)

Set-StrictMode -Version 3

$VerbosePreference = "Continue"

$credential = Get-Credential $credential
$username = $credential.Username
$password = $credential.GetNetworkCredential().Password

$script = @"

`$log = Join-Path `$env:TEMP Enable-RemotePsRemoting.output.txt
Remove-Item -Force `$log -ErrorAction SilentlyContinue
Start-Transcript -Path `$log

## Create a task that will run with full network privileges.
## In this task, we call Enable-PsRemoting
schtasks /CREATE /TN 'Enable Remoting' /SC WEEKLY /RL HIGHEST ``
    /RU $username /RP $password ``
    /TR "powershell -noprofile -command Enable-PsRemoting -Force" /F |
    Out-String
schtasks /RUN /TN 'Enable Remoting' | Out-String

`$securePass = ConvertTo-SecureString $password -AsPlainText -Force
`$credential =
    New-Object Management.Automation.PsCredential $username,`$securepass

## Wait for the remoting changes to come into effect
for(`$count = 1; `$count -le 10; `$count++)
{
    `$output = Invoke-Command localhost { 1 } -Cred `$credential ``
        -ErrorAction SilentlyContinue
    if(`$output -eq 1) { break; }

    "Attempt `$count : Not ready yet."
    Sleep 5
}

## Delete the temporary task
schtasks /DELETE /TN 'Enable Remoting' /F | Out-String
Stop-Transcript

"@

$commandBytes = [System.Text.Encoding]::Unicode.GetBytes($script)
$encoded = [Convert]::ToBase64String($commandBytes)

Write-Verbose "Configuring $computername"
```

```
$command = "powershell -NoProfile -EncodedCommand $encoded"
$null = Invoke-WmiMethod -Computer $computername -Credential $credential `
    Win32_Process Create -Args $command

Write-Verbose "Testing connection"
Invoke-Command $computername {
    Get-WmiObject Win32_ComputerSystem } -Credential $credential
```

For more information about running scripts, see Recipe 1.1, "Run Programs, Scripts, and Existing Tools".

## See Also

Recipe 1.1, "Run Programs, Scripts, and Existing Tools"

Recipe 28.1, "Access Windows Management Instrumentation and CIM Data"

Recipe 29.2, "Enable PowerShell Remoting on a Computer"

# 29.7. Program: Invoke a PowerShell Expression on a Remote Machine

PowerShell version 2 includes fantastic support for command execution on remote machines through its PowerShell Remoting features. These require only that the remote system have PowerShell available and have Remoting enabled.

If PowerShell Remoting is not available on a remote machine, many commands support their own remoting over WMI or DCOM. These do not require PowerShell Remoting to be configured on the remote system, but do require the specific protocol (WMI or DCOM) to be enabled.

If none of these prerequisites is possible, Example 29-3 offers an alternative. It uses PsExec (*http://technet.microsoft.com/en-us/sysinternals/bb897553*) to support the actual remote command execution.

This script offers more power than just remote command execution, however. As Example 29-2 demonstrates, it leverages PowerShell's capability to import and export strongly structured data, so you can work with the command output using many of the same techniques you use to work with command output on the local system. It demonstrates this power by filtering command output on the remote system but sorting it on the local system.

*Example 29-2. Invoking a PowerShell expression on a remote machine*

```
PS > $command = { Get-Process | Where-Object { $_.Handles -gt 1000 } }
PS > Invoke-RemoteExpression \\LEE-DESK $command | Sort Handles
```

```
Handles  NPM(K)   PM(K)   WS(K)  VM(M)  CPU(s)     Id ProcessName
-------  ------   -----   -----  -----  ------     -- -----------
   1025       8    3780    3772     32  134.42    848 csrss
   1306      37   50364   64160    322  409.23   4012 OUTLOOK
   1813      39   54764   36360    321  340.45   1452 iTunes
   2316     273   29168   41164    218  134.09   1244 svchost
```

Since this strongly structured data comes from objects on another system, PowerShell does not regenerate the functionality of those objects (except in rare cases). For more information about importing and exporting structured data, see Recipe 10.5, "Easily Import and Export Your Structured Data".

*Example 29-3. Invoke-RemoteExpression.ps1*

```
##############################################################################
##
## Invoke-RemoteExpression
##
## From Windows PowerShell Cookbook (O'Reilly)
## by Lee Holmes (http://www.leeholmes.com/guide)
##
##############################################################################

<#

.SYNOPSIS

Invoke a PowerShell expression on a remote machine. Requires PsExec from
http://live.sysinternals.com/tools/psexec.exe. If the remote machine
supports PowerShell version 2, use PowerShell Remoting instead.

.EXAMPLE

PS > Invoke-RemoteExpression LEE-DESK { Get-Process }
Retrieves the output of a simple command from a remote machine

.EXAMPLE

PS > (Invoke-RemoteExpression LEE-DESK { Get-Date }).AddDays(1)
Invokes a command on a remote machine. Since the command returns one of
PowerShell's primitive types (a DateTime object,) you can manipulate
its output as an object afterward.

.EXAMPLE

PS > Invoke-RemoteExpression LEE-DESK { Get-Process } | Sort Handles
Invokes a command on a remote machine. The command does not return one of
PowerShell's primitive types, but you can still use PowerShell's filtering
cmdlets to work with its structured output.

#>
```

```
param(
    ## The computer on which to invoke the command.
    $ComputerName = "$ENV:ComputerName",

    ## The script block to invoke on the remote machine.
    [Parameter(Mandatory = $true)]
    [ScriptBlock] $ScriptBlock,

    ## The username/password to use in the connection
    $Credential,

    ## Determines if PowerShell should load the user's PowerShell profile
    ## when invoking the command.
    [switch] $NoProfile
)

Set-StrictMode -Version 3

## Prepare the computername for PSExec
if($ComputerName -notmatch '^\\')
{
    $ComputerName = "\\$ComputerName"
}

## Prepare the command line for PsExec. We use the XML output encoding so
## that PowerShell can convert the output back into structured objects.
## PowerShell expects that you pass it some input when being run by PsExec
## this way, so the 'echo .' statement satisfies that appetite.
$commandLine = "echo . | powershell -Output XML "

if($noProfile)
{
    $commandLine += "-NoProfile "
}

## Convert the command into an encoded command for PowerShell
$commandBytes = [System.Text.Encoding]::Unicode.GetBytes($scriptblock)
$encodedCommand = [Convert]::ToBase64String($commandBytes)
$commandLine += "-EncodedCommand $encodedCommand"

## Collect the output and error output
$errorOutput = [IO.Path]::GetTempFileName()

if($Credential)
{
    ## This lets users pass either a username, or full credential to our
    ## credential parameter
    $credential = Get-Credential $credential
    $networkCredential = $credential.GetNetworkCredential()
    $username = $networkCredential.Username
    $password = $networkCredential.Password
```

```
    $output = psexec $computername /user $username /password $password `
        /accepteula cmd /c $commandLine 2>$errorOutput
}
else
{
    $output = psexec /acceptEula $computername cmd /c $commandLine 2>$errorOutput
}

## Check for any errors
$errorContent = Get-Content $errorOutput
Remove-Item $errorOutput

if($lastExitCode -ne 0)
{
    $OFS = "`n"
    $errorMessage = "Could not execute remote expression. "
    $errorMessage += "Ensure that your account has administrative " +
        "privileges on the target machine.`n"
    $errorMessage += ($errorContent -match "psexec.exe :")

    Write-Error $errorMessage
}

## Return the output to the user
$output
```

For more information about running scripts, see Recipe 1.1, "Run Programs, Scripts, and Existing Tools".

## See Also

Recipe 1.1, "Run Programs, Scripts, and Existing Tools"

Recipe 10.5, "Easily Import and Export Your Structured Data"

Recipe 29.1, "Find Commands That Support Their Own Remoting"

# 29.8. Test Connectivity Between Two Computers

## Problem

You want to determine the network availability of a computer or between two computers.

## Solution

Use the Test-Connection cmdlet to perform a traditional network ping:

```
PS > Test-Connection leeholmes.com
```

```
Source      Destination      IPV4Address      IPV6Address
------      -----------      -----------      -----------
LEE-DESK    leeholmes.com    66.186.25.131    {}
LEE-DESK    leeholmes.com    66.186.25.131    {}
LEE-DESK    leeholmes.com    66.186.25.131    {}
LEE-DESK    leeholmes.com    66.186.25.131    {}
```

Alternatively, the *ping.exe* utility continues to work:

```
PS > ping leeholmes.com

Pinging leeholmes.com [66.186.25.131] with 32 bytes of data:
Reply from 66.186.25.131: bytes=32 time=38ms TTL=115
Reply from 66.186.25.131: bytes=32 time=36ms TTL=115
Reply from 66.186.25.131: bytes=32 time=37ms TTL=115
Reply from 66.186.25.131: bytes=32 time=41ms TTL=115

Ping statistics for 66.186.25.131:
    Packets: Sent = 4, Received = 4, Lost = 0 (0% loss),
Approximate round trip times in milli-seconds:
    Minimum = 36ms, Maximum = 41ms, Average = 38ms
```

## Discussion

As a command-line shell, PowerShell of course continues to support traditional command-line utilities. *ping.exe* is one of the most common network diagnostic tools, and it works as expected from PowerShell.

The Test-Connection cmdlet offers the same features as *ping.exe* plus a great deal of additional functionality. Most ping utilities let you verify the connection between the current computer and a target computer, but the Test-Connection cmdlet lets you also specify the *source computer* for the network test.

Perhaps the most obvious benefit of the Test-Connection cmdlet is its object-based output—making filtering, sorting, and analysis immensely easier. For example, a simple script to monitor the average response time of a cluster of domains:

```
$topTen = "google.com","facebook.com","youtube.com","yahoo.com",
    "live.com","wikipedia.org","blogger.com","baidu.com","msn.com",
    "qq.com"

## Test all of the connections, grouping by address
$results = Test-Connection $topTen -ErrorAction SilentlyContinue | Group Address

## Go through each of the addresses
$averages = foreach($group in $results)
{
    ## Figure out the average response time
    $averageResponse = $group.Group |
        Measure-Object -Average ResponseTime | Select -Expand Average
```

```
## Create a new custom object to output the Address and ResponseTime
[PSCustomObject] @{
    Address = $group.Name;
    ResponseTime = $averageResponse
}
}

## Output the results
$averages | Sort ResponseTime | Select Address,ResponseTime
```

That script gives the following output:

```
Address         ResponseTime
-------         ------------
google.com                22
blogger.com             22.5
facebook.com           35.25
yahoo.com               37.5
youtube.com            86.25
wikipedia.org             99
baidu.com             203.25
qq.com                259.25
```

One thing to notice about this script's output is that not all of the top 10 websites are present. A ping request is a simple network-based handshake, but many websites block them to conserve network bandwidth or for perceived security hardening. When the Test-Connection cmdlet fails to make a connection, it generates the following error message:

```
Test-Connection : Testing connection to computer 'bing.com' failed: Error
due to lack of resources
```

To verify connectivity to these resources, you can use the -Test parameter of the Send-TcpRequest script given in Recipe 12.12, "Program: Interact with Internet Protocols":

```
PS > Send-TcpRequest bing.com -Test
True
PS > Send-TcpRequest bing.com -Test -Port 443
True
PS > Send-TcpRequest bing.com -Test -Port 23
False
```

For an effective use of the Test-Connection cmdlet to verify network resources before trying to manage them, see Recipe 29.9, "Limit Networking Scripts to Hosts That Respond".

## See Also

Recipe 12.12, "Program: Interact with Internet Protocols"

Recipe 29.9, "Limit Networking Scripts to Hosts That Respond"

# 29.9. Limit Networking Scripts to Hosts That Respond

## Problem

You have a distributed network management task, and want to avoid the delays caused by hosts that are offline or not responding.

## Solution

Use the `-Quiet` parameter of the `Test-Connection` to filter your computer set to only hosts that respond to a network ping:

```
$computers = "MISSING",$env:ComputerName,"DOWN","localhost"
$skipped = @()

foreach($computer in $computers)
{
    ## If the computer is not responding, record that we skipped it and
    ## continue. We can review this collection after the script completes.
    if(-not (Test-Connection -Quiet $computer -Count 1))
    {
        $skipped += $computer
    }

    ## Perform some batch of networked operations
    Get-CimInstance -Computer $computer Win32_OperatingSystem
}
```

## Discussion

One difficulty when writing scripts that manage a large collection of computers is that a handful of them are usually off or nonresponsive. If you don't address this situation, you are likely to run into many errors and delays as your script attempts to repeatedly manage a system that cannot be reached.

In most domains, a network ping is the most reliable way to determine the responsiveness of a computer. The `Test-Connection` cmdlet provides ping support in PowerShell, so the Solution builds on that.

For more information about the `Test-Connection` cmdlet, see Recipe 29.8, "Test Connectivity Between Two Computers".

## See Also

Recipe 29.8, "Test Connectivity Between Two Computers"

# 29.10. Enable Remote Desktop on a Computer

## Problem

You want to enable Remote Desktop on a computer.

## Solution

Set the fDenyTSConnections property of the Remote Desktop registry key to 0:

```
$regKey = "HKLM:\SYSTEM\CurrentControlSet\Control\Terminal Server"
Set-ItemProperty $regKey fDenyTSConnections 0
```

## Discussion

Remote Desktop is the de facto interactive management protocol, but can be difficult to enable automatically. Fortunately, its configuration settings come from the Windows Registry, so you can use PowerShell's registry provider to enable it.

To disable Remote Desktop, set the fDenyTSConnections property to 1.

To enable Remote Desktop on a remote computer, use PowerShell Remoting to change the registry properties, or remotely manage the registry settings directly. To see how to manage remote registry settings directly, see Recipe 21.12, "Work with the Registry of a Remote Computer".

## See Also

Recipe 21.12, "Work with the Registry of a Remote Computer"

# 29.11. Configure User Permissions for Remoting

## Problem

You want to control the users who are allowed to make remote connections to a machine.

## Solution

In PowerShell version 3, simply add users to the built-in Remote Management Users group:

```
PS > net localgroup "Remote Management Users" /add DOMAIN\User
The command completed successfully.
```

On machines based on PowerShell version 2, create a new Windows group to define which users can connect to the machine, and then use the Set-PSSession Configuration cmdlet to add this group to the permission list of the endpoint:

```
PS > net localgroup "PowerShell Remoting Users" /Add
The command completed successfully.

PS > net localgroup "PowerShell Remoting Users" Administrators /Add
The command completed successfully.

PS > Set-PSSessionConfiguration Microsoft.PowerShell -ShowSecurityDescriptorUI
```

## Discussion

Like many objects in Windows, the WS-Management endpoint that provides access to PowerShell Remoting has an associated access control list. In PowerShell version 3 by default, this access control list provides access to Administrators of the machine as well as the built-in Remote Management Users group.

In PowerShell version 2, the default access control list provides access only to Administrators of the machine. As you use PowerShell Remoting more often, you'll likely want more fine-grained control than that—similar to the type of control that you get from the existing Remote Desktop Users group. Enabling this control is a two-step process: first, create the group, and then add the group to the access control list of the endpoint.

For a one-off configuration, the -ShowSecurityDescriptorUI parameter of the Set-PSSessionConfiguration cmdlet lets you manage the access control list as you would manage a file, directory, or computer share.

To automate this process, though, you need to speak the language of security rules directly—a language called *SDDL*: the Security Descriptor Definition Language. This format is not really designed to be consumed by humans, but it is the format exposed by the -SecurityDescriptorSddl parameter of the Set-PSSessionConfiguration cmdlet. Although it is not user-friendly, you can use several classes from the .NET Framework to create a security rule or SDDL string. Example 29-4 demonstrates this approach.

*Example 29-4. Automating security configuration of PowerShell Remoting*

```
## Get the SID for the "PowerShell Remoting Users" group
$account = New-Object Security.Principal.NTAccount "PowerShell Remoting Users"
$sid = $account.Translate([Security.Principal.SecurityIdentifier]).Value

## Get the security descriptor for the existing configuration
$config = Get-PSSessionConfiguration Microsoft.PowerShell
$existingSddl = $config.SecurityDescriptorSddl

## Create a CommonSecurityDescriptor object out of the existing SDDL
## so that we don't need to manage the string by hand
```

```
$arguments = $false,$false,$existingSddl
$mapper = New-Object Security.AccessControl.CommonSecurityDescriptor $arguments

## Create a new access rule that adds the "PowerShell Remoting Users" group
$mapper.DiscretionaryAcl.AddAccess("Allow",$sid,268435456,"None","None")

## Get the new SDDL for that configuration
$newSddl = $mapper.GetSddlForm("All")

## Update the endpoint configuration
Set-PSSessionConfiguration Microsoft.PowerShell -SecurityDescriptorSddl $newSddl
```

For more information about working with the .NET Framework, see Recipe 3.8, "Work with .NET Objects". For more information about working with SDDL strings, see Recipe 18.16, "Manage Security Descriptors in SDDL Form".

### See Also

Recipe 3.8, "Work with .NET Objects"

Recipe 18.16, "Manage Security Descriptors in SDDL Form"

# 29.12. Enable Remoting to Workgroup Computers

## Problem

You want to connect to a machine in a workgroup or by IP address.

## Solution

Update the TrustedHosts collection on the *wsman:\localhost\client* path:

```
PS > $trustedHosts = Get-Item wsman:\localhost\client\TrustedHosts
PS > $trustedHosts.Value += ",RemoteComputer"
PS > Set-Item wsman:\localhost\client\TrustedHosts $trustedHosts.Value

WinRM Security Configuration.
This command modifies the TrustedHosts list for the WinRM client. The
computers in the TrustedHosts list might not be authenticated. The client
might send credential information to these computers. Are you sure that
you want to modify this list?
[Y] Yes  [N] No  [S] Suspend  [?] Help (default is "Y"): Y

PS > Get-Item wsman:\localhost\client\TrustedHosts


   WSManConfig: Microsoft.WSMan.Management\WSMan::localhost\Client
```

```
Name                     Value
----                     -----
TrustedHosts             Lee-Desk,RemoteComputer
```

## Discussion

One of the main aspects of client-side security in any remoting technology is being able to trust who you are connecting to. When you are at an Internet café, you can connect to your bank's website in a browser. If you use SSL, you are guaranteed that it's really your bank and not some fake proxy put up by an attacker who's manipulating the network traffic. This class of interception attack is called a *man-in-the-middle attack*.

PowerShell Remoting gives the same guarantee. When you connect to a computer inside of a domain, Kerberos authentication secures the connection. Kerberos authentication guarantees the identity of the endpoint—ensuring that no attacker can intercept your connection. When you're outside of a domain, SSL is the only standard way to guarantee this, which is why https is such an important protocol on the Internet.

There are two situations where built-in authentication mechanisms can't protect against man-in-the-middle attacks:

- Connecting to a host by IP (inside a domain or not)
- Using any authentication mechanism except for Kerberos, SSL, or CredSSP

Workgroup remoting (or cross-forest remoting) is an example of this. When you try to make a connection in either of these scenarios, PowerShell gives the error message:

```
PS > Enter-PSSession SomeComputer

Enter-PSSession : Connecting to remote server failed with the following
error message : The WinRM client cannot process the request. If the
authentication scheme is different from Kerberos, or if the client computer
is not joined to a domain, then HTTPS transport must be used or the destination
machine must be added to the TrustedHosts configuration setting. Use
winrm.cmd to configure TrustedHosts. Note that computers in the TrustedHosts
list might not be authenticated. You can get more information about that by
running the following command: winrm help config. For more information,
see the about_Remote_Troubleshooting Help topic.
```

While wordy, this error message exactly explains the problem.

Since PowerShell can't guarantee the identity of the remote computer in this situation, it fails safe and generates an error. All remoting protocols run into this problem:

- Remote Desktop: "…cannot verify the identity of the computer you want to connect to…"

- SSH: "The authenticity of the host…can't be established…"

The other protocols implement the equivalent of "I acknowledge this and want to continue," but PowerShell's experience is unfortunately more complex.

If you want to connect to a machine that PowerShell can't verify, you can update the `TrustedHosts` configuration setting. Its name is unfortunately vague, however, as it really means, "I trust my network during connections to this machine."

When you configure the `TrustedHosts` setting, you have three options: an explicit list (as shown in the Solution), `<local>` to bypass this message for all computers in the domain or workgroup, or `*` to disable the message altogether.

For more information, type **Get-Help about_Remote_Troubleshooting**.

# 29.13. Implicitly Invoke Commands from a Remote Computer

## Problem

You have commands on a remote computer that you want to invoke as though they were local.

## Solution

Use the `Import-PSSession` cmdlet to import them into the current session:

```
PS > $cred = Get-Credential

PS > $session = New-PSSession -ConfigurationName Microsoft.Exchange `
    -ConnectionUri https://ps.outlook.com/powershell/ -Credential $cred `
    -Authentication Basic -AllowRedirection


PS > Invoke-Command $session { Get-OrganizationalUnit } |
    Select DistinguishedName

DistinguishedName
-----------------
OU=leeholmes.com,OU=Microsoft Exchange Hosted Organizations,DC=prod,DC=...
OU=Hosted Organization Security Groups,OU=leeholmes.com,OU=Microsoft Ex...


PS > Import-PSSession $session -CommandName Get-OrganizationalUnit

ModuleType Name                        ExportedCommands
---------- ----                        ----------------
Script     tmp_1e510382-9a3d-43a5... Get-OrganizationalUnit
```

```
PS > Get-OrganizationalUnit | Select DistinguishedName

DistinguishedName
-----------------
OU=leeholmes.com,OU=Microsoft Exchange Hosted Organizations,DC=prod,DC=...
OU=Hosted Organization Security Groups,OU=leeholmes.com,OU=Microsoft Ex...
```

## Discussion

When you frequently work with commands from a remote system, the mental and conceptual overhead of continually calling the Invoke-Command and going through PowerShell's remoting infrastructure quickly adds up. When you write a script that primarily uses commands from the remote system, the majority of the script ends up being for the remoting infrastructure itself. When pipelining commands to one another, this gets even more obvious:

```
PS > Invoke-Command $session { Get-User } |
    Where-Object { $_.Identity -eq "lee@leeholmes.com" } |
    Invoke-Command $session { Get-Mailbox } |
    Select Identity,OriginatingServer,ExchangeVersion,DistinguishedName


Identity          OriginatingServer  ExchangeVersion  DistinguishedName
--------          -----------------  ---------------  -----------------
lee@leeholmes.com BL2PRD0103DC006... 0.10 (14.0.100.0) CN=lee@leeholm...
```

To address these issues, PowerShell Remoting supports the Import-PSSession cmdlet to let you import and seamlessly use commands from a remote session. This is especially helpful, for example, in scenarios such as Hosted Exchange. It's not reasonable to install an entire toolkit of commands just to manage your mailboxes in the cloud.

Once you've imported those commands, PowerShell enables *implicit remoting* on them:

```
PS > Import-PSSession $session -CommandName Get-Mailbox,GetUser

PS > Get-User | Where-Object { $_.Identity -eq "lee@leeholmes.com" } |
    Get-MailBox |
    Select Identity,OriginatingServer,ExchangeVersion,DistinguishedName


Identity          OriginatingServer  ExchangeVersion  DistinguishedName
--------          -----------------  ---------------  -----------------
lee@leeholmes.com BL2PRD0103DC006... 0.10 (14.0.100.0) CN=lee@leeholm...


PS > Get-Help Get-User -Examples

NAME
    Get-User
```

```
SYNOPSIS
    Use the Get-User cmdlet to retrieve all users in the forest that match
    the specified conditions.

    ------------------------- EXAMPLE 1 -------------------------
    This example retrieves information about users in the Marketing OU.

    Get-User -OrganizationalUnit "Marketing"
(...)
```

Expanding on this further, PowerShell even lets you export commands from a session into a module:

```
PS > $commands = "Get-Mailbox","Get-User"
PS > Export-PSSession $session -CommandName $commands -Module ExchangeCommands


    Directory: E:\Lee\WindowsPowerShell\Modules\ExchangeCommands


Mode                LastWriteTime     Length Name
----                -------------     ------ ----
-a---        2/19/2010   11:11 PM      13177 ExchangeCommands.psm1
-a---        2/19/2010   11:11 PM         99 ExchangeCommands.format.ps1xml
-a---        2/19/2010   11:11 PM        605 ExchangeCommands.psd1
```

When you import the module, PowerShell creates new implicit remoting commands for all commands that you exported. When you invoke a command, it recreates the remoting session (if required), and then invokes your command in that new session:

```
Windows PowerShell
Copyright (C) 2009 Microsoft Corporation. All rights reserved.

PS > Import-Module ExchangeCommands
PS > Get-User | Where-Object { $_.Identity -eq "lee@leeholmes.com" } |
    Get-MailBox |
    Select Identity,OriginatingServer,ExchangeVersion,DistinguishedName

Creating a new session for implicit remoting of "Get-User" command...

Identity            OriginatingServer ExchangeVersion  DistinguishedName
--------            ----------------- ---------------  -----------------
lee@leeholmes.com   BL2PRD0103DC006... 0.10 (14.0.100.0)  CN=lee@leeholm...
```

For more information about command-based remoting, see Recipe 29.4, "Invoke a Command on a Remote Computer". For more information about PowerShell modules, see Recipe 1.29, "Extend Your Shell with Additional Commands".

## See Also

Recipe 1.29, "Extend Your Shell with Additional Commands"

Recipe 29.4, "Invoke a Command on a Remote Computer"

# 29.14. Create Sessions with Full Network Access

## Problem

You want to create a PowerShell Remoting session (interactive, fan-out, or implicit) that has full access to network resources.

## Solution

Use the `-Authentication` parameter, and pick `CredSSP` as the authentication mechanism:

```
PS > Invoke-Command leeholmes1c23 {
    "Hello World"; dir \\lee-desk\c$ } -Authentication CredSSP -Cred Lee

Hello World

    Directory: \\lee-desk\c$

Mode                LastWriteTime     Length Name            PSComputerName
----                -------------     ------ ----            --------------
d----         2/5/2010  12:31 AM             inetpub         leeholmes1c23
d----        7/13/2009   7:37 PM             PerfLogs        leeholmes1c23
d-r--        2/16/2010   3:14 PM             Program Files   leeholmes1c23
(...)
```

## Discussion

When connecting to a computer using PowerShell Remoting, you might sometimes see errors running commands that access a network location:

```
PS > Invoke-Command leeholmes1c23 {
    "Hello World"; dir \\lee-desk\c$ } -Cred Lee

Hello World
Cannot find path '\\lee-desk\c$' because it does not exist.
    + CategoryInfo          : ObjectNotFound: (\\lee-desk\c$:String)
   [Get-ChildItem], ItemNotFoundException
    + FullyQualifiedErrorId : PathNotFound,Microsoft.PowerShell.Commands.
   GetChildItemCommand
```

When you remotely connect to a computer in a domain, Windows (and PowerShell Remoting) by default use an authentication mechanism called *Kerberos*. While you have full access to local resources when connected this way, security features of Kerberos prevent the remote computer from being able to use your account information to connect to additional computers.

This reduces the risk of connecting to a remote computer that has been compromised or otherwise has malicious software running on it. Without these protections, the malicious software can act on your behalf across the entire network—an especially dangerous situation if you are connecting with powerful domain credentials.

Although this Kerberos policy can be managed at the domain level by marking the computer "Trusted for Delegation," changing domain-level policies to accomplish ad hoc management tasks is a cumbersome process.

To solve this problem, PowerShell supports another authentication mechanism called *CredSSP*—the same authentication mechanism used by Remote Desktop and Terminal Services. Because of its security impact, you must explicitly enable support on both the client you are connecting from and the server you are connecting to.

 If you are making a connection back to the local computer rather than another computer on the network, you can instead use the -EnableNetworkAccess parameter of the remoting cmdlets to enable network access.

From the client side, specify -Role Client to the Enable-WsManCredSSP cmdlet. You can specify either specific computer names in the -DelegateComputer parameter or * to enable the setting for all target computers.

```
PS > Enable-WSManCredSSP -Role Client -DelegateComputer leeholmes1c23

CredSSP Authentication Configuration for WS-Management
CredSSP authentication allows the user credentials on this computer to be
sent to a remote computer. If you use CredSSP authentication for a
connection to a malicious or compromised computer, that computer will have
access to your username and password. For more information, see the
Enable-WSManCredSSP Help topic.
Do you want to enable CredSSP authentication?
[Y] Yes  [N] No  [S] Suspend  [?] Help (default is "Y"): Y
```

If you want to use CredSSP authentication within a workgroup (instead of a domain), one additional step is required. Authentication within a workgroup uses a protocol called *NTLM*, which doesn't offer the same security guarantees that Kerberos does—specifically, you can't guarantee the identity of the computer you are connecting to. This is the same caution that drives the TrustedHosts configuration requirement, as discussed in Recipe 29.12, "Enable Remoting to Workgroup Computers". To enable CredSSP over

NTLM connections, open *gpedit.msc*, and then navigate to Computer Configuration → Administrative Templates → System → Credentials Delegation. Enable the "Allow Delegating Fresh Credentials with NTLM-only Server Authentication" setting, and then add wsman/*computername* to the list of supported computers. In the previous example, this would be wsman/leeholmes1c23. As with the -DelegateComputer parameter, you can also specify wsman/* to enable the setting for all target computers.

From the server side, specify -Role Server to the Enable-WsManCredSSP cmdlet. You can invoke this cmdlet remotely, if needed:

```
PS > Enable-WsManCredSSP -Role Server

CredSSP Authentication Configuration for WS-Management
CredSSP authentication allows the server to accept user credentials from a
remote computer. If you enable CredSSP authentication on the server, the
server will have access to the username and password of the client computer
if the client computer sends them. For more information, see the
Enable-WSManCredSSP Help topic.
Do you want to enable CredSSP authentication?
[Y] Yes  [N] No  [S] Suspend  [?] Help (default is "Y"):
```

In PowerShell version 3, remotely enabling CredSSP is just as easy:

```
PS > Invoke-Command -ComputerName leeholmes1c23 {
    Enable-WsManCredSSP -Role Server }

CredSSP Authentication Configuration for WS-Management
CredSSP authentication allows the user credentials on this computer to be
sent to a remote computer. If you use CredSSP authentication for a
connection to a malicious or compromised computer, that computer will have
access to your username and password. For more information, see the
Enable-WSManCredSSP Help topic.
Do you want to enable CredSSP authentication?
[Y] Yes  [N] No  [S] Suspend  [?] Help (default is "Y"): Y
```

Ironically, remotely configuring CredSSP in PowerShell version 2 runs into the very same issues that CredSSP is designed to solve. To work around these, we can create a scheduled task to run the Enable-WsManCredSSP cmdlet (Example 29-5), as done in Recipe 29.6, "Program: Remotely Enable PowerShell Remoting".

*Example 29-5. Enable-RemoteCredSSP.ps1*

```
##############################################################################
##
## Enable-RemoteCredSSP
##
## From Windows PowerShell Cookbook (O'Reilly)
## by Lee Holmes (http://www.leeholmes.com/guide)
##
##############################################################################

<#
```

```
    .SYNOPSIS

    Enables CredSSP support on a remote computer. Requires that the machine
    have PowerShell Remoting enabled, and that its operating system is Windows
    Vista or later.

    .EXAMPLE

    PS > Enable-RemoteCredSSP <Computer>

    #>

    param(
        ## The computer on which to enable CredSSP
        $Computername,

        ## The credential to use when connecting
        $Credential = (Get-Credential)
    )

    Set-StrictMode -Version 3

    ## Call Get-Credential again, so that the user can type something like
    ## Enable-RemoteCredSSP -Computer Computer -Cred DOMAIN\user
    $credential = Get-Credential $credential
    $username = $credential.Username
    $password = $credential.GetNetworkCredential().Password

    ## Define the script we will use to create the scheduled task
    $powerShellCommand =
        "powershell -noprofile -command Enable-WsManCredSSP -Role Server -Force"
    $script = @"
    schtasks /CREATE /TN 'Enable CredSSP' /SC WEEKLY /RL HIGHEST ``
        /RU $username /RP $password ``
        /TR "$powerShellCommand" /F

    schtasks /RUN /TN 'Enable CredSSP'
    "@

    ## Create the task on the remote system to configure CredSSP
    $command = [ScriptBlock]::Create($script)
    Invoke-Command $computername $command -Cred $credential

    ## Wait for the remoting changes to come into effect
    for($count = 1; $count -le 10; $count++)
    {
        $output =
            Invoke-Command $computername { 1 } -Auth CredSSP -Cred $credential
        if($output -eq 1) { break; }

        "Attempt $count : Not ready yet."
```

```
    Sleep 5
}

## Clean up
$command = [ScriptBlock]::Create($script)
Invoke-Command $computername {
    schtasks /DELETE /TN 'Enable CredSSP' /F } -Cred $credential

## Verify the output
Invoke-Command $computername {
    Get-WmiObject Win32_ComputerSystem } -Auth CredSSP -Cred $credential
```

After completing these configuration steps, your remote sessions will have unrestricted network access.

## See Also

Recipe 29.6, "Program: Remotely Enable PowerShell Remoting"

Recipe 29.12, "Enable Remoting to Workgroup Computers"

# 29.15. Pass Variables to Remote Sessions

## Problem

You want to invoke a command on a remote computer but supply some of its information as a dynamic argument.

## Solution

Add $USING to the variable name when using a variable from your computer within the context of a remoting session:

```
PS > $s = New-PSSession
PS > $myNumber = 10
PS > Invoke-Command $s { 2 * $myNumber }
0
PS > Invoke-Command $s { 2 * $USING:myNumber }
20
```

## Discussion

When processing commands on a remote system, you sometimes need dynamic information from the local system—such as the value of a variable or something that changes for each invocation.

The solution gives an example of this approach. When you supply $myNumber by itself, that refers to $myNumber within the context of the remote session that $s represents. If you add the $USING: prefix, PowerShell takes the value of that variable from your local session—the one that created and controls $s.

The $USING: prefix was added in PowerShell version 3, and works even when connecting to a machine that supports only PowerShell version 2. If you are managing *from* a machine with PowerShell version 2 installed, the solution is a little more complex. As another example, consider trying to supply a credential to a remote script. Hardcoding usernames or passwords is a practice you should strive to avoid.

Example 29-6 solves this problem in PowerShell version 2. On a client computer, we request a credential from the user. We make a connection to RemoteComputer using that credential and invoke a command. The command itself makes yet another connection—this time to leeholmes1c23. That final command simply retrieves the computer name of the remote system. Rather than hardcode a username and password (or request them again), it uses the $cred variable passed in by the original call to Invoke-Command.

Use the -ArgumentList parameter of the Invoke-Command cmdlet.

*Example 29-6. Passing a credential to a remote computer in PowerShell version 2*

```
PS > $cred = Get-Credential

PS > $command = {
    param($cred)

    Invoke-Command leeholmes1c23 {
        "Hello from $($env:Computername)" } -Credential $cred
}

PS > Invoke-Command RemoteComputer $command -ArgumentList $cred -Credential $cred
Hello from LEEHOLMES1C23
```

To support this, the Invoke-Command cmdlet offers the -ArgumentList parameter. Variables supplied to this parameter will be converted into a version safe for remoting, which will then be made available to the commands inside of the -ScriptBlock parameter.

 Arguments that you supply to the -ArgumentList parameter go through a serialization process before being sent to the remote computer. Although their properties closely resemble the original objects, they no longer have methods. For more information about PowerShell serialization, see Recipe 29.4, "Invoke a Command on a Remote Computer".

As with arguments in other scripts, functions, and script blocks, the script block used in Invoke-Command can access arguments directly through the $args array, or through a param( ) statement to make the script easier to read. Unlike most param( ) statements, however, these parameter statements must all be positional. Named arguments (e.g., -ArgumentList "-Cred","$cred") are not supported, nor are advanced parameter attributes (such as [Parameter(Mandatory = $true)]).

For more information about arguments and param( ) statements, see Recipe 11.11, "Access Arguments of a Script, Function, or Script Block".

## See Also

Recipe 11.11, "Access Arguments of a Script, Function, or Script Block"

Recipe 29.4, "Invoke a Command on a Remote Computer"

# 29.16. Configure Advanced Remoting Quotas and Options

## Problem

You want to configure compression, profiles, proxy authentication, certificate verification, or culture information for a remote session.

## Solution

For client-side configuration settings, call the New-PSSessionOption cmdlet and provide values for parameters that you want to customize:

```
PS > $options = New-PSSessionOption -Culture "fr-CA"
PS > $sess = New-PSSession Lee-Desk -Cred Lee -SessionOption $options
PS > Invoke-Command $sess { Get-Date | Out-String }

20 février 2010 17:40:16
```

For server-side configuration settings, review the options under *WSMan:\localhost\ Shell* and *WSMan:localhost\Service*:

```
Set-Item WSMan:\localhost\shell\MaxShellsPerUser 10
```

## Discussion

PowerShell lets you define advanced client connection options through two paths: the New-PSSessionOption cmdlet and the $PSSessionOption automatic variable.

When you call the New-PSSession cmdlet, PowerShell returns an object that holds configuration settings for a remote session. You can customize all of the values through the cmdlet's parameters or set properties on the object that is returned.

Several of the options refer to timeout values: `OperationTimeout`, `Open Timeout`, `CancelTimeout`, and `IdleTimeout`. These parameters are generally not required (for example, even when invoking a long-running command), but they can be used to overcome errors when you encounter extremely slow or congested network conditions.

If you want to configure session options for every new connection, a second alternative is the `$PSSessionOption` automatic variable:

```
PS > $PSSessionOption

MaximumConnectionRedirectionCount : 5
NoCompression                     : False
NoMachineProfile                  : False
ProxyAccessType                   : None
ProxyAuthentication               : Negotiate
ProxyCredential                   :
SkipCACheck                       : False
SkipCNCheck                       : False
SkipRevocationCheck               : False
OperationTimeout                  : 00:03:00
NoEncryption                      : False
UseUTF16                          : False
IncludePortInSPN                  : False
OutputBufferingMode               : None
Culture                           :
UICulture                         :
MaximumReceivedDataSizePerCommand :
MaximumReceivedObjectSize         : 209715200
ApplicationArguments              :
OpenTimeout                       : 00:03:00
CancelTimeout                     : 00:01:00
IdleTimeout                       : -00:00:00.0010000
```

If you don't provide explicit settings during a connection attempt, PowerShell Remoting looks at the values in this variable for its defaults.

From the server perspective, all configuration sits in the *WSMan* drive. The most common configuration options come from the *WSMan:\localhost\Shell* path. These settings let you configure how many shells can be open simultaneously per user, how much memory they can use, and more.

```
PS > dir WSMan:\localhost\Shell

WSManConfig: Microsoft.WSMan.Management\WSMan::localhost\Shell
```

| Type | Name | SourceOfValue | Value |
| --- | --- | --- | --- |
| System.String | AllowRemoteShellAccess | | true |
| System.String | IdleTimeout | | 7200000 |

```
System.String    MaxConcurrentUsers                    10
System.String    MaxShellRunTime                       2147483647
System.String    MaxProcessesPerShell                  25
System.String    MaxMemoryPerShellMB                    1024
System.String    MaxShellsPerUser                      30
```

In addition to server-wide settings, you can further restrict these settings through configuration of individual endpoint configurations (plug-ins). If you want to increase the default values, you have to increase the quotas both at the server-wide level, as well as for the endpoint (such as the default Microsoft.PowerShell or Microsoft.Power Shell.Workflow endpoints) that users will connect to.

```
PS WSMan:\localhost\Plugin\Restrictive\Quotas> Set-Item MaxShellsPerUser 1

WARNING: The updated configuration is effective only if it is less than or equal
to the value of global quota WSMan:\localhost\Shell\MaxShellsPerUser. Verify the
value for the global quota using the PowerShell cmdlet "Get-Item WSMan:\localhost
\Shell\MaxShellsPerUser".

WARNING: The configuration changes you made will only be effective after the
WinRM service is restarted.  To restart the WinRM service, run the following
command: 'Restart-Service winrm'

PS WSMan:\localhost\Plugin\Restrictive\Quotas> dir

WSManConfig: Microsoft.WSMan.Management\WSMan::...\Plugin\Restrictive\Quotas
```

| Type | Name | SourceOfValue | Value |
| --- | --- | --- | --- |
| System.String | IdleTimeoutms | | 7200000 |
| System.String | MaxConcurrentUsers | | 5 |
| System.String | MaxProcessesPerShell | | 15 |
| System.String | MaxMemoryPerShellMB | | 1024 |
| System.String | MaxShellsPerUser | | 1 |
| System.String | MaxConcurrentCommandsPerShell | | 1000 |
| System.String | MaxShells | | 25 |
| System.String | MaxIdleTimeoutms | | 43200000 |

## See Also

Recipe 29.4, "Invoke a Command on a Remote Computer"

# 29.17. Invoke a Command on Many Computers

## Problem

You want to manage many computers simultaneously.

## Solution

Use the -ThrottleLimit and -AsJob parameters to configure how PowerShell scales out your commands:

```
PS > $sessions = $(
    New-PSSession localhost;
    New-PSSession localhost;
    New-PSSession localhost)

PS > $start = Get-Date
PS > Invoke-Command $sessions { Start-Sleep 2; "Test $pid" }
Test 720
Test 6112
Test 4792
PS > (Get-Date) - $start | Select TotalSeconds | Format-Table -Auto

TotalSeconds
------------
    2.09375


PS >
PS > $start = Get-Date
PS > Invoke-Command $sessions { Start-Sleep 2; "Test $pid" } -ThrottleLimit 1
Test 6112
Test 4792
Test 720
PS > (Get-Date) - $start | Select TotalSeconds | Format-Table -Auto

TotalSeconds
------------
    6.25
```

## Discussion

One of the largest difficulties in traditional networking scripts comes from managing many computers at once. Remote computer management is typically network-bound, so most scripts spend the majority of their time waiting for the network.

The solution to this is to scale. Rather than manage one computer at a time, you manage several. Not too many, however, as few machines can handle the demands of connecting to hundreds or thousands of remote machines at once.

Despite the benefits, writing a networking script that supports smart automatic throttling is beyond the capability of many and too far down "the big list of things to do" of most. Fortunately, PowerShell Remoting's main focus is to solve these common problems, and throttling is no exception.

By default, PowerShell Remoting connects to 32 computers at a time. After running your command on the first 32 computers in your list, it waits for commands to complete before running your command on additional computers. As each command completes, PowerShell invokes the next one waiting.

To demonstrate this automatic scaling, the Solution shows the difference between calling Invoke-Command with the default throttle limit and calling it with a throttle limit of one computer.

When working against many computers at a time, you might want to continue using your shell while these long-running tasks process in the background. To support background processing of tasks, the Invoke-Command cmdlet offers -AsJob, which lets you run your command as a PowerShell Job.

For more information about PowerShell Jobs, see Recipe 1.5, "Invoke a Long-Running or Background Command".

## See Also

Recipe 1.5, "Invoke a Long-Running or Background Command"

Recipe 29.4, "Invoke a Command on a Remote Computer"

# 29.18. Run a Local Script on a Remote Computer

## Problem

You have a local script and want to run it on a remote computer.

## Solution

Use the -FilePath parameter of the Invoke-Command cmdlet:

```
PS > Get-Content .\Get-ProcessByName.ps1
param($name)

Get-Process -Name $name

PS > Invoke-Command -Computername Lee-Desk `
    -FilePath .\Get-ProcessByname.ps1 -ArgumentList PowerShell `
    -Cred Lee

Handles  NPM(K)   PM(K)    WS(K) VM(M)   CPU(s)    Id Process   PSComputer
                                                      Name       Name
-------  ------   -----    ----- -----   ------    -- --------- ----------
    628      17   39084    58908   214     4.26  7540 powers... lee-des...
```

## Discussion

For quick one-off actions, the `-ScriptBlock` parameter of the `Invoke-Command` cmdlet lets you easily invoke commands against a remote computer:

```
PS > Invoke-Command Lee-Desk { Get-Process -n PowerShell } -Cred Lee

Handles  NPM(K)    PM(K)      WS(K) VM(M)   CPU(s)     Id Process   PSComputer
                                                          Name      Name
-------  ------    -----      ----- -----   ------     -- ---------  ---------
    628      17    39084      58908   214     4.26   7540 powers... lee-des...
```

When these commands become more complicated, however, writing them all in a script block becomes cumbersome. You have no syntax highlighting, line numbering, or any of the other creature comforts offered by writing script-based execution.

To let you write scripts against a remote computer instead, PowerShell offers the `-FilePath` parameter on the `Invoke-Command` cmdlet. When you use this parameter, PowerShell reads the script from disk and invokes its contents on the remote computer.

In this mode, PowerShell makes no attempt to address dependencies during this process. If your script requires any other scripts, commands, or environmental dependencies, ensure that they are available on the remote computer.

For one option on how to transfer items to a remote computer, see Recipe 29.19, "Program: Transfer a File to a Remote Computer".

## See Also

Recipe 29.4, "Invoke a Command on a Remote Computer"

Recipe 29.19, "Program: Transfer a File to a Remote Computer"

# 29.19. Program: Transfer a File to a Remote Computer

When you're working with remote computers, a common problem you'll face is how to bring your local tools and environment to that computer. Using file shares or FTP transfers is a common way to share tools between systems, but these options are not always available.

As a solution, Example 29-7 builds on PowerShell Remoting to transfer the file content over a regular PowerShell Remoting connection.

To do this, it reads the content of the file into an array of bytes. Then, it breaks that array into one-megabyte chunks. It streams each chunk to the remote system, which then recombines the chunks into the destination file. By breaking the file into large chunks, the script optimizes the network efficiency of PowerShell Remoting. By limiting these chunks to one megabyte, it avoids running into any quota issues.

*Example 29-7. Send-File.ps1*

```
##############################################################################
##
## Send-File
##
## From Windows PowerShell Cookbook (O'Reilly)
## by Lee Holmes (http://www.leeholmes.com/guide)
##
##############################################################################

<#

.SYNOPSIS

Sends a file to a remote session.

.EXAMPLE

PS > $session = New-PsSession leeholmes1c23
PS > Send-File c:\temp\test.exe c:\temp\test.exe $session

#>

param(
    ## The path on the local computer
    [Parameter(Mandatory = $true)]
    $Source,

    ## The target path on the remote computer
    [Parameter(Mandatory = $true)]
    $Destination,

    ## The session that represents the remote computer
    [Parameter(Mandatory = $true)]
    [System.Management.Automation.Runspaces.PSSession] $Session
)

Set-StrictMode -Version 3

$remoteScript = {
    param($destination, $bytes)

    ## Convert the destination path to a full filesystem path (to support
    ## relative paths)
    $Destination = $executionContext.SessionState.`
        Path.GetUnresolvedProviderPathFromPSPath($Destination)

    ## Write the content to the new file
    $file = [IO.File]::Open($Destination, "OpenOrCreate")
    $null = $file.Seek(0, "End")
    $null = $file.Write($bytes, 0, $bytes.Length)
    $file.Close()
```

```
}

## Get the source file, and then start reading its content
$sourceFile = Get-Item $source

## Delete the previously-existing file if it exists
Invoke-Command -Session $session {
    if(Test-Path $args[0]) { Remove-Item $args[0] }
} -ArgumentList $Destination

## Now break it into chunks to stream
Write-Progress -Activity "Sending $Source" -Status "Preparing file"

$streamSize = 1MB
$position = 0
$rawBytes = New-Object byte[] $streamSize
$file = [IO.File]::OpenRead($sourceFile.FullName)

while(($read = $file.Read($rawBytes, 0, $streamSize)) -gt 0)
{
    Write-Progress -Activity "Writing $Destination" `
        -Status "Sending file" `
        -PercentComplete ($position / $sourceFile.Length * 100)

    ## Ensure that our array is the same size as what we read
    ## from disk
    if($read -ne $rawBytes.Length)
    {
        [Array]::Resize( [ref] $rawBytes, $read)
    }

    ## And send that array to the remote system
    Invoke-Command -Session $session $remoteScript `
        -ArgumentList $destination,$rawBytes

    ## Ensure that our array is the same size as what we read
    ## from disk
    if($rawBytes.Length -ne $streamSize)
    {
        [Array]::Resize( [ref] $rawBytes, $streamSize)
    }

    [GC]::Collect()
    $position += $read
}

$file.Close()

## Show the result
Invoke-Command -Session $session { Get-Item $args[0] } -ArgumentList $Destination
```

For more information about running scripts, see Recipe 1.1, "Run Programs, Scripts, and Existing Tools".

## See Also

Recipe 1.1, "Run Programs, Scripts, and Existing Tools"

Recipe 29.4, "Invoke a Command on a Remote Computer"

# 29.20. Determine Whether a Script Is Running on a Remote Computer

## Problem

You have a script that needs to know whether it is running on a local or remote computer.

## Solution

Review the output of the $host.Name property. If it is ServerRemoteHost, it is running remotely. If it is anything else, it is running locally.

```
PS > $host.Name
ConsoleHost

PS > Invoke-Command leeholmes1c23 { $host.Name }
ServerRemoteHost
```

## Discussion

While your scripts should work no matter whether they are running locally or remotely, you might run into situations where you need to verify which environment your script is being launched under.

The $host automatic variable exposes information about the current host, of which PowerShell Remoting is one. When you access this variable in a remoting session, the value is ServerRemoteHost. Although the value on the console host is ConsoleHost, you should not depend on this as an indicator of a local script. There are many other PowerShell hosts—such as the PowerShell Integrated Scripting Environment (Windows PowerShell ISE Host), PowerGUI, PowerShell Plus, and more. Each has a customized host name, but none is ServerRemoteHost.

For more information about the $host automatic variable, see Recipe 13.9, "Access Features of the Host's User Interface".

## See Also

Recipe 13.9, "Access Features of the Host's User Interface"

# 29.21. Create a Task-Specific Remoting Endpoint

## Problem

You want to create a PowerShell endpoint that limits the commands that can be run.

## Solution

Use the `New-PSSessionConfigurationFile` command to create a session configuration, and then use the `Register-PSSessionConfiguration` cmdlet to create an endpoint based on that configuration.

```
PS > $s = New-PSSessionConfigurationFile -Path c:\temp\restricted.pssc `
    -VisibleCmdlets Get-Random -SessionType RestrictedRemoteServer
PS > Register-PSSessionConfiguration -Name Random `
    -Path c:\temp\restricted.pssc -Force
PS > $s = New-PSSession -ConfigurationName Random
PS > Invoke-Command $s { Get-Process }
The term 'Get-Process' is not recognized as the name of a cmdlet, function,
script file, or operable program. Check the spelling of the name, or if a path
was included, verify that the path is correct and try again.
    + CategoryInfo          : ObjectNotFound: (Get-Process:String) []
    + FullyQualifiedErrorId : CommandNotFoundException
    + PSComputerName        : localhost

PS > Invoke-Command $s { 1+1 }
The syntax is not supported by this runspace. This might be because it is in
no-language mode.
    + CategoryInfo          : ParserError: ( 1+1 :String) [], ParseException
    + FullyQualifiedErrorId : ScriptsNotAllowed
    + PSComputerName        : localhost

PS > Invoke-Command $s { Get-Random }
1967230856
```

## Discussion

In addition to its main feature of offering full and rich Remoting endpoints, PowerShell lets you configure a session to the other extreme as well. This is through a mechanism known as *restricted runspaces*.

Restricted runspaces let you control which commands you expose to the user, create proxy functions to wrap commands with more secure versions, and remove access to the PowerShell language altogether.

---

The most typical implementation of a restricted runspace is a developer's task: creating a custom assembly, building an *initial session state*, and more. When you create an initial session state, there are two types of commands: *public* and *private*. The main distinction is that users can call only public commands, while public commands can internally call both public and private commands. This lets you write a public function, for example, that calls many private PowerShell cmdlets to accomplish its task.

For administrators, there is a relatively simple alternative to the developer's approach: creating a custom endpoint that uses a session configuration file for its configuration tasks.

Session configuration files let you limit many aspects of a restricted runspace: its supported cmdlets, language mode, default variables, and more.

When you have more complex requirements than a session configuration file can handle, startup scripts offer a great opportunity to fill the gap.

 Many restricted runspaces implement what is known as a *Trusted Subsystem*. While the startup script validates that the connect user has access to a given command, the command itself runs under an alternate user account, usually one with elevated privileges. To create a session configuration that runs under these alternate or elevated credentials, use the -RunAsCredential parameter.

The implementation of this startup script is still a challenge, though. Which commands should you make public in order to support interactive remoting? Which parameters should you remove from the commands that you do expose?

Fortunately, the developer's API supports a command to answer this exact question. The CreateRestricted() method on the InitialSessionState class creates a minimal and secure startup environment. To create a startup script based on this information, you can examine the commands in the InitialSessionState object and clone that information in your restricted session.

After importing all of the proxy functions, the last step is to configure their proper visibility, disable access to scripts and applications, and then remove access to the PowerShell language.

Once you've built a script that can restrict a PowerShell session, call the Register-PSSessionConfiguration cmdlet to assign it a new endpoint name and configuration:

```
PS > Set-ExecutionPolicy RemoteSigned
PS > Register-PSSessionConfiguration -Name Inventory `
    -StartupScript 'C:\Program Files\Endpoints\Inventory.ps1'

Confirm
```

```
Are you sure you want to perform this action?
Performing operation "Register-PSSessionConfiguration" on Target "Name:
Inventory. This will allow administrators to remotely run Windows PowerShell
commands on this computer."
[Y] Yes  [A] Yes to All  [N] No  [L] No to All  [S] Suspend  [?] Help
(default is "Y"): Y


   WSManConfig: Microsoft.WSMan.Management\WSMan::localhost\Plugin

Name                      Type                  Keys
----                      ----                  ----
Inventory                 Container             {Name=Inventory}

Confirm
Are you sure you want to perform this action?
Performing operation ""Restart-Service"" on Target "Name: WinRM".
[Y] Yes  [A] Yes to All  [N] No  [L] No to All  [S] Suspend  [?] Help
(default is "Y"): Y


Enter-PSSession -Computer leeholmes1c23 -ConfigurationName Inventory
```

As with the Microsoft.PowerShell remoting endpoint, you can configure permissions, quotas, and more. For more information about endpoint configuration, see Recipe 29.11, "Configure User Permissions for Remoting" and Recipe 29.16, "Configure Advanced Remoting Quotas and Options".

Example 29-8 gives an example of a startup script, building an endpoint that exposes only a Get-Inventory command.

*Example 29-8. Inventory.ps1*

```
##############################################################################
##
## Inventory
##
## From Windows PowerShell Cookbook (O'Reilly)
## by Lee Holmes (http://www.leeholmes.com/guide)
##
##############################################################################

<#

.SYNOPSIS

Serves as the configuration script for a custom remoting endpoint that
exposes only the Get-Inventory custom command.

.EXAMPLE

PS >Register-PsSessionConfiguration Inventory `
```

```
    -StartupScript 'C:\Program Files\Endpoints\Inventory.ps1'
PS >Enter-PsSession leeholmes1c23 -ConfigurationName Inventory

[leeholmes1c23]: [Inventory] > Get-Command

CommandType     Name                          Definition
-----------     ----                          ----------
Function        Exit-PSSession                [CmdletBinding()]...
Function        Get-Command                   [CmdletBinding()]...
Function        Get-FormatData                [CmdletBinding()]...
Function        Get-Help                      [CmdletBinding()]...
Function        Get-Inventory                 ...
Function        Measure-Object                [CmdletBinding()]...
Function        Out-Default                   [CmdletBinding()]...
Function        prompt                        ...
Function        Select-Object                 [CmdletBinding()]...

[leeholmes1c23]: [Inventory] > Get-Inventory

SystemDirectory : C:\Windows\system32
Organization    :
BuildNumber     : 6002
RegisteredUser  : Lee Holmes
SerialNumber    : 89580-433-1295803-71477
Version         : 6.0.6002

[leeholmes1c23]: [Inventory] > 1+1
The syntax is not supported by this runspace. This might be because it is
in no-language mode.
    + CategoryInfo          :
    + FullyQualifiedErrorId : ScriptsNotAllowed

[leeholmes1c23]: [Inventory] > Exit-PsSession
PS >

#>

Set-StrictMode -Off

## Create a new function to get inventory
function Get-Inventory
{
    Get-WmiObject Win32_OperatingSystem
}

## Customize the prompt
function Prompt
{
    "[Inventory] > "
}
```

```
## Remember which functions we want to expose to the user
$exportedCommands = "Get-Inventory","Prompt"

## The System.Management.Automation.Runspaces.InitialSessionState class
## has a CreateRestricted() method that creates a default locked-down
## secure configuration for a remote session. This configuration only
## supports the bare minimum required for interactive remoting.
$issType = [System.Management.Automation.Runspaces.InitialSessionState]
$iss = $issType::CreateRestricted("RemoteServer")

## Add the commands to a hashtable so that we can access them easily
$issHashtable = @{}
foreach($command in $iss.Commands)
{
    $issHashtable[$command.Name + "-" + $command.CommandType] = $command
}

## Go through all of functions built into the restricted runspace and add
## them to this session. These are proxy functions to limit the functionality
## of commands that we need (such as Get-Command, Select-Object, etc.)
foreach($function in $iss.Commands |
    Where-Object { $_.CommandType -eq "Function" })
{
    Set-Content "function:\$($function.Name)" -Value $function.Definition
}

## Go through all of the commands in this session
foreach($command in Get-Command)
{
    ## If it was one of our exported commands, keep it Public
    if($exportedCommands -contains $command.Name) { continue }

    ## If the current command is defined as Private in the initial session
    ## state, mark it as private here as well.
    $issCommand = $issHashtable[$command.Name + "-" + $command.CommandType]
    if((-not $issCommand) -or ($issCommand.Visibility -ne "Public"))
    {
        $command.Visibility = "Private"
    }
}

## Finally, prevent all access to the PowerShell language
$executionContext.SessionState.Scripts.Clear()
$executionContext.SessionState.Applications.Clear()
$executionContext.SessionState.LanguageMode = "NoLanguage"
```

For more information about running scripts, see Recipe 1.1, "Run Programs, Scripts, and Existing Tools". For more information about proxy functions, see Recipe 11.23, "Program: Enhance or Extend an Existing Cmdlet".

---

## See Also

Recipe 1.1, "Run Programs, Scripts, and Existing Tools"

Recipe 11.23, "Program: Enhance or Extend an Existing Cmdlet"

Recipe 29.11, "Configure User Permissions for Remoting"

# Workflows

## 30.0. Introduction

When you're writing PowerShell scripts to automate administrative tasks, solutions of increasing scale and scope quickly fall within reach. Once you're automating solutions on the local system, PowerShell Remoting quickly lets you start duplicating those tasks across many machines. And once you're duplicating tasks across many machines, it's not long until you're orchestrating large-scale, coordinated, multimachine sequences.

Coordinating robust, long-running, reliable, multimachine sequences is a significant challenge in a networked environment. Remote connectivity needs to be ubiquitous and consistent. Machine connections need to be managed, pooled, and maintained. Network interruptions should be expected and recovered from. Tasks should let you suspend, unload, and resume them without losing either state or sequence.

And while solving all of that, you still need to be sure not to paint yourself into a corner with an obscure custom implementation. PowerShell will continue to add new functionality. The community will continue to extend PowerShell with new commands. Others are tackling these multimachine sequences and will share their results. Just as you benefit from shared PowerShell scripts, you should benefit from them sharing their efforts, as well.

Solving this complex nest of problems was one of the main focuses of PowerShell version 3.

# 30.1. Write a Workflow

## Problem

You want to write a workflow to automate a robust, long-running, multimachine PowerShell task.

## Solution

Use PowerShell's `workflow` keyword to define the task as a workflow:

```
workflow Get-ComputerStatus
{
    ## This workflow can be suspended and resumed at any point,
    ## as it doesn't have any portions where one step depends
    ## on system state prepared by a previous step.
    $PSPersistPreference = $true

    ## Get drive usage information
    "Current disk usage"
    "-----------------"
    $drives = Get-PSDrive

    ## Override persistence on a command that doesn't
    ## support it.
    $drives | Sort-Object -Property Free -Descending -PSPersist:$false

    ## See which non-system processes have consumed the
    ## most CPU
    "`nProcess CPU usage"
    "-----------------"
    InlineScript
    {
        $userProcesses = Get-Process |
            Where-Object Path -notlike ($env:WINDIR + "*")
        $userProcesses = $userProcesses | Sort CPU | Select Name,CPU,StartTime
        $userProcesses | Select -Last 10
    }

    ## Get licensing status
    "`nLicense status"
    "---------------"
    cscript $env:WINDIR\system32\slmgr.vbs /dlv
}

PS > Get-ComputerStatus -PSComputerName Server1,Server2
```

# Discussion

As mentioned in the Introduction, workflows are PowerShell's answer to the challenges of multimachine orchestration. Let's take a look at how PowerShell workflows accomplish some of the goals that need to be addressed in a multimachine orchestration platform:

*Robust*

PowerShell's workflow support builds on the core workflow engine exposed by Windows Workflow Foundation, a stable and well-proven component of the .NET Framework.

Being able to restart a workflow means being able to abandon and recreate that workflow's state (variables and current position) wherever the author wishes. PowerShell accomplishes this through reliable, filesystem-based persistence.

In a complex workflow, transient errors are commonplace. PowerShell workflows help address this by attempting to intelligently retry failed actions.

*Long-running*

To ensure that long-running commands don't monopolize the user's console, all workflows support running as PowerShell *jobs*.

Since most long-running jobs will eventually need to be interrupted, PowerShell offers easy support for checkpointing, suspending, and resuming workflows.

*Multimachine*

When dealing with multimachine scenarios, connection management becomes paramount. PowerShell handles all of this on behalf of the workflow: making connections when required, reusing connections when possible, and throttling connections if desired.

PowerShell workflows make remote support *ubiquitous*. Every PowerShell workflow and activity automatically gets support for over a dozen parameters that enable seamless multimachine processing.

*Reusable*

PowerShell's script-based workflow authoring syntax makes it easy to author and share workflows.

Since PowerShell's workflow support builds on the Windows Workflow Foundation engine, activities built for that ecosystem automatically work within PowerShell workflows.

Since PowerShell's workflow commands (such as cmdlets and `InlineScript`) are built as Windows Workflow Foundation activities, they can be used from any Windows Workflow Foundation–based application.

With those aspects of PowerShell workflows in focus, how do you write one?

In introducing workflows, PowerShell keeps its promise of letting you leverage what you already know. Writing and running a workflow isn't terribly different than what you're used to already: the PowerShell scripting language sits at the core of the workflow authoring experience.

## Writing a basic workflow

A basic workflow looks just like a function, but uses the `workflow` keyword. You will usually want to define workflows in a module, but you can also define them in a script that you dot-source:

```
workflow Invoke-MyFirstWorkflow
{
}
```

Workflows are best suited for sequences of chunky steps, so the `InlineScript` keyword lets you create islands of commands. Commands in the `InlineScript` block have full access to the PowerShell scripting language. You can use PowerShell's variable assignment syntax to save results, as well:

```
workflow Invoke-MyFirstWorkflow
{
    ## Run step 1
    InlineScript
    {
        $results = Get-Content log.txt | Where-Object { $_ -match "error" }
        foreach($result in $results) { ... }
    }

    ## Run step 2
    $step2 = InlineScript
    {
        $userProcesses = Get-Process |
            Where-Object Path -notlike ($env:WINDIR + "*")
        $userProcesses = $userProcesses | Sort CPU | Select Name,CPU,StartTime
        $userProcesses | Select -Last 10
    }
    $step2
}
```

If a phase of your workflow consists of a single command, you can invoke that command directly.

```
workflow Invoke-MyFirstWorkflow
{
    ## Run step 1
    InlineScript { ... }

    ## Run step 2
    InlineScript { ... }
```

```
## Run step 3
\\workflowserver\scripts\step3.ps1
}
```

At this point, you've got a workflow that runs but can't be suspended or resumed. When you write a workflow, it is important to consider at which points PowerShell can safely suspend your workflow. For more information about writing workflows that can be suspended and resumed, see Recipe 30.3, "Suspend and Resume a Workflow".

Given all of its power and similarity to traditional PowerShell scripting, it is also useful to consider when *not* to use a PowerShell workflow. If your scenario is not intended to be long-running or to stitch together multimachine scenarios, a PowerShell script may be better suited to your problem. Here are a few qualities of a problem or script that suggest a traditional PowerShell script might be the most appropriate choice:

*No need for recovery*
> If merely restarting the script is an acceptable recovery technique in your scenario, a workflow has little to offer over a traditional script.

*Detailed/fine-grained steps*
> Workflows are best suited to orchestration of *chunky* tasks. For example, building a server, patching it, and installing software. If you can't identify the major chunks of your scenario, you will probably be unable to identify the points where it is safe to suspend, resume, or restart your workflow. A workflow that you can't suspend, resume, or restart isn't much help at all! Two common indicators of detailed or fine-grained workflows are significant interaction with objects, and a complex hierarchy of functions and helper functions.

*Reliance on dynamic state*
> If your script depends heavily on dynamic state, then the script will not survive being suspended, restarted, or resumed. A common example of this is significant interaction with objects, methods, and properties. For example: you retrieve an object, call some methods on that live instance, and then pass it along to other commands. This is also a common indicator that your scenario may have too many detailed or fine-grained steps.

*Single-machine*
> If your scenario involves the management of just a single machine, you may find it easier to simply connect to that machine with PowerShell Remoting and automate the scenario with a script. This is an especially true indicator if the "single machine" is always the local machine. That said, long-running single-machine tasks can still benefit significantly from being written as a PowerShell workflow.

*Performance-critical*

> To guarantee the robustness of your workflows, PowerShell performs additional processing not done for traditional scripts. The most significant of these are process isolation, output serialization, and persistence. These steps add to the time it takes to execute your workflow, making it potentially unsuitable for performance-critical scenarios.

Given the differences in focus between a traditional script and workflow, there are two major impacts to your workflow scripting experience: conceptual and syntactic.

## Major conceptual differences between scripts and workflows

Workflow's focus on being a robust multimachine orchestration platform brings with it a set of differences that are primarily philosophical in nature. When you ask "how do I write this scripting concept in Workflow?", these are the kind of differences that end with the answer, "maybe I shouldn't."

*Checkpoints*

> One of the primary reasons for writing a workflow is to let users and the system suspend or resume it as required. This capability doesn't come for free. When you write a workflow, one of your foremost goals should be to understand where the system can safely suspend or resume your workflow. For more information about writing workflows that support being suspended or resumed, see Recipe 30.3, "Suspend and Resume a Workflow".

*Task orchestration and state separation*

> When you write a traditional PowerShell script, there's usually plenty of assumed context: you import modules, change PowerShell variables, and update files on the current system. Since workflows are primarily a vehicle for multimachine orchestration, they embody the concept of stateless, mobile code.
>
> Think of your workflow as a master controller that coordinates actions by shipping your code out to the nodes that it manages. When you use the Get-Process cmdlet in a workflow, your master controller doesn't run the Get-Process cmdlet and target it to a remote machine. Instead, it tells that remote machine to run the Get-Process cmdlet and return the results. After that, the remote computer completely cleans up its session so that commands don't accidentally take a dependency on things that wouldn't survive a reboot.
>
> A workflow/master controller sometimes manages the same machine it's running on, but think of that as an exception.

*Serialized results*

> One of the primary features of a workflow is that you can suspend it and resume it. However, PowerShell cmdlets (such as `Get-Process`) return live .NET objects that include methods and properties that can often update dynamically. PowerShell can't retain this type of functionality when it suspends and resumes your workflow.
>
> In addition to persistence guarantees, consistency is an important goal. When you use PowerShell Remoting to manage a remote machine (which workflows do), PowerShell serializes all objects by default before sending them back to the local machine.
>
> To resolve these issues, PowerShell workflows serialize the results from all command calls and actions. This ensures that the results can be persisted, and that both local and remote management is consistent.

*Background jobs*

> Given that workflows are intended to be long-running tasks, it wouldn't make much sense for them to hog your console window until complete. Instead, workflows run as background jobs. They have no direct access to the host (via `Read-Host` or `Write-Host`), and use the `*-Job` cmdlets for all interaction. For more information about the job-oriented nature of workflows, see Recipe 30.2, "Run a Workflow".

## Major syntactic differences between scripts and workflows

Given an understanding of the major philosophical and conceptual differences between scripts and workflows, there are some differences that are more syntactic—in the class of things you *type* differently, rather than things you *think* differently. For the most part, PowerShell workflows have an almost identical syntax to traditional scripts.

*Command differences*

> PowerShell workflows support two commands that are not supported in traditional PowerShell scripts: `Checkpoint-Workflow` (with an alias of `Persist`) to identify points where it is safe to suspend and resume, and `Suspend-Workflow`, which suspends the currently running workflow.
>
> In addition to supporting additional commands, some commands (such as `Invoke-History`) are intentionally not supported if they make little sense in a workflow context. PowerShell generates an error message when you try to use one of these.
>
> In a PowerShell workflow, commands support many additional parameters that their corresponding cmdlets do not. For more information about customizing these common parameters, see Recipe 30.6, "Customize an Activity's Connection Parameters".

*Language differences*

PowerShell workflows support three additional language statements: Inline Script, Parallel, and Sequence. For more information about InlineScript, see Recipe 30.4, "Invoke Islands of Traditional PowerShell Script". For more information about Parallel and Sequence, see Recipe 30.5, "Invoke Workflow Actions in Parallel".

PowerShell workflows do not support the begin, process, and end statements. To process pipeline input, use the $input automatic variable.

Switch statements are limited to primitive types and case-sensitive string comparisons. Parameter defaults are limited to primitive types. trap, break, and contin ue statements are not supported. Loop labels are not supported.

Comment-based help is not supported.

## See Also

Recipe 30.2, "Run a Workflow"

Recipe 30.3, "Suspend and Resume a Workflow"

Recipe 30.4, "Invoke Islands of Traditional PowerShell Script"

Recipe 30.5, "Invoke Workflow Actions in Parallel"

Recipe 30.6, "Customize an Activity's Connection Parameters"

# 30.2. Run a Workflow

## Problem

You want to run a workflow.

## Solution

Use the New-PSWorkflowSession cmdlet to connect to the Microsoft.PowerShell. Workflow endpoint on the server that will coordinate your workflow. Import the module that contains your workflow, and then invoke it as you would invoke any other Power-Shell command. Use the -AsJob parameter by default, unless you expect the workflow to be short-lived:

```
PS > $s = New-PSWorkflowSession -Computername WorkflowServer
PS > Invoke-Command $s { Import-Module C:\Workflows\Workflows.psm1 }
PS > Invoke-Command $s { Invoke-WorkflowMath -Number1 10 -Number2 20 -AsJob }
```

```
Id Name PSJobTypeName State    HasMoreData Command          PSComputerName
-- ---- ------------- -----    ----------- -------          --------------
9  Job9 PSWorkflowJob Running  True        Invoke-WorkflowMath WorkflowServer
```

## Discussion

As workflows go, Example 30-1 has very little reason to be written as a workflow. However, it provides a good demonstration of running and invoking workflows.

*Example 30-1. The Invoke-WorkflowMath module*

```
workflow Invoke-WorkflowMath
{
    param($Number1 = 12, $Number2 = 34)

    Get-CimInstance -Classname Win32_OperatingSystem
    Checkpoint-Workflow

    ## Multiply two numbers
    $Number1 * $Number2
    Checkpoint-Workflow

    Start-Sleep -Seconds 10

    ## Divide two numbers
    $Number1 / $Number2
}
```

After you define a workflow, it acts like most other PowerShell commands. As with scripts and cmdlets, Get-Command lets you filter workflows by name, noun, verb, or command type (in this case, Workflow). For simple experimentation, you can run a workflow as you would run a PowerShell command. This won't be the typical usage, though, as we'll get to shortly.

```
PS > Invoke-WorkflowMath

SystemDirectory        Organization         BuildNumber
---------------        ------------         -----------
C:\Windows\system32                         9200
408
0.352941176470588
```

Likewise, you can use Get-Command -Syntax to explore the workflow's parameters.

```
PS > Get-Command Invoke-WorkflowMath -Syntax

Invoke-WorkflowMath [[-Number1] <int>] [[-Number2] <int>]
    [<WorkflowCommonParameters>] ...
```

Although you can run a workflow just like a regular PowerShell command, this ties up your PowerShell console until the workflow completes. Any workflow where this is acceptable should probably not be written as a workflow. Instead, your preferred way to interact with workflows should always be through the \*-Job cmdlets. Use the -AsJob switch when you launch your workflow, and then use the Receive-Job, Suspend-Job, and Resume-Job cmdlets to retrieve output and manage its state.

When PowerShell creates a job for your workflow invocation, it creates one child job for each computer it processes. If you use the PSComputerName parameter to target 10 computers, the job that PowerShell returns will have 10 child jobs. In addition to the properties exposed by the parent job object, child jobs provide easy access to their results (such as Output and Progress) without having to use the Receive-Job to permanently consume those results.

When you run your workflow as a job, PowerShell connects to (or creates) the workflow engine in the *current PowerShell session*. If you launch your workflow in a regular PowerShell console window, this introduces a complication: you can't exit that window without terminating all running workflows. This creates a risky and error-prone approach to running commands that are intended to be robust and long-running.

For this reason, PowerShell defines a remoting configuration designed specifically for workflow invocation and management: Microsoft.PowerShell.Workflow.

Like a regular PowerShell Remoting session, you use Enter-PSSession or Invoke -Command to connect to it and invoke commands. Rather than using the New-PS Session cmdlet to create the connection, though, you use the New-PSWorkflowSes sion cmdlet. Unlike short-lived console sessions and regular remoting sessions, PowerShell keeps this session alive (by specifying the UseSharedProcess option when creating the endpoint) whether you are connected or not. This makes the workflow endpoint the ideal hosting environment for robust, long-running tasks.

 Despite this advice that workflows should be run on a dedicated workflow server, most examples in this chapter invoke workflows locally for demonstration purposes.

One thing you might notice when connecting to the workflow session is the relative lack of commands:

```
PS > $s = New-PSWorkflowSession -ComputerName WorkflowServer
PS > icm $s { Get-Process }
The term 'Get-Process' is not recognized as the name of a cmdlet,
function, script file, or operable program. Check the spelling of the
name, or if a path was included, verify that the path is correct and try
again.
    + CategoryInfo          : ObjectNotFound: (Get-Process:String) [],
    CommandNotFoundException
    + FullyQualifiedErrorId : CommandNotFoundException
    + PSComputerName        : WorkflowServer
```

The goal behind this difference is to make a clear distinction between the regular Mi crosoft.PowerShell endpoint and the Microsoft.PowerShell.Workflow endpoint. If you want to simply run commands, run them either in the current session, or in the regular Microsoft.PowerShell endpoint. If you want to run and manage workflows, then the Microsoft.PowerShell.Workflow endpoint has everything you require and should be used instead.

For more information about writing PowerShell workflows, see Recipe 30.1, "Write a Workflow".

## See Also

Recipe 30.1, "Write a Workflow"

# 30.3. Suspend and Resume a Workflow

## Problem

You want to write a workflow that users can suspend and resume, or want to suspend and resume a workflow that's already been written.

## Solution

Add calls to the Checkpoint-Workflow command in your workflow, or use $PSPersist Preference = $true if your workflow can be suspended and resumed at any point. Use the Suspend-Job and Resume-Job cmdlets to suspend and resume workflows.

```
workflow Invoke-MyFirstWorkflow
{
    ## Run step 1
    InlineScript { Start-Sleep -Seconds 5; "Done step 1" }

    Checkpoint-Workflow

    ## Run step 2
    InlineScript { Start-Sleep -Seconds 5; "Done step 2" }
}

PS > $j = Invoke-MyFirstWorkflow -AsJob
PS > Suspend-Job $j -Wait
PS > Receive-Job $j
Done step 1
PS > Resume-Job $j -Wait
PS > Receive-Job $j -Wait
Done step 2
```

## Discussion

When you write a workflow, it is important to consider at which points PowerShell can safely suspend your workflow. Any point that depends only on workflow variables or on system state that will survive a reboot is a safe place to suspend your workflow. In those places, add a call to the Checkpoint-Workflow command.

```
workflow Invoke-MyFirstWorkflow
{
    ## Run step 1
    InlineScript
    {
        "Starting step 1"
        Start-Sleep -Seconds 5
        "Ending step 1"
    }

    Checkpoint-Workflow

    ## Run step 2
    InlineScript
    {
        "Starting step 2"
        Start-Sleep -Seconds 5
        "Ending step 2"
    }

    Checkpoint-Workflow

    ## Run step 3
    \\workflowserver\scripts\step3.ps1
}
```

With checkpoints defined, you can now suspend and resume your workflow:

```
PS > $j = Invoke-MyFirstWorkflow -AsJob
PS > Suspend-Job $j

PS > $j

Id    Name         PSJobTypeName   State       HasMoreData
--    ----         -------------   -----       -----------
14    Job14        PSWorkflowJob   Suspended   True

PS > Receive-Job $j
Starting step 1
Ending step 1
PS > Resume-Job $j

PS > $j
```

```
Id      Name          PSJobTypeName    State     HasMoreData
--      ----          -------------    -----     -----------
14      Job14         PSWorkflowJob    Running   True

PS > Receive-Job $j
Starting step 2
Ending step 2

PS > Receive-Job $j
<Output from step3.ps1>
```

To have PowerShell wait for any of the * - Job cmdlets to get into the expected state before continuing, use the -Wait parameter.

 When you call the Suspend- Job cmdlet, PowerShell continues running the workflow that represents that job until it reaches the next defined persistence point. If the need is urgent, you can use Suspend-Job's -Force parameter. This should be avoided when possible, as the consequences may be grave. When given the -Force parameter, PowerShell forcefully terminates the workflow and will recover from the last saved checkpoint when resumed.

If you've authored every step of your workflow to rely only on workflow variables or on system state that survives reboots, you can use the $PSPersistPreference variable to have PowerShell checkpoint your workflow after every command. Be careful with this setting, as it tells PowerShell that it is safe for the user to suspend your workflow and restart the machine at any point.

```
workflow Invoke-MyFirstWorkflow
{
    $PSPersistPreference = $true

    ## Run step 1
    InlineScript
    {
        "Starting step 1"
        Start-Sleep -Seconds 5;
        "Ending step 1"
    }

    ## Run step 2
    InlineScript
    {
        "Starting step 2"
        Start-Sleep -Seconds 5;
        "Ending step 2"
    }
```

```
## Run step 3
\\workflowserver\scripts\step3.ps1
}
```

For more information about writing PowerShell workflows, see Recipe 30.1, "Write a Workflow".

## See Also

Recipe 30.1, "Write a Workflow"

# 30.4. Invoke Islands of Traditional PowerShell Script

## Problem

You are writing a workflow and want to include sections of traditional PowerShell scripting.

## Solution

Use the InlineScript keyword to define an island of traditional PowerShell script. If that script requires variables from your workflow, reference them with the $USING prefix.

```
workflow Invoke-Backup
{
    param([PSCredential] $FtpCredential)

    ## Each step is safe to persist after
    $PSPersistPreference = $true

    ## Create a backup
    Get-ChildItem -Path c:\ImportantDocuments |
        New-ZipFile -Path c:\temp\backup.zip

    ## And upload it to the server
    InlineScript
    {
        $credential = $USING:FtpCredential

        $wc = New-Object System.Net.WebClient
        $wc.Credentials = $credential.GetNetworkCredential()
        $wc.UploadFile("ftp://server.com/backups/backup.zip",
            "c:\temp\backup.zip")
    }
}
$cred = Get-Credential
Invoke-Backup -FtpCredential $cred
```

# Discussion

As mentioned in Recipe 30.1, "Write a Workflow", an important feature of realistic workflows is that they stitch together sequences of chunky tasks. Workflows that incorporate lots of fine-grained scripting techniques are very difficult to understand when it comes to placing appropriate persistence points, and incur an overhead not present in traditional PowerShell scripting.

However, what if those sequence of chunky tasks are themselves best expressed as PowerShell scripts?

For this reason, PowerShell workflows include the InlineScript keyword. Like all other activities, the InlineScript keyword automatically supports remote connectivity, multimachine targeting, automatic persistence points, and more. For example, to have the InlineScript target a specific computer during invocation (rather than the workflow target), use the -PSComputerName parameter.

```
workflow Invoke-InlineScriptTargeting
{
    ## Run on whatever computer is being targeted
    InlineScript
    {
        "Running on $USING:PSComputername"
    }

    ## Run on the workflow server
    InlineScript
    {
        "Running on $USING:PSComputername"
    } -PSComputerName localhost
}

PS > Invoke-InlineScriptTargeting -PSComputerName Computer1
Running on Computer1
Running on localhost
```

For a further discussion of common workflow parameters, see Recipe 30.6, "Customize an Activity's Connection Parameters".

When writing an InlineScript, it is important to remember that you're authoring mobile units of scripting. PowerShell packages your script, sends it to the target computer, and runs it there. As with the Invoke-Command cmdlet used for traditional PowerShell Remoting, PowerShell doesn't automatically ship variables to the remote machine. After all, what should happen to variable names that have an important meaning on both sides of the connection, like $pwd, $pid, or $error? As with the Invoke-Command cmdlet, you can add the $USING variable prefix to tell PowerShell that those variables represent references to workflow variables.

For more information about writing PowerShell workflows, see Recipe 30.1, "Write a Workflow".

## See Also

Recipe 30.1, "Write a Workflow"

Recipe 30.6, "Customize an Activity's Connection Parameters"

# 30.5. Invoke Workflow Actions in Parallel

## Problem

You are writing a workflow that can benefit from some of its tasks running simultaneously.

## Solution

Use the `parallel` or `foreach -parallel` statements to invoke actions in parallel. In a `parallel` statement, use the `sequence` statement to group statements that should be considered a unit.

```
workflow Invoke-Parallel
{
    parallel
    {
        ## Segment 1: Sleep for 5 seconds
        sequence
        {
            "Starting 5 second sleep"
            Start-Sleep -Seconds 5
            "Ending 5 second sleep"
        }

        ## Segment 2: Sleep for 4 seconds
        sequence
        {
            "Starting 4 second sleep"
            Start-Sleep -Seconds 4
            "Ending 4 second sleep"
        }

        ## Segment 3: Process 3 items in
        ## parallel, each of them sleeping for
        ## 2, 4, or 6 seconds
        foreach -parallel ($item in 1..3)
        {
            "Starting sleep for $item"
            Start-Sleep -Seconds (2 * $item)
```

```
            "Ending sleep for $item"
        }
    }
}
```

# Discussion

When you're writing a workflow, there are often pieces that you can invoke in parallel as a way to speed things up. For example, archiving an important backup directory at the same time that you clean up old files from other directories.

To enable this scenario, PowerShell workflows offer the `parallel` statement. In a `par allel` statement, PowerShell invokes each command enclosed by braces roughly at the same time. If there are two or more statements within the `parallel` block that should be invoked as a unit (sequentially, rather than in parallel), place them in a `sequence` block. In that case, PowerShell executes the commands *within* the sequence block sequentially, but the block itself runs in parallel with everything else in the `parallel` statement.

If you want to change or modify a variable defined outside of the `parallel` statement from within the `parallel` statement, you must use the `$WORKFLOW` variable prefix. This keeps parallel statements consistent with functions and script blocks in PowerShell, and those require the `$SCRIPT` variable prefix to modify script-level variables.

Be careful when changing shared workflow-level variables from within a `parallel` statement. Since the blocks run in parallel, there is no guarantee of the order in which the variable assignments will happen. This is commonly known as a *race condition*—a situation demonstrated by Example 30-2.

*Example 30-2. A workflow with a race condition*

```
workflow Invoke-WorkflowWithRaceCondition
{
    $counter = 0

    parallel
    {
        ## Segment 1 - retrieve the value of counter,
        ## wait for a while, add one to that value,
        ## and store the result
        sequence
        {
            $myValue = $counter
            Start-Sleep -Seconds 2
            $WORKFLOW:counter = $myValue + 1
        }

        ## Segment 2 - retrieve the value of counter,
        ## wait for a while, add one to that value,
        ## and store the result
```

```
    sequence
    {
        $myValue = $counter
        Start-Sleep -Seconds 2
        $WORKFLOW:counter = $myValue + 1
    }
}

## You might expect "2" here. However, since both
## segments read the value of $counter while it
## was "0", they both end up setting the result to "1".
"After 2 updates, counter is: $counter"
}

PS > Invoke-WorkflowWithRaceCondition
After 2 updates, counter is: 1
```

When it comes to parallel invocation, one of the most common opportunities comes from processing the items in a list. For example, these items may represent a list of computers to retrieve inventory from, or may represent the sources for some long-running calculations. If processing one item in the collection doesn't require the results of processing other items in the collection, you can use the foreach -parallel statement to process these items simultaneously.

```
workflow Invoke-ParallelDataProcessing
{
    $items = "Item1","Item2","Item3"

    ## Go through each item in the collection
    ## and process it.
    foreach -parallel ($item in $items)
    {
        "Processing item $item"
        Start-Sleep -Seconds 2
        "Done processing item $item"
    }
}

PS > Invoke-ParallelDataProcessing
Processing item Item3
Processing item Item2
Processing item Item1
Done processing item Item3
Done processing item Item2
Done processing item Item1
```

Unlike the parallel statement, the lines within the braces of the parallel -foreach statement are treated as a unit and are invoked sequentially. The benefits of this approach come from invoking all of those units simultaneously.

---

For more information about writing PowerShell workflows, see Recipe 30.1, "Write a Workflow".

## See Also

Recipe 30.1, "Write a Workflow"

# 30.6. Customize an Activity's Connection Parameters

## Problem

You are writing a workflow and want to customize the connectivity behavior of a specific command or activity.

## Solution

Provide values to any of the common activity parameters to customize their connectivity or workflow behavior.

```
workflow Invoke-InlineScriptTargeting
{
    ## Run on whatever computer is being targeted
    InlineScript
    {
        "Running on $USING:PSComputername"
    }

    ## Run on the workflow server
    InlineScript
    {
        "Running on $USING:PSComputername"
    } -PSComputerName localhost
}

PS > Invoke-InlineScriptTargeting -PSComputerName Computer1
Running on Computer1
Running on localhost
```

## Discussion

One of the sources of a workflow's power comes from the incredible ubiquity and consistency of its core functionality.

To start, each command you put in a workflow supports a large collection of common parameters. These are *parameter-level* workflow common parameters. As with any command in PowerShell, you can supply values to any of these parameters directly.

In addition, your workflow itself automatically gets many workflow common parameters. These are *workflow-level* common parameters, and let your users easily target your workflow at many machines. To coordinate this multimachine management, PowerShell uses these workflow-level common parameters as the values for the corresponding activity-level parameters unless explicit parameter values have been supplied in the workflow itself.

Table 30-1 describes these common parameters and how they relate to each other.

*Table 30-1. Workflow common parameters*

| Parameter | Meaning |
|-----------|---------|
| AppendOutput | *Parameter-level only*<br>Specifies that PowerShell should add the command's results to the variable used to hold the result rather than reset it (as would normally be expected by a variable assignment). This is rarely specified directly, as PowerShell does this automatically when you use the += operator in a workflow.<br><pre>workflow Invoke-AppendWorkflow<br>{<br>    $a = "Hello","World"<br>    $a += "How","Are","You"<br>    $a<br>}</pre> |
| AsJob | *Workflow-level only*<br>Determines whether PowerShell should return the job it creates and return control to the shell. The default is to simulate an interactive command by waiting for the job to complete. |
| Debug | *Workflow-level and parameter-level*<br>As with traditional PowerShell commands, specifies that PowerShell should enable the debug output stream for the specified command. |
| DisplayName | *Parameter-level only*<br>Defines the display name that should be used for the current activity when writing progress messages. |
| ErrorAction | *Workflow-level and parameter-level*<br>As with traditional PowerShell commands, defines how the workflow should react to error conditions. |
| Input | *Parameter-level only*<br>Defines the collection that should be used to represent the traditional PowerShell concept of pipeline input. This is rarely specified directly, as a more effective way of providing input to activities is through a pipeline:<br><pre>workflow Invoke-InputWorkflow<br>{<br>    "C","A","B" | Sort-Object<br>}</pre> |
| JobName | *Workflow-level only*<br>The job name to use for the job that PowerShell creates. The default is an autogenerated job name. |

| Parameter | Meaning |
|---|---|
| MergeErrorToOutput | *Parameter-level only*<br>Specifies that PowerShell should treat the command's errors as output. This is rarely specified directly, as PowerShell does this automatically when you use the stream redirection operator in a workflow. |
| PSActionRetryCount | *Parameter-level only*<br>The number of times that PowerShell should try invoking the specified command if initial invocation attempts result in an error. The default value of this parameter is 0. PowerShell does not report errors for retry attempts that fail unless they are over this limit. |
| PSActionRetryIntervalSec | *Parameter-level only*<br>The time (in seconds) that PowerShell should wait between command retry attempts. The default value of this parameter is one second. |
| PSActionRunningTimeoutSec | *Parameter-level only*<br>The maximum time (in seconds) that this command should be allowed to run. The default value of this parameter is unlimited. |
| PSAllowRedirection | *Workflow-level and parameter-level*<br>Determines whether PowerShell should allow remote connections to be redirected to another URI. The default is $false. |
| PSApplicationName | *Workflow-level and parameter-level*<br>The application name that should be used for remote connections. The default is WSMan. |
| PSAuthentication | *Workflow-level and parameter-level*<br>The authentication mechanism that should be used for remote connections. The default uses Kerberos in a domain environment and Negotiate in a workgroup. |
| PSAuthenticationLevel | *Workflow-level and parameter-level*<br>The authentication level that should be used for remote WMI connections. The default is Packet authentication. |
| PSCertificateThumbprint | *Workflow-level and parameter-level*<br>The certificate thumbprint that should be used to identify the user for remote connections. The default is to not use a certificate thumbprint. |
| PSComputerName | *Workflow-level and parameter-level*<br>The computer name(s) that should be used for remote connections. By default, PowerShell targets the current machine. |
| PSConfigurationName | *Workflow-level and parameter-level*<br>The application name that should be used for remote connections. The default is Microsoft.PowerShell. |
| PSConnectionRetryCount | *Workflow-level and parameter-level*<br>The number of times that PowerShell should try connecting to computers if initial connection attempts return an error. The default value of this parameter is 0. PowerShell does not report errors for connection attempts that fail unless they are over this limit. |
| PSConnectionRetryIntervalSec | *Workflow-level and parameter-level*<br>The time (in seconds) that PowerShell should wait between reconnection attempts. The default value of this parameter is one second. |

| Parameter | Meaning |
|---|---|
| PSConnectionUri | *Workflow-level and parameter-level*<br>The connection URI that should be used for remote connections. The default is `http://localhost:5985/WSMan`. |
| PSCredential | *Workflow-level and parameter-level*<br>The credential that PowerShell should use for remote connections. By default, PowerShell uses the credential of the user running the workflow. |
| PSDebug | *Parameter-level only*<br>Specifies the collection that holds any debug output generated by the command. This is rarely specified directly, as PowerShell populates this parameter automatically with a default collection to hold debug output. |
| PSDisableSerialization | *Parameter-level only*<br>Specifies that the activity should not serialize its output by default. Be careful when using this parameter, as most command output cannot be persisted properly when serialization is disabled.<br>This is required if your workflow needs to somehow deal with live objects. |
| PSElapsedTimeoutSec | *Workflow-level and parameter-level*<br>The maximum time (in seconds) that this workflow should be allowed to run. The default value of this parameter is unlimited. Time spent suspended in a workflow counts toward its elapsed time. |
| PSError | *Parameter-level only*<br>Specifies the collection that holds any error output generated by the command. This is rarely specified directly, as PowerShell populates this parameter automatically with a default collection to hold error output. |
| PSParameterCollection | *Workflow-level only*<br>A list of hashtables that define parameters for PowerShell to supply to your workflow for bulk invocation. For example:<br><br>```PS > $j = Invoke-WorkflowMath -AsJob`<br>`        -PSParameterCollection @{`<br>`    Number1 = 10; Number2 = 20}, @{ Number1 = 20;`<br>`                                    Number2 = 30 }```<br><br>```PS > Receive-Job $j.ChildJobs[0]```<br><br>```SystemDirectory        Organization        BuildNumber`<br>`---------------        ------------        -----------`<br>`C:\Windows\system32                        9200`<br>`200`<br>`0.5```<br><br>```PS > Receive-Job $j.ChildJobs[1]```<br><br>```SystemDirectory        Organization        BuildNumber`<br>`---------------        ------------        -----------`<br>`C:\Windows\system32                        9200`<br>`600`<br>`0.666666666666667``` |
| PSPersist | *Workflow-level, preference, and parameter* |

| Parameter | Meaning |
|-----------|---------|
| | When specified at the workflow or preference level, forces PowerShell to checkpoint the running workflow after every command unless that workflow (or its commands) has supplied an explicit PSPersist value. Be careful with this setting, as it tells PowerShell that it is safe to suspend the workflow and restart the machine at any point even if that was not the intention of the workflow author.<br><br>When specified at the parameter level, forces PowerShell to checkpoint the running workflow after the command completes.<br><br>This should be rarely specified directly at the parameter level, as the Checkpoint-Workflow command is a much clearer way to author this intent. |
| PSPort | *Workflow-level and parameter-level*<br>The port that should be used for remote connections. The default is 5985 and 5986 (for SSL-based connections). |
| PSProgress | *Parameter-level only*<br>Specifies the collection that holds any progress output generated by the command. This is rarely specified directly, as PowerShell populates this parameter automatically with a default collection to hold progress output. |
| PSProgressMessage | *Parameter-level only*<br>Defines the progress message to be displayed when executing this command. |
| PSPrivateMetadata | *Workflow-level and parameter-level*<br>Additional data to be associated with the workflow for later filtering. For example:<br><pre>PS > $j = Invoke-WorkflowMath -PSPrivateMetadata @{<br>    Hello = "World" } -AsJob<br>PS > Get-Job -Filter @{ Hello = "World2" }<br>PS > Get-Job -Filter @{ Hello = "World" }<br><br>Id    Name           PSJobTypeName    State<br>--    ----           -------------    -----<br>33    Job33          PSWorkflowJob    Completed</pre> |
| PSRemotingBehavior | *Parameter-level only*<br>Defines how remote connections should be handled by this command. A value of None means that the PSComputerName parameter (or workflow-level preference) should be ignored. A value of Custom means that the value of the PSComputerName parameter should be supplied to the command's actual -ComputerName parameter if it defines one. A value of PowerShell means that remote connectivity should be handled with a regular PowerShell Remoting connection. The default is PowerShell for most commands. |
| PSRequiredModules | *Parameter-level only*<br>Defines which modules PowerShell should load into the target session before invoking the command. This is required only when PowerShell's autoloading is not sufficient: for modules that aren't contained within the standard PSModulePath directories, or when the module defines a PowerShell provider required by the command. |
| PSRunningTimeoutSec | *Workflow-level only*<br>The maximum time (in seconds) that this workflow should be allowed to actively run. The default value of this parameter is unlimited. Time spent suspended in a workflow does not count toward its running time. |
| PSSessionOption | *Workflow-level and parameter-level* |

| Parameter | Meaning |
|---|---|
| | Any additional connections that should be used for remote connections, as defined by the New-PSSessionOption cmdlet. The default is no additional options. |
| PSUseSsl | *Workflow-level and parameter-level*<br>Determines whether PowerShell should connect to SSL endpoints when making remote connections. |
| PSVerbose | *Parameter-level only*<br>Specifies the collection that holds any verbose output generated by the command. This is rarely specified directly, as PowerShell populates this parameter automatically with a default collection to hold verbose output. |
| PSWarning | *Parameter-level only*<br>Specifies the collection that holds any warning output generated by the command. This is rarely specified directly, as PowerShell populates this parameter automatically with a default collection to hold warning output. |
| Result | *Parameter-level only*<br>Specifies the collection that holds any regular output generated by the command. This is rarely specified directly, as PowerShell populates this parameter automatically with a default collection to hold regular output. |
| UseDefaultInput | *Parameter-level only*<br>Specifies that the command should retrieve its input from the input collection maintained by the PowerShell workflow engine. This is rarely specified directly, as PowerShell populates this parameter when required. |
| Verbose | *Workflow-level and parameter-level*<br>As with traditional PowerShell commands, specifies that PowerShell should enable the verbose output stream for the specified command. |
| WarningAction | *Workflow-level and parameter-level*<br>As with traditional PowerShell commands, defines how the workflow should react to warning conditions. |

For any of the supported common parameters, PowerShell provides the values of these parameters through read-only automatic variables. For example, your workflow can access the $PSComputerName variable (among many others) to potentially react to (or log) its value while processing.

 If you want to use any of these variables from within the context of an InlineScript, be sure to use the $USING variable prefix. For more information about the $USING prefix in an InlineScript, see Recipe 30.4, "Invoke Islands of Traditional PowerShell Script".

To see all of the values at once, you can use the Get-PSWorkflowData command as an alternative to variable references to specific settings.

Since it is so easy to overwrite one of these variables by accidentally choosing the same variable name for a regular script, PowerShell prevents you from changing these values:

```
## This is not allowed within a workflow
$PSComputerName = "SomeOtherServer"
```

If you want to change the default values within your workflow, you can instead use the Set-PSWorkflowData activity. Beware that this changes the default for the remainder of the workflow. Because of that, you may find it useful to save the value before changing it, and then restore it when you're done:

```
workflow Invoke-ChangesComputerTarget
{
    $previousComputerName = $PSComputerName

    Set-PSWorkflowData -PSComputerName OtherServer
    Get-Process -Name PowerShell
    Set-PSWorkflowData -PSComputerName $previousComputerName
}
```

For more information about writing PowerShell workflows, see Recipe 30.1, "Write a Workflow".

## See Also

Recipe 30.1, "Write a Workflow"

# 30.7. Write a Workflow That Requires Human Intervention

## Problem

You have a long-running workflow that requires human intervention to continue.

## Solution

Send an email to the administrative contact signaling the need for human interaction, and then call the Suspend-Workflow command. If necessary, use a file as a communication mechanism.

```
workflow Invoke-SuspendWorkflow
{
    param($MailCredential)

    "Processing Step 1"

    ## Workflow detects an error condition
    $gotSomeError = $true

    Checkpoint-Workflow

    ## If we detected an error condition, notify the admin.
```

```
        if($gotSomeError)
        {
            $to = "admin@example.com"
            $from = "workflows@example.com"
            $smtpServer = "smtp.example.com"
            $inputPath = "c:\Workflows\$ParentJobId.input.txt"

            ## Send an alert by sending an email. Override the PSComputerName
            ## property so that this is not dispatched to other computers
            Send-MailMessage -To $to -From $from
                -Subject "Workflow ID $ParentJobId requires intervention" `
                -Body ("Workflow #$ParentJobId has detected an error and needs " +
                    "intervention. Supply required input in $inputPath and " +
                    "resume job #$ParentJobId.") `
                -SmtpServer $smtpServer -Credential $MailCredential -UseSSL `
                -PSComputerName $null

            ## Suspend and wait to be resumed
            Suspend-Workflow

            ## Get the response from the admin, overriding the PSComputerName
            ## parameter so that we're retrieving the input from the workflow server.
            $response = Get-Content -Path $inputPath -PSComputerName $null

            Checkpoint-Workflow

            ## Use the response to recover from the error
            "123 times $response is: $(123 * $response)"
        }
    }
```

## Discussion

When writing long-running workflows, you might find situations that require administrative intervention: data that can't be supplied through workflow parameters, or stages of the workflow that can't be resolved through automation. In these situations, you can notify the workflow administrator of the requirement for intervention through email. If email is a poor option, you can also use an alternate notification mechanism such as the Windows event log.

After sending the notification, call the Suspend-Workflow command. This suspends the current workflow. When the administrator resumes your workflow, execution continues after the call to Suspend-Workflow.

Example 30-3 shows the administrator's perspective of running and managing this workflow.

*Example 30-3. Running a workflow that suspends itself*

```
PS > $MailCredential = Get-Credential
PS > Invoke-SuspendWorkflow -MailCredential $MailCredential
```

```
Processing Step 1

Id     Name           PSJobTypeName   State      HasMoreData   Location
--     ----           -------------   -----      -----------   --------
34     Job34          PSWorkflowJob   Suspended  True          localhost

## After being suspended, administrator receives a mail
PS > Set-Content -Path c:\Workflows\34.input.txt -Value 321
PS > $j = resume-job -id 34
PS > $j | Receive-Job -Wait
123 times 321 is: 39483
```

If you use the Get-Content cmdlet to retrieve input from the administrator, be sure that you've properly secured the access controls on the path being used to hold the files. If an untrusted user has access to this path, he can provide (and potentially abuse) malicious input to workflows running with high privileges.

For more information about writing PowerShell workflows, see Recipe 30.1, "Write a Workflow".

## See Also

Recipe 30.1, "Write a Workflow"

# 30.8. Add Raw XAML to a Workflow

## Problem

You want to include a segment of literal XAML in a script-based workflow.

## Solution

Use the Invoke-Expression command with the -Language XAML parameter. Input you provide to the -Command parameter will be included directly in the resulting workflow:

```
workflow Invoke-InlineXaml
{
    Invoke-Expression -Language XAML `
        -Command '    <WriteLine>["Hello, World"]</WriteLine>'
}
```

## Discussion

When you write a workflow, PowerShell compiles the script that you type into a form used natively by the Windows Workflow Foundation engine, called XAML (Extensible Application Markup Language).

You can use the XamlDefinition property of your command to see how PowerShell converts your script into XAML:

```
PS > Get-Command Invoke-InlineXaml | Foreach-Object XamlDefinition
<Activity
    (...)
    >
    <Sequence>
        <WriteLine>["Hello, World"]</WriteLine>
        <Sequence.Variables>
            <Variable Name="WorkflowCommandName"
                x:TypeArguments="ns0:String" Default = "Invoke-InlineXaml" />
        </Sequence.Variables>
    </Sequence>
</Activity>
```

While PowerShell's scripting language should be sufficient for all workflows, you may find the need to write portions of your workflow in XAML directly. One potential example arises from converting a workflow that used to be written directly in XAML. To support this, PowerShell offers the -Language parameter to the Invoke-Expression command. When you supply an argument to the -Command parameter, PowerShell includes the exact XAML that you specify. Since PowerShell incorporates your XAML directly, you are also responsible for its correctness. PowerShell can't provide the usual detailed error detection and scripting support for XAML that it doesn't generate, so the error messages come directly from the Windows Workflow Foundation engine and are usually much more obscure.

For more information about writing PowerShell workflows, see Recipe 30.1, "Write a Workflow".

## See Also

Recipe 30.1, "Write a Workflow"

# 30.9. Reference Custom Activities in a Workflow

## Problem

You want to reference custom activities written for Windows Workflow Foundation.

## Solution

Use the -Assembly parameter of the #requires statement to reference an assembly that contains custom workflow activities. Then invoke that activity as though it were a command. Use PowerShell's parameter syntax to provide values for activity properties.

```
workflow Invoke-WorkflowActivity
{
```

---

```
    #requires -Assembly CustomActivityDll

    CustomActivity -Text "Hello World"
}
```

# Discussion

When you call a command in a workflow, PowerShell maps that call to Windows Work-flow Foundation's equivalent concept of a command: an *activity*.

For the most part, PowerShell activities should be able to handle everything you need to do in a workflow. That said, Windows Workflow Foundation is a mature technology that has its own ecosystem of workflow activities. Many of those activities provide useful features, and PowerShell makes it easy to work with those activities from a workflow.

This support for external activities comes from the -Assembly parameter of the #requires statement.

As an example, consider the WriteLine activity included in Windows Workflow Foundation. We can use the assembly's strong name to reference the activity:

```
workflow Invoke-WorkflowActivity
{
    #requires -Assembly "System.Activities,Version=4.0.0.0,
        Culture=neutral,PublicKeyToken=31bf3856ad364e35" ## do not break the line
    WriteLine -Text "Hello World"
}
```

The WriteLine activity isn't supported by default in script-based workflows, since it writes directly to the PowerShell console window. Given that workflows are intended to be run in remote sessions without access to an active console, writing to the output stream (via Write-Output or simply emitting objects) is the better way to accomplish the same goal.

The #requires statement supports three different ways to include activity DLLs:

*Relative path*
> If you specify a relative path (such as: #requires -Assembly CustomActivityDll), PowerShell loads the activity assembly from the root directory of the module that defines the workflow.

*Absolute path*
> If you specify an absolute path (such as: #requires -Assembly c:\Workflows \CustomActivityDll), PowerShell loads the activity assembly from that path.

*Strong name*
> If you specify the assembly's strong name, PowerShell looks in the systemwide GAC for that assembly.

Once you've referenced an activity assembly, you call its commands in the same way that you call other PowerShell commands.

When working with custom activities, you might stumble on *generic activities*. These are activities that require you to declare their output type. These are often documented on MSDN and elsewhere with text similar to `public sealed class PowerShell Value<T>`. To invoke a generic activity, place its type argument within square brackets:

```
workflow Invoke-GenericActivity
{
    $result = PowerShellValue[string] -Expression "'Hello world'"
    $result
}
```

For more information about writing PowerShell workflows, see Recipe 30.1, "Write a Workflow".

### See Also

Recipe 30.1, "Write a Workflow"

# 30.10. Debug or Troubleshoot a Workflow

## Problem

You want to diagnose or further understand the behavior of a running workflow.

## Solution

When debugging at implementation time, use `Write-Output` statements to trace important information in your workflow. As with PowerShell scripts, `Write-Output` is implied when a workflow generates output:

```
workflow Invoke-DebugWorkflow
{
    $a = 10
    $b = 20
    Write-Output "Current value of A is: $a"

    "All available variables:"
    InlineScript { dir variable: }
}
```

At runtime, review the workflow's `Progress` output to trace its execution.

```
PS > $j = Invoke-TestWorkflow -AsJob
PS > $j.ChildJobs[0].Progress

ActivityId       : 0
ParentActivityId : -1
```

```
Activity          : Get-Process
StatusDescription : Running
CurrentOperation  : 05df2fad-0a90-4576-aaef-867804d7f948:[localhost]:1.9:
                    Invoke-TestWorkflow line:2 char:2
PercentComplete   : -1
SecondsRemaining  : -1
RecordType        : Processing

(...)
```

For advanced diagnosis, review the output of $pshome\traces\PSTrace.etl after running Enable-PSWSManCombinedTrace and Disable-PSWSManCombinedTrace.

```
PS > Enable-PSWSManCombinedTrace
PS > Invoke-TestWorkflow
PS > Disable-PSWSManCombinedTrace
PS > $r = Get-WinEvent -Path $pshome\Traces\PSTrace.etl -Oldest
PS > $r | Where-Object ProviderName -eq Microsoft-Windows-PowerShell |
    Foreach-Object Message
(...)

Activity was queued for execution.
  WorkflowId: {FD87A839-5D23-4EC5-AEEF-82AD3E3A3360}
  ActivityName: Get-Process
Trace Information:
  :Activity DisplayName: Get-Process :ActivityInstanceState: Executing

(...)
```

## Discussion

When diagnosing a workflow, there are two primary types of debugging you'll do: authoring-time debugging, and runtime debugging.

### Authoring-time debugging

Debugging a workflow during development is what you'll do most often. In this situation, the questions on your mind will be along the lines of, "What is the value of this variable right now?" and "Is this portion of my workflow even being run?"

Since workflows run as background jobs, interactive debugging (as implemented beautifully for scripts in the PowerShell Integrated Scripting Environment) is not supported. Instead, the primary form of debugging at your disposal is the long-held staple of software: *trace statements*. If you need to determine the value of a variable, write a trace statement to output the value. If you need to find out if a branch of your workflow is being executed, write a trace statement in that branch that says "Got here!" or something similar.

## Runtime debugging

Once you've got a workflow written or deployed, how do you diagnose its behavior through runtime analysis alone?

The simplest way to diagnose a worklow's runtime behavior is through the job object that represents the workflow. If the workflow terminates with an error, you can access the `Reason` property of the `JobStateInfo` property to determine why:

```
PS > $j.ChildJobs[0].JobStateInfo.Reason | Format-List * -Force
Message        : Attempted to divide by zero.
(...)
```

If the workflow generated errors, you can access these through the `Error` collection:

```
PS > $j.ChildJobs[0].Error
Microsoft.PowerShell.Management\Get-Process : Cannot find a process with
the name "IDoNotExist". Verify the process name and call the cmdlet again.
At foo:1 char:1
(...)
```

If neither the exception nor error objects provide the information you need to diagnose your workflow, execution tracing is the next place to turn. For every workflow execution, PowerShell logs the progress of every command to the job's `Progress` stream. As demonstrated by the solution, this progress information includes the activity name, script position, execution status, and more. The `CurrentOperation` property includes the workflow GUID, computer the activity was run on, activity ID, and script position. With a little parsing, we can create a very useful script trace.

```
PS > $j.ChildJobs[0].Progress | Select Activity,StatusDescription,
    {($_.CurrentOperation -split ":",4)[3]} | ft -auto


Activity        StatusDescription ($_.CurrentOperation -split ":",4)[3]
--------        ----------------- ------------------------------------
Get-Process     Running           Invoke-DebugWorkflow line:3 char:3
Get-Process     Completed         Invoke-DebugWorkflow line:3 char:3
Get-Service     Running           Invoke-DebugWorkflow line:4 char:4
Get-Service     Completed         Invoke-DebugWorkflow line:4 char:4
Get-CimInstance Running           Invoke-DebugWorkflow line:5 char:5
Get-CimInstance Completed         Invoke-DebugWorkflow line:5 char:5
```

Even with this much detail, problems are sometimes rooted extremely deeply in the infrastructure. For example, PowerShell may run into problems during its automatic connection management. Or, it might start throttling connection attempts because your workflow has hit the per-computer connection limit.

For analysis at this level of detail, you can use the `PSDiagnostics` module. This module lets you monitor PowerShell's rich stream of Event Tracing for Windows (ETW) information. Comprehensive documentation of these events isn't possible, but the text of the message can often be insightful. To dump the diagnostic information into a text file for later viewing, run the following commands:

```
workflow Invoke-DebugWorkflow
{
    foreach -parallel ($item in 1..10)
    {
        InlineScript
        {
            "Starting $USING:item"
            Start-Sleep -Seconds 2
            "Ending $USING:item"
        } -PSComputername SomeComputerName
    }
}

PS > Enable-PSWSManCombinedTrace
PS > Invoke-DebugWorkflow
PS > Disable-PSWSManCombinedTrace
PS > $r = Get-WinEvent -Path $pshome\Traces\PSTrace.etl -Oldest
PS > $r | format-List > c:\temp\Invoke-DebugWorkflow.log
```

If you open *Invoke-DebugWorkflow.log* in a text editor, you can use the `Message` properties for analysis. For example, here are some messages that show PowerShell reusing
a connection it's made to a remote machine:

```
Message       : Trace Information:
                PSW ConnMgr: Creating new connection to service request
(...)
Message       : Trace Information:
                PowerShell activity: Finished running command.
(...)
Message       : Trace Information:
                PSW ConnMgr: Assigning existing connection to request
(...)
Message       : Trace Information:
                PowerShell activity: Finished running command.
```

Of course, a text editor isn't the only way to analyze these logs. Given that these event
logs are returned as fully structured objects, you can easily write scripts to automate the
analysis of these large data sets. For more information about analyzing ETW logfiles,
see Chapter 23.

As a final source of runtime knowledge, PowerShell workflows expose a fairly detailed
list of performance counters. These counters let you track the number of running workflows, number of remoting connections being used, and more. To see these counters,
use the `Get-Counter` cmdlet:

```
PS > Get-Counter -ListSet "PowerShell Workflow" | Foreach Paths

(...)
\PowerShell Workflow(*)\# of running workflow jobs
(...)

PS > Get-Counter "\PowerShell Workflow(*)\# of running workflow jobs"
```

```
Timestamp              CounterSamples
---------              --------------
8/24/2012 9:00:20 PM   \\computer\powershell workflow(7564)\
                        # of running workflow jobs : 1
```

For more information about working with performance counters, see Recipe 17.3, "Access Windows Performance Counters". For more information about writing PowerShell workflows, see Recipe 30.1, "Write a Workflow".

## See Also

Recipe 17.3, "Access Windows Performance Counters"

Recipe 30.1, "Write a Workflow"

Chapter 23, *Event Logs*

# 30.11. Use PowerShell Activities from a Traditional Windows Workflow Application

## Problem

You have a traditional Windows Workflow Foundation application and want to use PowerShell's cmdlets as activities.

## Solution

Add a reference to `Microsoft.PowerShell.Workflow.ServiceCore`, the appropriate `Microsoft.PowerShell.Activities` assembly, and invoke the PowerShell activity as you would any other Windows Workflow Foundation activity.

## Discussion

PowerShell's workflow engine builds entirely on Windows Workflow Foundation. When a workflow script calls the `Get-Process` cmdlet, PowerShell converts this to a call to the `Microsoft.PowerShell.Management.Activities.GetProcess` activity. In developing this support, PowerShell created traditional workflow activities for every single cmdlet in PowerShell, omitting those that didn't make sense in a workflow context.

As an example of this support, we can see how PowerShell compiles this simple workflow:

```
workflow Get-MyProcess
{
    Get-Process -Name PowerShell
}
```

Into the corresponding XAML:

```
<Activity
    x:Class="Microsoft.PowerShell.DynamicActivities.Activity_717311396"
    xmlns:ns3="clr-namespace:Microsoft.PowerShell.Management.Activities;
        assembly=Microsoft.PowerShell.Management.Activities"
    >
    <Sequence>
        <ns3:GetProcess>
            <ns3:GetProcess.Name>
                <ns2:InArgument x:TypeArguments="ns0:String[]">
                    <ns1:PowerShellValue x:TypeArguments="ns0:String[]"
                        Expression="'PowerShell'" />
                </ns2:InArgument>
            </ns3:GetProcess.Name>
        </ns3:GetProcess>
        <Sequence.Variables>
            <Variable Name="WorkflowCommandName" x:TypeArguments="ns0:String"
                Default = "Get-MyProcess" />
        </Sequence.Variables>
    </Sequence>
</Activity>
```

If you want to use PowerShell activities within your own traditional Windows Workflow Foundation–based application, you can add references to the core PowerShell activities assemblies just as PowerShell does.

PowerShell separates its activities into the following assemblies, roughly relating to the modules that define the corresponding cmdlets:

- `Microsoft.PowerShell.Activities`
- `Microsoft.PowerShell.Core.Activities`
- `Microsoft.PowerShell.Diagnostics.Activities`
- `Microsoft.PowerShell.Management.Activities`
- `Microsoft.PowerShell.Security.Activities`
- `Microsoft.WSMan.Management.Activities`
- `Microsoft.PowerShell.Workflow.ServiceCore`

These are registered in the Windows Global Assembly Cache (GAC), which means that Windows Workflow Foundation will discover them without issue using the earlier XAML syntax. However, the Visual Studio Workflow Designer understands only fully qualified paths when adding activity libraries to its toolbox. To find the full path to an assembly in the GAC, use the `System.Reflection.Assembly.LoadWithPartial Name()` method in PowerShell:

```
PS > $assembly = [Reflection.Assembly]::LoadWithPartialName(
    "Microsoft.PowerShell.Management.Activities")
PS > $assembly.Location
C:\Windows\Microsoft.Net\...\Microsoft.PowerShell.Management.Activities.dll
PS > $assembly.Location | clip
```

While it is useful to work with individual cmdlets exposed as activities, workflows are ideally sequences of chunky actions. The activity that enables this most effectively is the `InlineScript` activity, defined in the `Microsoft.PowerShell.Activities` DLL.

In addition to `InlineScript` being supremely useful, the `PowerShellValue` activity provides a handy alternative to the `VisualBasicValue` activity built into Windows Workflow. Rather than evaluate Visual Basic expressions, the `PowerShellValue` activity evaluates PowerShell expressions.

Perhaps not surprisingly, the activities written to represent PowerShell cmdlets were not all written by hand. To provide the incredible consistency and ubiquity of command functionality, PowerShell defines a `PSRemotingActivity` base class. If you'd like to expose a command in the same way that PowerShell does, simply derive from this base class. Rather than derive from it directly, you can use the code generator supplied by the `Microsoft.PowerShell.Activities.ActivityGenerator` class.

```
PS > [Microsoft.PowerShell.Activities.ActivityGenerator]::GenerateFromName(
    "Get-Process", "MyCompany.MyProduct.Activities")

using Microsoft.PowerShell.Activities;
using System.Management.Automation;
using System.Activities;
using System.Collections.Generic;
using System.ComponentModel;

namespace MyCompany.MyProduct.Activities
{
    /// <summary>
    /// Activity to invoke the Microsoft.PowerShell.Management\Get-Process
    /// command in a Workflow.
    /// </summary>
    [System.CodeDom.Compiler.GeneratedCode(
        "Microsoft.PowerShell.Activities.ActivityGenerator.GenerateFromName",
        "3.0")]
    (...)
```

For more information about writing PowerShell workflows, see Recipe 30.1, "Write a Workflow".

## See Also

Recipe 30.1, "Write a Workflow"

# Transactions

## 31.0. Introduction

*Transactions* describe a system's ability to support tentative or multistep changes. When you make changes within the context of a transaction, the system provides four main guarantees:

*Isolation*
> To observers not participating in the transaction, the commands inside the transaction have not impacted the system.

*Atomicity*
> Once you decide to finalize (*commit*) a transaction, either all of the changes take effect or none of them do.

*Consistency*
> Errors caused during a transaction that would cause an inconsistent system state are dealt with in order to bring the system back to a consistent state.

*Durability*
> Once the system has informed you of the transaction's successful completion, you can be certain that the changes are permanent.

As a real-world example of a transaction, consider a money transfer between two bank accounts. This might happen in two stages: subtract the money from the first account, and then add the money to the second account. In this situation, you have the exact same goals for robustness and correctness:

*Isolation*
> While the money transfer is taking place (but has not yet completed), the balance of both bank accounts appears unchanged.

*Atomicity*

At some point in the process, it's possible that we've subtracted the money from the first account but haven't added it yet to the second account. When we process the money transfer, it's critical that the system never show this intermediate state. Either all of the changes take effect or none of them do.

*Consistency*

If an error occurs during the money transfer, the system takes corrective action to ensure that it is not left in an intermediate state. Perhaps it accounts for a lack of funds by adding an overdraft charge or by abandoning the money transfer altogether. It should not, for example, take the funds from one account without depositing them into the second account.

*Durability*

Once the money transfer completes, you don't have to worry about a system error undoing all or part of it.

Although transactions are normally a developer topic, PowerShell exposes transactions as an end-user concept, opening a great deal of potential for consistent system management.

To start a transaction, call the Start-Transaction cmdlet. To use a cmdlet that supports transactions, specify the -UseTransaction parameter. Being explicit about this parameter is crucial, as many cmdlets that support transactions can work equally well without one. Because of that, PowerShell lets the cmdlet participate in the transaction only when you supply this parameter.

In Windows Vista and later, PowerShell's registry provider supports transactions as a first-class concept. You can see this in action in Recipe 21.6, "Safely Combine Related Registry Modifications".

```
PS > Set-Location HKCU:
PS > Start-Transaction

PS > mkdir TempKey -UseTransaction


    Hive: HKEY_CURRENT_USER

SKC  VC Name                        Property
---  -- ----                        --------
  0   0 TempKey                     {}

PS > New-Item TempKey\TempKey2 -UseTransaction


    Hive: HKEY_CURRENT_USER\TempKey
```

```
SKC  VC Name                           Property
---  -- ----                           --------
  0   0 TempKey2                        {}

PS > Get-ChildItem TempKey
Get-ChildItem : Cannot find path 'HKEY_CURRENT_USER\TempKey' because it
does not exist.

PS > Complete-Transaction
PS > Get-ChildItem TempKey


    Hive: HKEY_CURRENT_USER\TempKey

SKC  VC Name                           Property
---  -- ----                           --------
  0   0 TempKey2                        {}
```

Once you have completed the transactional work, call either the `Complete-Transaction` cmdlet to make it final or the `Undo-Transaction` cmdlet to discard the changes. While you may now be tempted to experiment with transactions on other providers (for example, the filesystem), be aware that only the registry provider currently supports them.

# 31.1. Safely Experiment with Transactions

## Problem

You want to experiment with PowerShell's transactions support but don't want to use the Registry Provider as your playground.

## Solution

Use PowerShell's `System.Management.Automation.TransactedString` object along with the `Use-Transaction` cmdlet to experiment with a string, rather than registry keys:

```
PS > Start-Transaction

Suggestion [1,Transactions]: Once a transaction is started, only commands that
get called with the -UseTransaction flag become part of that transaction.
PS >
PS > $transactedString = New-Object Microsoft.PowerShell.Commands.Management.
    TransactedString
PS > $transactedString.Append("Hello ")
PS >
PS > Use-Transaction -UseTransaction { $transactedString.Append("World") }
```

```
Suggestion [2,Transactions]: The Use-Transaction cmdlet is intended for
scripting of transaction-enabled .NET objects. Its ScriptBlock should contain
nothing else.
PS >
PS > $transactedString.ToString()
Hello
PS >
PS > Complete-Transaction
PS >
PS > $transactedString.ToString()
Hello World
PS >
```

## Discussion

PowerShell's transaction support builds on four core cmdlets: Start-Transaction, Use-Transaction, Complete-Transaction, and Undo-Transaction.

The Start-Transaction begins a transaction, creating a context where changes are visible to commands within the transaction, but not outside of it. For the most part, after starting a transaction, you'll apply commands to that transaction by adding the -UseTransaction parameter to a cmdlet that supports it. For example, when a PowerShell provider supports transactions, all of PowerShell's core cmdlets (Get-ChildItem, Remove-Item, etc.) let you specify the -UseTransaction parameter for actions against that provider.

The Use-Transaction cmdlet is slightly different. Although it still requires the -Use Transaction parameter to apply its script block to the current transaction, its sole purpose is to let you script against .NET objects that support transactions themselves. Since they have no way to supply a -UseTransaction parameter, PowerShell offers this generic cmdlet for any type of transactional .NET scripting.

 Other transaction-enabled cmdlets should not be called within the Use-Transaction script block. You still need to provide the -UseTransaction parameter to the cmdlet being called, and there's a chance that they might cause instability with your PowerShell-wide transactions.

To give users an opportunity to play with something a little less risky than the Windows Registry, PowerShell includes the Microsoft.PowerShell.Commands.Management. TransactedString class. This class acts like you'd expect any transacted command to act and lets you become familiar with how the rest of PowerShell's transaction cmdlets work together. Since this is a .NET object, it must be called from within the script block of the Use-Transaction cmdlet.

Finally, when you are finished performing tasks for the current transaction, call either the `Complete-Transaction` or the `Undo-Transaction` cmdlet. As compared to the solution, here's an example session where the `Undo-Transaction` cmdlet lets you discard changes made during the transaction:

```
PS > Start-Transaction

Suggestion [1,Transactions]: Once a transaction is started, only commands that
get called with the -UseTransaction flag become part of that transaction.
PS >
PS > $transactedString = New-Object Microsoft.PowerShell.Commands.Management.
TransactedString
PS > $transactedString.Append("Hello ")
PS >
PS > Use-Transaction -UseTransaction { $transactedString.Append("World") }

Suggestion [2,Transactions]: The Use-Transaction cmdlet is intended for
scripting of transaction-enabled .NET objects. Its ScriptBlock should contain
nothing else.
PS >
PS > $transactedString.ToString()
Hello
PS >
PS > Undo-Transaction
PS >
PS > $transactedString.ToString()
Hello
```

For more information about transactions in the Windows Registry, see Recipe 21.6, "Safely Combine Related Registry Modifications".

## See Also

Recipe 21.6, "Safely Combine Related Registry Modifications"

# 31.2. Change Error Recovery Behavior in Transactions

## Problem

You want to change how PowerShell responds to errors during the execution of a transacted cmdlet.

## Solution

Use the `-RollbackPreference` parameter of the `Start-Transaction` cmdlet to control what type of error will cause PowerShell to automatically undo your transaction:

```
HKCU:\ >Start-Transaction
HKCU:\ >New-Item Foo -UseTransaction
```

```
        Hive: HKEY_CURRENT_USER

SKC  VC Name                         Property
---  -- ----                         --------
  0   0 Foo                          {}

HKCU:\ >Copy IDoNotExist Foo -UseTransaction
Copy-Item : Cannot find path 'HKCU:\IDoNotExist' because it does not exist.

HKCU:\ >Complete-Transaction
Complete-Transaction : Cannot commit transaction. The transaction has been
rolled back or has timed out.

HKCU:\ >Start-Transaction -RollbackPreference TerminatingError

        Hive: HKEY_CURRENT_USER

SKC  VC Name                         Property
---  -- ----                         --------
  0   0 Foo                          {}

HKCU:\ >Copy IDoNotExist Foo -UseTransaction
Copy-Item : Cannot find path 'HKCU:\IDoNotExist' because it does not exist.

HKCU:\ >Complete-Transaction
HKCU:\ >Get-Item Foo

        Hive: HKEY_CURRENT_USER

SKC  VC Name                         Property
---  -- ----                         --------
  0   0 Foo                          {}
```

## Discussion

Errors in scripts are an extremely frequent cause of system inconsistency. If a script incorrectly assumes the existence of a registry key or other system state, this type of error tends to waterfall through the entire script. As the script continues, some of the operations succeed while others fail. When the script completes, you're in the difficult situation of not knowing exactly what portions of the script worked correctly.

Sometimes running the script again will magically make the problems go away. Unfortunately, it's just as common to face a painstaking manual cleanup effort.

Addressing these consistency issues is one of the primary goals of system transactions.

When PowerShell creates a new transaction, it undoes (*rolls back*) your transaction for any error it encounters that is operating in the context of that transaction. When PowerShell rolls back your transaction, the system impact is clear: no part of your transaction was made permanent, so your system is still entirely consistent.

Some situations are simply too volatile to depend on this rigid interpretation of consistency, though, so PowerShell offers the -RollbackPreference parameter on the Start-Transaction to let you configure how it should respond to errors:

Error
> PowerShell rolls back your transaction when any error occurs.

TerminatingError
> PowerShell rolls back your transaction only when a terminating error occurs.

Never
> PowerShell never automatically rolls back your transaction in response to errors.

For more information about PowerShell's error handling and error levels, see Chapter 15.

## See Also

Chapter 15, *Tracing and Error Management*

# Event Handling

## 32.0. Introduction

Much of system administration is reactionary: taking some action when a system service shuts down, when files are created or deleted, when changes are made to the Windows Registry, or even on a timed interval.

The easiest way to respond to system changes is to simply *poll* for them. If you're waiting for a file to be created, just check for it every once in a while until it shows up. If you're waiting for a process to start, just keep calling the Get-Process cmdlet until it's there.

This approach is passable for some events (such as waiting for a process to come or go), but it quickly falls apart when you need to monitor huge portions of the system—such as the entire registry or filesystem.

An an alternative to polling for system changes, many technologies support automatic notifications—known as *events*. When an application registers for these automatic notifications, it can respond to them as soon as they happen, rather than having to poll for them.

Unfortunately, each technology offers its own method of event notification: .NET defines one approach and WMI defines another. When you have a script that wants to generate its own events, neither technology offers an option.

PowerShell addresses this complexity by introducing a single, consistent set of event-related cmdlets. These cmdlets let you work with all of these different event sources. When an event occurs, you can let PowerShell store the notification for you in its event queue or use an Action script block to process it automatically:

```
PS > "Hello" > file.txt
PS > Get-Item file.txt

    Directory: C:\temp
```

```
Mode              LastWriteTime      Length Name
----              -------------      ------ ----
-a---         2/21/2010  12:57 PM        16 file.txt

PS > Get-Process notepad

Handles  NPM(K)    PM(K)     WS(K) VM(M)   CPU(s)    Id ProcessName
-------  ------    -----     ----- -----   ------    -- -----------
     64       3     1140      6196    63     0.06  3240 notepad

PS > Register-CimIndicationEvent Win32_ProcessStopTrace `
    -SourceIdentifier ProcessStopWatcher `
    -Action {
        if($EventArgs.NewEvent.ProcessName -eq "notepad.exe")
        {
            Remove-Item c:\temp\file.txt
        }
    }

PS > Stop-Process -n notepad
PS > Get-Item c:\temp\file.txt
Get-Item : Cannot find path 'C:\temp\file.txt' because it does not exist.
```

By building on PowerShell eventing, you can write scripts to quickly react to an ever-changing system.

# 32.1. Respond to Automatically Generated Events

## Problem

You want to respond automatically to a .NET, WMI, or engine event.

## Solution

Use the -Action parameter of the Register-ObjectEvent, Register-CimIndicationEvent, and Register-EngineEvent cmdlets to be notified when an event arrives and have PowerShell invoke the script block you supply:

```
PS > $timer = New-Object Timers.Timer
PS > $timer.Interval = 1000
PS > Register-ObjectEvent $timer Elapsed -SourceIdentifier Timer.Elapsed `
    -Action { $GLOBAL:lastRandom = Get-Random }

Id              Name          State      HasMoreData    Location
--              ----          -----      -----------    --------
2               Timer.Elapsed NotStarted False

PS > $timer.Enabled = $true
PS > $lastRandom
```

```
836077209
PS > $lastRandom
2030675971
PS > $lastRandom
1617766254
PS > Unregister-Event Timer.Elapsed
```

# Discussion

PowerShell's event registration cmdlets give you a consistent way to interact with many different event technologies: .NET events, WMI events, and PowerShell engine events.

By default, when you register for an event, PowerShell adds a new entry to the session-wide event repository called the *event queue*. You can use the Get-Event cmdlet to see events added to this queue, and the Remove-Event cmdlet to remove events from this queue.

In addition to its support for manual processing of events, you can also supply a script block to the -Action parameter of the event registration cmdlets. When you provide a script block to the -Action parameter, PowerShell automatically processes events when they arrive.

However, doing two things at once means multithreading. And multithreading? Thar be dragons! To prevent you from having to deal with multithreading issues, PowerShell tightly controls the execution of these script blocks. When it's time to process an action, it suspends the current script or pipeline, executes the action, and then resumes where it left off. It processes only one action at a time.

```
PS > $timer = New-Object Timers.Timer
PS > $timer.Interval = 1000
PS > Register-ObjectEvent $timer Elapsed -SourceIdentifier Timer.Elapsed `
    -Action { Write-Host "Processing event" }
$timer.Enabled = $true

PS > while($true) { Write-Host "Processing loop"; Sleep 1 }
Processing loop
Processing event
Processing loop
Processing event
Processing loop
Processing event
Processing loop
Processing event
Processing loop
(...)
```

Inside of the -Action script block, PowerShell gives your script access to five automatic variables:

**eventSubscriber**

The subscriber (event registration) that generated this event.

**event**

The details of the event itself: `MessageData`, `TimeGenerated`, etc.

**args**

The arguments and parameters of the event handler. Most events place the event sender and customized event information as the first two arguments, but this depends on the event handler.

**sender**

The object that fired the event (if any).

**eventArgs**

The customized event information that the event defines, if any. For example, the `Timers.Timer` object provides a `TimerElapsedEventArgs` object for this parameter. This object includes a `SignalTime` parameter, which identifies exactly when the timer fired. Likewise, WMI events define an object that places most of the information in the `$eventArgs.NewEvent` property.

In addition to the script block that you supply to the `-Action` parameter, you can also supply any objects you'd like to the `-MessageData` parameter during your event registration. PowerShell associates this data with any event notifications it generates for this event registration.

To prevent your script block from accidentally corrupting the state of scripts that it interrupts, PowerShell places it in a very isolated environment. Primarily, PowerShell gives you access to your event action through its job infrastructure. As with other PowerShell jobs, you can use the `Receive-Job` cmdlet to retrieve any output generated by your event action:

```
PS > $timer = New-Object Timers.Timer
PS > $timer.Interval = 1000
PS > Register-ObjectEvent $timer Elapsed -SourceIdentifier Timer.Elapsed `
    -Action {
        $SCRIPT:triggerCount = 1 + $SCRIPT:triggerCount
        "Processing Event $triggerCount"
    }
PS > $timer.Enabled = $true

Id              Name            State       HasMoreData     Location
--              ----            -----       -----------     --------
1               Timer.Elapsed   NotStarted  False

PS > Get-Job 1
```

---

```
Id              Name           State     HasMoreData    Location
--              ----           -----     -----------    --------
1               Timer.Elapsed  Running   True


PS > Receive-Job 1
Processing Event 1
Processing Event 2
Processing Event 3
(...)
```

For more information about working with PowerShell jobs, see Recipe 1.5, "Invoke a Long-Running or Background Command".

In addition to exposing your event actions through a job interface, PowerShell also uses a module to ensure that your -Action script block is not impacted by (and does not impact) other scripts running on the system. As with all modules, $GLOBAL variables are shared by the entire session. $SCRIPT variables are shared and persisted for all invocations of the script block. All other variables persist only for the current triggering of your event action. For more information about PowerShell modules, see Recipe 11.7, "Write Commands That Maintain State".

For more information about useful .NET and WMI events, see Appendix I.

## See Also

Recipe 1.5, "Invoke a Long-Running or Background Command"

Recipe 11.7, "Write Commands That Maintain State"

Appendix I, *Selected Events and Their Uses*

# 32.2. Create and Respond to Custom Events

## Problem

You want to create new events for other scripts to consume or want to respond automatically when they occur.

## Solution

Use the New-Event cmdlet to generate a custom event. Use the -Action parameter of the Register-EngineEvent cmdlet to respond to that event automatically.

```
PS > Register-EngineEvent -SourceIdentifier Custom.Event `
    -Action { Write-Host "Received Event" }

PS > $null = New-Event Custom.Event
Received Event
```

## Discussion

The New-Event cmdlet lets you create new custom events for other scripts or event registrations to consume. When you call the New-Event cmdlet, PowerShell adds a new entry to the sessionwide event repository called the *event queue*. You can use the Get-Event cmdlet to see events added to this queue, or you can use the Register-EngineEvent cmdlet to have PowerShell respond automatically.

One prime use of the New-Event cmdlet is to adapt complex events surfaced through the generic WMI and .NET event cmdlets. By writing task-focused commands to surface this adapted data, you can offer and work with data that is simpler to consume.

To accomplish this goal, use the Register-ObjectEvent or Register-Cim IndicationEvent cmdlets to register for one of their events. In the -Action script block, use the New-Event cmdlet to generate a new, more specialized event.

In this scenario, the event registrations that interact with .NET or WMI directly are merely "support" events, and users would not expect to see them when they use the Get-EventSubscriber cmdlet. To hide these event registrations by default, both the Register-ObjectEvent and Register-CimIndicationEvent cmdlets offer a -SupportEvent parameter.

Here is an example of two functions that notify you when a new process starts:

```
## Enable process creation events
function Enable-ProcessCreationEvent
{
    $identifier = "WMI.ProcessCreated"
    $query = "SELECT * FROM __instancecreationevent " +
                "WITHIN 5 " +
                "WHERE targetinstance isa 'win32_process'"
    Register-CimIndicationEvent -Query $query -SourceIdentifier $identifier `
        -SupportEvent -Action {
            [void] (New-Event "PowerShell.ProcessCreated" `
                -Sender $sender `
                -EventArguments $EventArgs.NewEvent.TargetInstance)
        }
}

## Disable process creation events
function Disable-ProcessCreationEvent
{
    Unregister-Event -Force -SourceIdentifier "WMI.ProcessCreated"
}
```

When used in the shell, the experience is much simpler than working with the WMI events directly:

```
PS > Enable-ProcessCreationEvent
PS > calc
PS > Get-Event

ComputerName      :
RunspaceId        : feeda302-4386-4360-81d9-f5455d74950f
EventIdentifier   : 2
Sender            : System.Management.ManagementEventWatcher
SourceEventArgs   :
SourceArgs        : {calc.exe}
SourceIdentifier  : PowerShell.ProcessCreated
TimeGenerated     : 2/21/2010 3:15:57 PM
MessageData       :

PS > (Get-Event).SourceArgs

(...)
Caption             : calc.exe
CommandLine         : "C:\Windows\system32\calc.exe"
CreationClassName   : Win32_Process
CreationDate        : 20100221151553.574124-480
CSCreationClassName : Win32_ComputerSystem
CSName              : LEEHOLMES1C23
Description         : calc.exe
ExecutablePath      : C:\Windows\system32\calc.exe
(...)

PS > Disable-ProcessCreationEvent
PS > notepad
PS > Get-Event

ComputerName      :
RunspaceId        : feeda302-4386-4360-81d9-f5455d74950f
EventIdentifier   : 2
Sender            : System.Management.ManagementEventWatcher
SourceEventArgs   :
SourceArgs        : {calc.exe}
SourceIdentifier  : PowerShell.ProcessCreated
TimeGenerated     : 2/21/2010 3:15:57 PM
MessageData       :
```

In addition to events that you create, *engine events* also represent events generated by the engine itself. In PowerShell version 2, the only defined engine event is Power Shell.Exiting. This lets you do some work when the PowerShell session exits. For an example of this, see Recipe 1.31, "Save State Between Sessions".

PowerShell treats engine events like any other type of event. You can use the `Register-EngineEvent` cmdlet to automatically react to these events, just as you can use the `Register-ObjectEvent` and `Register-CimIndicationEvent` cmdlets to react to .NET and WMI events, respectively. For information about how to respond to events automatically, see Recipe 32.1, "Respond to Automatically Generated Events".

## See Also

Recipe 1.31, "Save State Between Sessions"

Recipe 32.1, "Respond to Automatically Generated Events"

# 32.3. Create a Temporary Event Subscription

## Problem

You want to automatically perform an action when an event arrives but automatically remove the event subscription once that event fires.

## Solution

Use the `-MaxTriggerCount` parameter of the event registration command to limit PowerShell to one occurrence of the event:

```
PS > $timer = New-Object Timers.Timer
PS > $job = Register-ObjectEvent $timer Disposed -Action {
    [Console]::Beep(100,100) } -MaxTriggerCount 1
PS > Get-EventSubscriber
PS > $timer.Dispose()
PS > Get-EventSubscriber
PS > Remove-Job $job
```

## Discussion

When you provide a script block for the `-Action` parameter of `Register-ObjectEvent`, PowerShell creates an event subscriber to represent that subscription, and it also creates a job that lets you interact with the environment and results of that action. If the event registration is really a "throwaway" registration that you no longer want after the event gets generated, cleaning up afterward can be complex.

Fortunately, PowerShell supports the `-MaxTriggerCount` parameter that lets you configure a limit on how many times the event should trigger. Once the event subscription reaches that limit, PowerShell automatically unregisters that event subscriber.

When dealing with temporary event subscriptions, the solution demonstrates one additional step if your event subscription defines an -Action script block. PowerShell does not automatically remove the job associated with that action, as it may be holding important results. If you do not need these results, be sure to call the Remove-Job cmdlet as well.

For a script that combines both of these steps, see the Register-TemporaryEvent script included in this book's examples.

## See Also

Recipe 32.1, "Respond to Automatically Generated Events"

# 32.4. Forward Events from a Remote Computer

## Problem

You have a client connected to a remote machine through PowerShell Remoting, and you want to be notified when an event occurs on that machine.

## Solution

Use any of PowerShell's event registration cmdlets to subscribe to the event on the remote machine. Then, use the -Forward parameter to tell PowerShell to forward these events when they arrive:

```
PS > Get-Event
PS > $session = New-PSSession leeholmes1c23
PS > Enter-PSSession $session

[leeholmes1c23]: PS C:\> $timer = New-Object Timers.Timer
[leeholmes1c23]: PS C:\> $timer.Interval = 1000
[leeholmes1c23]: PS C:\> $timer.AutoReset = $false
[leeholmes1c23]: PS C:\> Register-ObjectEvent $timer Elapsed `
    -SourceIdentifier Timer.Elapsed -Forward
[leeholmes1c23]: PS C:\> $timer.Enabled = $true
[leeholmes1c23]: PS C:\> Exit-PSSession

PS > Get-Event

ComputerName    : leeholmes1c23
RunspaceId      : 053e6232-528a-4626-9b86-c50b8b762440
EventIdentifier : 1
Sender          : System.Timers.Timer
SourceEventArgs : System.Management.Automation.ForwardedEventArgs
```

```
SourceArgs        : {System.Timers.Timer, System.Timers.ElapsedEventArgs}
SourceIdentifier : Timer.Elapsed
TimeGenerated     : 2/21/2010 11:01:54 PM
MessageData       :
```

## Discussion

PowerShell's eventing infrastructure lets you define one of three possible actions when you register for an event:

- Add the event notifications to the event queue.
- Automatically process the event notifications with an -Action script block.
- Forward the event notifications to a client computer.

The -Forward parameter on all of the event registration cmdlets enables this third option. When you are connected to a remote machine that has this type of behavior enabled on an event registration, PowerShell will automatically forward those event notifications to your client machine. Using this technique, you can easily monitor many remote computers for system changes that interest you.

For more information about registering for events, see Recipe 32.1, "Respond to Automatically Generated Events". For more information about PowerShell Remoting, see Chapter 29.

## See Also

Recipe 32.1, "Respond to Automatically Generated Events"

Chapter 29, *Remoting*

# 32.5. Investigate Internal Event Action State

## Problem

You want to investigate the internal environment or state of an event subscriber's action.

## Solution

Retrieve the event subscriber, and then interact with the Subscriber.Action property:

```
PS > $null = Register-EngineEvent -SourceIdentifier Custom.Event `
    -Action {
        "Hello World"

        Write-Error "Got an Error"
```

```
            $SCRIPT:privateVariable = 10
    }

PS > $null = New-Event Custom.Event
PS > $subscriber = Get-EventSubscriber Custom.Event
PS > $subscriber.Action | Format-List

Module        : __DynamicModule_f2b39042-e89a-49b1-b460-6211b9895acc
StatusMessage :
HasMoreData   : True
Location      :
Command       :
                    "Hello World"
                    Write-Error "Got an Error"
                    $SCRIPT:privateVariable = 10

JobStateInfo : Running
Finished     : System.Threading.ManualResetEvent
InstanceId   : b3fcceae-d878-4c8b-a53e-01873f2cfbea
Id           : 1
Name         : Custom.Event
ChildJobs    : {}
Output       : {Hello World}
Error        : {Got an Error}
Progress     : {}
Verbose      : {}
Debug        : {}
Warning      : {}
State        : Running

PS > $subscriber.Action.Error
Write-Error : Got an Error
At line:4 char:20
+         Write-Error <<<<  "Got an Error"
    + CategoryInfo          : NotSpecified: (:) [Write-Error], WriteError
    Exception
    + FullyQualifiedErrorId : Microsoft.PowerShell.Commands.WriteError
    Exception,Microsoft.PowerShell.Commands.WriteErrorCommand
```

# Discussion

When you supply an -Action script block to any of the event registration cmdlets, PowerShell creates a PowerShell job to let you interact with that action. When interacting with this job, you have access to the job's output, errors, progress, verbose output, debug output, and warnings.

For more information about working with PowerShell jobs, see Recipe 1.5, "Invoke a Long-Running or Background Command".

In addition to the job interface, PowerShell's event system generates a module to isolate your script block from the rest of the system—for the benefit of both you and the system.

When you want to investigate the internal state of your action, PowerShell surfaces this state through the action's Module property. By passing the module to the invoke operator, you can invoke commands from within that module:

```
PS > $module = $subscriber.Action.Module
PS > & $module { dir variable:\privateVariable }

Name                            Value
----                            -----
privateVariable                 10
```

To make this even easier, you can use the Enter-Module script given by Recipe 11.9, "Diagnose and Interact with Internal Module State".

### See Also

Recipe 1.5, "Invoke a Long-Running or Background Command"

Recipe 11.9, "Diagnose and Interact with Internal Module State"

Recipe 32.1, "Respond to Automatically Generated Events"

## 32.6. Use a Script Block as a .NET Delegate or Event Handler

### Problem

You want to use a PowerShell script block to directly handle a .NET event or delegate.

### Solution

For objects that support a .NET delegate, simply assign the script block to that delegate:

```
$replacer = {
    param($match)

    $chars = $match.Groups[0].Value.ToCharArray()
    [Array]::Reverse($chars)
    $chars -join ''
}

PS > $regex = [Regex] "\w+"
PS > $regex.Replace("Hello World", $replacer)
olleH dlroW
```

To have a script block directly handle a .NET event, call that object's Add_*Event*( ) method:

```
$form.Add_Shown( { $form.Activate(); $textbox.Focus() } )
```

## Discussion

When working with some .NET developer APIs, you might run into a method that takes a delegate as one of its arguments. Delegates in .NET act as a way to provide custom logic to a .NET method that accepts them. For example, the solution supplies a custom delegate to the regular expression `Replace()` method to reverse the characters in the match—something not supported by regular expressions at all.

As another example, many array classes support custom delegates for searching, sorting, filtering, and more. In this example, we create a custom sorter to sort an array by the length of its elements:

```
PS > $list = New-Object System.Collections.Generic.List[String]
PS > $list.Add("1")
PS > $list.Add("22")
PS > $list.Add("3333")
PS > $list.Add("444")
PS > $list.Add("5")
PS > $list.Sort( { $args[0].Length - $args[1].Length } )
PS > $list
5
1
22
444
3333
```

Perhaps the most useful delegate per character is the ability to customize the behavior of the .NET Framework when it encounters an invalid certificate in a web network connection. This happens, for example, when you try to connect to a website that has an expired SSL certificate. The .NET Framework lets you override this behavior through a delegate that you supply to the `ServerCertificateValidationCallback` property in the `System.Net.ServicePointManager` class. Your delegate should return `$true` if the certificate should be accepted and `$false` otherwise. To accept all certificates during a development session, simply run the following statement:

```
[System.Net.ServicePointManager]::ServerCertificateValidationCallback = { $true }
```

In addition to delegates, you can also assign PowerShell script blocks directly to events on .NET objects.

Normally, you'll want to use PowerShell eventing to support this scenario. PowerShell eventing provides a very rich set of cmdlets that let you interact with events from many technologies: .NET, WMI, and the PowerShell engine itself. When you use PowerShell eventing to handle .NET events, PowerShell protects you from the dangers of having multiple script blocks running at once and keeps them from interfering with the rest of your PowerShell session.

However, when you write a self-contained script that uses events to handle events in a WinForms application, directly assigning script blocks to those events can be a much more lightweight development experience. For an example of this approach, see Recipe 13.10, "Program: Add a Graphical User Interface to Your Script".

For more information about PowerShell's event handling, see Recipe 32.1, "Respond to Automatically Generated Events".

## See Also

Recipe 13.10, "Program: Add a Graphical User Interface to Your Script"

Recipe 32.1, "Respond to Automatically Generated Events"

# References

Appendix A, *PowerShell Language and Environment*
Appendix B, *Regular Expression Reference*
Appendix C, *XPath Quick Reference*
Appendix D, *.NET String Formatting*
Appendix E, *.NET DateTime Formatting*
Appendix F, *Selected .NET Classes and Their Uses*
Appendix G, *WMI Reference*
Appendix H, *Selected COM Objects and Their Uses*
Appendix I, *Selected Events and Their Uses*
Appendix J, *Standard PowerShell Verbs*

# PowerShell Language and Environment

## Commands and Expressions

PowerShell breaks any line that you enter into its individual units (*tokens*), and then interprets each token in one of two ways: as a command or as an expression. The difference is subtle: expressions support logic and flow control statements (such as `if`, `foreach`, and `throw`), whereas commands do not.

You will often want to control the way that Windows PowerShell interprets your statements, so Table A-1 lists the options available to you.

*Table A-1. Windows PowerShell evaluation controls*

| Statement | Example | Explanation |
|---|---|---|
| Precedence control: ( ) | `PS > 5 * (1 + 2)`<br>`15`<br>`PS > (dir).Count`<br>`2276` | Forces the evaluation of a command or expression, similar to the way that parentheses are used to force the order of evaluation in a mathematical expression. |
| Expression subparse: $( ) | `PS > "The answer is (2+2)"`<br>`The answer is (2+2)`<br><br>`PS > "The answer is $(2+2)"`<br>`The answer is 4`<br><br>`PS > $value = 10`<br>`PS > $result = $(`<br>`   if($value -gt 0) { $true }`<br>`   else { $false })`<br>`PS > $result`<br>`True` | Forces the evaluation of a command or expression, similar to the way that parentheses are used to force the order of evaluation in a mathematical expression. However, a subparse is as powerful as a subprogram |

| Statement | Example | Explanation |
|---|---|---|
| | | and is required only when the subprogram contains logic or flow control statements. This statement is also used to expand dynamic information inside a string. |
| List evaluation: @( ) | ```
PS > "Hello".Length
5
PS > @("Hello").Length
1
PS > (Get-ChildItem).Count
12
PS > (Get-ChildItem *.txt).Count
PS > @(Get-ChildItem *.txt).Count
1
``` | Forces an expression to be evaluated as a list. If it is already a list, it will remain a list. If it is not, PowerShell temporarily treats it as one. |
| DATA evaluation: DATA { } | ```
PS > DATA { 1 + 1 }
2
PS > DATA { $myVariable = "Test" }
Assignment statements are not allowed in
restricted language mode or a Data section.
``` | Evaluates the given script block in the context of the PowerShell data language. The data language supports only data-centric features of the PowerShell language. |

# Comments

To create single-line comments, begin a line with the # character. To create a block (or multiline) comment, surround the region with the characters <# and #>.

```
# This is a regular comment

<# This is a block comment

function MyTest
{
    "This should not be considered a function"
}

$myVariable = 10;

Block comment ends
#>

# This is regular script again
```

# Help Comments

PowerShell creates help for your script or function by looking at its comments. If the comments include any supported help tags, PowerShell adds those to the help for your command.

Comment-based help supports the following tags, which are all case-insensitive:

.SYNOPSIS
> A short summary of the command, ideally a single sentence.

.DESCRIPTION
> A more detailed description of the command.

.PARAMETER *name*
> A description of parameter *name*, with one for each parameter you want to describe. While you can write a .PARAMETER comment for each parameter, PowerShell also supports comments written directly above the parameter (as shown in the solution). Putting parameter help alongside the actual parameter makes it easier to read and maintain.

.EXAMPLE
> An example of this command in use, with one for each example you want to provide. PowerShell treats the line immediately beneath the .EXAMPLE tag as the example command. If this line doesn't contain any text that looks like a prompt, PowerShell adds a prompt before it. It treats lines that follow the initial line as additional output and example commentary.

.INPUTS
> A short summary of pipeline input(s) supported by this command. For each input type, PowerShell's built-in help follows this convention:
>
> ```
> System.String
>     You can pipe a string that contains a path to Get-ChildItem.
> ```

.OUTPUTS
> A short summary of items generated by this command. For each output type, PowerShell's built-in help follows this convention:
>
> ```
> System.ServiceProcess.ServiceController
>     Get-Service returns objects that represent the services on the computer.
> ```

.NOTES
> Any additional notes or remarks about this command.

.LINK
> A link to a related help topic or command, with one .LINK tag per link. If the related help topic is a URL, PowerShell launches that URL when the user supplies the -Online parameter to Get-Help for your command.

Although these are all of the supported help tags you are likely to use, comment-based help also supports tags for some of Get-Help's more obscure features: .COMPONENT, .ROLE, .FUNCTIONALITY, .FORWARDHELPTARGETNAME, .FORWARDHELP CATEGORY, .REMOTEHELPRUNSPACE, and .EXTERNALHELP. For more information about these, type **Get-Help about_Comment_Based_Help**.

# Variables

Windows PowerShell provides several ways to define and access variables, as summarized in Table A-2.

*Table A-2. Windows PowerShell variable syntaxes*

| Syntax | Meaning |
|---|---|
| `$simpleVariable = "Value"` | A simple variable name. The variable name must consist of alphanumeric characters. Variable names are not case-sensitive. |
| `$variable1, $variable2 = "Value1","Value2"` | Multiple variable assignment. PowerShell populates each variable from the value in the corresponding position on the righthand side. Extra values are assigned as a list to the last variable listed. |
| `${arbitrary! @#@#`{var`}iable } = "Value"` | An arbitrary variable name. The variable name must be surrounded by curly braces, but it may contain any characters. Curly braces in the variable name must be escaped with a backtick (`). |
| `${c:\filename. extension}` | Variable "Get and Set Content" syntax. This is similar to the arbitrary variable name syntax. If the name corresponds to a valid PowerShell path, you can get and set the content of the item at that location by reading and writing to the variable. |
| `[datatype] $variable = "Value"` | Strongly typed variable. Ensures that the variable may contain only data of the type you declare. PowerShell throws an error if it cannot coerce the data to this type when you assign it. |
| `[constraint] $variable = "Value"` | Constrained variable. Ensures that the variable may contain only data that passes the supplied validation constraints.<br>`PS > [ValidateLength(4, 10)] $a = "Hello"`<br>The supported validation constraints are the same as those supported as parameter validation attributes. |
| `$SCOPE:variable` | Gets or sets the variable at that specific scope. Valid scope names are global (to make a variable available to the entire shell), script (to make a variable available only to the current script or persistent during module commands), local (to make a variable available only to the current scope and subscopes), and private (to make a variable available only to the current scope). The default scope is the *current* scope: global when defined interactively in the shell, script when defined outside any functions or script blocks in a script, and local elsewhere. |
| `New-Item Variable: \variable -Value value` | Creates a new variable using the variable provider. |
| `Get-Item Variable: \variable`<br>`Get-Variable variable` | Gets the variable using the variable provider or Get-Variable cmdlet. This lets you access extra information about the variable, such as its options and description. |

| Syntax | Meaning |
| --- | --- |
| New-Variable *variable* -Option *option* -Value *value* | Creates a variable using the New-Variable cmdlet. This lets you provide extra information about the variable, such as its options and description. |

 Unlike some languages, PowerShell rounds (rather than truncates) numbers when it converts them to the [int] data type:

```
PS > (3/2)
1.5
PS > [int] (3/2)
2
```

To have PowerShell truncate a number, see Chapter 6.

# Booleans

Boolean (true or false) variables are most commonly initialized to their literal values of $true and $false. When PowerShell evaluates variables as part of a Boolean expression (for example, an if statement), though, it maps them to a suitable Boolean representation, as listed in Table A-3.

*Table A-3. Windows PowerShell Boolean interpretations*

| Result | Boolean representation |
| --- | --- |
| $true | True |
| $false | False |
| $null | False |
| Nonzero number | True |
| Zero | False |
| Nonempty string | True |
| Empty string | False |
| Empty array | False |
| Single-element array | The Boolean representation of its single element |
| Multi-element array | True |
| Hashtable (either empty or not) | True |

# Strings

Windows PowerShell offers several facilities for working with plain-text data.

## Literal and Expanding Strings

To define a literal string (one in which no variable or escape expansion occurs), enclose it in single quotes:

```
$myString = 'hello `t $ENV:SystemRoot'
```

`$myString` gets the actual value of `hello `t $ENV:SystemRoot`.

To define an expanding string (one in which variable and escape expansion occur), enclose it in double quotes:

```
$myString = "hello `t $ENV:SystemRoot"
```

`$myString` gets a value similar to `hello   C:\WINDOWS`.

To include a single quote in a single-quoted string or a double quote in a double-quoted string, include two of the quote characters in a row:

```
PS > "Hello ""There""!"
Hello "There"!
PS > 'Hello ''There''!'
Hello 'There'!
```

> To include a complex expression inside an expanding string, use a subexpression. For example:
>
> ```
> $prompt = "$(get-location) >"
> ```
>
> `$prompt` gets a value similar to `c:\temp >`.
>
> Accessing the properties of an object requires a subexpression:
>
> ```
> $version =
>     "Current PowerShell version is: $($PSVersionTable.PSVersion.Major)"
> ```
>
> `$version` gets a value similar to `Current PowerShell version is: 3`.

## Here Strings

To define a *here string* (one that may span multiple lines), place the two characters `@"` at the beginning and the two characters `"@` on their own line at the end.

For example:

```
$myHereString = @"
This text may span multiple lines, and may
contain "quotes."
"@
```

Here strings may be of either the literal (single-quoted) or expanding (double-quoted) variety.

## Escape Sequences

Windows PowerShell supports escape sequences inside strings, as listed in Table A-4.

*Table A-4. Windows PowerShell escape sequences*

| Sequence | Meaning |
|---|---|
| `` `0 `` | The *null* character. Often used as a record separator. |
| `` `a `` | The *alarm* character. Generates a beep when displayed on the console. |
| `` `b `` | The *backspace* character. The previous character remains in the string but is overwritten when displayed on the console. |
| `` `f `` | A *form feed*. Creates a page break when printed on most printers. |
| `` `n `` | A *newline*. |
| `` `r `` | A *carriage return*. Newlines in PowerShell are indicated entirely by the `` `n `` character, so this is rarely required. |
| `` `t `` | A *tab*. |
| `` `v `` | A *vertical tab*. |
| `' '` (two single quotes) | A *single quote*, when in a literal string. |
| `" "` (two double quotes) | A *double quote*, when in an expanding string. |
| `` `any other character `` | That character, taken literally. |

# Numbers

PowerShell offers several options for interacting with numbers and numeric data.

## Simple Assignment

To define a variable that holds numeric data, simply assign it as you would other variables. PowerShell automatically stores your data in a format that is sufficient to accurately hold it:

```
$myInt = 10
```

`$myInt` gets the value of 10, as a (32-bit) integer:

```
$myDouble = 3.14
```

`$myDouble` gets the value of 3.14, as a (53-bit, 9 bits of precision) double.

To explicitly assign a number as a byte (8-bit) or short (16-bit) number, use the `[byte]` and `[int16]` casts:

```
$myByte = [byte] 128
$myShort = [int16] 32767
```

To explicitly assign a number as a long (64-bit) integer or decimal (96-bit, 96 bits of precision), use the long and decimal suffixes:

```
$myLong = 2147483648L
```

$myLong gets the value of 2147483648, as a long integer:

```
$myDecimal = 0.999D
```

$myDecimal gets the value of 0.999.

PowerShell also supports scientific notation, where e<*number*> represents multiplying the original number by the <*number*> power of 10:

```
$myPi = 3141592653e-9
```

$myPi gets the value of 3.141592653.

The data types in PowerShell (integer, long integer, double, and decimal) are built on the .NET data types of the same names.

## Administrative Numeric Constants

Since computer administrators rarely get the chance to work with numbers in even powers of 10, PowerShell offers the numeric constants of pb, tb, gb, mb, and kb to represent petabytes (1,125,899,906,842,624), terabytes (1,099,511,627,776), gigabytes (1,073,741,824), megabytes (1,048,576), and kilobytes (1,024), respectively:

```
PS > $downloadTime = (1gb + 250mb) / 120kb
PS > $downloadTime
10871.4666666667
```

## Hexadecimal and Other Number Bases

To directly enter a hexadecimal number, use the hexadecimal prefix 0x:

```
$myErrorCode = 0xFE4A
```

$myErrorCode gets the integer value 65098.

The PowerShell scripting language does not natively support other number bases, but its support for interaction with the .NET Framework enables conversion to and from binary, octal, decimal, and hexadecimal:

```
$myBinary = [Convert]::ToInt32("101101010101", 2)
```

$myBinary gets the integer value of 2901.

```
$myOctal = [Convert]::ToInt32("1234567", 8)
```

$myOctal gets the integer value of 342391.

```
$myHexString = [Convert]::ToString(65098, 16)
```

$myHexString gets the string value of fe4a.

```
$myBinaryString = [Convert]::ToString(12345, 2)
```

---

`$myBinaryString` gets the string value of 11000000111001.

 See "Working with the .NET Framework" (page 891) to learn more about using PowerShell to interact with the .NET Framework.

## Large Numbers

To work with extremely large numbers, use the `BigInt` class.

```
[BigInt]::Pow(12345, 123)
```

To do math with several large numbers, use the `[BigInt]` cast for all operands. Be sure to represent the numbers as strings before converting them to big integers; otherwise, data loss may occur:

```
PS > ([BigInt] "98123498123498123894") * ([BigInt] "98123498123498123894")
9628220883992139841085109029337773723236
```

## Imaginary and Complex Numbers

To work with imaginary and complex numbers, use the `System.Numerics.Complex` class:

```
PS > [System.Numerics.Complex]::ImaginaryOne *
    [System.Numerics.Complex]::ImaginaryOne | Format-List

Real      : -1
Imaginary : 0
Magnitude : 1
Phase     : 3.14159265358979
```

# Arrays and Lists

## Array Definitions

PowerShell arrays hold lists of data. The `@( )` (*array cast*) syntax tells PowerShell to treat the contents between the parentheses as an array. To create an empty array, type:

```
$myArray = @()
```

To define a nonempty array, use a comma to separate its elements:

```
$mySimpleArray = 1,"Two",3.14
```

Arrays may optionally be only a single element long:

```
$myList = ,"Hello"
```

Or, alternatively (using the array cast syntax):

```
$myList = @("Hello")
```

Elements of an array do not need to be all of the same data type, unless you declare it as a strongly typed array. In the following example, the outer square brackets define a strongly typed variable (as mentioned in "Variables" (page 864)), and `int[ ]` represents an array of integers:

```
[int[]] $myArray = 1,2,3.14
```

In this mode, PowerShell generates an error if it cannot convert any of the elements in your list to the required data type. In this case, it rounds 3.14 to the integer value of 3:

```
PS > $myArray[2]
3
```

 To ensure that PowerShell treats collections of uncertain length (such as history lists or directory listings) as a list, use the list evaluation syntax @(...) described in "Commands and Expressions" (page 861).

Arrays can also be multidimensional *jagged* arrays (arrays within arrays):

```
$multiDimensional = @(
    (1,2,3,4),
    (5,6,7,8)
)
```

`$multiDimensional[0][1]` returns 2, coming from row 0, column 1.

`$multiDimensional[1][3]` returns 8, coming from row 1, column 3.

To define a multidimensional array that is not jagged, create a multidimensional instance of the .NET type. For integers, that would be an array of `System.Int32`:

```
$multidimensional = New-Object "Int32[,]" 2,4
$multidimensional[0,1] = 2
$multidimensional[1,3] = 8
```

## Array Access

To access a specific element in an array, use the [ ] operator. PowerShell numbers your array elements starting at zero. Using `$myArray = 1,2,3,4,5,6` as an example:

```
$myArray[0]
```

returns 1, the first element in the array.

```
$myArray[2]
```

returns 3, the third element in the array.

```
$myArray[-1]
```

returns 6, the last element of the array.

```
$myArray[-2]
```

returns 5, the second-to-last element of the array.

You can also access ranges of elements in your array:

```
PS > $myArray[0..2]
1
2
3
```

returns elements 0 through 2, inclusive.

```
PS > $myArray[-1..2]
6
1
2
3
```

returns the final element, wraps around, and returns elements 0 through 2, inclusive. PowerShell wraps around because the first number in the range is positive, and the second number in the range is negative.

```
PS > $myArray[-1..-3]
6
5
4
```

returns the last element of the array through to the third-to-last element in the array, in descending order. PowerShell does not wrap around (and therefore scans backward in this case) because both numbers in the range share the same sign.

## Array Slicing

You can combine several of the statements in the previous section at once to extract more complex ranges from an array. Use the + sign to separate array ranges from explicit indexes:

```
$myArray[0,2,4]
```

returns the elements at indices 0, 2, and 4.

```
$myArray[0,2+4..5]
```

returns the elements at indices 0, 2, and 4 through 5, inclusive.

```
$myArray[,0+2..3+0,0]
```

returns the elements at indices 0, 2 through 3 inclusive, 0, and 0 again.

You can use the array slicing syntax to create arrays as well:

```
$myArray = ,0+2..3+0,0
```

# Hashtables (Associative Arrays)

## Hashtable Definitions

PowerShell *hashtables* (also called *associative arrays*) let you associate keys with values. To define a hashtable, use the syntax:

```
$myHashtable = @{}
```

You can initialize a hashtable with its key/value pairs when you create it. PowerShell assumes that the keys are strings, but the values may be any data type.

```
$myHashtable = @{ Key1 = "Value1"; "Key 2" = 1,2,3; 3.14 = "Pi" }
```

To define a hashtable that retains its insertion order, use the [ordered] cast:

```
$orderedHash = [ordered] @{}
$orderedHash["NewKey"] = "Value"
```

## Hashtable Access

To access or modify a specific element in an associative array, you can use either the array-access or property-access syntax:

```
$myHashtable["Key1"]
```

returns "Value1".

```
$myHashtable."Key 2"
```

returns the array 1,2,3.

```
$myHashtable["New Item"] = 5
```

adds "New Item" to the hashtable.

```
$myHashtable."New Item" = 5
```

also adds "New Item" to the hashtable.

# XML

PowerShell supports XML as a native data type. To create an XML variable, cast a string to the [xml] type:

```
$myXml = [xml] @"
<AddressBook>
```

```
    <Person contactType="Personal">
        <Name>Lee</Name>
        <Phone type="home">555-1212</Phone>
        <Phone type="work">555-1213</Phone>
    </Person>
    <Person contactType="Business">
        <Name>Ariel</Name>
        <Phone>555-1234</Phone>
    </Person>
</AddressBook>
"@
```

PowerShell exposes all child nodes and attributes as properties. When it does this, PowerShell automatically groups children that share the same node type:

```
$myXml.AddressBook
```

returns an object that contains a Person property.

```
$myXml.AddressBook.Person
```

returns a list of Person nodes. Each person node exposes contactType, Name, and Phone as properties.

```
$myXml.AddressBook.Person[0]
```

returns the first Person node.

```
$myXml.AddressBook.Person[0].ContactType
```

returns Personal as the contact type of the first Person node.

# Simple Operators

Once you have defined your data, the next step is to work with it.

## Arithmetic Operators

The arithmetic operators let you perform mathematical operations on your data, as shown in Table A-5.

The System.Math class in the .NET Framework offers many powerful operations in addition to the native operators supported by PowerShell:

```
PS > [Math]::Pow([Math]::E, [Math]::Pi)
23.1406926327793
```

See "Working with the .NET Framework" (page 891) to learn more about using PowerShell to interact with the .NET Framework.

*Table A-5. Windows PowerShell arithmetic operators*

| Operator | Meaning |
|---|---|
| + | The *addition operator:*<br>    `$leftValue + $rightValue`<br><br>When used with numbers, returns their sum.<br>When used with strings, returns a new string created by appending the second string to the first.<br>When used with arrays, returns a new array created by appending the second array to the first.<br>When used with hashtables, returns a new hashtable created by merging the two hashtables. Since hashtable keys must be unique, PowerShell returns an error if the second hashtable includes any keys already defined in the first hashtable.<br>When used with any other type, PowerShell uses that type's addition operator (`op_Addition`) if it implements one. |
| - | The *subtraction operator:*<br>    `$leftValue - $rightValue`<br><br>When used with numbers, returns their difference.<br>This operator does not apply to strings.<br>This operator does not apply to arrays.<br>This operator does not apply to hashtables.<br>When used with any other type, PowerShell uses that type's subtraction operator (`op_Subtraction`) if it implements one. |
| * | The *multiplication operator:*<br>    `$leftValue * $rightValue`<br><br>When used with numbers, returns their product.<br>When used with strings (`"=" * 80`), returns a new string created by appending the string to itself the number of times you specify.<br>When used with arrays (`1..3 * 7`), returns a new array created by appending the array to itself the number of times you specify.<br>This operator does not apply to hashtables.<br>When used with any other type, PowerShell uses that type's multiplication operator (`op_Multiply`) if it implements one. |
| / | The *division operator:*<br>    `$leftValue / $rightValue`<br><br>When used with numbers, returns their quotient.<br>This operator does not apply to strings.<br>This operator does not apply to arrays.<br>This operator does not apply to hashtables.<br>When used with any other type, PowerShell uses that type's division operator (`op_Division`) if it implements one. |
| % | The *modulus operator:*<br>    `$leftValue % $rightValue`<br><br>When used with numbers, returns the remainder of their division.<br>This operator does not apply to strings.<br>This operator does not apply to arrays.<br>This operator does not apply to hashtables.<br>When used with any other type, PowerShell uses that type's modulus operator (`op_Modulus`) if it implements one. |

| Operator | Meaning |
|---|---|
| += <br> -= <br> *= <br> /= <br> %= | *Assignment operators:* <br>     `$variable operator= value` <br><br> These operators match the simple arithmetic operators (+, -, *, /, and %) but store the result in the variable %= on the lefthand side of the operator. It is a short form for <br>     `$variable = $variable operator value.` |

## Logical Operators

The logical operators let you compare Boolean values, as shown in Table A-6.

*Table A-6. Windows PowerShell logical operators*

| Operator | Meaning |
|---|---|
| -and | *Logical AND:* <br>     `$leftValue -and $rightValue` <br><br> Returns `$true` if both lefthand and righthand arguments evaluate to `$true`. Returns `$false` otherwise. You can combine several -and operators in the same expression: <br>     `$value1 -and $value2 -and $value3 …` <br><br> PowerShell implements the -and operator as a short-circuit operator and evaluates arguments only if all arguments preceding it evaluate to `$true`. |
| -or | *Logical OR:* <br>     `$leftValue -or $rightValue` <br><br> Returns `$true` if the lefthand or righthand arguments evaluate to `$true`. Returns `$false` otherwise. You can combine several -or operators in the same expression: <br>     `$value1 -or $value2 -or $value3 ...` <br><br> PowerShell implements the -or operator as a short-circuit operator and evaluates arguments only if all arguments preceding it evaluate to `$false`. |
| -xor | *Logical exclusive OR:* <br>     `$leftValue -xor $rightValue` <br><br> Returns `$true` if either the lefthand or righthand argument evaluates to `$true`, but not if both do. Returns `$false` otherwise. |
| -not <br> ! | *Logical NOT:* <br>     `-not $value` <br><br> Returns `$true` if its righthand (and only) argument evaluates to `$false`. Returns `$false` otherwise. |

## Binary Operators

The binary operators, listed in Table A-7, let you apply the Boolean logical operators bit by bit to the operator's arguments. When comparing bits, a 1 represents `$true`, whereas a 0 represents `$false`.

## Table A-7. Windows PowerShell binary operators

| Operator | Meaning |
|----------|---------|
| -band | *Binary AND*: |

`$leftValue -band $rightValue`

Returns a number where bits are set to 1 if the bits of the lefthand and righthand arguments at that position are both 1. All other bits are set to 0.

For example:

```
PS > $boolean1 = "110110110"
PS > $boolean2 = "010010010"
PS > $int1 = [Convert]::ToInt32($boolean1, 2)
PS > $int2 = [Convert]::ToInt32($boolean2, 2)
PS > $result = $int1 -band $int2
PS > [Convert]::ToString($result, 2)
10010010
```

| -bor | *Binary OR*: |
|------|--------------|

`$leftValue -bor $rightValue`

Returns a number where bits are set to 1 if either of the bits of the lefthand and righthand arguments at that position is 1. All other bits are set to 0.

For example:

```
PS > $boolean1 = "110110110"
PS > $boolean2 = "010010010"
PS > $int1 = [Convert]::ToInt32($boolean1, 2)
PS > $int2 = [Convert]::ToInt32($boolean2, 2)
PS > $result = $int1 -bor $int2
PS > [Convert]::ToString($result, 2)
110110110
```

| -bxor | *Binary exclusive OR*: |
|-------|------------------------|

`$leftValue -bxor $rightValue`

Returns a number where bits are set to 1 if either of the bits of the lefthand and righthand arguments at that position is 1, but not if both are. All other bits are set to 0.

For example:

```
PS > $boolean1 = "110110110"
PS > $boolean2 = "010010010"
PS > $int1 = [Convert]::ToInt32($boolean1, 2)
PS > $int2 = [Convert]::ToInt32($boolean2, 2)
PS > $result = $int1 -bor $int2
PS > [Convert]::ToString($result, 2)
100100100
```

| -bnot | *Binary NOT*: |
|-------|---------------|

`-bnot $value`

Returns a number where bits are set to 1 if the bit of the righthand (and only) argument at that position is set to 1. All other bits are set to 0.

For example:

| Operator | Meaning |
|----------|---------|

```
PS > $boolean1 = "110110110"
PS > $int1 = [Convert]::ToInt32($boolean1, 2)
PS > $result = -bnot $int1
PS > [Convert]::ToString($result, 2)
11111111111111111111111001001001
```

-shl  *Binary shift left:*

     *$value* -slh *$count*

Shifts the bits of a number to the left *$count* places. Bits on the righthand side are set to 0.

For example:

```
PS > $int1 = 438
PS > [Convert]::ToString($int1, 2)
110110110

PS > $result = $int1 -shl 5
PS > [Convert]::ToString($result, 2)
11011011000000
```

-shr  *Binary shift right:*

     *$value* -slr *$count*

Shifts the bits of a number to the right *$count* places. For signed values, bits on the lefthand side have their sign preserved.

For example:

```
PS > $int1 = -2345
PS > [Convert]::ToString($int1, 2)
11111111111111111111011011010111

PS > $result = $int1 -shr 3
PS > [Convert]::ToString($result, 2)
11111111111111111111111011011010
```

# Other Operators

PowerShell supports several other simple operators, as listed in Table A-8.

*Table A-8. Other Windows PowerShell operators*

| Operator | Meaning |
|----------|---------|
| -replace | The *replace operator*: |

     *"target"* -replace *"pattern"*,*"replacement"*

Returns a new string, where the text in *"target"* that matches the regular expression *"pattern"* has been replaced with the replacement text *"replacement"*.

By default, PowerShell performs a case-insensitive comparison. The -ireplace operator makes this case-insensitivity explicit, whereas the -creplace operator performs a case-sensitive comparison.

If the regular expression pattern contains named captures or capture groups, the replacement string may reference those as well.

For example:

```
PS > "Hello World" -replace "(.*) (.*)",'$2 $1'
World Hello
```

| Operator | Meaning |
|---|---|
| | If *"target"* represents an array, the -replace operator operates on each element of that array.<br>For more information on the details of regular expressions, see Appendix B. |
| -f | The *format operator*:<br><br>    `"Format String" -f Values`<br><br>Returns a string where the format items in the format string have been replaced with the text equivalent of the values in the value array.<br>For example:<br><br>    `PS > "{0:n0}" -f 1000000000`<br>    `1,000,000,000`<br><br>The format string for the format operator is exactly the format string supported by the .NET String.Format method.<br>For more details about the syntax of the format string, see Appendix D. |
| -as | The *type conversion operator*:<br><br>    `$value -as [Type]`<br><br>Returns $value cast to the given .NET type. If this conversion is not possible, PowerShell returns $null.<br>For example:<br><br>    `PS > 3/2 -as [int]`<br>    `2`<br>    `PS > $result = "Hello" -as [int]`<br>    `PS > $result -eq $null`<br>    `True` |
| -split | The *unary split operator*:<br><br>    `-split "Input String"`<br><br>Breaks the given input string into an array, using whitespace (\s+) to identify the boundary between elements. It also trims the results.<br>For example:<br><br>    `PS > -split " Hello    World    "`<br>    `Hello`<br>    `World`<br><br>The *binary split operator*:<br><br>    `"Input String" -split "delimiter",maximum,options`<br>    `"Input String" -split { Scriptblock },maximum`<br><br>Breaks the given input string into an array, using the given *delimiter* or *script block* to identify the boundary between elements.<br>*Delimiter* is interpreted as a regular expression match. *Scriptblock* is called for each character in the input, and a split is introduced when it returns $true.<br>*Maximum* defines the maximum number of elements to be returned, leaving unsplit elements as the last item. This item is optional. Use "0" for unlimited if you want to provide options but not alter the maximum.<br>*Options* define special behavior to apply to the splitting behavior. The possible enumeration values are:<br><br>• SimpleMatch: Split on literal strings, rather than regular expressions they may represent.<br>• RegexMatch: Split on regular expressions. This option is the default.<br>• CultureInvariant: Does not use culture-specific capitalization rules when doing a case-insensitive split.<br>• IgnorePatternWhitespace: Ignores spaces and regular expression comments in the split pattern. |

| Operator | Meaning |
|---|---|

- **Multiline**: Allows the ^ and $ characters to match line boundaries, not just the beginning and end of the content.
- **Singleline**: Treats the ^ and $ characters as the beginning and end of the content. This option is the default.
- **IgnoreCase**: Ignores the capitalization of the content when searching for matches.
- **ExplicitCapture**: In a regular expression match, only captures named groups. This option has no impact on the -split operator.

For example:
```
PS > "1a2B3" -split "[a-z]+",0,"IgnoreCase"
1
2
3
```

| | |
|---|---|
| -join | The *unary join operator*: |

```
-join ("item1","item2",...,"item_n")
```

Combines the supplied items into a single string, using no separator. For example:
```
PS > -join ("a","b")
ab
```

The *binary join operator*:
```
("item1","item2",...,"item_n") -join Delimiter
```

Combines the supplied items into a single string, using *Delimiter* as the separator. For example:
```
PS > ("a","b") -join ", "
a, b
```

# Comparison Operators

The PowerShell comparison operators, listed in Table A-9, let you compare expressions against each other. By default, PowerShell's comparison operators are case-insensitive. For all operators where case sensitivity applies, the -i prefix makes this case insensitivity explicit, whereas the -c prefix performs a case-sensitive comparison.

*Table A-9. Windows PowerShell comparison operators*

| Operator | Meaning |
|---|---|
| -eq | The *equality operator*: |
| | $leftValue -eq $rightValue |
| | For all primitive types, returns $true if $leftValue and $rightValue are equal. When used with arrays, returns all elements in $leftValue that are equal to $rightValue. When used with any other type, PowerShell uses that type's Equals() method if it implements one. |
| -ne | The *negated equality operator*: |
| | $leftValue -ne $rightValue |
| | For all primitive types, returns $true if $leftValue and $rightValue are not equal. When used with arrays, returns all elements in $leftValue that are not equal to $rightValue. |

| Operator | Meaning |
|---|---|
| | When used with any other type, PowerShell returns the negation of that type's Equals() method if it implements one. |
| -ge | The *greater-than-or-equal operator*: |
| |     *$leftValue* -ge *$rightValue* |
| | For all primitive types, returns $true if *$leftValue* is greater than or equal to *$rightValue*. When used with arrays, returns all elements in *$leftValue* that are greater than or equal to *$right Value*. When used with any other type, PowerShell returns the result of that object's Compare() method if it implements one. If the method returns a number greater than or equal to zero, the operator returns $true. |
| -gt | The *greater-than operator*: |
| |     $leftValue -gt $rightValue |
| | For all primitive types, returns $true if *$leftValue* is greater than *$rightValue*. When used with arrays, returns all elements in *$leftValue* that are greater than *$rightValue*. When used with any other type, PowerShell returns the result of that object's Compare() method if it implements one. If the method returns a number greater than zero, the operator returns $true. |
| -in | The *in operator*: |
| |     *$value* -in *$list* |
| | Returns $true if the value *$value* is contained in the list *$list*. That is, if $item -eq $value returns $true for at least one item in the list. This is equivalent to the -contains operator with the operands reversed. |
| -notin | The *negated in operator*: |
| | Returns $true when the -in operator would return $false. |
| -lt | The *less-than operator*: |
| |     *$leftValue* -lt *$rightValue* |
| | For all primitive types, returns $true if *$leftValue* is less than *$rightValue*. When used with arrays, returns all elements in *$leftValue* that are less than *$rightValue*. When used with any other type, PowerShell returns the result of that object's Compare() method if it implements one. If the method returns a number less than zero, the operator returns $true. |
| -le | The *less-than-or-equal operator*: |
| |     *$leftValue* -le *$rightValue* |
| | For all primitive types, returns $true if *$leftValue* is less than or equal to *$rightValue*. When used with arrays, returns all elements in *$leftValue* that are less than or equal to *$rightValue*. When used with any other type, PowerShell returns the result of that object's Compare() method if it implements one. If the method returns a number less than or equal to zero, the operator returns $true. |
| -like | The *like operator*: |
| |     *$leftValue* -like *Pattern* |
| | Evaluates the pattern against the target, returning $true if the simple match is successful. When used with arrays, returns all elements in *$leftValue* that match *Pattern*. The -like operator supports the following simple wildcard characters: |
| | ? |
| |     Any single unspecified character |

| Operator | Meaning |
|---|---|
| | * |
| | Zero or more unspecified characters |
| | [a-b] |
| | Any character in the range of a–b |
| | [ab] |
| | The specified characters a or b |
| | For example: |
| | ```
PS > "Test" -like "[A-Z]e?[tr]"
True
``` |
| -notlike | The *negated like operator*: |
| | Returns $true when the -like operator would return $false. |
| -match | The *match operator*: |
| | ```
"Target" -match Regular Expression
``` |
| | Evaluates the regular expression against the target, returning $true if the match is successful. Once complete, PowerShell places the successful matches in the $matches variable. |
| | When used with arrays, returns all elements in *Target* that match *Regular Expression*. |
| | The $matches variable is a hashtable that maps the individual matches to the text they match. 0 is the entire text of the match, 1 and on contain the text from any unnamed captures in the regular expression, and string values contain the text from any named captures in the regular expression. |
| | For example: |
| | ```
PS > "Hello World" -match "(.*) (.*)"
True
PS > $matches[1]
Hello
``` |
| | For more information on the details of regular expressions, see Appendix B. |
| -notmatch | The *negated match operator*: |
| | Returns $true when the -match operator would return $false. |
| | The -notmatch operator still populates the $matches variable with the results of match. |
| -contains | The *contains operator*: |
| | ```
$list -contains $value
``` |
| | Returns $true if the list specified by $list contains the value $value—that is, if $item -eq $value returns $true for at least one item in the list. This is equivalent to the -in operator with the operands reversed. |
| -notcontains | The *negated contains operator*: |
| | Returns $true when the -contains operator would return $false. |
| -is | The *type operator*: |
| | ```
$leftValue -is [type]
``` |
| | Returns $true if $value is (or extends) the specified .NET type. |
| -isnot | The *negated type operator*: |
| | Returns $true when the -is operator would return $false. |
```

# Conditional Statements

Conditional statements in PowerShell let you change the flow of execution in your script.

## if, elseif, and else Statements

```
if(condition)
{
    statement block
}
elseif(condition)
{
    statement block
}
else
{
    statement block
}
```

If *condition* evaluates to $true, PowerShell executes the statement block you provide. Then, it resumes execution at the end of the if/elseif/else statement list. PowerShell requires the enclosing braces around the statement block, even if the statement block contains only one statement.

 See "Simple Operators" (page 873) and "Comparison Operators" (page 879) for a discussion on how PowerShell evaluates expressions as conditions.

If *condition* evaluates to $false, PowerShell evaluates any following (optional) else if conditions until one matches. If one matches, PowerShell executes the statement block associated with that condition, and then resumes execution at the end of the if/ elseif/else statement list.

For example:

```
$textToMatch = Read-Host "Enter some text"
$matchType = Read-Host "Apply Simple or Regex matching?"
$pattern = Read-Host "Match pattern"
if($matchType -eq "Simple")
{
    $textToMatch -like $pattern
}
elseif($matchType -eq "Regex")
{
    $textToMatch -match $pattern
}
```

```
else
{
    Write-Host "Match type must be Simple or Regex"
}
```

If none of the conditions evaluate to $true, PowerShell executes the statement block associated with the (optional) else clause, and then resumes execution at the end of the if/elseif/else statement list.

## switch Statements

```
switch options expression
{
    comparison value          { statement block }
    -or-
    { comparison expression }  { statement block }
    (...)
    default                    { statement block }
}
```

or:

```
switch options -file filename
{
    comparison value          { statement block }
    -or
    { comparison expression }  { statement block }
    (...)
    default                    { statement block }
}
```

When PowerShell evaluates a switch statement, it evaluates *expression* against the statements in the switch body. If *expression* is a list of values, PowerShell evaluates each item against the statements in the switch body. If you specify the -file option, Power-Shell treats the lines in the file as though they were a list of items in *expression*.

The *comparison value* statements let you match the current input item against the pattern specified by *comparison value*. By default, PowerShell treats this as a case-insensitive exact match, but the options you provide to the switch statement can change this, as shown in Table A-10.

*Table A-10. Options supported by PowerShell switch statements*

| Option | Meaning |
| --- | --- |
| -casesensitive<br>-c | *Case-sensitive match.*<br>With this option active, PowerShell executes the associated statement block only if the current input item exactly matches the value specified by *comparison value*. If the current input object is a string, the match is case-sensitive. |
| -exact<br>-e | *Exact match*<br>With this option active, PowerShell executes the associated statement block only if the current input item |

| Option | Meaning |
|---|---|
| | exactly matches the value specified by *comparison value*. This match is case-insensitive. This is the default mode of operation. |
| -regex <br> -r | *Regular-expression match* <br> With this option active, PowerShell executes the associated statement block only if the current input item matches the regular expression specified by *comparison value*. This match is case-insensitive. |
| -wildcard <br> -w | *Wildcard match* <br> With this option active, PowerShell executes the associated statement block only if the current input item matches the wildcard specified by *comparison value*. <br> The wildcard match supports the following simple wildcard characters: <br> ? <br>     Any single unspecified character <br> * <br>     Zero or more unspecified characters <br> [a-b] <br>     Any character in the range of a–b <br> [ab] <br>     The specified characters a or b <br> This match is case-insensitive. |

The { *comparison expression* } statements let you process the current input item, which is stored in the $_ (or $PSItem) variable, in an arbitrary script block. When it processes a { *comparison expression* } statement, PowerShell executes the associated statement block only if { *comparison expression* } evaluates to $true.

PowerShell executes the statement block associated with the (optional) default statement if no other statements in the switch body match.

When processing a switch statement, PowerShell tries to match the current input object against each statement in the switch body, falling through to the next statement even after one or more have already matched. To have PowerShell discontinue the current comparison (but retry the switch statement with the next input object), include a continue statement as the last statement in the statement block. To have PowerShell exit a switch statement completely after it processes a match, include a break statement as the last statement in the statement block.

For example:

```
$myPhones = "(555) 555-1212","555-1234"

switch -regex ($myPhones)
{
  { $_.Length -le 8 }  { "Area code was not specified"; break }
  { $_.Length -gt 8 }  { "Area code was specified" }
  "\((555)\).*"        { "In the $($matches[1]) area code" }
}
```

produces the output:

```
Area code was specified
In the 555 area code
Area code was not specified
```

 See "Looping Statements" (page 885) for more information about the break statement.

By default, PowerShell treats this as a case-insensitive exact match, but the options you provide to the switch statement can change this.

# Looping Statements

Looping statements in PowerShell let you execute groups of statements multiple times.

## for Statement

```
:loop_label for (initialization; condition; increment)
{
    statement block
}
```

When PowerShell executes a for statement, it first executes the expression given by *initialization*. It next evaluates *condition*. If *condition* evaluates to $true, Power-Shell executes the given statement block. It then executes the expression given by *in crement*. PowerShell continues to execute the statement block and *increment* statement as long as *condition* evaluates to $true.

For example:

```
for($counter = 0; $counter -lt 10; $counter++)
{
    Write-Host "Processing item $counter"
}
```

The break and continue statements (discussed later in this appendix) can specify the *loop_label* of any enclosing looping statement as their target.

## foreach Statement

```
:loop_label foreach (variable in expression)
{
    statement block
}
```

When PowerShell executes a foreach statement, it executes the pipeline given by *ex pression*—for example, Get-Process | Where-Object {$_.Handles -gt 500} or 1..10. For each item produced by the expression, it assigns that item to the variable specified by *variable* and then executes the given statement block. For example:

```
$handleSum = 0;
foreach($process in Get-Process |
    Where-Object { $_.Handles -gt 500 })
{
    $handleSum += $process.Handles
}
$handleSum
```

The break and continue statements (discussed later in this appendix) can specify the *loop_label* of any enclosing looping statement as their target. In addition to the foreach statement, PowerShell also offers the Foreach-Object cmdlet with similar capabilities. For more information, see Recipe 4.4, "Repeat Operations with Loops".

## while Statement

```
:loop_label while(condition)
{
    statement block
}
```

When PowerShell executes a while statement, it first evaluates the expression given by *condition*. If this expression evaluates to $true, PowerShell executes the given statement block. PowerShell continues to execute the statement block as long as *condition* evaluates to $true. For example:

```
$command = "";
while($command -notmatch "quit")
{
    $command = Read-Host "Enter your command"
}
```

The break and continue statements (discussed later in this appendix) can specify the *loop_label* of any enclosing looping statement as their target.

## do … while Statement/do … until Statement

```
:loop_label do
{
    statement block
} while(condition)
```

or

```
:loop_label do
{
    statement block
} until(condition)
```

When PowerShell executes a do … while or do … until statement, it first executes the given statement block. In a do … while statement, PowerShell continues to execute the statement block as long as *condition* evaluates to $true. In a do … until statement, PowerShell continues to execute the statement as long as *condition* evaluates to $false. For example:

```
$validResponses = "Yes","No"
$response = ""
do
{
    $response = read-host "Yes or No?"
} while($validResponses -notcontains $response)
"Got it."

$response = ""
do
{
    $response = read-host "Yes or No?"
} until($validResponses -contains $response)
"Got it."
```

The break and continue statements (discussed later in this appendix) can specify the *loop_label* of any enclosing looping statement as their target.

## Flow Control Statements

PowerShell supports two statements to help you control flow within loops: break and continue.

### break

The break statement halts execution of the current loop. PowerShell then resumes execution at the end of the current looping statement, as though the looping statement had completed naturally. For example:

```
for($counter = 0; $counter -lt 5; $counter++)
{
    for($counter2 = 0; $counter2 -lt 5; $counter2++)
    {
        if($counter2 -eq 2)
        {
            break
        }
```

```
        Write-Host "Processing item $counter,$counter2"
    }
}
```

produces the output:

```
Processing item 0,0
Processing item 0,1
Processing item 1,0
Processing item 1,1
Processing item 2,0
Processing item 2,1
Processing item 3,0
Processing item 3,1
Processing item 4,0
Processing item 4,1
```

If you specify a label with the break statement—for example, break outer_loop—
PowerShell halts the execution of that loop instead. For example:

```
:outer_loop for($counter = 0; $counter -lt 5; $counter++)
{
    for($counter2 = 0; $counter2 -lt 5; $counter2++)
    {
        if($counter2 -eq 2)
        {
            break outer_loop
        }

        Write-Host "Processing item $counter,$counter2"
    }
}
```

produces the output:

```
Processing item 0,0
Processing item 0,1
```

## continue

The continue statement skips execution of the rest of the current statement block.
PowerShell then continues with the next iteration of the current looping statement, as
though the statement block had completed naturally. For example:

```
for($counter = 0; $counter -lt 5; $counter++)
{
    for($counter2 = 0; $counter2 -lt 5; $counter2++)
    {
        if($counter2 -eq 2)
        {
            continue
        }
```

```
        Write-Host "Processing item $counter,$counter2"
    }
}
```

produces the output:

```
Processing item 0,0
Processing item 0,1
Processing item 0,3
Processing item 0,4
Processing item 1,0
Processing item 1,1
Processing item 1,3
Processing item 1,4
Processing item 2,0
Processing item 2,1
Processing item 2,3
Processing item 2,4
Processing item 3,0
Processing item 3,1
Processing item 3,3
Processing item 3,4
Processing item 4,0
Processing item 4,1
Processing item 4,3
Processing item 4,4
```

If you specify a label with the continue statement—for example, continue outer_loop
—PowerShell continues with the next iteration of that loop instead.

For example:

```
:outer_loop for($counter = 0; $counter -lt 5; $counter++)
{
    for($counter2 = 0; $counter2 -lt 5; $counter2++)
    {
        if($counter2 -eq 2)
        {
            continue outer_loop
        }

        Write-Host "Processing item $counter,$counter2"
    }
}
```

produces the output:

```
Processing item 0,0
Processing item 0,1
Processing item 1,0
Processing item 1,1
Processing item 2,0
Processing item 2,1
```

```
Processing item 3,0
Processing item 3,1
Processing item 4,0
Processing item 4,1
```

# Workflow-Specific Statements

Within a workflow, PowerShell supports four statements not supported in traditional PowerShell scripts: InlineScript, Parallel, Sequence, and foreach -parallel.

## InlineScript

The InlineScript keyword defines an island of PowerShell script that will be invoked as a unit, and with traditional PowerShell scripting semantics. For example:

```
workflow MyWorkflow
{
    ## Method invocation not supported in a workflow
    ## [Math]::Sqrt(100)

    InlineScript
    {
        ## Supported in an InlineScript
        [Math]::Sqrt(100)
    }
}
```

## Parallel/Sequence

The Parallel keyword specifies that all statements within the statement block should run in parallel. To group statements that should be run as a unit, use the Sequence keyword:

```
workflow MyWorkflow
{
    Parallel
    {
        InlineScript { Start-Sleep -Seconds 2; "One thing run in parallel" }
        InlineScript { Start-Sleep -Seconds 4; "Another thing run in parallel" }
        InlineScript { Start-Sleep -Seconds 3; "A third thing run in parallel" }

        Sequence
        {
            Start-Sleep -Seconds 1
            "A fourth"
            "and fifth thing run as a unit, in parallel"
        }
    }
}
```

### Foreach -Parallel

Acts like PowerShell's traditional `foreach` statement, but processes each element of the collection in parallel:

```
workflow MyWorkflow
{
    $items = 1..10
    foreach -parallel ($item in $items)
    {
        $sleep = Get-Random -Max 200
        Start-Sleep -Milliseconds $sleep
        $item
    }
}
```

# Working with the .NET Framework

One feature that gives PowerShell its incredible reach into both system administration and application development is its capability to leverage Microsoft's enormous and broad .NET Framework.

Work with the .NET Framework in PowerShell comes mainly by way of one of two tasks: calling methods or accessing properties.

## Static Methods

To call a static method on a class, type:

```
[ClassName]::MethodName(parameter list)
```

For example:

```
PS > [System.Diagnostics.Process]::GetProcessById(0)
```

gets the process with the ID of 0 and displays the following output:

```
Handles  NPM(K)    PM(K)      WS(K) VM(M)  CPU(s)     Id ProcessName
-------  ------    -----      ----- -----  ------     -- -----------
      0       0        0         16     0              0 Idle
```

## Instance Methods

To call a method on an instance of an object, type:

```
$objectReference.MethodName(parameter list)
```

For example:

```
PS > $process = [System.Diagnostics.Process]::GetProcessById(0)
PS > $process.Refresh()
```

This stores the process with ID of 0 into the $process variable. It then calls the Refresh() instance method on that specific process.

## Explicitly Implemented Interface Methods

To call a method on an explicitly implemented interface:

```
([Interface] $objectReference).MethodName(parameter list)
```

For example:

```
PS > ([IConvertible] 123).ToUint16($null)
```

## Static Properties

To access a static property on a class, type:

```
[ClassName]::PropertyName
```

or:

```
[ClassName]::PropertyName = value
```

For example, the [System.DateTime] class provides a Now static property that returns the current time:

```
PS > [System.DateTime]::Now
Sunday, July 16, 2006 2:07:20 PM
```

Although this is rare, some types let you set the value of some static properties.

## Instance Properties

To access an instance property on an object, type:

```
$objectReference.PropertyName
```

or:

```
$objectReference.PropertyName = value
```

For example:

```
PS > $today = [System.DateTime]::Now
PS > $today.DayOfWeek
Sunday
```

This stores the current date in the $today variable. It then calls the DayOfWeek instance property on that specific date.

## Learning About Types

The two primary avenues for learning about classes and types are the Get-Member cmdlet and the documentation for the .NET Framework.

### The Get-Member cmdlet

To learn what methods and properties a given type supports, pass it through the `Get-Member` cmdlet, as shown in Table A-11.

*Table A-11. Working with the Get-Member cmdlet*

| Action | Result |
| --- | --- |
| `[typename]` \| `Get-Member -Static` | All the static methods and properties of a given type. |
| `$objectReference` \| `Get-Member -Static` | All the static methods and properties provided by the type in `$objectReference`. |
| `$objectReference` \| `Get-Member` | All the instance methods and properties provided by the type in `$objectReference`. If `$objectReference` represents a collection of items, PowerShell returns the instances and properties of the types contained by that collection. To view the instances and properties of a collection itself, use the `-InputObject` parameter of `Get-Member`: <br> `Get-Member -InputObject $objectReference` |
| `[typename]` \| `Get-Member` | All the instance methods and properties of a `System.Runtime` Type object that represents this type. |

### .NET Framework documentation

Another source of information about the classes in the .NET Framework is the documentation itself, available through the search facilities here (*http://msdn.microsoft.com*).

Typical documentation for a class first starts with a general overview, and then provides a hyperlink to the members of the class—the list of methods and properties it supports.

> To get to the documentation for the members quickly, search for them more explicitly by adding the term "members" to your MSDN search term:
>
> `classname members`

The documentation for the members of a class lists their constructors, methods, properties, and more. It uses an S icon to represent the static methods and properties. Click the member name for more information about that member, including the type of object that the member produces.

# Type Shortcuts

When you specify a type name, PowerShell lets you use a short form for some of the most common types, as listed in Table A-12.

*Table A-12. PowerShell type shortcuts*

| Type shortcut | Full classname |
|---|---|
| [Adsi] | [System.DirectoryServices.DirectoryEntry] |
| [AdsiSearcher] | [System.DirectoryServices.DirectorySearcher] |
| [Float] | [System.Single] |
| [Hashtable] | [System.Collections.Hashtable] |
| [Int] | [System.Int32] |
| [IPAddress] | [System.Net.IPAddress] |
| [Long] | [System.Collections.Int64] |
| [PowerShell] | [System.Management.Automation.PowerShell] |
| [PSCustomObject] | [System.Management.Automation.PSObject] |
| [PSModuleInfo] | [System.Management.Automation.PSModuleInfo] |
| [PSObject] | [System.Management.Automation.PSObject] |
| [Ref] | [System.Management.Automation.PSReference] |
| [Regex] | [System.Text.RegularExpressions.Regex] |
| [Runspace] | [System.Management.Automation.Runspaces.Runspace] |
| [RunspaceFactory] | [System.Management.Automation.Runspaces.RunspaceFactory] |
| [ScriptBlock] | [System.Management.Automation.ScriptBlock] |
| [Switch] | [System.Management.Automation.SwitchParameter] |
| [Wmi] | [System.Management.ManagementObject] |
| [WmiClass] | [System.Management.ManagementClass] |
| [WmiSearcher][ | [System.Management.ManagementObjectSearcher] |
| [Xml] | [System.Xml.XmlDocument] |
| [*TypeName*] | [System.*TypeName*] |

# Creating Instances of Types

```
$objectReference = New-Object TypeName parameters
```

Although static methods and properties of a class generate objects, you will often want to create them explicitly yourself. PowerShell's New-Object cmdlet lets you create an instance of the type you specify. The parameter list must match the list of parameters accepted by one of the type's constructors, as documented on MSDN.

For example:

```
$webClient = New-Object Net.WebClient
$webClient.DownloadString("http://search.msn.com")
```

If the type represents a generic type, enclose its type parameters in square brackets:

```
PS > $hashtable = New-Object "System.Collections.Generic.Dictionary[String,Bool]"
PS > $hashtable["Test"] = $true
```

Most common types are available by default. However, many types are available only after you load the library (called the *assembly*) that defines them. The MSDN documentation for a class includes the assembly that defines it.

To load an assembly, use the -AssemblyName parameter of the Add-Type cmdlet:

```
PS > Add-Type -AssemblyName System.Web

PS > [Web.HttpUtility]::UrlEncode("http://www.bing.com")
http%3a%2f%2fwww.bing.com
```

## Interacting with COM Objects

PowerShell lets you access methods and properties on COM objects the same way you would interact with objects from the .NET Framework. To interact with a COM object, use its ProgId with the -ComObject parameter (often shortened to -Com) on New-Object:

```
PS > $shell = New-Object -Com Shell.Application
PS > $shell.Windows() | Select-Object LocationName,LocationUrl
```

For more information about the COM objects most useful to system administrators, see Appendix H.

## Extending Types

PowerShell supports two ways to add your own methods and properties to any type: the Add-Member cmdlet and a custom types extension file.

### The Add-Member cmdlet

The Add-Member cmdlet lets you dynamically add methods, properties, and more to an object. It supports the extensions shown in Table A-13.

*Table A-13. Selected member types supported by the Add-Member cmdlet*

| Member type | Meaning |
| --- | --- |
| AliasProperty | A property defined to alias another property: |
| | ```
PS > $testObject = [PsObject] "Test"
PS > $testObject | Add-Member "AliasProperty" Count Length
PS > $testObject.Count
4
``` |
| CodeProperty | A property defined by a System.Reflection.MethodInfo. |
| | This method must be public, static, return results (nonvoid), and take one parameter of type PsObject. |
| NoteProperty | A property defined by the initial value you provide: |
```

| Member type | Meaning |
|---|---|
| | ```PS > $testObject = [PsObject] "Test"``` |
| | ```PS > $testObject | Add-Member NoteProperty Reversed tseT``` |
| | ```PS > $testObject.Reversed``` |
| | ```tseT``` |
| ScriptProperty | A property defined by the script block you provide. In that script block, $this refers to the current instance: |
| | ```PS > $testObject = [PsObject] ("Hi" * 100)``` |
| | ```PS > $testObject | Add-Member ScriptProperty IsLong {``` |
| | ```    $this.Length -gt 100``` |
| | ```}``` |
| | ```PS > $testObject.IsLong``` |
| | |
| | ```True``` |
| PropertySet | A property defined as a shortcut to a set of properties. Used in cmdlets such as Select-Object: |
| | ```PS > $testObject = [PsObject] [DateTime]::Now``` |
| | ```PS > $collection = New-Object `` |
| | ```    Collections.ObjectModel.Collection``1[System.String]``` |
| | ```$collection.Add("Month")``` |
| | ```$collection.Add("Year")``` |
| | ```$testObject | Add-Member PropertySet MonthYear $collection``` |
| | ```$testObject | select MonthYear``` |
| | |
| | ```Month                              Year``` |
| | ```-----                              ----``` |
| | ```    3                              2010``` |
| CodeMethod | A method defined by a System.Reflection.MethodInfo. This method must be public, static, and take one parameter of type PsObject. |
| ScriptMethod | A method defined by the script block you provide. In that script block, $this refers to the current instance, and $args refers to the input parameters: |
| | ```PS > $testObject = [PsObject] "Hello"``` |
| | ```PS > $testObject | Add-Member ScriptMethod IsLong {``` |
| | ```    $this.Length -gt $args[0]``` |
| | ```}``` |
| | ```PS > $testObject.IsLong(3)``` |
| | ```True``` |
| | |
| | ```PS > $testObject.IsLong(100)``` |
| | ```False``` |

## Custom type extension files

While the Add-Member cmdlet lets you customize individual objects, PowerShell also supports configuration files that let you customize all objects of a given type. For example, you might want to add a Reverse() method to all strings or a HelpUrl property (based on the MSDN Url Aliases) to all types.

PowerShell adds several type extensions to the file *types.ps1xml*, in the PowerShell in-stallation directory. This file is useful as a source of examples, but you should not modify it directly. Instead, create a new one and use the `Update-TypeData` cmdlet to load your customizations. The following command loads *Types.custom.ps1xml* from the same di-rectory as your profile:

```
$typesFile = Join-Path (Split-Path $profile) "Types.Custom.Ps1Xml"
Update-TypeData -PrependPath $typesFile
```

For more information about custom type extensions files, see Recipe 3.17, "Add Custom Methods and Properties to Types".

# Writing Scripts, Reusing Functionality

When you want to start packaging and reusing your commands, the best place to put them is in scripts, functions, and script blocks. A *script* is a text file that contains a sequence of PowerShell commands. A *function* is also a sequence of PowerShell com-mands but is usually placed within a script to break it into smaller, more easily under-stood segments. A script block is a function with no name. All three support the same functionality, except for how you define them.

## Writing Commands

### Writing scripts

To write a script, write your PowerShell commands in a text editor and save the file with a *.ps1* extension.

### Writing functions

Functions let you package blocks of closely related commands into a single unit that you can access by name.

```
function SCOPE:name(parameters)
{
    statement block
}
```

or:

```
filter SCOPE:name(parameters)
{
    statement block
}
```

Valid scope names are global (to create a function available to the entire shell), script (to create a function available only to the current script), local (to create a function available only to the current scope and subscopes), and private (to create a function available only to the current scope). The default scope is the local scope, which follows the same rules as those of default variable scopes.

The content of a function's statement block follows the same rules as the content of a script. Functions support the $args array, formal parameters, the $input enumerator, cmdlet keywords, pipeline output, and equivalent return semantics.

A common mistake is to call a function as you would call a method:

```
$result = GetMyResults($item1, $item2)
```

PowerShell treats functions as it treats scripts and other commands, so this should instead be:

```
$result = GetMyResults $item1 $item2
```

The first command passes an array that contains the items $item1 and $item2 to the GetMyResults function.

A filter is simply a function where the statements are treated as though they are contained within a process statement block. For more information about process statement blocks, see "Cmdlet keywords in commands" (page 906).

Commands in your script can access only functions that have already been defined. This can often make large scripts difficult to understand when the beginning of the script is composed entirely of helper functions. Structuring a script in the following manner often makes it more clear:

```
function Main
{
    (...)
    HelperFunction
    (...)
}

function HelperFunction
{
    (...)
}

. Main
```

### Writing script blocks

```
$objectReference =
{
    statement block
}
```

PowerShell supports script blocks, which act exactly like unnamed functions and scripts. Like both scripts and functions, the content of a script block's statement block follows the same rules as the content of a function or script. Script blocks support the $args array, formal parameters, the $input enumerator, cmdlet keywords, pipeline output, and equivalent return semantics.

As with both scripts and functions, you can either invoke or dot-source a script block. Since a script block does not have a name, you either invoke it directly (& { "Hello"}) or invoke the variable (& $objectReference) that contains it.

## Running Commands

There are two ways to execute a command (script, function, or script block): by invoking it or by dot-sourcing it.

### Invoking

Invoking a command runs the commands inside it. Unless explicitly defined with the GLOBAL scope keyword, variables and functions defined in the script do not persist once the script exits.

 By default, a security feature in PowerShell called the Execution Policy prevents scripts from running. When you want to enable scripting in PowerShell, you must change this setting. To understand the different execution policies available to you, type Get-Help about_signing. After selecting an execution policy, use the Set-ExecutionPolicy cmdlet to configure it:

```
Set-ExecutionPolicy RemoteSigned
```

If the command name has no spaces, simply type its name:

```
c:\temp\Invoke-Commands.ps1 parameter1 parameter2 ...
Invoke-MyFunction parameter1 parameter2 ...
```

You can use either a fully qualified path or a path relative to the current location. If the script is in the current directory, you must explicitly say so:

```
.\Invoke-Commands.ps1 parameter1 parameter2 ...
```

If the command's name has a space (or the command has no name, in the case of a script block), you invoke the command by using the invoke/call operator (&) with the command name as the parameter.

```
& "C:\Script Directory\Invoke-Commands.ps1" parameter1 parameter2 ...
```

Script blocks have no name, so you place the variable holding them after the invocation operator:

```
$scriptBlock = { "Hello World" }
& $scriptBlock parameter1 parameter2 ...
```

If you want to invoke the command within the context of a module, provide a reference to that module as part of the invocation:

```
$module = Get-Module PowerShellCookbook
& $module Invoke-MyFunction parameter1 parameter2 ...
& $module $scriptBlock parameter1 parameter2 ...
```

### Dot-sourcing

Dot-sourcing a command runs the commands inside it. Unlike simply invoking a command, variables and functions defined in the script *do* persist after the script exits.

You invoke a script by using the dot operator (.) and providing the command name as the parameter:

```
. "C:\Script Directory\Invoke-Commands.ps1" Parameters
. Invoke-MyFunction parameters
. $scriptBlock parameters
```

When dot-sourcing a script, you can use either a fully qualified path or a path relative to the current location. If the script is in the current directory, you must explicitly say so:

```
. .\Invoke-Commands.ps1 Parameters
```

If you want to dot-source the command within the context of a module, provide a reference to that module as part of the invocation:

```
$module = Get-Module PowerShellCookbook
. $module Invoke-MyFunction parameters
. $module $scriptBlock parameters
```

### Parameters

Commands that require or support user input do so through parameters. You can use the Get-Command cmdlet to see the parameters supported by a command:

```
PS > Get-Command Stop-Process -Syntax

Stop-Process [-Id] <int[]> [-PassThru] [-Force] [-WhatIf] [-Confirm] [...]
Stop-Process -Name <string[]> [-PassThru] [-Force] [-WhatIf] [-Confirm] [...]
Stop-Process [-InputObject] <Process[]> [-PassThru] [-Force] [-WhatIf] [...]
```

In this case, the supported parameters of the Stop-Process command are Id, Name, InputObject, PassThru, Force, WhatIf, and Confirm.

To supply a value for a parameter, use a dash character, followed by the parameter name, followed by a space, and then the parameter value.

```
Stop-Process -Id 1234
```

If the parameter value contains spaces, surround it with quotes:

```
Stop-Process -Name "Process With Spaces"
```

If a variable contains a value that you want to use for a parameter, supply that through PowerShell's regular variable reference syntax:

```
$name = "Process With Spaces"
Stop-Process -Name $name
```

If you want to use other PowerShell language elements as a parameter value, surround the value with parentheses:

```
Get-Process -Name ("Power" + "Shell")
```

You only need to supply enough of the parameter name to disambiguate it from the rest of the parameters.

```
Stop-Process -N "Process With Spaces"
```

If a command's syntax shows the parameter name in square brackets (such as [-Id]), then it is *positional* and you may omit the parameter name and supply only the value. PowerShell supplies these unnamed values to parameters in the order of their position.

```
Stop-Process 1234
```

Rather than explicitly providing parameter names and values, you can provide a hashtable that defines them and use the *splatting operator*:

```
$parameters = @{
    Path = "c:\temp"
    Recurse = $true
}

Get-ChildItem @parameters
```

To define the default value to be used for the parameter of a command (if the parameter value is not specified directly), assign a value to the `PSDefaultParameterValues` hashtable. The keys of this hashtable are command names and parameter names, separated by a colon. Either (or both) may use wildcards. The values of this hashtable are either simple parameter values, or script blocks that will be evaluated dynamically.

```
PS > $PSDefaultParameterValues["Get-Process:ID"] = $pid
PS > Get-Process

PS > $PSDefaultParameterValues["Get-Service:Name"] = {
    Get-Service -Name * | Foreach-Object Name | Get-Random }
PS > Get-Service
```

## Providing Input to Commands

PowerShell offers several options for processing input to a command.

### Argument array

To access the command-line arguments by position, use the argument array that PowerShell places in the `$args` special variable:

```
$firstArgument = $args[0]
$secondArgument = $args[1]
$argumentCount = $args.Count
```

### Formal parameters

To define a command with simple parameter support:

```
param(
    [TypeName] $VariableName = Default,
    ...
)
```

To define one with support for advanced functionality:

```
[CmdletBinding(cmdlet behavior customizations)]
param(
    [Parameter(Mandatory = $true, Position = 1, ...)]
    [Alias("MyParameterAlias")]
    [...]
    [TypeName] $VariableName = Default,
    ...
)
```

Formal parameters let you benefit from some of the many benefits of PowerShell's consistent command-line parsing engine.

PowerShell exposes your parameter names (for example, `$VariableName`) the same way that it exposes parameters in cmdlets. Users need to type only enough of your parameter name to disambiguate it from the rest of the parameters.

---

If you define a command with simple parameter support, PowerShell attempts to assign the input to your parameters by their position if the user does not type parameter names.

When you add the [CmdletBinding()] attribute, [Parameter()] attribute, or any of the validation attributes, PowerShell adds support for advanced parameter validation.

## Command behavior customizations

The elements of the [CmdletBinding()] attribute describe how your script or function interacts with the system.

SupportsShouldProcess = $true

> If $true, enables the -WhatIf and -Confirm parameters, which tells the user that your command modifies the system and can be run in one of these experimental modes. When specified, you must also call the $psCmdlet.ShouldProcess() method before modifying system state. When not specified, the default is $false.

DefaultParameterSetName = *name*

> Defines the default parameter set name of this command. This is used to resolve ambiguities when parameters declare multiple sets of parameters and the user input doesn't supply enough information to pick between available parameter sets. When not specified, the command has no default parameter set name.

ConfirmImpact = *"High"*

> Defines this command as one that should have its confirmation messages (generated by the $psCmdlet.ShouldProcess() method) shown by default. More specifically, PowerShell defines three confirmation impacts: Low, Medium, and High. PowerShell generates the cmdlet's confirmation messages automatically whenever the cmdlet's impact level is greater than the preference variable. When not specified, the command's impact is Medium.

## Parameter attribute customizations

The elements of the [Parameter()] attribute mainly define how your parameter behaves in relation to other parameters. All elements are optional.

Mandatory = $true

> Defines the parameter as mandatory. If the user doesn't supply a value to this parameter, PowerShell automatically prompts him for it. When not specified, the parameter is optional.

Position = *position*

> Defines the position of this parameter. This applies when the user provides parameter values without specifying the parameter they apply to (e.g., *Argument2* in Invoke-MyFunction -*Param1 Argument1 Argument2*). PowerShell supplies these values to parameters that have defined a Position, from lowest to highest. When not specified, the name of this parameter must be supplied by the user.

**ParameterSetName** = *name*

Defines this parameter as a member of a set of other related parameters. Parameter behavior for this parameter is then specific to this related set of parameters, and the parameter exists only in the parameter sets that it is defined in. This feature is used, for example, when the user may supply only a Name *or* ID. To include a parameter in two or more specific parameter sets, use two or more [`Parameter()`] attributes. When not specified, this parameter is a member of all parameter sets.

**ValueFromPipeline** = `$true`

Declares this parameter as one that directly accepts pipeline input. If the user pipes data into your script or function, PowerShell assigns this input to your parameter in your command's `process {}` block. When not specified, this parameter does not accept pipeline input directly.

**ValueFromPipelineByPropertyName** = `$true`

Declares this parameter as one that accepts pipeline input if a property of an incoming object matches its name. If this is true, PowerShell assigns the value of that property to your parameter in your command's `process {}` block. When not specified, this parameter does not accept pipeline input by property name.

**ValueFromRemainingArguments** = `$true`

Declares this parameter as one that accepts all remaining input that has not otherwise been assigned to positional or named parameters. Only one parameter can have this element. If no parameter declares support for this capability, PowerShell generates an error for arguments that cannot be assigned.

## Parameter validation attributes

In addition to the [`Parameter()`] attribute, PowerShell lets you apply other attributes that add behavior or validation constraints to your parameters. All validation attributes are optional.

**[Alias("** *name* **")]**

Defines an alternate name for this parameter. This is especially helpful for long parameter names that are descriptive but have a more common colloquial term. When not specified, the parameter can be referred to only by the name you originally declared.

**[AllowNull()]**

Allows this parameter to receive `$null` as its value. This is required only for mandatory parameters. When not specified, mandatory parameters cannot receive `$null` as their value, although optional parameters can.

`[AllowEmptyString()]`

Allows this string parameter to receive an empty string as its value. This is required only for mandatory parameters. When not specified, mandatory string parameters cannot receive an empty string as their value, although optional string parameters can. You can apply this to parameters that are not strings, but it has no impact.

`[AllowEmptyCollection()]`

Allows this collection parameter to receive an empty collection as its value. This is required only for mandatory parameters. When not specified, mandatory collection parameters cannot receive an empty collection as their value, although optional collection parameters can. You can apply this to parameters that are not collections, but it has no impact.

`[ValidateCount(`*lower limit, upper limit*`)]`

Restricts the number of elements that can be in a collection supplied to this parameter. When not specified, mandatory parameters have a lower limit of one element. Optional parameters have no restrictions. You can apply this to parameters that are not collections, but it has no impact.

`[ValidateLength(`*lower limit, upper limit*`)]`

Restricts the length of strings that this parameter can accept. When not specified, mandatory parameters have a lower limit of one character. Optional parameters have no restrictions. You can apply this to parameters that are not strings, but it has no impact.

`[ValidatePattern("`*regular expression*`")]`

Enforces a pattern that input to this string parameter must match. When not specified, string inputs have no pattern requirements. You can apply this to parameters that are not strings, but it has no impact.

`[ValidateRange(`*lower limit, upper limit*`)]`

Restricts the upper and lower limit of numerical arguments that this parameter can accept. When not specified, parameters have no range limit. You can apply this to parameters that are not numbers, but it has no impact.

`[ValidateScript( {` *script block* `} )]`

Ensures that input supplied to this parameter satisfies the condition that you supply in the script block. PowerShell assigns the proposed input to the `$_` (or `$PSItem`) variable, and then invokes your script block. If the script block returns `$true` (or anything that can be converted to `$true`, such as nonempty strings), PowerShell considers the validation to have been successful.

```
[ValidateSet("First Option", "Second Option", …, "Last Option")]
```
Ensures that input supplied to this parameter is equal to one of the options in the set. PowerShell uses its standard meaning of equality during this comparison: the same rules used by the -eq operator. If your validation requires nonstandard rules (such as case-sensitive comparison of strings), you can instead write the validation in the body of the script or function.

```
[ValidateNotNull()]
```
Ensures that input supplied to this parameter is not null. This is the default behavior of mandatory parameters, so this is useful only for optional parameters. When applied to string parameters, a $null parameter value gets instead converted to an empty string.

```
[ValidateNotNullOrEmpty()]
```
Ensures that input supplied to this parameter is not null or empty. This is the default behavior of mandatory parameters, so this is useful only for optional parameters. When applied to string parameters, the input must be a string with a length greater than one. When applied to collection parameters, the collection must have at least one element. When applied to other types of parameters, this attribute is equivalent to the [ValidateNotNull()] attribute.

## Pipeline input

To access the data being passed to your command via the pipeline, use the input enumerator that PowerShell places in the $input special variable:

```
foreach($element in $input)
{
    "Input was: $element"
}
```

The $input variable is a .NET enumerator over the pipeline input. Enumerators support streaming scenarios very efficiently but do not let you access arbitrary elements as you would with an array. If you want to process their elements again, you must call the Reset() method on the $input enumerator once you reach the end.

If you need to access the pipeline input in an unstructured way, use the following command to convert the input enumerator to an array:

```
$inputArray = @($input)
```

## Cmdlet keywords in commands

When pipeline input is a core scenario of your command, you can include statement blocks labeled begin, process, and end:

```
param(...)

begin
```

```
    {
        ...
    }
    process
    {
        ...
    }
    end
    {
        ...
    }
```

PowerShell executes the begin statement when it loads your command, the process statement for each item passed down the pipeline, and the end statement after all pipeline input has been processed. In the process statement block, the $_ (or $PSItem) variable represents the current pipeline object.

When you write a command that includes these keywords, all the commands in your script must be contained within the statement blocks.

### $MyInvocation automatic variable

The $MyInvocation automatic variable contains information about the context under which the script was run, including detailed information about the command (*MyCom mand*), the script that defines it (*ScriptName*), and more.

## Retrieving Output from Commands

PowerShell provides three primary ways to retrieve output from a command.

### Pipeline output

```
        any command
```

The return value/output of a script is any data that it generates but does not capture. If a command contains:

```
    "Text Output"
    5*5
```

then assigning the output of that command to a variable creates an array with the two values Text Output and 25.

### Return statement

```
    return value
```

The statement:

```
    return $false
```

is simply a short form for pipeline output:

```
$false
return
```

### Exit statement

```
exit errorlevel
```

The **exit** statement returns an error code from the current command or instance of PowerShell. If called anywhere in a script (inline, in a function, or in a script block), it exits the script. If called outside of a script (for example, a function), it exits PowerShell. The **exit** statement sets the $LastExitCode automatic variable to *errorLevel*. In turn, that sets the $? automatic variable to $false if *errorLevel* is not zero.

 Type **Get-Help about_automatic_variables** for more information about automatic variables.

# Help Documentation

PowerShell automatically generates help content out of specially tagged comments in your command:

```
<#

.SYNOPSIS
Runs a ...

.EXAMPLE
PS > ...

#>

param(
    ## Help content for the Param1 parameter
    $Param1
)
```

Help-specific comments must be the only comments in a comment block. If PowerShell discovers a nonhelp comment, it discontinues looking for comments in that comment block. If you need to include nonhelp comments in a comment block, place them in a separate block of comments. The following are the most typical help comments used in a comment block:

.SYNOPSIS
 A short summary of the command, ideally a single sentence.

.DESCRIPTION
 A more detailed description of the command.

**.PARAMETER** *name*

A description of parameter *name*, with one for each parameter you want to describe. While you can write a .PARAMETER comment for each parameter, PowerShell also supports comments written directly above the parameter. Putting parameter help alongside the actual parameter makes it easier to read and maintain.

**.EXAMPLE**

An example of this command in use, with one for each example you want to provide. PowerShell treats the line immediately beneath the .EXAMPLE tag as the example command. If this line doesn't contain any text that looks like a prompt, PowerShell adds a prompt before it. It treats lines that follow the initial line as additional output and example commentary.

**.INPUTS**

A short summary of pipeline input(s) supported by this command. For each input type, PowerShell's built-in help follows this convention:

```
System.String
    You can pipe a string that contains a path to Get-ChildItem.
```

**.OUTPUTS**

A short summary of items generated by this command. For each output type, PowerShell's built-in help follows this convention:

```
System.ServiceProcess.ServiceController
    Get-Service returns objects that represent the services on the computer.
```

**.NOTES**

Any additional notes or remarks about this command.

**.LINK**

A link to a related help topic or command, with one .LINK tag per link. If the related help topic is a URL, PowerShell launches that URL when the user supplies the -Online parameter to Get-Help for your command.

# Managing Errors

PowerShell supports two classes of errors: *nonterminating* and *terminating*. It collects both types of errors as a list in the $error automatic variable.

## Nonterminating Errors

Most errors are *nonterminating errors,* in that they do not halt execution of the current cmdlet, script, function, or pipeline. When a command outputs an error (via Power-Shell's error-output facilities), PowerShell writes that error to a stream called the *error output stream.*

You can output a nonterminating error using the Write-Error cmdlet (or the WriteError() API when writing a cmdlet).

The $ErrorActionPreference automatic variable lets you control how PowerShell handles nonterminating errors. It supports the following values, shown in Table A-14.

*Table A-14. ErrorActionPreference automatic variable values*

| Value | Meaning |
| --- | --- |
| Ignore | Do not display errors, and do not add them to the $error collection. Only supported when supplied to the ErrorAction parameter of a command. |
| SilentlyContinue | Do not display errors, but add them to the $error collection. |
| Stop | Treat nonterminating errors as terminating errors. |
| Continue | Display errors, but continue execution of the current cmdlet, script, function, or pipeline. This is the default. |
| Inquire | Display a prompt that asks how PowerShell should treat this error. |

Most cmdlets let you configure this explicitly by passing one of these values to the ErrorAction parameter.

## Terminating Errors

A *terminating error* halts execution of the current cmdlet, script, function, or pipeline. If a command (such as a cmdlet or .NET method call) generates a structured exception (for example, if you provide a method with parameters outside their valid range), PowerShell exposes this as a terminating error. PowerShell also generates a terminating error if it fails to parse an element of your script, function, or pipeline.

You can generate a terminating error in your script using the throw keyword:

```
throw message
```

 In your own scripts and cmdlets, generate terminating errors only when the fundamental intent of the operation is impossible to accomplish. For example, failing to execute a command on a remote server should be considered a nonterminating error, whereas failing to connect to the remote server altogether should be considered a terminating error.

You can intercept terminating errors through the try, catch, and finally statements, as supported by many other programming languages:

```
try
{
    statement block
}
catch [exception type]
```

```
{
    error handling block
}
catch [alternate exception type]
{
    alternate error handling block
}
finally
{
    cleanup block
}
```

After a try statement, you must provide a catch statement, a finally statement, or both. If you specify an exception type (which is optional), you may specify more than one catch statement to handle exceptions of different types. If you specify an exception type, the catch block applies only to terminating errors of that type.

PowerShell also lets you intercept terminating errors if you define a trap statement before PowerShell encounters that error:

```
trap [exception type]
{
    statement block
    [continue or break]
}
```

If you specify an exception type, the trap statement applies only to terminating errors of that type.

Within a catch block or trap statement, the $_ (or $PSItem) variable represents the current exception or error being processed.

If specified, the continue keyword tells PowerShell to continue processing your script, function, or pipeline after the point at which it encountered the terminating error.

If specified, the break keyword tells PowerShell to halt processing the rest of your script, function, or pipeline after the point at which it encountered the terminating error. The default mode is break, and it applies if you specify neither break nor continue.

# Formatting Output

*Pipeline | Formatting Command*

When objects reach the end of the output pipeline, PowerShell converts them to text to make them suitable for human consumption. PowerShell supports several options to help you control this formatting process, as listed in Table A-15.

*Table A-15. PowerShell formatting commands*

| Formatting command | Result |
|---|---|
| Format-Table *Properties* | Formats the properties of the input objects as a table, including only the object properties you specify. If you do not specify a property list, PowerShell picks a default set.<br>In addition to supplying object properties, you may also provide advanced formatting statements:<br><pre>PS > Get-Process \| `<br>   Format-Table -Auto Name,`<br>   @{Label="HexId";<br>     Expression={ "{0:x}" -f $_.Id}<br>     Width=4<br>     Align="Right"<br>     }</pre>The advanced formatting statement is a hashtable with the keys Label and Expression (or any short form of them). The value of the expression key should be a script block that returns a result for the current object (represented by the $_ variable).<br>For more information about the Format-Table cmdlet, type **Get-Help Format-Table**. |
| Format-List *Properties* | Formats the properties of the input objects as a list, including only the object properties you specify. If you do not specify a property list, PowerShell picks a default set.<br>The Format-List cmdlet supports advanced formatting statements as used by the Format-Table cmdlet.<br>The Format-List cmdlet is the one you will use most often to get a detailed summary of an object's properties.<br>The command Format-List * returns all properties, but it does not include those that PowerShell hides by default. The command Format-List * -Force returns all properties.<br>For more information about the Format-List cmdlet, type **Get-Help Format-List**. |
| Format-Wide *Property* | Formats the properties of the input objects in an extremely terse summary view. If you do not specify a property, PowerShell picks a default.<br>In addition to supplying object properties, you can also provide advanced formatting statements:<br><pre>PS > Get-Process \| `<br>   Format-Wide -Auto `<br>   @{ Expression={ "{0:x}" -f $_.Id} }</pre>The advanced formatting statement is a hashtable with the key Expression (or any short form of it). The value of the expression key should be a script block that returns a result for the current object (represented by the $_ variable).<br>For more information about the Format-Wide cmdlet, type **Get-Help Format-Wide**. |

## Custom Formatting Files

All the formatting defaults in PowerShell (for example, when you do not specify a formatting command, or when you do not specify formatting properties) are driven by the *\*.Format.Ps1Xml* files in the installation directory in a manner similar to the type extension files mentioned in Recipe 3.17, "Add Custom Methods and Properties to Types".

To create your own formatting customizations, use these files as a source of examples, but do not modify them directly. Instead, create a new file and use the `Update-FormatData` cmdlet to load your customizations. The `Update-FormatData` cmdlet applies your changes to the current instance of PowerShell. If you wish to load them every time you launch PowerShell, call `Update-FormatData` in your profile script. The following command loads *Format.custom.ps1xml* from the same directory as your profile:

```
$formatFile = Join-Path (Split-Path $profile) "Format.Custom.Ps1Xml"
Update-FormatData -PrependPath $typesFile
```

To add formatting information without using format files, see Recipe 3.18, "Define Custom Formatting for a Type".

# Capturing Output

There are several ways to capture the output of commands in PowerShell, as listed in Table A-16.

*Table A-16. Capturing output in PowerShell*

| Command | Result |
| --- | --- |
| `$variable = Command` | Stores the objects produced by the PowerShell command into `$variable`. |
| `$variable = Command \| Out-String` | Stores the visual representation of the PowerShell command into `$variable`. This is the PowerShell command after it's been converted to human-readable output. |
| `$variable = NativeCommand` | Stores the (string) output of the native command into `$variable`. PowerShell stores this as a list of strings—one for each line of output from the native command. |
| `Command -OutVariable variable` | For most commands, stores the objects produced by the PowerShell command into `$variable`. The parameter `-OutVariable` can also be written `-Ov`. |
| `Command > File` | Redirects the visual representation of the PowerShell (or standard output of a native command) into `File`, overwriting `File` if it exists. Errors are not captured by this redirection. |
| `Command >> File` | Redirects the visual representation of the PowerShell (or standard output of a native command) into `File`, appending to `File` if it exists. Errors are not captured by this redirection. |
| `Command 2> File` | Redirects the errors from the PowerShell or native command into `File`, overwriting `File` if it exists. |

| Command | Result |
|---|---|
| `Command n> File` | Redirects stream number *n* into `File`, overwriting `File` if it exists. Supported streams are 2 for error, 3 for warning, 4 for verbose, 5 for debug, and * for all. |
| `Command 2>> File` | Redirects the errors from the PowerShell or native command into `File`, appending to `File` if it exists. |
| `Command n>> File` | Redirects stream number *n* into `File`, appending to `File` if it exists. Supported streams are 2 for error, 3 for warning, 4 for verbose, 5 for debug, and * for all. |
| `Command> File 2>&1` | Redirects both the error and standard output streams of the PowerShell or native command into `File`, overwriting `File` if it exists. |
| `Command>> File 2>&1` | Redirects both the error and standard output streams of the PowerShell or native command into `File`, appending to `File` if it exists. |

# Common Customization Points

As useful as it is out of the box, PowerShell offers several avenues for customization and personalization.

## Console Settings

The Windows PowerShell user interface offers several features to make your shell experience more efficient.

### Adjust your window size

In the System menu (right-click the title bar at the top left of the console window), select Properties→Layout. The Window Size options let you control the actual window size (how big the window appears on screen), whereas the Screen Buffer Size options let you control the virtual window size (how much content the window can hold). If the screen buffer size is larger than the actual window size, the console window changes to include scrollbars. Increase the virtual window height to make PowerShell store more output from earlier in your session. If you launch PowerShell from the Start menu, PowerShell launches with some default modifications to the window size.

### Make text selection easier

In the System menu, click Options→QuickEdit Mode. QuickEdit mode lets you use the mouse to efficiently copy and paste text into or out of your PowerShell console. By default, PowerShell launches with QuickEdit mode enabled.

### Use hotkeys to operate the shell more efficiently

The Windows PowerShell console supports many hotkeys that help make operating the console more efficient, as shown in Table A-17.

*Table A-17. Windows PowerShell hotkeys*

| Hotkey | Meaning |
|---|---|
| Windows key-r, and then type **powershell** | Launch Windows PowerShell. |
| Up arrow | Scan backward through your command history. |
| Down arrow | Scan forward through your command history. |
| Page Up | Display the first command in your command history. |
| Page Down | Display the last command in your command history. |
| Left arrow | Move cursor one character to the left on your command line. |
| Right arrow | Move cursor one character to the right on your command line. If at the end of the line, inserts a character from the text of your last command at that position. |
| Home | Move the cursor to the beginning of the command line. |
| End | Move the cursor to the end of the command line. |
| Ctrl-left arrow | Move the cursor one word to the left on your command line. |
| Ctrl-right arrow | Move the cursor one word to the right on your command line. |
| Alt-space, e, l | Scroll through the screen buffer. |
| Alt-space, e, f | Search for text in the screen buffer. |
| Alt-space, e, k | Select text to be copied from the screen buffer. |
| Alt-space, e, p | Paste clipboard contents into the Windows PowerShell console. |
| Alt-space, c | Close the Windows PowerShell console. |
| Ctrl-c | Cancel the current operation. |
| Ctrl-break | Forcibly close the Windows PowerShell window. |
| Ctrl-home | Deletes characters from the beginning of the current command line up to (but not including) the current cursor position. |
| Ctrl-end | Deletes characters from (and including) the current cursor position to the end of the current command line. |
| F1 | Move cursor one character to the right on your command line. If at the end of the line, inserts a character from the text of your last command at that position. |
| F2 | Creates a new command line by copying your last command line up to the character that you type. |
| F3 | Complete the command line with content from your last command line, from the current cursor position to the end. |
| F4 | Deletes characters from your cursor position up to (but not including) the character that you type. |
| F5 | Scan backward through your command history. |
| F7 | Interactively select a command from your command history. Use the arrow keys to scroll through the window that appears. Press the Enter key to execute the command, or use the right arrow key to place the text on your command line instead. |
| F8 | Scan backward through your command history, only displaying matches for commands that match the text you've typed so far on the command line. |

| Hotkey | Meaning |
|---|---|
| F9 | Invoke a specific numbered command from your command history. The numbers of these commands correspond to the numbers that the command-history selection window (F7) shows. |
| Alt-F7 | Clear the command history list. |

 While useful in their own right, the hotkeys listed in Table A-17 become even more useful when you map them to shorter or more intuitive keystrokes using a hotkey program such as the free AutoHotkey (*http://www.autohotkey.com*).

## Profiles

Windows PowerShell automatically runs the four scripts listed in Table A-18 during startup. Each, if present, lets you customize your execution environment. PowerShell runs anything you place in these files as though you had entered it manually at the command line.

*Table A-18. Windows PowerShell profiles*

| Profile purpose | Profile location |
|---|---|
| Customization of all PowerShell sessions, including PowerShell hosting applications for all users on the system | *InstallationDirectory\profile.ps1* |
| Customization of *PowerShell.exe* sessions for all users on the system | *InstallationDirectory\ Microsoft. PowerShell _profile.ps1* |
| Customization of all PowerShell sessions, including PowerShell hosting applications | *<My Documents>\WindowsPowerShell\profile.ps1* |
| Typical customization of *PowerShell.exe* sessions | *<My Documents>\WindowsPowerShell\ Microsoft.PowerShell _profile.ps1* |

PowerShell makes editing your profile script simple by defining the automatic variable $profile. By itself, it points to the "current user, PowerShell.exe" profile. In addition, the $profile variable defines additional properties that point to the other profile locations:

```
PS > $profile | Format-List -Force


AllUsersAllHosts         : C:\Windows\System32\WindowsPowerShell\v1.0\
                           profile.ps1
AllUsersCurrentHost      : C:\Windows\System32\WindowsPowerShell\v1.0\
                           Microsoft.PowerShell_profile.ps1
CurrentUserAllHosts      : E:\Lee\WindowsPowerShell\profile.ps1
CurrentUserCurrentHost   : E:\Lee\WindowsPowerShell\Microsoft.PowerShell_
                           profile.ps1
```

To create a new profile, type:

```
New-Item -Type file -Force $profile
```

To edit this profile, type:

```
notepad $profile
```

## Prompts

To customize your prompt, add a `prompt` function to your profile. This function returns a string. For example:

```
function Prompt
{
    "PS [$env:COMPUTERNAME] >"
}
```

For more information about customizing your prompt, see also Recipe 1.8, "Customize Your Shell, Profile, and Prompt".

## Tab Completion

You can define a `TabExpansion2` function to customize the way that Windows PowerShell completes properties, variables, parameters, and files when you press the Tab key.

Your `TabExpansion` function overrides the one that PowerShell defines by default, though, so you may want to use its definition as a starting point:

```
Get-Content function:\TabExpansion2
```

For more information about customizing tab expansion, see Recipe 1.17, "Understand and Customize PowerShell's Tab Completion".

## User Input

You can define a `PSConsoleHostReadLine` function to customize the way that the Windows PowerShell console host (not the ISE) reads input from the user. This function is responsible for handling all of the user's keypresses, and finally returning the command that PowerShell should invoke.

For more information about overriding user input, see Recipe 1.9, "Customize PowerShell's User Input Behavior".

## Command Resolution

You can intercept PowerShell's command resolution behavior in three places by assigning a script block to one or all of the `PreCommandLookupAction`, `PostCommandLookupAction`, or `CommandNotFoundAction` properties of `$executionContext.SessionState.InvokeCommand`.

PowerShell invokes the `PreCommandLookupAction` after the user types a command name, but before it has tried to resolve the command. It invokes the `PostCommandLoo kupAction` once it has resolved a command, but before it executes the command. It invokes the `CommandNotFoundAction` when a command is not found, but before it generates an error message. Each script block receives two arguments: `CommandName` and `CommandLookupEventArgs`.

```
$executionContext.SessionState.InvokeCommand.CommandNotFoundAction = {
    param($CommandName, $CommandLookupEventArgs)

    (...)
}
```

If your script block assigns a script block to the `CommandScriptBlock` property of the `CommandLookupEventArgs` or assigns a `CommandInfo` to the `Command` property of the `CommandLookupEventArgs`, PowerShell will use that script block or command, respectively. If your script block sets the `StopSearch` property to `true`, PowerShell will do no further command resolution.

For more information about overriding user input, see Recipe 1.10, "Customize PowerShell's Command Resolution Behavior".

# Regular Expression Reference

Regular expressions play an important role in most text parsing and text matching tasks. They form an important underpinning of the -split and -match operators, the switch statement, the Select-String cmdlet, and more. Tables B-1 through B-9 list commonly used regular expressions.

*Table B-1. Character classes: patterns that represent sets of characters*

| Character class | Matches |
| --- | --- |
| . | Any character except for a newline. If the regular expression uses the SingleLine option, it matches any character.<br>`PS > "T" -match '.'`<br>`True` |
| [*characters*] | Any character in the brackets. For example: [aeiou].<br>`PS > "Test" -match '[Tes]'`<br>`True` |
| [^*characters*] | Any character not in the brackets. For example: [^aeiou].<br>`PS > "Test" -match '[^Tes]'`<br>`False` |
| [*start-end*] | Any character between the characters *start* and *end*, inclusive. You may include multiple character ranges between the brackets. For example, [a-eh-j].<br>`PS > "Test" -match '[e-t]'`<br>`True` |
| [^*start-end*] | Any character not between any of the character ranges *start* through *end*, inclusive. You may include multiple character ranges between the brackets. For example, [^a-eh-j].<br>`PS > "Test" -match '[^e-t]'`<br>`False` |

| Character class | Matches |
|---|---|
| \p{character class} | Any character in the Unicode group or block range specified by {character class}.<br><br>```PS > "+" -match '\p{Sm}'```<br>```True``` |
| \P{character class} | Any character not in the Unicode group or block range specified by {character class}.<br><br>```PS > "+" -match '\P{Sm}'```<br>```False``` |
| \w | Any word character. Note that this is the *Unicode* definition of a word character, which includes digits, as well as many math symbols and various other symbols.<br><br>```PS > "a" -match '\w'```<br>```True``` |
| \W | Any nonword character.<br><br>```PS > "!" -match '\W'```<br>```True``` |
| \s | Any whitespace character.<br><br>```PS > "`t" -match '\s'```<br>```True``` |
| \S | Any nonwhitespace character.<br><br>```PS > " `t" -match '\S'```<br>```False``` |
| \d | Any decimal digit.<br><br>```PS > "5" -match '\d'```<br>```True``` |
| \D | Any character that isn't a decimal digit.<br><br>```PS > "!" -match '\D'```<br>```True``` |

*Table B-2. Quantifiers: expressions that enforce quantity on the preceding expression*

| Quantifier | Meaning |
|---|---|
| <none> | One match.<br><br>```PS > "T" -match 'T'```<br>```True``` |
| * | Zero or more matches, matching as much as possible.<br><br>```PS > "A" -match 'T*'```<br>```True```<br>```PS > "TTTTT" -match '^T*$'```<br>```True``` |

| Quantifier | Meaning |
|---|---|
| | `PS > 'ATTT' -match 'AT*'; $Matches[0]`<br>`True`<br>`ATTT` |
| + | One or more matches, matching as much as possible.<br>`PS > "A" -match 'T+'`<br>`False`<br>`PS > "TTTTT" -match '^T+$'`<br>`True`<br><br>`PS > 'ATTT' -match 'AT+'; $Matches[0]`<br>`True`<br>`ATTT` |
| ? | Zero or one matches, matching as much as possible.<br>`PS > "TTTTT" -match '^T?$'`<br>`False`<br><br>`PS > 'ATTT' -match 'AT?'; $Matches[0]`<br>`True`<br>`AT` |
| {*n*} | Exactly *n* matches.<br>`PS > "TTTTT" -match '^T{5}$'`<br>`True` |
| {*n*,} | *n* or more matches, matching as much as possible.<br>`PS > "TTTTT" -match '^T{4,}$'`<br>`True` |
| {*n*,*m*} | Between *n* and *m* matches (inclusive), matching as much as possible.<br>`PS > "TTTTT" -match '^T{4,6}$'`<br>`True` |
| *? | Zero or more matches, matching as little as possible.<br>`PS > "A" -match '^AT*?$'`<br>`True`<br><br>`PS > 'ATTT' -match 'AT*?'; $Matches[0]`<br>`True`<br>`A` |
| +? | One or more matches, matching as little as possible.<br>`PS > "A" -match '^AT+?$'`<br>`False`<br><br>`PS > 'ATTT' -match 'AT+?'; $Matches[0]`<br>`True`<br>`AT` |
| ?? | Zero or one matches, matching as little as possible.<br>`PS > "A" -match '^AT??$'`<br>`True` |

| Quantifier | Meaning |
|---|---|
| | ```
PS > 'ATTT' -match 'AT??'; $Matches[0]
True
A
``` |
| {n}? | Exactly n matches.<br>```
PS > "TTTTT" -match '^T{5}?$'
True
``` |
| {n,}? | n or more matches, matching as little as possible.<br>```
PS > "TTTTT" -match '^T{4,}?$'
True
``` |
| {n,m}? | Between n and m matches (inclusive), matching as little as possible.<br>```
PS > "TTTTT" -match '^T{4,6}?$'
True
``` |

*Table B-3. Grouping constructs: expressions that let you group characters, patterns, and other expressions*

| Grouping construct | Description |
|---|---|
| (text) | Captures the text matched inside the parentheses. These captures are named by number (starting at one) based on the order of the opening parenthesis.<br>```
PS > "Hello" -match '^(.*)llo$'; $matches[1]
True
He
``` |
| (?<name>) | Captures the text matched inside the parentheses. These captures are named by the name given in *name*.<br>```
PS > "Hello" -match '^(?<One>.*)llo$'; $matches.One
True
He
``` |
| (?<name1-name2>) | A balancing group definition. This is an advanced regular expression construct, but lets you match evenly balanced pairs of terms. |
| (?:) | Noncapturing group.<br>```
PS > "A1" -match '((A|B)\d)'; $matches
True

Name                           Value
----                           -----
2                              A
1                              A1
0                              A1

PS > "A1" -match '((?:A|B)\d)'; $matches
True
``` |
```

| Grouping construct | Description | |
| --- | --- | --- |
| | Name | Value |
| | ---- | ----- |
| | 1 | A1 |
| | 0 | A1 |
| `(?imnsx-imnsx:)` | Applies or disables the given option for this group. Supported options are:<br>i    case-insensitive<br>m   multiline<br>n   explicit capture<br>s   singleline<br>x   ignore whitespace<br><br>`PS > "Te`nst" -match '(T e.st)'`<br>`False`<br>`PS > "Te`nst" -match '(?sx:T e.st)'`<br>`True` | |
| `(?=)` | Zero-width positive lookahead assertion. Ensures that the given pattern matches to the right, without actually performing the match.<br>`PS > "555-1212" -match '(?=...-)(.*)'; $matches[1]`<br>`True`<br>`555-1212` | |
| `(?!)` | Zero-width negative lookahead assertion. Ensures that the given pattern does not match to the right, without actually performing the match.<br>`PS > "friendly" -match '(?!friendly)friend'`<br>`False` | |
| `(?<=)` | Zero-width positive lookbehind assertion. Ensures that the given pattern matches to the left, without actually performing the match.<br>`PS > "public int X" -match '^.*(?<=public )int .*$'`<br>`True` | |
| `(?<!)` | Zero-width negative lookbehind assertion. Ensures that the given pattern does not match to the left, without actually performing the match.<br>`PS > "private int X" -match '^.*(?<!private )int .*$'`<br>`False` | |
| `(?>)` | Nonbacktracking subexpression. Matches only if this subexpression can be matched completely.<br>`PS > "Hello World" -match '(Hello.*)orld'`<br>`True`<br>`PS > "Hello World" -match '(?>Hello.*)orld'`<br>`False`<br><br>The nonbacktracking version of the subexpression fails to match, as its complete match would be "Hello World". | |

*Table B-4. Atomic zero-width assertions: patterns that restrict where a match may occur*

| Assertion | Restriction |
| --- | --- |
| ^ | The match must occur at the beginning of the string (or line, if the Multiline option is in effect). |

| Assertion | Restriction |
|---|---|
| | ```PS > "Test" -match '^est'```<br>```False``` |
| $ | The match must occur at the end of the string (or line, if the Multiline option is in effect).<br>```PS > "Test" -match 'Tes$'```<br>```False``` |
| \A | The match must occur at the beginning of the string.<br>```PS > "The`nTest" -match '(?m:^Test)'```<br>```True```<br>```PS > "The`nTest" -match '(?m:\ATest)'```<br>```False``` |
| \Z | The match must occur at the end of the string, or before \n at the end of the string.<br>```PS > "The`nTest`n" -match '(?m:The$)'```<br>```True```<br>```PS > "The`nTest`n" -match '(?m:The\Z)'```<br>```False```<br>```PS > "The`nTest`n" -match 'Test\Z'```<br>```True``` |
| \z | The match must occur at the end of the string.<br>```PS > "The`nTest`n" -match 'Test\z'```<br>```False``` |
| \G | The match must occur where the previous match ended. Used with System.Text.RegularExpressions.Match.NextMatch(). |
| \b | The match must occur on a word boundary: the first or last characters in words separated by nonalphanumeric characters.<br>```PS > "Testing" -match 'ing\b'```<br>```True``` |
| \B | The match must not occur on a word boundary.<br>```PS > "Testing" -match 'ing\B'```<br>```False``` |

*Table B-5. Substitution patterns: patterns used in a regular expression replace operation*

| Pattern | Substitution |
|---|---|
| $number | The text matched by group number *number*.<br>```PS > "Test" -replace "(.*)st",'$1ar'```<br>```Tear``` |
| ${name} | The text matched by group named *name*.<br>```PS > "Test" -replace "(?<pre>.*)st",'${pre}ar'```<br>```Tear``` |
| $$ | A literal $. |

| Pattern | Substitution |
|---|---|
| | ```
PS > "Test" -replace ".",'$$'
$$$$
``` |
| $& | A copy of the entire match.<br>```
PS > "Test" -replace "^.*$",'Found: $&'
Found: Test
``` |
| $` | The text of the input string that precedes the match.<br>```
PS > "Test" -replace "est$",'Te$`'
TTeT
``` |
| $' | The text of the input string that follows the match.<br>```
PS > "Test" -replace "^Tes",'Res$''
Restt
``` |
| $+ | The last group captured.<br>```
PS > "Testing" -replace "(.*)ing",'$+ed'
Tested
``` |
| $_ | The entire input string.<br>```
PS > "Testing" -replace "(.*)ing",'String: $_'
String: Testing
``` |

*Table B-6. Alternation constructs: expressions that let you perform either/or logic*

| Alternation construct | Description |
|---|---|
| \| | Matches any of the terms separated by the vertical bar character.<br>```
PS > "Test" -match '(B|T)est'
True
``` |
| (?(*expression*)*yes*\|*no*) | Matches the *yes term* if expression matches at this point. Otherwise, matches the *no term*. The *no term* is optional.<br>```
PS > "3.14" -match '(?(\d)3.14|Pi)'
True
PS > "Pi" -match '(?(\d)3.14|Pi)'
True
PS > "2.71" -match '(?(\d)3.14|Pi)'
False
``` |
| (?(*name*)*yes*\|*no*) | Matches the *yes term* if the capture group named name has a capture at this point. Otherwise, matches the *no term*. The *no term* is optional.<br>```
PS > "123" -match '(?<one>1)?(?(one)23|234)'
True
PS > "23" -match '(?<one>1)?(?(one)23|234)'
False
PS > "234" -match '(?<one>1)?(?(one)23|234)'
True
``` |
```

*Table B-7. Backreference constructs: expressions that refer to a capture group within the expression*

| Backreference construct | Refers to |
|---|---|
| \\*number* | Group number *number* in the expression.<br>```PS > "\|Text\|" -match '(.)Text\1'```<br>```True```<br>```PS > "\|Text+" -match '(.)Text\1'```<br>```False``` |
| \k<*name*> | The group named *name* in the expression.<br>```PS > "\|Text\|" -match '(?<Symbol>.)Text\k<Symbol>'```<br>```True```<br>```PS > "\|Text+" -match '(?<Symbol>.)Text\k<Symbol>'```<br>```False``` |

*Table B-8. Other constructs: other expressions that modify a regular expression*

| Construct | Description |
|---|---|
| (?*imnsx-imnsx*) | Applies or disables the given option for the rest of this expression.<br>Supported options are:<br>  i   case-insensitive<br>  m   multiline<br>  n   explicit capture<br>  s   singleline<br>  x   ignore whitespace<br><br>```PS > "Te`nst" -match '(?sx)T e.st'```<br>```True``` |
| (?# ) | Inline comment. This terminates at the first closing parenthesis.<br>```PS > "Test" -match '(?# Match 'Test')Test'```<br>```True``` |
| # *[to end of line]* | Comment form allowed when the regular expression has the Ignor eWhitespace option enabled.<br>```PS > "Test" -match '(?x)Test # Matches Test'```<br>```True``` |

*Table B-9. Character escapes: character sequences that represent another character*

| Escaped character | Match |
|---|---|
| <*ordinary characters*> | Characters other than . $ ^ { [ ( | ) * + ? \ match themselves. |
| \a | A bell (alarm) \u0007. |
| \b | A backspace \u0008 if in a [ ] character class. In a regular expression, \b denotes a word boundary (between \w and \W characters) except within a [ ] character class, where \b refers to the backspace character. In a replacement pattern, \b always denotes a backspace. |
| \t | A tab \u0009. |

| Escaped character | Match |
| --- | --- |
| \r | A carriage return \u000D. |
| \v | A vertical tab \u000B. |
| \f | A form feed \u000C. |
| \n | A new line \u000A. |
| \e | An escape \u001B. |
| \ddd | An ASCII character as octal (up to three digits). Numbers with no leading zero are treated as backreferences if they have only one digit, or if they correspond to a capturing group number. |
| \xdd | An ASCII character using hexadecimal representation (exactly two digits). |
| \cC | An ASCII control character; for example, \cC is Control-C. |
| \udddd | A Unicode character using hexadecimal representation (exactly four digits). |
| \ | When followed by a character that is not recognized as an escaped character, matches that character. For example, \* is the literal character *. |

# XPath Quick Reference

Just as regular expressions are the standard way to interact with plain text, XPath is the standard way to interact with XML. Because of that, XPath is something you are likely to run across in your travels. Several cmdlets support XPath queries: `Select-Xml`, `Get-WinEvent`, and more. Tables C-1 and C-2 give a quick overview of XPath concepts.

For these examples, consider this sample XML:

```
<AddressBook>
  <Person contactType="Personal">
    <Name>Lee</Name>
    <Phone type="home">555-1212</Phone>
    <Phone type="work">555-1213</Phone>
  </Person>
  <Person contactType="Business">
    <Name>Ariel</Name>
    <Phone>555-1234</Phone>
  </Person>
</AddressBook>
```

*Table C-1. Navigation and selection*

| Syntax | Meaning |
|--------|---------|
| / | Represents the root of the XML tree.<br>For example:<br><br>`PS > $xml | Select-Xml "/" | Select -Expand Node`<br><br>`AddressBook`<br>`-----------`<br>`AddressBook` |
| /Node | Navigates to the node named *Node* from the root of the XML tree.<br>For example: |

| Syntax | Meaning |
|--------|---------|
|        | ```
PS > $xml | Select-Xml "/AddressBook" | Select -Expand Node

Person
------
{Lee, Ariel}
``` |
| */Node/*/Node2* | Navigates to the noded named *Node2* via *Node*, allowing any single node in between.<br>For example:<br>```
PS > $xml | Select-Xml "/AddressBook/*/Name" | Select -Expand Node

#text
-----
Lee
Ariel
``` |
| *//Node* | Finds all nodes named *Node*, anywhere in the XML tree.<br>For example:<br>```
PS > $xml | Select-Xml "//Phone" | Select -Expand Node

type                          #text
----                          -----
home                          555-1212
work                          555-1213
                              555-1234
``` |
| .. | Retrieves the parent node of the given node.<br>For example:<br>```
PS>$xml | Select-Xml "//Phone" | Select -Expand Node

type                          #text
----                          -----
home                          555-1212
work                          555-1213
                              555-1234


PS>$xml | Select-Xml "//Phone/.." | Select -Expand Node

contactType        Name            Phone
-----------        ----            -----
Personal           Lee             {Phone, Phone}
Business           Ariel           555-1234
``` |
| @*Attribute* | Accesses the value of the attribute named *Attribute*.<br>For example:<br>```
PS > $xml | Select-Xml "//Phone/@type" | Select -Expand Node

#text
-----
home
work
``` |
```

*Table C-2. Comparisons*

| Syntax | Meaning |
|--------|---------|
| [ ] | Filtering, similar to the `Where-Object` cmdlet. |

For example:

```
PS > $xml | Select-Xml "//Person[@contactType = 'Personal']" |
    Select -Expand Node

contactType                Name                  Phone
-----------                ----                  -----
Personal                   Lee                   {Phone, Phone}


PS > $xml | Select-Xml "//Person[Name = 'Lee']" | Select -Expand Node

contactType                Name                  Phone
-----------                ----                  -----
Personal                   Lee                   {Phone, Phone}
```

| Syntax | Meaning |
|--------|---------|
| and | Logical *and*. |
| or | Logical *or*. |
| not( ) | Logical *negation*. |
| = | *Equality*. |
| != | *Inequality*. |

# .NET String Formatting

## String Formatting Syntax

The format string supported by the format (-f) operator is a string that contains format items. Each format item takes the form of:

```
{index[,alignment][:formatString]}
```

*index* represents the zero-based index of the item in the object array following the format operator.

*alignment* is optional and represents the alignment of the item. A positive number aligns the item to the right of a field of the specified width. A negative number aligns the item to the left of a field of the specified width.

```
PS > ("{0,6}" -f 4.99), ("{0,6:##.00}" -f 15.9)
  4.99
 15.90
```

*formatString* is optional and formats the item using that type's specific format string syntax (as laid out in Tables D-1 and D-2).

## Standard Numeric Format Strings

Table D-1 lists the standard numeric format strings. All format specifiers may be followed by a number between 0 and 99 to control the precision of the formatting.

*Table D-1. Standard numeric format strings*

| Format specifier | Name | Description | Example |
|---|---|---|---|
| C or c | Currency | A currency amount. | PS > "{0:C}" -f 1.23<br>$1.23 |

| Format specifier | Name | Description | Example |
|---|---|---|---|
| D or d | Decimal | A decimal amount (for integral types). The precision specifier controls the minimum number of digits in the result. | PS > "{0:D4}" -f 2 <br> 0002 |
| E or e | Scientific | Scientific (exponential) notation. The precision specifier controls the number of digits past the decimal point. | PS > "{0:E3}" -f [Math]::Pi <br> 3.142E+000 |
| F or f | Fixed-point | Fixed-point notation. The precision specifier controls the number of digits past the decimal point. | PS > "{0:F3}" -f [Math]::Pi <br> 3.142 |
| G or g | General | The most compact representation (between fixed-point and scientific) of the number. The precision specifier controls the number of significant digits. | PS > "{0:G3}" -f [Math]::Pi <br> 3.14 <br> PS > "{0:G3}" -f 1mb <br> 1.05E+06 |
| N or n | Number | The human-readable form of the number, which includes separators between number groups. The precision specifier controls the number of digits past the decimal point. | PS > "{0:N4}" -f 1mb <br> 1,048,576.0000 |
| P or p | Percent | The number (generally between 0 and 1) represented as a percentage. The precision specifier controls the number of digits past the decimal point. | PS > "{0:P4}" -f 0.67 <br> 67.0000 % |
| R or r | Roundtrip | The Single or Double number formatted with a precision that guarantees the string (when parsed) will result in the original number again. | PS > "{0:R}" -f (1mb/2.0) <br> 524288 <br> PS > "{0:R}" -f (1mb/9.0) <br> 116508.44444444444 |
| X or x | Hexadecimal | The number converted to a string of hexadecimal digits. The case of the specifier controls the case of the resulting hexadecimal digits. The precision specifier controls the minimum number of digits in the resulting string. | PS > "{0:X4}" -f 1324 <br> 052C |

# Custom Numeric Format Strings

You can use custom numeric strings, listed in Table D-2, to format numbers in ways not supported by the standard format strings.

*Table D-2. Custom numeric format strings*

| Format specifier | Name | Description | Example |
|---|---|---|---|
| 0 | Zero placeholder | Specifies the precision and width of a number string. Zeros not matched by digits in the original number are output as zeros. | PS > "{0:00.0}" -f 4.12341234 <br> 04.1 |

| Format specifier | Name | Description | Example |
|---|---|---|---|
| # | Digit placeholder | Specifies the precision and width of a number string. # symbols not matched by digits in the input number are not output. | `PS > "{0:##.#}" -f 4.12341234` <br> `4.1` |
| . | Decimal point | Determines the location of the decimal. | `PS > "{0:##.#}" -f 4.12341234` <br> `4.1` |
| , | Thousands separator | When placed between a zero or digit placeholder before the decimal point in a formatting string, adds the separator character between number groups. | `PS > "{0:#,#.#}" -f 1234.121234` <br> `1,234.1` |
| , | Number scaling | When placed before the literal (or implicit) decimal point in a formatting string, divides the input by 1,000. You can apply this format specifier more than once. | `PS > "{0:##,,.000}" -f 1048576` <br> `1.049` |
| % | Percentage placeholder | Multiplies the input by 100, and inserts the percent sign where shown in the format specifier. | `PS > "{0:%##.000}" -f .68` <br> `%68.000` |
| E0 <br> E+0 <br> E-0 <br> e0 <br> e+0 <br> e-0 | Scientific notation | Displays the input in scientific notation. The number of zeros that follow the E define the minimum length of the exponent field. | `PS > "{0:##.#E000}" -f 2.71828` <br> `27.2E-001` |
| ' text ' <br> " text " | Literal string | Inserts the provided text literally into the output without affecting formatting. | `PS > "{0:#.00'##'}" -f 2.71828` <br> `2.72##` |
| ; | Section separator | Allows for conditional formatting. <br> If your format specifier contains no section separators, the formatting statement applies to all input. <br> If your format specifier contains one separator (creating two sections), the first section applies to positive numbers and zero, and the second section applies to negative numbers. <br> If your format specifier contains two separators (creating three sections), the sections apply to positive numbers, negative numbers, and zero. | `PS > "{0:POS;NEG;ZERO}" -f -14` <br> `NEG` |
| Other | Other character | Inserts the provided text literally into the output without affecting formatting. | `PS > "{0:$## Please}" -f 14` <br> `$14 Please` |

# .NET DateTime Formatting

DateTime format strings convert a `DateTime` object to one of several standard formats, as listed in Table E-1.

*Table E-1. Standard DateTime format strings*

| Format specifier | Name | Description | Example |
|---|---|---|---|
| d | Short date | The culture's short date format. | PS > "{0:d}" -f [DateTime] "01/23/4567"<br>1/23/4567 |
| D | Long date | The culture's long date format. | PS > "{0:D}" -f [DateTime] "01/23/4567"<br>Friday, January 23, 4567 |
| f | Full date/short time | Combines the long date and short time format patterns. | PS > "{0:f}" -f [DateTime] "01/23/4567"<br>Friday, January 23, 4567 12:00 AM |
| F | Full date/long time | Combines the long date and long time format patterns. | PS > "{0:F}" -f [DateTime] "01/23/4567"<br>Friday, January 23, 4567 12:00:00 AM |
| g | General date/short time | Combines the short date and short time format patterns. | PS > "{0:g}" -f [DateTime] "01/23/4567"<br>1/23/4567 12:00 AM |
| G | General date/long time | Combines the short date and long time format patterns. | PS > "{0:G}" -f [DateTime] "01/23/4567"<br>1/23/4567 12:00:00 AM |
| M or m | Month day | The culture's MonthDay format. | PS > "{0:M}" -f [DateTime] "01/23/4567"<br>January 23 |
| o | Round-trip date/time | The date formatted with a pattern that guarantees the string (when parsed) will result in the original DateTime again. | PS > "{0:o}" -f [DateTime] "01/23/4567"<br>4567-01-23T00:00:00.0000000 |
| R or r | RFC1123 | The standard RFC1123 format pattern. | PS > "{0:R}" -f [DateTime] "01/23/4567"<br>Fri, 23 Jan 4567 00:00:00 GMT |

| Format specifier | Name | Description | Example |
|---|---|---|---|
| s | Sortable | Sortable format pattern. Conforms to ISO 8601 and provides output suitable for sorting. | PS > "{0:s}" -f [DateTime] "01/23/4567" <br> 4567-01-23T00:00:00 |
| t | Short time | The culture's ShortTime format. | PS > "{0:t}" -f [DateTime] "01/23/4567" <br> 12:00 AM |
| T | Long time | The culture's LongTime format. | PS > "{0:T}" -f [DateTime] "01/23/4567" <br> 12:00:00 AM |
| u | Universal sortable | The culture's UniversalSortable DateTime format applied to the UTC equivalent of the input. | PS > "{0:u}" -f [DateTime] "01/23/4567" <br> 4567-01-23 00:00:00Z |
| U | Universal | The culture's FullDateTime format applied to the UTC equivalent of the input. | PS > "{0:U}" -f [DateTime] "01/23/4567" <br> Friday, January 23, 4567 8:00:00 AM |
| Y or y | Year month | The culture's YearMonth format. | PS > "{0:Y}" -f [DateTime] "01/23/4567" <br> January, 4567 |

# Custom DateTime Format Strings

You can use the custom DateTime format strings listed in Table E-2 to format dates in ways not supported by the standard format strings.

Single-character format specifiers are by default interpreted as a standard DateTime formatting string unless they are used with other formatting specifiers. Add the % character before them to have them interpreted as a custom format specifier.

*Table E-2. Custom DateTime format strings*

| Format specifier | Description | Example |
|---|---|---|
| d | Day of the month as a number between 1 and 31. Represents single-digit days without a leading zero. | PS > "{0:%d}" -f <br> [DateTime] "01/02/4567" <br> 2 |
| dd | Day of the month as a number between 1 and 31. Represents single-digit days with a leading zero. | PS > "{0:dd}" -f <br> [DateTime] "01/02/4567" <br> 02 |

| Format specifier | Description | Example |
|---|---|---|
| ddd | Abbreviated name of the day of week. | PS > "{0:ddd}" -f<br>    [DateTime] "01/02/4567"<br>Fri |
| dddd | Full name of the day of the week. | PS > "{0:dddd}" -f<br>    [DateTime] "01/02/4567"<br>Friday |
| f | Most significant digit of the seconds fraction (milliseconds). | PS > $date = Get-Date<br>PS > $date.Millisecond<br>93<br>PS > "{0:%f}" -f $date<br>0 |
| ff | Two most significant digits of the seconds fraction (milliseconds). | PS > $date = Get-Date<br>PS > $date.Millisecond<br>93<br>PS > "{0:ff}" -f $date<br>09 |
| fff | Three most significant digits of the seconds fraction (milliseconds). | PS > $date = Get-Date<br>PS > $date.Millisecond<br>93<br>PS > "{0:fff}" -f $date<br>093 |
| ffff | Four most significant digits of the seconds fraction (milliseconds). | PS > $date = Get-Date<br>PS > $date.Millisecond<br>93<br>PS > "{0:ffff}" -f $date<br>0937 |
| fffff | Five most significant digits of the seconds fraction (milliseconds). | PS > $date = Get-Date<br>PS > $date.Millisecond<br>93<br>PS > "{0:fffff}" -f $date<br>09375 |
| ffffff | Six most significant digits of the seconds fraction (milliseconds). | PS > $date = Get-Date<br>PS > $date.Millisecond<br>93<br>PS > "{0:ffffff}" -f $date<br>093750 |
| fffffff | Seven most significant digits of the seconds fraction (milliseconds). | PS > $date = Get-Date<br>PS > $date.Millisecond<br>93<br>PS > "{0:fffffff}" -f $date<br>0937500 |
| F<br>FF<br>FFF<br>(...) | Most significant digit of the seconds fraction (milliseconds).<br>When compared to the lowercase series of 'f' specifiers, displays nothing if the number is zero. | PS > "{0:\|F FF FFF FFFF\|}" -f<br>    [DateTime] "01/02/4567"<br>\|    \| |

| Format specifier | Description | Example |
|---|---|---|
| FFFFFFF | | |
| %g or gg | Era (e.g., A.D.). | PS > "{0:gg}" -f [DateTime] <br> "01/02/4567" <br> A.D. |
| %h | Hours, as a number between 1 and 12. Single digits do not include a leading zero. | PS > "{0:%h}" -f <br> [DateTime] "01/02/4567 4:00pm" <br> 4 |
| hh | Hours, as a number between 01 and 12. Single digits include a leading zero. Note: this is interpreted as a standard DateTime formatting string unless used with other formatting specifiers. | PS > "{0:hh}" -f <br> [DateTime] "01/02/4567 4:00pm" <br> 04 |
| %H | Hours, as a number between 0 and 23. Single digits do not include a leading zero. | PS > "{0:%H}" -f <br> [DateTime] "01/02/4567 4:00pm" <br> 16 |
| HH | Hours, as a number between 00 and 23. Single digits include a leading zero. | PS > "{0:HH}" -f <br> [DateTime] "01/02/4567 4:00am" <br> 04 |
| K | DateTime.Kind specifier that corresponds to the kind (i.e., Local, Utc, or Unspecified) of input date. | PS > "{0:%K}" -f <br> [DateTime]::Now.ToUniversalTime() <br> Z |
| m | Minute, as a number between 0 and 59. Single digits do not include a leading zero. | PS > "{0:%m}" -f [DateTime]::Now <br> 7 |
| mm | Minute, as a number between 00 and 59. Single digits include a leading zero. | PS > "{0:mm}" -f [DateTime]::Now <br> 08 |
| M | Month, as a number between 1 and 12. Single digits do not include a leading zero. | PS > "{0:%M}" -f <br> [DateTime] "01/02/4567" <br> 1 |
| MM | Month, as a number between 01 and 12. Single digits include a leading zero. | PS > "{0:MM}" -f <br> [DateTime] "01/02/4567" <br> 01 |
| MMM | Abbreviated month name. | PS > "{0:MMM}" -f <br> [DateTime] "01/02/4567" <br> Jan |
| MMMM | Full month name. | PS > "{0:MMMM}" -f <br> [DateTime] "01/02/4567" <br> January |
| s | Seconds, as a number between 0 and 59. Single digits do not include a leading zero. | PS > $date = Get-Date <br> PS > "{0:%s}" -f $date <br> 7 |

| Format specifier | Description | Example |
|---|---|---|
| ss | Seconds, as a number between 00 and 59. Single digits include a leading zero. | `PS > $date = Get-Date`<br>`PS > "{0:ss}" -f $date`<br>`07` |
| t | First character of the a.m./p.m. designator. | `PS > $date = Get-Date`<br>`PS > "{0:%t}" -f $date`<br>`P` |
| tt | a.m./p.m. designator. | `PS > $date = Get-Date`<br>`PS > "{0:tt}" -f $date`<br>`PM` |
| y | Year, in (at most) two digits. | `PS > "{0:%y}" -f`<br>`   [DateTime] "01/02/4567"`<br>`67` |
| yy | Year, in (at most) two digits. | `PS > "{0:yy}" -f`<br>`   [DateTime] "01/02/4567"`<br>`67` |
| yyy | Year, in (at most) four digits. | `PS > "{0:yyy}" -f`<br>`   [DateTime] "01/02/4567"`<br>`4567` |
| yyyy | Year, in (at most) four digits. | `PS > "{0:yyyy}" -f`<br>`   [DateTime] "01/02/4567"`<br>`4567` |
| yyyyy | Year, in (at most) five digits. | `PS > "{0:yyyy}" -f`<br>`   [DateTime] "01/02/4567"`<br>`04567` |
| z | Signed time zone offset from GMT. Does not include a leading zero. | `PS > "{0:%z}" -f [DateTime]::Now`<br>`-8` |
| zz | Signed time zone offset from GMT. Includes a leading zero. | `PS > "{0:zz}" -f [DateTime]::Now`<br>`-08` |
| zzz | Signed time zone offset from GMT, measured in hours and minutes. | `PS > "{0:zzz}" -f [DateTime]::Now`<br>`-08:00` |
| : | Time separator. | `PS > "{0:y/m/d h:m:s}" -f`<br>`   [DateTime] "01/02/4567 4:00pm"`<br>`67/0/2 4:0:0` |
| / | Date separator. | `PS > "{0:y/m/d h:m:s}" -f`<br>`   [DateTime] "01/02/4567 4:00pm"`<br>`67/0/2 4:0:0` |
| " text "<br>' text ' | Inserts the provided text literally into the output without affecting formatting. | `PS > "{0:'Day: 'dddd}" -f`<br>`   [DateTime]::Now`<br>`Day: Monday` |

| Format specifier | Description | Example |
|---|---|---|
| %c | Syntax allowing for single-character custom formatting specifiers. The % sign is not added to the output. | PS > "{0:%h}" -f<br>    [DateTime] "01/02/4567 4:00pm"<br>4 |
| Other | Inserts the provided text literally into the output without affecting formatting. | PS > "{0:dddd!}" -f [DateTime]::Now<br>Monday! |

# Selected .NET Classes and Their Uses

Tables F-1 through F-16 provide pointers to types in the .NET Framework that usefully complement the functionality that PowerShell provides. For detailed descriptions and documentation, search here (*http://msdn.microsoft.com*) for the official documentation.

*Table F-1. Windows PowerShells*

| Class | Description |
| --- | --- |
| `System.Management.Automation.PSObject` | Represents a PowerShell object to which you can add notes, properties, and more. |

*Table F-2. Utility*

| Class | Description |
| --- | --- |
| `System.DateTime` | Represents an instant in time, typically expressed as a date and time of day. |
| `System.Guid` | Represents a globally unique identifier (GUID). |
| `System.Math` | Provides constants and static methods for trigonometric, logarithmic, and other common mathematical functions. |
| `System.Random` | Represents a pseudorandom number generator, a device that produces a sequence of numbers that meet certain statistical requirements for randomness. |
| `System.Convert` | Converts a base data type to another base data type. |
| `System.Environment` | Provides information about, and means to manipulate, the current environment and platform. |
| `System.Console` | Represents the standard input, output, and error streams for console applications. |
| `System.Text.RegularExpressions.Regex` | Represents an immutable regular expression. |
| `System.Diagnostics.Debug` | Provides a set of methods and properties that help debug your code. |
| `System.Diagnostics.EventLog` | Provides interaction with Windows event logs. |

| Class | Description |
|---|---|
| `System.Diagnostics.Process` | Provides access to local and remote processes and enables you to start and stop local system processes. |
| `System.Diagnostics.Stopwatch` | Provides a set of methods and properties that you can use to accurately measure elapsed time. |
| `System.Media.SoundPlayer` | Controls playback of a sound from a *.wav* file. |

*Table F-3. Collections and object utilities*

| Class | Description |
|---|---|
| `System.Array` | Provides methods for creating, manipulating, searching, and sorting arrays, thereby serving as the base class for all arrays in the Common Language Runtime. |
| `System.Enum` | Provides the base class for enumerations. |
| `System.String` | Represents text as a series of Unicode characters. |
| `System.Text.StringBuilder` | Represents a mutable string of characters. |
| `System.Collections.Specialized.OrderedDictionary` | Represents a collection of key/value pairs that are accessible by the key or index. |
| `System.Collections.ArrayList` | Implements the IList interface using an array whose size is dynamically increased as required. |

*Table F-4. The .NET Framework*

| Class | Description |
|---|---|
| `System.AppDomain` | Represents an application domain, which is an isolated environment where applications execute. |
| `System.Reflection.Assembly` | Defines an Assembly, which is a reusable, versionable, and self-describing building block of a Common Language Runtime application. |
| `System.Type` | Represents type declarations: class types, interface types, array types, value types, enumeration types, type parameters, generic type definitions, and open or closed constructed generic types. |
| `System.Threading.Thread` | Creates and controls a thread, sets its priority, and gets its status. |
| `System.Runtime.InteropServices.Marshal` | Provides a collection of methods for allocating unmanaged memory, copying unmanaged memory blocks, and converting managed to unmanaged types, as well as other miscellaneous methods used when interacting with unmanaged code. |
| `Microsoft.CSharp.CSharpCodeProvider` | Provides access to instances of the C# code generator and code compiler. |

## Table F-5. Registry

| Class | Description |
|---|---|
| Microsoft.Win32.Registry | Provides RegistryKey objects that represent the root keys in the local and remote Windows Registry and static methods to access key/value pairs. |
| Microsoft.Win32.RegistryKey | Represents a key-level node in the Windows Registry. |

## Table F-6. Input and Output

| Class | Description |
|---|---|
| System.IO.Stream | Provides a generic view of a sequence of bytes. |
| System.IO.BinaryReader | Reads primitive data types as binary values. |
| System.IO.BinaryWriter | Writes primitive types in binary to a stream. |
| System.IO.BufferedStream | Adds a buffering layer to read and write operations on another stream. |
| System.IO.Directory | Exposes static methods for creating, moving, and enumerating through directories and subdirectories. |
| System.IO.FileInfo | Provides instance methods for the creation, copying, deletion, moving, and opening of files, and aids in the creation of FileStream objects. |
| System.IO.DirectoryInfo | Exposes instance methods for creating, moving, and enumerating through directories and subdirectories. |
| System.IO.File | Provides static methods for the creation, copying, deletion, moving, and opening of files, and aids in the creation of FileStream objects. |
| System.IO.MemoryStream | Creates a stream whose backing store is memory. |
| System.IO.Path | Performs operations on String instances that contain file or directory path information. These operations are performed in a cross-platform manner. |
| System.IO.TextReader | Represents a reader that can read a sequential series of characters. |
| System.IO.StreamReader | Implements a TextReader that reads characters from a byte stream in a particular encoding. |
| System.IO.TextWriter | Represents a writer that can write a sequential series of characters. |
| System.IO.StreamWriter | Implements a TextWriter for writing characters to a stream in a particular encoding. |
| System.IO.StringReader | Implements a TextReader that reads from a string. |
| System.IO.StringWriter | Implements a TextWriter for writing information to a string. |
| System.IO.Compression.DeflateStream | Provides methods and properties used to compress and decompress streams using the Deflate algorithm. |
| System.IO.Compression.GZipStream | Provides methods and properties used to compress and decompress streams using the GZip algorithm. |
| System.IO.FileSystemWatcher | Listens to the filesystem change notifications and raises events when a directory or file in a directory changes. |

*Table F-7. Security*

| Class | Description |
|---|---|
| `System.Security.Principal.WindowsIdentity` | Represents a Windows user. |
| `System.Security.Principal.WindowsPrincipal` | Allows code to check the Windows group membership of a Windows user. |
| `System.Security.Principal.WellKnownSidType` | Defines a set of commonly used security identifiers (SIDs). |
| `System.Security.Principal.WindowsBuiltInRole` | Specifies common roles to be used with `IsInRole`. |
| `System.Security.SecureString` | Represents text that should be kept confidential. The text is encrypted for privacy when being used and deleted from computer memory when no longer needed. |
| `System.Security.Cryptography.TripleDESCryptoServiceProvider` | Defines a wrapper object to access the cryptographic service provider (CSP) version of the TripleDES algorithm. |
| `System.Security.Cryptography.PasswordDeriveBytes` | Derives a key from a password using an extension of the PBKDF1 algorithm. |
| `System.Security.Cryptography.SHA1` | Computes the SHA1 hash for the input data. |
| `System.Security.AccessControl.FileSystemSecurity` | Represents the access control and audit security for a file or directory. |
| `System.Security.AccessControl.RegistrySecurity` | Represents the Windows access control security for a registry key. |

*Table F-8. User interface*

| Class | Description |
|---|---|
| `System.Windows.Forms.Form` | Represents a window or dialog box that makes up an application's user interface. |
| `System.Windows.Forms.FlowLayoutPanel` | Represents a panel that dynamically lays out its contents. |

*Table F-9. Image manipulation*

| Class | Description |
|---|---|
| `System.Drawing.Image` | A class that provides functionality for the `Bitmap` and `Metafile` classes. |
| `System.Drawing.Bitmap` | Encapsulates a GDI+ bitmap, which consists of the pixel data for a graphics image and its attributes. A bitmap is an object used to work with images defined by pixel data. |

## Table F-10. Networking

| Class | Description |
|---|---|
| System.Uri | Provides an object representation of a uniform resource identifier (URI) and easy access to the parts of the URI. |
| System.Net.NetworkCredential | Provides credentials for password-based authentication schemes such as basic, digest, Kerberos authentication, and NTLM. |
| System.Net.Dns | Provides simple domain name resolution functionality. |
| System.Net.FtpWebRequest | Implements a File Transfer Protocol (FTP) client. |
| System.Net.HttpWebRequest | Provides an HTTP-specific implementation of the WebRequest class. |
| System.Net.WebClient | Provides common methods for sending data to and receiving data from a resource identified by a URI. |
| System.Net.Sockets.TcpClient | Provides client connections for TCP network services. |
| System.Net.Mail.MailAddress | Represents the address of an electronic mail sender or recipient. |
| System.Net.Mail.MailMessage | Represents an email message that can be sent using the SmtpClient class. |
| System.Net.Mail.SmtpClient | Allows applications to send email by using the Simple Mail Transfer Protocol (SMTP). |
| System.IO.Ports.SerialPort | Represents a serial port resource. |
| System.Web.HttpUtility | Provides methods for encoding and decoding URLs when processing web requests. |

## Table F-11. XML

| Class | Description |
|---|---|
| System.Xml.XmlTextWriter | Represents a writer that provides a fast, noncached, forward-only way of generating streams or files containing XML data that conforms to the W3C Extensible Markup Language (XML) 1.0 and the namespaces in XML recommendations. |
| System.Xml.XmlDocument | Represents an XML document. |

## Table F-12. Windows Management Instrumentation (WMI)

| Class | Description |
|---|---|
| System.Management.ManagementObject | Represents a WMI instance. |
| System.Management.ManagementClass | Represents a management class. A management class is a WMI class such as Win32_LogicalDisk, which can represent a disk drive, or Win32_Process, which represents a process such as an instance of Notepad.exe. The members of this class enable you to access WMI data using a specific WMI class path. For more information, see "Win32 Classes" in the Windows Management Instrumentation documentation in the MSDN Library here (*http://msdn.microsoft.com/library*). |
| System.Management.ManagementObjectSearcher | Retrieves a collection of WMI management objects based on a specified query. This class is one of the more commonly used entry points to retrieving management information. For example, it can be used to enumerate |

| Class | Description |
|---|---|
|  | all disk drives, network adapters, processes, and many more management objects on a system or to query for all network connections that are up, services that are paused, and so on. When instantiated, an instance of this class takes as input a WMI query represented in an Ob jectQuery or its derivatives, and optionally a Man agementScope representing the WMI namespace to execute the query in. It can also take additional advanced options in an EnumerationOptions. When the Get method on this object is invoked, the ManagementOb jectSearcher executes the given query in the specified scope and returns a collection of management objects that match the query in a ManagementOb jectCollection. |
| System.Management.ManagementDateTimeConverter | Provides methods to convert DMTF datetime and time intervals to CLR-compliant DateTime and Time Span formats, and vice versa. |
| System.Management.ManagementEventWatcher | Subscribes to temporary event notifications based on a specified event query. |

*Table F-13. Active Directory*

| Class | Description |
|---|---|
| System.DirectoryServices.DirectorySearcher | Performs queries against Active Directory. |
| System.DirectoryServices.DirectoryEntry | The DirectoryEntry class encapsulates a node or object in the Active Directory hierarchy. |

*Table F-14. Database*

| Class | Description |
|---|---|
| System.Data.DataSet | Represents an in-memory cache of data. |
| System.Data.DataTable | Represents one table of in-memory data. |
| System.Data.SqlClient.SqlCommand | Represents a Transact-SQL statement or stored procedure to execute against a SQL Server database. |
| System.Data.SqlClient.SqlConnection | Represents an open connection to a SQL Server database. |
| System.Data.SqlClient.SqlDataAdapter | Represents a set of data commands and a database connection that are used to fill the DataSet and update a SQL Server database. |
| System.Data.Odbc.OdbcCommand | Represents a SQL statement or stored procedure to execute against a data source. |
| System.Data.Odbc.OdbcConnection | Represents an open connection to a data source. |
| System.Data.Odbc.OdbcDataAdapter | Represents a set of data commands and a connection to a data source that are used to fill the DataSet and update the data source. |

## Table F-15. Message queuing

| Class | Description |
| --- | --- |
| `System.Messaging.MessageQueue` | Provides access to a queue on a Message Queuing server. |

## Table F-16. Transactions

| Class | Description |
| --- | --- |
| `System.Transactions.Transaction` | Represents a transaction. |

# WMI Reference

The Windows Management Instrumentation (WMI) facilities in Windows offer thousands of classes that provide information of interest to administrators. Table G-1 lists the categories and subcategories covered by WMI and can be used to get a general idea of the scope of WMI classes. Table G-2 provides a selected subset of the most useful WMI classes. For more information about a category, search the official WMI documentation here (*http://msdn.microsoft.com*).

*Table G-1. WMI class categories and subcategories*

| Category | Subcategory |
| --- | --- |
| Computer system hardware | Cooling device, input device, mass storage, motherboard, controller and port, networking device, power, printing, telephony, video, and monitor |
| Operating system | COM, desktop, drivers, filesystem, job objects, memory and page files, multimedia audio/visual, networking, operating system events, operating system settings, processes, registry, scheduler jobs, security, services, shares, Start menu, storage, users, Windows NT event log, Windows product activation |
| WMI Service Management | WMI configuration, WMI management |
| General | Installed applications, performance counter, security descriptor |

*Table G-2. Selected WMI classes*

| Class | Description |
| --- | --- |
| CIM_DataFile | Represents a named collection of data or executable code. Currently, the provider returns files on fixed and mapped logical disks. In the future, only instances of files on local fixed disks will be returned. |
| Win32_BaseBoard | Represents a baseboard, which is also known as a motherboard or system board. |
| Win32_BIOS | Represents the attributes of the computer system's basic input/output services (BIOS) that are installed on a computer. |

| Class | Description |
|---|---|
| Win32_BootConfiguration | Represents the boot configuration of a Windows system. |
| Win32_CacheMemory | Represents internal and external cache memory on a computer system. |
| Win32_CDROMDrive | Represents a CD-ROM drive on a Windows computer system. Be aware that the name of the drive does not correspond to the logical drive letter assigned to the device. |
| Win32_ComputerSystem | Represents a computer system in a Windows environment. |
| Win32_ComputerSystemProduct | Represents a product. This includes software and hardware used on this computer system. |
| Win32_DCOMApplication | Represents the properties of a DCOM application. |
| Win32_Desktop | Represents the common characteristics of a user's desktop. The properties of this class can be modified by the user to customize the desktop. |
| Win32_DesktopMonitor | Represents the type of monitor or display device attached to the computer system. |
| Win32_DeviceMemoryAddress | Represents a device memory address on a Windows system. |
| Win32_Directory | Represents a directory entry on a Windows computer system. A *directory* is a type of file that logically groups data files and provides path information for the grouped files. Win32_Directory does not include directories of network drives. |
| Win32_DiskDrive | Represents a physical disk drive as seen by a computer running the Windows operating system. Any interface to a Windows physical disk drive is a descendant (or member) of this class. The features of the disk drive seen through this object correspond to the logical and management characteristics of the drive. In some cases, this may not reflect the actual physical characteristics of the device. Any object based on another logical device would not be a member of this class. |
| Win32_DiskPartition | Represents the capabilities and management capacity of a partitioned area of a physical disk on a Windows system (for example, Disk #0, Partition #1). |
| Win32_DiskQuota | Tracks disk space usage for NTFS filesystem volumes. A system administrator can configure Windows to prevent further disk space use and log an event when a user exceeds a specified disk space limit. An administrator can also log an event when a user exceeds a specified disk space warning level. This class is new in Windows XP. |
| Win32_DMAChannel | Represents a direct memory access (DMA) channel on a Windows computer system. DMA is a method of moving data from a device to memory (or vice versa) without the help of the microprocessor. The system board uses a DMA controller to handle a fixed number of channels, each of which can be used by one (and only one) device at a time. |
| Win32_Environment | Represents an environment or system environment setting on a Windows computer system. Querying this class returns environment variables found in *HKLM\System\CurrentControlSet\Control\Sessionmanager\Environment* as well as *HKEY_USERS\<user sid>\Environment*. |
| Win32_Group | Represents data about a group account. A group account allows access privileges to be changed for a list of users (for example, Administrators). |

| Class | Description |
|---|---|
| Win32_IDEController | Manages the capabilities of an integrated device electronics (IDE) controller device. |
| Win32_IRQResource | Represents an interrupt request line (IRQ) number on a Windows computer system. An interrupt request is a signal sent to the CPU by a device or program for time-critical events. IRQ can be hardware- or software-based. |
| Win32_LoadOrderGroup | Represents a group of system services that define execution dependencies. The services must be initiated in the order specified by the Load Order Group, as the services are dependent on one another. These dependent services require the presence of the antecedent services to function correctly. The data in this class is derived by the provider from the registry key *System \CurrentControlSet\Control\GroupOrderList*. |
| Win32_LogicalDisk | Represents a data source that resolves to an actual local storage device on a Windows system. |
| Win32_LogicalMemoryConfiguration | Represents the layout and availability of memory on a Windows system. Beginning with Windows Vista, this class is no longer available in the operating system. Windows XP and Windows Server 2003: This class is no longer supported. Use the Win32_OperatingSystem class instead. Windows 2000: This class is available and supported. |
| Win32_LogonSession | Describes the logon session or sessions associated with a user logged on to Windows NT or Windows 2000. |
| Win32_NetworkAdapter | Represents a network adapter of a computer running on a Windows operating system. |
| Win32_NetworkAdapterConfiguration | Represents the attributes and behaviors of a network adapter. This class includes extra properties and methods that support the management of the TCP/IP and Internetworking Packet Exchange (IPX) protocols that are independent from the network adapter. |
| WIN32_NetworkClient | Represents a network client on a Windows system. Any computer system on the network with a client relationship to the system is a descendant (or member) of this class (for example, a computer running Windows 2000 Workstation or Windows 98 that is part of a Windows 2000 domain). |
| Win32_NetworkConnection | Represents an active network connection in a Windows environment. |
| Win32_NetworkLoginProfile | Represents the network login information of a specific user on a Windows system. This includes but is not limited to password status, access privileges, disk quotas, and login directory paths. |
| Win32_NetworkProtocol | Represents a protocol and its network characteristics on a Win32 computer system. |
| Win32_NTDomain | Represents a Windows NT domain. |
| Win32_NTEventlogFile | Represents a logical file or directory of Windows NT events. The file is also known as the event log. |
| Win32_NTLogEvent | Used to translate instances from the Windows NT event log. An application must have SeSecurityPrivilege to receive events from the security event log; otherwise, "Access Denied" is returned to the application. |

| Class | Description |
|---|---|
| Win32_OnBoardDevice | Represents common adapter devices built into the motherboard (system board). |
| Win32_OperatingSystem | Represents an operating system installed on a computer running on a Windows operating system. Any operating system that can be installed on a Windows system is a descendant or member of this class. Win32_Oper atingSystem is a singleton class. To get the single instance, use @ for the key.<br>Windows Server 2003, Windows XP, Windows 2000, and Windows NT 4.0: If a computer has multiple operating systems installed, this class returns only an instance for the currently active operating system. |
| Win32_OSRecoveryConfiguration | Represents the types of information that will be gathered from memory when the operating system fails. This includes boot failures and system crashes. |
| Win32_PageFileSetting | Represents the settings of a page file. Information contained within objects instantiated from this class specifies the page file parameters used when the file is created at system startup. The properties in this class can be modified and deferred until startup. These settings are different from the runtime state of a page file expressed through the associated class Win32_PageFileUsage. |
| Win32_PageFileUsage | Represents the file used for handling virtual memory file swapping on a Win32 system. Information contained within objects instantiated from this class specifies the runtime state of the page file. |
| Win32_PerfRawData_PerfNet_Server | Provides raw data from performance counters that monitor communications using the WINS Server service. |
| Win32_PhysicalMemoryArray | Represents details about the computer system physical memory. This includes the number of memory devices, memory capacity available, and memory type (for example, system or video memory). |
| Win32_PortConnector | Represents physical connection ports, such as DB-25 pin male, Centronics, or PS/2. |
| Win32_PortResource | Represents an I/O port on a Windows computer system. |
| Win32_Printer | Represents a device connected to a computer running on a Microsoft Windows operating system that can produce a printed image or text on paper or another medium. |
| Win32_PrinterConfiguration | Represents the configuration for a printer device. This includes capabilities such as resolution, color, fonts, and orientation. |
| Win32_PrintJob | Represents a print job generated by a Windows application. Any unit of work generated by the Print command of an application that is running on a computer running on a Windows operating system is a descendant or member of this class. |
| Win32_Process | Represents a process on an operating system. |

| Class | Description |
|---|---|
| Win32_Processor | Represents a device that can interpret a sequence of instructions on a computer running on a Windows operating system. On a multiprocessor computer, one instance of the Win32_Processor class exists for each processor. |
| Win32_Product | Represents products as they are installed by Windows Installer. A product generally correlates to one installation package. For information about support or requirements for installation of a specific operating system, visit this site (*http://msdn.microsoft.com*) and search for "Operating System Availability of WMI Components." |
| Win32_QuickFixEngineering | Represents system-wide Quick Fix Engineering (QFE) or updates that have been applied to the current operating system. |
| Win32_QuotaSetting | Contains setting information for disk quotas on a volume. |
| Win32_Registry | Represents the system registry on a Windows computer system. |
| Win32_ScheduledJob | Represents a job created with the AT command. The Win32_ScheduledJob class does not represent a job created with the Scheduled Task Wizard from the Control Panel. You cannot change a task created by WMI in the Scheduled Tasks UI.<br>Windows 2000 and Windows NT 4.0: You can use the Scheduled Tasks UI to modify the task you originally created with WMI. However, although the task is successfully modified, you can no longer access the task using WMI. Each job scheduled against the schedule service is stored persistently (the scheduler can start a job after a reboot) and is executed at the specified time and day of the week or month. If the computer is not active or if the scheduled service is not running at the specified job time, the schedule service runs the specified job on the next day at the specified time.<br>Jobs are scheduled according to Universal Coordinated Time (UTC) with bias offset from Greenwich Mean Time (GMT), which means that a job can be specified using any time zone. The Win32_ScheduledJob class returns the local time with UTC offset when enumerating an object, and converts to local time when creating new jobs. For example, a job specified to run on a computer in Boston at 10:30 p.m. Monday PST will be scheduled to run locally at 1:30 a.m. Tuesday EST. Note that a client must take into account whether daylight saving time is in operation on the local computer, and if it is, then subtract a bias of 60 minutes from the UTC offset. |
| Win32_SCSIController | Represents a SCSI controller on a Windows system. |
| Win32_Service | Represents a service on a computer running on a Microsoft Windows operating system. A service application conforms to the interface rules of the Service Control Manager (SCM), and can be started by a user automatically at system start through the Services Control Panel utility or by an application that uses the service functions included in the Windows API. Services can start when there are no users logged on to the computer. |
| Win32_Share | Represents a shared resource on a Windows system. This may be a disk drive, printer, interprocess communication, or other shareable device. |
| Win32_SoftwareElement | Represents a software element, part of a software feature (a distinct subset of a product, which may contain one or more elements). Each software |

| Class | Description |
|---|---|
| | element is defined in a Win32_SoftwareElement instance, and the association between a feature and its Win32_SoftwareFeature instance is defined in the Win32_SoftwareFeatureSoftwareEle ments association class. For information about support or requirements for installation on a specific operating system, visit this site (*http:// msdn.microsoft.com*) and search for "Operating System Availability of WMI Components." |
| Win32_SoftwareFeature | Represents a distinct subset of a product that consists of one or more software elements. Each software element is defined in a Win32_SoftwareEle ment instance, and the association between a feature and its Win32_SoftwareFeature instance is defined in the Win32_Soft wareFeatureSoftwareElements association class. For information about support or requirements for installation on a specific operating system, visit this site (*http://msdn.microsoft.com*) and search for "Operating System Availability of WMI Components." |
| WIN32_SoundDevice | Represents the properties of a sound device on a Windows computer system. |
| Win32_StartupCommand | Represents a command that runs automatically when a user logs on to the computer system. |
| Win32_SystemAccount | Represents a system account. The system account is used by the operating system and services that run under Windows NT. There are many services and processes within Windows NT that need the capability to log on internally—for example, during a Windows NT installation. The system account was designed for that purpose. |
| Win32_SystemDriver | Represents the system driver for a base service. |
| Win32_SystemEnclosure | Represents the properties that are associated with a physical system enclosure. |
| Win32_SystemSlot | Represents physical connection points, including ports, motherboard slots and peripherals, and proprietary connection points. |
| Win32_TapeDrive | Represents a tape drive on a Windows computer. Tape drives are primarily distinguished by the fact that they can be accessed only sequentially. |
| Win32_TemperatureProbe | Represents the properties of a temperature sensor (e.g., electronic thermometer). |
| Win32_TimeZone | Represents the time zone information for a Windows system, which includes changes required for the daylight saving time transition. |
| Win32_UninterruptiblePowerSupply | Represents the capabilities and management capacity of an uninterruptible power supply (UPS). Beginning with Windows Vista, this class is obsolete and not available, because the UPS service is no longer available. This service worked with serially attached UPS devices, not USB devices. Windows Server 2003 and Windows XP: This class is available, but not usable, because the UPS service fails. Windows Server 2003, Windows XP, Windows 2000, and Windows NT 4.0: This class is available and implemented. |
| Win32_UserAccount | Contains information about a user account on a computer running on a Windows operating system. |

| Class | Description |
|---|---|
| | Because both the `Name` and `Domain` are key properties, enumerating `Win32_UserAccount` on a large network can affect performance negatively. Calling `GetObject` or querying for a specific instance has less impact. |
| `Win32_VoltageProbe` | Represents the properties of a voltage sensor (electronic voltmeter). |
| `Win32_VolumeQuotaSetting` | Relates disk quota settings with a specific disk volume. Windows 2000/NT: This class is not available. |
| `Win32_WMISetting` | Contains the operational parameters for the WMI service. This class can have only one instance, which always exists for each Windows system and cannot be deleted. Additional instances cannot be created. |

# Selected COM Objects and Their Uses

As an extensibility and administration interface, many applications expose useful functionality through COM objects. Although PowerShell handles many of these tasks directly, many COM objects still provide significant value.

Table H-1 lists a selection of the COM objects most useful to system administrators.

*Table H-1. COM identifiers and descriptions*

| Identifier | Description |
| --- | --- |
| Access.Application | Allows for interaction and automation of Microsoft Access. |
| Agent.Control | Allows for the control of Microsoft Agent 3D animated characters. |
| AutoItX3.Control | (nondefault) Provides access to Windows Automation via the AutoIt administration tool. |
| CEnroll.CEnroll | Provides access to certificate enrollment services. |
| Certificate Authority.Request | Provides access to a request to a certificate authority. |
| COMAdmin.COMAdminCatalog | Provides access to and management of the Windows COM+ catalog. |
| Excel.Application | Allows for interaction and automation of Microsoft Excel. |
| Excel.Sheet | Allows for interaction with Microsoft Excel worksheets. |
| HNetCfg.FwMgr | Provides access to the management functionality of the Windows Firewall. |
| HNetCfg.HNetShare | Provides access to the management functionality of Windows Connection Sharing. |
| HTMLFile | Allows for interaction and authoring of a new Internet Explorer document. |
| InfoPath.Application | Allows for interaction and automation of Microsoft InfoPath. |
| InternetExplorer. Application | Allows for interaction and automation of Microsoft Internet Explorer. |
| IXSSO.Query | Allows for interaction with Microsoft Index Server. |
| IXSSO.Util | Provides access to utilities used along with the IXSSO.Query object. |
| LegitCheckControl.LegitCheck | Provide access to information about Windows Genuine Advantage status on the current computer. |

| Identifier | Description |
|---|---|
| MakeCab.MakeCab | Provides functionality to create and manage cabinet (*.cab*) files. |
| MAPI.Session | Provides access to a Messaging Application Programming Interface (MAPI) session, such as folders, messages, and the address book. |
| Messenger.MessengerApp | Allows for interaction and automation of Messenger. |
| Microsoft.FeedsManager | Allows for interaction with the Microsoft RSS feed platform. |
| Microsoft.ISAdm | Provides management of Microsoft Index Server. |
| Microsoft.Update.AutoUpdate | Provides management of the auto update schedule for Microsoft Update. |
| Microsoft.Update.Installer | Allows for installation of updates from Microsoft Update. |
| Microsoft.Update.Searcher | Provides search functionality for updates from Microsoft Update. |
| Microsoft.Update.Session | Provides access to local information about Microsoft Update history. |
| Microsoft.Update.SystemInfo | Provides access to information related to Microsoft Update for the current system. |
| MMC20.Application | Allows for interaction and automation of Microsoft Management Console (MMC). |
| MSScriptControl.ScriptControl | Allows for the evaluation and control of WSH scripts. |
| Msxml2.XSLTemplate | Allows for processing of XSL transforms. |
| Outlook.Application | Allows for interaction and automation of your email, calendar, contacts, tasks, and more through Microsoft Outlook. |
| OutlookExpress.MessageList | Allows for interaction and automation of your email through Microsoft Outlook Express. |
| PowerPoint.Application | Allows for interaction and automation of Microsoft PowerPoint. |
| Publisher.Application | Allows for interaction and automation of Microsoft Publisher. |
| RDS.DataSpace | Provides access to proxies of Remote DataSpace business objects. |
| SAPI.SpVoice | Provides access to the Microsoft Speech API. |
| Scripting.FileSystemObject | Provides access to the computer's filesystem. Most functionality is available more directly through PowerShell or through PowerShell's support for the .NET Framework. |
| Scripting.Signer | Provides management of digital signatures on WSH files. |
| Scriptlet.TypeLib | Allows the dynamic creation of scripting type library (*.tlb*) files. |
| ScriptPW.Password | Allows for the masked input of plain-text passwords. When possible, you should avoid this, preferring the Read-Host cmdlet with the -AsSecureString parameter. |
| SharePoint.OpenDocuments | Allows for interaction with Microsoft SharePoint Services. |
| Shell.Application | Provides access to aspects of the Windows Explorer Shell application, such as managing windows, files and folders, and the current session. |
| Shell.LocalMachine | Provides access to information about the current machine related to the Windows shell. |
| Shell.User | Provides access to aspects of the current user's Windows session and profile. |
| SQLDMO.SQLServer | Provides access to the management functionality of Microsoft SQL Server. |
| Vim.Application | (nondefault) Allows for interaction and automation of the VIM editor. |

| Identifier | Description |
| --- | --- |
| WIA.CommonDialog | Provides access to image capture through the Windows Image Acquisition facilities. |
| WMPlayer.OCX | Allows for interaction and automation of Windows Media Player. |
| Word.Application | Allows for interaction and automation of Microsoft Word. |
| Word.Document | Allows for interaction with Microsoft Word documents. |
| WScript.Network | Provides access to aspects of a networked Windows environment, such as printers and network drives, as well as computer and domain information. |
| WScript.Shell | Provides access to aspects of the Windows Shell, such as applications, shortcuts, environment variables, the registry, and the operating environment. |
| WSHController | Allows the execution of WSH scripts on remote computers. |

# Selected Events and Their Uses

PowerShell's eventing commands give you access to events from the .NET Framework, as well as events surfaced by Windows Management Instrumentation (WMI). Table I-1 lists a selection of .NET events. Table I-2 lists a selection of WMI events.

*Table I-1. Selected .NET events*

| Type | Event | Description |
| --- | --- | --- |
| System.AppDomain | AssemblyLoad | Occurs when an assembly is loaded. |
| System.AppDomain | TypeResolve | Occurs when the resolution of a type fails. |
| System.AppDomain | ResourceResolve | Occurs when the resolution of a resource fails because the resource is not a valid linked or embedded resource in the assembly. |
| System.AppDomain | AssemblyResolve | Occurs when the resolution of an assembly fails. |
| System.AppDomain | ReflectionOnlyAssemblyResolve | Occurs when the resolution of an assembly fails in the reflection-only context. |
| System.AppDomain | UnhandledException | Occurs when an exception is not caught. |
| System.Console | CancelKeyPress | Occurs when the Control modifier key (Ctrl) and C console key (C) are pressed simultaneously (Ctrl-C). |
| Microsoft.Win32.SystemEvents | DisplaySettingsChanging | Occurs when the display settings are changing. |
| Microsoft.Win32.SystemEvents | DisplaySettingsChanged | Occurs when the user changes the display settings. |

| Type | Event | Description |
|---|---|---|
| Microsoft.Win32.SystemEvents | InstalledFontsChanged | Occurs when the user adds fonts to or removes fonts from the system. |
| Microsoft.Win32.SystemEvents | LowMemory | Occurs when the system is running out of available RAM. |
| Microsoft.Win32.SystemEvents | PaletteChanged | Occurs when the user switches to an application that uses a different palette. |
| Microsoft.Win32.SystemEvents | PowerModeChanged | Occurs when the user suspends or resumes the system. |
| Microsoft.Win32.SystemEvents | SessionEnded | Occurs when the user is logging off or shutting down the system. |
| Microsoft.Win32.SystemEvents | SessionEnding | Occurs when the user is trying to log off or shut down the system. |
| Microsoft.Win32.SystemEvents | SessionSwitch | Occurs when the currently logged-in user has changed. |
| Microsoft.Win32.SystemEvents | TimeChanged | Occurs when the user changes the time on the system clock. |
| Microsoft.Win32.SystemEvents | UserPreferenceChanged | Occurs when a user preference has changed. |
| Microsoft.Win32.SystemEvents | UserPreferenceChanging | Occurs when a user preference is changing. |
| System.Net.WebClient | OpenReadCompleted | Occurs when an asynchronous operation to open a stream containing a resource completes. |
| System.Net.WebClient | OpenWriteCompleted | Occurs when an asynchronous operation to open a stream to write data to a resource completes. |
| System.Net.WebClient | DownloadStringCompleted | Occurs when an asynchronous resource-download operation completes. |
| System.Net.WebClient | DownloadDataCompleted | Occurs when an asynchronous data download operation completes. |
| System.Net.WebClient | DownloadFileCompleted | Occurs when an asynchronous file download operation completes. |
| System.Net.WebClient | UploadStringCompleted | Occurs when an asynchronous string-upload operation completes. |
| System.Net.WebClient | UploadDataCompleted | Occurs when an asynchronous data-upload operation completes. |
| System.Net.WebClient | UploadFileCompleted | Occurs when an asynchronous file-upload operation completes. |

| Type | Event | Description |
|------|-------|-------------|
| System.Net.WebClient | UploadValuesCompleted | Occurs when an asynchronous upload of a name/value collection completes. |
| System.Net.WebClient | DownloadProgressChanged | Occurs when an asynchronous download operation successfully transfers some or all of the data. |
| System.Net.WebClient | UploadProgressChanged | Occurs when an asynchronous upload operation successfully transfers some or all of the data. |
| System.Net.Sockets.SocketAsyncEventArgs | Completed | The event used to complete an asynchronous operation. |
| System.Net.NetworkInformation.NetworkChange | NetworkAvailabilityChanged | Occurs when the availability of the network changes. |
| System.Net.NetworkInformation.NetworkChange | NetworkAddressChanged | Occurs when the IP address of a network interface changes. |
| System.IO.FileSystemWatcher | Changed | Occurs when a file or directory in the specified path is changed. |
| System.IO.FileSystemWatcher | Created | Occurs when a file or directory in the specified path is created. |
| System.IO.FileSystemWatcher | Deleted | Occurs when a file or directory in the specified path is deleted. |
| System.IO.FileSystemWatcher | Renamed | Occurs when a file or directory in the specified path is renamed. |
| System.Timers.Timer | Elapsed | Occurs when the interval elapses. |
| System.Diagnostics.EventLog | EntryWritten | Occurs when an entry is written to an event log on the local computer. |
| System.Diagnostics.Process | OutputDataReceived | Occurs when an application writes to its redirected StandardOutput stream. |
| System.Diagnostics.Process | ErrorDataReceived | Occurs when an application writes to its redirected StandardError stream. |
| System.Diagnostics.Process | Exited | Occurs when a process exits. |
| System.IO.Ports.SerialPort | ErrorReceived | Represents the method that handles the error event of a SerialPort object. |
| System.IO.Ports.SerialPort | PinChanged | Represents the method that will handle the serial pin changed event of a SerialPort object. |
| System.IO.Ports.SerialPort | DataReceived | Represents the method that will handle the data received event of a SerialPort object. |

| Type | Event | Description |
|---|---|---|
| System.Manage ment.Automation.Job | StateChanged | Event fired when the status of the job changes, such as when the job has completed in all runspaces or failed in any one runspace. This event is introduced in Windows PowerShell 2.0. |
| System.Manage ment.Automation.Debugger | DebuggerStop | Event raised when Windows PowerShell stops execution of the script and enters the debugger as the result of encountering a breakpoint or executing a step command. This event is introduced in Windows PowerShell 2.0. |
| System.Management.Automa tion.Debugger | BreakpointUpdated | Event raised when the breakpoint is updated, such as when it is enabled or disabled. This event is introduced in Windows PowerShell 2.0. |
| System.Management.Automa tion.Runspaces.Runspace | StateChanged | Event that is raised when the state of the runspace changes. |
| System.Management.Automa tion.Runspaces.Runspace | AvailabilityChanged | Event that is raised when the availability of the runspace changes, such as when the runspace becomes available and when it is busy. This event is introduced in Windows PowerShell 2.0. |
| System.Management.Automa tion.Runspaces.Pipeline | StateChanged | Event raised when the state of the pipeline changes. |
| System.Management.Automa tion.PowerShell | InvocationStateChanged | Event raised when the state of the pipeline of the PowerShell object changes. This event is introduced in Windows PowerShell 2.0. |
| System.Management.Automa tion.PSDataCollection[T] | DataAdded | Event that is fired after data is added to the collection. This event is introduced in Windows PowerShell 2.0. |
| System.Management.Automa tion.PSDataCollection[T] | Completed | Event that is fired when the Com plete method is called to indicate that no more data is to be added to the collection. This event is introduced in Windows PowerShell 2.0. |

| Type | Event | Description |
|---|---|---|
| System.Management.Automa tion.Runspaces.RunspacePool | StateChanged | Event raised when the state of the runspace pool changes. This event is introduced in Windows PowerShell 2.0. |
| System.Management.Automa tion.Runspaces.PipelineRead er[T] | DataReady | Event fired when data is added to the buffer. |
| System.Diagnostics.Event ing.Reader.EventLogWatcher | EventRecordWritten | Allows setting a delegate (event handler method) that gets called every time an event is published that matches the criteria specified in the event query for this object. |
| System.Data.Com mon.DbConnection | StateChange | Occurs when the state of the event changes. |
| System.Da ta.SqlClient.SqlBulkCopy | SqlRowsCopied | Occurs every time that the number of rows specified by the Notify After property have been processed. |
| System.Data.SqlClient.SqlCom mand | StatementCompleted | Occurs when the execution of a Transact-SQL statement completes. |
| System.Data.SqlClient.SqlCon nection | InfoMessage | Occurs when SQL Server returns a warning or informational message. |
| System.Data.SqlClient.SqlCon nection | StateChange | Occurs when the state of the event changes. |
| System.Data.SqlClient.SqlDa taAdapter | RowUpdated | Occurs during Update after a command is executed against the data source. The attempt to update is made, so the event fires. |
| System.Data.SqlClient.SqlDa taAdapter | RowUpdating | Occurs during Update before a command is executed against the data source. The attempt to update is made, so the event fires. |
| System.Data.SqlClient.SqlDa taAdapter | FillError | Returned when an error occurs during a fill operation. |
| System.Data.SqlClient.SqlDe pendency | OnChange | Occurs when a notification is received for any of the commands associated with this SqlDepend ency object. |

*Table I-2. Selected WMI Events*

| Event | Description |
| --- | --- |
| __InstanceCreationEvent | This event class generically represents the creation of instances in WMI providers, such as Processes, Services, Files, and more.<br>A registration for this generic event looks like:<br>```<br>$query = "SELECT * FROM __InstanceCreationEvent " +<br>        "WITHIN 5 " +<br>        "WHERE targetinstance is a<br>        'Win32_UserAccount'<br>Register-CimIndicationEvent -Query $query<br>``` |
| __InstanceDeletionEvent | This event class generically represents the removal of instances in WMI providers, such as Processes, Services, Files, and more.<br>A registration for this generic event looks like:<br>```<br>$query = "SELECT * FROM __InstanceDeletionEvent " +<br>        "WITHIN 5 " +<br>        "WHERE targetinstance is a<br>        'Win32_UserAccount'<br>Register-CimIndicationEvent -Query $query<br>``` |
| __InstanceModificationEvent | This event class generically represents the modification of instances in WMI providers, such as Processes, Services, Files, and more.<br>A registration for this generic event looks like:<br>```<br>$query = "SELECT * FROM __InstanceModificationEvent "<br>        + "WITHIN 5 " +<br>        "WHERE targetinstance is a<br>        'Win32_UserAccount'<br>Register-CimIndicationEvent -Query $query<br>``` |
| Msft_WmiProvider_OperationEvent | The Msft_WmiProvider_OperationEvent event class is the root definition of all WMI provider events. A provider operation is defined as some execution on behalf of a client via WMI that results in one or more calls to a provider executable. The properties of this class define the identity of the provider associated with the operation being executed and is uniquely associated with instances of the class Msft_Providers. Internally, WMI can contain any number of objects that refer to a particular instance of __Win32Provider since it differentiates each object based on whether the provider supports per-user or per-locale instantiation and also depending on where the provider is being hosted. Currently TransactionIdentifier is always an empty string. |
| Win32_ComputerSystemEvent | This event class represents events related to a computer system. |
| Win32_ComputerShutdownEvent | This event class represents events when a computer has begun the process of shutting down. |
| Win32_IP4RouteTableEvent | The Win32_IP4RouteTableEvent class represents IP route change events resulting from the addition, removal, or modification of IP routes on the computer system. |
| RegistryEvent | The registry event classes allow you to subscribe to events that involve changes in hive subtrees, keys, and specific values. |
| RegistryKeyChangeEvent | The RegistryKeyChangeEvent class represents changes to a specific key. The changes apply only to the key, not its subkeys. |

| Event | Description |
|---|---|
| RegistryTreeChangeEvent | The RegistryTreeChangeEvent class represents changes to a key and its subkeys. |
| RegistryValueChangeEvent | The RegistryValueChangeEvent class represents changes to a single value of a specific key. |
| Win32_SystemTrace | The SystemTrace class is the base class for all system trace events. System trace events are fired by the kernel logger via the event tracing API. |
| Win32_ProcessTrace | This event is the base event for process events. |
| Win32_ProcessStartTrace | The ProcessStartTrace event class indicates a new process has started. |
| Win32_ProcessStopTrace | The ProcessStopTrace event class indicates a process has terminated. |
| Win32_ModuleTrace | The ModuleTrace event class is the base event for module events. |
| Win32_ModuleLoadTrace | The ModuleLoadTrace event class indicates a process has loaded a new module. |
| Win32_ThreadTrace | The ThreadTrace event class is the base event for thread events. |
| Win32_ThreadStartTrace | The ThreadStartTrace event class indicates a new thread has started. |
| Win32_ThreadStopTrace | The ThreadStopTrace event class indicates a thread has terminated. |
| Win32_PowerManagementEvent | The Win32_PowerManagementEvent class represents power management events resulting from power state changes. These state changes are associated with either the Advanced Power Management (APM) or the Advanced Configuration and Power Interface (ACPI) system management protocols. |
| Win32_DeviceChangeEvent | The Win32_DeviceChangeEvent class represents device change events resulting from the addition, removal, or modification of devices on the computer system. This includes changes in the hardware configuration (docking and undocking), the hardware state, or newly mapped devices (mapping of a network drive). For example, a device has changed when a WM_DEVICECHANGE message is sent. |
| Win32_SystemConfigurationChangeEvent | The Win32_SystemConfigurationChangeEvent is an event class that indicates the device list on the system has been refreshed, meaning a device has been added or removed or the configuration changed. This event is fired when the Windows message "DevMgrRefreshOn<ComputerName>" is sent. The exact change to the device list is not contained in the message, and therefore a device refresh is required in order to obtain the current system settings. Examples of configuration changes affected are IRQ settings, COM ports, and BIOS version, to name a few. |
| Win32_VolumeChangeEvent | The Win32_VolumeChangeEvent class represents a local drive event resulting from the addition of a drive letter or mounted drive on the computer system (e.g., CD-ROM). Network drives are not currently supported. |

# Standard PowerShell Verbs

Cmdlets and scripts should be named using a *Verb-Noun* syntax—for example, Get-ChildItem. The official guidance is that, with rare exception, cmdlets should use the standard PowerShell verbs. They should avoid any synonyms or concepts that can be mapped to the standard. This allows administrators to quickly understand a set of cmdlets that use a new noun.

 To quickly access this list (without the definitions), type **Get-Verb**.

Verbs should be phrased in the present tense, and nouns should be singular. Tables J-1 through J-6 list the different categories of standard PowerShell verbs.

*Table J-1. Standard Windows PowerShell common verbs*

| Verb | Meaning | Synonyms |
|---|---|---|
| Add | Adds a resource to a container or attaches an element to another element | Append, Attach, Concatenate, Insert |
| Clear | Removes all elements from a container | Flush, Erase, Release, Unmark, Unset, Nullify |
| Close | Removes access to a resource | Shut, Seal |
| Copy | Copies a resource to another name or container | Duplicate, Clone, Replicate |
| Enter | Sets a resource as a context | Push, Telnet, Open |
| Exit | Returns to the context that was present before a new context was entered | Pop, Disconnect |
| Find | Searches within an unknown context for a desired item | Dig, Discover |
| Format | Converts an item to a specified structure or layout | Layout, Arrange |
| Get | Retrieves data | Read, Open, Cat, Type, Dir, Obtain, Dump, Acquire, Examine, Find, Search |

| Verb | Meaning | Synonyms |
| --- | --- | --- |
| Hide | Makes a display not visible | Suppress |
| Join | Joins a resource | Combine, Unite, Connect, Associate |
| Lock | Locks a resource | Restrict, Bar |
| Move | Moves a resource | Transfer, Name, Migrate |
| New | Creates a new resource | Create, Generate, Build, Make, Allocate |
| Open | Enables access to a resource | Release, Unseal |
| Pop | Removes an item from the top of a stack | Remove, Paste |
| Push | Puts an item onto the top of a stack | Put, Add, Copy |
| Redo | Repeats an action or reverts the action of an Undo | Repeat, Retry, Revert |
| Remove | Removes a resource from a container | Delete, Kill |
| Rename | Gives a resource a new name | Ren, Swap |
| Reset | Restores a resource to a predefined or original state | Restore, Revert |
| Select | Creates a subset of data from a larger data set | Pick, Grep, Filter |
| Search | Finds a resource (or summary information about that resource) in a collection (does not actually retrieve the resource but provides information to be used when retrieving it) | Find, Get, Grep, Select |
| Set | Places data | Write, Assign, Configure |
| Show | Retrieves, formats, and displays information | Display, Report |
| Skip | Bypasses an element in a seek or navigation | Bypass, Jump |
| Split | Separates data into smaller elements | Divide, Chop, Parse |
| Step | Moves a process or navigation forward by one unit | Next, Iterate |
| Switch | Alternates the state of a resource between different alternatives or options | Toggle, Alter, Flip |
| Unlock | Unlocks a resource | Free, Unrestrict |
| Use | Applies or associates a resource with a context | With, Having |
| Watch | Continually monitors an item | Monitor, Poll |

*Table J-2. Standard Windows PowerShell communication verbs*

| Verb | Meaning | Synonyms |
| --- | --- | --- |
| Connect | Connects a source to a destination | Join, Telnet |
| Disconnect | Disconnects a source from a destination | Break, Logoff |
| Read | Acquires information from a nonconnected source | Prompt, Get |
| Receive | Acquires information from a connected source | Read, Accept, Peek |
| Send | Writes information to a connected destination | Put, Broadcast, Mail |
| Write | Writes information to a nonconnected destination | Puts, Print |

*Table J-3. Standard Windows PowerShell data verbs*

| Verb | Meaning | Synonyms |
|------|---------|----------|
| Backup | Backs up data | Save, Burn |
| Checkpoint | Creates a snapshot of the current state of data or its configuration | Diff, StartTransaction |
| Compare | Compares a resource with another resource | Diff, Bc |
| Compress | Reduces the size or resource usage of an item | Zip, Squeeze, Archive |
| Convert | Changes from one representation to another when the cmdlet supports bidirectional conversion or conversion of many data types | Change, Resize, Resample |
| ConvertFrom | Converts from one primary input to several supported outputs | Export, Output, Out |
| ConvertTo | Converts from several supported inputs to one primary output | Import, Input, In |
| Dismount | Detaches a name entity from a location in a namespace | Dismount, Unlink |
| Edit | Modifies an item in place | Change, Modify, Alter |
| Expand | Increases the size or resource usage of an item | Extract, Unzip |
| Export | Stores the primary input resource into a backing store or interchange format | Extract, Backup |
| Group | Combines an item with other related items | Merge, Combine, Map |
| Import | Creates a primary output resource from a backing store or interchange format | Load, Read |
| Initialize | Prepares a resource for use and initializes it to a default state | Setup, Renew, Rebuild |
| Limit | Applies constraints to a resource | Quota, Enforce |
| Merge | Creates a single data instance from multiple data sets | Combine, Join |
| Mount | Attaches a named entity to a location in a namespace | Attach, Link |
| Out | Sends data to a terminal location | Print, Format, Send |
| Publish | Make a resource known or visible to others | Deploy, Release, Install |
| Restore | Restores a resource to a set of conditions that have been predefined or set by a checkpoint | Repair, Return, Fix |
| Save | Stores pending changes to a recoverable store | Write, Retain, Submit |
| Sync | Synchronizes two resources with each other | Push, Update |
| Unpublish | Removes a resource from public visibility | Uninstall, Revert |
| Update | Updates or refreshes a resource | Refresh, Renew, Index |

*Table J-4. Standard Windows PowerShell diagnostic verbs*

| Verb | Meaning | Synonyms |
|------|---------|----------|
| Debug | Examines a resource, diagnoses operational problems | Attach, Diagnose |
| Measure | Identifies resources consumed by an operation or retrieves statistics about a resource | Calculate, Determine, Analyze |
| Ping | Determines whether a resource is active and responsive (in most instances, this should be replaced by the verb Test) | Connect, Debug |
| Repair | Recovers an item from a damaged or broken state | Fix, Recover, Rebuild |
| Resolve | Maps a shorthand representation to a more complete one | Expand, Determine |

| Verb | Meaning | Synonyms |
|------|---------|----------|
| Test | Verify the validity or consistency of a resource | Diagnose, Verify, Analyze |
| Trace | Follow the activities of the resource | Inspect, Dig |

*Table J-5. Standard Windows PowerShell lifecycle verbs*

| Verb | Meaning | Synonyms |
|------|---------|----------|
| Approve | Gives approval or permission for an item or resource | Allow, Let |
| Assert | Declares the state of an item or fact | Verify, Check |
| Complete | Finalizes a pending operation | Finalize, End |
| Confirm | Approves or acknowledges a resource or process | Check, Validate |
| Deny | Disapproves or disallows a resource or process | Fail, Halt |
| Disable | Configures an item to be unavailable | Halt, Hide |
| Enable | Configures an item to be available | Allow, Permit |
| Install | Places a resource in the specified location and optionally initializes it | Setup, Configure |
| Invoke | Calls or launches an activity that cannot be stopped | Run, Call, Perform |
| Register | Adds an item to a monitored or publishing resource | Record, Submit, Journal, Subscribe |
| Request | Submits for consideration or approval | Ask, Query |
| Restart | Stops an operation and starts it again | Recycle, Hup |
| Resume | Begins an operation after it has been suspended | Continue |
| Start | Begins an activity | Launch, Initiate |
| Stop | Discontinues an activity | Halt, End, Discontinue |
| Submit | Adds to a list of pending actions or sends for approval | Send, Post |
| Suspend | Pauses an operation, but does not discontinue it | Pause, Sleep, Break |
| Uninstall | Removes a resource from the specified location | Remove, Clear, Clean |
| Unregister | Removes an item from a monitored or publishing resource | Unsubscribe, Erase, Remove |
| Wait | Pauses until an expected event occurs | Sleep, Pause, Join |

*Table J-6. Standard Windows PowerShell security verbs*

| Verb | Meaning | Synonyms |
|------|---------|----------|
| Block | Restricts access to a resource | Prevent, Limit, Deny |
| Grant | Grants access to a resource | Allow, Enable |
| Protect | Limits access to a resource | Encrypt, Seal |
| Revoke | Removes access to a resource | Remove, Disable |
| Unblock | Removes a restriction of access to a resource | Clear, Allow |
| Unprotect | Removes restrictions from a protected resource | Decrypt, Decode |

# Index

## Symbols

& (ampersand)
    invoke operator, 20, 21
    preceding accelerator key, 399
    in regular expressions, 925

<...> (angle brackets), in regular expressions, 922, 926

<#...#> (angle brackets, pound sign), enclosing comments, 862

* (asterisk)
    multiplication operator, 207, 874
    in regular expressions, 920, 921
    in XPath queries, 930

*= (asterisk, equal), multiplication assignment operator, 208, 875

@ (at sign)
    preceding variables passed as parameters, 336, 356
    in XPath queries, 930

@{...} (at sign, braces), hashtable cast syntax, 238, 872

@"..."@ (at sign, double quotes), enclosing here strings, 177, 180, 866

@(...) (at sign, parentheses)
    array cast syntax, 225, 869
    list evaluation, 862

\ (backslash), in regular expressions, 920, 924, 926

` (backtick)
    escape character, 178, 867
    in regular expressions, 925

{...} (braces)
    escaping complex variable names, 125
    in regular expressions, 920, 921

^ (caret), in regular expressions, 919, 923

: (colon)
    preceding stream in filename, 584
    in regular expressions, 922

:: (colon, double), accessing static methods or properties, 133, 134, 136

, (comma), unary comma operator, 145

.\ (current directory), 20, 21

$_ (current object variable), ix

$ (dollar sign)
    preceding variable names, viii, 123, 864
    in regular expressions, 924

${...} (dollar sign, braces)
    enclosing arbitrary variable name, 864
    Get-Content variable syntax, 259

$(...) (dollar sign, parentheses), expression evaluation, 861

$? (dollar sign, question mark), dollar hook variable, 444–445

. (dot notation)
    accessing methods or properties, viii, 133, 135, 137
    in regular expressions, 919

*We'd like to hear your suggestions for improving our indexes. Send email to index@oreilly.com.*

sourcing functions or scripts, 352–354
"..." (double quotes), enclosing expanding
  strings, 176, 866
= (equal sign)
  in regular expressions, 923
  equality operator, 931
! (exclamation point)
  not operator, 875
  in regular expressions, 923
!= (exclamation point, equal), inequality operator, 931
/ (forward slash)
  division operator, 207, 874
  in XPath queries, 929
/= (forward slash, equal), division assignment
  operator, 208, 875
< (left angle bracket), in regular expressions, 923
- (minus sign), subtraction operator, 207, 874
-= (minus sign, equal), subtraction assignment
  operator, 208, 875
(...) (parentheses)
  enclosing New-Object call, 138
  in regular expressions, 922
  specifying precedence, 208, 861
% (percent sign), modulus operator, 207, 874
%= (percent sign, equal), modulus assignment
  operator, 208, 875
+ (plus sign)
  addition operator, 207, 874
  combining arrays, 231
  in regular expressions, 921, 925
+= (plus sign, equal), addition assignment operator, 208, 875
# (pound sign)
  auto-completion of history commands, 55,
    68, 68
  preceding comments, 862
  in regular expressions, 926
? (question mark), in regular expressions, 921,
  922, 925, 926
> (right angle bracket)
  in redirection operators, 79, 81, 913
  in regular expressions, 923
' (single quote), in regular expressions, 925
'...' (single quotes)
  enclosing commands containing special
    characters, 20, 24
  enclosing literal strings, 176, 180, 866

[...] (square brackets)
  enclosing array indexes, 227, 870
  enclosing class name, 133, 134, 136
  enclosing constraints, 864
  enclosing generic parameters, 141
  enclosing type name, 864
  in regular expressions, 919
  in XPath queries, 931
_ (underscore), in regular expressions, 925
--% (verbatim argument marker), 24, 25
| (vertical bar)
  pipeline character, ix, 89
  in regular expressions, 925
0x prefix for numbers, 214, 220

A

Abs() method, Math class, 209
absolute value, 209
Abstract Syntax Tree (AST) API, 297, 300
accelerator key, 399
Access.Application COM object, 959
ACL (Access Control List)
  getting, 587–589, 611
  for registry keys, 611–614
  setting, 589, 612–614
ACos() method, Math class, 209
-Action parameter
  for breakpoints, 432–434
  for events, 845, 846, 847, 849
Active Directory, 669–670
  classes for, 948
  computer accounts
    properties of, listing, 694
    searching for, 692
  groups
    adding users to, 688–689
    creating, 683–685
    listing users belonging to, 691
    owner of, determining, 687
    properties of, listing, 686–687
    properties of, modifying, 688
    removing users from, 689
    searching for, 685–686
    type of, setting, 684
  organizational units
    children of, listing, 676
    creating, 673–674
    deleting, 675
    listing users in, 691

properties of, listing, 674
properties of, modifying, 675–675
system requirements for, 669
testing scripts, 670–672
user accounts
creating, 677
importing, 678–680
listing group memberships of, 690
properties of, listing, 681
properties of, modifying, 682
searching for, 680
Active Directory Application Mode (ADAM),
670–672
Active Directory Lightweight Directory Services
(AD LDS), 670–672
Active Directory module, 669
Active Directory Service Interface (ADSI), xiv,
669
activities (see workflows)
ActivityGenerator class, 836
AD LDS (Active Directory Lightweight Directo-
ry Services), 670–672
AD provider (AD: drive), 669, 676
ADAM (Active Directory Application Mode),
670–672
Add verb, 971
Add() method, [adsi] type shortcut, 688–689
Add-Computer cmdlet, 695–696
Add-Event() method, 857
Add-ExtendedFileProperties script, 591–593
Add-FormatData script, 159
Add-History cmdlet, 65
Add-Member cmdlet, 147–149, 895
Add-ObjectCollector script, 109–110
Add-ons submenu, ISE, 555
Add-PsSnapin cmdlet, 84
Add-RelativePathCapture script, 354–355
Add-Type cmdlet, 490, 492, 495, 500–502, 503–
507, 586
AddDays() method, DateTime class, 563
addition assignment operator (+=), 208, 875
addition operator (+), 207, 231, 874
administrative constants, 218–219, 868
administrative templates, 524
administrator rights
temporary, running a command with, 534–
536
testing for, 480–481

ADSI (Active Directory Service Interface), xiv,
669
[adsi] type shortcut, 670, 894
[adsisearcher] type shortcut, 670, 680, 685, 691,
692, 894
Agent.Control COM object, 959
[Alias()] attribute, 332, 904
aliases
adding to personal profile script, 36
for cmdlets, vii, 59–61
for parameters, 61–64
removing, 37
scope of, 128–130
AliasProperty member type, 157, 895
[AllowEmptyCollection()] attribute, 332, 905
[AllowEmptyString()] attribute, 332, 905
[AllowNull()] attribute, 332, 904
AllScope scope, 129
AllSigned execution policy, 517
alternate data streams for files, 584–586
ampersand (&)
invoke operator, 20, 21
preceding accelerator key, 399
in regular expressions, 925
and operator, 931
-and operator, 165, 875
angle brackets (<…>), in regular expressions,
922, 926
angle brackets, pound sign (<#…#>), enclosing
comments, 862
AppDomain class, 944
-AppendOutput parameter, workflows, 820
applications (see executables)
Approve verb, 974
$args array, 325–329, 337, 784, 848, 902
-ArgumentList parameter, Invoke-Command
cmdlet, 784
arguments (see parameters)
arithmetic operators, 207–209, 873–875
array cast syntax (@(…)), 225, 869
Array class, 944
ArrayList class, 236–237, 944
capturing command output in, 109–110
creating instance of, 224
arrays, 223, 869–872
(see also lists)
accessing items in, 226–228, 870
adding items to, 236–237
associative (see hashtables)

combining, 231

command output stored in, 224

comparing, 233

creating, 223–225

determining if item is in, 230

fixed size, 224

importing and exporting to a file, 289–291

jagged, 225–226, 870

multidimensional, 225–226, 870

removing items from, 234–235, 236–237

searching for items greater or less than a value, 235–236

searching for items matching a value, 232

slicing, 871

sorting, 229–230

strongly typed, 224

working with each item in, 228–229

-as operator, 878

ASin() method, Math class, 209

-AsJob parameter

for remoting, 788–789

for workflows, 808–811, 820

-AsSecureString parameter, Read-Host cmdlet, 529–530

assemblies, loading, 138, 895

Assembly class, 944

-Assembly parameter, #requires statement, 828–830

AssemblyLoad event, 963

AssemblyResolve event, 963

Assert verb, 974

associations (see shell associations)

associative arrays (see hashtables)

AST (Abstract Syntax Tree) API, 297, 300

asterisk (*)

multiplication operator, 207, 874

in regular expressions, 920, 921

in XPath queries, 930

asterisk, equal (*=), multiplication assignment operator, 208, 875

-At parameter, New-ScheduledTaskTrigger cmdlet, 712

at sign (@)

preceding variables passed as parameters, 336, 356

in XPath queries, 930

at sign, braces (@{...}), hashtable cast syntax, 238, 872

at sign, double quotes (@"..."@), enclosing here strings, 177, 180, 866

at sign, parentheses (@(...))

array cast syntax, 225, 869

list evaluation, 862

ATan() method, Math class, 209

-AtLogOn parameter, New-ScheduledTaskTrigger cmdlet, 712

atomicity, 605, 837

-AtStartup parameter, New-ScheduledTaskTrigger cmdlet, 712

attrib.exe program, 565

-Attributes parameter, Get-ChildItem cmdlet, 561, 562

Attributes property, files, 565–566

-Authentication parameter, Invoke-Command cmdlet, 779–783

auto-completion, vii, 55–59, 68

AutoItX3.Control COM object, 959

automatic parameters, 338

automatic variables

in Action scripts, 847

$error variable, 909

$errorActionPreference variable, 910

$host variable, 793

$input variable, 808

$lastExitCode variable, 444–445, 908

listing, 123

$myInvocation variable, 467–472, 907

$profile variable, 916

$PSBoundParameters variable, 337

$psCmdlet variable, 338

$PSDebugContext variable, 435

$psISE variable, 552

$psISE.Options variable, 549

$PSSessionOption variable, 785

$PSVersionTable variable, 479–480

$pwd variable, 476

AvailabilityChanged event, 966

awk utility, 196

(see also -split operator)

# B

background jobs (see jobs)

backslash (\), in regular expressions, 920, 924, 926

backtick (`)

escape character, 178, 867

in regular expressions, 925

Backup verb, 973
backups, of event logs, 643–644
-band operator, 876
bases, converting numbers between, 219–221
batch files
    environment variable changes in, retaining,
        126–128
    running in interactive shell, 19–22
begin keyword, 347–351, 808, 906
BigInt class, 211, 869
binary files
    hexadecimal representation of, 277–280
    parsing, 267–269
binary numbers, 214–218, 220, 868
binary operators, 875–877
BinaryReader class, 269, 945
BinaryWriter class, 945
BitConverter class, 267
Bitmap class, 946
Block verb, 974
-bnot operator, 876
booleans, 865
-bor operator, 876
braces ({...})
    escaping complex variable names, 125
    in regular expressions, 920, 921
break statement, 170, 808, 887, 911
breakpoints
    conditional
        for code coverage analysis, 440–442
        on errors, 430–432
        on specific actions, 432–434
    current state during, 434–437
    enabling and disabling, 430
    in ISE, 547–549
    removing, 430
    setting, 428–430
    types of, 428–430
BreakpointUpdated event, 966
BufferedStream class, 945
-bxor operator, 876
Bypass execution policy, 517
Byte encoding, 267, 269

C

C#
    generating with PowerShell, 204
    writing portions of scripts in, 503–504
"c", preceding comparison operators, 165

calculated properties, 149, 571
calculations (see math and calculations)
CancelAllJobs() method, print queues, 717
CancelKeyPress event, 963
capitalization, 408
caret (^), in regular expressions, 919, 923
case of strings, converting, 191–193
catch statement, 452, 454, 910
CEnroll.Cenroll COM object, 959
certificate drive, 539, 542
certificate store
    accessing, 539–540
    adding and removing certificates, 542
    navigating, xvi
    searching, 540–541
CertificateAuthority.Request COM object, 959
Changed event, 965
ChangeExtension() method, Path class, 271
Checkpoint verb, 973
Checkpoint-Computer cmdlet, 706–708
Checkpoint-Workflow cmdlet, 807, 811–814
checkpoints in workflows, 806, 811–814
Children property, [adsi] type shortcut, 676
CIM (Common Information Model), xiii, 729
    converting VBScripts to PowerShell, 743–
        747
    instances
        properties of, modifying, 732–734
        retrieving, 730
    methods, invoking, 730
CimClassProperties property, WMI classes, 741
CimCmdlets module, 729
CIM_DataFile WMI class, 951
classes, 134
    (see also objects)
    auto-completion of, 56
    extending, 896
    listing constructors for, 146
    listing methods and properties for, 145–147,
        893
    .NET clases
        shortening names for, 141–142
    .NET classes, 943–949
        defining or extending, 500–502
    static methods of (see static methods)
    static properties of (see static properties)
    type shortcuts for, 893
Clear verb, 971
Clear() method, $error variable, 448

Clear-Content cmdlet, 564–565
Clear-EventLog cmdlet, 648–650
Clear-History cmdlet, 65
ClearLog() method, GlobalSession class, 650
clipboard, reading and writing to, 246
Close verb, 971
CLR (Common Language Runtime), version of, 479
.cmd file extension, 19
    (see also batch files)
[CmdletBinding()] attribute, 328, 338, 903
cmdlets, vii–vii
    (see also commands)
    as activities in workflows, 834–836
    aliases for, vii, 59–61
    auto-completion for, vii, 55, 68
    checking possible results of, x–x
    creating, 507–510
    defined, vii
    extending, 356
    finding, 43–45
    help on, 45–47
    information about, xi
    naming conventions for, vii, 44, 971–974
    parameters for
        default values for, 26–28
        dynamic, 540
        positional, vii
        wildcards in, vii
    running in interactive shell, 23–23
    running outside PowerShell, 52–54
code
    coverage of, analyzing, 440–442
    generating, 202–205
    reusing (see functions; modules; script
        blocks; scripts)
code examples, xxiii
code-signing certificates
    accessing from certificate store, 539–540
    certificate rules for, 526
    Microsoft Certificate Services, 525
    searching for, 540–541
    self-signed certificate, 522–523
    signing scripts using, 520–522
CodeMethod member type, 896
CodeProperty member type, 895
-CodeSign parameter, Get-ChildItem cmdlet, 540

colon (:)
    preceding stream in filename, 584
    in regular expressions, 922
colon, double (::), accessing static methods or
    properties, 133, 134, 136
colorized script content, 251–256
colors in ISE, customizing, 549–551
COM objects, 959–961
    accessing, xiv, 895
    creating, 143, 483–484
COMAdmin.COMAdminCatalog COM object, 959
comma (,), unary comma operator, 145
command history
    auto-completion of commands in, 55, 68
    auto-completion of IDs in, 55
    clearing, 65
    creating scripts from, 66–67
    displaying, 64, 65
    displaying IDs for, 38
    importing commands to, 65
    maximum number of commands in, 64, 65
    running commands from, 64, 65, 68–69
    saving between sessions, 85–87
    saving to a file, 64
-Command parameter, PowerShell.exe, 52, 84, 701
CommandNotFoundAction property, 43, 354–355, 918
commands
    breakpoints on, 429
    customizing behavior of, 40–43, 917–918
    debug output for, 450–451
    DOS, in interactive shell, v
    duration of execution, 244–245
    dynamically-named, calling, 354–355
    errors generated by, 445–448
    finding, 43–45
    functions (see functions)
    help for, writing, 908–909
    help on, 45–47
    importing from modules, 82–83
    invocation of, information about, 466–470
    monitoring for changed results, 32–34
    notification of completion, 35–35
    output from, 907–908
        capturing in ArrayList, 109–110
        comparing output of two commands,
            627–629

converting to XML, 286–287
exporting to CSV files, 291–292
filtering, 90–91, 94–96
filtering interactively, 96–98
formatting, 911–913
formatting as a web page, 387
grouping in hashtable, 91–94
loading into Excel, 295–297
piping to another command (see pipelines)
redirecting to a file, 79–81
searching for a pattern, 69–70
storing in a file, 913
storing in a variable, 122–123, 913
storing in an array, 224
streaming, 200–202
viewing in interactive grid, 70–72
working with each item in, 99–101
parameters for, 900–906
aliases for, 61–64
argument values for, 21–22, 325–329
auto-completion for, 55
environment variables as values for, 26
errors from, troubleshooting, 24–26
script blocks as, 334–336
validating arguments for, 330–334
variables for, 22
verbatim argument marker (--%) for, 25
PowerShell commands (see cmdlets)
progress output for, 450–451
running as background jobs, 28–31
scripts (see scripts)
status of, on completion, 443–445
syntax for, 861–862
Unix, in interactive shell, v
verbose output for, 450–451
comments
help content in, 340–342, 863–864, 908–909
syntax for, 862
Common Information Model (see CIM)
Common Language Runtime (CLR), version of, 479
CommonSecurityDescriptor class, 543
Compare verb, 973
Compare-Object cmdlet, 234, 627–631
Compare-Property script, 95
comparison operators, 163–165, 879–881
Complete verb, 974

Complete-Transaction cmdlet, 604–606, 839, 841
Completed event, 965, 966
Complex class, 212
complex numbers, 212, 869
Compress verb, 973
computer accounts, Active Directory
properties of, listing, 694
searching for, 692
-ComputerName parameter
for event logs, 635, 650–651
finding all cmdlets supporting, 750–751
Get-Hotfix cmdlet, 710
for sessions, 761
computers
adding to domain, 695–696
adding to workgroup, 695–696
DHCP lease for, renewing, 720–721
hibernating or suspending, 709
hotfixes, determining if installed on, 710
IP addresses for, listing, 723
network connectivity between, testing, 768–771
remote (see remote computers; Remoting)
removing from domain, 696–697
renaming, 697
restarting, 708–709
restore points for, managing, 706–708
scheduled jobs on, 710–714
shutting down, 708–709
startup and shutdown scripts for, 699–701
static IP address for, assigning, 721–722
system information about, 718–720
conditional statements, 165–170, 882–885
-Confirm parameter, x, 338–340
Confirm verb, 974
Connect verb, 972
Connect-PSSession cmdlet, 761–762
consistency, 605, 837
Console class, 943
console pane, ISE, 547
constructors
creating objects using, 138
listing for a class, 146
contact information for this book, xxiv
-contains operator, 230, 881
Contains() method, String class, 183
continue statement, 808, 888, 911
Control-Space key, customizing, 55

conventions used in this book, xxii
Convert class, 943
Convert verb, 973
Convert-TextObject script, 196–200, 264–267
ConvertFrom verb, 973
ConvertFrom-Csv cmdlet, 293
ConvertFrom-Json cmdlet, 294–295
ConvertFrom-SecureString cmdlet, 537–538
ConvertTo verb, 973
ConvertTo-Csv cmdlet, 204
ConvertTo-HTml cmdlet, 204
ConvertTo-Html cmdlet, 387
ConvertTo-Json cmdlet, 294–295
ConvertTo-SecureString cmdlet, 530, 537–538
ConvertTo-Xml cmdlet, 204, 286–287
Cooked Mode, 39
Copy verb, 971
Copy-History cmdlet, 66
Cos() method, Math class, 209
Create() method, [adsi] type shortcut, 673, 677, 684
Created event, 965
-Credential parameter, Invoke-WebRequest cmdlet, 366
credentials (see user credentials)
CredSSP authentication, 756, 779–783
-creplace operator, 272–274
CSharpCodeProvider class, 944
CSV files
    exporting command output to, 291–292
    importing data from, 292–293
    loading into Excel, 295–297
    reading, 102, 103
current directory, specifying, 20, 21
CurrentUser scope, 518

**D**

-Daily parameter, New-ScheduledTaskTrigger cmdlet, 712
data, 627
    (see also files)
    comparing, 627–631
    IO classes for, 945
    standard PowerShell verbs for, 973
:$DATA stream, 585
DATA {…} evaluation, 862
database
    classes for, 948
    querying, 485–487

DataReady event, 967
DataReceived event, 965
DataSet class, 948
DataTable class, 948
DateAdded event, 966
dates and times
    files modified based on, listing, 563–564
    formatting, 194–196, 407, 937–942
    statistical operations on, 214
    system date and time, 243
DateTime class, ix, 937–942, 943
Debug class, 943
-Debug parameter
    as standard parameter, 327, 451
    workflows, 820
Debug verb, 973
Debug-Process cmdlet, 661–662
DebuggerStop event, 966
debugging, 421–422
    breakpoints
        conditional, on errors, 430–432
        conditional, on specific actions, 432–434
        current state during, 434–437
        enabling and disabling, 430
        removing, 430
        setting, 428–430
        types of, 428–430
    code coverage, analyzing, 440–442
    debug output for commands, 450–451
    errors
        analyzing, 448–449
        displaying, 445–448
        double-hop problem, 755, 760, 763
        handling, 452–455
        notifying caller of, 455
        running executables in PowerShell, 24–26
        in transactions, handling, 841–843
        types of, 448, 909–911
    in ISE, 547–549
    processes, 661–662
    progress output for commands, 450–451
    status of previous command, 443–445
    tracing script execution, 424–427
    verbose output for commands, 450–451
    warnings
        enabling, 422–424
        handling, 452–455
        notifying caller of, 455

watching value of expressions, 437–439
workflows, 830–834
Write-Host cmdlet for, 421
$debugPreference variable, 450, 451
default statement, 884
-DefinitionName parameter, Start-Job cmdlet, 712
DeflateStream class, 945
degrees, converting to radians, 211
delegates, .NET Framework, 856–858
Deleted event, 965
DeleteTree() method, [adsi] type shortcut, 676
Deny verb, 974
.DESCRIPTION help tag, 863, 908
-Description parameter, Get-Hotfix cmdlet, 710
DHCP
    enabling, 722
    lease for, renewing, 720–721
diagnostics
    duration of command execution, 244–245
    events related to, 965, 967
    log files, parsing, 264–267
    standard PowerShell verbs for, 973
digital signatures, verifying, 527–529
directories
    ACL for
        getting, 587–589
        setting, 589
    creating, 576–577
    disk usage statistics for, 570–572
    listing files in, 561–562
    moving, 579–580
    removing, 577–578
    renaming, 578–579
Directory class, 945
-Directory parameter, Get-ChildItem cmdlet, 562
DirectoryEntry class, 948
DirectoryInfo class, 562, 945
DirectorySearcher class, 948
Disable verb, 974
Disable-ComputerRestore cmdlet, 706–708
Disable-PsBreakpoint cmdlet, 430
Disable-PSWSManCombinedTrace cmdlet, 831
Disconnect verb, 972
Disconnect-PSSession cmdlet, 761–762
disk usage statistics, 570–572
Dismount verb, 973
-DisplayName parameter, workflows, 820

DisplaySettingsChanged event, 963
DisplaySettingsChanging event, 963
Distributed Management Task Force (DMTF), 729
distribution group, Active Directory
    adding users to, 688–689
    creating, 683–685
    listing members of, 691
    owner of, determining, 687
    properties of
        listing, 686–687
        modifying, 688
    removing users from, 689
    searching for, 685–686
division assignment operator (/=), 208, 875
division operator (/), 207, 874
DLLs
    accessing, 505–507
    version information for, 573–574
DMTF (Distributed Management Task Force), 729
Dns class, 947
do statement, 170–172, 886
dollar sign ($)
    preceding variable names, viii, 864
    in regular expressions, 924
dollar sign ($),
    preceding variable names, 123
dollar sign, braces (${...})
    enclosing arbitrary variable name, 864
    Get-Content variable syntax, 259
dollar sign, parentheses ($(...)), expression evaluation, 861
dollar sign, question mark ($?), dollar hook variable, 444–445
domain
    adding computers to, 695–696
    removing computers from, 696–697
-DomainName parameter, Add-Computer cmdlet, 695
DOS commands, running in interactive shell, v
dot notation (.)
    accessing methods or properties, viii, 133, 135, 137
    in regular expressions, 919
    sourcing functions or scripts, 352–354, 900
double quotes ("..."), enclosing expanding strings, 176, 866
double-hop problem, 755, 760, 763

DownloadDataCompleted event, 964
DownloadFileCompleted event, 964
DownloadProgressChanged event, 965
DownloadStringCompleted event, 964
drives
    AD provider (AD: drive), 669, 676
    custom, creating, 580–582
    environment provider (env: drive), 123, 124,
        463, 464
    removing, 581
    scope of, 128–130, 319
durability, 837
dynamic parameters, 540
dynamic variables, 130–133

## E

Edit verb, 973
Elapsed event, 965
else statement, 165–167, 882
elseif statement, 165–167, 882
email
    checking status of mailbox, 391
    protocols for, 391
    sending, 388–389
Enable verb, 974
Enable-BreakOnError script, 430–432
Enable-ComputerRestore cmdlet, 706–708
Enable-HistoryPersistence script, 85
Enable-PsBreakpoint cmdlet, 430
Enable-PSRemoting cmdlet, 752–753, 763
Enable-PSWSManCombinedTrace cmdlet, 831
Enable-RemotePSRemoting script, 763–765
Enable-WSManCredSSP cmdlet, 780
-EnableNetworkAccess parameter, remoting,
    756, 780
-EncodedCommand parameter, PowerShell.exe,
    54
encoding of files, 273, 275–277, 407
end keyword, 347–351, 808, 906
Enter verb, 971
Enter-Module script, 322–323
Enter-PSSession cmdlet, 754–756
enterprise-wide security, 523–525
EntryWritten event, 965
Enum class, 944
Environment class, 465, 466, 943
environment provider (env: drive), 123, 124,
    463, 464

environment variables
    accessing, 123–126, 463–465
    as command parameter values, 26
    listing, 123
    retaining changes made in batch files, 126–
        128
-eq operator, 233, 879
equal sign (=)
    in regular expressions, 923
    equality operator, 931
Error collection, workflows, 832
$error variable, 445–448, 909
-ErrorAction parameter
    as standard parameter, 327
    workflows, 820
$errorActionPreference variable, 452, 454, 910
ErrorDataReceived event, 965
ErrorReceived event, 965
errors, 421
    (see also debugging)
    analyzing, 448–449
    double-hop problem, 755, 760, 763
    listing for current session, 445–448
    notifying caller of, 455
    running executables in PowerShell, 24–26
    in scripts, handling, 452–455
    in transactions, handling, 841–843
    types of, 448, 909–911
-ErrorVariable parameter, as standard parame-
    ter, 327
$errorView variable, 446, 447
escape character (`), 178
escape sequences, 178
    preventing conflicts with, 164, 570
    in regular expressions, 926
    in strings, 867
event logs, 633
    backing up, 643–644
    browsing, in Windows Event Viewer, 634
    clearing, 648–650
    creating, 644–645
    listing, 633–635
    newest entries of, retrieving, 635–636
    querying after backing up, 643–644
    on remote computers, accessing, 650–651
    removing, 644–645
    retention policy for, 645, 648–650
    running scripts based on specific events in,
        646–648

searching based on frequency, 641–643
searching for specific text in, 636–640
writing to, 646–646
event queue, 850
$event variable, 848
$eventArgs variable, 848
EventLog class, 943
EventRecordWritten event, 967
events
    Action script block for, 845, 846, 847
    custom, creating, 849–852
    forwarding from remote computer, 853–854
    handling, 845–849
    internal event action state of, 854–856
    .NET events, 856–858, 963–967
    polling for, 845
    PowerShell.Exiting event, 85, 87
    subscriber of, 848, 852, 854
    temporary subscription for, 852–853
    WMI, 968–969
$eventSubscriber variable, 848
.EXAMPLE help tag, 863, 909
Excel, loading CSV data into, 295–297
Excel.Application COM object, 959
Excel.Sheet COM object, 959
exclamation point (!)
    not operator, 875
    in regular expressions, 923
exclamation point, equal (!=), inequality operator, 931
-Exclude parameter, Get-ChildItem cmdlet, 567
.exe file extension, 19
executables
    associated with a document, launching, 655–656
    binary output from, redirecting, 111–115
    errors from, troubleshooting, 24–26
    including PowerShell scripting in, 510–513
    installed, listing, 704–705
    Registry keys for, determining, 622–625
    running in interactive shell, 19–22
    uninstalling, 705–706
    version information for, 573–574
execution policy
    modifying for remote computer, 614
    scoping of, 517
    setting, 516–519
$executionContext variable, 560

$executionContext.SessionState.Invoke-
    Command variable, 41–43, 917
-ExecutionPolicy parameter, PowerShell.exe, 54,
    517, 701
exit statement, 313, 908
Exit verb, 971
Exited event, 965
Exiting event, 325
Expand verb, 973
expanding strings, 176, 179–180, 866
Export verb, 973
Export-CliXml cmdlet, 64, 286, 289–291, 292,
    537–538, 643, 644
Export-Counter cmdlet, 490
Export-Csv cmdlet, 291–292, 295–297
Export-ModuleMember cmdlet, 320–321
expressions
    subexpressions (see subexpressions)
    syntax for, 861–862

## F

-f operator, 142, 182–183, 194, 202–205, 220,
    878, 933–935
$false literal, 865
fan-out remoting, 750, 757
fDenyTSConnections property, 772
File class, 945
-File parameter, PowerShell.exe, 52, 84, 701
file sets, verifying integrity of, 630–631
FileInfo class, 562, 945
filenames
    auto-completion of, 56
    special characters in, 569–570
    very long, accessing, 582–583
-FilePath parameter, Invoke-Command cmdlet,
    789–790
files
    ACL for
        getting, 587–589
        setting, 589
    alternate data streams of, 584–586
    attributes of, modifying, 565–566
    binary files
        hexadecimal representation of, 277–280
        parsing, 267–269
    comparing, 629
    CSV files
        exporting command output to, 291–292
        importing data from, 292–293

loading into Excel, 295–297
    reading, 102, 103
deleting from FTP sites, 367
disk usage statistics for, 570–572
downloading from FTP site or website, 365–366
encoding of, 273, 275–277, 407
erasing contents from, 564–565
extended properties of, adding, 591–593
finding
    based on modification date, 563–564
    matching a pattern, 561, 566–569
hard links for, 593–595
hashes of, 574–576
importing and exporting structured data to, 289–291
IO classes for, 945
JSON data, converting to and from, 294–295
listing for a directory, 561–562
locked, moving or removing, 586–587
log files, parsing, 264–267
monitoring for new content, 572–573
moving, 579–580
reading all at once, 259, 260, 261
reading by lines, 101–105, 124, 259–261
reading by specified strings, 260
redirecting command output to, 79–81
removing, 577–578
renaming, 578–579
searching, 261–264
searching and replacing text, 271–274
temporary, creating, 270–271
transferring to remote computer, 790–793
unblocking, 583–584
uploading to FTP sites, 366–368
version information for, 573–574
XML files
    accessing properties of, 281–284
    converting command output to, 286–287
    modifying data in, 287–289
    XPath queries on, 284–286
ZIP archives, creating, 595–597
FileSystemSecurity class, 946
FileSystemWatcher class, 945
FillError event, 967
filter keyword, 351
-Filter parameter, Get-ChildItem cmdlet, 568
-Filter* parameters, Get-WinEvent cmdlet, 638–640

finally statement, 452, 454, 910
Find verb, 971
FindAll() method, [adsisearcher] type shortcut, 681, 685, 691, 693
FindOne() method, [adsisearcher] type shortcut, 681, 685, 693
[Float] type shortcut, 894
flow control statements (see comparison operators; conditional statements)
FlowLayoutPanel class, 946
folders (see directories)
fonts used in this book, xxii
for statement, 170–172, 228, 885
-Force parameter
    Enable-PSRemoting cmdlet, 753
    Format-List cmdlet, 447
    Restart-Computer cmdlet, 709
    Stop-Computer cmdlet, 709
    Suspend-Job cmdlet, 813
foreach statement, 101, 170–172, 228, 816–819, 886, 891
Foreach-Object cmdlet, 99–106, 170–172, 228, 311
Form class, 946
Format verb, 971
Format-Hex script, 277–280
Format-List cmdlet, 43, 118–119, 447, 552, 912
Format-String script, 203–205
Format-Table cmdlet, 120–122, 149, 912
Format-Wide cmdlet, 912
formatting
    command output, 911–913
    customizing for an object, 158–159
    dates and times, 194–196
    lists, 43, 118–119
    strings, 177, 181–183, 203–205
    tables, 120–122, 149
    views for, 159
formatting files, signing, 520–522
-Forward parameter, multiple cmdlets, 853
forward slash (/)
    division operator, 207, 874
    in XPath queries, 929
forward slash, equal (/=), division assignment operator, 208, 875
FTP sites
    deleting files from, 367
    downloading files from, 365–366
    uploading files to, 366–368

FtpWebRequest class, 947
functions
    calling, 307, 898, 899–902
    custom tags for, 343–345
    debugging (see debugging)
    exit code for, 313
    help for, adding, 340–342
    in personal profile script, 36
    internal to a module, accessing, 322–323
    invocation of, information about, 466–470
    Main function, 352–354
    maintaining state between calls of, 317–319
    packaging in modules, 314–317
    pipeline input to, accessing, 345–347
    pipeline-oriented filter for, 351
    pipeline-oriented regions for, 347–351
    removing, 37
    return value of, 307, 311–313
    scope of, 128–130
    writing, 306–308, 897

# G

GB constant (gigabytes), viii, 218, 868
-ge operator, 164, 235, 880
generic objects, creating instances of, 140–141
Get verb, 971
Get-Acl cmdlet, 588–589, 611
Get-AclMisconfiguration script, 588–589
Get-ADComputer cmdlet, 694
Get-ADOrganizationalUnit cmdlet, 675
Get-ADUser cmdlet, 681, 682
Get-AliasSuggestion script, 59
Get-AuthenticodeSignature cmdlet, 528
Get-Characteristics script, 267–269
Get-ChildItem cmdlet, 36, 124, 559, 561–562,
    563–564, 566, 567
Get-CimAssociatedInstance cmdlet, 741
Get-CimClass cmdlet, 741
Get-CimInstance cmdlet, 167, 660, 664, 714,
    729, 730–732, 743–747
Get-Clipboard script, 246–248
Get-Command cmdlet, xi, 43–45, 49, 750–751,
    900
Get-CommandForContext function, 344
Get-ComputerRestorePoint cmdlet, 706–708
Get-Content cmdlet, 101, 124, 259–261, 464,
    572
Get-Counter cmdlet, 488–490, 833
Get-Credential cmdlet, 531–532, 533

Get-Date cmdlet, 194–196, 243, 407, 563
Get-DetailedSystemInformation script, 718–720
Get-DiskUsage script, 570–572
Get-Event cmdlet, 850
Get-EventLog cmdlet, 633–643
Get-EventSubscriber cmdlet, 850
Get-FileEncoding script, 275–277
Get-FileHash script, 630–631
Get-Help cmdlet, xi, 45–47, 48, 49, 340
Get-History cmdlet, xii, 64, 65, 66
Get-Hotfix cmdlet, 710
Get-InstalledSoftware script, 704–705
Get-Item cmdlet, 561–562, 864
Get-ItemProperty cmdlet, 600–601
Get-Job cmdlet, 29
Get-Location cmdlet, 476–477, 560
Get-MachineStartupShutdownScript script,
    699–701
Get-Member cmdlet, xi, 143–145, 552, 893
Get-Module cmdlet, 84, 85
Get-PageUrls script, 380
Get-ParameterAlias script, 61–64
Get-PfxCertificate cmdlet, 542
Get-Process cmdlet, viii, 23, 117, 653, 654–655,
    806, 834
Get-PsCallStack cmdlet, 437
Get-PSDrive cmdlet, 570
Get-PsSnapin cmdlet, 84
Get-PSWorkflowData cmdlet, 824
Get-Random cmdlet, 248–250
Get-RemoteRegistryChildItem script, 614–622
Get-RemoteRegistryKeyProperty script, 614–
    622
Get-ScheduledJob cmdlet, 711
Get-ScheduledTask cmdlet, 713
Get-ScriptCoverage script, 440–442
Get-ScriptPerformanceProfile script, 456–461
Get-Service cmdlet, 663–665
Get-UserLogonLogoffScript script, 698–699
Get-Variable cmdlet, 864
Get-Verb cmdlet, 308–309, 971
Get-WinEvent cmdlet, 636, 638–640, 643
Get-WmiClassKeyProperty script, 736–737
Get-WmiObject cmdlet, 742–743
GetEnumerator() method, Hashtable class, 239–
    241
GetEnvironmentVariable() method, Environ-
    ment class, 465

GetFolderPath() method, Environment class, 473–475

GetNetworkCredential() method, PsCredential class, 530, 531

GetNewClosure() method, script blocks, 334–336

GetOwner() method, Win32_Process class, 659

GetRelated() method, WMI instances, 741

GetTempFilename() method, Path class, 270–271

gigabytes, GB constant for, viii, 218, 868

Global scope, 128, 129, 319, 478–479

Grant verb, 974

Graphical User Interface (GUI), 415–418

grep utility, 196

    (see also Select-String cmdlet)

Group Policy settings, 524

Group verb, 973

Group-Object cmdlet, 92–94, 641, 641

-gt operator, 235, 880

GUI (Graphical User Interface), 415–418

Guid class, 943

GZipStream class, 945

## H

hard links, 593–595

hash of a file, 574–576

[Hashtable] type shortcut, 894

hashtables, 872–872

    accessing items in, 872

    creating, 238–239, 872

    grouping command output in, 91–94

    importing and exporting to a file, 289–291

    parameters passed using, 336–337, 356

    sorting, 239–241

help

    on commands, 45–47

    online version of, 45

    searching text of, 49–50

    updating content of, 46, 47–48

    writing for user-defined commands, 340–342, 863–864, 908–909

here strings, 177, 180, 866

hexadecimal format of binary data, 277–280

hexadecimal numbers, 214–218, 220, 868

Hide verb, 972

history of commands (see command history)

HKEY_CURRENT_USER hive, Registry, 518

HKEY_LOCAL_MACHINE hive, Registry, 518

HNetCfg.FwMgr COM object, 703, 959

HNetCfg.HNetShare COM object, 959

HNetCfg.RsMgr COM object, 702

host application, accessing, 414–415

$host variable, 793

$host.Name property, 793

$host.UI.RawUI variable, 414–415

$host.UI.RawUI.WindowTitle variable, 37

hotfixes, determining if installed, 710

hotkeys, 914–916

HTMLFile COM object, 959

HTTP protocol, 391

HttpUtility class, 947

HttpWebRequest class, 947

## I

if statement, 165–167, 882

Image class, 946

imaginary numbers, 212, 869

implicit remoting, 750, 776–778

Import verb, 973

Import-ADUser script, 678–680, 684

Import-CliXml cmdlet, 65, 289–291, 293, 537–538, 644

Import-Counter cmdlet, 490

Import-Csv cmdlet, 102, 103, 292–293

Import-LocalizedData cmdlet, 410–412

Import-Module cmdlet, 82–83, 315, 317

Import-PSSession cmdlet, 776–778

-in operator, 880

-Include parameter, Get-ChildItem cmdlet, 562, 567

IndexOf() method, String class, 183

-InDisconnectedSession parameter, Invoke-Command cmdlet, 762

InfoMessage event, 967

InfoPath.Application COM object, 959

Initialize verb, 973

InlineScript keyword, 804, 814–816, 836, 890

-Input parameter, workflows, 820

$input variable, 345–347, 808, 906

.INPUTS help tag, 863, 909

Install verb, 974

InstalledFontsChanged event, 964

instance methods, 135, 891

    (see also methods)

instance properties, 137, 892

    (see also properties)

__InstanceCreationEvent class, 968

__InstanceDeletionEvent class, 968
__InstanceModificationEvent class, 968
instances of a class (see objects)
[Int] type shortcut, 894
Integrated Scripting Environment (see ISE)
Intellisense, customizing, 55
interactive remoting, 750, 754–756
interactive shell, iv–vii
  batch files, running, 19–22
  cmdlets
    default values for parameters, 26–28
    running, 23–23
  commands
    monitoring for changed results, 32–34
    running as background jobs, 28–31
  console window title for, 37
  customized, running commands from, 84–
    85
  customizing, 36–38, 914–916
  DOS commands, running, v
  executables
    running, 19–22
    troubleshooting, 24–26
  extending with additional commands, 82–83
  history of commands in (see command his-
    tory)
  hotkeys for, 914–916
  input mechanism used by, customizing, 39–
    40, 917
  jobs
    notification of completion, 35–35
    running and managing, 28–31
  launching, iv
  launching in specific location, 50–51
  prompt for, 36, 917
  recording transcript of session, 81
  running cmdlets or scripts outside of, 52–54
  saving state of, 85–87
  scripts, running, 19–22
  Tab completion, customizing, 55–59, 917
  text selection in, 914
  Unix commands in, v
  viewing colorized scripts in, 251–256
  window size, 914
  Windows tools in, vi
internationalization, 405–409
  capitalization, 192, 408
  date and time formatting, 195, 407
  of messages to user, 409–412

number formatting, 407
  sorting rules, 409
  testing script blocks for, 412–413
  text encoding, 407
Internet (see email; FTP sites; websites)
Internet Explorer
  configuration of, modifying, 608–609
  security zones, configuring, 606–608, 609
  UncAsIntranet setting, 519–520
Internet protocols, 391–395
InternetExplorer.Application COM object, 959
InvocationInfo property, $error variable, 447
InvocationStateChanged event, 966
invoke operator (&), 20, 21
Invoke verb, 974
Invoke-BinaryProcess script, 111–115
Invoke-CimMethod cmdlet, 660, 730, 731, 734–
  735, 744–747
Invoke-CmdScript script, 126–128
Invoke-Command cmdlet, 756–760, 784, 788–
  789, 789–790
Invoke-DebugWorkflow.log file, 833
Invoke-ElevatedCommand script, 534–536
Invoke-Expression cmdlet, 22, 827
Invoke-History cmdlet, 64, 65, 68–69
Invoke-Inline script, 503–504
Invoke-Item cmdlet, 295–297
Invoke-RemoteExpression script, 765–768
Invoke-RestMethod cmdlet, 294, 383–384
Invoke-ScriptBlock script, 309–311
Invoke-ScriptBlockClosure script, 334–336
Invoke-SqlCommand script, 485
Invoke-WebRequest cmdlet, 294, 365–366, 368–
  373, 376–379, 389–390
Invoke-WindowsApi script, 497
IO classes, 945
[IPAddress] type shortcut, 894
IP addresses
  listing, 723
  static, assigning, 721–722
ipconfig program, vi, 720–721, 723
-is operator, 881
ISE (Integrated Scripting Environment), 545–
  547
  Add-ons submenu, customizing, 555
  colors used in, customizing, 549–551
  console pane, 547
  Control-Space key, customizing, 55
  debugging, 547–549

editing personal profile script, 36
extending features of, 552–553
remote computer, connecting to, 551
scripting pane, 546
IsInRole() method, WindowsPrincipal class, 480–481
IsLeapYear() method, DateTime class, ix
-isnot operator, 881
isolation, 837
IsReadOnly property, files, 565
IXSSO.Query COM object, 959
IXSSO.Util COM object, 959

**J**

jagged arrays, 225–226, 870
-JobName parameter, workflows, 820
jobs
    event actions using, 848
    notification of completion, 35–35
    running and managing, 28–31
    scheduled, 710–714
    workflows running as, 803, 807
JobStateInfo property, workflows, 832
-join operator, 190–191, 879
Join verb, 972
Join-Path cmdlet, 477, 477, 560
JSON data, converting to and from, 294–295
JSON REST-based web APIs, 383–384

**K**

KB constant (kilobytes), 218, 868
Kerberos authentication, 780
keypress, reading, 398–399
Kill() method, Process object, viii
kilobytes, KB constant for, 218, 868

**L**

$lastExitCode variable, 444–445, 908
LastWriteTime property, files, 563–564
LDAP filter
    searching for Active Directory groups, 685
    searching for Active Directory user accounts, 681
    searching for computer accounts, 693
-le operator, 235, 880
left angle bracket (<), in regular expressions, 923

LegitCheckControl.LegitCheck COM object, 959
Length property, String object, viii
libraries, loading, 138, 895
life cycles, 974
-like operator, 164, 183, 233, 880
Limit verb, 973
Limit-EventLog cmdlet, 645, 648–650
.LINK help tag, 863, 909
Links property, web page results, 379
-List parameter, Get-EventLog cmdlet, 633–635, 635
lists, 223
    (see also arrays)
    comparing, 233
    creating, 223–225
    determining if item is in, 230
    filtering items in, 90–91, 94–96
    filtering items in, interactively, 96–98
    formatting, 43, 118–119
    sorting, 229–230
    statistical properties of, 213–214
    working with each item in, 99–101
literal (nonexpanding) strings, 176, 180–181, 866
-LiteralPath parameter, Get-ChildItem cmdlet, 569–570
LoadWithPartialName() method, Assembly class, 506
Local scope, 129
Local Security Policy MMC snap-in, 526
LocalMachine scope, 518
Lock verb, 972
locked files, moving or removing, 586–587
log files, parsing, 264–267
    (see also event logs)
Log Parser, Microsoft, 267
logical operators, 163–165, 875
logon and logoff scripts, 698–699, 701
[Long] type shortcut, 894
looping statements, 170–172, 228–229, 885–891
lowercase, converting strings to, 191–193
LowMemory event, 964
-lt operator, 235, 880

**M**

Machine scope, 465, 466
MailAddress class, 947
MailMessage class, 947

Main function, 352–354
MakeCab.MakeCab COM object, 960
ManagedBy property, [adsi] type shortcut, 687
ManagementClass class, 947
ManagementDateTimeConverter class, 948
ManagementEventWatcher class, 948
ManagementObject class, 947
ManagementObjectSearcher class, 947
MAPI.Session COM object, 960
Marshal class, 530, 944
-match operator, 164, 183, 185, 233, 881
math and calculations
    absolute value, 209
    administrative constants for, 218–219, 868
    arithmetic operators, 207–209, 873–875
    bases, converting numbers between, 219–
        221
    on binary numbers, 214–218
    calculated properties, 149, 571
    complex numbers, 212
    extremely large numbers, 211
    on hexadecimal numbers, 214–218
    imaginary numbers, 212
    order of operations, 208
    power operation, 209
    precedence, 208
    random numbers, generating, 248–250
    roots, 209, 210
    rounding results of, 208
    statistical properties of lists, 213–214
    trigonometric operations, 209, 211
    truncating results of, 208
    widening results of, 208
Math class, 209–212, 873, 943
-MaxEvents parameter, Get-WinEvent cmdlet,
    636
$MaximumErrorCount variable, 447
$MaximumHistoryCount variable, 64, 65
-MaxTriggerCount parameter, multiple cmdlets,
    852–853
MB constant (megabytes), viii, 218, 868
md function, 576–577
MD5 file hash, 574–576
Measure verb, 973
Measure-Command cmdlet, 244–245
Measure-Object cmdlet, 213–214
megabytes, MB constant for, viii, 218, 868
Member property, [adsi] type shortcut, 691

member types
    AliasProperty type, 157, 895
    CodeMethod type, 896
    CodeProperty type, 895
    NoteProperty type, 148, 895
    PropertySet type, 896
    ScriptMethod type, 157, 896
    ScriptProperty type, 156, 896
-MemberDefinition parameter, Add-Type
    cmdlet, 490, 495, 503–504
MemberOf property, [adsi] type shortcut, 690
members (see methods; properties)
MemoryStream class, 945
menu, displaying to user, 399–401
Merge verb, 973
-MergeErrorToOutput parameter, workflows,
    821
MessageQueue class, 949
Messenger.MessengerApp COM object, 960
methods, 134
    accessing, viii, 133, 135
    adding to a class, 154–158, 896
    adding to objects, 147–149, 895
    on explicitly-implemented interface, 892
    instance methods, invoking, 891
    listing for a class, 145–147
    listing for an object, 143–145
    preventing output to pipeline from, 312
    static methods
        accessing, 133, 134
        invoking, 891
        shortening class name for, 141–142
    WMI, invoking, 734–735
Microsoft Certificate Services, 525
Microsoft Log Parser, 267
Microsoft.FeedsManager COM object, 960
Microsoft.ISAdm COM object, 960
Microsoft.Update.AutoUpdate COM object, 960
Microsoft.Update.Installer COM object, 960
Microsoft.Update.Searcher COM object, 960
Microsoft.Update.Session COM object, 960
Microsoft.Update.SystemInfor COM object, 960
minus sign (-), subtraction operator, 207, 874
minus sign, equal (-=), subtraction assignment
    operator, 208, 875
mkdir function, 576–577
MMC20.Application COM object, 960
Mode property, files, 565
module manifest, 315

modules
    creating, 314–317
    detecting loaded modules, 84, 85
    exporting session commands into, 778
    exporting specific commands from, 320–321
    importing, 82–83, 315, 315, 778
    internal variables and functions of, accessing, 322–323
    loading, 317
    location of, 315, 315, 316
    maintaining state using, 317–319
    naming conventions for, 315
    parameters for, 317
    removing, cleanup tasks for, 324–325
    signing, 520–522
modulus assignment operator (%=), 208, 875
modulus operator (%), 207, 874
Monad project, xix
Mount verb, 973
Move verb, 972
Move-Item cmdlet, 579–580
Move-LockedFile script, 586–587
MoveFileEx API, 586–587
Msft_WmiProvider_OperationEvent class, 968
msinfo32.exe program, 718
MSScriptControl.ScriptControl COM object, 960
Msxm12.XSLTemplate COM object, 960
MTA (multi-threaded apartment) mode, 418–420
-MTA switch, PowerShell, 418
multi-threaded apartment (MTA) mode, 418–420
multidimensional arrays, 225–226, 870
multiplication assignment operator (*=), 208, 875
multiplication operator (*), 207, 874
$myInvocation variable, 467–472, 907

N

namespaces
    navigating, xv–xvi
    storing in a variable to shorten class name, 141–142
naming conventions
    cmdlets, 44, 971–974
    modules, 315
    scripts, 304–306, 308–309, 971–974
-ne operator, 234, 879

.NET Framework
    classes, 943–949
        defining or extending, 500–502
        shortening names for, 141–142
    delegates, 856–858
    documentation for, 145–147
    events, 856–858, 963–967
    objects, 133–137
    support for, viii, xii
.NET SDK libraries, accessing, 505–507
network
    classes for, 947
    connectivity, testing, 768–771
network adapters, properties of, 724–725
NetworkAddressChanged event, 965
NetworkAvailabilityChanged event, 965
NetworkCredential class, 531, 947
New verb, 972
New-ADOrganizationalUnit cmdlet, 674
New-ADUser cmdlet, 677
New-CommandWrapper script, 108, 109–110, 356
New-DynamicVariable script, 131–133
New-Event cmdlet, 849–852
New-EventLog cmdlet, 644–645
New-FilesystemHardLink script, 593–595
New-Item cmdlet, 36, 606–608, 864
New-ItemProperty cmdlet, 602–603, 606–608
New-ModuleManifest cmdlet, 315
New-Object cmdlet, 138–140, 894
    constructor parameter list for, 146
    creating ArrayLists, 224
    creating arrays, 224
    creating COM objects, 143, 484
    creating DLL objects, 505–507
    creating generic objects, 141
    creating multidimensional arrays, 226
New-PSDrive cmdlet, 319, 580–583
New-PSSession cmdlet, 755, 759
New-PSSessionConfigurationFile cmdlet, 794–798
New-PSSessionOption cmdlet, 785–787
New-PSWorkflowSession cmdlet, 808–811
New-ScheduledJobOption cmdlet, 713
New-ScheduledTaskTrigger cmdlet, 712
New-SelfSignedCertificate script, 522–523
New-Variable cmdlet, 865
New-WebserviceProxy cmdlet, 385–387
New-ZipFile script, 595–597

-Newest parameter, Get-EventLog cmdlet, 635–636

nonterminating errors, 448, 909

-NoProfile parameter, PowerShell.exe, 53

not operator, 931

not operator (!), 875

-not operator, 164, 875

-notcontains operator, 881

notepad tool, vii

NoteProperty member type, 148, 895

.NOTES help tag, 863, 909

-notin operator, 880

-notlike operator, 234, 881

-notmatch operator, 234, 881

NTLM authentication, 780

$null literal, 865

numbers, 867–869

    administrative numeric constants, 218–219, 868

    assigning, 867

    binary, 214–218, 220, 868

    complex, 212, 869

    formatting, 407, 933–935

    hexadecimal, 214–218, 220, 868

    imaginary, 212, 869

    octal, 220, 868

    type conversions of, 865

    very large, 869

## O

objects, viii–viii, 117

    COM objects, 959–961

        accessing, xiv, 895

        creating, 143, 483–484

    comparing, 627–631

    converting strings to, 196–200

    creating instances of, 138–140, 894

    current, referencing, ix

    custom, creating, 150–153

    formatting for, customizing, 158–159

    generic, creating instances of, 140–141

    in interactive shell, viii, xii

    for ISE, 552–553

    listing members of, 143–145

    methods of (see methods)

    .NET objects, 133–137

    properties of (see properties)

    in scripts, xii

    viewing in interactive grid, 72–79

octal numbers, 220, 868

OdbcCommand class, 948

OdbcConnection class, 948

OdbcDataAdapter class, 948

-Once parameter, New-ScheduledTaskTrigger cmdlet, 712

OnChange event, 967

OnRemove event, modules, 324–325

Open verb, 972

OpenReadCompleted event, 964

OpenWriteCompleted event, 964

operating system requirements, xxii

operators

    arithmetic operators, 207–209, 873–875

    auto-completion of, 56

    binary operators, 875–877

    case-sensitivity of, 165

    comparison operators, 163–165, 879–881

    logical operators, 163–165, 875–875

    preceded by "c", 165

or operator, 931

-or operator, 875

OrderedDictionary class, 944

OU (organizational unit)

    children of, listing, 676

    creating, 673–674

    deleting, 675

    listing users in, 691

    properties of

        listing, 674

        modifying, 675–675

Out verb, 973

Out-Default cmdlet, 108

Out-File cmdlet, 79–81

Out-GridView cmdlet, 70, 96, 416–418

Out-Host cmdlet, 403

Out-String cmdlet, 69, 185

-OutBuffer parameter, as standard parameter, 327

-OutFile parameter, Invoke-WebRequest cmdlet, 365

Outlook.Application COM object, 960

OutlookExpress.MessageList COM object, 960

-OutputAssembly parameter, Add-Type cmdlet, 502

OutputDataReceived event, 965

.OUTPUTS help tag, 863, 909

-OutVariable parameter, as standard parameter, 327

# P

P/Invoke Windows API definitions, 497
PaletteChanged event, 964
parallel statement, 816–819, 890
param statement, 325–328, 784
[Parameter() attribute], 330–334
[Parameter()] attribute, 903
.PARAMETER help tag, 863, 909
parameters
    argument values for
        accessing, 325–329
        specifying, 21–22
        validating, 330–334
    automatic, 338
    default values for, 26–28
    dynamic, 336–337, 356, 540
    environment variables as values for, 26
    errors from, troubleshooting, 24–26
    for modules, 317
    positional, vii
    script blocks as, 334–336
    splatting, 337, 356
    standard parameters, 327
    variables for, 22
    verbatim argument marker (--%) for, 25
parentheses ((…))
    enclosing New-Object call, 138
    in regular expressions, 922
    specifying precedence, 208, 861
ParentProcessId property, Win32_Process class, 660–661
ParsedHtml property, web page results, 373–375
PasswordDeriveBytes class, 946
passwords (see user credentials)
Path class, 945
-Path parameter, Add-Type cmdlet, 502, 505–507
-Path parameter, Get-ChildItem cmdlet, 567
$PATH variable, 465
paths
    building from subpaths, 477
    common system paths, location of, 473–475
    of current location, determining, 476–477, 560
    of current script, determining, 471–472
    modifying, 465
    relative path navigation, 355
    UNC paths, running scripts from, 519–520
    very long, accessing, 582–583

patterns (see regular expressions)
pause command, 172–174
PB constant (petabytes), 218, 868
percent sign (%), modulus operator, 207, 874
percent sign, equal (%=), modulus assignment operator, 208, 875
performance counters, 488–490, 833
performance of scripts, 456–461
Perl scripts, running in interactive shell, 19–22
permissions
    for administrator (see administrator rights)
    for Remoting, 772–774
    Windows enforcing, 515
-Persist parameter, New-PSDrive cmdlet, 581, 582–583
PersistentState module, 318
personal profile script, 36–38, 916
petabytes, PB constant for, 218
PinChanged event, 965
Ping verb, 973
ping.exe program, 769
pipeline character (|), ix, 89
pipelines, ix, 89–90
    functions using, filter for, 351
    input from, accessing, 345–347, 906
    intercepting stages of, 108
    output from, 907
        binary, redirecting, 111–115
        capturing in ArrayList, 109–110
        filtering, 90–91, 94–98
        grouping in hashtables, 91–94
        storing in a variable, 122–123
    scripts processing, regions for, 347–351
    steppable, 356
    working with list items, 99–106
plus sign (+)
    addition operator, 207, 874
    combining arrays, 231
    in regular expressions, 921, 925
plus sign, equal (+=), addition assignment operator, 208, 875
polling, 845
Pop verb, 972
Pop-Location cmdlet, 600
POP3 protocol, 391
PoshCode, 83
positional breakpoints, 428
positional parameters, for cmdlets, vii
PostCommandLookupAction property, 42, 918

pound sign (#)
    auto-completion of history commands, 55, 68, 68
    preceding comments, 862
    in regular expressions, 926
Pow() method, Match class, 209
PowerModeChanged event, 964
PowerPoint.Application COM object, 960
powers
    administrative constants based on, 219
    calculating, 209
PowerShell, iii–iv
    cmdlets (see cmdlets)
    commands (see commands)
    functions (see functions)
    history of, xix
    installing, xxii
    interactive shell (see interactive shell)
    scripts (see scripts)
    version of, determining, 479–480
PowerShell Community Extensions, 83
PowerShell Hosting features, 510–513
PowerShell Remoting (see Remoting)
PowerShell SDK, 508, 511
[PowerShell] type shortcut, 894
PowerShell.exe, iv, 414
    -Command parameter, 52, 84, 701
    -EncodedCommand parameter, 54
    -ExecutionPolicy parameter, 54, 517, 701–701
    -File parameter, 52, 84, 701–701
    -NoProfile parameter, 53
    -PSConsoleFile parameter, 84
    running based on specific events, 647–648
    -WindowStyle parameter, 53
PowerShell.Exiting event, 85, 87, 851
PreCommandLookupAction property, 41, 918
print queues
    managing, 717–718
    statistics for, listing, 715–717
printers, information about, 714
Private scope, 129
process keyword, 347–351, 808, 906
Process Monitor, 622–625
Process object, viii, 117, 654, 944
Process scope, 517
process statement, 898
processes, 653
    currently running, listing, 654–655

debugging, 661–662
    owner of, determining, 659
    parent of, determining, 660–661
    starting, 655–657
    starting as another user, 532–534
    stopping, 658–659
ProcessStartInfo object, 656
$profile variable, 36–38, 916
profiles (see personal profile script)
programs (see executables)
progress output for commands, 404–405, 450–451, 830, 832
$progressPreference variable, 451
prompt function, 36, 37, 60, 917
properties, 134
    accessing, 133, 137
    adding to a class, 154–158, 896
    adding to objects, 147–149, 895
    calculated properties, 149, 571
    displaying as a list, 118–119
    displaying as a table, 120–122
    instance properties, 892
    listing for a class, 145–147
    listing for an object, 143–145
    static properties, 133, 136, 892
PropertySet member type, 896
Protect verb, 974
providers, xv–xvi
    AD provider (AD: drive), 669, 676
    environment provider (env: drive), 123, 124, 463, 464
proxy command APIs, 356
ps command, 653
.ps1 file extension, 19, 303, 897
    (see also scripts)
-PSActionRetryCount parameter, workflows, 821
-PSActionRetryIntervalSec parameter, workflows, 821
-PSActionRunningTimeoutSec parameter, workflows, 821
-PSAllowRedirection parameter, workflows, 821
-PSApplicationName parameter, workflows, 821
-PSAuthentication parameter, workflows, 821
-PSAuthenticationLevel parameter, workflows, 821
$PSBoundParameters variable, 337
-PSCertificateThumbprint parameter, workflows, 821

$psCmdlet variable, 338–340

$PSCommandPath variable, 467–468, 471–472

-PSComputerName parameter, workflows, 821

PSComputerName property, Invoke-Command cmdlet, 758

-PSConfigurationName parameter, workflows, 821

-PSConnectionRetryCount parameter, workflows, 821

-PSConnectionRetryIntervalSec parameter, workflows, 821

-PSConnectionUri parameter, workflows, 822

-PSConsoleFile parameter, PowerShell.exe, 84

PSConsoleHostReadLine function, 39–40, 917

PsCredential class, 530, 531, 532, 537

-PSCredential parameter, workflows, 822

PSCustomObject class, 150–153

[PSCustomObject] type shortcut, 894

-PSDebug parameter, workflows, 822

$PSDebugContext variable, 435–437

PSDefaultParameterValues hashtable, 26, 27, 902

PSDiagnostics module, 832

-PSDisableSerialization parameter, workflows, 822

-PSElapsedTimeoutSec parameter, workflows, 822

-PSError parameter, workflows, 822

$psISE variable, 552–553

$psISE.CurrentPowerShellTab.AddOnsMenu.Submenus variable, 555

$psISE.Options variable, 549–551

.psm1 file extension, 314

$PSModuleAutoLoadingPreference variable, 82

[PSModuleInfo] type shortcut, 894

$PSModulePath variable, 83, 315

PSObject class, 943

[PSObject] type shortcut, 894

-PSParameterCollection parameter, workflows, 822

-PSPersist parameter, workflows, 822

$PSPersistPreference variable, 811, 813

-PSPort parameter, workflows, 823

-PSPrivateMetadata parameter, workflows, 823

-PSProgress parameter, workflows, 823

-PSProgressMessage parameter, workflows, 823

PSRemotingActivity class, 836

-PSRemotingBehavior parameter, workflows, 823

-PSRequiredModules parameter, workflows, 823

-PSRunningTimeoutSec parameter, workflows, 823

$PSScriptRoot variable, 467–468, 472–473

-PSSessionOption parameter, workflows, 823

$PSSessionOption variable, 785–787

-PSUSeSsi parameter, workflows, 824

-PSVerbose parameter, workflows, 824

$PSVersionTable variable, 479–480

-PSWarning parameter, workflows, 824

Publish verb, 973

Publisher.Application COM object, 960

Push verb, 972

Push-Location cmdlet, vi, 600

Put() method, [adsi] type shortcut, 675, 682, 688

$pwd variable, 476

## Q

-Query parameter, Set-CimInstance cmdlet, 733

question mark (?), in regular expressions, 921, 922, 925, 926

-Quiet parameter, Test-Connection cmdlet, 771

## R

radians, converting to degrees, 211

Random class, 943

random numbers, generating, 248–250

RDS.DataSpace COM object, 960

Read verb, 972

Read-Host cmdlet, 398, 529–530

ReadAllLines() method, File class, 259

ReadAllText() method, File class, 259

ReadKey() method, console, 172–174, 398–399

Receive verb, 972

Receive-Job cmdlet, 29, 810, 848

Receive-PSSession cmdlet, 762

-Recurse parameter, Get-ChildItem cmdlet, 561

redirection operators, 79

Redo verb, 972

[Ref] type shortcut, 894

ReflectionOnlyAssemblyResolve event, 963

reg.exe program, 599

Regex class, 943

[Regex] type shortcut, 894

Register verb, 974

Register-CimIndicationEvent cmdlet, 846, 850

Register-EngineEvent cmdlet, 846, 849–852

Register-ObjectEvent cmdlet, 846, 850

Register-PSSessionConfiguration cmdlet, 794–798

Register-ScheduledJob cmdlet, 711–714

Register-TemporaryEvent cmdlet, 35

Registry, 599
    CurrentUser scope settings, 518
    events related to, 968
    keys in
        ACL for, 611–614
        adding, 606–608
        adding values to, 602–603
        determining for a program, 622–625
        for Internet Explorer, 606–609
        modifying multiple keys in a transaction, 604–606
        modifying values of, 601–602, 608–609
        removing, 603–604, 607
        removing values of, 601–602
        viewing, 600–601
    LocalMachine scope settings, 518
    navigating, xv–xvi, 599–600
    on remote computer, working with, 614–622
    searching, 609–611
    transactions used with, 838

Registry class, 945

Registry Editor, 599

RegistryEvent class, 968

RegistryKey class, 945

RegistryKeyChangeEvent class, 968

RegistrySecurity class, 946

RegistryTreeChangeEvent class, 969

RegistryValueChangeEvent class, 969

regular expressions, 919–927
    converting case of strings using, 192
    finding files based on, 566–569
    replacing text in files using, 273
    replacing text in strings using, 186–187
    searching files using, 261, 262–263
    searching strings using, 183, 184
    splitting strings using, 187, 188

relative path navigation, 355

remote computers
    commands, invoking on, 750–751, 765–768
    connecting to, 551
    DHCP lease, renewing, 721
    enabling PowerShell Remoting on, 753
    event logs on, accessing, 650–651
    forwarding events from, 853–854
    hotfixes, determining if installed on, 710
    IP addresses, listing, 723
    Registry on, working with, 614–622
    renaming, 697
    services on
        configuring, 667
        listing, 665

Remote Desktop, 615, 772

Remote Management Users group, 772–774

Remote Registry service, 614

RemoteSigned execution policy, 517

Remoting, 749–750
    advanced configuration for, 785–787
    commands not requiring, 750–751, 765–768
    connecting to remote session, 754–756
    disconnecting from remote sessions, 760–762
    enabling for a computer, 752–753
    enabling for workgroup computers, 774–776
    enabling remotely, 763–765
    fan-out remoting, 750, 757
    features enabled by default, 749
    full network access for, 779–783
    implicit remoting, 750, 776–778
    interactive remoting, 750, 754–756
    invoking a command on multiple computers, 787–789
    invoking a commands on a remote computer, 756–760
    network resources used by, 755, 756, 760, 763
    passing variables to remote sessions, 783–785
    reconnecting to remote sessions, 760–762
    running local script on remote computer, 789–790
    scripts running on remote computer, determining, 793
    security issues regarding, 749, 775
    task-specific endpoint for, 794–798
    transferring files to remote computer, 790–793
    user permissions for, 772–774

Remove verb, 972

Remove() method, [adsi] type shortcut, 689

Remove-ADOrganizationalUnit cmdlet, 676

Remove-Computer cmdlet, 696–697

Remove-EventLog cmdlet, 644–645

Remove-Item cmdlet, 37, 542, 577–578, 603–604, 607

Remove-ItemProperty cmdlet, 601–602
Remove-Job cmdlet, 29
Remove-PsBreakpoint cmdlet, 430
Remove-PSDrive cmdlet, 581
Rename verb, 972
Rename-Computer cmdlet, 697
Rename-Item cmdlet, 578–579
Renamed event, 965
Repair verb, 973
repetitive text, generating, 202–205
-replace operator, 186–187, 196, 877
Replace() method, String class, 185, 202
reports, creating using streaming, 200–202
Request verb, 974
-RequireNetwork parameter, New-
    ScheduledJobOption cmdlet, 713
#requires statement, 828–830
Reset verb, 972
Resolve verb, 973
Resolve-Error script, 448–449
Resolve-Path cmdlet, 477, 560
ResourceResolve event, 963
REST-based web APIs, 383–384
Restart verb, 974
Restart-Computer cmdlet, 696, 697, 708–709
Restart-Service cmdlet, 665
restore points, managing, 706–708
Restore verb, 973
Restore-Computer cmdlet, 706–708
Restricted execution policy, 517
restricted runspaces, 794
-Result parameter, workflows, 824
Resume verb, 974
Resume-Job cmdlet, 810, 811–814
Resume-Service cmdlet, 665
retention policy for event logs, 648–650
return statement, 312, 907
Revoke verb, 974
right angle bracket (>)
    in redirection operators, 79, 81, 913
    in regular expressions, 923
-RollbackPreference parameter, Start-
    Transaction cmdlet, 841–843
root function, 210
RowUpdated event, 967
RowUpdating event, 967
[Runspace] type shortcut, 894
[RunspaceFactory] type shortcut, 894

## S

SAPI.SpVoice COM object, 960
Save verb, 973
scheduled jobs, 710–714
scheduled tasks, 713
schtasks.exe program, 647–648, 714
$SCOPE: syntax, 864
scoping, 128–130, 864
    AllScope scope, 129
    CurrentUser scope, 518
    of drives, 319
    of execution policy, 517
    Global scope, 128, 129, 319, 478–479
    Local scope, 129
    LocalMachine scope, 518
    Machine scope, 465, 466
    Private scope, 129
    Process scope, 517
    Script scope, 128, 129, 318, 353
    of Set-StrictMode cmdlet, 424
    User scope, 465, 466
    of variables in script block parameters, 334–
        336
    of WMI instances, 741
screen scraping, 368–373
script blocks
    calling, 899, 899–902
    custom tags for, 343–345
    as default parameter value, 27
    invocation of, information about, 466–470
    as parameters, 334–336
    pipeline input to, accessing, 345–347
    pipeline-oriented regions for, 347–351
    testing with other culture settings, 412–413
    writing, 309–311, 899
Script scope, 128, 129, 318, 353
-ScriptBlock parameter, Invoke-Command
    cmdlet, 790
[ScriptBlock] type shortcut, 894
scripting pane, ISE, 546
Scripting.FileSystemObject COM object, 960
Scripting.Signer COM object, 960
Scriptlet.TypeLib COM object, 960
ScriptMethod member type, 157, 896
ScriptProperty member type, 156, 896
ScriptPW.Password COM object, 960
scripts
    Active Directory scripts, testing, 670–672
    ad hoc development of, xii

code coverage of, analyzing, 440–442
colorized, viewing in interactive shell, 251–256
commands in, xii
compared to workflows, 805–808
creating from command history, 66–67
debugging (see debugging)
enabling execution of, 304, 516–519, 899
exit code for, 313
filename of, determining, 471–472
help for, adding, 340–342
invocation of, information about, 466–470
location of, determining, 471–473
logon and logoff scripts, 698–699, 701
maintaining state between calls of, 317–319
naming conventions for, 304–306, 308–309, 971–974
parsing and interpreting, 297–300
performance of, analyzing, 456–461
personal profile script, 36–38
pipeline input to, accessing, 345–347
pipeline-oriented regions for, 347–351
return value of, 311–313
running, 304, 899–902
running based on specific event log entries, 646–648
running in interactive shell, 19–22
running outside PowerShell, 52–54
running with elevated privileges, 534–536
signing, 520–522
snippets of, inserting, 553–555
software restriction policies for, 526–527
startup and shutdown scripts, 699–701
structure of, Main function for, 352–354
VBScripts
    converting to PowerShell, 702
    running in interactive shell, 19–22
in workflows, 814–816
writing, 303–306, 897
writing portions in C#, 503–504
SDDL (Security Descriptor Definition Language, 543
Search verb, 972
Search-Help script, 49–50
Search-Registry script, 609–611
Search-StartMenu script, 250–251
Search-WmiNamespace script, 737–740
searching
    arrays, 232, 235

files, 261–264, 271–274
    Registry, 609–611
    strings, 183–185
SecureString class, 529–530, 531, 946
security, 515
    certificate store
        accessing, 539–540
        adding and removing certificates, 542
        navigating, xvi
        searching, 540–541
    classes for, 946
    digital signatures, verifying, 527–529
    enterprise-wide, 523–525
    execution policy for scripts, 516–519
    Internet-based scripts, removing warnings
        for, 519–520
    for Remoting, 749, 775
    running commands with elevated privileges,
        534–536
    SDDL for, 543
    self-signed certificate, creating, 522–523
    signing scripts, 520–522
    software restriction policies, 526–527
    standard PowerShell verbs for, 974
    starting processes as another user, 532–534
    user credentials, storing on disk, 537–538
    of user's sensitive data, 529–532
    Windows features for, 515
security descriptor (see ACL (Access Control
    List))
Security Descriptor Definition Language
    (SDDL), 543
security group, Active Directory
    adding users to, 688–689
    creating, 683–685
    listing members of, 691
    owner of, determining, 687
    properties of
        listing, 686–687
        modifying, 688
    removing users from, 689
    searching for, 685–686
security zones, Internet Explorer, 606–608, 609
sed utility, 196
    (see also -replace operator)
Select verb, 972
Select-FilteredObject script, 96–98
Select-Object cmdlet, 121, 149
Select-String cmdlet, 69, 196, 261–264

Select-TextOutput script, 69
Select-Xml cmdlet, 284–286
self-signed certificate, 522–523
Send verb, 972
Send-File script, 790–793
Send-MailMessage cmdlet, 388–389
Send-TcpRequest script, 770
$sender variable, 848
sequence statement, 890
SerialPort class, 947
ServiceController object, 664
services, 663
    configuring, 666
    currently running, listing, 663–665
    managing, 665–666
    stopping, 665–666
SessionEnded event, 964
SessionEnding event, 964
SessionSwitch event, 964
-SessionVariable parameter, Invoke-
    WebRequest cmdlet, 376–379
Set verb, 972
Set-Acl cmdlet, 590, 612–614
Set-ADOrganizationalUnit cmdlet, 675
Set-Alias cmdlet, 36
Set-AuthenticodeSignature cmdlet, 520–522,
    539
Set-CimInstance cmdlet, 732–734
Set-Clipboard script, 246–248
Set-Content cmdlet, 464, 585
Set-ExecutionPolicy cmdlet, 516–519
Set-ItemProperty cmdlet, 601–602, 608–609
Set-Location cmdlet, 51, 599–600
Set-NetConnectionProfile cmdlet, 753
Set-PsBreakpoint cmdlet, 428–430, 432–434
Set-PsBreakpointLastError script, 432
Set-PsDebug cmdlet, 425–427
Set-PSSessionConfiguration cmdlet, 773–774
Set-PSWorkflowData activity, 825
Set-RemoteRegistryKeyProperty script, 614–622
Set-ScheduledJob cmdlet, 713
Set-Service cmdlet, 666
Set-StrictMode cmdlet, 423–424
Set-WmiInstance cmdlet, 734
SetEnvironmentVariable() method, Environ-
    ment class, 465, 466
SetInfo() method, [adsi] type shortcut, 675, 682,
    688
SetPassword() method, [adsi] type shortcut, 683

SHA1 class, 946
SHA1 file hash, 574–576
SHA256 file hash, 574–576
SharePoint.OpenDocuments COM object, 960
shell associations, 656
Shell.Application COM object, 960
Shell.LocalMachine COM object, 960
Shell.User COM object, 960
-shl operator, 877
Show verb, 972
Show-ColorizedContent script, 251–256
Show-EventLog cmdlet, 634
Show-Object script, 72–79
Show-UI project, 416
-shr operator, 877
shutdown scripts, 699–701
signtool.exe program, 521
Sin() method, Math class, 209
single quote ('), in regular expressions, 925
single quotes ('…')
    enclosing commands containing special
        characters, 20, 24
    enclosing literal strings, 176, 180, 866
single-threaded apartment (STA) mode, 419
Skip verb, 972
-SkipNetworkProfileCheck parameter, Enable-
    PSRemoting cmdlet, 753
SMTP protocol, 391
SmtpClient class, 947
SmtpMail class, 391
snapins, 82, 84, 84
snippets, 553–555
software restriction policies, 526–527
Sort() method, Array class, 230
Sort-Object cmdlet, 229–230, 239–241
sorting rules, 409
SoundPlayer class, 944
special characters
    in commands, 24
    executables using, problems with, 24–26
    in filenames, 569–570
    in commands, 20
    in strings, 178–179
special variable syntax, 125
splatting, 337, 356
-split operator, 187–189, 878
Split verb, 972
Split-Path cmdlet, 472

SQL
    classes for, 948
    events related to, 967
    querying data source using, 485–487
SqlCommand class, 948
SqlConnection class, 948
SqlDataAdapter class, 948
SQLDMO.SQLServer COM object, 960
SqlRowsCopied event, 967
Sqrt() method, Math class, 209
square brackets ([…])
    enclosing array indexes, 227, 870
    enclosing class name, 133, 134, 136
    enclosing constraints, 864
    enclosing generic parameters, 141
    enclosing type name, 864
    in regular expressions, 919
    in XPath queries, 931
square root, 209
STA (single-threaded apartment) mode, 419
standard PowerShell verbs, 308–309
Start menu, searching, 250–251
Start verb, 974
Start() method, Process class, 656, 657
Start-Job cmdlet, 29
Start-Process cmdlet, 533, 655–657
Start-ProcessAsUser script, 533–534
Start-Sleep cmdlet, 172–174
Start-Transaction cmdlet, 604–606, 838, 840, 841–843
Start-Transcript cmdlet, 81
startup scripts, 699–701
state, maintainting, 317–319
StateChange event, 967
StateChanged event, 966, 967
StatementCompleted event, 967
static methods, 891
    (see also methods)
    accessing, 133, 134
    shortening class name for, 141–142
static properties, 133, 136, 892
    (see also properties)
statistical properties of lists, 213–214
-Step parameter, Set-PsDebug cmdlet, 425
Step verb, 972
steppable pipelines, 356
SteppablePipeline objects, 356
Stop verb, 974
Stop-Computer cmdlet, 708–709

Stop-Process cmdlet, viii, 658–659
Stop-Service cmdlet, 665–666
Stop-Transcript cmdlet, 81
Stopwatch class, 944
Stream class, 945
-Stream parameter, for multiple cmdlets, 584–586
streaming, 200–202
StreamReader class, 269, 945
StreamWriter class, 945
strict mode, 423–424
String class, 944
StringBuilder class, 200–202, 944
StringInfo class, 408
StringReader class, 945
strings, 865–867
    case of, converting, 191–193
    combining, 190–191
    concatenating, 182
    converting to objects, 196–200
    creating, 175–177
    dynamic information in, 179–180
    escape sequences for, 867
    expanding, 176, 179–180, 866
    formatted items in, 181–183
    formatting, 177, 203–205, 933–935
    here strings, 177, 866
    literal (nonexpanding), 176, 180–181, 866
    multiline, 177
    parsing, 196–200
    replacing text in, 185–187
    searching, 183–185
    special characters in, escaping, 178–179
    splitting, 187–189
    trimming, 193
StringWriter class, 945
structured commands (see cmdlets)
subexpressions in strings, evaluating, 179–180
Submit verb, 974
subtraction assignment operator (-=), 208, 875
subtraction operator (-), 207, 874
-SupportEvent parameter, multiple cmdlets, 850
Suspend verb, 974
Suspend-Job cmdlet, 810, 811–814
Suspend-Service cmdlet, 665
Suspend-Workflow cmdlet, 807, 825–827
switch statement, 167–170, 808, 883
[Switch] type shortcut, 894
Switch verb, 972

Sync verb, 973
synonyms, for PowerShell verbs, 971–974
.SYNOPSIS help tag, 863, 908
Sysinternals Process Monitor, 622–625
system paths
    common, location of, 473–475
    modifying, 465
    tools directory in, 21
system requirements, xxii
[System.ComponentModel.Description()] attribute, 343
System.Diagnostics.Process object (see Process object)
%SYSTEMROOT% variable, 481

**T**

Tab completion, vii, 55–59, 68, 917
TabExpansion2 function, 55–59
tables, formatting, 120–122, 149
Tan() method, Math class, 209
tasks, scheduled (see scheduled tasks)
TB constant (terabytes), 218, 868
TCP (Transmission Control Protocol), 391–395
TcpClient class, 947
Technet Script Center Gallery, 83
Telnet protocol, 391
temporary files, 270–271
terabytes, TB constant for, 218, 868
terminating errors, 448, 910
Test verb, 974
Test-Connection cmdlet, 768–771
text (see commands: output from; files; strings)
TextReader class, 945
TextWriter class, 945
Thread class, 944
threading
    events related to, 969
    MTA mode, 418–420
-ThrottleLimit parameter
    Get-WmiObject cmdlet, 742–743
    Invoke-Command cmdlet, 788–789
    Restart-Computer cmdlet, 709
    Stop-Computer cmdlet, 709
throw statement, 456, 910
TimeChanged event, 964
times (see dates and times)
ToInt32() method, Convert class, 215, 220
Tokenizer API, 297, 298, 440–442
ToLower() method, String class, 191–193

ToString() method, 194, 215, 220
ToUpper() method, String class, 191–193
-Trace parameter, Set-PsDebug cmdlet, 425
Trace verb, 974
Trace-Command cmdlet, 25
tracing script execution, 424–427
TransactedString object, 839–841
Transaction class, 949
transactions, 837–843
    discarding changes made in, 839, 841–843
    ending, 839, 841
    error recovery in, 841–843
    Registry modifications using, 604–606
    starting, 838, 840
transcript of interactive shell session, 81
Transmission Control Protocol (TCP), 391–395
trap statement, 452, 455, 808, 911
trigonometric operations, 209, 211
Trim() method, String class, 193
TripleDESCryptoServiceProvider class, 946
$true literal, 865
trunc function, 209
Trusted Subsystem, 795
TrustedHosts collection, 774–776
try statement, 452, 454, 910
Type class, 944
type conversion operator, 878
type shortcuts, 893
-TypeDefinition parameter, Add-Type cmdlet, 500–502
TypeResolve event, 963
types (see classes)

**U**

unary comma operator (,), 145
Unblock verb, 974
Unblock-File cmdlet, 520, 583–584
UNC paths, running scripts from, 519–520
UncAsIntranet setting, Internet Explorer, 519–520
underscore (_), in regular expressions, 925
Undo-Transaction cmdlet, 839, 841
UnhandledException event, 963
Unicode, 407
Uninstall verb, 974
Unix commands, running in interactive shell, v
Unlock verb, 972
Unprotect verb, 974
Unpublish verb, 973

Unregister verb, 974
Unregister-ScheduledJob cmdlet, 711
Unrestricted execution policy, 517
-Unsecure parameter, Add-Computer cmdlet, 696
Update verb, 973
Update-FormatData cmdlet, 159, 913
Update-Help cmdlet, 47–48
Update-TypeData cmdlet, 154–158, 896
UploadDataCompleted event, 964
UploadFileCompleted event, 964
UploadProgressChanged event, 965
UploadStringCompleted event, 964
UploadValues Completed event, 965
uppercase, converting strings to, 191–193
Uri class, 947
URLs, extracting from web pages, 379–382
Use verb, 972
Use-Culture script, 412–413
Use-Transaction cmdlet, 839–841
-UseDefaultInput parameter, workflows, 824
user accounts, Active Directory
    adding users to groups, 688–689
    creating, 677
    importing, 678–680
    listing for an organizational unit, 691
    listing group memberships of, 690
    properties of
        listing, 681
        modifying, 682
    removing users from, 689
    searching for, 680
user credentials
    requesting securely, 531–532
    starting processes as another user, 532–534
    storing on disk, 537–538
user interaction
    GUI for, 415–418
    host application, accessing, 414–415
    input mechanism in interactive shell, customizing, 39–40
    internationalization of, 405–413
    menu for user, displaying, 399–401
    messages for user, displaying, 401–404, 409–412
    progress updates, displaying, 404–405
    reading user input
        by keypress, 398–399
        by line, 397–398

User scope, 465, 466
-UserAgent parameter, Invoke-WebRequest cmdlet, 373
UserPreferenceChanged event, 964
UserPreferenceChanging event, 964
users
    administrator (see administrator rights)
    logon and logoff scripts for, 698–699, 701–701
    permissions for (see permissions)
    profile for (see personal profile script)
-UseTransaction parameter, multiple cmdlets, 838
$USING: variable prefix, 783, 814–816, 824

## V

[ValidateCount()] attribute, 333, 905
[ValidateLength()] attribute, 333, 905
[ValidateNotNull()] attribute, 334, 906
[ValidateNotNullOrEmpty()] attribute, 334, 906
[ValidatePattern()] attribute, 333, 905
[ValidateRange()] attribute, 333, 905
[ValidateScript()] attribute, 333, 905
[ValidateSet()] attribute, 333, 906
variables
    assigning, 864
    auto-completion of, 56
    automatic (see automatic variables)
    at breakpoints, examining, 434–437
    breakpoints on, 429
    complex names of, escaping, 125
    constraints for, 864
    dollar sign ($) preceding, viii
    dynamic, 130–133
    environment variables
        accessing, 123–126, 463–465
        as command parameter values, 26
        listing, 123
        retaining changes made in batch files, 126–128
    for parameters, 22
    global (see Global scope)
    in script block parameters, 334–336
    internal to a module, accessing, 322–323
    namespaces stored in, to shorten class name, 141–142
    nonexisting, warnings regarding, 423
    passing to remote sessions, 783–785
    scope of, 128–130, 864

special variable syntax, 125
storing command output in, 122–123
in strings, substitution of, 179–180
syntax for, 864–865
VBScripts, 727
converting to PowerShell, 702
running in interactive shell, 19–22
WMI, converting to PowerShell, 743–747
verb-noun pattern, for cmdlets, vii
verbatim argument marker (--%), 24, 25
verbose output for commands, 450–451
-Verbose parameter
as standard parameter, 327, 451
workflows, 824
$verbosePreference variable, 451
verbs, 308–309, 971–974
version information for files, 573–574
VersionInfo property, files, 573–574
vertical bar (|)
pipeline character, ix, 89
in regular expressions, 925
views, for formatting, 159
Vim.Application COM object, 960

**W**

-Wait parameter
Get-Content cmdlet, 572
*Job cmdlets, 813
Restart-Computer cmdlet, 709
Wait verb, 974
Wait-Job cmdlet, 29
Wait-Process cmdlet, 659
-WarningAction parameter
as standard parameter, 327
workflows, 824
$warningPreference variable, 452, 453
warnings (see debugging)
-WarningVariable parameter, as standard parameter, 327
Watch verb, 972
Watch-Command cmdlet, 32–34
Watch-DebugExpression script, 437–439
wbemtest.exe program, 727
web services, connecting to, 385–387
WebClient class, 366, 367, 368, 391, 947
WebRequest class, 367
-WebSession parameter, Invoke-WebRequest cmdlet, 376–379

website resources
Active Directory module, 670
administrative templates, 524
code examples, xxiii
commands and scripts to extend PowerShell, 83
community implementation of PSConsole-HostReadLine function, 40
converting VBScript to PowerShell, 702
"How to Create a Windows PowerShell Cmdlet", MSDN topic, 508
Internet Explorer security zones, 608, 609
LDAP search filter syntax, 681
Microsoft Certificate Services, 525
Microsoft Log Parser, 267
.NET Framework classes, 943
.NET Framework documentation, 145, 893
P/Invoke Windows API definitions, 497
PowerShell download, xxii
SDDL format, 544
Sysinternals Process Monitor, 622
Windows Firewall API, 702
websites
adding to an Internet Explorer security zone, 606–608
command output formatted as web page, 387
cookies, managing, 377
downloading files from, 365–366, 583
downloading web pages from, 368–373
form detection and submission, 377
links, extracting, 379–382
monitoring, 389–390
parsing web pages from, 373–375
redirections, managing, 377
REST-based APIs, interacting with, 383–384
scripting interaction with, 375–379
-Weekly parameter, New-ScheduledTaskTrigger cmdlet, 712
WellKnownSidType class, 946
wevtutil.exe program, 643, 644
-WhatIf parameter, x, 338–340
Where-Object cmdlet, 90–91, 94–96, 233, 563–564, 567, 568, 636–639, 641
while statement, 170–172, 886
WIA.CommonDialog COM object, 961
wildcards
in cmdlet parameters, vii
finding files using, 561, 566–570
string searches using, 183, 184

Win32_BaseBoard WMI class, 951
Win32_BIOS WMI class, 951
Win32_BootConfiguration WMI class, 952
Win32_CacheMemory WMI class, 952
Win32_CDROMDrive WMI class, 952
Win32_ComputerShutdownEvent class, 968
Win32_ComputerSystem WMI class, 952
Win32_ComputerSystemEvent class, 968
Win32_ComputerSystemProduct WMI class, 955
Win32_DCOMApplication WMI class, 952
Win32_Desktop WMI class, 952
Win32_DesktopMonitor WMI class, 952
Win32_DeviceChangeEvent class, 969
Win32_DeviceMemoryAddress WMI class, 952
Win32_Directory WMI class, 952
Win32_DiskDrive WMI class, 952
Win32_DiskPartition WMI class, 952
Win32_DiskQuota WMI class, 952
Win32_DMAChannel WMI class, 952
Win32_Environment WMI class, 952
Win32_Group WMI class, 952
Win32_IDEController WMI class, 953
Win32_IP4RouteTableEvent class, 968
Win32_IRQResource WMI class, 953
Win32_LoadOrderGroup WMI class, 953
Win32_LogicalDisk WMI class, 953
Win32_LogicalMemoryConfiguration WMI class, 953
Win32_LogonSession WMI class, 953
Win32_ModuleLoadTrace event class, 969
Win32_ModuleTrace event class, 969
Win32_NetworkAdapter WMI class, 953
Win32_NetworkAdapterConfiguration WMI class, 722, 723, 724–725, 953
WIN32_NetworkClient WMI class, 953
Win32_NetworkConnection WMI class, 953
Win32_NetworkLoginProfile WMI class, 953
Win32_NetworkProtocol WMI class, 953
Win32_NTDomain WMI class, 953
Win32_NTEventLogFile class, 644
Win32_NTEventlogFile WMI class, 953
Win32_NTLogEvent WMI class, 953
Win32_OnBoardDevice WMI class, 954
Win32_OperatingSystem WMI class, 954
Win32_OSRecoveryConfiguration WMI class, 954
Win32_PageFileSetting WMI class, 954
Win32_PageFileUsage WMI class, 954

Win32_Perf* classes, 488
Win32_PerfFormattedData_Spooler_Print-Queue WMI class, 715–717
Win32_PerfRawData_PerfNet_Server WMI class, 954
Win32_PhysicalMemoryArray WMI class, 954
Win32_PortConnector WMI class, 954
Win32_PortResource WMI class, 954
Win32_PowerManagementEvent class, 969
Win32_Printer WMI class, 714, 717–718, 954
Win32_PrinterConfiguration WMI class, 954
Win32_PrintJob WMI class, 954
Win32_Process class, 659, 660–661
Win32_Process WMI class, 954
Win32_Processor WMI class, 952
Win32_ProcessStartTrace event class, 969
Win32_ProcessStopTrace event class, 969
Win32_ProcessTrace event class, 969
Win32_Product WMI class, 955
Win32_QuickFixEngineering WMI class, 955
Win32_QuotaSetting WMI class, 955
Win32_Registry WMI class, 955
Win32_ScheduledJob WMI class, 955
Win32_SCSIController WMI class, 955
Win32_Service WMI class, 955
Win32_Share WMI class, 955
Win32_SoftwareElement WMI class, 955
Win32_SoftwareFeature WMI class, 956
WIN32_SoundDevice WMI class, 956
Win32_StartupCommand WMI class, 956
Win32_SystemAccount WMI class, 956
Win32_SystemConfigurationChangeEvent class, 969
Win32_SystemDriver WMI class, 956
Win32_SystemEnclosure WMI class, 956
Win32_SystemSlot WMI class, 956
Win32_SystemTrace event class, 969
Win32_TapeDrive WMI class, 956
Win32_TemperatureProbe WMI class, 956
Win32_ThreadStartTrace event class, 969
Win32_ThreadStopTrace event class, 969
Win32_ThreadTrace event class, 969
Win32_TimeZone WMI class, 956
Win32_UninterruptiblePowerSupply WMI class, 956
Win32_UserAccount WMI class, 956
Win32_VoltageProbe WMI class, 957
Win32_VolumeChangeEvent class, 969
Win32_VolumeQuotaSetting WMI class, 957

Win32_WMISetting WMI class, 957
Windows API functions, 490–500
Windows clipboard, reading and writing to, 246–248
Windows Event Viewer
  browsing event logs, 634
  filtering event logs, 639
  viewing backed-up event logs, 644
Windows Explorer
  clearing downloaded warning flag, 583–584
  extended file properties from, 591–593
  launching interactive shell from, 51
Windows Firewall
  enabling or disabling, 702
  opening or closing ports in, 702
Windows Management Framework, iv, 750
Windows Management Instrumentation (see WMI)
Windows performance counters (see performance counters)
Windows PowerShell (see PowerShell)
Windows Registry (see Registry)
Windows security features, 515
Windows Start menu, searching, 250–251
WindowsBuiltInRole class, 946
WindowsIdentity class, 946
WindowsPrincipal class, 480–481, 946
-WindowStyle parameter, PowerShell.exe, 53
WMI (Windows Management Instrumentation), xiii, 727–729
  classes, 951–957
    accessing from specific namespace, 731
    finding, 731, 737–740
    key properties, determining, 736–737
    methods of, invoking, 731, 734–735
    properties of, listing, 741
    qualifiers of, listing, 741
  converting VBScripts to PowerShell, 743–747
  events, 968–969
  instances
    associators of, determining, 741
    methods of, invoking, 730, 734–735
    properties of, modifying, 732–734
    querying, 741
    retrieving, 730
    scoping options, 741
  large-scale operations, 742–743
  .NET classes for, 947

performance counters, 488
[Wmi] type shortcut, 730, 731, 743–747, 894
wmic.exe program, 727
[WmiClass] type shortcut, 731, 735, 744–747, 894
[WmiSearcher] type shortcut, 730, 731, 743–747, 894
WMPlayer.OCX COM object, 961
Word.Application COM object, 961
Word.Document COM object, 961
workflow keyword, 802, 804
workflows, 801
  checkpoints in, 806, 811–814
  commands not supported in, 807, 810
  compared to scripts, 805–808
  connection parameters for, 819–825
  creating, 802–808
  custom activities in, 828–830
  debugging, 830–834
  performance counters for, 833
  PowerShell cmdlets as activities in, 834–836
  requiring human interaction, 825–827
  resuming, 811–814
  running, 804, 808–811
  running as jobs, 803, 807
  scripts in, 814–816
  statements invoked in parallel, 816–819, 890
  statements not supported in, 808
  statements specific to, 890
  suspending, 811–814
  XAML in, 827
-WorkGroupName parameter, Add-Computer cmdlet, 695
workgroups
  adding computers to, 695–696
  enabling Remoting for, 774–776
Write verb, 972
Write-Debug cmdlet, 402, 450
Write-Error cmdlet, 456, 910
Write-EventLog cmdlet, 646
Write-Host cmdlet, 37, 402, 403, 421
Write-Output cmdlet, 313, 401, 830
Write-Progress cmdlet, 404–405, 451
Write-Verbose cmdlet, 402, 450
Write-Warning cmdlet, 456
WriteDebug() method, 450
WriteProgress() method, 451
WriteVerbose() method, 450
WScript.Network COM object, 961

WScript.Shell COM object, 473, 474, 961
WSHController COM object, 961
WSMan (WS-Management service), 753, 786
WSMAN (WS-Management service), 773

# X

XAML, 827, 835
XelectXmlInfo objects, 285
XML data type, 872–873
XML files, xiii
    accessing properties of, 281–284
    converting command output to, 286–287
    modifying data in, 287–289
    XPath querys on, 284–286

XML REST-based web APIs, 383–384
[xml] type shortcut, 281–284, 872
[Xml] type shortcut, 894
XmlDocument class, 283, 947
XmlElement class, 283
XmlTextWriter class, 947
-xor operator, 875
XPath queries, 284–286
    filtering event logs using, 640
    syntax for, 929–931

# Z

ZIP archives, creating, 595–597

## About the Author

**Lee Holmes** is a developer on the Microsoft Windows PowerShell team, and has been an authoritative source of information about PowerShell since its earliest betas. His vast experience with Windows PowerShell enables him to integrate both the "how" and the "why" into discussions. Lee's involvement with the PowerShell and administration community (via newsgroups, mailing lists, and blogs) gives him a great deal of insight into the problems faced by all levels of administrators and PowerShell users alike.

## Colophon

The animal on the cover of *Windows PowerShell Cookbook, Third Edition*, is a box turtle (*Terrapene carolina carolina*). This box turtle is native to North America, specifically northern parts of the United States and Mexico. The male turtle averages about six inches long and has red eyes; the female is a bit smaller and has yellow eyes. This turtle is omnivorous as a youth but largely herbivorous as an adult. It has a domed shell that is hinged on the bottom and which snaps tightly shut if the turtle is in danger. Box turtles usually stay within the area in which they were born, rarely leaving a 750 foot radius. When mating, male turtles sometimes shove and push one another to win a female's attention. During copulation, it is possible for the male turtle to fall backward, be unable to right himself, and starve to death.

Although box turtles can live for more than 100 years, their habitats are seriously threatened by land development and roads. Turtles need loose, moist soil in which to lay eggs and burrow during their long hibernation season. Experts strongly discourage taking turtles from their native habitats—not only will it disrupt the community's breeding opportunities, but turtles become extremely stressed outside of their known habitats and may perish quickly.

The cover image is from *Dover Pictorial Images*. The cover font is Adobe ITC Garamond. The text font is Adobe Minion Pro; the heading font is Adobe Myriad Condensed; and the code font is Dalton Maag's Ubuntu Mono.

# Get even more for your money.

**Join the O'Reilly Community, and register the O'Reilly books you own. It's free, and you'll get:**

- $4.99 ebook upgrade offer
- 40% upgrade offer on O'Reilly print books
- Membership discounts on books and events
- Free lifetime updates to ebooks and videos
- Multiple ebook formats, DRM FREE
- Participation in the O'Reilly community
- Newsletters
- Account management
- 100% Satisfaction Guarantee

**Signing up is easy:**

1. **Go to: oreilly.com/go/register**
2. **Create an O'Reilly login.**
3. **Provide your address.**
4. **Register your books.**

Note: English-language books only

**To order books online:**

oreilly.com/store

**For questions about products or an order:**

orders@oreilly.com

**To sign up to get topic-specific email announcements and/or news about upcoming books, conferences, special offers, and new technologies:**

elists@oreilly.com

**For technical questions about book content:**

booktech@oreilly.com

**To submit new book proposals to our editors:**

proposals@oreilly.com

**O'Reilly books are available in multiple DRM-free ebook formats. For more information:**

oreilly.com/ebooks

# O'REILLY®

Spreading the knowledge of innovators     oreilly.com

CPSIA information can be obtained
at www.ICGtesting.com
Printed in the USA
BVOW08s0941310118
506848BV00023B/975/P